Contents

Population figures in this guide are based on the 1990 US census.

Addresses, telephone numbers, opening hours and prices given in this guide are accurate at the time of publication. We apologize for any inconveniences resulting from outdated information. Please send us your comments:

Michelin Travel Publications
Editorial Department
PO Box 19001, Greenville SC 29602-9001.

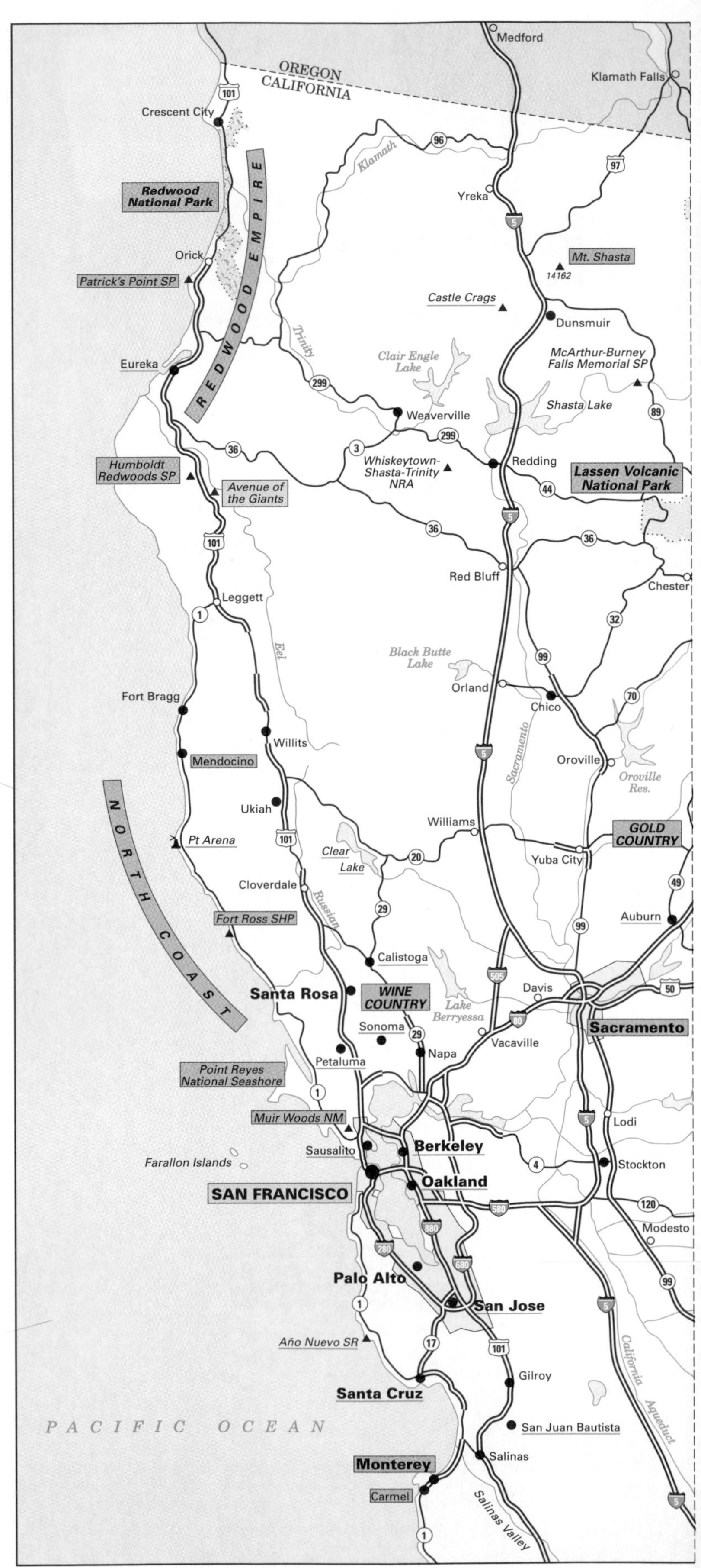

OREGON
CALIFORNIA
Medford
Klamath Falls
Crescent City
Redwood National Park
REDWOOD EMPIRE
Klamath
Yreka
Orick
Patrick's Point SP
Mt. Shasta
14162
Castle Crags
Dunsmuir
Trinity
Clair Engle Lake
McArthur-Burney Falls Memorial SP
Eureka
Shasta Lake
Weaverville
Whiskeytown-Shasta-Trinity NRA
Redding
Lassen Volcanic National Park
Humboldt Redwoods SP
Avenue of the Giants
Red Bluff
Chester
Leggett
Eel
Black Butte Lake
Orland
Chico
Fort Bragg
Willits
Mendocino
Sacramento
Oroville
Oroville Res.
NORTH COAST
Ukiah
Williams
Pt Arena
GOLD COUNTRY
Clear Lake
Yuba City
Cloverdale
Russian
Auburn
Fort Ross SHP
Calistoga
Santa Rosa
WINE COUNTRY
Davis
Lake Berryessa
Sacramento
Sonoma
Vacaville
Napa
Petaluma
Point Reyes National Seashore
Muir Woods NM
Lodi
Sausalito
Berkeley
Farallon Islands
Stockton
Oakland
SAN FRANCISCO
Modesto
Palo Alto
San Jose
Año Nuevo SR
Gilroy
Santa Cruz
California Aqueduct
PACIFIC OCEAN
San Juan Bautista
Salinas
Monterey
Carmel
Salinas Valley

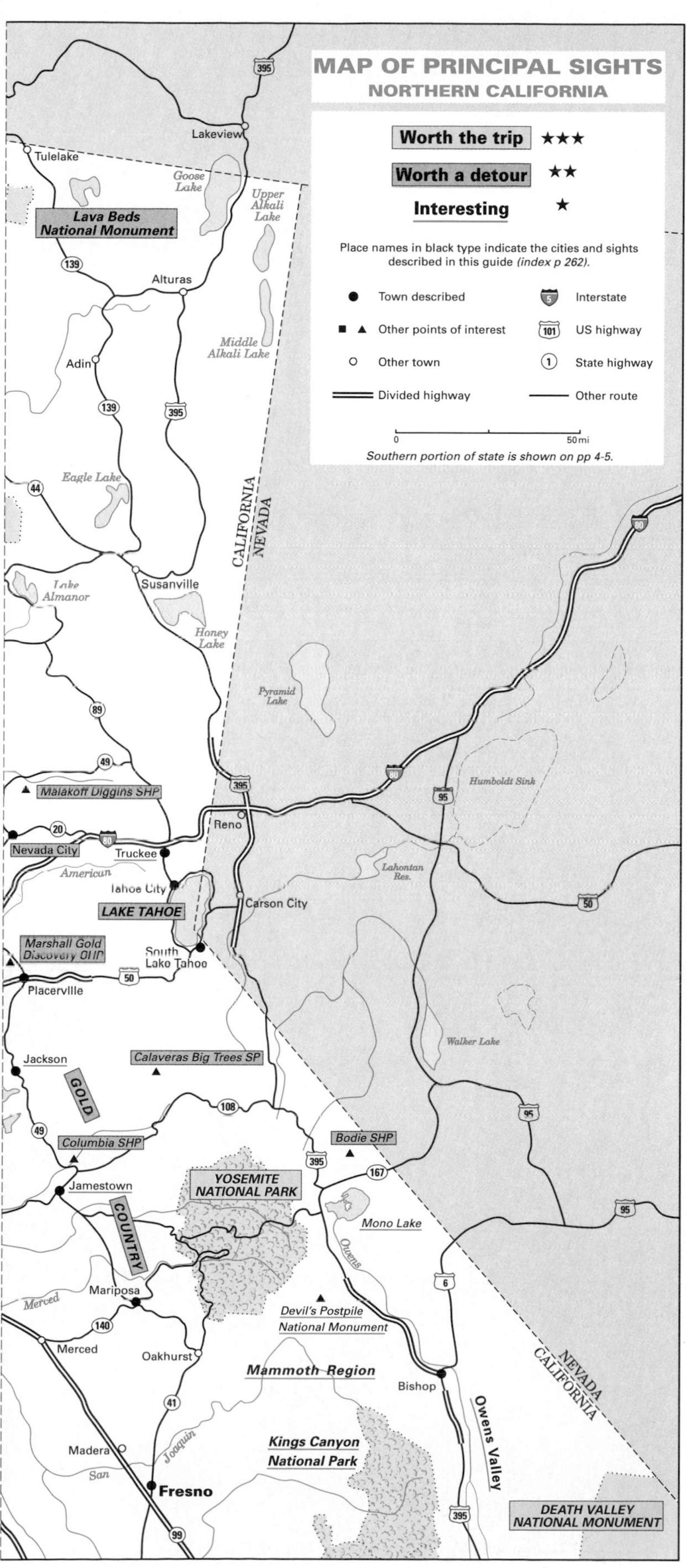

MAP OF PRINCIPAL SIGHTS
NORTHERN CALIFORNIA
Worth the trip ★★★
Worth a detour ★★
Interesting ★
Place names in black type indicate the cities and sights described in this guide (index p 262).
Town described
Other points of interest
Other town
Divided highway
Interstate
US highway
State highway
Other route
0
50mi
Southern portion of state is shown on pp 4-5.
Lakeview
Tulelake
Goose Lake
Upper Alkali Lake
Lava Beds National Monument
Alturas
Adin
Middle Alkali Lake
Eagle Lake
Susanville
Lake Almanor
Honey Lake
Pyramid Lake
CALIFORNIA
NEVADA
Humboldt Sink
Malakoff Diggins SHP
Reno
Nevada City
Truckee
American
Tahoe City
Lahontan Res.
Carson City
LAKE TAHOE
Marshall Gold Discovery SHP
South Lake Tahoe
Placerville
Walker Lake
Jackson
Calaveras Big Trees SP
GOLD
COUNTRY
Columbia SHP
Bodie SHP
Jamestown
YOSEMITE NATIONAL PARK
Mono Lake
Owens
Merced
Mariposa
Devil's Postpile National Monument
Oakhurst
Mammoth Region
Bishop
Owens Valley
Madera
Joaquin
San
Kings Canyon National Park
Fresno
DEATH VALLEY NATIONAL MONUMENT

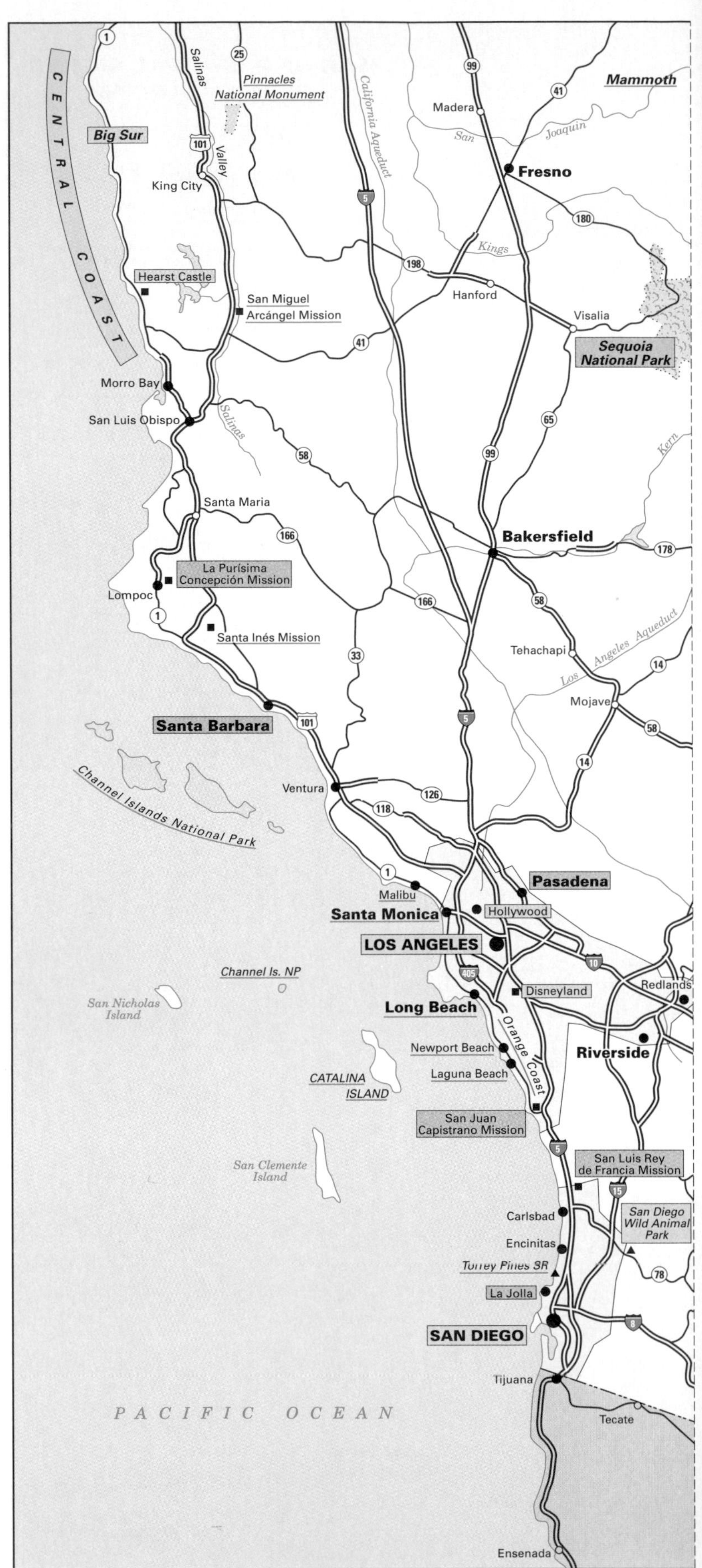

CENTRAL COAST
Big Sur
Salinas
Valley
Pinnacles National Monument
California Aqueduct
Madera
Mammoth
San Joaquin
Fresno
King City
Kings
Hearst Castle
San Miguel Arcángel Mission
Hanford
Visalia
Sequoia National Park
Morro Bay
San Luis Obispo
Salinas
Kern
Santa Maria
Bakersfield
La Purísima Concepción Mission
Lompoc
Santa Inés Mission
Tehachapi
Los Angeles Aqueduct
Mojave
Santa Barbara
Channel Islands National Park
Ventura
Malibu
Pasadena
Santa Monica
Hollywood
LOS ANGELES
Channel Is. NP
Disneyland
Redlands
San Nicholas Island
Long Beach
Orange Coast
Riverside
Newport Beach
Laguna Beach
CATALINA ISLAND
San Juan Capistrano Mission
San Clemente Island
San Luis Rey de Francia Mission
Carlsbad
San Diego Wild Animal Park
Encinitas
Torrey Pines SR
La Jolla
SAN DIEGO
Tijuana
PACIFIC OCEAN
Tecate
Ensenada

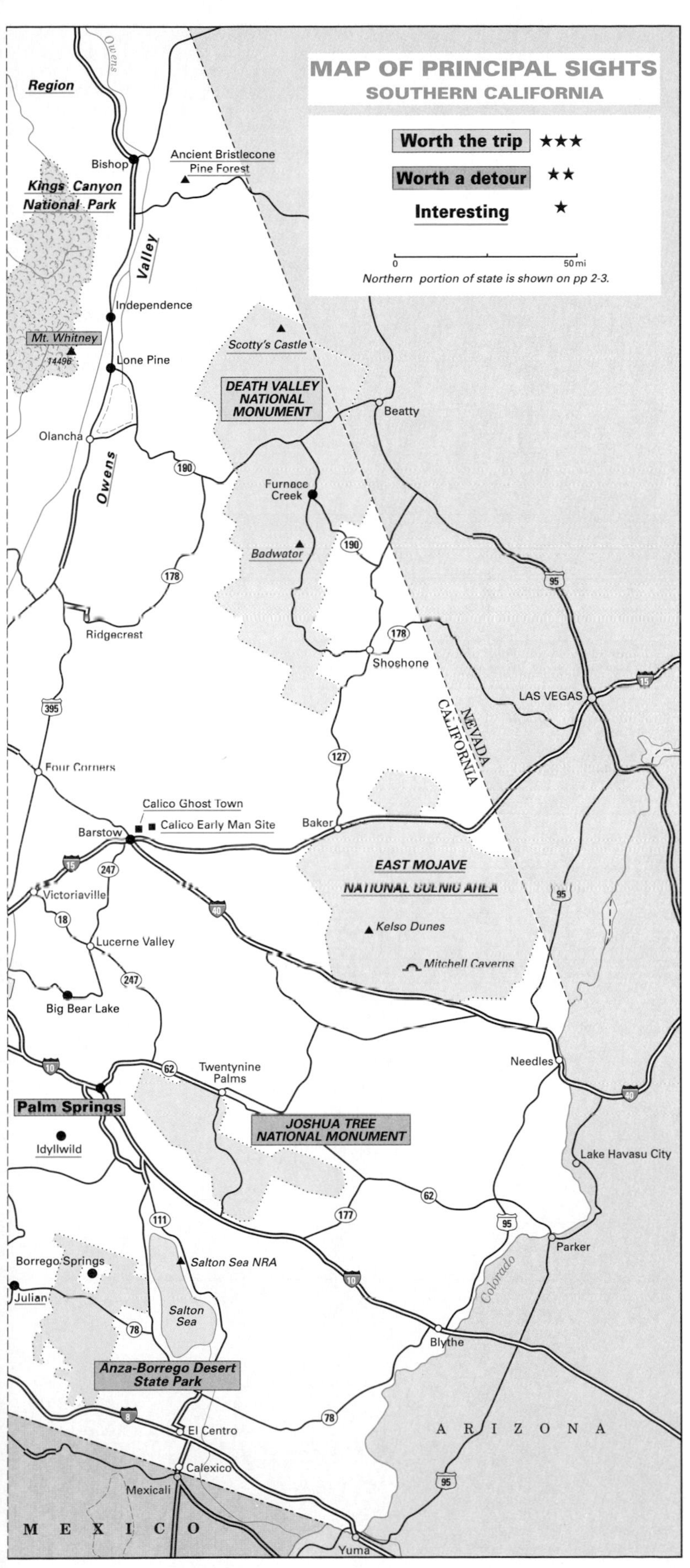

MAP OF PRINCIPAL SIGHTS
SOUTHERN CALIFORNIA
Worth the trip ★★★
Worth a detour ★★
Interesting ★
0
50 mi
Northern portion of state is shown on pp 2-3.
Region
Kings Canyon National Park
Bishop
Ancient Bristlecone Pine Forest
Owens
Valley
Independence
Mt. Whitney
14496
Lone Pine
Scotty's Castle
DEATH VALLEY NATIONAL MONUMENT
Beatty
Olancha
Owens
190
Furnace Creek
Badwater
190
178
95
Ridgecrest
178
Shoshone
15
LAS VEGAS
395
NEVADA
CALIFORNIA
127
Four Corners
Calico Ghost Town
Calico Early Man Site
Barstow
Baker
15
247
EAST MOJAVE
Victoriaville
40
95
18
Kelso Dunes
Lucerne Valley
Mitchell Caverns
247
Big Bear Lake
10
62
Twentynine Palms
Needles
Palm Springs
40
JOSHUA TREE NATIONAL MONUMENT
Idyllwild
Lake Havasu City
62
111
177
95
Parker
Borrego Springs
Salton Sea NRA
10
Julian
Salton Sea
Colorado
78
Blythe
Anza-Borrego Desert State Park
8
78
El Centro
A R I Z O N A
Calexico
Mexicali
95
M E X I C O
Yuma

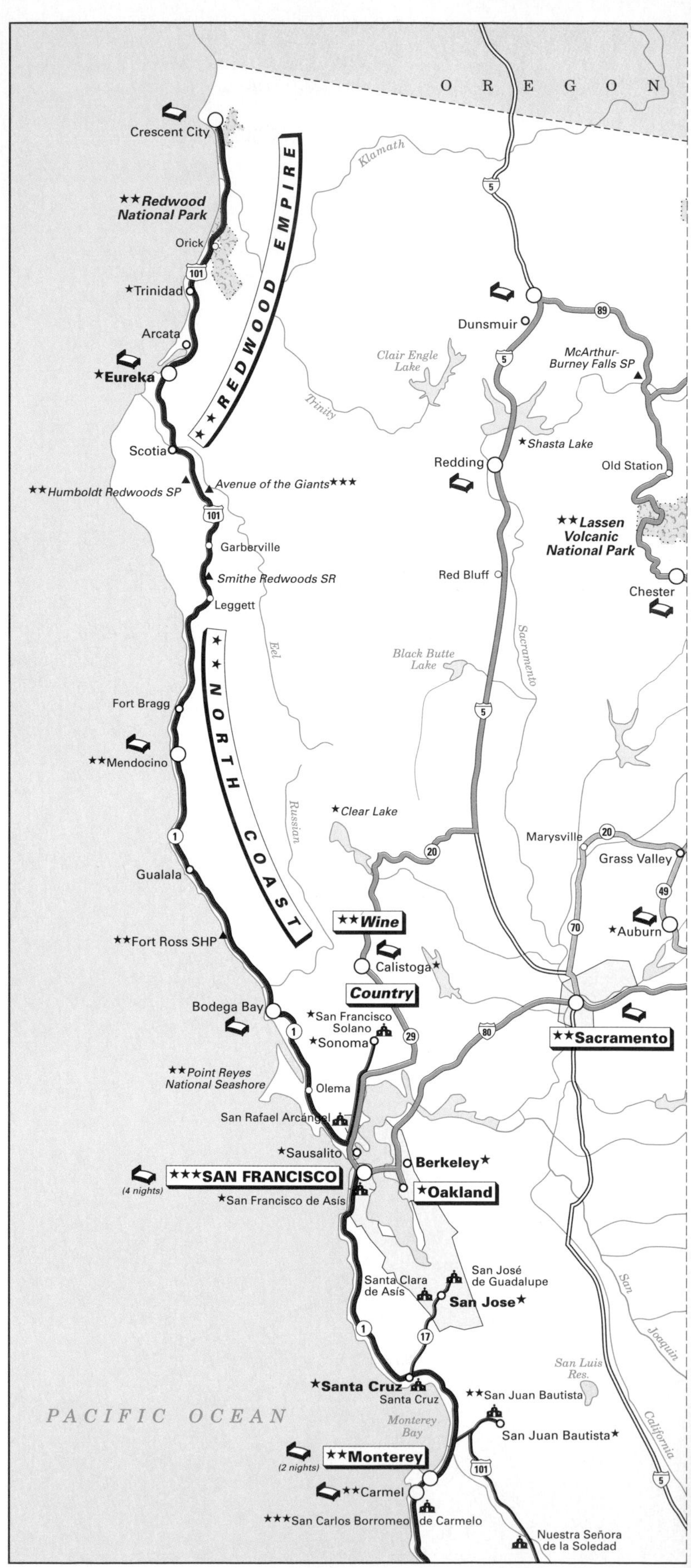

OREGON
Crescent City
Klamath
REDWOOD EMPIRE
★★Redwood National Park
Orick
101
★Trinidad
Arcata
★Eureka
5
Dunsmuir
89
Clair Engle Lake
McArthur-Burney Falls SP
Trinity
Scotia
★Shasta Lake
Redding
Old Station
★★Humboldt Redwoods SP
Avenue of the Giants★★★
★★Lassen Volcanic National Park
Garberville
Smithe Redwoods SR
Red Bluff
Chester
Leggett
NORTH COAST
Eel
Black Butte Lake
Sacramento
Fort Bragg
★★Mendocino
Russian
★Clear Lake
Marysville
20
Grass Valley
1
Gualala
49
★★Wine
70
★Auburn
★★Fort Ross SHP
Calistoga★
Country
Bodega Bay
★San Francisco Solano
★Sonoma
29
80
★★Sacramento
★★Point Reyes National Seashore
Olema
San Rafael Arcángel
★Sausalito
Berkeley★
★★★SAN FRANCISCO
(4 nights)
★Oakland
★San Francisco de Asís
San José de Guadalupe
Santa Clara de Asís
San Jose★
San
17
Joaquin
San Luis Res.
★Santa Cruz
Santa Cruz
★★San Juan Bautista
PACIFIC OCEAN
Monterey Bay
San Juan Bautista★
California
★★Monterey
(2 nights)
★★Carmel
★★★San Carlos Borromeo de Carmelo
Nuestra Señora de la Soledad

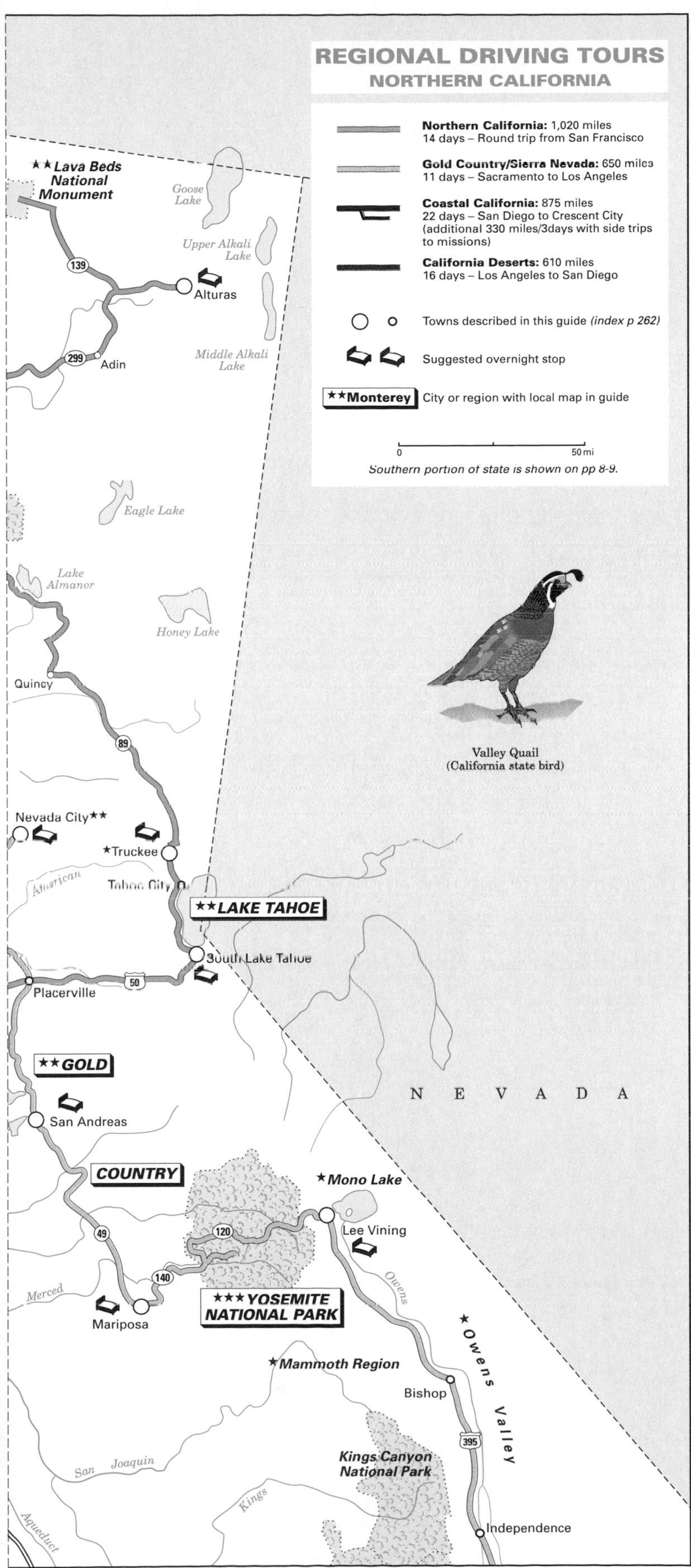

Valley Quail
(California state bird)

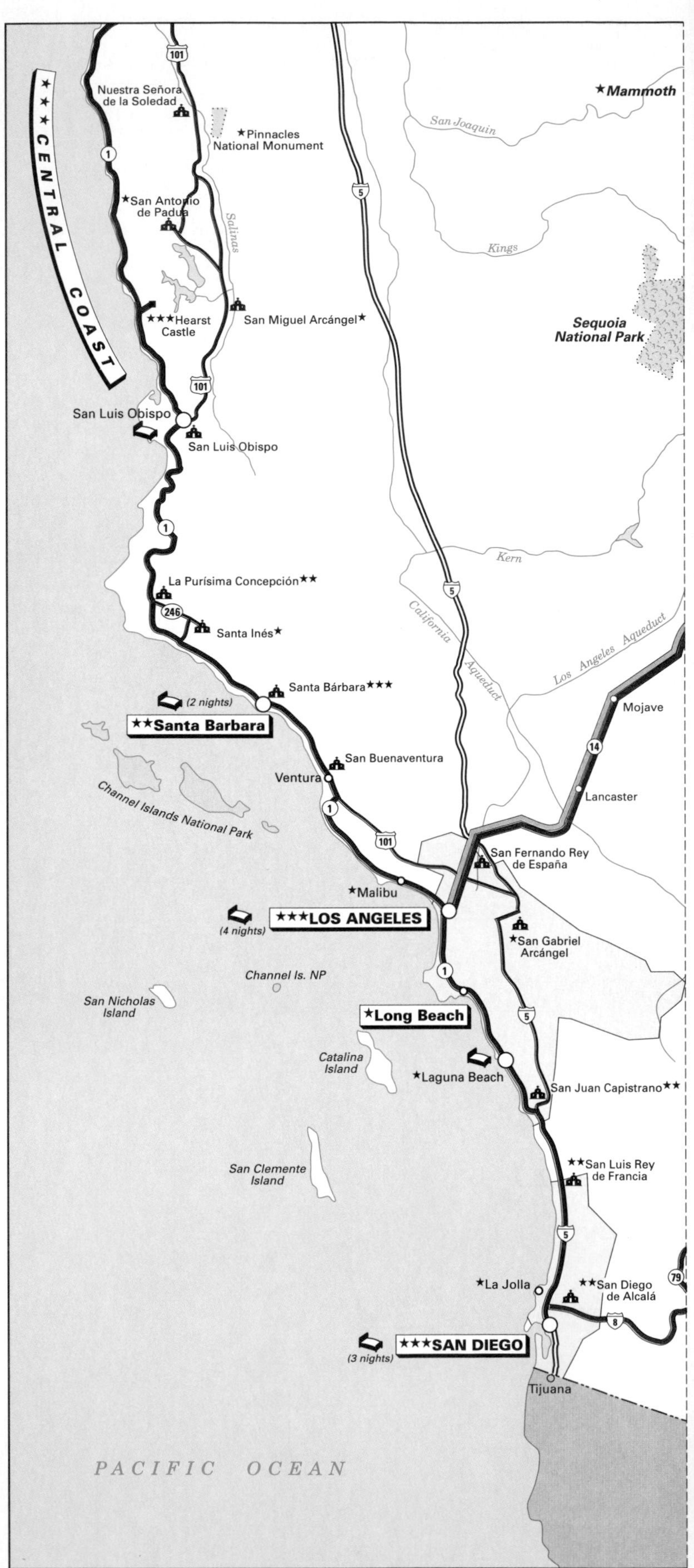
★★★CENTRAL COAST
Nuestra Señora de la Soledad
★Pinnacles National Monument
★Mammoth
San Joaquin
★San Antonio de Padua
Salinas
Kings
★★★Hearst Castle
San Miguel Arcángel★
Sequoia National Park
San Luis Obispo
San Luis Obispo
Kern
La Purísima Concepción★★
California Aqueduct
Santa Inés★
Los Angeles Aqueduct
Santa Bárbara★★★
(2 nights)
★★Santa Barbara
Mojave
San Buenaventura
Ventura
Lancaster
Channel Islands National Park
San Fernando Rey de España
★Malibu
★★★LOS ANGELES
(4 nights)
★San Gabriel Arcángel
Channel Is. NP
San Nicholas Island
★Long Beach
Catalina Island
★Laguna Beach
San Juan Capistrano★★
★★San Luis Rey de Francia
San Clemente Island
★La Jolla
★★San Diego de Alcalá
★★★SAN DIEGO
(3 nights)
Tijuana
PACIFIC OCEAN
101
1
5
246
14
8
79

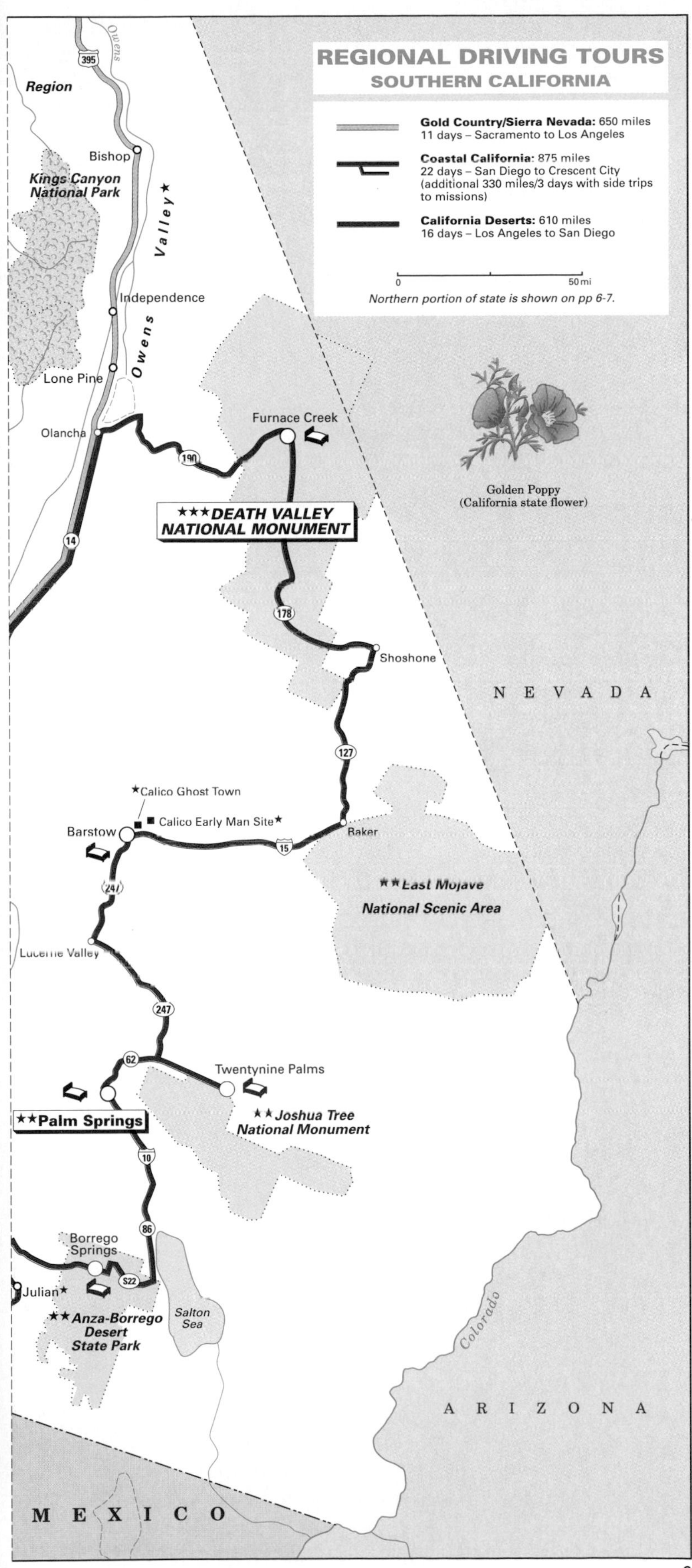

Golden Poppy (California state flower)

DISTANCE CHART

(distances given in miles; to estimate kilometers, multiply by 1.6)

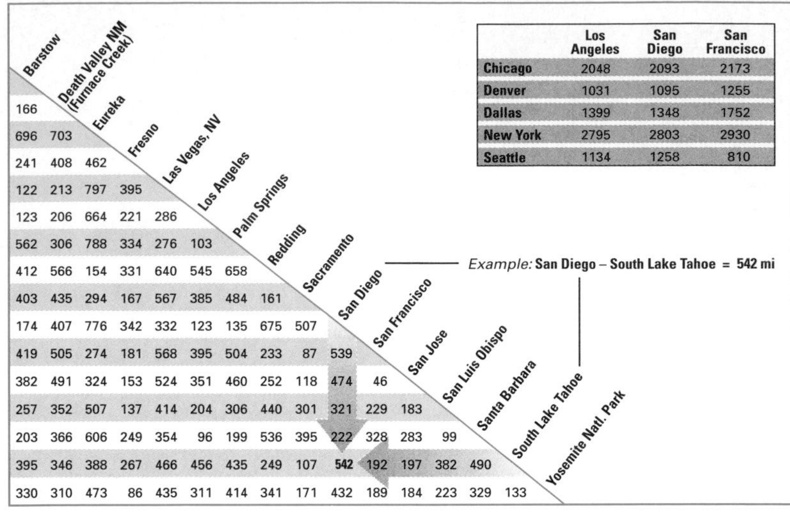

	Barstow	Death Valley NM (Furnace Creek)	Eureka	Fresno	Las Vegas, NV	Los Angeles	Palm Springs	Redding	Sacramento	San Diego	San Francisco	San Jose	San Luis Obispo	Santa Barbara	South Lake Tahoe
Death Valley NM (Furnace Creek)	166														
Eureka	696	703													
Fresno	241	408	462												
Las Vegas, NV	122	213	797	395											
Los Angeles	123	206	664	221	286										
Palm Springs	562	306	788	334	276	103									
Redding	412	566	154	331	640	545	658								
Sacramento	403	435	294	167	567	385	484	161							
San Diego	174	407	776	342	332	123	135	675	507						
San Francisco	419	505	274	181	568	395	504	233	87	539					
San Jose	382	491	324	153	524	351	460	252	118	474	46				
San Luis Obispo	257	352	507	137	414	204	306	440	301	321	229	183			
Santa Barbara	203	366	606	249	354	96	199	536	395	222	328	283	99		
South Lake Tahoe	395	346	388	267	466	456	435	249	107	**542**	192	197	382	490	
Yosemite Natl. Park	330	310	473	86	435	311	414	341	171	432	189	184	223	329	133

Example: **San Diego – South Lake Tahoe = 542 mi**

	Los Angeles	San Diego	San Francisco
Chicago	2048	2093	2173
Denver	1031	1095	1255
Dallas	1399	1348	1752
New York	2795	2803	2930
Seattle	1134	1258	810

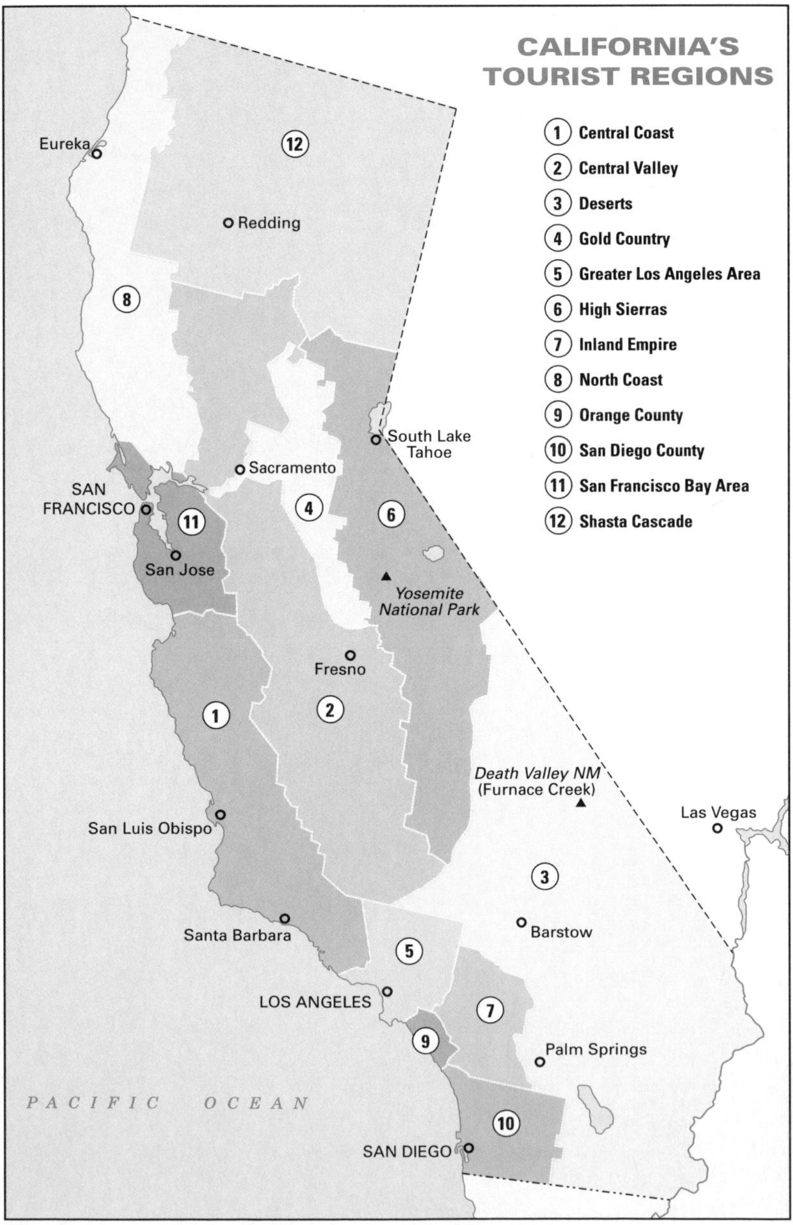

CALIFORNIA'S TOURIST REGIONS
1 Central Coast
2 Central Valley
3 Deserts
4 Gold Country
5 Greater Los Angeles Area
6 High Sierras
7 Inland Empire
8 North Coast
9 Orange County
10 San Diego County
11 San Francisco Bay Area
12 Shasta Cascade
Eureka
Redding
South Lake Tahoe
Sacramento
SAN FRANCISCO
San Jose
Yosemite National Park
Fresno
Death Valley NM (Furnace Creek)
Las Vegas
San Luis Obispo
Santa Barbara
Barstow
LOS ANGELES
Palm Springs
PACIFIC OCEAN
SAN DIEGO

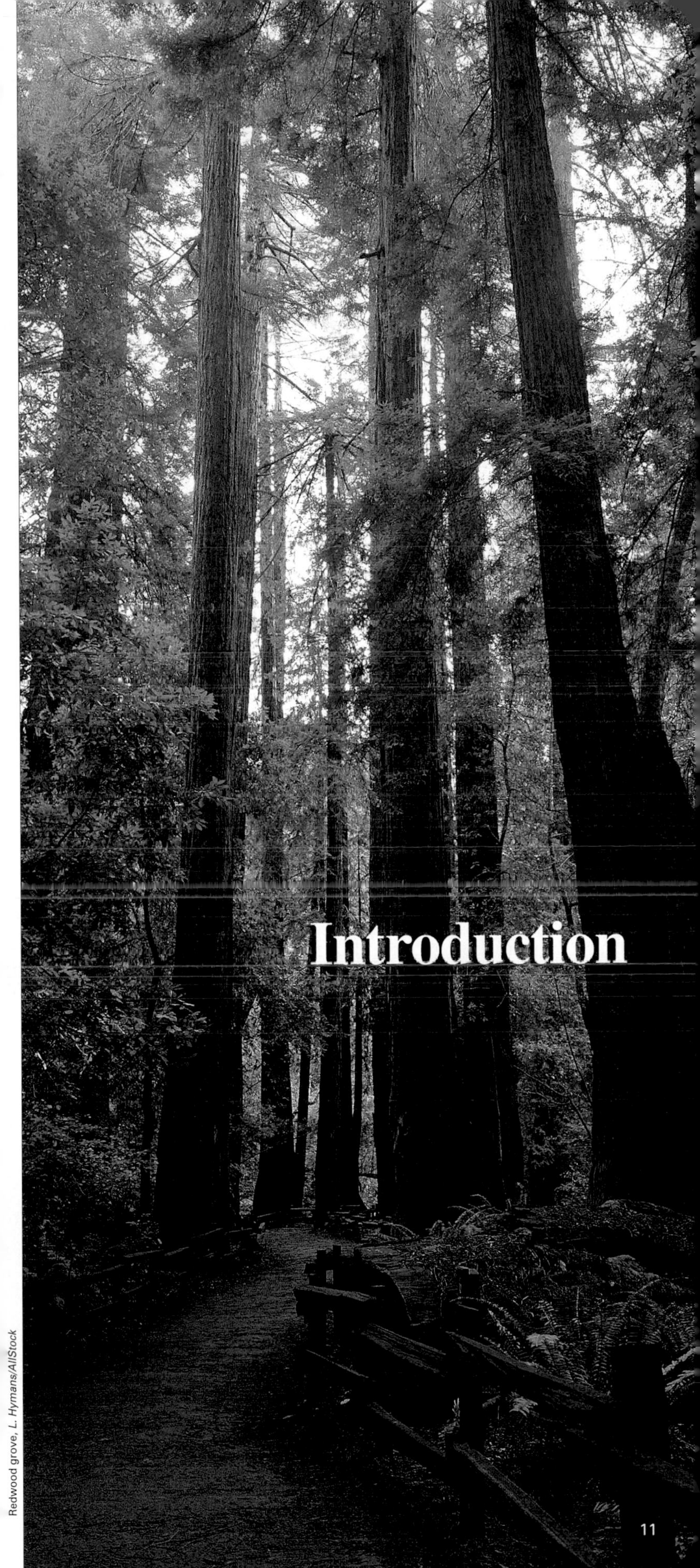

Introduction

Redwood grove, *L. Hymans/AllStock*

CALIFORNIA'S LANDSCAPES

The third largest state (163,707sq mi), California is bounded naturally by the Pacific Ocean on the west and the Colorado River on the southeast; the northern boundary with Oregon, the eastern with Nevada and the southern with Mexico are surveyors' straight lines. California stretches some 850mi from its southeast to northwest corners, and the distance from the coast to its land borders averages 200mi. At 14,494ft, MT WHITNEY, near Lone Pine, is the highest point in the contiguous 48 states while the lowest point in the Western Hemisphere (282ft below sea level) is found at Badwater in DEATH VALLEY.

Geologic Foundations

The western US was formed, and is today greatly affected, by the opposite motion of two **plates**, giant solidified sections of the earth's crust that move about atop the molten material of the earth's mantle. About 400 million years ago, the eastern edge of the Pacific plate, which extends nearly to Asia, slipped beneath the North American plate's western edge in a process known as subduction. As the overriding edge of the North American plate continued to move westward over the Pacific plate, sections of the earth's crust along the contact zone compressed and crumpled, creating mountain ranges; smaller, outlying land masses, or **terranes**, coalesced with the North American plate. This accretion of crust fragments over tens of millions of years has added some 500mi of new land to western North America; California consists of the most recent and most unstable of these accreted terranes. Over the past 25 million years, the Pacific plate began to rotate counterclockwise, and shifted direction. Today it is heading generally northwest, while the North American plate continues to move steadily west.

Earthquakes – California's area of greatest tectonic instability is the **San Andreas rift zone**, running from the Imperial Valley in southeastern California to Cape Mendocino on the north coast. The San Andreas fault, as well as California's other fault systems, is created by the motion of the Pacific and North American plates as they slide past each other at an average speed of 2in per year. Movements along faults can occur frequently (and imperceptibly), but occasionally the slide is impeded by rigid materials such as granite, and pressure increases as the plates strain to move. When the obstruction gives way, the pent-up pressure is released in an **earthquake**, a sudden lurch that causes the earth along the fault to shudder and tremble.

The Richter Scale

In the 1940s, Charles Richter, a seismologist at the California Institute of Technology, devised a scale to measure the amount of energy released by an earthquake. Each whole-number increase on the scale represents a 10-fold increase in the amount of ground vibration.

Some of California's 20C Earthquakes

San Francisco (San Francisco Bay Area)	1906	8.3
Lompoc (Central Coast)	1925	7.5
Imperial Valley (Deserts)	1940	7.1
Kern County (Central Valley)	1952	7.7
Eureka (North Coast)	1980	7.0
Whittier Narrows (Greater Los Angeles Area)	1987	6.8
Loma Prieta (San Francisco Bay Area)	1989	7.1
Petrolia/Ferndale (North Coast)	1992	7.1
Yucca Valley (Deserts)	1992	7.6
Northridge (Greater Los Angeles Area)	1994	6.8

Volcanoes – The volcanic region of northern California, marked by lava beds, hot springs, geysers, fumaroles and volcanic cones, results from the tremendous heat and pressure at the center of the earth. Pressure is created by the subducted edge of the Pacific plate as it is pushed deeper toward the earth's superheated core, where it melts and expands. This molten material is then forced upward, sometimes exploding through the crust. The openings, or vents, and the cones of material that build up around them, are known as **volcanoes**. Volcanic cones of several types exist in California. Composite volcanoes (such as MT SHASTA) result from repeated eruptions of thick lava from the same vent over hundred of thousands of years. The cone is thus composed of many layers of lava, cinders and ash. Composite volcanoes tend to erupt violently and grow precipitously upward. Shield volcanoes form when more fluid types of lava erupt smoothly from a vent, flowing long distances over the surface and creating a relatively flat cone such as that of the Mt Harkness in LASSEN VOLCANIC NATIONAL PARK. Cinder cone volcanoes form as lava spews upward, solidifying and shattering into fragments that rain down to build a cone of cinders around the vent. Schonchin Butte, in LAVA BEDS NATIONAL MONUMENT, is an example of a cinder cone.

Regional Landscapes

California's rough-and-tumble geologic history has resulted in a remarkable diversity of landscapes within the state, from the lushly forested, fog-draped slopes of the northern coastal mountain ranges to the flat, shade-forsaken deserts.

The Coast Ranges – With most peaks and ridgetops between 2,000ft and 5,000ft, this rugged belt of mountains is between 50mi and 75mi wide, and extends some 500mi from the Oregon border to Santa Barbara County. The Coast Ranges began to uplift about 25 million years ago as the edge of the North American plate crumpled and folded with the pressure of the Pacific plate. The rugged, steep slopes plunging abruptly into the sea are met on the south by long ridges and small, fertile valleys that generally run northwest to southeast. The region owes its diverse geomorphic composition to the fact that it consists of many different accreted land masses, some of which are thought to have originated thousands of miles away.

The Coast Ranges are bisected by the **San Francisco Bay**, the only sea-level break through the mountains between the Central Valley *(below)* and the Pacific Ocean. The rivers draining the western slope of the Sierra Nevada and the flat plains of the Central Valley join and pass to the sea through this break. When the immobilization of vast amounts of water in continental glaciation lowered sea level by some 300ft (the prevailing situation as recently as 15,000 years ago), what is now the bay was a typical elongated Coast Range valley. As the glaciers melted, sea level rose to its present level and drowned this valley, creating one of the world's great natural harbors. San Francisco Bay today covers some 496sq mi.

The Central Valley – Between the Sierra Nevada on the east and the Coast Ranges on the west, tectonic plate movements have made a great trough in the earth's crust. Much of this space has been filled up with sediment washed down from the surrounding mountains, creating an area of immensely fertile flat land about 400mi long and averaging 50mi wide. The northern and southern portions of this great, elongated grassland bear the names of the rivers that drain them: the **Sacramento Valley** in the north and the **San Joaquin Valley** in the south. The two rivers meet just inland from San Francisco Bay to form the **Delta**, under natural conditions a tidal marsh but now engineered into a maze of agricultural islands resembling Dutch polders. With some seven million acres under irrigation, the Central Valley is today considered among the most productive and varied agricultural regions in the world *(p 19)*.

The Cascade Range and the Modoc Plateau – California's Cascade mountains, (among them MT LASSEN and MT SHASTA) form the southern end of the Cascade Range, a line of volcanoes that extends through the Pacific Northwest into British Columbia. The Cascades were created about five million years ago by volcanic activity *(p 12)* that shows no sign of abating. Mt Shasta is a geologic twin of Washington's Mt St Helens, which erupted violently in 1980, and is subject to the same type of catastrophic eruption. Inland from Mt Lassen and Mt Shasta, in the far northeastern corner of California, lies the Modoc plateau, a relatively flat region created by great outpourings of lava that continued until as recently as 30,000 years ago. The lava beds of the Modoc plateau are punctuated by cinder cones that are no more than 1,000 years old.

The Sierra Nevada – Roughly paralleling the Central Valley along its eastern border, the majestic Sierra Nevada (Spanish for "snowy range") is one of the highest mountain ranges in the contiguous 48 states. The mountains comprise an enormous block of granite that began to uplift about ten million years ago and today tilts gently to the west. Eroding forces of rivers and glaciers have etched deep canyons into the western slope, creating the stunningly beautiful formations encompassed within YOSEMITE NATIONAL PARK and SEQUOIA AND KINGS CANYON NATIONAL PARKS. The range breaks off steeply to the east, and the 10,000ft vertical sweep from the OWENS VALLEY floor to the Sierra crest near Mt Whitney is probably the highest escarpment in the US. The Sierra crest bifurcates into an eastern and western summit ridge in two areas: in the south, where it is divided by the canyon of the Kern River; and in the middle, where a deep basin has filled with water to form LAKE TAHOE. The southern portion of the range, between Tioga Pass and Walker Pass, is often called the **High Sierra**. Broad expanses above the timberline include Mt Whitney and several small glaciers, as well as many shaded slopes where snow remains through the summer.

The Deserts – The Cascade, Sierra Nevada, Transverse and Peninsular ranges *(p 16)* form an effective barrier to atmospheric moisture carried by prevailing westerly winds from the Pacific Ocean. The areas lying in this **rain shadow** receive less than 10in of precipitation per year, and are thus defined as desert.

Three types of desert exist in California, their differences stemming largely from variations in elevation. Ranging along the state's eastern border and encompassing the Modoc Plateau *(above)* is the California portion of the **Great Basin Desert**, a vast area of interior drainage that comprises most of Nevada and portions of neighboring states.

Superstock

California's Desert

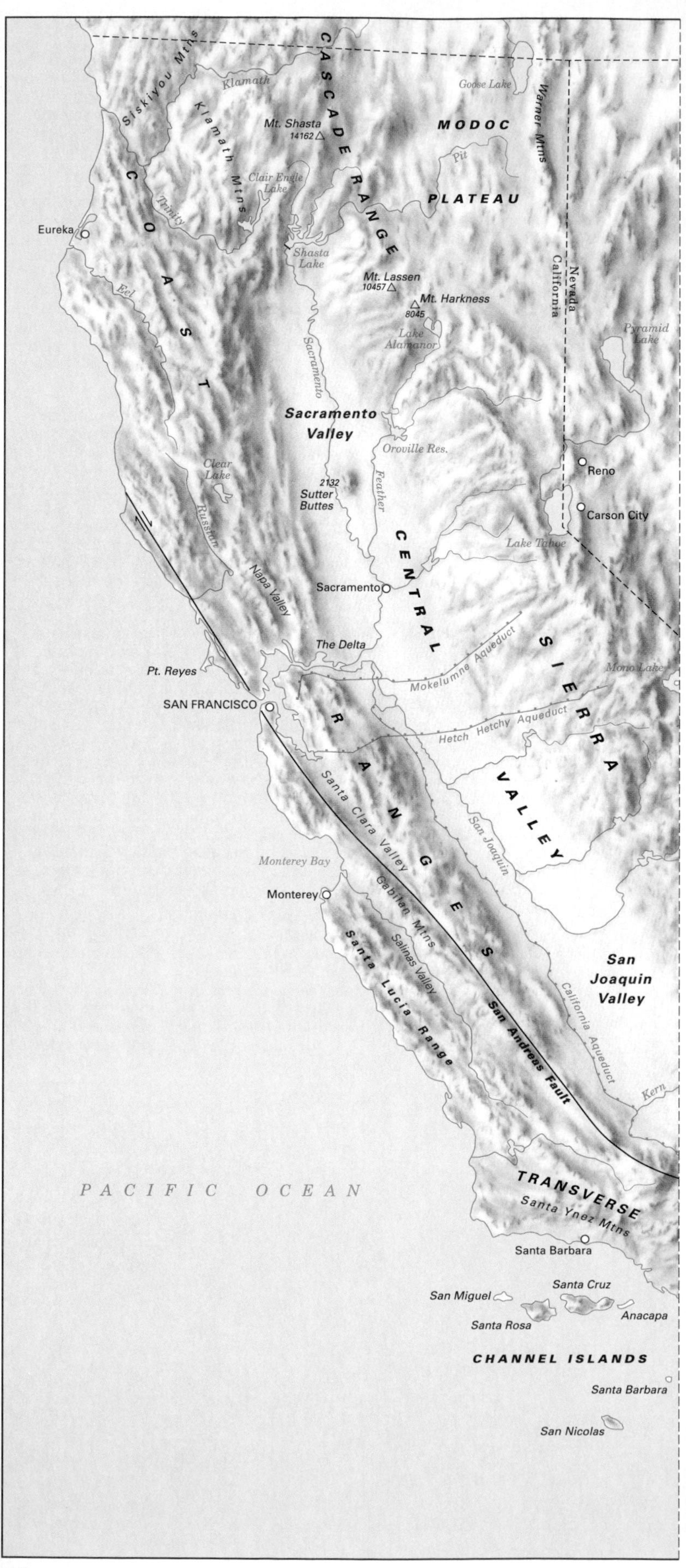

Siskiyou Mtns
CASCADE RANGE
Klamath
Goose Lake
Warner Mtns
Mt. Shasta
14162
MODOC
Klamath Mtns
Pit
Clair Engle Lake
PLATEAU
Trinity
Eureka
Shasta Lake
Mt. Lassen
10457
Nevada
California
Mt. Harkness
8045
Eel
Pyramid Lake
Lake Almanor
Sacramento
COAST
Sacramento Valley
Oroville Res.
Reno
Clear Lake
2132
Sutter Buttes
Feather
Carson City
Russian
CENTRAL
Lake Tahoe
Napa Valley
Sacramento
The Delta
Mokelumne Aqueduct
Mono Lake
Pt. Reyes
SAN FRANCISCO
RANGES
SIERRA
Hetch Hetchy Aqueduct
VALLEY
Santa Clara Valley
San Joaquin
Monterey Bay
Monterey
Gabilan Mtns
Santa Lucia Range
Salinas Valley
San Joaquin Valley
San Andreas Fault
California Aqueduct
Kern
PACIFIC OCEAN
TRANSVERSE
Santa Ynez Mtns
Santa Barbara
Santa Cruz
San Miguel
Anacapa
Santa Rosa
CHANNEL ISLANDS
Santa Barbara
San Nicolas

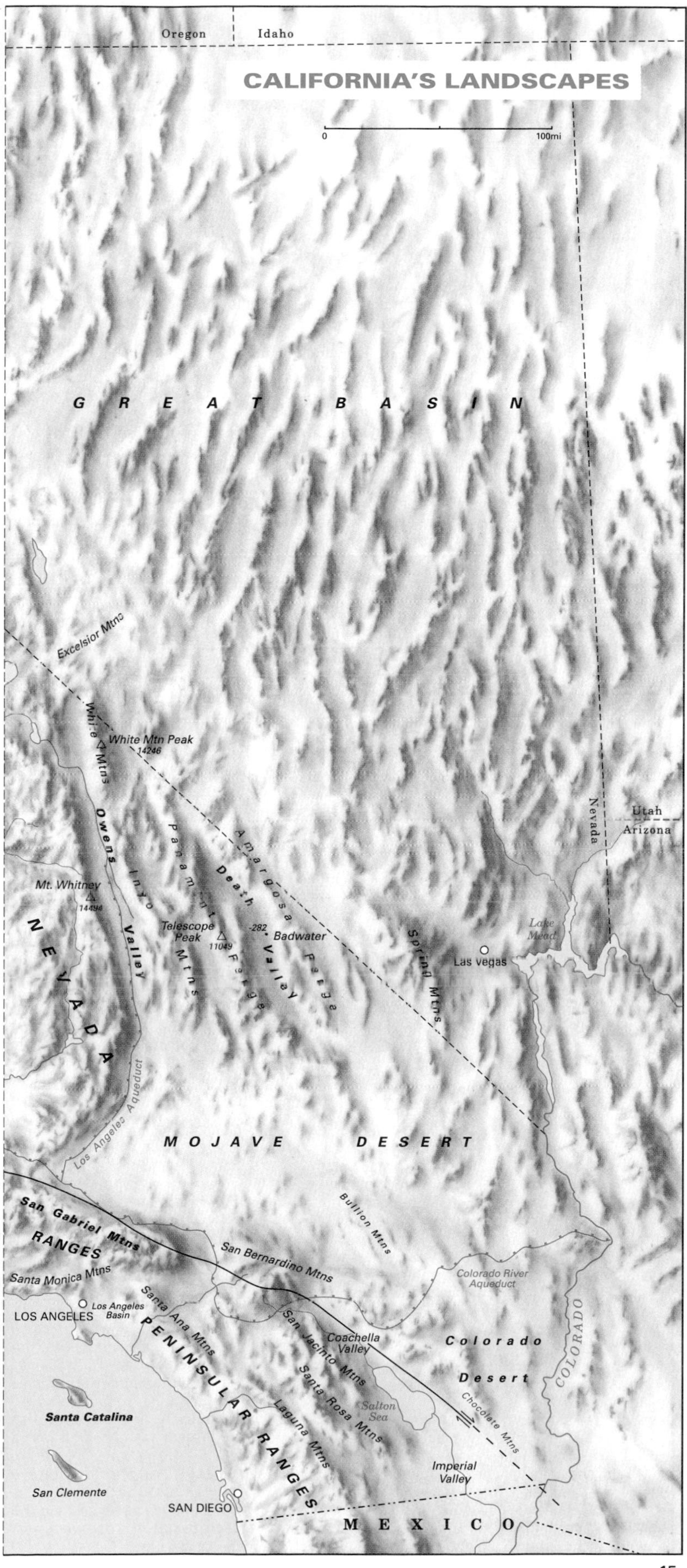

CALIFORNIA'S LANDSCAPES
0
100mi
Oregon
Idaho
GREAT BASIN
Excelsior Mtns
White Mtns
White Mtn Peak
14246
Owens Valley
Inyo Mtns
Mt. Whitney
14494
NEVADA
Panamint Range
Telescope Peak
11049
Death Valley
-282
Badwater
Amargosa Range
Spring Mtns
Las Vegas
Lake Mead
Nevada
Utah
Arizona
Los Angeles Aqueduct
MOJAVE DESERT
Bullion Mtns
San Gabriel Mtns
RANGES
San Bernardino Mtns
Santa Monica Mtns
Los Angeles Basin
LOS ANGELES
Santa Ana Mtns
PENINSULAR RANGES
San Jacinto Mtns
Coachella Valley
Santa Rosa Mtns
Colorado River Aqueduct
Colorado Desert
COLORADO
Salton Sea
Chocolate Mtns
Santa Catalina
Laguna Mtns
San Clemente
Imperial Valley
SAN DIEGO
MEXICO

The Great Basin is semi-arid bush land rather than true desert, but DEATH VALLEY, where elevations sink to 282ft below sea level, is the hottest and driest desert in the US. Mountain ranges here, among them the Panamint and Amargosa ranges fringing DEATH VALLEY NATIONAL MONUMENT, contain some of California's loftiest peaks, including Telescope Peak (11,049ft) and White Mountain Peak (14,246ft). To the south, occupying most of San Bernardino County and portions of adjoining counties, is the **Mojave Desert**, nicknamed the "high desert" because its elevation averages 3,500ft, although broad areas lie above 4,000ft. The Mojave receives between 10in and 15in of rain a year, and temperatures are relatively cool, resulting in less evaporation and more plant life. Southernmost of the three and situated in the eastern portions of Riverside and San Diego counties and all of Imperial County is the **Colorado Desert**, also called the "low desert," ranging from 2,000ft to below sea level around the Salton Sea. The Colorado Desert generally receives less than 5in of rain per year, and is subject to blistering summer temperatures.

The Transverse Ranges – The south end of the Coast Ranges *(p 12)* merges with this east-west line of mountains that began to uplift as long as 25 million years ago, although most rapidly through the last 3 million years. Although composed of granite like the Sierra Nevada, the Transverse Ranges reveal fewer signs of glaciation and erosion, owing to their more southerly location.
The ranges lie along fault lines that extend from the San Andreas fault system. Individual ranges include the Santa Ynez Mountains, which create a spectacular backdrop for SANTA BARBARA; the Santa Monica Mountains bordering the basin of Los Angeles; the San Gabriel Mountains; and the San Bernardino Mountains, whose snowy peaks loom over Los Angeles. The Transverse Ranges continue out to sea to form the CHANNEL ISLANDS.

The Peninsular Ranges – Actually the coast ranges of the far south, these mountains are the northern end of the range that forms the backbone of Mexico's narrow Baja California peninsula. Dominating the coastal landscape of San Diego, Orange and Riverside counties are the Santa Ana Mountains, San Jacinto Mountains and the Santa Rosa Mountains; several peaks, including Mt San Jacinto, top 10,000ft. Striking granite outcrops and boulder fields are characteristic features.
On the west side of the Peninsular and Transverse ranges and in the angle between them lies a broad area of coastal plain that continues inland as far as the southern deserts. These coastal lowlands (which include the Los Angeles Basin) enjoy a dry, sunny climate tempered by ocean winds, and today harbor vast metropolitan regions, including Los Angeles, SAN DIEGO and the cities of the Inland Empire.

Climate

Coastal California enjoys a Mediterranean climate, generally characterized by warm, dry summers and cool winters. Rain generally falls between November and April; the northern coastal mountains receive as much as 100in a year, while the driest areas around Death Valley typically receive less than 2in a year. Summer rain is rare along the coast and in the Central Valley, where persistently high atmospheric pressure suppresses convection and the formation of rain clouds, and diverts moist westerly winds far to the north. In winter, the incidence of high pressure moves south and allows moisture-laden westerlies to blow through. In regions above 2,000ft, an higher percentage of precipitation falls as snow.
Seasonal variation of temperature along the coast is remarkably slight *(p 251)*. In San Diego, the average daily high in August, the warmest month, is 77°F, in January 65°F. Comparable figures for Los Angeles are 76°F and 63°F.
Inland the summers become much hotter, though winters remain mild. Winter cold is restrained by the great mountain wall of the Sierra Nevada and the Cascade Range, which blocks the cold air masses of the continental interior and allows the relatively balmy winds off the Pacific to dominate. The potential heat of the dry, clear summer is dramatically tamed along the coast by the cold **California current** flowing south just offshore. This current, the eastern portion of a great clockwise swirl in the northern half of the Pacific Ocean, brings cold water down from Alaska.

Water Resources

About 75 percent of the state's precipitation falls north of Sacramento, while 75 percent of the demand for water comes from the portion of the state lying south of the capital city. To compensate, California has developed massive water storage and transportation systems that move about 60 percent of its water requirements from the sources to the areas of demand, making possible the phenomenal growth of metropolitan Southern California and the massive irrigation system that transformed the Central Valley from a vast grassland into one of the nation's most productive agricultural regions. In recent years, water has become the subject of dispute among urban, agricultural and environmental interest groups.
Major urban water systems began in 1913 with the opening of **Los Angeles Aqueduct**, built to that city from the east side of the Sierra Nevada in Owens Valley, 240mi away. The **Colorado River Aqueduct**, opened in 1941, carries water about the same distance from Lake Havasu, on the state's southeastern border, to the San Diego area. Coordinated control of the entire Sierra Nevada/Central Valley river system began in the 1930s with the Federally-funded **Central Valley Project**, which included huge structures like Shasta Dam, and hundreds of miles of irrigation canals. In 1972 Southern California began to get water through the **State Water Project** via the California Aqueduct from Oroville Reservoir in the Sacramento Valley, 440mi away. Created in the 1960s, the state project provides irrigation water for large areas in the Central Valley and pumps water over the Tehachapi Mountains for urban Southern California. Oakland and other East Bay cities received water from the Sierra Nevada via the **Mokelumne Aqueduct** beginning in 1929, and San Francisco began to receive water from Yosemite National Park through the **Hetch Hetchy Aqueduct** in 1934.

Flora

California's natural vegetation reflects the diversity of climatic environments that results from the great variety of elevations within the state as well as the presence of the Pacific Ocean.

The lower western slopes of the northern Coast Ranges are the realm of the coast redwood *(p 149)*. Other conifers here include Douglas fir and ponderosa pine. In the southern Coast Ranges and Bay Area, coniferous forests give way to **chaparral**, a community of bushy, 6ft-high plants that form dense thickets and enter a state of fire-prone dormancy during the summer, but grow back quickly after fires from a subsurface burl on the root system. Chaparral occupies a great area in the drier southern Coast Ranges as well as the Transverse and Peninsular ranges.

Running the length of the Sierra Nevada at elevations between 2,500ft and 7,000ft is a large belt of conifers—great forests of ponderosa pine, sugar pine, Douglas fir and incense cedar. Scattered groves of giant sequoias *(p 226)* occur in the southern half of the range. The lower western slopes of the Sierra Nevada are covered with chaparral and scattered oak woodlands, which give way to conifers and alpine vegetation at higher elevations.

The margins of the Central Valley at the feet of both the Sierra Nevada and the Coast ranges are characterized by open oak woodland. The grass, flushed bright green with the winter rains, dries to golden in summer. The wide spacing of the oaks is thought to be the result of root competition for scarce water; coast live oak, interior live oak, and valley oak are the most common species.

Plants in both high and low deserts are adapted to the permanent drought conditions of these regions. Most common is the creosote bush, a ground-covering shrub that extends its roots deeply into the earth to secure adequate water, as does the Joshua tree *(p 68)*. The **ocotillo**, denizen of the low desert, sheds its leaves during dry periods, but flowers as soon as there is adequate rain.

Cholla

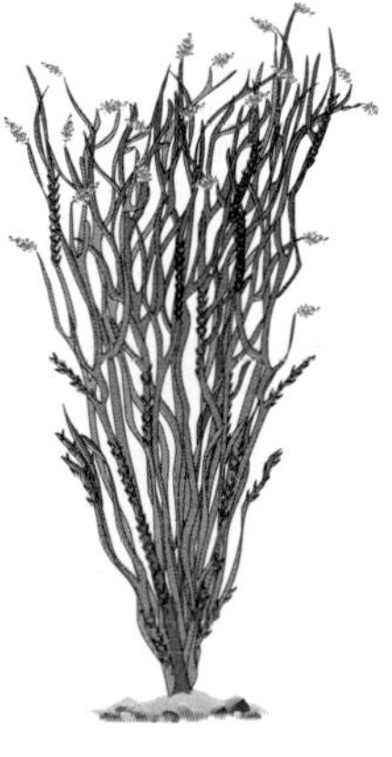
Ocotillo

The **cholla** cactus stores water whenever it is available and protects itself from thirsty animals with its fuzzy-looking, but painfully sharp spines. The **fan palm** thrives in oases and areas along fault lines, where water seeps to the surface. The desert's colorful wildflowers are drought-evading, their seeds lying dormant—sometimes for decades—until enough rain falls to overcome resistance to germination.

Fauna

Animal life in California has been greatly affected by the enormous increase in human population during the past two centuries. Some species are extinct, others are endangered, and others, driven to the verge of extinction, have staged remarkable comebacks aided by conservation organizations.

Grizzly bears, which survive only on the state flag *(illustration p 1)*, once roamed throughout California except in the desert; the last one was shot in 1922. Black bears, smaller and less fierce, are still common in mountainous areas. The **bighorn sheep** declined because of grazing competition and transference of diseases from domestic sheep; the small remaining population lives in desert mountain areas. The **California condor**, a vulture with a 9ft wingspan (the largest of any North American bird), is close to extinction. The birds consumed meat that ranchers had poisoned in order to kill coyotes, and by 1987 their number was down to 27, all in captivity, where they were being encouraged to breed for eventual release to the wild. Nearly gone from California in 1900, varieties of **deer** are once again numerous. Tule elk, once common in the Central Valley, have been successfully reestablished in some areas, such as POINT REYES NATIONAL SEASHORE. The larger Roosevelt elk now thrive in the redwood parks on the far north coast *(p 154)*. Pronghorn antelope have recovered in the thinly populated backcountry of the Modoc Plateau. Not near extinction but greatly reduced in number are the many species of waterfowl—including whistling swans, snow geese, mallards, redhead ducks, ibis and herons—that darkened the skies over the Central Valley 150 years ago before dams were built in the foothills and levees along the riverbanks. The greatly reduced wetland habitat now supports a proportionately reduced population of the waterfowl that sojourn in California.

The state's rich population of marine mammals includes **gray whales**, which can be seen from many points along the coast *(p 261)* as they migrate north in spring and south in the fall to their winter quarters in Baja California. Permanent residents along the coast include winsome sea otters and aggressive sea lions.

From photo J. Warden/Travel Image

Sea Lion

ECONOMY

The great diversity of economic activity in California was established early in the state's history, when isolation from the rest of the country made importation of goods expensive and encouraged local enterprise in every field. Today bolstered by abundant natural resources and a diversified industrial base, the economy of California alone ranks seventh largest among the world's major industrial nations. The nation's most populous state produced 13 percent of the US Gross Domestic Product in 1989, leading the US in enterprises as varied as agriculture, aerospace and entertainment.

Aerospace – California's enormous economic growth in the decades following World War II is attributed largely to the expansion of its aerospace industry, producing airplanes, missiles, spacecraft and related equipment. The aircraft industry was well established in Southern California before World War II, owing to risk-taking attitudes of regional investors and a temperate climate that allowed flight-testing year-round. After the war, rockets and space vehicles were added to the industry's product lines. In 1990 California received about a fifth of the nation's total value of defense contracts. The end of the Cold War, however, has dealt heavy blows to the industry, resulting in severe job losses and impelling the surviving aerospace firms to adapt production to the civilian market.

Computer Industry – The burgeoning of California's electronics industry over the past 50 years began with Federal spending during the Cold War and has continued, supported by increasing demand for personal computers, integrated circuits and other

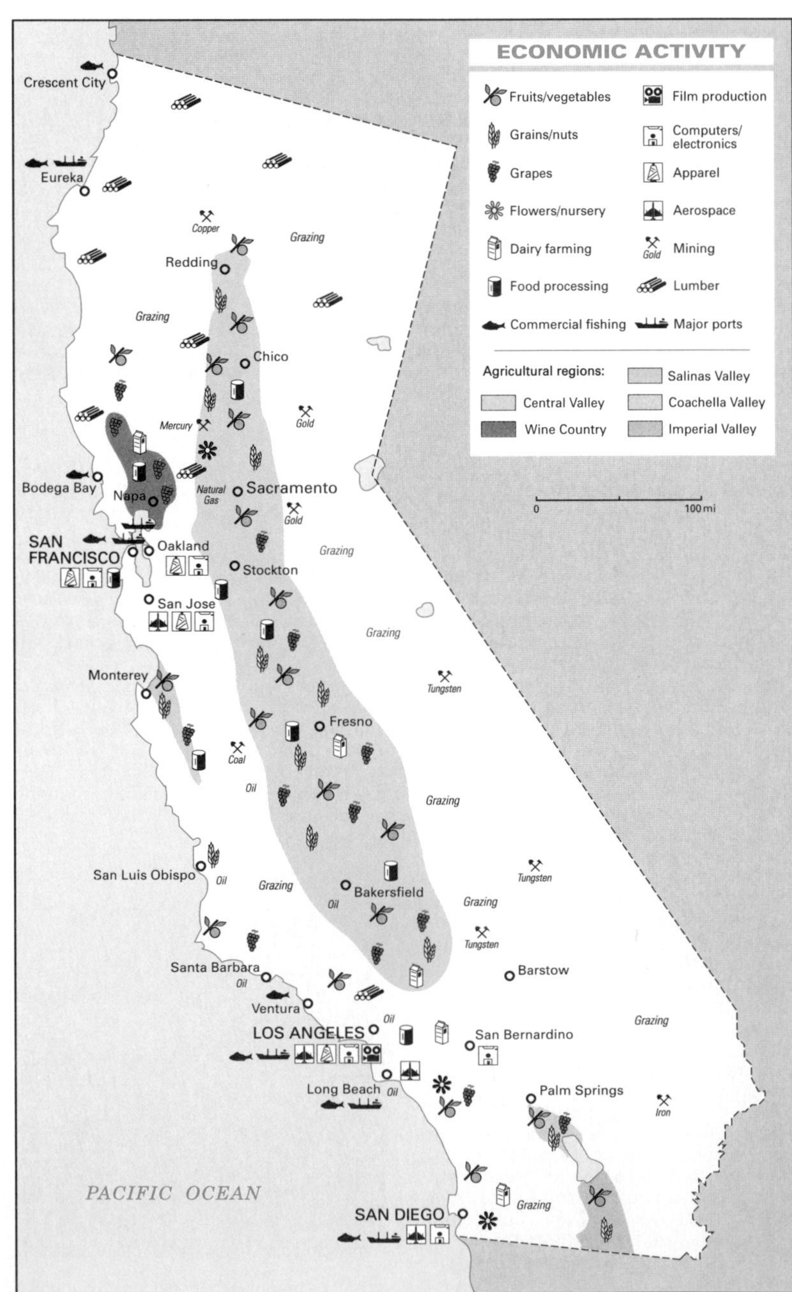

products of advancing technology. California's major research institutions, among them the California Institute of Technology in PASADENA and Stanford University in PALO ALTO, became seedbeds for small, innovative electronics concerns that were the heart of the early semiconductor and computer companies. Today **Silicon Valley**, formerly an orchard district northwest of SAN JOSE, is a world-renowned center for research and development in computers and electronics. As of 1989, some 5,500 computer, electronics and information technology companies were based in California.

Entertainment – Formerly a quiet suburb of LOS ANGELES, Hollywood became the nation's leading center for motion picture production in the 1920s when major film studios moved here from Chicago and New York. When the advent of television eroded movie ticket sales in the 1950s, the industry responded by making fewer, but bigger films, by producing features for television, and eventually by amalgamating with television, the recording business and publishing to form giant media/entertainment conglomerates. Today well over half of US feature films are produced in California. The industry, which typically employs workers and specialists from a wide variety of fields, generated an estimated $7.9 billion in 1991.

Tourism – Some 283 million people visit California annually for business and pleasure, making it the leading US travel destination. Drawn by the state's appealing Mediterranean climate, spectacular natural features and myriad tourist attractions, residents of and visitors to California spent some $53 billion in 1992, benefitting lodging, dining, retail trade, travel, transportation, entertainment, recreation and many other industries, and supporting nearly 750,000 jobs.

Agriculture – With over 200 commercially grown crops and 8 of the top 10 US agricultural counties, California is the nation's number one farm state. Tremendous productivity has resulted from irrigation on a grand scale; a benign climate that creates a year-round growing season in some areas; and a tendency towards mechanization and specialization that imparts an industrial intensity to the growing of crops. Nearly all of the nation's almonds, artichokes, dates, figs, kiwifruit, olives and pistachios are produced here, in addition to most of the US production in apricots, broccoli, Brussels sprouts, garlic, grapes, lettuce, nectarines, plums, strawberries and walnuts. The vast Central Valley is California's principal farming area; others include the SALINAS VALLEY, and the Imperial and Coachella valleys in the southeastern corner of the state. The grape-growing districts in the WINE COUNTRY are the most famous of many small, highly productive fruit and vegetable districts in Coast Range valleys, and cattle ranching remains important in the unirrigated hills and plateaus of the state.

Manufacturing – Glamour industries like entertainment and tourism may obscure the fact that California is the nation's leading manufacturing state. Prior to the 1869 completion of the transcontinental railroad, the state's geographic isolation was a stimulus to manufacturers, who sought to produce equipment and other goods more cheaply than they could be shipped around Cape Horn. Mining equipment began to be produced in San Francisco in the 1850s, followed by farm machinery in STOCKTON; canning and other forms of food-processing became important in the early 20C. Automobile assembly, airplane manufacturing and shipbuilding increased through the 1930s, and boomed during World War II. California's apparel industry began in San Francisco in 1850 with the manufacture of heavy denim trousers for miners by Levi Strauss; today San Francisco and Los Angeles are outranked only by New York City in apparel manufacturing, and Los Angeles is a major center for fashion design. Other important manufactured products are chemical and petroleum products, plastics, paper, machinery of all kinds, and home furnishings.

Natural Resources – California is second only to Oregon in the nation's lumber production. **Logging** and **lumbering** dominate the economies of towns located amid the northern Coast Ranges and the Cascade Range. Redwood, Douglas fir, ponderosa pine and sugar pine are among the commercially important trees. However, deforestation has become an acute problem, and the viability of the logging industry has in recent years been challenged by conservation groups dedicated to protecting remaining old-growth redwood forests along the North Coast. Federal, state and county forest protection measures, including the creation of 18 national forests and of REDWOOD NATIONAL PARK, have slowed logging activity and produced the expected economic consequences, offset to a degree by tourism.

With over 1,000mi of coastline, California is a leading state in **commercial fishing**; mackerel, salmon, squid, tuna, anchovies and sole are among the important ocean species. Crab, mussels, oysters and clams are also prevalent, and in recent years, sea urchins for export to Japan have become a significant catch along the northern coast. Los Angeles is now by far the largest fishing port, with 232 million pounds landed in 1989; other centers include CRESCENT CITY and the area around VENTURA.

Greatly diminished from its supreme importance during the Gold Rush *(p 60)*, **mining** remains a significant contributor to California's economy. The state accounts for almost all of the nation's production of evaporite minerals such as borax and trona (sodium carbonate), and important iron ore and tungsten deposits have been exploited in the Mojave Desert. Commercially important oil fields near BAKERSFIELD, Coalinga, and Los Angeles were tapped around the turn of the century, and rocker arms can still be seen pumping away offshore near LONG BEACH and other coastal areas.

Services – As befits the nation's most populous state, the service sector is the stronghold of California's economy. Well over a quarter of the state's jobs are in such industries as health care, finance, government, administration, business services, personal services, education and professional services. In addition, **real estate** and **construction** have grown with the state's intermittent population surges. To some extent, growth in this sector has been based on nothing more than the anticipation of further growth, fueling a speculative real estate market that keeps housing costs high compared with the rest of the country.

TIME LINE

20,000-15,000 BC Human migration from Asia into North America via the Bering land bridge.

1492 Christopher Columbus lands in the region of the present-day Bahamas.

1542 **Juan Rodríguez Cabrillo**, a Portuguese explorer in the service of Spain, enters San Diego Bay.

1564 Manila galleons begin landing in Alta California en route to and from trade in the Philippines.

1577 Explorer **Francis Drake** anchors near Point Reyes to repair his ship, and claims Alta California for England *(p 145)*.

1602 **Sebastián Vizcaíno**, a Spanish explorer, anchors in Monterey Bay.

1728-1741 Explorers in the service of Russia discover the Bering Strait, the Aleutian Islands and Alaska.

1768 English mariner Capt James Cook lands on Nootka Sound, in present-day British Columbia, and claims the territory for England.

1769 The Sacred Expedition, led by **Padre Junípero Serra** and **Gaspar de Portolá**, sets out from Mexico to establish the mission chain in Alta California. Foundation of SAN DIEGO DE ALCALÁ, the first of California's 21 missions. Sgt José Ortega, leading a detachment of the Portolá expedition, records his impressions of San Francisco Bay.

1774 Juan Bautista de Anza forges the **Anza Trail**, an overland route from Sonora, Mexico, to the SAN GABRIEL ARCÁNGEL MISSION.

1776 Foundation of SAN FRANCISCO.

1781 LOS ANGELES is founded by a group of settlers led by Felipe de Neve *(p 81)*.

1812 FORT ROSS is established on the North Coast, marking the southernmost Russian presence in North America.

1818 Spain abandons claims to Oregon Territory; **Adams-Onís Treaty** (1819) establishes northern boundary of Alta California along the 42nd parallel.

1821 **Mexican independence** from Spain is achieved.

1822 Spain cedes California to Mexico.

1824 Land grant system, begun by the Spanish government, accelerates.

1827 American trapper Jedediah Smith is the first white man to travel overland from the eastern US to California.

1833-34 **Secularization** of the mission chain decreed by the Mexican government.

1839 Swiss immigrant **John Sutter** establishes New Helvetia and builds Sutter's Fort in present-day SACRAMENTO.

1841 The **Bidwell-Bartleson Party**, organized to blaze a trail across the Rocky Mountains, arrives in California, opening the way for settlers of the Great Westward Migration.

1846 Declaration of the **Mexican War**; US and Mexico vie for possession of California and Texas. American settlers stage the **Bear Flag Revolt** in SONOMA and proclaim the short-lived Bear Flag Republic. One month later, Commodore John Sloat raises the American flag over MONTEREY and claims Alta California for the US, establishing military rule.

1847 Capt José María Flores and Gov Pío Pico surrender to American forces in the **Cahuenga Capitulation**, completing the US conquest of California.

California's first newspaper, the *California Star*, is published in San Francisco by Sam Brannan *(p 38)*.

1848 **Treaty of Guadalupe Hidalgo** is signed, concluding the Mexican War.

James Marshall discovers gold in the tailrace of John Sutter's sawmill at Coloma *(p 64)*, sparking the California **Gold Rush** of 1849.

1849 California's Constitutional Convention meets at Colton Hall in Monterey; the constitution is ratified by popular vote on November 13.

1850 California enters the Union as the 31st state.

Some 45,000 people head west to California along the California Trail during the height of the Great Westward Migration.

1859 The **Comstock Lode** silver deposits are discovered in neighboring Nevada; the resultant wealth fuels commerce and manufacturing in San Francisco and Los Angeles.

1854 State capital is transferred from Benicia to Sacramento.

1861 Establishment of the first **transcontinental telegraph**.

1868 The College of California in OAKLAND is taken over by the state, chartered and renamed the **University of California**. The campus is moved to BERKELEY in 1873.

1869 The Central Pacific and Union Pacific railroads are joined at Promontory, Utah, creating the first **transcontinental railroad** link.

1873 **Modoc War** arises from conflict between Modoc Natives and American settlers.

1878 Navel orange trees from Brazil thrive in the area around RIVERSIDE, giving birth to California's citrus industry.

1882 **Chinese Exclusion Act** is passed by the Federal Government to restrict immigration of Orientals to the US (act repealed in 1943).

1890 YOSEMITE NATIONAL PARK and SEQUOIA NATIONAL PARK are created by congressional act.

1891 Stanford University is established in PALO ALTO.

1905 Produce wholesaler A.P. Giannini, an Italian immigrant, founds the Bank of Italy, later called the Bank of America, in San Francisco.

1906 **Great Earthquake and Fire** devastate San Francisco *(p 185)*; the earthquake is estimated at 8.3 on the Richter scale.

1911 The current California state flag *(illustration p 1)* is adopted by the state legislature.

1913 **Los Angeles Aqueduct** *(p 84)* brings water from the OWENS VALLEY to Los Angeles.

Hollywood's first feature film, *The Squaw Man*, is shot in a barn at the corner of Selma and Vine Streets.

1914-1918 **World War I.**

1915 **Panama-Pacific International Exposition** in San Francisco celebrates the city's recovery from the 1906 earthquake. **Panama-California International Exposition** opens in SAN DIEGO.

1927 Hollywood's first commercially successful talkie is released: *The Jazz Singer*, starring Al Jolson, ends the era of silent films.

1929 Stock market crash signals the beginning of the Great Depression.

1932 **Summer Olympic Games** are held in Los Angeles.

1935 **Central Valley Project** is completed, bringing water from the Sacramento and San Joaquin rivers to irrigate the Central Valley.

1936-1937 Openings of the **San Francisco-Oakland Bay Bridge** *(p 131)* and the **Golden Gate Bridge** *(p 205)* bring increased development to Northern California and the Bay Area.

1939 US enters **World War II**. California's aviation industry booms.

1942 President Franklin D. Roosevelt signs Executive Order 9066, stipulating internment of Japanese-Americans; thousands are herded to MANZANAR.

1947 The "Hollywood Ten," a group of prominent personalities in the film industry, are blacklisted for their refusal to testify before the Congressional Committee on Un-American Activities.

1955 Great fanfare heralds the opening of DISNEYLAND, situated in the orange groves of rural Anaheim.

1958 Major league baseball: the Brooklyn Dodgers relocate to Los Angeles and the New York Giants move to San Francisco.

1961 The **Beach Boys**, heartthrob singers of the "California sound," are formed. Their hit singles, including *Surfin' USA*, spread the California Dream across the US.

1963 *Beach Party*, starring Frankie Avalon and Annette Funicello, gives rise to a wave of movies based on "what happens when 10,000 kids meet on 5,000 beach blankets."

1964 Free Speech Movement sit-ins at the University of California, Berkeley lead to mass arrests of student protesters.

1965 Watts Riots rage through an African-American enclave in suburban Los Angeles in response to the repeal of the Rumford Fair Housing Act forbidding racial discrimination. 34 people are killed.

1967 San Francisco's Haight-Ashbury district welcomes hippies to the "summer of love."

1968 Robert F. Kennedy is assassinated in Los Angeles *(p 99)*.

1969 **Richard Nixon**, a native of Yorba Linda and former US Senator (1950-1952), takes office as the 36th US President.

late 1960s California surpasses New York as the nation's most populous state, with nearly 20 million inhabitants.

1972 **Proposition 20** is passed, authorizing a state commission to regulate coastal development.

1974 **Edmund G. (Jerry) Brown** is elected governor of California on the Democratic ticket. Brown's father, Edmund G. Brown Sr, served as governor from 1959-1967.

1978 **Proposition 13** is passed by California voters; the initiative limits property taxes to one percent of the property's assessed value in 1976.

San Francisco mayor and gay-rights sympathizer **George Moscone** and openly gay City Supervisor **Harvey Milk** are assassinated by disgruntled City Supervisor Dan White. White's sentence of just 5 years' imprisonment touches off massive gay "White Night" riots.

1980 **Ronald Reagan**, former movie star and governor of California (1966-75), is elected 39th US President.

1983 The first California condor *(p 17)* hatched in captivity breaks through its shell at the San Diego Zoo *(p 170)*.

1984 **Summer Olympic Games** are held in Los Angeles.

1989 **Loma Prieta earthquake**, measuring 7.1 on the Richter scale, strikes south of the San Francisco Bay Area.

1992 **Riots** occur in South Central Los Angeles, sparked by the verdict of the Rodney King civil rights trial.

1993 Dianne Feinstein and Barbara Boxer join the US Senate; California is the first state to have two women senators simultaneously in office.

1994 **Northridge earthquake**, measuring 6.8 on the Richter scale, strikes the San Fernando Valley north of Los Angeles.

HISTORICAL NOTES

PREHISTORIC AND NATIVE CALIFORNIANS

At least 7,000 years ago, the area of North America that now includes California was first populated by descendants of the peoples who crossed the Bering land bridge from Asia between 20,000 and 15,000 BC. By the time Europeans first visited the Pacific Coast in the mid-16C, a Native population estimated as high as 310,000 was divided into almost 500 self-governing tribelets speaking more than 300 dialects of some 80 mutually unintelligible tongues. Chief among the tribal groups were the **Pomo** in the coastal lands near present-day MENDOCINO; the **Maidu** in the volcanic regions near Lassen Peak; the **Miwok** in the Sierra Nevada and its western foothills; the **Salinan** along the Central Coast around MONTEREY; the **Chumash** in what are now the areas of SANTA BARBARA and VENTURA; the **Gabrieleño** in the LOS ANGELES area; and the **Cahuilla**, inland from present-day SAN DIEGO. Occupying a landscape whose generally scant rainfall made agriculture difficult, tribal peoples supported themselves by hunting and fishing, and by gathering naturally available foodstuffs such as acorns and mesquite beans. Thus tied to the natural world and its seasons, they were largely migrant, establishing thousands of widely scattered small and large villages statewide, concentrated largely in coastal areas, more sparsely in the arid interior and hardly at all in the high mountain regions.

Simple though their lives were, the Native Californians developed sophisticated cultures and social orders. They practiced complex religions based on nature and its phenomena, and the men of the tribe cured themselves of physical and spiritual ailments in airtight sweat lodges. In many parts of the state, tribes set fires to control the growth of grasses, promoting more abundant yields of wild crops. Basketry reached a fine art, providing vessels for food gathering, preparation and storage. Some coastal tribes fashioned seaworthy plank boats. Strings of shell beads provided a common currency by which foods could be exchanged among tribes in times of need.

HISPANIC CALIFORNIA

Early European Encroachment – Owing to the voyages of Christopher Columbus to the Caribbean beginning in 1492, much of the New World fell under the flag of Spain. Having glimpsed the Pacific Ocean from Panama in 1513 and conquered Mexico in 1521, the *conquistadores* were eager to push north and west.

In 1535 Spanish general Hernando Cortés (1485-1547) explored the narrow sea known today as the Gulf of California, stepping ashore near the present-day site of La Paz, Mexico. Thinking the peninsula on which he landed, which would later become the Mexican state of Baja California, was actually an island, he named it "California" after an imaginary island described in the 1510 novel *Las sergas de Esplandián (The Adventures of Esplandian)* by Garcí Ordóñez de Montalvo.

Seeking the fabled **Strait of Anian**, a deep-water link between the Atlantic and Pacific, the Spanish Crown dispatched Portuguese explorer **Juan Rodríguez Cabrillo** to sail northward along the Pacific Coast in June, 1542. During a 7-month voyage in which he became the first European explorer of **Alta California** (the upper part of California north of the Baja Peninsula), Cabrillo landed in present-day SAN DIEGO; on CATALINA ISLAND and the CHANNEL ISLANDS; at the future sites of SAN PEDRO and SANTA MONICA; and as far north as FORT ROSS, failing en route to notice the entrance to San Francisco Bay.

For more than 40 years after Cabrillo's journey, Spain neglected its claims to California, providing entree for English privateer Francis Drake to land his ship, the *Golden Hinde*, at Point Reyes in 1577 *(p 145)*. England never took possession of the area Drake claimed as Nova Albion (New England), but his landing aroused Spain to protect the territory, sending Pedro Unamuno in 1587 and Sebastián Rodríguez in 1595 to sail along the shore in search of an anchorage and supply port for Spanish galleons. In 1602 **Sebastián Vizcaíno** dropped anchor in Monterey Bay; his exaggerated description of the exposed cove eventually provoked the first European sighting of San Francisco Bay by members of the Sacred Expedition 167 years later *(p 184)*.

The Mission Chain – In 1697 Jesuit priests established in Baja California the first of a chain of Catholic missions that would set a pattern for Spain's eventual colonization of all of California. Each mission typically consisted of a church, residences for its priests, schools and dormitories for its Native converts (neophytes), and thousands of acres of surrounding farmland. As it grew and became established, each mission was intended to be secularized as a *pueblo*, or town, for neophytes and Spanish colonists.

With the Jesuits fallen from favor and the Spanish government alarmed by the appearance of Russian settlements along the northern Pacific Coast, in 1767 the Crown turned to the Franciscan order to extend Spanish control northward into Alta California. Appointed head of the new missions was **Padre Junípero Serra** (1713-1784). A diminutive 54-year-old priest, Serra was born, educated and ordained on the Spanish island of Majorca, where he taught philosophy for 15 years at the Lullian University. He began his missionary work in Mexico in 1749, gaining a well-deserved reputation as a worker whose intensity, asceticism and tirelessness were made all the more dramatic by the fact that he was lame for the last 35 years of his life.

In the spring of 1769, the **Sacred Expedition** left Baja California, its two land columns and three supply ships

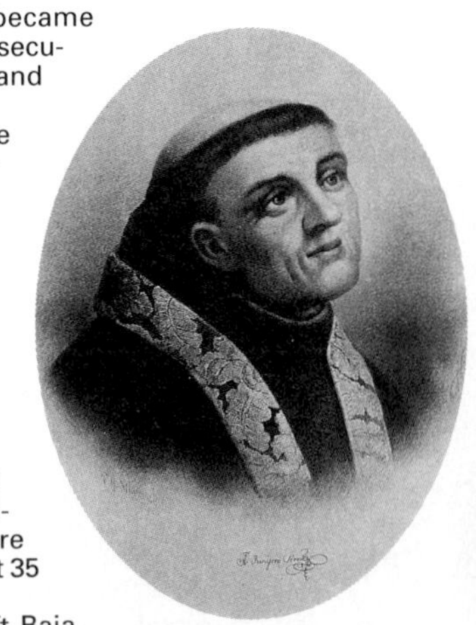

Bancroft Library

Padre Junípero Serra

destined for San Diego. The long, difficult overland journey was made more difficult when one of the supply ships was lost at sea and the other two were late in arriving. Approximately half of the 300 priests, soldiers and settlers died en route and, faced with starvation, the expedition nearly turned back. But the second column, headed by Serra and **Gaspar de Portolá** (1723-1786), eventually named Spanish governor of Alta California, finally founded the territory's first mission at San Diego in July 1769. Over the next 54 years, 20 more missions would be established in a chain stretching from San Diego north to Sonoma. Located a day's travel apart, the outposts were linked by a trail known as **El Camino Réal**, "the Royal Highway," a route largely traced today by California Highway 101.

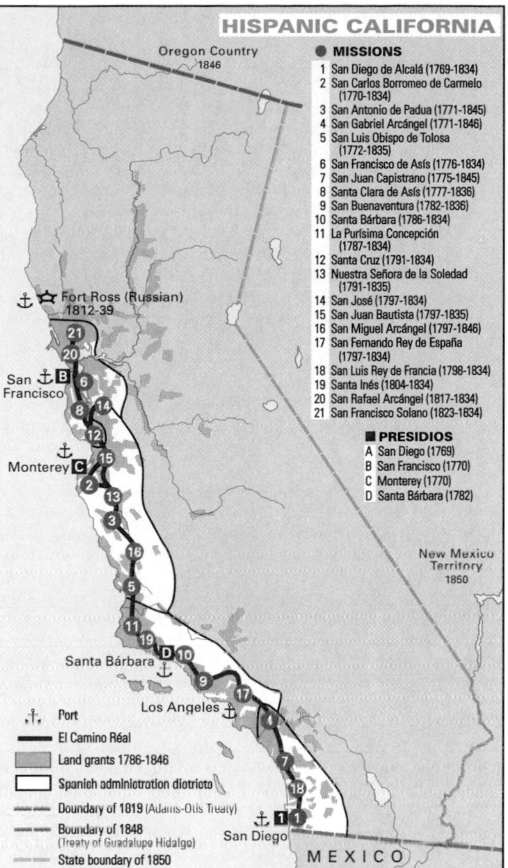

Source: California Patterns *by D. Hornbeck, 1983*

Neophytes living within the mission compound were schooled in the Spanish language and the Catholic faith; the padres also taught them such trades as farming, brickmaking, blacksmithing, weaving, spinning, tanning and winemaking. But life was far from idyllic in the missions. Supplies and equipment from Mexico sometimes arrived late or fell scarce. Earthquakes leveled adobe brick buildings. Many Natives died from such European diseases as measles, chicken pox, diphtheria, pneumonia, tuberculosis and syphilis; still others suffered physical or sexual abuse at the hands of settlers. Revolts broke out among the neophytes, and unconverted Natives outside mission lands frequently harassed those who lived within. At San Diego, Santa Bárbara, Monterey and SAN FRANCISCO, military garrisons known as **presidios** were built to safeguard the Spanish holdings against both foreign and Native attacks.

Though conversion of Natives began slowly, by 1833 some 88,000 neophytes had been baptized and 31,000 lived within mission landholdings. In 1834, still grappling with the political and economic turmoil following its independence from Spain 13 years earlier *(below)*, the Mexican congress voted to secularize the missions of Alta California. The state's governor at the time, José Figueroa (1792-1835), himself partly of Native descent, issued proclamations of secularization that would prevent land-grabbing of mission property, but his orders were not strictly followed. In 1845-1846 his successor as governor, Pío Pico (1801-1894) sold off 15 of the missions to private buyers, and all mission property eventually passed into private ownership. Mission buildings were used for a wide range of secular and profane purposes, and many fell into disrepair. Not until 1865 did some of the chapels and grounds revert to religious use, when President Abraham Lincoln signed executive orders returning them to the Catholic Church. Since the beginning of the 20C, many of the missions have been restored as legacies of California's Spanish past, their chapels in use today as local parish churches.

Mexican Period – Bridling against rule from distant Spain, colonists of New Spain (Mexico) broke out in revolt against their mother country in 1810, finally gaining independence in 1821. The new republic adopted a laissez-faire attitude toward Alta California, appointing a succession of governors who promoted the colonization of the territory by granting huge parcels of land to loyal subjects and ambitious foreigners. These **land grants** formed the basis of vast cattle ranches, or *ranchos*. Some grants were bought up by wealthy families to form holdings of 300,000 acres or more; the Pico family of Southern California controlled more than half a million acres.

Out of these vast and lonely pastures came the cattle hides—"California bank notes"—and tallow that lured Yankee clipper ships from New York and Boston around Cape Horn on trading expeditions such as that described by Richard Henry Dana in *Two Years Before the Mast* (1840). The merchant ships in turn brought manufactured goods for California's growing population, and carried back east tales of a gracious, hospitable way of life: leisurely roundups, exciting rodeos and week-long fiestas centered on the sprawling adobe ranch houses. The romantic era of the California *ranchos* lasted only briefly during the 1830s and 1840s, but their style endures in the architecture of some areas of modern California, and in the names of such great landholding families as Pico, Estudillo, Alvarado, Vallejo, Castro and Sepúlveda, which grace towns and thoroughfares from San Diego to Sonoma County.

Exploration and Statehood – Much of California's growth during the final years of Mexican rule came from immigration by US citizens seeking land grants. During the same period, California attracted adventurous and enterprising explorers and settlers. A party led by Jedediah Smith (1799-1831) crossed the Mojave Desert in 1826; the following year, they became the first white men to cross the Sierras. In 1827 James Ohio Pattie followed a desert route into California along the Gila River. In 1833-1834, sixty trappers led by Joseph Walker pioneered a route over the central Sierras, blazing what was later called the **Oregon Trail**—the preferred immigrant trail and one of several passages into the state that collectively became known as the **California Trail**.

The 1840s saw the first wagon trains bring settlers overland, following the 24-week trek of the Bidwell-Bartleson Party from Missouri in 1841. The perils inherent in such journeys were tragically dramatized by the Donner Party *(p 230)*, a group of 87 men, women and children who were trapped by heavy snows in the eastern Sierra during the fierce winter of 1846-1847.

Mexican fears grew that the US might annex California, and American immigration was banned in 1845. The government was particularly threatened by surveys across the Sierra conducted by **John C. Frémont** (1813-1890), a US Army topographical engineer who was sometimes guided by legendary scout **Kit Carson** (1809-1868). In March 1846, the armed foreigners were ordered out of California, and Frémont defiantly raised the US flag on Gabilan Peak before retreating into Oregon.

Three months later, after the **Mexican War** broke out in Texas between the US and Mexico, Americans hoisted above the Mexican barracks in Sonoma a flag displaying a brown bear and lone star; in what became known as the Bear Flag Revolt, Frémont announced an independent California Republic. Within weeks, John D. Sloat captured the California capital at Monterey, declaring the territory a US possession. War with Mexico in California ended in January 1847, and the **Treaty of Guadalupe Hidalgo** ceded California and other Mexican possessions in the Southwest to the US in February 1848. In September 1849, 48 elected delegates met at Monterey to draft and adopt a state constitution, and US President Millard Fillmore formally granted California statehood on September 9, 1850.

The Gold Rush and the Great Migration – A few weeks before the formal peace with Mexico, flecks of gold were discovered in the sand at John Sutter's lumber mill on the American River in the Sierra foothills *(p 60)*. News of the discovery drew international attention, and by the following year, fortune hunters, known ever since as "Forty-Niners," began to pour by land and sea into California from the eastern US, Europe, Australia, Asia and South America. Along with thousands of would-be miners came still more tradesmen, money-lenders, innkeepers, teamsters, preachers, gamblers, prostitutes and criminals.

Following statehood, the opportunities inherent in California's vast expanses also drew other settlers than those seeking quick fortunes in the mines. In 1850 alone, it is estimated that 45,000 people immigrated along the California Trail. The state's Caucasian population, estimated at 15,000 in 1848, had grown to almost 100,000 in 1850.

After the surface gold that drew so many people to the state was depleted, thousands of fortune-hunters returned home or moved on to other opportunities. California's diverse and growing population raised cattle, farmed, mined and built booming commercial cities, including San Francisco, SACRAMENTO, STOCKTON and Marysville. By 1860 the state population exceeded 380,000, and there were ten times as many cattle as had existed in 1848. Wheat became the major crop of the Sacramento and San Joaquin valleys, and California's year-round production of virtually every kind of non-tropical fruit and vegetable began in the coastal valleys and the Los Angeles basin.

The discovery of the vast **Comstock Lode** of silver near Virginia City, Nevada, in 1859 gave still further impetus to California's growth. Yielding about $400 million in two decades, it pumped capital into the industrial development of the region and created a powerful San Francisco-based financial elite of mine owners, entrepreneurs and bankers: the "Bonanza Firm" mine-owning foursome of John W. Mackay, James Fair, James C. Flood and William S. O'Brien; Bank of California founders William C. Ralston, William Sharon and Darius Ogden Mills; Adolph Sutro, who would become mayor and largest property owner in San Francisco *(p 207)*; and mining magnate George Hearst, founder of the Hearst family fortune *(p 66)*.

The Railroads – Despite its growth, prosperity and statehood, California's links to the US east of the Mississippi remained both tenuous and arduous: four-horse overland coaches; ox-drawn wagons; sailing routes around Cape Horn; weekly steamships with land connections across Nicaragua or Panama; the short-lived Pony Express mail service; and finally, in 1861, the establishment of the transcontinental telegraph.

The Civil War (1861-1865), during which a steady flow of California gold and Comstock silver was essential to the Union campaign, increased national demand for a transcontinental railroad. In 1857 railroad construction engineer **Theodore D. Judah** (1826-1863) developed and published his plan for building a railroad through Dutch Flat and Donner Pass in the Sierra Nevada. Financiers Collis P. Huntington, Mark Hopkins, Leland Stanford *(p 140)* and Charles Crocker, whose subsequent wealth and power brought them the popular nickname of "the **Big Four**," signed on to Judah's plan and established the Central Pacific Railroad Company in 1861.

With the US Congress granting land for 20mi in either direction of the route and providing generous subsidies as high as $48,000 per mile for track laid in steep terrain, the **Central Pacific Railroad** began its eastward construction from Sacramento on January 8, 1863. As many as 15,000 low-paid Chinese laborers laid track in a frantic race to meet the westward-bound **Union Pacific Railroad**, eventually joining tracks at Promontory, Utah, on May 10, 1869, for the driving of the final Golden Spike linking East and West. Other railroads built in the decades that followed provided still stronger ties to the nation, including the Southern Pacific Railroad and the Santa Fe Railroad links between San Francisco, Los Angeles, Arizona, New Mexico and Colorado.

The Close of the 19C – While fostering growth, the railroads flooded California with laborers who faced unemployment once construction was completed. A nationwide depression and anti-foreign attitudes fostered acts of mob violence against Chinese immigrants in the 1870s, as well as Federal Chinese Exclusion Acts *(p 192)*. Racial tensions also found tragic outlet in 1872 and 1873 in the US Army's crushing of an uprising by the Modoc tribe *(p 78)*.
California continued to lure immigrants, sometimes trapping them in boom-and-bust land speculation cycles, as in Southern California in the 1880s. The 1875 depression led to the failure of many banks. Despite another panic in 1893, California faced the 20C with its economic output more than double that of a decade before.

THE TWENTIETH CENTURY

Population Booms – The beginning of the 20C found California with a population of almost 1.5 million people. During the decades that followed, the state grew almost twice as quickly as the rest of the nation, achieving a 1920 population of more than 3.4 million and reaching almost 10.6 million in 1950.
Much of this growth was fueled by the state's burgeoning industries, predominantly in Southern California. Improvements in agricultural techniques during the 1890s and the advent of cooperative marketing through the founding in 1905 of the California Fruit Growers Exchange boosted citrus growing. Oil drilling spread in the early years of the century across Los Angeles and neighboring counties, with production rising from 4.32 million barrels in 1900 to 105.72 million in 1920. Before World War I, the movie industry found year-round clement weather and a diversity of natural backdrops in and around the Los Angeles suburb of Hollywood *(p 101)*, transforming that sleepy burg into the self-proclaimed movie capital of the world. Fine weather and spectacular scenery also fueled a growing tourist industry statewide.
Two world wars boosted the aircraft and ship-building industries, fed the economies of towns near military bases and swelled the population further with service men and women who decided to make California their home after demobilizing. The population more than doubled from 6.9 million in 1940 to over 15.6 million in 1960, and by 1980 it had risen to more than 23.6 million.

Contemporary California – Such phenomenal growth has dramatically impacted many aspects of the state's history in the 20C. California's water supplies, for example, have been sorely stressed. Although the greatest percentage of the population and the most extensive agricultural activity are concentrated in Southern California, approximately 75 percent of the state's water flows from streams in the north. Schemes to divert water, such as the Central Valley and Owens River projects and the State Water Project *(p 16)*, have remained heated political issues throughout the century.
Spurred by a constant influx of new citizens, the state has become a hotbed for political action and change. In 1911 political reforms first introduced in 1903 were adopted statewide, giving Californians the right to exercise the **initiative**, whereby a petition signed by 8 percent of voters could place a proposed statute, ordinance or constitutional amendment on the ballot; the **referendum**, by which government measures could be put to a popular vote; and the **recall**, through which voters could remove an elected official from office. The passage of a gasoline tax in 1923 raised funds for the construction of a state highway system, literally paving the way for Californians' love affair with the automobile. In the fall of 1964, the **Free Speech Movement** on the campus of UC Berkeley established a say in political and social causes for students nationwide. From the early 1960s until his death in 1993, **Cesar Chavez** organized and fought for the rights of farm workers in California's agricultural regions. In June 1978, the Jarvis-Gann initiative, passed as **Proposition 13**, expressed the electorate's desire to curb state taxation of private individuals.

California's Future – Since the 1970s, California's population growth has tapered, and some surveys indicate that more people may now be leaving the state than settling here. Highlighted by the harsh spotlight of national and international media, the dream that drew so many to California has been declared to be shattered. Like so much of the rest of the US and the world, the state grapples with the economic, social and environmental plagues of the late 20C. The recession of the early 1990s and Federal spending cuts hurt the state's defense industry, contributing to massive unemployment and a severe economic downturn. In some areas, pollution fouls the air, lakes, rivers and coastal waters; acid rain threatens the Central Valley and the Sierra Nevada, and offshore oil spills, such as that which occurred in the Santa Barbara Channel in 1969, occasionally blacken the coastline. Rioting in Los Angeles and its suburbs following the first verdicts in the 1992 Rodney King civil rights trial placed severe social inequities in sharp relief. Immigration remains a sensitive topic as boat people arrive from Asia and Hispanics stream across the Mexican border. Even the state itself seems to be tearing apart politically, its elected officials debating the possibility of partitioning California into two or three separate and more easily governable bodies.
Nature can also be unpredictable. Statewide drought has led to strict water rationing. Acts of arson have scourged neighborhoods in Oakland (October 1992), Malibu (November 1993) and elsewhere, only to be followed by flooding and mudslides come the rainy season. Serious earthquakes such as those at Loma Prieta near San Francisco (October 1989) and the Los Angeles suburb of Northridge (January 1994) leave residents dreading the long-predicted "Big One" along the San Andreas Fault.
Responses to such challenges include the 1960 formation of the Motor Vehicle Pollution Control Board, charged with monitoring carbon monoxide emissions from automobiles; works by organizations such as the Sierra Club, TreePeople and Save the Whales, which fight to save the environment; and development of new construction techniques and building codes designed to increase resistance to fire and earthquakes. The decades-long discussions about partitioning the state promise to continue into the 21C, the lack of resolution perhaps acknowledging the fact that there could only ever be one California.

ARCHITECTURE

A benign Mediterranean climate, abundant natural building materials, waves of immigrants, and recurring collisions between romance and reality have all shaped California's architectural mosaic.

Native and Spanish Architecture – Little architectural evidence remains of the peoples who occupied California prior to the arrival of the Spanish, owing to the transitory nature of their constructions. The first of many imported building traditions arrived as the Spanish padres, soldiers and settlers, bent on colonizing Alta California, erected forts (presidios), farming communities (pueblos) and religious edifices (missions). Though Padre Junípero Serra *(p 22)* established nine missions prior to his death in 1784, it was a successor, Padre Fermín Lasuén, who developed the California mission style.

Based on Spanish and, more specifically, Mexican monastery prototypes, the California mission complex generally took the form of a large, rectangular garden courtyard surrounded by a narrow, adobe-walled church and arcaded structures containing padres' living quarters *(convento)*, barracks, workshops, infirmary, and housing for unmarried Indian women and young children. The church typically occupied the northeast corner of the courtyard; its signature element became its bell tower or *campanario*—a simple, high front wall with arched openings for bells. Outbuildings included more workshops and neophyte dwellings.

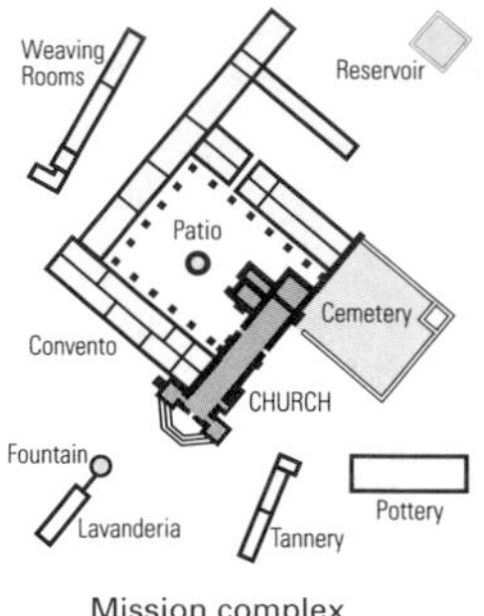

Mission complex

For their primary building material, the Franciscans turned to **adobe**, a plentiful local black clay. Adobe bricks were made by filling molds with a mixture of mud and straw, which was then sun-dried. Walls were several feet thick and narrowed toward the top. Overhanging tile roofs and lime plastering kept the bricks from deteriorating in wet weather. Inspiration for the details of design and ornamentation came from many sources, including Antiquity (SANTA BARBARA MISSION) and the Baroque and Moorish architecture of Spain (CARMEL MISSION). The missions' arcaded walkways and bell towers reappeared in many Mission Revival buildings of the late 19C-early 20C.

19C – California's Mexican settlers typically built rectangular, 1-story, adobe-walled structures with floors of packed earth and flat roofs covered in tar *(brea)*. Houses of the wealthy, such as the Casa Estudillo in San Diego and the Casa de la Guerra in SANTA BARBARA, opened to a courtyard along a covered porch or *corredor*.

Anglo architectural influences first appeared during the 1830s, with the 2-story, veranda-wrapped Larkin House in MONTEREY, which combined adobe and redwood frame construction with glazed, double-hung windows and fireplaces. The house's distinctive stacked balconies and shingle roof characterize the **Monterey Colonial** style.

The Gold Rush of 1849 *(p 60)* caused an abrupt shift from Hispanic to American architecture. Settlers arriving in the aftermath of the Great Westward Migration constructed wood-frame houses with materials and embellishments shipped from abroad or from the eastern US, including chimney bricks, mantelpieces and Gothic-Revival style ornamentation. Other pioneers shipped entire houses of pre-fabricated sheet metal or wood from faraway places like Boston, London and Canton.

As the century progressed into the Victorian era, wooden, balloon-frame construction for residences came into vogue, reaching a climax in distinctive rows of houses built from the 1870s through the 1890s in San Francisco and other cities of Northern California, where redwood lumber was readily available. Known popularly as **Victorians**, such houses displayed a hodgepodge of loosely defined and overlapping architectural styles and resulted from rapidly evolving industrial processes, tastes and merchandising techniques. Pattern-book and millwork catalogue publishers contributed to the rich stylistic soup preferred by an increasingly fashion-conscious middle class.

Victorians were built in a range of styles. The **Italianate** style, prevalent through the 1870s, employed flat-front or bay-windowed designs with relatively simple classical details like keystones. Such houses were essentially wooden versions of the brick or brownstone row houses popular in Eastern cities. A more skeletal, "stick-like" ornamental emphasis, considered a variant of the American Stick Style, appeared in the 1880s. In its time, it was known by various names, including **Eastlake**, after the English author and furniture designer Charles Eastlake. Increasing verticality and rectangularity, and a new vocabulary of machined, wood strip ornament that is often indistinguishable from furniture treatments were hallmarks. The so-called **Queen Anne** style produced some of California's most picturesque Victorian houses during the 1880s and 1890s, including the Carson Mansion in EUREKA. Irregular plans and elevations, towers and turrets, high chimneys, bulging bays, recessed balconies and gables of all sizes abounded.

20C – Beaux Arts Classicism came into vogue in California, as in the rest of the country, after it was popularized at the Chicago Fair of 1893, and reached its apogee in the San Francisco Civic Center *(p 199)*. With the arrival of steel frame construction, downtown commercial buildings—still clad in brick or stone for fireproofing—rose to ten stories or more. Hinting at technological possibilities to come were two precedent-shattering designs:

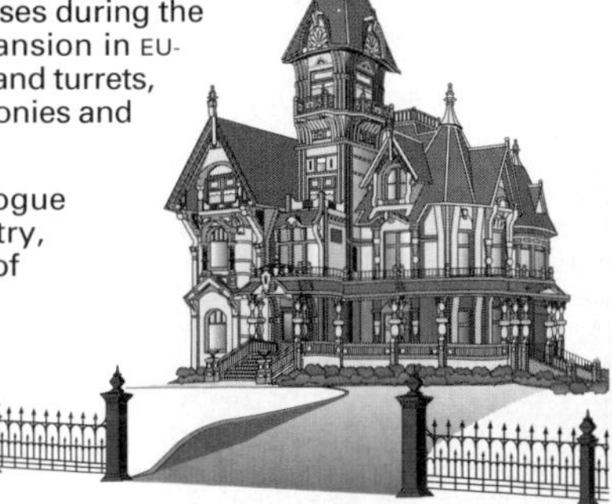
Carson Mansion

the glass-roofed atrium of George Wyman's Bradbury Building (1893) in Los Angeles *(p 92)*, and the glass "curtain wall" facade of Willis Polk's Hallidie Building (1917) in San Francisco.

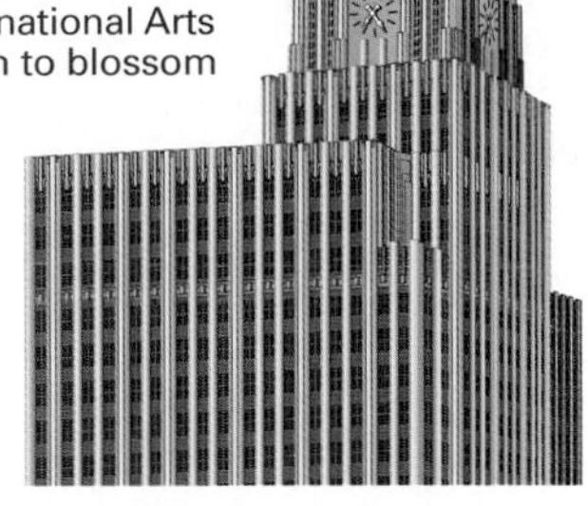

Eastern Columbia Building

By the turn of the century, the high ideals of the international Arts and Crafts Movement had migrated west and begun to blossom in the work of such local architects as Charles and Henry Greene and Bernard Maybeck. The Greenes' Japan-influenced emphasis on meticulous craftsmanship, structural expression, and the wedding of house and garden produced the landmark Gamble House in PASADENA, and spawned California's first architectural export: the **bungalow**. Countless variations of the California bungalow—a 1-story wood or stucco-sheathed house with a pergola or porch opening to a garden—were built from pattern books across the country during the first two decades of the century. A more radical, sculptural approach to house design arrived during the late 1910s, when Southern California's halcyon environment inspired preeminent US architect Frank Lloyd Wright to create some of his most inventive designs, including the Hollyhock House *(p 105)* in Los Angeles.

The early 1920s saw the rise of the **Spanish Colonial Revival** style, stimulated by enthusiastic public response to the unabashedly romantic, stage-set buildings of San Diego's 1915 Panama-California Exposition. There, New York architect Bertram Goodhue took his inspiration directly from the elaborately ornamented, domed, tiled and stucco-walled Spanish Colonial architecture of Mexico. After a severe earthquake in 1923, Santa Barbara embraced the fashion by rebuilding its major institutional structures along Spanish Colonial Revival lines.

Throughout the US in the late 1920s, an increasingly industrialized society set architects searching for ways to express modernity without historical reference. **Art Deco** or **Moderne**, with its elegant lines, shiny surfaces and highly stylized ornamentation, was eagerly adopted by the automobile and movie-industry culture of Southern California as a fitting expression of its glamorous image. Early Art Deco ornament generally followed cubistic or zig-zag patterns, as in Bullocks Wilshire department store *(p 99)* in Los Angeles, while later structures borrowed the concept of streamlining from the automobile and airplane industries.

Other approaches eliminated applied ornament, allowing the structure to express its function. This philosophy formed the basis for the **International Style**, which first appeared in California in the primarily residential work of such architects as Richard Neutra, who emigrated from Vienna in the 1920s, and Rudolph Schindler.

Taking the idea of architectural packaging to its logical conclusion were the many idiosyncratic vernacular roadside eateries that took the form of such unlikely objects as a zeppelin or a hat, the most renowned example being the Brown Derby restaurant in Los Angeles *(now demolished)*. Vernacular structures formed the basis of a type of architecture dubbed **California Crazy**, whose most recent incarnation is the binocular-shaped Chiat-Day-Mojo building (1991, Frank Gehry) in Venice.

B. Boehner

California Crazy

Post-World War II – California construction boomed prodigiously after the war, as aviation and other industries expanded and the incoming population reached a flood tide. The state functioned as a laboratory for experimentation in residential architecture, especially around Los Angeles and the San Francisco Bay Area, where architects perfected the modern, flowing, open-plan house. The subdivision **ranch house**, popularized by Los Angeles designer-developer Cliff May, became synonymous with California during the 1950s and early 1960s, and was rapidly adopted throughout the US. Descended from the California bungalow *(above)*, the often sprawling ranch house was long and low, with a two-car garage, and combined modern built-in appliances with a vague hint of Spanish California romance. Worlds apart esthetically, but sharing a common ancestry in California barn architecture, is the shed-roofed condominium complex at Sea Ranch *(p 129)*, designed in 1965 by Charles Moore and his associates. Sea Ranch's particular quality of blending with its surroundings spawned a new style that was adopted for beach and resort construction throughout the US.

Recent Trends – The downtown areas of Los Angeles, San Diego and San Francisco have been remade several times since the 1950s, sprouting ever-taller buildings in a wide variety of styles, from corporate International Style through post-Modern and beyond. Renowned Los Angeles-based architect Frank Gehry expresses California's experimental nature in his work both at home and abroad, using ordinary materials like plywood or chain link fencing in innovative and often sculptural ways. World-renowned architects who have left their marks on the state include Louis Kahn (the Salk Institute in LA JOLLA); Michael Graves (Clos Pegase winery in the WINE COUNTRY, Disney Studios Headquarters in BURBANK); Cesar Pelli (the Pacific Design Center in Los Angeles); and Philip Johnson (101 California Street in San Francisco). More recently, an international team of architects led by Fumihiko Maki has designed San Francisco's new art and park complex at Yerba Buena Gardens, and celebrated architect Richard Meier's new complex for the J. Paul Getty Museum *(p 115)* is slated to open before the turn of the century.

ARTS

California's legendary light, landscape and climate, along with influences of myriad indigenous and immigrant cultures, have contributed to unique and vital developments in visual art produced in the state, giving rise to its growing reputation as an international art capital.

Native and Hispanic Art – Diverse and distinct Native American cultures flourished in California for more than 7,000 years prior to the arrival of Europeans. Pictographs by early cultures remain at LAVA BEDS NATIONAL MONUMENT and Chumash Painted Cave near SANTA BARBARA, while featherwork regalia and elaborately patterned basketry flourished throughout California.

Spanish Colonial arts were introduced into the region by the padres of the mission chain established after 1769. The wall and ceiling murals of churches at SAN JUAN BAUTISTA MISSION and SAN MIGUEL ARCÁNGEL MISSION reveal a mingling of indigenous motifs and symbolism with neoclassical, Spanish Colonial aesthetic traditions; the blend is also evident in paintings, silverwork, church implements, textiles and furnishings of the period.

19C Influences – The influx of people and wealth that ensued in the wake of the Gold Rush set the stage for the presence of imported art in California. The vast fortunes of railroad magnates and other "bonanza kings" gave rise to important private collections (including the Huntington Art Collections in PASADENA and the Crocker Art Museum in SACRAMENTO) and introduced art from Europe and the eastern US, enabling Impressionism, eclecticism and genre painting to influence art in the state. Late-19C artists, including painter Albert Bierstadt and photographer Carleton Watkins, were drawn to California and inspired by the state's magnificent vistas to create heroic landscapes that gave many people living in the East their first look at the wonders of California. A growing public interest in art was fueled during the last quarter of the century by the founding of the California School of Fine Arts (today known as the San Francisco Art Institute, *p 197*); the M.H. de Young Museum *(p 201)*; and the Southwest Museum *(p 93)*.

Early 20C – Early in the century, art colonies were formed in CARMEL, LA JOLLA, LONG BEACH and other picturesque coastal communities. California Impressionists and painters of the **Plein-air movement**, including Franz Bischoff, and later Oakland's Society of Six, created sparkling landscapes inspired by the region's unique light and natural features. With the growth of Los Angeles in the late 1910s and the burgeoning of the entertainment industry, Southern California art embraced a more modern and abstract profile, perhaps most notably in the work of Stanton Macdonald-Wright, who adapted Cubist forms to create a style which he dubbed Synchromist. Noted primitive and modern art collector Walter Arensberg was at the center of a growing art community that included ceramist Beatrice Wood. During the 1930s, abstraction, surrealism and social realism characterized the works of painters and muralists. Mexican painter Diego Rivera completed several murals in SAN FRANCISCO, and Orozco and Siqueiros each painted murals in LOS ANGELES. These works inspired the realism of the WPA murals *(p 197)* as well as the murals of California's contemporary barrios and urban communities.

During the early part of the century, California's dramatic natural landscapes attracted such sharp-focus photographers as Edward Weston and Ansel Adams, who is particularly noted for his transcending portrayals of YOSEMITE NATIONAL PARK. Other photographers, among them Dorothea Lange and Imogen Cunningham, documented California's inhabitants.

Post World War II – As the mid-20C approached, San Francisco Art Institute visiting faculty members Clyfford Still and Mark Rothko inspired an explosion of abstract painting by their students, who included Sam Francis and Robert Motherwell. In response, such painters as Elmer Bischoff, Richard Diebenkorn and David Park created a painterly representational movement known as **Bay Area Figuration**. The impact of the popular culture inspired 1960s "Pop" artists and photorealists (Ed Ruscha, Wayne Thiebaud, Robert Bechtle), followed by a wave of conceptualism (Bruce Nauman, William T. Wiley).

In Southern California during the postwar period, several art museums, including the Los Angeles County Museum of Art *(p 100)*, expanded significantly. Los Angeles painters explored hard-edged abstraction (John McLaughlin, Lorser Feitelson), influencing a "finish fetish" focus on surface and light evident in the perceptualist works of Robert Irwin and James Turrel. An influential art scene developed in the 1950s around the Ferus Gallery, launching the careers of Edward Kienholz and Ed Moses. Subsequent decades brought several new museums and galleries to the Los Angeles area, including the J. Paul Getty Museum *(p 115)*, the Armand Hammer Museum *(p 108)* and the Museum of Contemporary Art *(p 91)*, which have made that city an important international art center. Noted artists working in the area, including David Hockney, Jonathan Borofsky and Guillermo Gómez-Peña, helped focus artworld attention on Southern California.

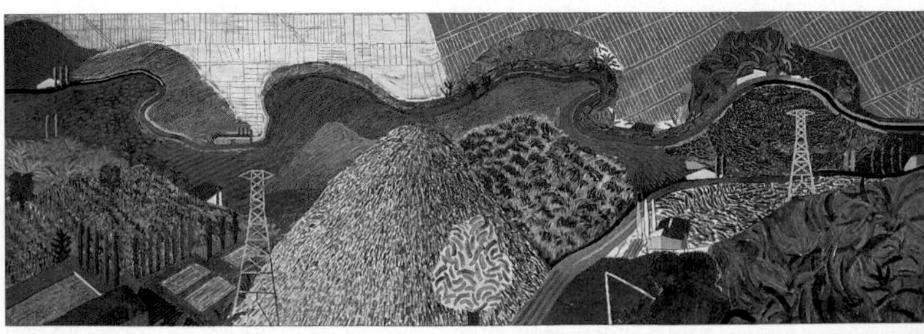

Mulholland Drive: The Road to the Studio (1980)
by David Hockney

California's contemporary art scene is defined by its pluralism and eclecticism. Multicultural arts centers such as San Francisco's Yerba Buena Gardens, and spaces for large installations, among them the Santa Monica Museum of Art, have appeared in the last several years. Performance artists such as Chris Burden continue to expand current conceptions of art, and innovative work can be seen at such venues as the Sushi Gallery in SAN DIEGO and Highways in SANTA MONICA, or at numerous new spaces in San Francisco's South of Market district.

Performing Arts – The state continues to be a recognized source of pop music, a trend which began in the 1960s with the hit songs of such groups as the Beach Boys and the Mamas and the Papas. Classical music enjoys an avid following statewide, satisfied primarily by the regular performance schedules of high-caliber orchestras in Los Angeles and San Francisco; other orchestras thrive in the smaller cities. The Los Angeles Music Center Opera, the San Francisco Opera and the San Diego Opera mount major performance seasons, and the San Francisco Ballet maintains a resident dance company.
Drawn by a creative, sunny environment as well as by Hollywood's siren song, many actors and writers practice their art and craft on the California's stages, creating a thriving theater scene. Nationally recognized repertory programs of classics and original works are presented in San Francisco, Los Angeles, Pasadena, Berkeley, La Jolla and San Diego.

LITERATURE

Early Voices – No Native California tribes practiced writing; but many passed rich legacies of oral myths down through the generations, to be recorded by 19C and 20C historians and anthropologists, notably Alfred L. Kroeber, author of the *Handbook of the Indians of California* (1925). Vivid impressions of the Natives and their lands may also be found in diaries kept by 18C explorers, among them Padre Juan Crespí's journal of the Sacred Expedition of 1769 *(p 81)* and Padre Francisco Garcés' memoir of a trek through the Mojave Desert and Tehachapi Mountains in 1776.
English-language accounts of travel and life in Hispanic California form the state's earliest indigenous literature; most notable is *Two Years Before the Mast* (1840s) by Richard Henry Dana, describing life at sea along the California coast. The Gold Rush fueled an increase in publishing, spurring the rapid growth of the state's first two newspapers: *The Californian*, launched in 1846, and the *California Star*, first published in 1848 by Sam Brannan *(p 38)*. Several literary journals appeared at the same time, including the *Golden Era* (1852), which published early works by Bret Harte, **Mark Twain** (1835-1910), and poets Joaquin Miller and Charles Warren Stoddard. These and others gained national and international reputations describing the rough-and-ready life of mid to late-19C California. In short stories such as "The Luck of Roaring Camp" and "The Outcasts of Poker Flat," Harte sharply etched a larger-than-life picture of Gold Rush country in readers' minds. Twain, who sojourned in SAN FRANCISCO and the GOLD COUNTRY in the early 1860s, published sketches of the region in *The Overland Monthly* and included vivid descriptions of the state in his books *Roughing It* and *Innocents Abroad*, as well as in his famous yarn "The Celebrated Jumping Frog of Calaveras County."
Among many others who memorably chronicled the state were San Francisco journalist and short-story writer Ambrose Bierce, naturalist John Muir *(p 241)* and Scottish writer **Robert Louis Stevenson** *(p 238)*, who lived briefly in the Napa Valley. In Southern California, Helen Hunt Jackson wrote the phenomenally popular *Ramona* (1884), romanticizing life in the mission era.

20C – The social consciousness that pervaded early-20C American literature found voice in many California writers, including novelist Frank Norris and poet Edwin Markham. Oakland native **Jack London** (1876-1916) wrote more than two dozen highly personal adventure novels espousing his socialist ideals *(p 239)*. Pasadena-based novelist Upton Sinclair (1878-1968) campaigned against social inequities in some 90 published works. Novels and short stories by **John Steinbeck** (1902-1968), who in 1962 became California's only Nobel Prize winner for literature *(p 160)*, wrote compassionately of the working people of the Central Valley and Monterey in such works as *Tortilla Flat* (1935), *Of Mice and Men* (1937) and *The Grapes of Wrath* (1939). The dark side of Hollywood's dream factories was probed by screenwriter Nathaniel West (1903-1940) in his apocalyptic novel *The Day of the Locust* (1939), while Raymond Chandler (1888-1959) departed from traditional detective fiction with four novels featuring hardboiled Los Angeles private eye Philip Marlowe.
Award-winning Fresno-born **William Saroyan** (1908-1981) bestowed everyday life and ordinary people with magical beauty in his many novels, short stories and plays. Poet Robinson Jeffers (1887-1962) celebrated CARMEL and its surroundings, underscoring mankind's insignificance within nature's greater scheme. Prolific novelist and historian Wallace Stegner (1909-1993) evoked the power of the American West, winning a Pulitzer Prize for *Angle of Repose* (1971).
Disaffection with American society following World War II found expression among a group of San Francisco writers and other artists self-described as the "Beat Generation," *(p 197)* possessing, in the words of novelist **Jack Kerouac** (1922-1969) "an inner knowledge . . . a kind of 'beatness.' " The passionate beat voice was perhaps best captured in the works of such poets as Lawrence Ferlinghetti (b. 1919) and Allen Ginsberg (b. 1926), which challenged and often met with the disapproval of mainstream society.
Today, a new generation of writers runs the gamut of subjects and styles, from best-selling novels by Maxine Hong Kingston (b. 1940) and Amy Tan (b. 1952) that forge epic ties between California and Asia to quirky tales of life in Los Angeles by San Fernando Valley-based novelist T. Coraghessan Boyle (b. 1948), emotionally charged poetry and prose by African-American writer Wanda Coleman (b. 1946) to the innovative, nationally acclaimed verse of Fresno-born Chicano poet Gary Soto (b. 1952). Newer California writers find voice in serious and experimental literary magazines and journals, including Berkeley's *The Threepenny Review* and San Francisco's *Zyzzyva*.

FOOD AND WINE

Distinguished California food essayist M.F.K. Fisher described her native state's approach to eating as "an agreeable tolerance of all that is good," summing up the regional cuisine's dedication to freshness and quality and its warmhearted acceptance of myriad ethnic traditions. Without traveling more than a few miles in most cities or good-sized towns, California residents and visitors can readily sample cuisines from around the world. The state's Mexican, Italian, Chinese, Japanese and Thai restaurants show particular distinction.

California Cuisine – As a direct result of such global influences, so-called California cuisine combines a potpourri of American, French, Asian and Latino culinary styles. Alice Waters, founder of the acclaimed Chez Panisse restaurant in BERKELEY, is generally acknowledged to be the cuisine's founder, and Michael McCarty further popularized it in Southern California at his Michael's restaurant in the Los Angeles coastal community of SANTA MONICA. The appellation appears today on hundreds, if not thousands of menus throughout the state.

California cuisine is distinguished by a reliance on outstanding local ingredients, including seafood from the Pacific; vegetables, fruits and poultry from the San Joaquin Valley and other regions; and countless items from small, specialist producers of gourmet quality ingredients ranging from fresh goat cheeses to organically raised lamb, from rare species of banana to bite-size baby vegetables.

Such foods are generally prepared quickly and simply, their presentation on the plate as beautiful as a still-life painting. Main-course meats and seafood are most likely to be grilled over the hot coals of a barbecue, a method well suited to the state's outdoor lifestyle; in recent years, many cooks have opted to cook over mesquite wood, which yields a searing and fragrant heat, or over other scented woods. Salads, often meals in themselves, display an extravagance of locally grown produce, sometimes garnished with meat, poultry or seafood; they are also often graced with California **avocado**, an ingredient so common that it once enjoyed the nickname "Indian butter." Avocado also appears frequently in sandwiches and mashed with lemon or lime juice and chilies to make the popular Mexican dip guacamole.

Desserts in this health-conscious state tend to be such light but flavorful offerings as fresh fruit salads or sorbets; but the state's chefs also take pride in creating riches to tempt the most unrepentant sweet tooth or chocolate addiction.

World-Class Wines – As fresh-tasting and flavorful as its native foods and regional cuisine, California's own wines are a natural companion to any meal eaten in the state. In recent decades, they have also won the state's wine industry worldwide acclaim for their quality *(p 234)*.

Along with fertile earth, wine grapes need a long growing season of hot days and cool nights, which several regions in California provide abundantly *(map p 18)*. While Napa and Sonoma counties, together known as the WINE COUNTRY, are the premiere winemaking region, they produce only five percent of California wines. Excellent vintages also come from Mendocino County, northwest of the Wine Country; the Livermore Valley east of SAN FRANCISCO; the MONTEREY area; the Santa Ynez Valley inland from SANTA BARBARA; and the Temecula Valley in Riverside County, north of SAN DIEGO.

California's current wine production is based primarily on descendants of *Vitis vinifera* cuttings introduced in the 19C *(p 233)*; the strains have been tested and adapted over subsequent generations, with tremendous strides in the science of agriculture and vinification made in this century by the Department of Enology at the University of California, Davis. Best adapted to California growing conditions is the Cabernet Sauvignon, a small, blue-black grape from the Médoc district of France's Bordeaux region that produces a rich, full red wine. The Burgundy region's Pinot Noir grape is used primarily in the making of California sparkling wine. Other red wine grapes from Europe include the Cabernet Franc, Petite-Sirah and the Napa Gamay (derived from France's Gamay Beaujolais).

Some of California's finest white wines are made from the Chardonnay, premier white grape of France's Chablis and Burgundy regions. Chardonnay produces a richly flavored, fruity, dry wine, further characterized by the taste of the oak barrels in which it is often aged. The Sauvignon Blanc, used in the making of French Sauternes and Pouilly-Fumé, is a lighter-tasting grape that grows well in cooler areas. The Pinot Blanc, of the same family as Burgundy's Pinot Noir, is an important ingredient in many sparkling wines. Other white European varieties include Riesling and Chenin Blanc.

FURTHER READING

A Companion to California edited by James D. Hart *(University of California Press, 1987)*

A Natural History of California by Allan A. Schoenherr *(University of California Press, 1992)*

California Architecture: Historic American Buildings Survey by Sally B. Woodbridge *(Chronicle Books, 1988)*

The Missions of California by Melba Levick and Stanley Young *(Chronicle Books, 1988)*

Two Years Before the Mast by Richard Henry Dana (1840)

The Grapes of Wrath by John Steinbeck (1939)

The Silverado Squatters by Robert Louis Stevenson (1883)

The Celebrated Jumping Frog of Calaveras County by Mark Twain (1867)

Sierra Club Books (series): 17 titles about California

Story Behind the Scenery Books (series): 9 titles about California

CALIFORNIANS

If the US as a whole has been described as a great melting pot, California resembles nothing so much as an enormous stew in which peoples of vastly diverse ethnic, racial and cultural backgrounds live side by side, retaining their distinctive characters. The state's 31.5 million inhabitants (as of January 1993) come from a wide variety of backgrounds, with Caucasians making up less than two-thirds of the population, Asians or Pacific peoples more than 9 percent, and African Americans more than 7 percent; over 25 percent of Californians are Latinos of various races.

This diversity is not consistent statewide. A much higher percentage of Latinos live in Southern California, for example, reflecting that region's closer ties to Mexico and Central America; larger Asian enclaves may be found to the north, particularly in the San Francisco Bay Area. Throughout the state are found tight-knit communities that steadfastly maintain the lifestyles of different lands, from the Laotian population of FRESNO, to the Basques of Bakersfield, to San Francisco's world-renowned Chinatown *(p 192)*. The great metropolitan centers of LOS ANGELES, SAN FRANCISCO and SAN DIEGO possess far greater ethnic diversity, attracting steady streams of hopeful immigrants from across the nation and around the world; while smaller towns and rural areas can seem almost Midwestern in their homogeneity.

Opportunity Seekers – Diverse though they are, Californians have always been drawn by the state's reputation as a land of opportunity, a place to wipe one's slate clean and start anew. Inaccessible and distant, the territory attracted a slow trickle of Easterners during the early years of the Great Westward Migration in the early 19C. That trickle grew to a flood following the Gold Rush; after gold fever died down, the transcontinental railroads completed in the 1860s continued to channel a steady stream of settlers seeking new lives in a beneficent climate amidst magnificent scenery. Land booms, agriculture, the aircraft and defense industries, Hollywood, the Silicon Valley electronics boom: many and seemingly (until recent years) endless opportunities have drawn people to California, and that draw remains strong, even as the state and its industries suffer severely through the recession of the 1990s.

Opposites and Extremes – California's pioneers seized the chance to forge a new kind of society in which independence, resourcefulness and a willingness to accept people in all their diversity were qualities prized above all. English author Rudyard Kipling described the typical Californian of the 1880s as someone who "is devoid of fear, carries himself like a man, and has a heart as big as his boots." Over the course of another century, that big-hearted and tolerant spirit has attracted more settlers still, as people of all persuasions have found acceptance in California's vastness.

That diversity and tolerance may dazzle or disorient outsiders or newcomers first confronted by bikini-clad rollerbladers on Venice Beach's Oceanfront Walk or Gay Pride paraders on the streets of San Francisco. Personal freedom is prized in California. And visitors who assume that freedom translates solely as liberalism should bear in mind that California is the birthplace not only of the Free Speech Movement but also of Orange County's ultra-right-wing John Birch Society; that Californians elected as governor not only New Age Democrat Jerry Brown but also conservative Ronald Reagan.

Diversity in California takes many forms. Though the state's mythic reputation seems merely myth amid the crushing poverty of South Central Los Angeles or in the simple, rural communities of the Central Valley, the myth nonetheless springs fully to life along the legendary beaches, in the chic boutiques of Beverly Hills, on the slopes surrounding Lake Tahoe, or in the vineyards and tasting rooms of the Wine Country. Politically, culturally, and socially, California is a land—and Californians a people—of opposites and extremes, at once steadfastly resisting and irresistibly inviting definition.

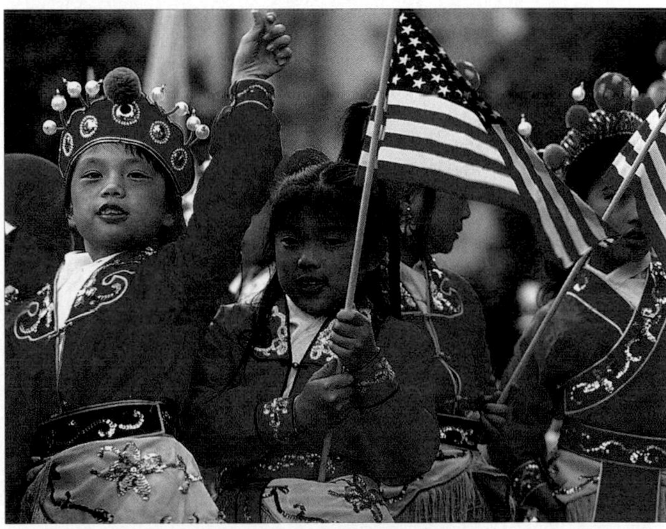

Golden Dragon Parade in Los Angeles

M. Kazmers/Dembinsky Photo Assoc.

Sights

★★ ANZA-BORREGO DESERT STATE PARK San Diego County

Map of Principal Sights p 5

Situated in the eastern region of San Diego County, this 6,000-acre state park encompasses rocky mountains, intricately carved badlands, canyons concealing shady palm groves, and relics of historic transportation routes. The park is named for the Spanish military explorer who traversed the region in 1774, and for the elusive "borregos" or bighorn sheep *(Ovis canadensis)* that roam here.

From Savanna to Desert – The Peninsular Ranges to the west began uplifting some 5 million years ago, and their rise continues today, faster than weathering and erosion can wear them down. The upheaval has broken, stretched and twisted the earth's surface into the rugged surface we see today. As the rising mountains impeded, then cut off the flow of moisture from the Pacific Ocean, the subtropical savanna vegetation gave way to hardier plants adapted for desert survival. The water-loving California fan palms that formerly flourished widely are now found only in canyons, where runoff and ground water are available to their roots.

Rock art and mortar holes found within the park attest to the presence of the Native Kumeyaay here. The hunter-gatherer people's way of life was disrupted in the late 18C and early 19C when Spanish, and later Yankee and European settlers established migrant trails through the region. In 1776, Borrego Valley became part of the **Anza Trail**, the principal overland route connecting Spain's California settlements with Mexico. Pioneered by Juan Bautista de Anza in 1774, the route was abandoned by the Spanish in 1781 in favor of sea routes, owing to Native uprisings near the Colorado River. In 1846, during the Mexican War, the Mormon Battalion laid out an east-west trail and thousands of gold seekers followed in their footsteps on what became known as the **Southern Emigrant Trail**, a route that followed a series of meadows and watering points through the mountains, far to the south of a more direct route from the East, thus reducing the difficulties of crossing the open desert between the Colorado River and the Pacific Ocean. The Butterfield Overland Mail, the first regular overland postal connection between California and eastern states, adopted this route for four years just before the Civil War. When the eastern part of the trail came under Confederate control during the war, operations were shifted north to a route through central Nevada.

The park, originally named Borrego Palms Desert State Park, was created in 1933, largely through federal grants and donation of lands purchased by local benefactors. Acquisitions and administrative changes expanded it to its present size, and today it ranks as the largest state park in the 48 contiguous states.

Visiting Anza-Borrego – *Open daily year-round.* ⚠ ♿ ☎619-767-5311. Anza-Borrego Desert State Park is located approximately 80mi northeast of SAN DIEGO via I-15 and Highway 78. Privately owned lands lie within the park boundaries; the town of Borrego Springs (pop 2,244) offers a full range of amenities. We recommend beginning the visit with a stop at the **visitor center** *(1.5mi west of traffic circle on Palm Canyon Dr in Borrego Springs; open daily Oct–May, rest of the year weekends only;* ♿*).* The numerous trail guides and tour pamphlets available here greatly enhance a visit to the park. Nestled beneath rocks and vegetation, the attractive stone structure also houses a natural history museum, park information desk, bookstore and slide show *(15min).*

Although many of the park's main attractions can be visited by car, several areas are accessible only by 4-wheel drive vehicle.

VISIT *At least 1 day*

★ **Borrego Palm Canyon** – *3mi round-trip. Trailhead in campground about 2mi north of visitor center. Brochure recommended.* The most popular of Anza-Borrego's 25 palm groves is accessible by a moderately difficult nature trail that ascends an alluvial fan *(p 46)*, and rounds a corner to reveal the green oasis of fan palms in the mouth of the canyon ahead. Palm Canyon Creek creates a waterfall and pool in the shade of the oasis and commonly flows as late as spring.

★ **Erosion Road Auto Tour** – *14mi along Hwy S22 east of Borrego Springs; begin at milepost 22.* Highway S22, one of the park's main roads, traverses the rolling plains at the foot of the Santa Rosa Mountains; ten marked points along the way identify landscape evidence of geologic forces that formed and continue to shape the area. Near the base of the Santa Rosa Range is the San Jacinto Fault, the most active in California; mountains here are uplifting rapidly, some 4in per 100 years. At mile 32.6, recent fault movement is indicated by the low range of hills on the north side of the road. At mile 29.3, a sandy side road *(4-wheel drive vehicle strongly recommended)* leads 4mi to Font's Point, from which a panoramic **view**★★ extends over the Borrego Badlands.

Split Mountain Road – *Drive east on Hwy 78 past eastern boundary of park to crossroads settlement of Ocotillo Wells, then south on Split Mountain Rd.* South of Ocotillo Wells *(5.8mi)*, a gravel road leads to the Elephant Trees Nature Trail. Named for the skin-like appearance of their outer trunks, elephant trees *(Bursera microphylla)* were used by area's Native inhabitants for medicinal purposes. The trees were thought by non-Native botanists to be extinct until they were discovered growing here in 1937. Highlighting many other desert plants, the trail offers a chance to experience the low desert flora in a relatively isolated setting.

Continuing south *(.9mi)*, Split Mountain Road crosses the dry wash of Fish Creek. A right turn leads up the wash into the Anza-Borrego backcountry *(4-wheel drive vehicle required).* Some 3.6mi further, a remarkable anticlinal fold structure can be seen in the west wall of the canyon. At mile 4.1, a foot trail *(.5mi)* leads uphill to **Wind Caves**, an outcrop of sandstone conglomerate eroded into a bizarre, miniature landscape of deep hollows, pockets and natural bridges.

Narrows Earth Trail – *.5mi loop. Trailhead 12.2mi south of Borrego Springs on Hwy S3, 4.7mi east on Hwy 78.* A short trail through a small canyon reveals several types of rock formed by various geologic processes. Numbered posts offer explanations of large- and small-scale geologic forces present in the area, including faulting and erosion.

Southern Portion – *Proceed south on Hwy 78 from its intersection with Hwy S3; at Scissors Crossing, turn left onto Hwy S2.* This stretch of Highway S2 roughly follows the path of the Southern Emigrant Trail *(p 34)*; in some places, the ruts left by thousands of trudging feet, clopping hooves and creaking wheels are still plainly visible. At **Foot & Walker Pass** *(mile 22.9)*, stagecoach passengers often had to alight and push the vehicle over the steep terrain. A monument overlooking the narrow valley of Vallecito Wash at **Box Canyon** *(mile 25.7)* points out the trails made by the Mormon Battalion and the Butterfield stagecoach; both trails are easily accessible on foot from this point.

Vallecito Stage Station – *Mile 34.8.* A major stop on the Butterfield stage route, the station was an oasis for passengers, drivers and horses alike. The original adobe buildings disintegrated from disuse, and the present building is a replica constructed in 1934.

Located in the southeastern portion of the park, the **Carrizo Badlands Overlook** *(mile 52.7)* offers a splendid **panorama**★ of jagged ridges; the vast field of eroded sediments is all that remains of a lush grassland that 1 million years ago supported saber-toothed tigers, mastodons and camels.

C. Curran

Spring bloom in Anza-Borrego

BAKERSFIELD Central Valley — Pop 174,820

Map of Principal Sights p 4 Tourist Office ☎805-325-5051

Sprawling, rambunctious Bakersfield was founded in the 1860s when discovery of gold in the bed of the Kern River brought an influx of settlers to the area. Irrigation from canal projects on the Kern River and the development of engines to pump underground water led to rapid agricultural development in the late 19C, with cotton becoming an especially important crop in the mid-1920s. In the early 20C, petroleum production boomed in Kern County, and machines continue to pump at a large oil field on the northern edge of the city. Since the 1950s, Bakersfield has enjoyed a reputation as California's capital of country and western music.

SIGHT *2hrs*

★ **Kern County Museum and Pioneer Village** – *3801 Chester Ave, about 1mi north of downtown. Open daily year-round. Closed Jan 1, Thanksgiving Day, Dec 24, 25, 31. $5. ☎805-561-2132.* A substantial collection of artifacts and a 15-acre assemblage of historic structures offer an excellent depiction of life in Kern County from the 1860s to the 1930s. Stop in the main museum building to view exhibits that change periodically, before proceeding to the outdoor display of more than 50 buildings either moved here for preservation from their original locations in Kern County, or reconstructed from photographs. Some of the more unusual structures include a sheepherder's cabin, a ranch chuck wagon and an 1891 Victorian home. Particularly noteworthy is a large collection of oil-drilling equipment, featuring an early 20C wooden oil derrick; and an exhibition hall devoted to the technology of oil exploration and extraction.

★ BERKELEY San Francisco Bay Area — Pop 102,724

Map p 36 Tourist Office ☎510-549-7040

This dynamic university city has an unending appetite for political activism, energetic intellectualism and cultural diversity. Spreading up into the Berkeley Hills, the town also boasts beautiful old neighborhoods with stunning views to the west of SAN FRANCISCO and its bay.

From Cow Town to "Cal" Town – Like OAKLAND, the site of present-day Berkeley served as pasture land for MISSION DOLORES before becoming part of Luís María Peralta's Rancho San Antonio *(p 131)* in the 1820s. Berkeley remained an unnamed rural area with only one real town, Ocean View, until the establishment of the university here in the 1860s. In 1866 the fledgling community was named for English bishop and philosopher George Berkeley, author of the oft-quoted line, "Westward the course of empire takes its way." For the next four decades the town grew up steadily around "Cal," as the university is called, and in 1906 the San Francisco earthquake brought a tidal wave of exurbanites, who poured out of the devastated city and settled permanently in the East Bay.

Throughout the 20C, Berkeley has enjoyed the reputation of a well-planned university town, home to academics and intellectuals. Gracious old residences surround the campus and climb into the Berkeley Hills. Commercial arteries radiating from the university, particularly **Telegraph, College** and **University Avenues,** offer a plethora of curio and craft shops, bookstores, cafes and restaurants. The immense variety of fine restaurants and eateries in Berkeley, including California cuisine originator Alice Waters' renowned Chez Panisse, has earned the city the moniker "Gourmet Ghetto."

★★ UNIVERSITY OF CALIFORNIA, BERKELEY

The first, and still the most prestigious campus of California's acclaimed university system, the Berkeley campus is memorable for its luxuriant grounds, varied architecture, noteworthy museums and atmosphere of liberalism and social awareness. The university owes its creation to scholars from the eastern US, who arrived in California in the mid-19C and established the Christian, non-sectarian College of California in Oakland. In 1860, finding Oakland's lusty boomtown atmosphere inauspicious, they dedicated a new college site on the bucolic banks of Strawberry Creek east of Ocean View, and several years later hired acclaimed landscape architect Frederick Law Olmsted to design the campus. Lack of funds prevented the realization of Olmsted's plan, however, and in 1868, the college's trustees turned the institution over to the state. Renamed the University of California, it welcomed its first students to North and South halls, in the lush Berkeley Hills, in 1873.

At the turn of the century, noted philanthropist and university regent **Phoebe Apperson Hearst**, mother of William Randolph Hearst *(p 66)*, helped finance a campus expansion, "with landscape gardening and architecture forming one composition." Supported by Hearst monies and state funds, architects John Galen Howard, Bernard Maybeck and Julia Morgan *(p 67)* rapidly added new structures to the university campus as its prestige as an academic center grew.

The 1960s anti-war and civil rights movements catapulted Berkeley into the national spotlight as a center of student activism. Today, Cal continues to attract a politically active and ethnically diverse student body, now numbering some 30,000. The university is recognized as one of the nation's leading institutions of higher education: among its 1,400 faculty members are 15 Nobel laureates and 21 winners of the National Medal of Science. Its professors and graduate students regularly garner prestigious academic prizes and research grants, and the school is the nation's leading granter of PhDs. Cuts in state funding and the seismic retrofitting of university buildings have both left their marks on campus life, but Berkeley remains on the cutting edge of social thinking and academic research.

Visit *3hrs*

BART: Berkeley. Visitor information and campus maps available at the information center in the Student Union (Bancroft Way and Telegraph Ave) and the visitor center (101 University Hall, 2200 University Ave). Guided tours of the campus (1hr 30min) year-round Mon, Wed, Fri. Closed major holidays. ♿. ☎510-642-4636.

Though the campus totals 1,232 acres and stretches high into the Berkeley Hills, the developed core of the university lies in the 178 acres situated along the north and south forks of picturesque Strawberry Creek. The campus is notable for its fine oak, bay, eucalyptus, pine and cedar trees. **Sather Gate** (1910), a filigreed wrought-iron and stone portal designed by John Galen Howard, fronts **Sproul Plaza**, a main gathering area for students.

★ **Sather Tower** – *Open daily year-round. Access to top of Tower $.50. ☎510-642-5215.* Berkeley's landmark "Campanile" (1914), also the work of John Galen Howard, is modeled after the bell tower in St Mark's Square, Venice. A memorial to university benefactor Jane K. Sather, the 307ft tower houses 61 bells that chime throughout the day. The panoramic **view** from the observation platform encompasses the hills, the campus and San Francisco Bay.

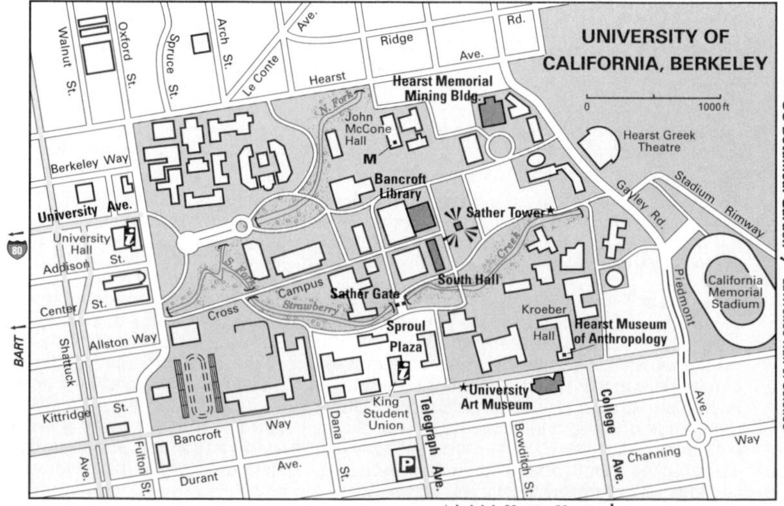

Below the tower's southwest face sits **South Hall** (1873), a stately Second Empire structure that is the oldest building on campus. A small hall in the **Bancroft Library** features changing exhibits from the renowned collection of early California manuscripts and artifacts; the acorn-size **gold nugget** that began the 1849 Gold Rush is also displayed in an office here *(open year-round Mon–Sat; closed major holidays; ♿ ☎510-642-6481)*. The 1907 Beaux-Arts **Hearst Memorial Mining Building**, another work by Howard, is notable for its ornate, skylit main hall. The **Museum of Paleontology [M]** consists of fossil exhibits—including the 100 million-year-old **skull** of a Triceratops—scattered through the lower two floors of John McCone Hall *(open Sep–May daily, rest of the year Mon–Fri; closed major holidays; ♿ ☎510-642-1821)*.

Hearst Museum of Anthropology – *103 Kroeber Hall, Bancroft Way & College Ave. Open daily year-round. Closed major & university holidays. $2. ♿ 🅿 ☎510-643-7648.* This institution boasts a permanent **collection★** of some 4 million artifacts from throughout the world, that ranks the Hearst among the country's most significant research museums of anthropology. Changing exhibits from the collection of artifacts from pre-dynastic and early dynastic Egypt, ancient Peru and Native California supplement a permanent display of tools made by **Ishi**, the last survivor of the Stone Age culture Yahi people. Ishi was discovered in 1911 in the Central Valley town of Oroville and worked with Berkeley anthropologists until his death in 1916.

★ **University Art Museum** – *2626 Bancroft Way. Open year-round Wed–Sun. Closed major holidays. $5. ✗ ♿ ☎510-642-0808.* Housed in a dramatic, semicircular structure (1970), Berkeley's art museum was born in the mid-1960s when painter and professor **Hans Hofmann** (1880-1966) donated 50 of his works and $250,000 to the university on condition that they be used to found an art museum. The expanding permanent collections are displayed in ten cantilevered exhibit "terraces" that allow visitors to view works of art from various vantage points.

The museum is also a noted showplace for traveling exhibits of international caliber and special exhibits *(galleries 1, 2, 3 & B)*. Works from the 7,000-piece permanent collection focus on 20C American art *(galleries 4, 5 & 6)*, while selections of Hofmann's works are displayed on a rotating basis *(gallery A)*. The museum also maintains an extensive Asian collection *(galleries C & D)*.

The lower level houses the renowned **Pacific Film Archive**, with some 6,000 films emphasizing Japanese, Soviet and American art cinema *(public showings daily)*. An outdoor **sculpture garden** wraps around the north and west sides of the building.

★★ **University of California Botanical Garden** – *Centennial Dr, first left off Stadium Rimway. Open year-round daily 9am–4:45pm. Closed Dec 25. ♿ ☎510-642-3343.* More than 10,000 species of plants grace the slopes of Strawberry Canyon in a sylvan setting above the main campus and overlooking the bay. Since 1890, university botanical facilities have nurtured exotic plants collected from the wild. This 33-acre site, established in the 1920s, is organized in gardens representing the flora of Meso-America, Asia, southern Africa, the Mediterranean/Europe, New Zealand, Australia, North America and California, the latter especially notable for its **pygmy forest** *(p 129)*. Three greenhouses are devoted to desert and rain forest plants; ferns and insectivorous plants; and tropical plants. A sequoia forest and redwood grove are located across Centennial Drive.

Lawrence Hall of Science – *Top of Centennial Dr. Open daily year-round. Closed major holidays. $5. ✗ ♿ 🅿 ☎510-642-5132.* Dramatically situated on the slopes below Grizzly Peak, this museum-in-the-round (1968) is dedicated to teaching schoolchildren such topics as physiology, lasers and dinosaurs through high-tech, interactive exhibits. The Lawrence Memorial Room traces the achievements of **Ernest O. Lawrence**, the university's first Nobel Laureate (1939), whose cyclotron advanced the field of nuclear physics. Outdoor exhibits include a **wind organ** with 36 12ft pipes, and Sunstones II, an 18ft sculpture that serves as an astronomical calendar. The rear patio **view★** overlooks much of the Bay Area.

ADDITIONAL SIGHT *Map p 183*

★ **Judah L. Magnes Museum** – *2911 Russell St. BART: Berkeley. Open year-round Sun–Thu. Closed major & Jewish holidays. ♿ 🅿 ☎510-549-6950.* Housed in an early-20C brick mansion set amid shaded grounds, this museum of Jewish history and art was named for a prominent San Francisco rabbi. Its changing exhibits *(main level)* highlight the works of contemporary Jewish artists and photographers, and permanent exhibits display ceremonial and cultural items *(upper level)*. Housed within the museum is the **Western Jewish History Center**, a comprehensive archive on the Jewish presence in the American West.

EXCURSION *Map p 183*

★ **John Muir National Historic Site** – *1 hr. 22mi northeast of Berkeley. Follow I-80 north, then Hwy 4 east to Martinez. Open year-round Wed–Sun. Closed Jan 1, Thanksgiving Day, Dec 25. $2. ♿ ☎510-228-8860.* This Italianate frame residence was home to legendary conservationist John Muir *(p 241)* from 1890 until his death in 1914. Built in 1882 by Muir's father-in-law, Dr John Strenzel, the home was part of Muir's 2,600-acre fruit ranch, but is furnished with early-20C period pieces that reflect the stylish inclinations of the Strenzel family and convey little of Muir's own simple taste. The desk and chair in his "scribble den" are the only furnishings that belonged to Muir personally.

The ranch occupied lands formerly owned by Vicente Martinez as part of an early 19C land grant; a short trail leads through the nearly 9-acre grounds to the pleasant **Martinez Adobe** (1849). A film on Muir's life is shown in the visitor center.

★ CALISTOGA North Coast Pop 4,468

Map p 236 Tourist Office ☎707-942-6333

Founded in 1859, this residential and resort town in the shadow of Mt St Helena (4,343 ft) is the northern hub of the NAPA VALLEY. Thermal activity in the area, manifested in a multitude of geysers and hot springs, fueled Calistoga's development as a resort where tourists flocked to "take the waters." Legend has it that Calistoga's founder Sam Brannan stumbled upon the town's name by confusedly declaring it "The Calistoga of Sarafornia" (Saratoga of California) after upstate New York's famed Saratoga Hot Springs. Still renowned today for its numerous spas, Calistoga unites the flavor of the late-19C frontier era with 20C modernity.

California's First Millionaire – Born in Maine, **Sam Brannan** (1819-1888) traveled throughout most of the US as a journeyman printer and newspaperman. A convert to the Church of Jesus Christ of Latter-Day Saints, Brannan led a group of some 240 fellow Mormons on an 1845 sea expedition to establish a colony on the West Coast. The colony never materialized, but Brannan remained in Yerba Buena, later renamed SAN FRANCISCO, and in 1847 founded the city's first newspaper, the *California Star*. Brannan is credited with inciting the Gold Rush of 1849 by proclaiming, in San Francisco, the discovery of gold at COLOMA. Ever the entrepreneur, he spotted unlimited opportunities for resort development in Calistoga, where local Natives had long sworn by the medicinal properties of the area's natural hot springs. Flamboyant and opportunistic, Brannan was reputedly a heavy drinker; his fortunes ran out near the end of his life, and he died in poverty near San Diego.

SIGHTS *1/2 day*

★ **Sharpsteen Museum** – *1311 Washington St, 2 blocks north of Lincoln Ave. Open daily year-round. Closed Thanksgiving Day, Dec 25.* ♿ *☎707-942-5911.* The highlight of this small museum is an intriguing assemblage of miniature **dioramas** recreating scenes of Calistoga's colorful past. Founded in 1979 by Ben Sharpsteen, retired Walt Disney Studios producer, the museum also features a collection of early 19C photos; a restored stagecoach; and assorted artifacts pertaining to the town's history. Adjoining the museum is a **cottage** from Sam Brannan's resort, relocated from its original site and fully refurbished to reflect the period of Calistoga's heyday.

Railroad Depot – *1458 Lincoln Ave.* Fronting busy **Lincoln Avenue**, Calistoga's main thoroughfare, is this historic station (1868). Erected to serve the Napa Valley Railroad Company, the building ceased to function as a depot in 1929. Today the renovated structure houses shops, a restaurant and a visitor center.

★★ **Old Faithful Geyser** – *From downtown drive east on Lincoln Ave; bear left on Grant St and continue 1mi. Turn left on Tubbs Lane. Entrance on the right. Open Apr-Oct daily 9am-6pm, rest of the year 5pm. $5.* ✗ *☎707-942-6463.* Located at the foot of Mt St Helena, this privately owned geyser is one of the world's three known "faithful" geysers, so named for their regular eruptions (the others are located in Yellowstone National Park and in New Zealand). At 40min intervals the geyser spews a column of superheated water some 60ft into the air in a splendid shower of droplets and steam lasting 3-5min.

Calistoga's Mud Baths and Mineral Springs

Volcanic activity in the northern Napa Valley has produced numerous geysers and hot springs, many of which have been harnessed to fuel Calistoga's renowned spas. A basic mud bath package, including mud bath, herbal wrap and mineral whirlpool bath, lasts approximately 1hr and costs $30-$40.

***Calistoga Spa** 1006 Washington St ☎707-942-6296.*

***Dr. Wilkinson's** 1507 Lincoln Ave ☎707-942-4636.*

***Golden Haven Hot Springs** 1713 Lake St ☎707-942-6793.*

***Indian Springs** 1712 Lincoln Ave ☎707-942-4913.*

EXCURSIONS

★ **Petrified Forest** – *2 hrs. 6mi. From Calistoga drive north on Hwy 128 and turn left on Petrified Forest Dr. Open daily year-round. Closed Thanksgiving Day, Dec 25. $3. ☎707-942-6667.* A circuit trail through this small, privately owned forest winds past the stone remnants of fallen giant redwoods that were petrified more than 3 million years ago when Mt St Helena erupted, covering the surrounding area with ash and molten lava. Among the highlights is The Giant, an ancient redwood measuring 60ft long and 6ft in diameter. A small exhibit and nature store are located at the entrance to the forest.

Robert Louis Stevenson State Park – *7mi. From Calistoga (Lincoln Ave) drive east and north on Hwy 29. Parking area on the left. Open daily year-round. ☎707-942-4575. Facility information p 257.* This largely undeveloped park provides an excellent opportunity for hikers to explore the rugged, picturesque slopes of Mt St Helena. From the parking area, a 5mi trail climbs through dense woods, its hairpin turns switching back and forth across the steep incline to the summit. The trail passes the site, near an abandoned silver mine, of the cabin where Robert Louis Stevenson *(p 237)* and his wife, Fanny Osborne Stevenson, spent their honeymoon in 1880. The Scotland-born author's book, *The Silverado Squatters*, was inspired by this sojourn in the Napa Valley. After 1mi, the trail emerges from the forest to join an unpaved access road to the summit; from this road, sweeping **views**★★ extend over the northern Napa Valley.

★★ CARMEL Central Coast Pop 4,239

Map p 40 Tourist Office ☎408-624-1711

One of California's most picturesque villages, Carmel-by-the-Sea (as it is officially known) arcs along the coastline just below the point of the Monterey Peninsula. A charming square mile of carefully tended cottages nestled under a canopy of pine, oak and cypress, Carmel has long attracted artists, writers and celebrities.

"Bohemia-by-the-Sea" – The village was originally planned in the 1880s as a seaside resort for Catholics. By the turn of the century, however, that venture had failed, and Frank Devendorf, a young real estate speculator from SAN JOSE, had purchased the land and begun planning a community that would preserve the pristine beauty of the natural setting and attract "people of aesthetic taste."

In 1905, aspiring poet George Sterling settled in Carmel and enticed fellow writers and artists to the area. Soon the quaint village developed a reputation as a bohemian retreat, with Sterling hosting abalone parties for literary figures Jack London, Upton Sinclair and Joaquin Miller. Through the 20C, the village has been home to an artistic crowd that has included photographers Edward Weston and Ansel Adams, writer Lincoln Steffens and poet Robinson Jeffers *(p 40)*.

Carmel's charmingly eclectic cottages and village ambience are protected by a strict 1929 zoning ordinance stating that commercial development will "forever be subordinate to the residential character of the community." By law, no sidewalks, street lights or mailboxes mar the effect in residential areas. However, a number of upscale boutiques, galleries, inns and restaurants are concentrated in the commercial area *(Ocean, Sixth and Seventh Aves between Junipero Ave and Monte Verde St)*.

Scenic Road, a thoroughfare shared by joggers, walkers and motorists, winds south along the beachfront for 1.5mi, ending at the Carmel River State Beach *(accessible off Ocean Ave; one-way southbound for first .7mi)*.

SIGHTS *1/2 day*

★★★ **San Carlos Borromeo de Carmelo Mission** – *West end of Rio Rd. Open Jul–Aug Mon–Sat 9:30am–7:30pm, Sun 10am–7:30pm, rest of the year Mon–Sat 9:30am–4:30pm, Sun 10am–4pm. Closed Easter Sunday, Thanksgiving Day, Dec 25.* ♿ ☎*408-624-1271.* Headquarters of the California missions during their expansive early years, the Carmel mission resonates with the visionary spirit of its founder, Padre Junípero Serra, whose remains lie interred here in the church sanctuary. The stately old chapel and rebuilt mission grounds, today surrounded by a residential area, continue to serve as a parish church and school.

Birth, Death and Resurrection – In 1771, when Padre Serra decided to move the mission out of the presidio at MONTEREY, he chose this site near the Carmel River "because of the extreme and excellent quality of the land and the water." Named in honor of the canonized 16C cardinal St Charles Borromeo, the frontier outpost struggled for several years, but Serra's tenacity eventually brought prosperity. With Serra in residence, the mission also served as headquarters for the chain of California missions that the padre was founding. When Serra died here in 1784, the mission supported some 700 Native Americans and Spaniards.

The mission continued to expand under the energetic direction of Padre Fermín Lasuén. Construction on the current stone church was undertaken from 1793 to 1797 to replace an adobe chapel built in 1782. Manuel and Santiago Ruíz, brother stonemasons, came from Mexico to design the church and oversee its construction. At Lasuén's death in 1803, the headquarters of the mission chain was removed to SANTA BARBARA, and the Carmel mission began a slow decline. Mission life here ended after secularization in 1834, and the resident padre moved to a church in Monterey. Though Mass continued to be offered here intermittently, the structures gradually fell into ruin. For 30 years the chapel stood roofless, until in 1884, a pitched shingle roof was erected to preserve its remains. In 1931 **Harry Downie**, a local craftsman, began a 50-year preservation effort that resulted in one of the most authentically restored missions in the state. In 1960 Pope John XXIII conferred the status of Minor Basilica on the chapel.

Church – Built of rough-hewn sandstone, the facade is offset by two asymmetrical, Moorish-style bell towers and an intriguing star window. The church is unique among the churches of the mission chain for its interior, supported by a series of graceful catenary arches, which slope upward more steeply than a traditional barrel vault. The walls are hung with 18C oil paintings original to the church; **Our Lady of Sorrows** *(right of the reredos)* is the work of Nicholas Rodríguez, founder of the Royal Academy in Mexico City. The elaborate **reredos** was crafted by Downie and modeled after one in MISSION DOLORES. The

J. Randklev/AllStock

San Carlos Borromeo de Carmelo Mission

graves of Padres Serra and Lasuén are below the reredos. The side chapel of Our Lady of Bethlehem contains a **statue** of the Virgin that accompanied Serra on his 1769 journey from Mexico. The baptistry contains its original stone font.

Padres Quarters – This adobe reconstruction is entered through the Serra Room, which is dominated by a 20C cenotaph dedicated to the padre by sculptor Jo Mora. Silver altar pieces brought to the mission by Serra are also on display. Beyond the chapel lie re-creations of rooms from the original mission. Notable are the library, containing antique volumes dating from 1534 to 1830; and Serra's cell, where the weary padre died at age 71. The walled complex encloses lovely gardens, an expansive reconstructed quadrangle, and the old cemetery.

★★ **Carmel City Beach** – *Heavy surf; swimming not recommended.* This wide, pristine sweep of white sand is pounded by the rolling turquoise breakers of **Carmel Bay.** To the south, the rocky finger of POINT LOBOS extends into the Pacific, while the north cliffs of the bay are topped by the greens of the renowned Pebble Beach Golf Club. Sea otters are easily spotted bobbing between the breakers, and gray whales can be glimpsed offshore during the migratory seasons *(Dec-Apr).*

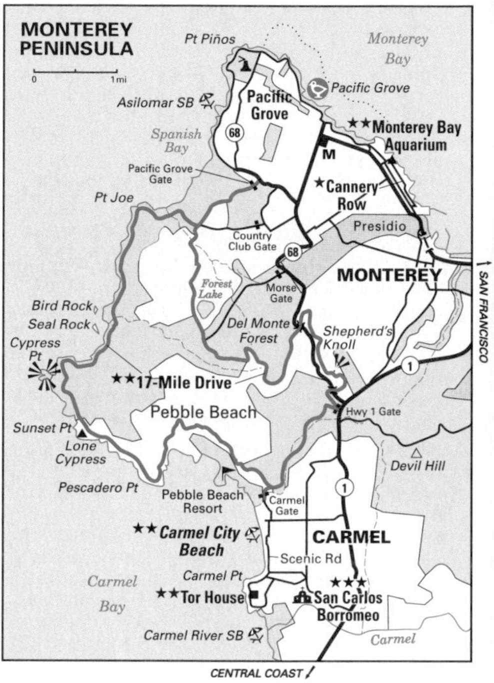

★★ **Tor House** – *Stewart Way, off Scenic Rd, 1.1mi south of Ocean Ave. Visit by guided tour (1hr) only, year-round Fri & Sat 10am–3pm. Closed Jan 1, Dec 25. $5. Reservations required. ☏408-624-1813 (Mon–Thu).* Overlooking Carmel Bay, this enchanting stone complex embodies the spirit of its builder, poet Robinson Jeffers, whose writing was inspired by the raw beauty of the Pacific coast. Jeffers and his wife settled in Carmel in 1914, and in 1918 work was begun on a small home on the "tor," or rock promontory, of Carmel Point. Over the years Jeffers expanded Tor House into a cluster of low stone buildings. Furnished with Jeffers' belongings, today the home comprises the original small parlor, a vaulted dining room, and the small bedroom where Jeffers died in 1962 at age 75. The whimsical **Hawk Tower** contains his desk and chair. Gaelic motifs and artifacts from around the world are embedded throughout the complex.

EXCURSION

★★ **17-Mile Drive** – *Map above. Access via Carmel Gate, on N. San Antonio off Ocean Ave; Hwy 1 Gate; and Samuel B. Morse Gate, off Hwy 68. Description p 124.*

★ CATALINA ISLAND Greater Los Angeles Area

Map of Principal Sights p 4

Lying approximately 26mi off the California coast south of LOS ANGELES, this mountainous 76sq mi island is a popular getaway for Southern Californians, who are drawn to its charming harbor town of Avalon, its unspoiled wilderness interior, and the boating and fishing off its 54mi coastline.

An Isolated Outpost – Visited in 1542 by Portuguese explorer Juan Rodríguez Cabrillo, the island was claimed for Spain on November 24, 1602, by Sebastián Vizcaíno, who named it Santa Catalina to honor the following day's feast of Saint Catherine. The island's Native population of approximately 2,000 peaceful Gabrieleños dwindled through epidemics and resettlement by mission priests; few if any remained by 1832.

European and American interest in isolated Santa Catalina increased in the early 19C. The island was sold for $200,000 in 1887 to entrepreneur George Shatto, who developed a resort village on a site his sister named Avalon. In 1919 the island (today known as Catalina) was sold for $3 million to Chicago chewing gum magnate William Wrigley Jr; from 1921 to 1951, it served as the spring training site of Wrigley's Chicago Cubs baseball team. The 24 buffalo used in the filming of Cecil B. De Mille's *The Vanishing American* (1924) were left behind and engendered a wild herd now numbering some 300 animals. Western novelist Zane Grey settled in Avalon, building a hillside adobe house that today operates as a bed & breakfast. Today converted into a country inn, the stately Wrigley mansion (1921), overlooks the prosperous town of Avalon from its perch in the southeastern hills, 350ft above crescent-shaped Avalon Bay. Much of Catalina remains in its natural state. In 1975, the Wrigley family transferred ownership of 86 percent of the island (42,135 acres) to the Catalina Conservancy, which is dedicated to safeguarding its natural beauty and promoting controlled public use.

Practical Information

Area Code: 310

Getting There – Passenger ferries depart daily year-round (schedule may vary Nov–Feb). 1-2hrs one-way ($34 average round-trip). **Catalina Express** departs from San Pedro (20mi from Los Angeles; I-110 south to Terminal Island/Long Beach exit to Harbor Blvd); and from Long Beach (21mi from Los Angeles; I-5 east to I-710 south to Golden Shore exit, follow signs to terminal) ☎519-1212. **Catalina Cruises** departs from Long Beach ☎253-9800. **Catalina Passenger Service** departs from Newport Beach (45mi from Los Angeles, I-5 east to Hwy 55 south to Newport Blvd to Balboa Blvd east; follow signs to Balboa Pavilion) ☎714-673-5245. **Island Express Helicopter Service** departs daily year-round from Long Beach & San Pedro harbors ☎491-5550. Greyhound **bus** station (Long Beach): 464 W. Third St (1mi north of terminal) ☎800-231-2222. Los Angeles **Metrorail** Blue Line to Long Beach station (4mi north of terminal).

Getting Around – Rental cars are unavailable on the island. Shuttle service (passengers only) between Avalon and Two Harbors daily Jun–mid-Sept $14.50, rest of the year call for service. **Catalina Safari Bus** ☎510-0303. **Catalina Cab Co** ☎510-0025. Golf cart rentals ($30/hr), bike rentals ($5-$9/hr) ☎510-0111. Sea and land tours of the island: **Santa Catalina Island Co** PO Box 737, Avalon CA 90704 ☎510-2500 (advance reservations strongly suggested); **Catalina Adventure Tours** PO Box 1314, Avalon CA 90704 ☎510-2888.

Visitor Information – **Catalina Island Chamber of Commerce & Visitors Bureau**, #1 Green Pier, Avalon CA 90704 ☎510-1520. Boating information: **Catalina Harbor Dept** Box 5044-HG, Two Harbors CA 90704-5044 ☎510-2683.

Accommodations – Advance reservations strongly suggested. Accommodations include modest hotels, bed & breakfasts ($100/day double), cottages and beach houses. Lodging directory available (free) from the Chamber of Commerce & Visitors Bureau *(above)*. **Catalina Island Accommodations** ☎510-3000. For cottage and beach house rental agencies contact the Chamber of Commerce. Camping by permit only; contact **Catalina Camping Reservations**, PO Box 5044, Two Harbors CA 90704 ☎531-2228.

SIGHTS *1 day*

Avalon – Pop 2,918. Hugging the hillsides surrounding Avalon Bay, Catalina's only town is a tightly packed assortment of pastel-colored houses and bungalows, hotels, restaurants and souvenir shops. With automobiles restricted on the island, Avalon's streets are thronged with pedestrians and rented golf carts. From the **Pleasure Pier**, glass-bottomed boats depart to view undersea life along the coastline, and other tours visit sea lion colonies and track schools of flying fish. Bus tours to the island's wilderness interior, the Catalina Airport and the Wrigley family's Arabian horse ranch depart from the center of town *(Tour Plaza between Catalina and Sumner Aves opposite 3rd St)*.

★★ **Casino Building** – *1 Casino Way. Visit by guided tour (45min) only, May–Oct Mon–Fri noon–3pm, weekends & holidays 4pm; rest of the year Mon–Fri noon–2pm, weekends & holidays 4pm. Reservations required. $7.50. ♿ ☎310-510-2500.* Dominating Avalon from a point on the bay's northwestern end is Catalina's most prominent architectural landmark, a 140ft-tall circular Art Deco building (1928-29) with Spanish and Moorish flourishes. Built as a tourist attraction by William Wrigley Jr, the casino enjoyed its heyday in the 1930s and 1940s, when dancing enthusiasts flocked to its ornate ballroom for entertainment by such big-band legends as Benny Goodman, Kay Kyser and Freddy Martin; music from the casino was radio broadcast live throughout the US.

Walking tours depart from the box office loggia, decorated with Art Deco undersea murals by John Gabriel Beckman. Additional Beckman murals depicting Southern California history and scenery decorate the walls of the 1,184-seat Avalon Theatre, which screens first-run feature films. The theater boasts an elliptical ceiling covered with some 60,000 squares of silver leaf, and a full-scale pipe organ. The ornate **Avalon Ballroom**, still a dance venue, features the world's largest circular dance floor, an open, cantilever-supported 10,000sq ft surface of cushioned maple, white oak and rosewood. Facing the bay on the casino's lowest level, a small **museum** presents exhibits on Catalina's history, natural history and archaeology *(open daily year-round; $1; ♿ ☎310-510-2414)*.

Wrigley Memorial and Botanical Garden – *1400 Avalon Canyon Rd. Open daily year-round. $1. ♿ ☎310-510-2288.* Tucked into the head of Avalon Canyon, 1.3mi inland from the bay, this 38-acre garden highlights Catalina's native plants, along with cacti and succulents. The 130ft Spanish-style memorial, built in 1934 of reinforced concrete made with aggregate quarried and crushed on Catalina, honors William Wrigley Jr. Steps lead to a platform beneath its 80ft tower, offering **views** of Avalon.

★★★ CENTRAL COAST Central Coast

Map p 43

Novelist Henry Miller once described the breathtaking length of coast between MONTEREY and Morro Bay as "the face of the earth as the Creator intended it to look." With its steep, craggy slopes punctuated by pockets of white sand, the area's rugged beauty has inspired painters, poets, photographers and writers.

A Forbidding Geography – Mountains that run the length of the Central Coast once formed part of the ocean floor. Over the past 25 million years, shifting of the earth's crust gradually thrust them upward to form the Coast Ranges. The southern ranges, which are relatively young compared to their northern counterparts *(p 12)*, consist of a granitic block bounded on the east and west by Franciscan rocks (named for sedimentary deposits found near the city of SAN FRANCISCO). The San Andreas and Nacimiento faults separate the zones of softer sedimentary rock from the granite block, which today forms the Santa Lucia Mountains.

Fierce winter storms and the lack of sheltered anchorages along this forbidding coast warded off explorers for more than a century. Although Sebastián Vizcaíno landed briefly in Monterey Bay in 1602 *(p 22)*, the Costanoan, Esselen and Salinan tribes who were the region's earliest inhabitants did not make contact with Europeans until 1770, when Gaspar de Portolá and Padre Junípero Serra landed on the Monterey Peninsula and built a mission at the current site of CARMEL.

South of the peninsula, a handful of hardy homesteaders in the 1880s tried logging (the southern limit of the coast redwood's range lies in southern Monterey County) and limestone mining in the Santa Lucia Mountains. Industry boomed, and the region's population swelled until local natural resources were exhausted in the early 1900s. In 1919 workers began blasting the **Cabrillo Highway**—designated the nation's first Scenic Highway between 1965 and 1985—out of the western slopes of the mountains that plummet into the Pacific from heights topping 5,000ft.

Visiting the Central Coast – Moderating influences of the Pacific Ocean ensure mild temperatures year-round. Between November and April, as much as 60in of rain soaks the area. Although the summer months are dry, fog frequently shrouds the shoreline. The warmest days usually occur in September and October, when temperatures sometimes reach 80°F. Even so, it's advisable to keep a sweater handy while traveling through at any time of year.

Although points along this coast present excellent opportunities for whale-watching *(p 261)*, the terrain becomes quite rugged south of Carmel, and accessible beaches *(p 258)* north of San Simeon are few. The village of Big Sur offers lodgings, restaurants and one gas station; amenities are scarce between Big Sur and San Simeon.

DRIVING TOUR *2 1/2 days. 118mi.*

Leave Monterey by the Pacific Coast Highway (Hwy 1) south.

From Monterey to Big Sur

★★ **Carmel** – *3mi. 1/2 day. Description p 39.*

★★ **Point Lobos State Reserve** – *3.5mi. Entrance off Hwy 1. Sea Lion Point, Bird Island and Whalers Cove areas can be reached by car; the rest of the reserve is accessible by hiking trails. Open Jun–Sept daily 9am–7pm, rest of the year 5pm. $6/car. ♿ ☏408-624-4909.* This small but dramatic peninsula defines the southern end of Carmel Bay. Early Spanish explorers named the site Punta de los Lobos Marinos ("point of the sea wolves"), because the baying of resident sea lions reminded them of the howling of wolves. Deeded to the state in 1933, the site now comprises 1,250 acres, including 750 submerged acres of the nation's first underwater reserve.

Visitors can explore sights along a variety of short, easy shoreline paths, such as **Sea Lion Point Trail** *(.6mi round-trip; bring binoculars)* and **Cypress Grove Trail** *(.8mi round-trip)*; the latter loops past the gnarled forms of one of the last two naturally occurring stands of Monterey Cypress trees left on earth (the other can be seen along the 17-MILE DRIVE). **Bird Island Trail** *(.8mi round-trip)* winds above the crystal aquamarine waters and blanched sands of tiny **China Cove**★. Having served alternately in the 19C as a whaling station, abalone cannery and granite quarry, **Whalers Cove** is the site of a 19C cabin for Chinese fishermen that now contains cultural history exhibits *(open Jun–Sept daily 10am–4pm, rest of the year noon–4pm).*

★★★ Big Sur

This spectacular coastline, loosely defined as extending 90mi from south of Carmel to San Simeon, has historically represented as much a state of mind as a physical location. Its mystique lives on today, in silent redwood canyons and along granite ridges that plunge to the frothy sea, in the words of poet Robinson Jeffers, "Like the steep necks of a herd of horses . . . at thirst in summer . . . "

The Native Esselen had occupied this wilderness for some 1,800 years when the Spanish arrived in the 1770s and christened the raw land south of their Carmel Mission El País Grande del Sur ("the big country to the south"). The first Yankee homesteaders trickled into the area in the mid-1800s to establish cattle ranches in the back country. By the turn of the century, Big Sur bustled with activity occasioned by newly formed industries, including tanbark harvesting, redwood logging and lime smelting.

Until the 1930s, the only access to Big Sur was via Old Coast Road, a former wagon trail that winds for some 10mi behind the hills. Completion of the coast highway in 1937 opened the area to visitors, and to hippies who fled here in the 1960s to escape the "establishment." Today, local resorts and the area's several state parks employ many Big Sur residents. Ranchers occupy the isolated canyons of the Big Sur hills, and artists and writers continue to seek their muses in the coast's haunting beauty.

Numerous turnouts on the highway provide opportunities to stop and enjoy the dramatic scenery. A lovely **beach★** at **Garrapata State Park** *(3mi from Point Lobos; parking on shoulder only)* is one of the few accessible beaches along this stretch of coast, where the road climbs as high as 1,000ft above the ocean. Spanning the deep canyon cut by Bixby Creek, the 714ft-long **Bixby Creek Bridge** *(7mi from Garrapata State Park)* affords a stunning **view★** of the coastline from the overlook on its north side.

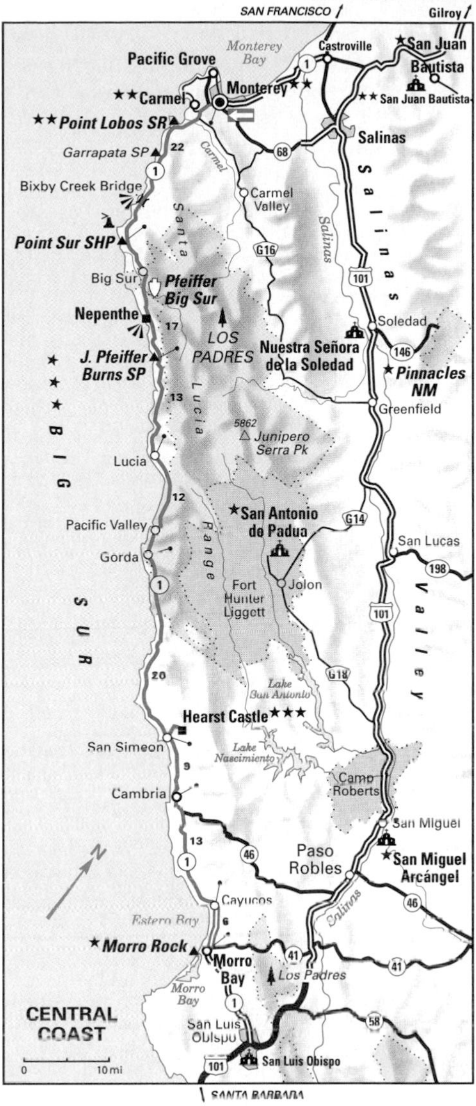

Point Sur State Historic Park – *5mi from Bixby Creek Bridge. Visit by guided tour (2hr) only, year-round Sat & Sun. Closed during inclement weather. $5. ☎408-667-2315.* Perched 272ft above the surf on a volcanic rock connected to the mainland by a sandbar, Point Sur Light Station was built in 1889. Visitors can get a taste of life on this lonely outpost by touring the original stone lighthouse (now automated), and the keeper's houses and workshops.

Pfeiffer Big Sur State Park – *6.5mi; entrance on left. Open daily year-round. $6/car. ⛺ (reservations suggested) ♿ ☎408-667-2315. Facility information p 257.* Over 800 acres of redwoods, conifers and oak trees fringe the banks of the Big Sur River in this popular park, named after Big Sur's first permanent European settlers. A trail *(1mi round-trip)* ascends through redwood groves to the point where **Pfeiffer Falls★** tumble 60ft into Pfeiffer-Redwood Creek. Other park trails provide access to the 164,000-acre Ventana Wilderness that stretches eastward from the Big Sur coast.

Pfeiffer Beach – *1.5mi. From Hwy 1, turn right on narrow Sycamore Canyon Rd (unmarked); 2mi to parking lot. Open daily year-round. ☎408-667-2315.* Sunbathers here enjoy views of wave-eroded sea stacks just off the shore of this secluded cove, where Pfeiffer Creek flows into the ocean.

Nepenthe – *1.7mi. Open daily year-round. ✂ ♿ ☎408-667-2345.* Greek mythology describes "nepenthe" as a potion used to obliterate pain and sorrow. It is an apt name for the restaurant that offers sweeping **views★★★** from its cliffside terraces 800ft above the blue Pacific. The log cabin that originally stood on this site was purchased in 1944 by Orson Welles for his wife, Rita Hayworth.
Tucked back in the trees, the rustic redwood **Henry Miller Memorial Library** *(entrance on the left, .3mi past Nepenthe)* houses books and memorabilia written and owned by the novelist (1891-1980), who lived in Big Sur for 18 years *(open year-round, hours vary; contribution requested; ♿ ☎408-667-2100).*

Julia Pfeiffer Burns State Park – *8mi; entrance on left. Open daily year-round. ⛺ ♿ ☎408-667-2315. Facility information p 257.* Occupying 1,800 acres of the rugged southern section of the Big Sur coast, this park bears the name of the daughter of pioneers Michael and Barbara Pfeiffer. From the parking lot alongside burbling McWay Creek, **Waterfall Trail** *(.5mi round-trip)* leads under the highway and out along the bluffs, where visitors are treated to a unique **view★** of McWay Creek plunging some 80ft to join the jade waters of the Pacific.
South of Julia Pfeiffer Burns State Park, the road rides the edge of the continent for 35 desolate miles; the only signs of humanity are the tiny settlements of Lucia, Pacific Valley and Gorda. Along this rugged stretch of coast, **views** abound of granite slopes falling into the turquoise ocean. As it approaches San Simeon, the highway descends and straightens, and rocky cliffs yield to rolling pastureland.

From San Simeon to Morro Bay

★★★ **Hearst Castle** – *51mi. 1 day Description p 66.*

Hidden back off the west side of Highway 1, the languid beach town of **Cambria** *(9mi)* served in the 19C as a key shipping port for the local mining industry.

Morro Bay – Pop 9,664. *19mi from Cambria. Take Main St exit off Hwy 1.* Life in this small fishing port centers around the Embarcadero, which runs for 1.5mi along the bay. Now lined with shops and restaurants, the Embarcadero once hosted scores of schooners that ferried local dairy and farm products to market in San Francisco in the 1870s. By the mid-20C, commercial fishing supplanted trade as the principal industry. Although fishermen still haul bountiful catches of albacore, salmon and lingcod from the offshore waters, tourism now reigns as the town's main source of revenue.
The bay's most distinctive geographic feature is 576ft **Morro Rock**★ *(take Main St to right on Beach St and follow signs)*, one of the "Seven Sisters," a series of seven extinct volcanic peaks extending along a 12mi line from SAN LUIS OBISPO to Morro Bay. Called El Moro by Spanish explorer Juan Rodríguez Cabrillo *(p 22)*, who sighted the dome-shaped promontory in 1542, Morro Rock now harbors the nests of endangered peregrine falcons in its lofty crevices.

Morro Bay State Park Museum of Natural History – *State Park Rd (follow Main St extended). Open daily year-round. Closed Jan 1, Thanksgiving Day, Dec 25. $2. ♿ ☎805-772-2694. Facility information p 257.* Set in a fragrant eucalyptus grove overlooking Morro Bay's bustling harbor, this small museum houses exhibits relating to regional geology, cultural history and marine life. A Discovery Center features hands-on displays.

★ CHANNEL ISLANDS NATIONAL PARK Central Coast

Map of Principal Sights p 4

Encompassing the northernmost five of the eight Channel Islands that extend along the coast of Southern California between SANTA BARBARA and SAN DIEGO, this unique national park harbors rich plant, animal and marine life, including many species not found on the mainland. With public access tightly controlled, largely unspoiled Anacapa, Santa Cruz, Santa Rosa, San Miguel and Santa Barbara islands offer an experience of coastal life as it might have existed throughout the southern part of the state several centuries ago.

Historical Notes – The islands are actually the top of submerged mountains; the northern four of the five are considered a westward extension of the Santa Monica Mountains, which, as part of the Transverse Ranges, were rotated counterclockwise into their present position and east-west alignment by the movements of the Pacific and North American plates along the San Andreas fault *(p 12)*. The islands' current names were fixed in 1793 by Capt George Vancouver, an English explorer, but the first European to visit and document them was Juan Rodríguez Cabrillo *(p 22)*, who passed here in 1542 (an injury he incurred the following year while landing on San Miguel or Santa Rosa led to his death; his unmarked grave is believed to be on one of the islands). Fur traders in the late 18C and 19C threatened the abundant populations of otters, seals and sea lions, and about this same time, the Chumash and Gabrieleño Natives who had existed on the islands for some 6,000 years were relocated to mainland missions. Sheep and cattle ranches were established by the mid-19C, and thrived into the 20C, particularly on Santa Rosa.

Practical Information

Area Code: 805

Getting There – Boat transportation to all islands provided by **Island Packers** 1867 Spinnaker Dr, Ventura CA 93001 ♿ ☎642-1393. Departures from Ventura Marina, Ventura. Advance reservations recommended for all boat crossings. For detailed information, see individual island descriptions *(p 45)*. From **Los Angeles** (58mi), I-101 north to Victoria Ave exit; turn left. Turn right onto Olivas Park to Ventura Marina, follow signs to National Park. Closest Greyhound **bus** station: 291 East Thompson Blvd, Ventura ☎800-231-2222. Amtrak **train**/bus service from Los Angeles into Ventura Station (Harbor Blvd and Figueroa St) ☎800-872-7245. **Air** service available to Santa Rosa and Santa Cruz Islands, Channel Islands Aviation, 305 Durley Ave, Camarillo CA 93101 ☎987-1301.

Visitor Information – The park is open year-round daily 8am–5pm. **Channel Islands National Park Visitor Center** is located at Ventura Marina ☎658-5730. Mailing address: Superintendent, Channel Islands National Park, 1901 Spinnaker Dr, Ventura CA 93001. Weather on the islands can vary year-round from windy and cold to hot and humid; it is advisable to be prepared for both. Facilities on the islands include campsites, pit toilets and picnic tables. It is recommended that each visitor bring an extra pair of shoes (waves can be high during on & off loading), 1 gallon of drinking water per day, and food (lunch boxes for sale near Island Packers office). All trash must be packed out. For boating information, contact the National Park Service.

Accommodations – Rustic **camping** available on Anacapa, Santa Barbara, Santa Rosa and San Miguel Islands by advance permit only; contact Park Superintendent *(above)*. Permits granted up to 90 days in advance. Campers must provide all needed camping equipment, cooking water and stoves. Owing to unpredictable weather, landings cannot be guaranteed; packing an additional day's ration is recommended.

In 1938 Anacapa and Santa Barbara islands were declared the Channel Islands National Monument, and in 1980, the five islands and the ocean within 1mi of their shores were declared a national park, though a portion of Santa Cruz remains under private ownership. Also in 1980, 6mi bands around each island were designated as national marine sanctuaries.

Today Channel Islands National Park is visited by sightseers drawn to its natural beauty; campers in search of blissful isolation; and divers seeking the beauty of its crystal-clear waters, kelp beds, rich marine life and remains of offshore shipwrecks.

VISIT *1 day per island*

Anacapa – *Departures to East Anacapa daily year-round, West Anacapa Jun–Labor Day, Dec–Apr (days vary). One-way 1hr 30min. Total duration (cruise & visit) 6-8hrs. $37.* ⚠. Lying just 14mi off the coast of VENTURA, Anacapa Island comprises three sparsely vegetated islets. Endangered brown pelicans breed on its inaccessible western reaches, and the entire island is home to Western gulls, black oyster-catchers and cormorants. A ranger station and lighthouse are located on relatively flat East Anacapa; off its coast stands water-eroded Arch Rock.

Santa Cruz – *Departures to Scorpion Ranch (East Santa Cruz) year-round Tue, Fri–Sun. $42.* ⚠. *Departures to West Santa Cruz Apr–Labor Day (days vary). $49. One-way 2hrs. Total duration (cruise & visit) 8-10hrs.* The largest of the Channel Islands offers a diverse landscape of wooded mountain slopes and beach-fringed cliffs. Santa Cruz's deep central valley indicates that it was formed of two separate land masses now joined together. **Painted Cave**, the state's largest sea cave, is visible by boat on the island's northwestern shore. Diverse animal species make their home on Santa Cruz, including island foxes, spotted skunks, sheep, feral pigs, two species of mice and nine species of bat.

Santa Rosa – *Departures Jun–Labor Day, Dec–Apr (days vary). One-way 3hrs 30min. Total duration (cruise & visit) 11-12hrs. $52.* ⚠. Reached by a sometimes rough ocean crossing, the second-largest island has sandy beaches and an inland terrain of grassy rolling hills with oaks and Torrey pines *(p 70)*. Animal life includes over 195 bird species.

San Miguel – *Departures Jan, Apr, Jun–Oct (days vary). One-way 6hrs. Total duration (cruise & visit) 17 hrs. $62, $215 (2-day excursion, includes meals & berth).* ⚠. The windswept, relatively flat westernmost island highlights a caliche forest, the calcium-carbonate castings of ancient trees; and, at Point Bennett on its western tip, the only place in the world where six different species of seals and sea lions breed in large numbers.

Santa Barbara – *Departures weekends year-round. One-way 3hrs. Total duration (cruise & visit) 11-12hrs. $49.* ⚠. The smallest island, 33mi south of Anacapa, is a breeding ground for sea lions and elephant seals, and offers excellent bird-watching.

CHICO Central Valley — Pop 40,079

Map of Principal Sights p 2 — Tourist Office ☎916-891-5556

This attractive farming hub and college town is located near the north end of the Sacramento Valley "rice belt," where the natural marshes of riverine lowlands have been cultivated to grow rice. Pleasant **Bidwell Park★**, with its gardens and groves of huge oak trees along Big Chico Creek, provides a verdant connector between the center of town and the Sierra Nevada foothills to the east. Home to several light industrial concerns, Chico is the main business center between REDDING and SACRAMENTO and site of a popular campus of California State University.

SIGHT *1hr*

Bidwell Mansion State Historic Park – *525 Esplanade. Visit by guided tour (45min) only, daily year-round. Closed Jan 1, Thanksgiving Day, Dec 25. $2.* ♿ *☎916-895-6144.* This rose-colored, Italianate mansion at the edge of the California State University campus was built in 1867 by successful businessman and politician **John Bidwell** (1819-1900), who arrived in California in 1841 as a leader of one of the first parties of Americans to cross overland from the Missouri frontier. While in the employ of John Sutter *(p 156)*, Bidwell discovered placer gold deposits on the Feather River in mid-1848; he eventually accumulated enough wealth to purchase 22,000 acres of land, on which he experimented with cultivation of fruits, nuts and other crops that became mainstays of Central Valley agriculture. Bidwell founded the town of Chico in 1860 and was active in state politics before serving a term in the US House of Representatives (1865-1867). In 1964 the state park system acquired the Bidwell mansion; restoration occurred during the 1970s.

Today refurbished in the style of the late 19C, the house offers glimpses into Bidwell's life and times; displays present the history and development of Chico.

EXCURSION

Oroville Chinese Temple – *1/2hr. 21mi southeast of Chico in Oroville. 1550 Broderick St. Visit by guided tour (1hr) only, Feb–mid-Dec daily. Closed Easter Sunday, Thanksgiving Day. $2. ☎916-538-2415.* This compound (1863) comprising a Taoist temple, a smaller Buddhist temple, a Confucian family chapel, a Tapestry Hall of Chinese folk arts and a garden featuring plants of Chinese origin is one of the few remaining vestiges of the 10,000 Chinese gold miners who lived in the Oroville area in the late 19C. The temple was nearly destroyed by floods in 1907, but was restored and rededicated in 1949.

★★★ DEATH VALLEY NATIONAL MONUMENT Deserts

Map p 49

This sunblasted realm of stone, sand and wide-open spaces stretching along California's eastern border with Nevada has the lowest elevations and highest temperatures in the Western Hemisphere. Far from population centers and major highways, Death Valley confronts the visitor with the silent, stark grandeur of earth-forming processes unobscured by vegetation or scars of human encroachment.

A Tilted Basin – Death Valley is not precisely a valley, but a deep basin with no outlet, formed progressively as a block of the earth's crust sagged and sank, leaving adjoining blocks standing high on either side to form the Panamint and the Amargosa ranges. This process began about 3 million years ago and continues today, more rapidly on the east side than on the west, making the basin floor tilt down to the east. The mountains are flanked by **alluvial fans**, delta-like deposits built up as debris washes out of canyons during flash floods. Fans on the west side are larger, because the tilt of the basin causes debris to flow farther. During the past 2 million years, episodes of moister climate have filled the basin with a series of fresh-water lakes, of which the largest, Lake Manly, reached a depth of 600ft about 12,000 years ago. The lakes left layers of sediments on the basin floor that were later exposed by movements along faults and carved by erosion into badlands.

Today the basin stretches 130mi long, and ranges from 5mi to 25mi in width; elevations within the park range from 11,049ft above sea level to –282ft. The Sierra Nevada range blocks most incoming moisture from the Pacific Ocean. Furnace Creek Ranch, site of the park headquarters and a center for food, lodging and other amenities, receives an average of 1.65in of rain per year. The sun shines relentlessly in the dry clear air and heats the almost bare ground of the basin floor to some of the highest average temperatures on earth. Furnace Creek's average daily high in July is 116.2°F, and the basin's highest recorded temperature of 134° has been exceeded only in the Libyan Sahara Desert.

Flora and Fauna – Stands of limber pine and bristlecone pine, the park's only trees, grow in the heights of the Panamint Mountains. Lower elevations support various kinds of sparse, bushy vegetation, depending on the availability of water and salt content of the soil. Cactus, usually associated with desert vegetation, is not prominent in Death Valley; the pungent creosote bush is the most common plant over wide areas. Desert holly grows near the drier, saltier soils of the basin bottom, and in spots where groundwater is not too saline, thickets of mesquite thrive. In highly saline areas, often on the edges of saltwater pools, only pickleweed grows. Some 200sq mi of salt pan in the very bottom of the basin are completely barren of any plant life. After unusually wet winters, tiny seeds that may have lain dormant for years sprout, bedecking the area with wildflowers.

Death Valley's larger animals—bighorn sheep, feral burros, deer, mountain lions, bobcats, coyotes and foxes—are elusive. More commonly seen are jackrabbits, rodents and lizards. The sidewinder rattlesnake lives here, but flees from humans. Many animals of all sizes are nocturnal, and their tracks are easier to see (especially in sand dunes early in the morning) than the animals themselves.

Practical Information

Area Code: 619

Desert safety tips p 255

Getting There – To Furnace Creek (center of park on Hwy 190): from **Los Angeles** (252mi) I-10 east to I-15 north to Hwy 127 north to Hwy 178 west; from **San Francisco** (476mi); I-80 east to I-580 east to I-205 east to Hwy 99 south to Hwy 178 east to Hwy 190 east; from **Las Vegas** (140mi) US-95 north to Hwy 373 south (becomes Hwy 127) to Hwy 190 west. Radiator water at Hwy 190 and Hwy 374 entrances and at Furnace Creek. Closest airport: Las Vegas (LAS) 123mi east. Closest Greyhound (☎800-231-2222) and Amtrak (☎800-872-7245) stations: Barstow (160mi south); rental car agency branches *(p 253)*.

Getting Around – Death Valley is best visited by car. Gas available at Furnace Creek, Scotty's Castle and Stovepipe Wells. Stay on marked roads when traveling by car. Notify a park ranger station before exploring Titus Canyon and other jeep roads, where 4-wheel drive vehicles are recommended.

Visitor Information – Open daily year-round. $5/car entrance fee. **Furnace Creek Visitor Center** open daily year-round. **Beatty Ranger Station** (Hwy 374, Beatty NV) open daily year-round ☎702-553-2200. **Shoshone Ranger Station** (Hwy 127, Shoshone) hours vary ☎852-4308. Mailing address: Superintendent, Death Valley National Monument, Death Valley CA 92328 ☎786-2331. **Eastern Sierra InterAgency Visitor's Center** (Lone Pine), information on area parks and public lands, open year-round daily 9am–5pm; closed Jan 1, Dec 25; ☎876-6222.

Accommodations – Accommodations available in the park at Furnace Creek Ranch ($98) ☎786-2345, Furnace Creek Inn ($235) ☎786-2361, and Stovepipe Wells Motel ($58) ☎786-2387; advance reservations strongly recommended. **Campsites** available by self-registration; no reservations accepted (except at Furnace Creek, Oct–Apr, through MISTIX ☎800-365-2267). Limited camping available Apr–Oct. Registration recommended for **backcountry camping**. Accommodations also available in: Beatty NV (10mi east), Lone Pine (60mi west), Shoshone (22mi east) and Trona (27mi west). *All rates quoted are average prices for a double room.*

Useful Numbers

Police/Fire	**911**
Emergency (24 hours)	786-2330
Road Service (repair and towing, daily 8am–4pm)	786-2232

Borax Boom – For at least 10,000 years, the basin was visited seasonally by various hunting and gathering groups, including Shoshone and Paiute. Two parties of gold-seeking emigrants looking for a pass around the snowy Sierras in December 1849 were the first non-Natives to enter the area; the extreme hunger and thirst they suffered during their passage through the basin led them to bestow on it the name "Death Valley."

The basin saw several mining booms in the late 19C, but the only mineral of lasting economic importance was borax (a salt containing the element boron) left behind by the evaporation of ancient lakes. As early as 1873, commercial interests were aware of the presence of borax here, but the difficulty of transporting it out discouraged mining until 1883, when William T. Coleman established a 20-mule team wagon route stretching 165mi across the desert from the Harmony Borax Works *(p 48)* to the Southern Pacific railroad station at Mojave. Five years later, a rich borax strike at Calico *(p 57)*, only 12mi from the railroad, eclipsed the Death Valley deposits, and the mules and wagons were moved there. Borax mining recommenced in Death Valley in 1907 and continued until 1927, this time using the Death Valley Railroad (since abandoned) to transport concentrate to the connecting Tonopah and Tidewater Railroad at Death Valley Junction on the basin's eastern rim.

Management of the Tonapah and Tidewater conceived the idea of supplementing the railroad's income by promoting tourism at the Furnace Creek oasis, and opened the Furnace Creek Inn in 1927. Although rail ticket sales were poor, by the early 1930s tourists were venturing into the basin by automobile. The hotel prospered, and less expensive cabin accommodations were added at the ranch. The increase in tourism to the region, together with the final demise of borax mining, led to the basin's designation as a national monument in 1933, and political support is growing for upgrading Death Valley to national park status.

SOUTH OF FURNACE CREEK *1/2 day. 77mi.*

Leave Shoshone by Hwy 178 west.

Named for a nearby mine, **Jubilee Pass** (1,290ft) offers the first view of Death Valley to visitors entering the monument from the south on Highway 178. Across the basin floor, Shoreline Butte exhibits terrace-like shorelines created by wave action in the lakes that filled Death Valley during the Ice Age.

★ **Badwater** – *55mi.* This shallow pool of alkali water, 279.8ft below sea level, is virtually the nadir of the Americas. *(The ultimate low points, measuring 282ft below sea level, are unmarked, 3.3mi and 4.6mi away out on the salt flat.)* Even in this extreme location life goes on: pickleweed grows at the water's edge and several species of aquatic insects thrive.

The **Devil's Golf Course** *(6mi north of Badwater; 1.3mi to end of dirt road)*, a jagged chaos of low salt pinnacles, is continuously re-created as salty ground water rises to the surface through capillary action and evaporates, leaving salt crystals behind.

★ **Artist's Drive** – *2.3mi.* This one-way scenic drive winds 9mi across alluvial fans at the base of the Amargosa Range. The landscape is splashed with colors from volcanic ash and ancient lake deposits, and all occur in one remarkable spot, **Artist's Palette**★★, about midway through the drive. The reds, pinks, and yellows are produced by iron compounds, the greens by mica and copper, and the purples by manganese. **Mushroom Rock**, on the east side of the highway just north of the exit from Artist's Drive, is an outcrop of basalt sculpted the blowing sand and expanding salt crystals that lodge in its cracks.

★★ **Golden Canyon** – *3mi from Artist's Drive exit.* A gently ascending trail *(2mi round-trip)* winds through a rugged canyon created by flash floods cutting through the tilted deposits of an ancient alluvial fan. As the trail ascends, the rocky walls give way to softer lake sediments that have eroded less precipitously, forming gentle badlands. After 1mi the trail divides, the right fork going 2mi through the badlands to Zabriskie Point, and the left fork continuing .5mi to the base of a cliff called the Red Cathedral for its fancied resemblance to Gothic architecture. *Late afternoon visit recommended for best light effects.*

FURNACE CREEK *Junction of Hwys 178 and 190.*

Today Death Valley's principal concentration of lodging and amenities, this pleasant oasis created by a naturally occurring spring is the historic center of human activity in the basin. Permanent settlement began in 1874 when the Greenland Ranch was established here to grow produce and alfalfa hay for the miners and mules working in the Panamint Range. When William Coleman launched the Harmony Borax Works nearby in 1883, he bought the ranch and increased production. In 1927 the elegantly appointed **Furnace Creek Inn**, a vaguely Moorish stone structure in a palm grove .5mi to the east, became the main consumer of ranch-produced goods. A grove of date palms, now a prominent part of the landscape, was established in 1924, and is still producing dates for sale.

Tent-houses, cabins and the world's lowest golf course (some of its greens lie 215ft below sea level) were opened here in the 1930s, and since then **Furnace Creek Ranch** has grown into a popular winter resort. The **Borax Museum**★ *(on grounds of Furnace Creek Ranch; open daily year-round)* occupies a small wooden building (1885) that served as an office and bunkhouse in 20-Mule Team Canyon *(p 48)* before being moved here in 1954. Today it houses a display of borax mining tools and a good collection of minerals gathered in and near Death Valley. In the shade of tamarisk trees outside are larger items of mining and transportation equipment, including a mine locomotive and 20-mule team wagons.

★ **Death Valley Museum** – *Just north of Furnace Creek Ranch. Open daily year-round.* ♿ This small museum provides an excellent introduction to Death Valley geology, natural history, ethnography and mining history, and displays a remarkable three-dimensional relief map of the park. Housed in the same building is the National Park Service Furnace Creek **visitor center**, offering a well-stocked bookstore, and a full range of naturalist programs. The center is a good place to stock up on brochures detailing the natural history of individual sights in the park.

Excursions from Furnace Creek

★★ **Zabriskie Point** – *4.5mi from Furnace Creek by Hwy 190 east.* This point overlooking Golden Canyon badlands from the east offers a splendid **view★★★** of multicolored lake sediments uplifted and tilted by tectonic movements and eroded by rain and wind. The distinctive, tooth-like prominence is Manly Beacon, named for William Manly, one of the unlucky party of goldseekers who stumbled into the basin in 1849. The point is named for Christian Zabriskie, a prominent figure in Death Valley borax mining.

About 1.2mi further east on Hwy 190 is the entrance to a one-way 2.9mi scenic drive through **20-Mule Team Canyon [A]** that cuts through the same badlands. Deposits of high-grade borax, naturally concentrated by sedimentation, were mined here in the early 20C.

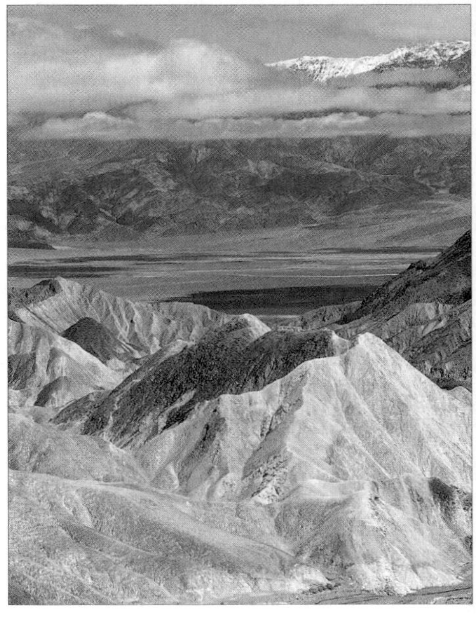

View from Zabriskie Point

★★★ **Dante's View** – *24mi from Furnace Creek by Hwy 190 east and Dante's View Rd.* From its 5,475ft perch atop a peak of the Amargosa Range (Death Valley's eastern wall), Dante's View offers the most comprehensive and renowned **view★★★** of the enormous basin and the geologic processes that have shaped it. The shallow, salt-edged pools of Badwater lie directly below.

Surmounting the Panamint Range across the basin is the park's highest point, 11,049ft Telescope Peak, which is capped with snow much of the year. Below the peak and slightly to the right is the large alluvial fan of Hanaupah Canyon, which coalesces with other fans to form a composite alluvial apron, or *bajada*, along the west side of the basin. *Early morning visit recommended for best visibility.*

★★ **Titus Canyon Road** – *Allow 1/2 day. 98mi round-trip from Furnace Creek. Drive north on Hwy 190 and take the Beatty Cutoff to Daylight Pass and Nevada Rte 374. The road begins at an inconspicuously marked turn-off on the north side of the highway, 35mi from Furnace Creek. 4-wheel drive vehicle recommended.* One of the most spectacular drives in the monument, this one-lane dirt road traverses a stupendous landscape of layered cliffs, peaks of tilted and twisted sediments, and remnants of great volcanic eruptions. Crossing the Grapevine Mountains via White Pass and Red Pass, the road dips en route into rugged Titanothere Canyon (named for an extinct rhinoceros-like mammal found here in fossil form). From a high point at 5,250ft, the road winds and squeezes its way through the narrow passages of Titus Canyon down to sea level in Death Valley. The explanatory brochure is recommended for an understanding of the terrain's geologic complexity *(available at Furnace Creek Visitor Center only).* Near the top of Titus Canyon is the ghost town of Leadfield, which experienced a 6-month mining boom in the mid-1920s. *Early morning visit recommended for best light.*

NORTH OF FURNACE CREEK

Leave Furnace Creek by Hwy 190, which extends north of Furnace Creek, intersecting with park road to northern Death Valley and Nevada Rte 267.

Harmony Borax Works – *1.7mi.* The remains of a borax processing plant and a restored 20-mule team borax wagon commemorate the borax boom of the 1880s, when Chinese laborers toiled over the basin floor on foot, scraping the ulexite form of borax ("cottonball") off the ground and carrying it back to this point for the first stage of refining and concentration. 20-mule team wagons then hauled the concentrate on a three-week (round-trip) journey to the Mojave railroad station.

Some 12mi north of the borax works, **Salt Creek** and the surrounding marsh form an intense patch of life amidst dry rock and sand. A boardwalk nature trail extends out into the marsh, a saltwater oasis formed by groundwater in the creek bed forced up by an impermeable rock layer. Visible during the late winter and early spring, the Salt Creek Pupfish *(Cyprinodon salinus)*, a tiny descendent of fish present in a freshwater lake that filled Death Valley 20,000 years ago, is known to exist only here.

Mosaic Canyon – *2mi round-trip trail; trailhead 2.3mi from Stovepipe Wells gravel access road.* Named for the *breccia* (natural concrete with embedded angular pieces of older rock) exposed along its walls, the canyon is also noteworthy for a layer of dolomite that has been metamorphosed into a rosy-ivory marble and then smoothed and fluted by passage of water. The most attractive formations are in the first .5mi of the 2mi trail.

An extensive field of **sand dunes** lies north of Highway 190 *(accessible on foot either from the highway or via a turn-off 6mi east of Stovepipe Wells).* These dunes are formed as sand and other material is carried on winds from the surrounding mountains; crosswinds and swirling currents over time have caused the sand to drop here. *Early morning visit recommended, for best light and viewing of animal tracks.*

★ **Scotty's Castle** – *55mi north of Furnace Creek. Interior visit by guided tour (1hr) only, daily year-round. $6. Long waits during peak season.* ✗ ♿ ☎*619-786-2392.* Begun in 1924, this eclectic, Spanish-Moorish complex of house and grounds was commissioned by Albert Johnson, a Chicago insurance magnate seeking a quiet and healthful retreat. Johnson was a friend and financial backer of Walter Scott, a former rodeo cowboy and gold prospector who claimed vast wealth from a secret gold mine in Death Valley. Scott, known as "Death Valley Scotty," managed to live well for years on nothing more than his extraordinary talents for self-promotion and yarn-spinning.

Johnson sank $2.5 million into this architectural extravaganza, in one of the most unlikely settings imaginable. The grounds were never completed, but the interior was finished in a luxurious, if rustic fashion with highly crafted furniture and fittings and noteworthy tile and woodwork. The cavernous **Great Hall** is appointed with heavy, stuffed leather furniture and features a humidity-producing interior rock fountain. Photographs and the storyteller's own clothes hang in Scotty's bedroom, while a collection of dinnerware from Mexico, Spain and Italy adorns the dining room. The tour concludes in the lavishly appointed **music room**, with its massive 1121-pipe theater organ and impressive arched-beam ceiling.

★ **Ubehebe Crater** – *57mi north of Furnace Creek; 8mi west of Scotty's Castle.* This natural cauldron, 600ft deep and 2,640ft wide, with orange and gray layered walls, was created not more than a few thousand years ago by a titanic steam explosion caused by groundwater heated and pressurized by magma deep below the surface. Debris from the explosion lies scattered over 6sq mi.

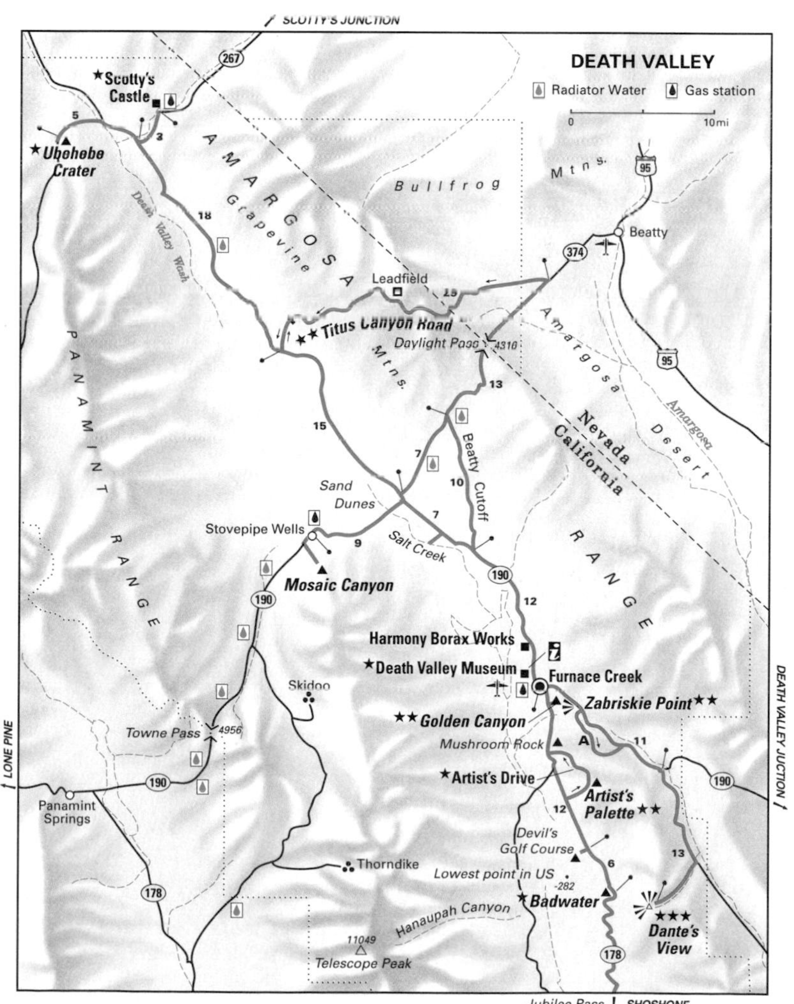

★★★ DISNEYLAND Orange County

Map pp 54-55

Since 1955, the "Magic Kingdom" has been America's ultimate fantasyland, a place of pilgrimage that children dream of visiting. Though larger Disney theme parks have now opened around the world, California's 90-acre Disneyland embodies the original vision of its creator, **Walt Disney**. Its rides, cartoon characters and "lands" perpetuate the fairytale enchantment symbolized by the name Disney.

The Story Behind the Dream – Born in Chicago, Walter Elias Disney (1901-1967) moved to a Missouri farm with his family at the age of five and spent four idyllic years there. His ever restless father, Elias, then moved the family to Kansas City, where Walt spent the remainder of his boyhood. As a child, Walt showed little talent for schoolwork but a great deal of imagination. Always interested in drawing, he completed several courses at the Kansas City Art Institute and in 1919 took a job in the budding field of animation with a Kansas City cartoon company. The entrepreneurial Disney quickly began producing his own cartoons, and in 1922 founded a production company called Laugh-O-Grams. As with many of Disney's early endeavors, the company fared well artistically but was a financial failure. By 1923 the business was bankrupt, and Disney, aged 21, headed for California.

"When You Wish Upon a Star" – In HOLLYWOOD, Disney quickly established another cartoon business, putting his older brother Roy in charge of finances. Their partnership lasted a lifetime. In 1928 the Disney Brothers Studio gained fame with the debut of *Steamboat Willie*, starring a newly created character named **Mickey Mouse**. With the innovation that would characterize future Disney productions, the feature combined animation with the new technology of sound. The studio soon produced other artistic and commercial triumphs, including the first Technicolor cartoon, *Flowers and Trees*, which won Disney his first of 32 Oscars. By the mid-1930s the studio was undertaking its boldest concept yet: a feature-length animated cartoon. Amid industry skepticism, *Snow White* opened in 1937 to instant success, and the studio's next two endeavors, live-action adventures and nature films, were equally well received.

A Magic Kingdom – In the early 1950s, with his film interests well established, Disney again let his imagination rove. Disillusioned with the tawdriness of amusement parks of the day, he began planning his own. Purchasing a 180-acre tract of orange groves in then-rural Anaheim, Disney and a staff of "imagineers"—engineers, architects, writers and artists—set about designing a "Magic Kingdom." On July 17, 1955, the barely completed park opened to national fanfare and 90 minutes of live television coverage, hosted in part by then-actor Ronald Reagan.

In keeping with Disney's decree that Disneyland will "never be complete," the park has undergone continual expansion and updating. In the early 1960s the technology for **audio-animatronics**, life-like robotic figures, was developed by Disney's "imagineers" for the 1964 New York World's Fair and subsequently put to widespread use throughout the park. Soon after, Disney also began work on a new Magic Kingdom, Walt Disney World, and adjacent to it, a Experimental Prototype Community of Tomorrow (EPCOT), in Orlando, Florida. But at age 67, one year before the opening of his new park, Walt Disney died of cancer.

The Disney Empire – Today Disney Studios is a major force in the US film industry, regularly producing films both critically acclaimed and financially successful. In addition to film and television, the vast Disney enterprises include two theme parks abroad: Tokyo Disneyland (1983); and Euro Disney (1992), located outside Paris *(see Michelin Green Guide to Euro Disney)*. Ambitious plans for the coming decade call for a new American history theme park outside Washington, DC, and for the expansion of the Anaheim complex into a Disneyland Resort, adding more hotels, gardens, and WESTCOT, a new version of EPCOT.

Over the years, critics have pointed out that Disney theme parks and films portray an idealized, unrealistic view of the world; Walt Disney himself realized that he was somewhat limited artistically by the rose-colored Disney mystique. But that mystique has apparently earned an unassailable place in the hearts of a devoted public worldwide, and Disneyland continues to welcome millions of visitors a year to what it calls "the happiest place on earth."

Disneyland Thrills

Several of Disneyland's fast-moving thrill rides have age and height restrictions. The following carry a warning to pregnant women and guests with other physical conditions:

Star Tours *(p 52)*

Space Mountain *(p 52)*

Matterhorn Bobsleds *(p 53)*

Splash Mountain *(p 56)*

Big Thunder Mountain Railroad *(p 56)*

Practical Information

Area Code: 714

When to Go – Disneyland is busiest from Dec 25–Jan 1. Other holidays also attract large crowds, as do summer months (Jun–Aug). During these periods, attendance can reach 60,000 a day. The least crowded period falls between Thanksgiving and Dec 25, followed by September and October, then January. Saturday is the busiest day of the week, while Friday and Sunday are least crowded. Some rides and eating facilities may be closed in the off-season.

Getting There

By Car – Located 25mi south of **Los Angeles.** Take I-5 south; exit at Harbor Blvd and follow signs.

By Air – Closest airports: **Orange County/John Wayne Airport** (SNA) 14mi south; **Los Angeles International Airport** (LAX) 35mi northwest; **Long Beach Municipal Airport** (LBG) 20mi west. Shuttles to Disneyland-area hotels average $10/one-way.

By Bus and Train – Greyhound (☎800-231-2222) bus terminal: 2080 S. Harbor Blvd, Anaheim (8mi from park). Amtrak (☎800-872-7245) station: 2150 East Katella Ave, Anaheim (2mi from park).

Accommodations – Information available from the **Anaheim Area Visitor & Convention Bureau,** PO Box 4270, Anaheim CA 92803 ☎999-8999. Reservations strongly recommended 6 months in advance for hotel rooms and campsites, especially during busy seasons *(above)*. Numerous lodging facilities are located within a 5mi radius of the park; accommodations range from elegant hotels ($151/day), to budget motels ($78/day). The Disneyland Hotel, owned by the Walt Disney Company, averages $120-$215/day and is accessible from the park by the Disneyland Monorail. Many area hotels and motels offer shuttle service to Disneyland. *All rates quoted are average prices for a double room.*

Camping – Several full service campgrounds are located on S. West St (within walking distance of the park); contact the Visitor & Convention Bureau *(above)* for more information.

Visitor Information – For general information, contact **Disneyland Guest Relations,** PO Box 3232, Anaheim CA 92803 ☎999-4565. Guest Relations Center located in City Hall , west side of Town Square in Main Street, USA.
The park is open Easter week, Jul–Aug, mid–late Dec daily 8–1am, rest of the year Mon–Fri 10am–6pm Sat & Sun 9am–midnight ♿. One-day ($28.75, child $23), two-day ($52.50, child $42) & three-day ($71.25, child $57) tickets (known as Disneyland Passports) are available; free for children under 2. Tickets allow unlimited access to all Disneyland attractions; season tickets available. Parking $5. Behind-the-scenes guided tours (3hrs 30min) depart from the south side of City Hall; tickets ($38.75, child $31, includes same privileges as one-day tickets) available at Guest Relations Center *(above)*.
Most visitor services (baby facilities, first aid, lost & found, storage lockers, banking services) are located around Town Square and elsewhere in Main Street, USA. Automated tellers, kennels, and stroller and wheelchair rentals are available outside the park near the main entrance gates.
Same-day **re-entry** to the park is allowed with a valid ticket & hand stamp (available at exits).

Planning your Visit – Visitors with limited time can see Disneyland's main attractions in one day; however, a 2- or 3-day visit is preferable, particularly for families with young children.
On the day of visit, arrive when ticket booths open, about an hour before the official opening time. When purchasing a ticket, you'll receive a Disneyland souvenir guide, with a detailed map of the park, and **Disneyland Today**, a listing of show times. While waiting for the park to open, plan a strategy. If you wish to see the Golden Horseshoe Jamboree, head immediately to Frontierland for tickets to one of the day's performances. If you're in for some thrills, remember that the roller coasters, Star Tours, Haunted Mansion and Pirates of the Caribbean acquire long lines as the day progresses, so head for those first. Otherwise, save them for the last hour before closing, when crowds are thinner.

Showtime – A variety of live-performance stage shows are presented in the park throughout the day. All are on a first-come, first-served basis, with the exception of the Golden Horseshoe Jamboree. Afternoons, when many rides have long lines, are good times to take in the shows. For show times, check the *Disneyland Today* brochure. In addition to stage shows, entertainers stroll throughout the park giving impromptu live performances.

When to Eat – Disneyland theme restaurants and cafeterias get very crowded during peak mealtimes of 11:30am–2pm and 5–8pm. Spend less time in line by planning to eat outside these hours. Or, you may elect to exit the park and eat at one of the many restaurants along Harbor Blvd near the park. Be sure to have your hand stamped at the park exit for re-entry *(above)*.

Disney by Night – The Disney magic works best when darkness falls. Crowds abate at dinnertime, then pick up again for the nightly extravaganzas Fantasmic!, Fantasy in the Sky, and the Main Street Electrical Parade. Most rides continue to run during the entertainment, and lines are shorter then. Particularly attractive by night are Storybook Land, Skyways to Tomorrowland and Fantasyland, the Matterhorn, Big Thunder Mountain Railroad and Splash Mountain.

VISIT

Roughly elliptical in shape, Disneyland is organized into eight distinct sections: Main Street, U.S.A.; Tomorrowland; Fantasyland; Mickey's Toontown; Frontierland; Critter Country; New Orleans Square; and Adventureland. These areas radiate out from the central plaza. The shops, eateries, attractions and costumed "cast members" (ride attendants, shopkeepers and other staff) in each section echo the dominant theme of their "land."

★ Main Street, USA

This idyllic re-creation of an early 20C main street gives visitors their first taste of the Magic Kingdom. Tidy, brick Victorian storefronts hold old-fashioned shops, while horse-drawn trolleys, fire engines and a double-decker omnibus ferry passengers up and down *(stops at Town Square and Central Plaza).* Minstrels often stroll the street, and the patriotic **Livin' in the USA Cavalcade** parades through in the afternoons. The Plaza Gardens also feature live entertainment. Evenings bring the **Main Street Electrical Parade**, a charming parade of lights featuring characters from Disney film classics *(Check* Disneyland Today *for schedules).* **Fantasy in the Sky** features a flying appearance by Tinkerbell, and a fireworks display.
In designing Main Street, Walt Disney used a film device called "forced perspective." Upper stories of buildings are not as high as lower ones, giving them a taller appearance, and Sleeping Beauty's Castle is built to a smaller scale, making it seem farther away.

Disneyland Railroad – Passengers can board steam trains here that circle the park, making stops at New Orleans Square, Mickey's Toontown and Tomorrowland. The railroad travels through a re-creation of the Grand Canyon and a Primeval World populated by audio-animatronic animals. At New Orleans Square, the Telegraph Cable Office taps out Walt Disney's opening speech for the park. Two of the current trains (nos. 3 and 4) were formerly working steam trains.

The Walt Disney Story – This combination museum/theater traces the construction of Disneyland and the Disney empire through photographs. Re-created here are Walt Disney's casual "working office" at the Burbank studios and his "formal" office, containing the baby grand piano on which composer Leopold Stokowski played parts of the *Fantasia* score for the animator's approval. The theater features Disney's crowning audio-animatronic success, **Great Moments With Mr. Lincoln**, first created for the 1964 World's Fair. Gesturing on stage, an eerily lifelike Abe delivers a speech.

Main Street Cinema – Six small screens in an arcade-style room continuously show Disney animated classics in black and white from the 1920s-1930s, among them *Steamboat Willie (p 50).*

★★★ Tomorrowland

The first impression of Tomorrowland is that of motion: various "modern" conveyances glide overhead, suspended from cables or supported by elevated tracks. The future, however, has overtaken Tomorrowland and its curving white structures and 1960s-style image of the modern era now look like a vision from the past. Tomorrowland features some of Disneyland's most innovative rides, among them Star Tours and Space Mountain. The **Tomorrowland Terrace** mounts live performances, and at **EPCOT Poll Person of the Century**, visitors can cast their votes for the person they feel has had the greatest effect on the 20C. The winner of the 10-year Disney poll will be announced on New Year's Day, 2000.
A good overview of this land can be had either from **PeopleMover**, a trolley-like car that snakes its way along an elevated track above and through most Tomorrowland's rides; or from the **Disneyland Monorail**, a silent, elevated train touted as "America's first daily-operating monorail." In operation since 1959, it whisks passengers between Tomorrowland and the Disneyland Hotel.

Star Tours – This futuristic popular attraction was jointly conceived by Disneyland "imagineers" and *Star Wars* creator George Lucas. The adventure begins in the Tomorrowland Spaceport, where *Star Wars* droids C3PO and R2D2 are hard at work preparing for takeoff. Travelers then board a StarSpeeder for a voyage to the Moon of Endor. Excellent special effects, particularly through the large "window" in the craft, result in the ride of a lifetime.

Space Mountain – Since it opened in 1977, this roller coaster enclosed in a futuristic mountain has been one of the park's most popular rides. Space Mountain is not for the faint-of-heart: thrill-seeking visitors are hurtled through space in near-darkness, plunging through sudden, atmospheric comet showers and past faintly twinkling stars.

Magic Eye Theater – Special effects such as 3-D are a highlight of films specially produced by Disney for presentation in this large-screen theater; special viewing glasses provided at the entrance enhance the 3-D experience.

Circle-Vision – The nine huge screens here present changing films generally devoted to scenic areas of the world. Viewers, standing surrounded by the screen surfaces, have the sensation of actually being inside the movie.

Submarine Voyage – Passenger-laden submarines descend into the bright blue depths of a brilliantly colored lagoon for a "20,000 Leagues Under the Sea" voyage past corals and fishes, and under the polar ice cap. Watch out for the giant squid, and consider this: the mermaids were once played by live actresses.

Rocket Jets – These somewhat old-fashioned rockets circle a central missile, offering whirling, aerial views down on Tomorrowland.

Mission to Mars – Space travel was a national obsession when this ride opened in 1975 as the Flight to the Moon. Today passengers begin with a visit to officials in mission control, before boarding a "space craft" for a flight to the red planet.

Tomorrowland Autopia – Originally designed to teach young people how to drive safely, this ride gives both young and experienced drivers the chance to motor little sports cars around a pleasantly shaded track.

Skyway to Fantasyland – Cable gondolas gliding 60ft above the ground offer **views** of Tomorrowland and a peek inside the Matterhorn before arriving above the storybook rooftops of Fantasyland.

*** Fantasyland

With the fairytale air of an old European village, Fantasyland was Disney's personal favorite, and the area today appeals to adults with a taste for whimsy, as well as to young children just exposed to the Disney classics through re-release and videotape. The **Videopolis**, an open-air amphitheater, features first-rate, Broadway-style stage productions *(Check* Disneyland Today *for schedule).*
For a quick trip from fantasy to future, visitors can hop aboard the **Skyway to Tomorrowland**, the return portion of the Skyway to Fantasyland *(above).*

Sleeping Beauty Castle – Today a worldwide symbol of Disney, this small-scale castle, with its gold-leafed turrets and encircling moat, serves as a majestic entrance to Fantasyland. **Snow White's Grotto** *(right of castle entrance)* features a carved Carrara marble version of the young girl surrounded by the loyal dwarfs. Along a narrow corridor in the castle interior, dioramas trace the tale of Sleeping Beauty.

Matterhorn Bobsleds – Rollercoaster-style sleds wind up and through the Matterhorn mountain, a Disney landmark. Once at the top, the sleds make a swirling downhill dash through ice caves and past an abominable snowman.

King Arthur Carrousel [A] – An attractive carousel with antique white horses and gilded trim dominates the center of Fantasyland. The ride is accompanied by Disney tunes pumping out of the calliope.

It's a Small World – Perhaps Disneyland's most recognized ride, this international fantasy was conceived for the 1964 World's Fair, and embodies a rather idealized view of international relations. The facade is an aggregation of moving parts and architectural images from many lands—the Taj Mahal, the Eiffel Tower, Big Ben, and more. Inside, boats float visitors past 500 audio-animatronic children and animals representing nearly 100 nations, all singing a repetitive theme song.

Disney Animated Classics – Fantasyland celebrates Disney's greatest film successes, with both carnival-style rides and enclosed, or "dark" rides based on animated features, in which special vehicles transport visitors through the narrative as storybook images unfold before them. In **Peter Pan's Flight [B]**, pirate-ship gondolas fly riders out of the Darling childrens' bedroom and above a charming, fiber-optic version of London by night before plunging into a Never Never Land adventure where Captain Hook, Smee, and the Lost Boys await in their galleon. Board the caterpillar cars of **Alice in Wonderland [C]** for a twisting trip through a colorful fantasyland populated by the Queen of Hearts, her playing-card knights, the Mad Hatter, and of course, that elusive White Rabbit. In jaunty vintage sportscars, those who brave **Mr. Toad's Wild Ride [D]** hurtle through the picturesque English countryside and into London's foggy back streets, where surprises lurk around every corner. **Snow White's Scary Adventures [E]** takes visitors from the dwarfs' cozy cottage to an encounter with the Wicked Queen, Snow White's evil stepmother, and on to a happy ending. In **Pinocchio's Daring Adventure [F]**, visitors are whisked from Geppetto's charming toymaking shop to accompany the puppet/boy on his misadventures, while Jiminy Cricket keeps a watchful eye on everyone. Join in the **Mad Tea Party [G]**, a teacup tilt-a-whirl of colorful cups and saucers swirling madly about, with riders controlling their spin by a wheel in the center of each cup.

For Little Dreamers – Fantasyland features several carnival-type rides particularly suited for the very young. **Dumbo the Flying Elephant [H]** has been a longtime favorite with small visitors, who can make their Dumbos soar up and down by manipulating a knob in front of the seat. Young mariners take command on the **Motor Boat Cruise**, where small "motor boats" give riders the illusion that they are steering themselves through Gummi Bear Glen. The **Storybook Land Canal Boats** glide past a series of scale-model miniatures depicting such scenes as Mr. Toad's abode and Alice's home; Storybook Land can also be toured aboard the **Casey Jr. Circus Train**. *Storybook scenes are particularly magical by night.*

** Mickey's Toontown

Disneyland's newest "land" is an exclusive residential address for Disney cartoon characters that has, as the story goes, existed since the 1930s when cartoon characters decided to live here, away from the bustle of Hollywood. Walt Disney himself was purportedly the only human allowed to visit. But today, everyone is welcome to explore the neighborhood's curving streets, buildings and interactive attractions, all of which display the garish colors and skewed perspective of an animated cartoon. The **Jolly Trolley**, Toontown's public transportation, continuously huffs, chuffs and sways its way through the village, and Toontown residents are regularly on hand to meet visitors and give a live-performance welcome blast *(check the bandstand in Toontown Square for schedule).*

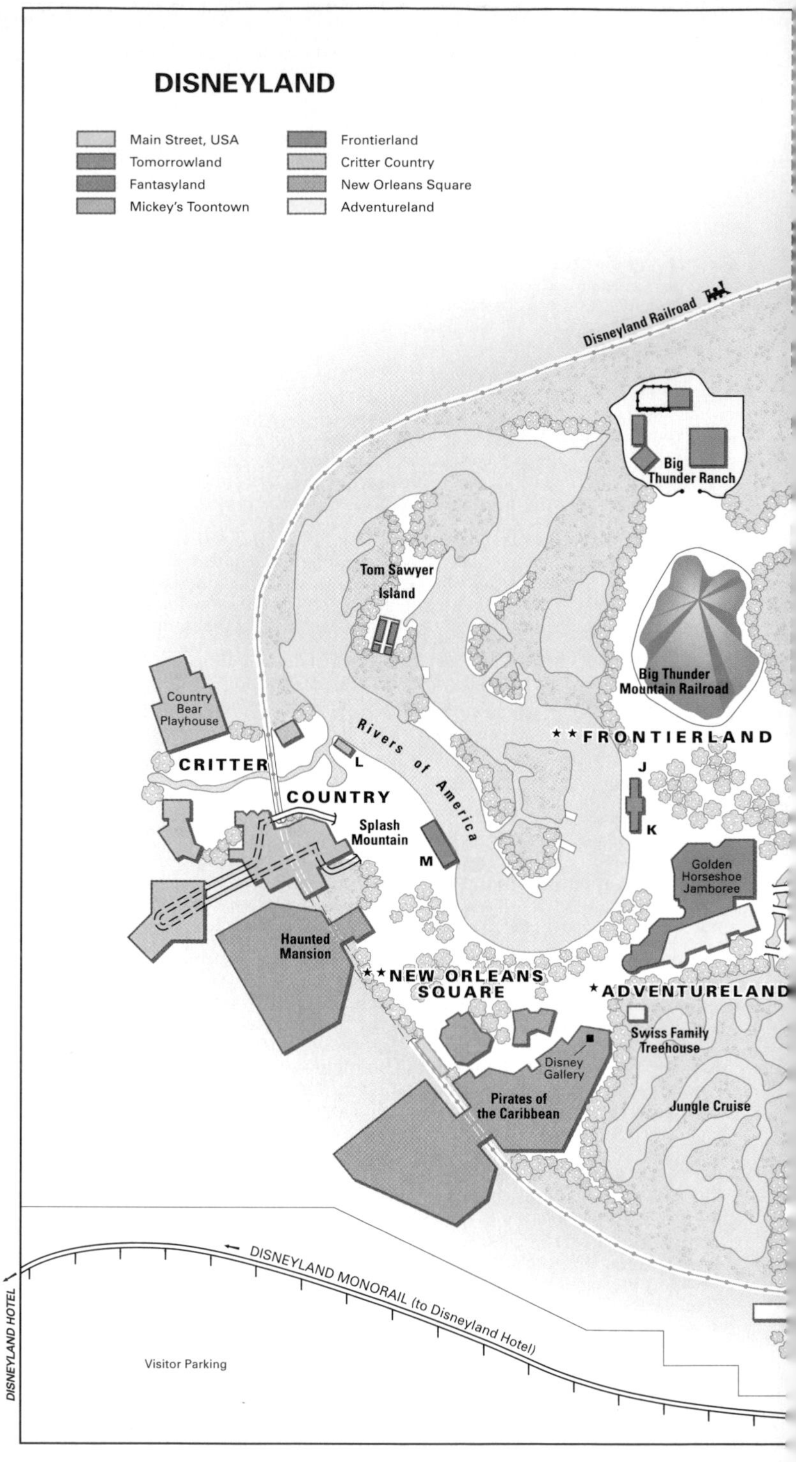

Mickey's House – Stroll through Mickey's modest, red-roofed home at your own pace to investigate the lifestyle of a celebrity mouse. Visitors are treated to a quick screening of clips from Mickey's movies before stepping through to the set, where the star himself is on hand for introductions and photographs.

Minnie's House – The residence of Mickey's erstwhile sweetheart offers an array of housekeeping activities, including baking a cake, washing dishes and making the teakettle boil. Try on Minnie's perfume and open the refrigerator door to see what she has on hand for dinner.

Goofy's Bounce House – Small-size visitors will enjoy bouncing energetically off the walls and furniture of Goofy's inflatable dwelling. Afterward, climb up to the bridge of Donald Duck's boat, the **Miss Daisy**, for a bird's-eye view of Toontown.

Chip 'n Dale's Tree Slide and Acorn Crawl – A spiral staircase and two slides let visitors explore the rascally chipmunks' house, nestled in the branches of a Toonesque tree, while younger visitors play in a winter hoard of oversize acorns.

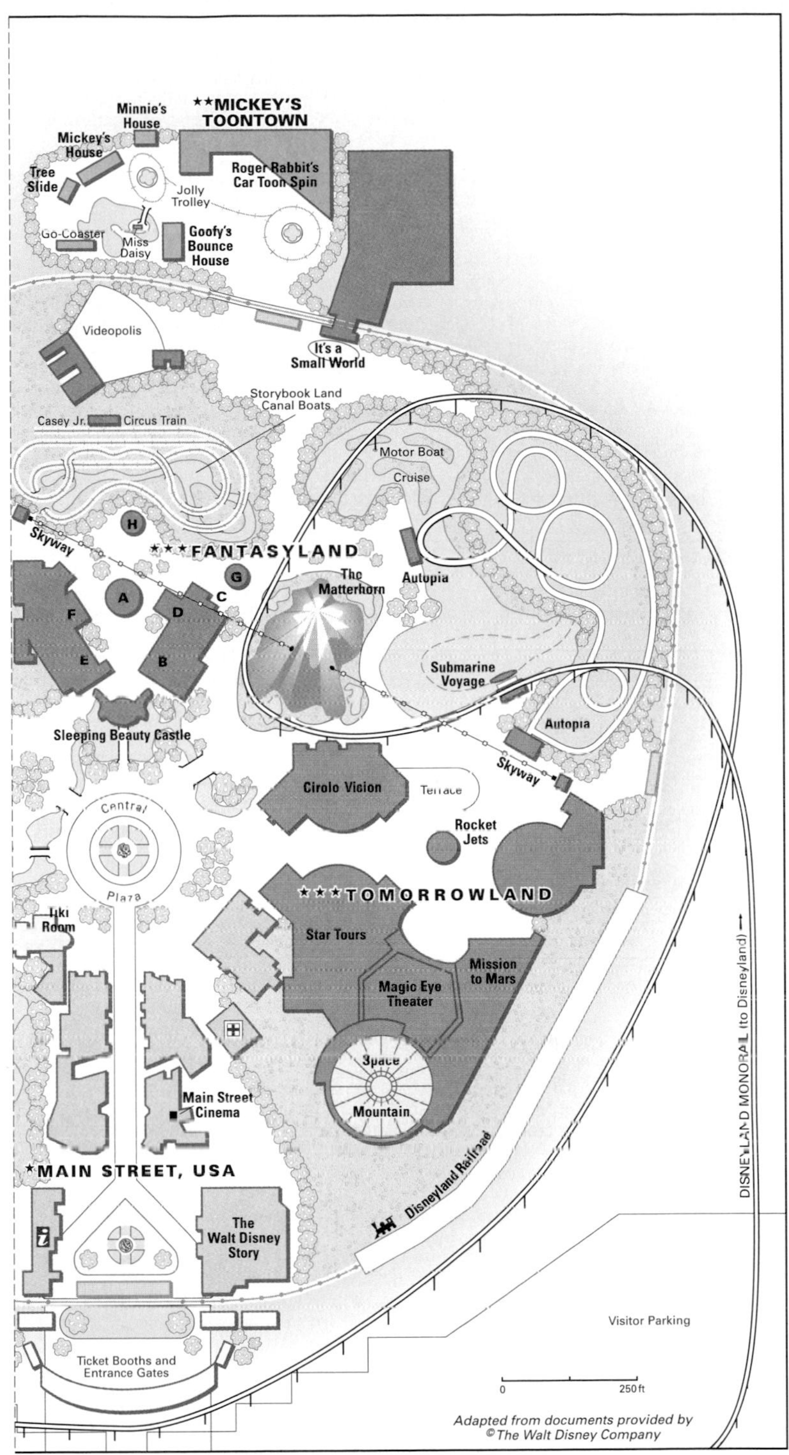

Adapted from documents provided by ©The Walt Disney Company

Nearby, the chipmunks' friend Gadget has recycled oversize toys into **Gadget's Go-Coaster**, which offers pint-size thrills on its short ride.

Roger Rabbit's Car Toon Spin – Follow the skid marks to the Toontown Cab Co. building for a menacing adventure in the darkened recesses of Toontown.

★★ Frontierland

The legend of the Old West lives on in this frontier town, with its board walkways, country stores, and saloons. The town borders the Rivers of America *(p 56)*, which circle Tom Sawyer Island. At night, the river rides shut down and visitors crowd the shoreline to see **Fantasmic!**, a fiber optic show *(22min)* that presents Disney animation at its pyrotechnic, innovative best. The fantasia of laser images projected onto "mist screens" stars Mickey Mouse, the witch Maleficent, and other favorite Disney characters.

The **Golden Horseshoe Jamboree**, a dance hall-style revue, is performed several times daily in Frontierland's Golden Horseshoe Saloon.

Big Thunder Mountain Railroad – This impressive reddish mountain dominates the landscape in this part of the park, its crags and caves scaled by one of Disneyland's most thrilling roller coasters. Boarding a runaway train in an old mining town, passengers speed through a terrain of hoodoos, caves and canyons, and down into a rickety old mine shaft.

Big Thunder Ranch – The 2-acre "spread" features a log homestead, a blacksmith and harness shop, and barnyard full of pettable buddies, among them goats, sheep, horses and cows.

Rivers of America – Those in search of riverine adventure have their pick of five different kinds of vessels plying the waters of Disneyland's "river." For a glimpse of Mississippi River history, board the **Mark Twain Steamboat [J]**, an elegant 105ft reconstruction of an graceful old paddle wheeler. Along the way, you'll encounter audio-animatronic animals and an Indian village. Navigating a similar route is the **Sailing Ship Columbia [K]**, a finely crafted 3-masted windjammer that offers a taste of life aboard an 18C merchant ship. Visitors can paddle themselves around the river, accompanied by coonskin-capped guides, in **Davy Crockett's Explorer Canoes [L]** *(board in Critter Country, below)*. Log **rafts** offer transportation to Tom Sawyer Island, where the especially energetic can explore Injun Joe's cave, the stockaded Fort Wilderness, a swinging footbridge, a treehouse, and more. The island can also be reached by the southern-style **Mike Fink Keelboats [N]**.

Critter Country

This small, bucolic corner of the park, nestled at the edge of a wooded area, is home to a host of audio-animatronic critters. Originally known as Bear Country, it was renamed when the park's newest thriller, Splash Mountain *(below)*, opened here in 1989. Performances change seasonally at the **Country Bear Playhouse**, where the wonderfully playful "Bear-itones," a troupe of audio-animatronic bears, sing, tell jokes and delight the crowds. *Check* Disneyland Today *for schedule.*

Splash Mountain – Riders board bark dugouts for a languid float through the swamps and bayous inside this mountain, as Brer Rabbit, Brer Fox and other characters from the Disney classic *Song of the South* (1946) serenade the passengers. At the mountain's top awaits one of the biggest thrills in Disneyland: a 52ft flume that hurtles the dugouts down a 47° slope to a monstrous splash at the bottom.

★★ New Orleans Square

This squeaky-clean version of New Orleans' French Quarter features a narrow, twisting street of pastel, stuccoed shop facades and ornate, wrought-iron balustrades. Musicians regularly stroll through, performing fine Dixieland jazz tunes. True to the city that inspired it, the square's atmosphere is more languid than that of the rest of the park.

Pirates of the Caribbean – Considered among the most popular amusement park rides ever created, this piratical adventure features excellent scenery, details, and action. Boarding boats, visitors first weave through a swamp before entering a Caribbean village peopled by buccaneers, pigs, parrots, and more. Disney's imagineers used their own faces as models for the pirates' features.
Above the entrance to Pirates of the Caribbean is the **Disney Gallery**, a salon-style gallery originally intended as a private apartment for Walt Disney and his wife Lilly. Today it displays and sells artwork related to Disneyland, and cartoon cels from Disney animated features.

Haunted Mansion – Looming ominously over New Orleans Square, this elegant "deserted" mansion is home to 999 ghosts and ghouls. From the **stretch room**, where heights and dimensions are not as they appear, visitors board small black "doom buggies" for an eerie trip among holographic images and haunting, if humorous, special effects.

★ Adventureland

The Polynesian motif of this little area is immediately obvious in the thatched roofs and massive tusk entrance gate. Little changed since the 1960s, Adventureland derives its particular charm from its early Disneyland feel. Stores here sell an interesting assortment of curios from "exotic" lands, and live performers periodically entertain diners in the Tahitian Terrace. The **Enchanted Tiki Room**, one of the first applications of audio-animatronics, stars funny, fantastical tropical birds and flowers with enough charisma to inspire the audience to sing along with them. *Check* Disneyland Today *for schedule.*

Jungle Cruise – Since opening day, visitors have been able to cruise through an overgrown river forest aboard safari boats. Combining features of the jungles of Africa and Asia, the riverfront is populated by mechanized crocodiles, hippos, elephants and tigers. Boat pilots offer a pun-laced narration throughout the trip. Walt Disney initially planned to use live animals in this attraction but was dissuaded by zoologists.

Swiss Family Treehouse – Visitors can climb through this sprawling, 80ft artificial banyan, which re-creates the appealing arboreal home of the indefatigable Swiss Family Robinson.

EXCURSION

★ **Crystal Cathedral** – *In Garden Grove. From Disneyland, drive south on Harbor Blvd; turn left on Chapman Blvd and left on Lewis St. 12141 Lewis St. Visit by guided tour (40min) only, daily year-round. Closed major holidays. ♿ ☎714-971-4000.* The inspiration for this star-shaped, glass-walled cathedral was born in the 1950s when evangelist Robert H. Schuller began preaching sermons at a local drive-in theater. In 1961 Schuller commissioned architect Richard Neutra, an Austrian-born practitioner of the International Style, to design the Garden Grove Community Church, a "drive-in church" with 1400 parking spaces, that enabled visitors to view the pulpit and participate in the service from their cars. By 1975 Neutra's structure could no longer accommodate the growing church. Philip Johnson conceived the present glass sanctuary (1980), which seats 3,000 and accommodates drive-in worshippers via a large video screen. The awe-inspiring spaciousness of the interior is achieved by the use of a lacelike framework of white steel trusses sheathed in more than 11,000 individual window panes. The adjacent Tower of Hope (1967), topped by a 236ft cross, was designed by Dion Neutra, son of Richard Neutra.

★ EAST MOJAVE NATIONAL SCENIC AREA Deserts

Map of Principal Sights p 5

This roughly pie-shaped area of some 1.5 million acres is situated near the Nevada state line between LOS ANGELES and Las Vegas. Administered by the US Bureau of Land Management, the vast expanse is punctuated by precipitous mountain ranges, dry lake beds, lava mesas, sand dunes, cinder cones and limestone caverns. Elevations ranging from 900 to 7929ft are home to some 700 species of plants and nearly 300 species of animals. A threadbare carpet of creosote bush covers the lowlands, while open forests of pine and juniper, and extensive stands of Joshua trees thrive in higher, cooler areas.

The eastern Mojave Desert has long been crossed by important transportation routes. Native American trading parties followed the Mojave River—usually dry but with water just below the surface in its sandy bed—between population centers on the Pacific Coast and the Colorado River. Early Spanish travelers, including the great Franciscan padre-explorer **Francisco Garcés** in 1776, followed in their footsteps. The Santa Fe Railroad from Chicago to Los Angeles crossed just south of the region in 1885, and the Union Pacific's line between Salt Lake City and Los Angeles came through in 1905, with Kelso Station as a division point for crew changes. There were occasional mining booms in the late 19C and early 20C, but the only sustained economic activity was ranching in the moister, higher elevations. Ranching continues today, but recreation, including hiking, backpacking and rock climbing, is of increasing importance to the region's economy.

Visiting the Region – East Mojave National Scenic Area (EMNSA) is very sparsely populated, and large sections are accessible only by 4-wheel drive vehicle. The city of **Barstow**, located about 80mi west, offers abundant lodging, food and fuel, and is the location of the BLM-operated **California Desert Information Center**, which functions as an off-site visitor center *(831 Barstow Road/Hwy 247 between Main St and I-40; open daily year-round; closed Jan 1, Dec 25; ♿ ☎619-256-8313)*. The small town of Baker, on the EMNSA's northern boundary, is another major service center.

SIGHTS *At least 1 day*

★ **Calico Ghost Town** – *Outside boundaries of EMNSA. From Barstow drive 8mi east on I-15 to Ghost Town Road exit; north 3mi to entrance gate. Open daily year-round. Closed Dec 25. $5. ⛺ ✕ ♿ ☎619-254-2122.* The vestiges of a historic silver and borax boom town have been restored and augmented to form a popular tourist attraction. Silver was discovered here in 1881, and the community of Calico was established as a mining supply center. By 1896 silver mining had become less profitable, owing to a drop in the price of the metal, and the town would probably have perished but for the discovery of borax deposits in the area. Borax mining powered the town's economy until 1907. The mines around Calico produced a total of between $13 and $20 million in silver and $9 million in borax, and the town reached a peak population of 3,000 in 1894. Calico was fast sinking into ruins when it was acquired in 1951 by Walter Knott, creator of Knott's Berry Farm *(p 112)*, who restored some of its Old West flavor before deeding it to San Bernardino County.

Visit – A long flight of steps *(a short incline railway accommodates those who would rather ride)* leads from the parking lot to the town's main street, now paved and reserved for pedestrians browsing in Calico's shops and historic buildings. **Lil's Saloon**, the Town Office, Lucy Lane's Home, the R&D Store and the **General Store** are original structures; the others have been rebuilt. The narrow-gauge **Calico & Odessa Railroad** offers short rides *(10min)* accompanied by historical narration, that circumscribe the hill just east of town.

★ **Calico Early Man Site** – *Outside boundaries of EMNSA. From Barstow drive 15mi east on I-15 to Minneola Road exit; continue north and east to end of 2.4mi dirt road.* On this barren desert hillside, deep pits excavated in strata laid down 200,000 years ago have revealed what may be crude scrapers and choppers made by very ancient humans, who lived on the game-rich shores of a lake that occupied the lowlands to the east and south. The site offers an excellent introduction to the physical organization and technical aspects of a major archaeological dig.

The veracity of artifacts found here upholds a theory that there may have been an earlier species of man in the Americas before *Homo sapiens*, which is thought to have entered the North American continent via the Bering land bridge about 13,000 BC. Louis S. B. Leakey, the excavator of some of the world's oldest human remains in East Africa's Olduvai Gorge, believed that the Calico site was a stone tool workshop, and directed excavations here from 1964 until his death in 1972.

Visit – *By guided tour (1hr) only, year-round Wed–Sun. Closed major holidays. Contributions requested. ☎619-256-8313.* Begin at the small, rustic visitor center, where several excavated artifacts are on view. Tours led by site archaeologists depart from the miner's shack that Leakey used as his field headquarters, and offer a close-up look at three large and several smaller excavation pits, some as deep as 30ft and protected from the elements by open shelters.

Kelso Dunes – *From Barstow drive 63mi east to Baker on I-15, then south 33mi to Kelso on Kelbaker Rd. Access on foot from a dirt road that turns off Kelbaker Rd 7.4mi south of the Union Pacific tracks. Evening or early morning visit recommended for best light.* Some of California's highest sand dunes, measuring 600ft above the valley floor, have accumulated in this spot where mountains weaken the prevailing winds that blow sand and dust in from the dry Mojave River sink to the northwest. The dunes may be seen to good advantage for several miles along Kelbaker Road northwest of the town of Kelso.

Mitchell Caverns – *Within the boundaries of the Providence Mountains State Recreation Area. From Barstow, drive east 80mi on I-40 ; take Essex Rd exit and continue 16mi northwest to end of road. Visit by guided tour (1hr 30min) only, mid-Sept–mid-Jun daily; rest of the year weekends and holidays. $4. ⚠ ♿ ☎805-942-0662. Warm clothing suggested.* Concealed within a desert mountainside, six limestone cavern chambers reveal beautiful, colorful and curious dripstone and flowstone formations, including stalactites, stalagmites, cave columns, cave shields, cave mushrooms and coral pipes. The predominantly fossil formations were created by percolating groundwater millions of years ago when the climate was wetter, before the rising San Gabriel and Sierra Nevada ranges cut off the flow of moist air from the Pacific Ocean.

★ EUREKA **North Coast** Pop 27,025

Map p 152 Tourist Office ☎707-443-5097

Smokestacks of several pulp mills line the shores of the city whose name (Greek for "I have found it") serves as California's state motto. Established on the tidal flats of Humboldt Bay by land companies in 1850, Eureka soon surpassed its northern neighbor Arcata *(p 151)* as the shipping hub of the mining, and later the lumber industry. The city's large deep-water harbor has ensured Eureka's standing as a major port since it became the county seat in 1856. Commercial fishing and processing of local timber still generate the bulk of the city's revenues.
Skirmishes between local Natives and settlers during the early 1850s led to the construction of a military post on Humboldt Heights in 1853. Conflicts escalated until 1864, when tensions eased and reservation land in the Hoopa Valley was set aside for the remaining Natives. **Fort Humboldt State Historic Park** now occupies the bluff on the southern edge of town where the original garrison once stood *(3431 Fort Ave; open daily year-round; ♿ ☎707-445-6567).*

SIGHTS *1/2 day*

★ **Old Town** – *Second and Third Sts between E and M Sts, adjacent to the waterfront.* On the western end of this 10-block historic district sits the ornate Victorian **Carson Mansion★★** *(Second and M Sts; not open to the public)*, built in 1886 for lumber magnate William Carson. Now a private men's club, the 3-story redwood mansion—the city's most photographed landmark—reflects the prosperity that Eureka experienced in its heyday *(illustration p 26)*.
Old Town contains fine examples of late-19C cast-iron architecture, such as the Buhne Building/Art Center *(211 G St)*, as well as other notable turn-of-the-century Victorian residences *(Third St between J and K Sts)*. Works by North Coast artists can be viewed at the Humboldt Cultural Center *(422 First St)* and at the whimsical **Wooden Sculpture Garden** *(317 Second St)* by the late Eureka sculptor Romano Gabriel.

★ **Clarke Memorial Museum** – *240 E St. Open year-round Tue–Sat. Closed major holidays. Contribution requested. ♿ ☎707-443-1947.* This glazed terra-cotta Classical Revival structure (1912) once served as a bank. It now houses a well-organized collection of objects and photographs relating to the city's history. A separate wing displays a fine group of over 1,200 Hoopa, Yurok and Karuk artifacts, including baskets, stonework and a log canoe.

Sequoia Park Zoo – *3414 West St. Open year-round Tue–Sun. ✗ ♿ ☎707-441-4263.* Adjacent to a small redwood forest, this modest, well-maintained zoo began as a deer park in 1907. Today it features a walk-through aviary and petting zoo in addition to its assemblage of animals.

Additional Sights – Lying in the bay just off the coast of Old Town, **Woodley Island** *(take Hwy 255 from R St)* maintains a rustic charm enhanced by its modern marina complex. Continuing on Highway 225 across the Samoa Bridge, the visitor reaches the Samoa Peninsula, site of the **Samoa Cookhouse** *(take Hwy 255 across the Samoa Bridge; turn left on Samoa Rd and take first left at sign)*, the last establishment of its kind in the West. Founded in 1900 to feed hungry lumberjacks, the camp-style restaurant exhibits antique logging equipment and photographs that recount the early days of the timber industry *(open daily year-round; ♿ ☎707-442-1659)*.

FRESNO **Central Valley** Pop 354,202

Map of Principal Sights p 3 Tourist Office ☎209-233-0836

California's eighth largest city is the seat of Fresno County, which leads the nation in agricultural output. Fully five percent of the world's grape harvest is produced here, along with oranges, figs, olives, vegetables, cotton, turkeys, beef cattle and dairy cattle. The city of Fresno was founded after the Gold Rush, and its proximity to the region's agricultural abundance led naturally to its development as a center of the food processing industry. Throughout the 20C it has grown as a major service, shipping and distribution center. A large campus of the California State University system is located here, and important medical facilities further diversify the local economy.

Fresno enjoys an ethnically diverse population: the city became a center of Armenian immigration a century ago, and presently boasts the country's largest concentration of Hmongs, a tribal people from Laos. The **Fresno Metropolitan Museum** *(1555 Van Ness Ave)* features a permanent gallery devoted to the city's most famous native son, Armenian-American author **William Saroyan** *(open daily year-round; closed major holidays; $4; ♿ ☎209-441-1444)*. The **Fresno Art Museum** *(2233 N. First St, in Radio Park)* mounts exhibits from its collection of French post-Impressionist prints and drawings, Mexican art from the pre-Columbian era to the present, California and Asian art and American sculpture *(open year-round Tue–Sun; closed major holidays, first 2 weeks Aug & first week Sept; $2; ♿ ☎209-441-4220)*.

SIGHTS *1/2 day*

Chaffee Zoological Gardens – *894 W. Belmont Ave in Roeding Park, about 2mi northwest of downtown. Open daily year-round. $4.50. ✕ ♿ ☎209-498-2671.* Set amid an attractive park, this pleasant, 18-acre zoo harbors some 400 species of animals. Successes from the zoo's program of breeding rare and endangered species include Sumatran tigers, sable antelopes and Galapagos tortoises; tropical birds fly about within a walk-through rain forest exhibit.

Meux Home Museum – *1007 R St, at corner of Tulare St. Visit by guided tour (45min) only, Feb–Dec Fri–Sun. Closed Dec 24 & 25. $3. ♿ ☎209-233-8007.* This elaborate Victorian mansion (1889) was considered the finest in Fresno at the time of its construction. The house was built by Dr Thomas R. Meux, an ex-Confederate Army surgeon who settled here after the Civil War. The house was restored as a museum in 1973, and is today appointed with period decorations and furnishings; Victorian era plants and flowers flourish in the gardens.

Kearney Mansion Museum – *7160 W. Kearney Blvd, in Kearney Park. Visit by guided tour only (40min), year-round Fri–Sun. Closed Jan 1, Easter Sunday, Dec 25. $3. ☎209-441-0862.* This lovely, French Renaissance-style residence was erected in 1903 by pioneer developer Theodore Kearney, who employed extensive canal systems to convert large tracts of land surrounding Fresno from pasture to intensively cultivated orchards and vineyards. Today the mansion exhibits many of its original furnishings, including Art Nouveau-style light fixtures and wall coverings imported from France.

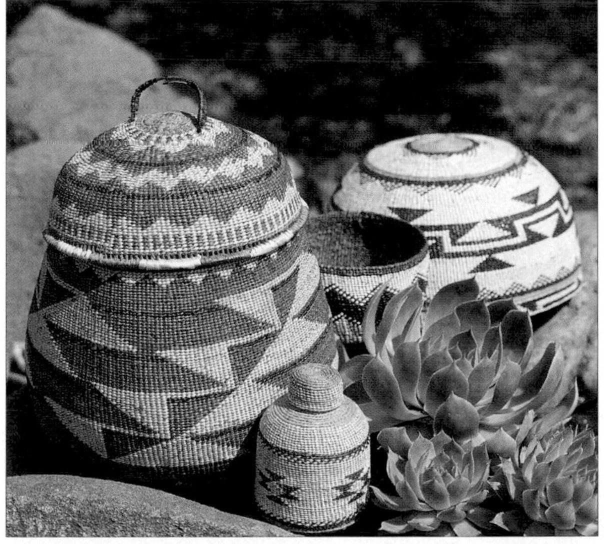

N. Kerby

Native American baskets

★★ GOLD COUNTRY Gold Country

Map p 64

The long, narrow strip of steeply rolling foothills extending between the western flank of the lofty Sierra Nevada range and the eastern edge of the Central Valley plain was the setting of the California Gold Rush of 1849. The frenzied 15 years following the discovery of gold in the American River brought waves of fortune-hunters—most of whom hoped to strike it rich and return home—and of immigrants seeking a better life in the western US. The rush placed California at the forefront of America's economic frontier for several decades. Nicknamed the "Mother Lode" after a large quartz vein, the region is now a quiet backcountry of scenic vistas and residential communities, many of which retain the flavor of the 19C.

HISTORICAL NOTES

Largely ignored during the Spanish and Mexican periods, the region remained unsettled during the early 19C, its virgin grasslands and forests of pine and oak home to such Native hunter-gatherer peoples as the Miwok and Maidu.
In 1839 Swiss immigrant John Sutter arrived in California and began the chain of events that so transformed the region. Sutter, a businessman and landowner, founded the settlement of New Helvetia at the site of present-day SACRAMENTO, intending to establish a vast agricultural estate in the Central Valley. To produce lumber for his many construction projects, Sutter entered into partnership in 1847 with **James Marshall** to erect a sawmill along the South Fork of the American River about 45mi northeast of New Helvetia.
On the morning of January 24, 1848, during an inspection of the nearly completed sawmill, Marshall discovered flakes of metal glittering in the tailrace, or channel leading from the waterwheel back to the river. He immediately informed Sutter, and together they concluded that the flakes were pure gold.

Historic Urban Plans

View of Coloma in 1857

Sutter tried to keep news of the discovery from spreading, fearing that his lands would be overrun with fortune hunters if the word got out. Though sworn to secrecy, Marshall was unable to stay silent, and soon members of his construction crew began to neglect the mill, roaming the riverbanks and digging out gold nuggets with pocket knives.
As legend has it, Sam Brannan *(p 38)*, observing that raw gold was being used as payment at his general store in New Helvetia, shrewdly stocked the store with provisions and supplies, then traveled to SAN FRANCISCO where he strode into Portsmouth Square, waving a medicine bottle full of nuggets and shouting "Gold! Gold in the American River!"

Gold Fever – By May of 1848, many California towns were virtually deserted as residents headed for the Sierra foothills in search of gold. Word of the discovery reached the eastern US by September. President James K. Polk, in an effort to justify US efforts to acquire the territory, publicized its unmined riches in a December address to Congress, and the rush began in earnest.
Throughout the year 1849, swarms of gold seekers, or "Forty-niners," as they were called, traveled from the eastern US by land via the California Trail *(p 24)* or by sea around Cape Horn. Others made their way south by ship to Panama, crossed overland to the Pacific Ocean and headed north by ship to California. Fortune hunters also arrived from Europe, South America, Australia and China, settling in the camps that dotted the region wherever gold was discovered.
The Gold Rush peaked around 1852 when the number of miners flooding the region neared 90,000, and slowly abated throughout the remainder of the 1850s as placer gold became more difficult to find. The developing hardrock mining industry offered employment, but these jobs, lacking the get-rich-quick results of placer and hydraulic mining, were less enticing to feverish Forty-niners and were often filled by immigrants from such European mining regions as Cornwall and Serbia. Within a decade, a steady mining industry was in place and the rush was over. It is estimated that more than 106 million troy ounces of gold were extracted from the region during the period between 1848 and 1867.
Many historic Gold Rush boom towns grew into present-day business centers and county seats; others dwindled into bucolic hamlets, or disappeared altogether. Time has softened and obscured the scars of mining on the landscape, and the Gold Country today presents an aspect more pastoral than industrial.

MINING FOR GOLD

Gold was concentrated in quartz veins by sub-surface geochemical processes about 100 million years ago, during the formation of the Sierran granite massif. Over the next 50 million years, nuggets and flakes of gold ore were released from their granite prison by erosion and concentrated in stream gravels that were later covered by flows of lava from erupting volcanoes. In the last few million years, the entire mountain range was elevated further and tilted to the west, allowing erosion to carve a new pattern of streams down through the lava and ancient gravel layers, liberating some of the gold into present-day stream beds.
Thus by the 19C, gold deposits existed in three forms: loosely mixed with the sand and gravel in rivers and streams; immobilized in buried riverbeds; and locked in quartz veins deep within the earth. The three principal methods of gold mining correspond to these settings.

Pans, Monitors and Buried Treasure – The process of agitating stream gravels to separate gold ore from non-gold-bearing sand and rock is known as **placer** (PLASS-er) mining. Panning, the simplest form of placer mining, entails swirling water and gravel around in a large pan, washing sand and rock over the edge and leaving the heavier gold fragments settled in the bottom. More efficient rockers and sluice boxes also harnessed moving water and gravity to separate the flecks of gold. Stories of rich placer deposits fueled the early influx of prospectors, but within a decade most Gold Country streams had been picked clean of surface gold.
Hydraulic mining grew from the discovery that further ore deposits lay buried in the ancient streambeds outcropping high on the region's hillsides. In 1853 miners near Nevada City began using streams of water to loosen these outcrops, washing the gravel down to where the gold could be recovered. During the heyday of hydraulic mining, whole hillsides were washed away by miners armed with huge water nozzles known as **monitors**. The resultant mud and gravel clogged river channels, causing serious floods as far away as the Central Valley, and by 1884, environmental damage was so severe that hydraulic mining was forbidden by court order. Today, more than a century later, the yet unvegetated scars of hydraulic mining are visible in many areas of the Gold Country.
The method employed to recover gold ore contained within buried quartz veins was called **hardrock** mining. Teams of miners tunneled deep into the earth to blast apart the veins and bring the rubble to the surface, where the gold was extracted through both physical and chemical processes. The capital investment and engineering expertise required for industrial quartz mining and milling brought a measure of economic and social stability to the chaotically settled region, and several important companies such as Sutter Creek's Central Eureka Mine and Grass Valley's Empire Mine *(p 65)* remained in operation for nearly a century.
Hardrock mining engendered the invention of two important devices: the **stamp mill**, which employed piston-like stampers to crush ore prior to gold extraction, and the **Pelton wheel**, devised by Lester Pelton in 1878 to power mining machinery. The wheel operated by force of a high-pressure stream of water aimed into rounded, bisected cups attached to its rim, a device that efficiently harnessed the stream's force by holding more water within the cup. Today stamp mills and Pelton wheels are visible in rusting retirement throughout the Gold Country.

Visiting the Gold Country – Summer afternoons in the region can be quite hot, although evenings are usually comfortable. Winter is often chilly and rainy, with snow occurring as low as 2,000ft above sea level, but the season offers interludes of mild dry weather as well. The best times to visit are spring, when the winter rains have turned the hillsides green; and autumn, when the height of the tourist season has passed and deciduous trees present their glorious colors.
Most sights lie along or near Highway 49, "The Golden Chain" traversing nine counties on its route between Mariposa and Sierra City. Towns and cities along the way offer a variety of accommodations ranging from chain motels to charming bed & breakfasts and inns.

DRIVING TOUR *3 days. 326mi (not including excursions). Begin on Hwy 49 in Mariposa.*

1 From Mariposa to Angels Camp *1 day. 76mi.*

Mariposa – Pop 1,152. Formerly a Gold Rush boom town of 5000 residents, Mariposa ("butterfly" in Spanish) is now a bustling county seat. Built in 1854, the handsome Greek Revival **courthouse** *(Bullion St between 9th and 10th Sts)* is said to be the West's oldest continuously functioning county courthouse.

★★ **California State Mining and Mineral Museum** – *1.5mi south of intersection of Hwys 49 and 140, in the county fairgrounds. Open May–Sept Mon, Wed–Sun 10am–6pm; rest of the year Wed–Sun 10am–4pm. Closed Jan 1, Thanksgiving Day, Dec 25. $3.50.* ✗ ☎*209-742-7625.* Home of the state **mineral collection** of some 20,000 specimens, the museum offers changing exhibits of gold samples, and eye-catching displays of mineralogical splendors and oddities. A working model of a 1904 Union Iron Works stamp mill highlights presentations on mining technology and California mining history.

Mariposa Museum and History Center – *West side of Hwy 49 at 12th St. Open daily Apr–Nov. Feb–Mar, Dec weekends only. Closed Thanksgiving Day, Dec 25. Contribution requested.* ♿ ☎*209-966-2924.* This small museum is densely packed with artifacts and memorabilia from daily life in 1850s Mariposa. Linking and unifying the exhibits are excerpts from letters written by a young pioneer to his family in New England. The museum also showcases the life of John C. Frémont *(p 24)*.

Coulterville – *33mi.* Situated in a sloping valley amid majestic hills, tiny Coulterville was home to some 1,000 Chinese immigrants during the height of the Gold Rush. The stately **Hotel Jeffery** and several other 19C buildings survive along Main Street, and local history exhibits are housed at the **Northern Mariposa County History Center** *(Hwy 49 and Main St; open Tue–Sun Apr–Oct; Nov–Mar weekends only; contribution requested; ♿ ☎209-878-3015).*

★ **Jamestown** – Pop 2,178. *25mi.* Founded in 1848, this attractive town sports original false-front buildings and boardwalks along Main Street. "Jimtown," as it is affectionately nicknamed, is known for its numerous restaurants.

★ **Railtown 1897 State Historic Park** – *5th and 9th Aves just east of Main St. Open daily year-round. Closed Jan 1, Thanksgiving Day, Dec 25. Narrated steam train excursions depart Mar–Nov weekends (round-trip 1hr). $9. ♿ ☎209-984-3953.* This complex of workshops and facilities served as a maintenance station for the historic Sierra Railway. Founded in 1897 and still in operation today, the railway linked the gold mines of the Mother Lode with supply and financial centers to the east and west. Departing from the visitor center in the former freight house, guided tours *(50min)* allow a thorough exploration of the park's historic working steam **roundhouse★**, with its belt-driven workshops and its cache of four turn-of-the-century steam engines. An excellent slide show *(17min)* presents the history of the Sierra Railway.

Railtown 1897 SHP

Roundhouse

Sonora – Pop 4,153. *4mi.* Established in 1848 by miners from the Mexican state of Sonora, this attractive commercial center and seat of Tuolumne County combines 19C charm with 20C vitality. Economic prosperity and longevity resulted in the variety of architectural styles that enlivens Sonora's hilly, curving streets. Housed in the former county jail, the **Tuolumne County Museum and History Center★** features a fine collection of historical photographs from the 19C along with artifacts and exhibits on mining, lumbering, and immigrant wagon trails over the Sierra Nevada *(158 W. Bradford St, 3 blocks west of Washington St; open Memorial Day–Labor Day Tue–Sun, rest of the year Tue–Sat; ♿ ☎209-532-1317).*

★★ **Columbia State Historic Park** – *4mi.* Founded in 1850, the boom town of Columbia survived several conflagrations and a lengthy decline as nearby gold deposits were exhausted during the late 19C. In 1945, Main Street and Broadway were purchased by the state and preserved as a charming historic park.

Visit – *Open year-round daily 8:30am–4:30pm. Closed Thanksgiving Day, Dec 25. ✗ ☎209-532-0150.* With cars banned from the 12 square blocks of park-owned streets, and costumed park employees traversing the tree-shaded brick sidewalks in re-creation of daily life between 1850 and 1870, Columbia paints an authentic picture of a Gold Rush boom town. Several structures, among them the Wells Fargo depot and the Masonic lodge, are maintained as museums, while others are operated as private concessions under state regulation to maintain historical authenticity. Live performances are presented in the elegant theater of the **Fallon Hotel**, and the restored **City Hotel** boasts a dining room noted for its fine cuisine. The **Museum** *(State and Main Sts)*, housed in a former miner supply store (1854), presents exhibits on local history, and features a collection of some 20 large mineral specimens. A slide show *(13min)* provides a good introduction to historic Columbia.

★ **Hidden Treasure Mine** – *Open May–Labor Day daily, rest of the year Mon, Thu–Sun. Closed Jan 1, Thanksgiving Day, Dec 25, during inclement weather. $7. Vans depart from the corner of Main St and Washington. ✗ ☎209-532-9693.* The Gold Country's only functioning hardrock mine open to the public penetrates a hillside overlooking a steep, scenic canyon. Guides narrate a miner's history of Columbia during the twisting, turning ride *(4.5mi)* to the mine, where all don hardhats before entering the 800ft tunnel for glimpses an ancient vein of gold-bearing ore.

Angels Camp – Pop 2,409. *15mi.* The setting for Mark Twain's short story *The Celebrated Jumping Frog of Calaveras County*, this picturesque town commemorates the tale with an annual frog-jumping contest in May. The **City Museum** presents some 50 buggies, surreys, and other horse-drawn vehicles along with mining exhibits and assorted Gold Rush artifacts *(Hwy 49, .5mi north of downtown; open daily Apr–end of Nov, rest of the year Wed–Sun. Closed major holidays. $1; ♿ ☎209-736-2963).*

★ **Murphys** – *Excursion: 18mi round-trip from Angels Camp via Hwy 4.* Pop 1,517. This charming community is graced by tall trees and mid-19C brick and stone buildings. Among those lining Main Street are the still-operating **Murphys Hotel★** (1856), with a historic guest list of such illustrious figures as Mark Twain, Ulysses S. Grant,

J.P. Morgan and Horatio Alger; and the **Old Timers Museum**, presenting the droll history of E Clampus Vitus, a fraternal order that originated during the Gold Rush to satirize the exclusivity of such established organizations as the Masons and the Odd Fellows *(open year-round Fri–Sun; $.50; ☎209-728-1160).*

Mercer Caverns – *1.3mi from Main St via Sheep Ranch Rd. Visit by guided tour (45min) only, daily year-round. Closed Thanksgiving Day, Dec 25. $5. ☎209-728-2101.* Visitors descend 160ft through a series of chambers containing spectacular examples of limestone formations, including stalactites, stalagmites and calcite curtains awash in color.

★★ **Calaveras Big Trees State Park** – *Excursion: 48mi round-trip from Angels Camp via Hwy 4 (15mi northeast of Murphys). Open daily year-round dawn–dusk. $5/car. ♿ ☎209-795-2334.* This lush preserve of some 6,000 pine-forested acres in the western foothills of the Sierra Nevada harbors two remarkable groves of giant sequoia trees *(p 226)*.

The startling size of these gargantuan botanical wonders attracted worldwide attention to the **North Grove** in the early 1850s, when tourists arrived in droves and several trees were destroyed for display elsewhere. Today, a well-maintained, self-guided trail *(1mi)* winds gently through the grove, where some 150 giant sequoias coexist with pine trees, dogwoods and other forest vegetation. The more remote South Grove *(1mi from end of paved road at Beaver Creek)* has been left in its natural state; a 3.5mi loop trail offers a rare opportunity to experience the untouched primeval forest.

2 From San Andreas to Auburn *1 day. 47mi.*

San Andreas – Pop 2,115. *12mi from Angels Camp.* Founded in 1848 by Mexican settlers and today the seat of Calaveras County, sleepy San Andreas was the scene of the 1883 trial of Charles E. Bolton, better known as **Black Bart**. A prominent San Francisco socialite, Bolton robbed 28 stagecoaches between 1875 and 1883. The "gentleman robber" was found guilty at the San Andreas trial and served nearly six years in the state prison at San Quentin.

★ **Calaveras County Museum** – *30 N. Main St. Open daily year-round. Closed Jan 1, Dec 25. $.50. ♿ ☎209-754-6579.* Located on the second floor of the renovated Hall of Records, this contemporary museum highlights the history of the Native Miwok people, as well as lumbering, mining and agriculture in Calaveras County. A special feature is an excellent exhibit of the area's geologic history.

A short stroll through the pleasant walled garden behind the building leads to a row of **jail cells**, where Black Bart was incarcerated during his trial.

Mokelumne Hill – *8mi.* Today a minuscule village set atop a mountainous ridge blessed with lovely views, "Moke Hill," for a brief period in the early 1850s, boasted a population of 15,000 and served as the center of one of California's richest placer gold districts. A large concentration of French immigrants settled here, and the historic **Hotel Leger** (1851), originally the Hotel de France, remains in operation today.

★ **Jackson** – Pop 3,545. *8mi.* Seat of Amador County, this bustling town was founded in 1849 as a placer mining camp. By 1859 hardrock operations had begun on the rich quartz vein that renders Amador County second only to Nevada County in total gold output.

Today Jackson reflects a pleasing balance of the old and new, especially evident in the 19C architecture along Main Street. The **National Hotel** *(foot of Main St)* claims to be the oldest continually operating hotel in California (1863). From a scenic overlook about 1.5mi north of town on Highway 49, the **view** encompasses the rusting headframes of the defunct Kennedy and Argonaut mines.

★ **Amador County Museum** – *225 Church St. Open year-round Wed–Sun. Contribution requested. ☎209-223-6386.* Set atop a small knoll some two blocks northeast of the business district, this historic brick home (1859), with its many artifacts and thematic displays, offers a charming introduction to daily life in Jackson from the Gold Rush to the 1920s. An adjacent building *(visit by 30min guided tour only, weekends year-round; $1)* contains working models of the Kennedy Mine headframe and tailing wheels *(below)*, and the attractively landscaped property is crowned by two majestic cedar trees.

Crowning a small rise across Church Street is the small, white **St Sava Serbian Orthodox Church**, founded in 1894 to serve Jackson's immigrant Serbian population. The church is the "mother church" of Serbian Orthodoxy in the US.

Kennedy Mine Tailing Wheels – *N. Main St, 1mi north of downtown. Information kiosk at edge of parking lot. Open daily year-round. ☎209-223-0350.* Built in 1912, these 58ft wooden wheels were designed to transport rubble and debris, via a series of inclined flumes, over two ridges from the Kennedy Mine to a holding pond. Accessed by rugged trails, the wheels are now collapsing into ruin, ghostly reminders of a once-burgeoning industry.

★ **Indian Grinding Rock State Historic Park** – *Excursion: 24mi round-trip from Jackson by Hwy 88 and Volcano Rd. Open daily year-round. Closed Jan 1, Thanksgiving Day, Dec 25. $5/car. ☎209-626-7488.* Prior to the Gold Rush, Native Miwoks lived in this peaceful grove of pine trees, today transformed as a small park that offers visitors a unique opportunity to experience Native culture firsthand. Well worth seeing is the flat limestone outcrop pitted with hundreds of *chaw'se*, or mortar holes, used for grinding acorns into meal. Nearby are re-created Miwok bark dwellings and a ceremonial roundhouse that still hosts local tribal gatherings. A small regional museum is dedicated to Sierra Nevada indigenous peoples.

★ **Sutter Creek** – Pop 1,835. *4mi from Jackson.* Today one of the Gold Country's most charming small communities, Sutter Creek began in 1848 as a placer mining camp. John Sutter stayed here briefly, but left when his panning efforts in the area proved unsuccessful. Stability arrived in the mid-1850s with the establishment of the Central Eureka hardrock mine just south of town. The mine operated for nearly a century and the prosperity it brought to Sutter Creek is reflected today along attractive **Main Street**, where antique and specialty shops occupy original 19C storefronts.

Amador City – Pop 196. *2mi.* California's smallest incorporated city, this charming village nestled along Highway 49 as it bends through a small valley was founded in 1848 by José Maria Amador, a Mexican soldier. Amador City is today known for its antique shops and for the elegant brick **Imperial Hotel** (1879).

Placerville – Pop 8,355. *29mi.* The placer mining camp founded here in 1848 was dubbed "Hangtown," owing to its residents' propensity to visit quick retribution on malefactors. Situated on present-day US-50, then the principal route over the Sierra Nevada linking California with the Nevada silver mines, the community developed as a transportation hub and was renamed Placerville in 1854. Today the city is the bustling seat of El Dorado County. Its 20C outskirts surround a nucleus of 19C buildings that retain their historical charm, among them the brick-and-fieldstone structure housing the **Historical Society Museum** *(524 Main St; open May–Sept Fri–Sun, rest of the year weekends only; contribution requested; ☎916-626-0773).* Especially pleasant during the fall harvest season is the **Apple Hill** district, a rolling expanse of orchards and farms anchored by Highway 50 east of Placerville. Visitors can meander along the highway and its scenic back roads, sampling local produce and baked goods from roadside stands, bakeries, restaurants and wineries.

El Dorado County Historical Museum – *100 Placerville Dr, in county fairgrounds (2.5mi west of town). Open year-round Wed–Sun. Closed Dec 24–Jan 1. Contribution requested. ♿ ☎916-621-5865.* Among the great variety of exhibits are a splendidly appointed and restored **Concord coach** that crossed the Sierra Nevada via Placerville; a re-created country store; and a large outdoor display of mining and railroad equipment, including an operable Shay locomotive (1907).

Gold Bug Mine – *1mi north of Hwy 50 on Bedford Ave. Open daily May–mid-Sept; mid-Mar–Apr & mid-Sept–Oct weekends only. $1. ☎916-642-5232.* Operated from 1928 to the beginning of World War II by local residents, this hardrock mine is today owned by the city and open to the public. A taped narration of the mine's history accompanies visitors through the 300ft mine tunnel for a view of the quartz vein that lured miners to sink some 250 shafts in the immediate vicinity.

★★ **Marshall Gold Discovery State Historic Park** – *8mi.* Nestled at the foot of a grass-covered hill on the banks of the American River, at the site where James Marshall stumbled across his first nuggets of gold *(p 60)*, this 276-acre state historic park commemorates the town of Coloma, site of California's gold discovery. Coloma was founded in 1847 when Marshall and John Sutter selected the site for the location of Sutter's new sawmill. The town served as the seat of easily-mined El Dorado County during the rush's frenzied heyday, but sank into relative obscurity as the supply of placer gold was exhausted. In 1856 the county seat was moved to Placerville, and Coloma became an agricultural village.

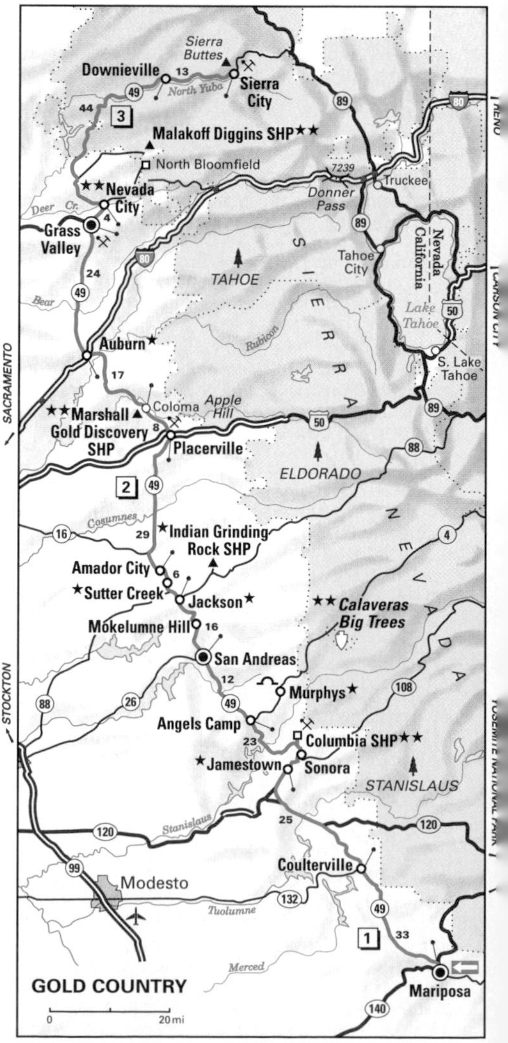

Today some 70 percent of Coloma (pop 200) is preserved within the park boundaries. Historic structures line peaceful Main, Back and Brewery Streets, and the modest rapids of this celebrated stretch of the American River invite kayakers and rafters, as well as panners, to try their luck.

Visit – *Open May–Sept daily 10am–5pm, rest of the year 10:30am–4:30pm. $5/car. ♿ ☎ 916-622-3470.* Begin in the **visitor center**, where exhibits and an excellent video presentation *(12min)* summarize the geology of gold and the history of the Gold Rush, describing the ruinous effect of the discovery on the fortunes of both Marshall and Sutter. Mining equipment, including monitors, stamp mills and horse-drawn mills are on display next to the center, and a small path leads to two restored **Chinese stores**, originally owned by members of Coloma's Chinese immigrant population.
The replicated wood-frame **sawmill**, reconstructed from Marshall's original drawings, stands upstream from the original mill site. Visitors can try panning for gold on the river's opposite bank, accessed by a narrow bridge *(pans available at visitor center)*.
A narrow road passes the buildings of historic Coloma, many of them survivors of the Gold Rush era, before winding up the adjacent hill where sits Marshall's restored cabin; his grave, at the hill's summit, is marked by a large bronzed monument overlooking the gold discovery site.

★ **Auburn** – Pop 10,592. *17mi.* Today the Gold Country's largest town, Auburn was founded in 1848 when a band of prospectors led by French immigrant Claude Chana set out from Sigard's Ranch near present-day Sacramento to join the diggings at Coloma *(above)*. Camping here beside a stream for the night, Chana tried his luck with a pan or two, and discovered three nuggets of gold. He and his band went no further, and the tent camp they founded grew into a major transportation center. The Southern Pacific Railroad passes through Auburn, and its location at the junction of Highway 49 and the main route between Sacramento and LAKE TAHOE (present-day I-80) enabled the city to escape the post-Gold Rush decline common to other boom towns.

Old Town – Auburn's original nucleus of settlement is today a charming conglomeration of antique stores, specialty shops and restaurants, many located in buildings dating to the mid-19C. Particularly noteworthy are the red and white striped **Old Firehouse** (1891); and a monumental **statue** of Claude Chana *(above)*. Overlooking Old Town from an adjacent hill is the Placer County **courthouse**, a striking, domed structure in the neoclassical style (1898).

Gold Country Museum – *1273 High St in the county fairgrounds. From Old Town drive north on Sacramento St, cross Auburn-Folsom Rd and continue .5mi east to fairgrounds entrance. Open year-round Tue–Sun. Closed Jan 1, Dec 25. $1 admission includes Bernhard Museum. ♿ ☎916-889-4134.* This small, informative museum invites visitors to explore a simulated mine shaft and mineral exhibits highlighting the mining, processing and uses of gold. Located within walking distance is the **Bernhard Museum**, built in 1851 as a hotel and presently restored as a Victorian-era house museum and winery complex *(291 Auburn-Folsom Rd; visit by 45min guided tour only, year-round Tue–Sun; closed Jan 1, Dec 25; ♿ ☎916-889-4156)*.

3 From Grass Valley to Sierra City *1 day. 58mi.*

Grass Valley – Pop 9,048. *24mi from Auburn.* This small but active commercial center owed its long prosperity to important innovations in deep mining technology that were developed and applied here at the Empire, North Star and Idaho-Maryland Mines. Laborers were recruited from regions as distant as Cornwall, England, with its centuries-old tin mining industry; Cornish "pasties" (meat pies) remain a local specialty today.
Much of the area around Main and Mill streets was rebuilt after a fire swept the town in 1855; of note is the opulent **Holbrooke Hotel** *(W. Main St)*; built in 1862, the hostelry welcomed presidents Ulysses S. Grant, James A. Garfield, Benjamin Harrison and Grover Cleveland during the late 19C.

★★ **Empire Mine State Historic Park** – *1.5mi southeast of downtown by Mill and Empire Sts. Open daily year-round. $2. ♿ ☎916-273-8522.* California's largest and richest deep mine comprised 365mi of underground tunnels and produced 5.8 million troy ounces of gold during its century of operation (1852-1957). In the main shaft, visitors may stand on a platform located some 30ft below the surface for a gaze into the blackness of the mile-deep pit. Clustered about the mouth of the shaft is an assortment of equipment, processing buildings and administrative offices. The **visitor center** features a poignant photographic exhibit commemorating the hard life of the Cornish miners, and contained within the park are the handsome, redwood-paneled house and landscaped grounds of William Bourn, owner of the mine from 1879 to 1929.

★ **North Star Mining Museum** – *South of downtown on Mill St, just beyond the Hwy 20 viaduct. Open daily May–Oct. Contribution requested. ♿ ☎916-273-2455.* The North Star Mine's historic stone powerhouse (1885) has been refurbished as one of the region's most comprehensive museums of mining technology. Especially noteworthy is a working Cornish water pump *(coin-activated)* that was used to remove water from the mine's deepest levels, and a Pelton wheel *(p 61)*, said to be the world's largest.

★★ **Nevada City** – Pop 2,855. *4mi.* A favorite destination for lovers of 19C architecture, this picturesque town is a relaxing haven of shops and restaurants, and home to several performing arts groups. A concentration of placer claims on Deer Creek led to the founding of the community, first incorporated in 1851 simply as Nevada; the "City" was added later to avoid confusion with Nevada Territory, created in 1862. Today Nevada City's charming, well-preserved business district is highlighted by **Broad Street**, which slopes gently down from the square-towered Methodist church (1864) to the filigree-balconied **National Hotel★** (1856). The attractive Art Deco Nevada County **courthouse** (1937) overlooks the downtown area from an adjacent hill, and the charming, 2-story Victorian **firehouse** *(214 Main St)* built in 1861, today holds a collection of local artifacts, including the altar from a mid-19C Chinese joss house.

★★ **Malakoff Diggins State Historic Park** – *Excursion: 54mi round-trip from Nevada City. Take Hwy 49 north 11mi and turn right on Tyler Foote Crossing Rd and bear left on Cruzon Grade Rd; follow signs. Open daily year-round. $5/car. ♿ ☎916-265-2740.* Hydraulic operations began on this site in 1855, and 25 years later the Malakoff diggings had become California's largest hydraulic mine operation. Today, more than a century after hydraulic mining was forbidden by court order *(p 61)*, the eroded walls of the vast **Malakoff Pit** remain bare of vegetation, forming a raw badland amid lush mountain forests. A few Gold Rush-era buildings survive, grouped in a pleasant tree-shaded setting at the site of the historic North Bloomfield; the village reached a population of 1,200 in the early 1880s. A film of a hydraulic monitor in action is shown in the small museum *(open daily Jun–Aug, rest of the year weekends only)*, and a short drive *(2mi)* leads past the Hiller Tunnel, from which mine tailings drained from Malakoff Pit into the south fork of the North Yuba River, to several lookout points on the pit's south rim.

Downieville – *44mi from Nevada City.* Isolated deep in a forested canyon at the confluence of the Yuba and Downie rivers, Downieville is graced by a narrow Main Street lined with 19C structures, many of them of brick or stone with iron shutters. The town is one of the smallest county seats in the US, and the homes of its inhabitants perch on the steep slopes rising from the rivers. The **Sierra County Museum** *(Main St)*, occupying an old store constructed of schist boulders, houses artifacts and photographs from mining days *(open daily Memorial Day–1st weekend in Oct; contribution requested; ☎916-289-3261)*.

Sierra City – *13mi.* The highest of the Gold Country towns enjoys a spectacular **setting** at the foot of the craggy, 8590ft summits of the Sierra Buttes. The tiny community survived several calamitous avalanches of snow and ice that rushed down its precipitous slopes, killing residents and employees of the Sierra Buttes mine. Today, Sierra City's few homes overlook the business district from the surrounding mountainsides.

★ **Kentucky Mine Historical Park and Museum** – *1mi north of Sierra City by Hwy 49. Open Memorial Day–Sept Wed–Sun. Oct weekends only.* Last worked in 1953, the Kentucky Mine is a unique attraction—a hardrock gold mine with a operable ore-processing stamp mill. Guided tours depart from the mine's portal, proceed across an ore-cart trestle and down through the levels of the mill, with stops to explain each step in the milling and extraction process.

★★★ HEARST CASTLE Central Coast

Map p 43

Overlooking the Pacific Ocean from high atop a crest of the Santa Lucia mountains near the seaside village of San Simeon, this expansive 127-acre estate and the opulent mansion crowning it embody the flamboyant image of **William Randolph Hearst**. Eclectically designed and lavishly embellished with the newspaper magnate's world-class collection of Mediterranean art and antiques, the castle attracts some one million visitors annually.

Building an Empire – The only child of George and Phoebe Apperson Hearst inherited his father's hunger for money as well as his mother's passion for travel and the arts. A frontier miner, George Hearst made his fortune from rich veins of ore in the western US. While the elder Hearst traveled back and forth from the mines, William was left with his mother, an intellectual woman who valued education. Under her tutelage, young Will was exposed to a world of art and culture that whetted his appetite for what would later become an obsession for collecting art.
After being suspended from Harvard for failing to attend classes, Hearst took a job with Joseph Pulitzer's sensational newspaper, the *New York World.* A year later, in 1887, the budding journalist convinced his father to put him at the helm of the *San Francisco Examiner*, which the elder Hearst had acquired in 1880. Thus began a media empire that at its height employed 38,000 people and included 26 newspapers, 16 magazines, 11 radio stations, 5 news services and a movie company. In 1902, Hearst successfully ran for a seat in the US House of Representatives, serving two consecutive terms, but ended his foray into politics in 1912 after two failed attempts to win the US presidency as an independent candidate.

The title character of Orson Welles' 1941 masterpiece **Citizen Kane** *was loosely modeled on William Randolph Hearst.*
Hearst unsuccessfully attempted to suppress the film prior to its release.

La Cuesta Encantada – Boyhood camping vacations at San Simeon ranch, which his father had purchased in 1865, instilled in Hearst a lifelong love of this site. He and his wife, vaudeville actress Millicent Willson, and their five sons often vacationed at "Camp Hill," where they erected a luxurious tent village. When Hearst inherited the San Simeon lands in 1919, he hired San Francisco architect **Julia Morgan**—the first woman ever to be accepted in the architecture program at France's famed Ecole des Beaux-Arts—to design a "bungalow" on the site. Over the next 27 years, the project snowballed from a modest country residence to *La Cuesta Encantada,* "The Enchanted Hill," as Hearst named his palatial estate.

With Hearst's collaboration, Morgan drafted plans for the imposing main house, called **La Casa Grande**, and three guest houses, all inspired by the southern Mediterranean Revival style. From La Casa Grande's twin Spanish Colonial towers with their Arabesque grillwork and Belgian carillon bells, to the Etruscan colonnades that complement the Greco-Roman temple facade of the Neptune Pool, the design emerged as a mélange of eclectic elements that defies strict classification. (When questioned once about the many styles represented in Hearst's mansion, Morgan retorted, "I call it 'pleasing my client.'")

Refectory

... Blades/Hearst Monument

Hearst's estate became a study in superlatives. The 65,000sq ft main house, the grandest private residence in the nation at the time, contained 115 rooms, including 24 bedrooms, 41 bathrooms, two libraries, a billiard room, beauty salon and theater, all resplendent with works from Hearst's art holdings, one of the most extensive private collections in the US. The estate also boasted the world's largest privately owned zoo (with some 100 species of domestic and exotic animals), and the country's most capacious heated pool.

Secluded San Simeon served as a playground for Hearst, his mistress Marion Davies (a starlet he met in 1915) and a host of Hollywood glitterati, among them Gloria Swanson, Charlie Chaplin, Greta Garbo and Cary Grant. In 1947 a heart attack forced the millionaire to leave the hill and move to LOS ANGELES. The man *Life* magazine described as a "one-man fireworks display" died four years later at the age of 88. The Hearst Corporation deeded the 127-acre estate to the State of California in 1957; the family still owns the working ranch land surrounding the castle.

The Collection – Hearst's zeal for collecting art was born during an 18-month trip to Europe with his mother when he was 10 years old. Impact and impression were the yardsticks he used to measure his purchases, which he expected Morgan to incorporate into the estate's ever-changing design (plans for a formal art gallery were never realized). During the 1920s, Hearst amassed enough treasures to fill six warehouses. Dealers in auction houses in New York and London scoured the continents for now-priceless antiquities, textiles, sculptures, paintings and antique ceilings. Highlights of the castle's collection include silver and furnishings, **16C tapestries**, Florentine Renaissance terra-cotta sculpture, and a superb group of ancient **Greek vases** that line the shelves of Hearst's 5,000-volume library.

VISIT *1 day*

47mi north of San Luis Obispo via Hwy 1; 98mi south of Monterey by Hwy 1.

Purchase tickets at visitor center (opens at 8am). Visit by guided tour only (1hr 45min), year-round daily 8:20am–3:20pm. Closed Jan 1, Thanksgiving Day, Dec 25. $14. ✗ ♿ ☎805-927-2093. In order to see the estate, visitors must take one (or more) of four different tours. Least strenuous and most comprehensive of the four, Tour 1 is recommended for first-time visitors. All tours depart by bus from the **visitor center**, the east wing of which is devoted to an exhibit depicting the many facets of Hearst and his monument. During the ride *(10min)* up to **La Casa Grande**, lovely **views** stretch past oak hollows to the sea glimmering miles below, and a recorded narrative provides a brief history of the family and estate.

Guides lead groups through the buildings and grounds; visitors are not permitted to roam the site or to linger during or after tours. All tours entail walking at least .5mi and climbing over 150 stair steps, and include a look at Hearst's two spectacular swimming pools: the outdoor **Neptune Pool★**, with its graceful Classical design, and the indoor **Roman Pool★**, lined with gold-inlaid Venetian glass tiles.

Tour 1 – *150 stairs. Recommended for first-time visitors.* Hearst Castle's most spectacular features are revealed on this tour, including the Assembly Room, Refectory, Morning Room, Billiard Room, Theater and the 18-room Casa del Sol guest cottage. Lined with choir stalls from a 14C Spanish cathedral, the **Refectory** contains a remarkable display of antique silver. A rare example of a Flemish *mille fleurs* tapestry (c.1500) hangs in the **Billiard Room**.

Tour 2 – *377 stairs.* Doge's Suite, the Cloisters—including the **Della Robbia Room**—the **Library**, Hearst's private Gothic Suite and Study, as well as the Pantry and cavernous Kitchen are included.

Tour 3 – *316 stairs.* Completed during Hearst's final years at the castle, the three floors of bedroom suites serve as a showcase for antique Spanish ceilings and priceless Oriental carpets. The 10-room Casa del Monte guest cottage and a short *(8min)* film about the estate's construction are also featured.

Tour 4 – *Apr–Oct only. 306 stairs.* On the grounds and gardens tour, visitors will discover the **Hidden Terrace**, a spidery network of stairs that was concealed by construction in the 1930s, as well as Hearst's wine cellar, the Neptune Pool dressing rooms and the 18-room Casa del Mar, the largest of the three guest cottages and the first building on the site to be completed.

★★ JOSHUA TREE NATIONAL MONUMENT Deserts

Map of Principal Sights p 5

Named for a tree-like member of the Yucca genus whose long, strangely contorted branches made early Mormon travelers think of Joshua pointing to the promised land, this 850sq mi park preserves within its boundaries two very distinct types of desert: the high (Mojave) and low (Colorado). The transition from one to the other can be experienced in a short drive. The monument is also known for its picturesque hills of rounded monzogranite boulders.

Two Distinct Landscapes – The monumental piles of quartz monzogranite boulders visible throughout much of the park were formed 135 million years ago when flows of molten rock pushed up towards the surface, failed to break through, and cooled slowly underground. Erosion eventually removed the softer overlying rock, exposed the solidified masses, enlarged the cracks formed when the rock cooled, and rounded the remaining chunks into the smooth formations seen today.

The **Joshua tree** *(Yucca brevifolia)* is characteristic of the high, cool Mojave Desert (above 3,000ft), and is distinguished from other types of yucca by its height (as tall as 40ft). The trees propagate both by seed and by sending out long underground runners, and colonize broad areas to form sparse "forests."

The monument's eastern portion comprises hotter, drier Colorado desert (below 3,000ft), characterized by broad, flat spaces, tall spindly ocotillo bushes and fuzzy cholla cacti. The road from the northwestern part of the monument down to the Cottonwood Springs entrance in its southeastern corner *(38mi)* crosses a transition zone where characteristics of both types of desert are mingled.

The Chemehuevi, Serrano and Cahuilla hunter-gatherers and farmers who originally occupied this land were forced out by a flurry of white settlers who arrived here when gold strikes were discovered in the 1870s and 1880s. The ore had petered out by the early 20C, and for a brief period, cattle ranches thrived here. The area was designated a national monument in 1936.

Visiting Joshua Tree – *Open daily year-round. $5/car. ♿ ☎619-367-7511.* Joshua Tree is located approximately 140mi from LOS ANGELES via I-10 and Highway 62 (Twentynine Palms Highway). Towns along Highway 62 offer a full range of amenities. The **Oasis Visitor Center** *(.5mi south of Hwy 62 in the town of Twentynine Palms; follow signs; open daily year-round; closed Dec 25; ♿)* offers a small museum, bookstore, and information desk. The south entrance and **Cottonwood Visitor Center** *(same hours as Oasis Visitor Center)* are accessible from PALM SPRINGS via I-10 *(50mi)* and Cottonwood Springs Road. Campsites are the only accommodation available within the park; food and water are not available within the park.

VISIT *1 day*

★ **Geology Tour Road** – *From Oasis Visitor Center drive 13.6mi; follow signs. Brochure available at visitor center. 4-wheel drive vehicle suggested.* Penetrating the park's scenic backcountry, this rugged dirt road *(18mi)* is marked with 16 stops that highlight evidence of the geological forces present in this region.

Joshua trees

Quartz monzogranite boulders display horizontal grooves several feet above ground that were formed by blowing sand before erosion had lowered the ground level. The black basalt of Malapai Hill, a near-volcano, rises to the west. At Squaw Tank, grinding holes made by generations of Native Americans are visible, as are linear dikes formed by molten rock intrusions into joints in the monzogranite. The road then descends an alluvial fan into Pleasant Valley, a *graben*, or sinking valley formed by virtual movement on the Blue Cut fault. Remains of abandoned gold mines are visible in this fault scarp.

★ **Keys View** – *From Oasis Visitor Center drive 19mi on main park road, turn left and continue 6.2mi.* This perch on the crest of the Little San Bernardino Mountains at 5,185ft offers a sweeping **view★★** of Coachella Valley, from the Palm Springs area to the Salton Sea. To the south and west loom Mt San Jacinto (10,804ft) and San Gorgonio Peak (11,499ft), the highest point in southern California. Both peaks are snow-covered for much of the year. *Morning visit recommended for best light.*

★ **Cholla Cactus Garden** – *17mi from Oasis Visitor Center via main park road and Pinto Basin Rd.* The deceptively soft and fuzzy-looking cholla *(Opuntia bigelovii)* grows here in great abundance owing to favorable groundwater conditions. Cholla spines penetrate the skin easily and are painful and difficult to remove. About 1.5mi further east, the **Ocotillo Patch** harbors a splendid stand of this tall shrub *(Fouquieria splendens)*. A member of the low desert plant community, the ocotillo looks like a bundle of thorny sticks most of the year, but sports a fur of brilliant green leaves after rains, and bright orange flag-like flowers in spring *(illustration p 17)*.

★ **Walks among the Rocks** – *Brochures available at Oasis Visitor Center.* These short nature trails, several with interpretive signs identifying desert plants, provide easy access to mysteriously attractive quartz monzogranite formations.

★ **Hidden Valley Nature Trail** – *1mi loop. Trailhead 21.5mi from Oasis Visitor Center on the main park road.* An easy trail winds through a natural enclosure formed by hills of monzogranite, said to have been used by cattle rustlers in the 1880s for hiding stolen cattle. Today the area is a mecca for rock climbers.

★ **Skull Rock Nature Trail** – *3mi round-trip. Trailhead 9mi from Oasis Visitor Center on the main park road.* This moderate trail winds across open country to a rock that resembles a human skull, then crosses the road and becomes more difficult as it ascends a dry wash. Formations here reveal remarkable dikes, light-colored bands formed when molten rock was forced into cracks in already existing monzogranite.

Indian Cove Nature Trail – *.5mi round-trip. From Twentynine Palms drive west 5mi on Hwy 62; turn left and proceed 2.7mi. Trailhead is at the west edge of the camping area.* This easy trail passes the monzogranite formations, and winds through a typical Mojave Desert wash, offering a view far out into the desert to the north.

Cap Rock Nature Trail – *.4mi round-trip. Trailhead at intersection of the main park loop road and the spur road to Keys View.* This paved, level trail circumnavigates a typical monzogranite dome. Next to the parking lot, another dome sports a balanced boulder that resembles the bill of a baseball cap.

★★ LA JOLLA San Diego County

Map of Principal Sights p 4

Tourist Office ☎619-454-1444

SAN DIEGO'S most upscale, sunkissed suburb, the community of La Jolla (la-HOY-ya) hugs some of Southern California's most breathtakingly beautiful shoreline 12mi northwest of downtown. The glittering community's name is generally taken to mean "the jewel," from the identically pronounced Spanish word *la joya*.

Nature Enhanced – Prior to the 1880s, the chaparral- and sagebrush-covered slopes were prized by San Diegans as a day-trip and picnic site with spectacular ocean views. In 1886, Frank Botsford and George Heald recognized the area's potential for growth. They bought up much of La Jolla, planting eucalyptus, cedar and palm trees and laying out streets that followed the land's natural contours. Among La Jolla's earliest settlers were members of the publishing millionaire Scripps family. **Ellen Browning Scripps** in particular contributed greatly to its character, safeguarding its coastline and parks and commissioning architect **Irving Gill** to design many graceful buildings that continue to enhance the area's character.

La Jolla today maintains an affluent, yet relaxed ambience. Mediterranean villas behold the Pacific from lushly landscaped hillsides surrounding a shopping village centering on **Prospect Street**, where Mediterranean-style buildings conceal chic boutiques and restaurants. North of town are such academic and research enclaves as the University of California, San Diego; the Scripps Institute of Oceanography; and the Salk Institute *(p 70)*, all originally drawn here by the area's unspoiled beauty. On the university campus is the nationally acclaimed La Jolla Playhouse.

SIGHTS *1 day*

★★ **Museum of Contemporary Art, San Diego** – *700 Prospect St. Closed for renovation until 1996. ☎619-454-3541.* Distinguished by its rectilinear Prospect Street colonnade, the museum was established in 1941 and occupies the remodeled home (1916, Irving Gill) of Ellen Browning Scripps. Visiting shows and selections from a permanent collection of artworks created since the 1950s fill spacious white galleries. The **sunroom** is most spectacular, offering ocean views through its picture windows. A **sculpture garden** is arrayed on the slope below.

Further renovation of the original site, masterminded by architect Robert Venturi, will add more space and completely restore the facade of Gill's original structure.

★★ **La Jolla Cove** – The rugged beauty of the California coast is readily accessible in this small, cliff-fringed cove downslope from Prospect Street. Snorkelers bob face-down in clear, tranquil waters, while beside the cove, **Scripps Park** attracts sunbathers, picnickers and artists attempting to capture the **views**★★ of ocean-facing bluffs stretching north and south.

A short stroll to the north along **Coast Walk**, the waves have carved out the seven **La Jolla Caves**; one of them, Sunny Jim Cave, may be reached via La Jolla Cave and Shell Shop *(1325 Coast Blvd; open daily year-round; closed Thanksgiving Day, Dec 25; $1.25; access to caves via 145 stairs ☏619-454-6080).*

★★ **Stephen Birch Aquarium-Museum** – *2300 Expedition Way. Open year-round daily 9am–5pm. Closed Thanksgiving Day, Dec 25. $6.50.* ✂ ♿ *☏619-534-3474.* Rising on a bluff above La Jolla's coastline, the 49,400sq ft contemporary Mission-style complex encompasses a state-of-the-art aquarium and the largest museum in the nation devoted solely to oceanography.

The founders of the Marine Biological Association of San Diego included in their 1903 bylaws a commitment to create a public aquarium and museum. Renamed the Scripps Institution for Biological Research in 1912 for local benefactors E.W. and Ellen Browning Scripps, the association eventually acquired a 170-acre stretch of coastline north of La Jolla where, operating since 1925 as the Scripps Institution of Oceanography (SIO), they established a research campus and a succession of ever-larger public aquarium-museums.

The present facility, named to recognize funding from the Stephen and Mary Birch Foundation, opened in September 1992. It overlooks the SIO campus, now part of the University of California, San Diego.

Aquarium – Ocean life from the Pacific Northwest, Southern California, Mexico, and the tropical western Pacific is displayed in 33 separate viewing tanks housing some 3,500 fish from 280 different species. A highlight is the **kelp forest**, a 50,000-gallon tank containing a giant kelp environment; open to natural sunlight and gently agitated by a wave-making machine, the exhibit features towering sea plants, senorita fish, garibaldis, blacksmiths, sheepheads and California morays.The 10in-thick acrylic window weighs 10 tons. In a plaza just off the building's central galleria, a small **tide pool** provides a closeup look at shoreline marine life.

★ **Hall of Oceanography** – Under the umbrella title "Exploring the Blue Planet," the regularly updated interactive exhibits and displays cover the history of oceanography; the physics of seawater; the ocean's effect on climate and weather; the ocean floor; undersea life; and the future of oceanographic research. A **submersible ride** *(12min)* simulates a deep-sea dive, and a series of galleries is devoted to changing exhibits.

★★ **Salk Institute** – *10010 N. Torrey Pines Rd. Open year-round Mon–Fri. Closed major holidays.* ✂ ♿ *☏619-453-4100.* A leading world center for biological research and a unique marriage of science and architecture, the Salk Institute for Biological Studies occupies a 27-acre site overlooking the Pacific.

Having pioneered the development of vaccines against influenza and polio in the late 1940s and early 1950s, **Dr Jonas Salk** (b. 1914) set out to establish "a crucible for creativity" where scientists could work together "in an environment that would prompt them to consider the wider implications of their discoveries for the future." In December 1959, he and leading modernist architect **Louis Kahn** (1901-1974) together began conceiving a building to house such a center. Completed in 1962, the Salk Institute now employs some 200 scientists conducting research in six biomedical fields: neuroscience, cancer studies, molecular medicine, human genetics, AIDS and plant biology.

Kahn's elegant design is widely recognized as an outstanding achievement in 20C architecture. The 411,580sq-ft complex consists of two identical 6-story buildings of reinforced concrete, teak and steel; 2 stories lie underground, yet gain ample natural illumination from large light wells. In both structures, each of three "working levels" housing vast, glass-walled laboratories, administrative offices, conference rooms and lecture halls, is surmounted by an "interstitial level" containing utility functions. Facing each other across a travertine courtyard through which flows a narrow channel of water, the buildings frame a view of the sea; the striking La Jolla coastline is visible to the south.

★ **Torrey Pines State Reserve** – *N. Torrey Pines Rd, 2mi north of Genesee Ave. Open daily year-round. $4/car.* ♿ *☏619-755-2063.* Established in 1921, this 1,750-acre reserve is dedicated to the preservation of one of the world's rarest pine trees. Thought to be remnants of an ancient forest that was disrupted by glaciers, fewer than 5,000 Torrey pines *(Pinus torreyana)* survive, and occur naturally only here and on the island of Santa Rosa, one of the CHANNEL ISLANDS. The gnarled, wind-twisted trees were recognized as a distinct species in 1850 by Columbia University botanist C.C. Parry, who named them for his former professor, Dr John Torrey.

The reserve occupies an isolated bluff overlooking the Pacific, a stunning **setting** in which multi-colored sandstone cliffs carved by water and wind action serve as a backdrop for lovely Torrey Pines State Beach. In the early 1920s, Ellen Browning Scripps *(p 69)*, who had purchased and donated for public use some 1,000 acres of land supporting the precious trees, commissioned the Hopi-style adobe Torrey Pines Lodge (1923, Richard Requa). Formerly a restaurant, the structure today houses a **visitor center** with a small museum of local natural history.

From here, the well-marked **Fleming Trail** *(.6mi)* offers ocean views and passes several stands of Torrey Pines. Other trails explore the blufftop, offering **views**★★ of the cliffs and the sea, before leading down to the beach. Encompassed within the reserve is Los Peñasquitos Lagoon, a 600-acre lagoon and salt marsh that serves as a nesting site for 13 endangered species of birds.

★★ LA PURÍSIMA CONCEPCIÓN MISSION Central Coast

Map of Principal Sights p 4

Cradled in a tranquil valley just outside the town of Lompoc, La Purísima is recognized as being among the best restored of California's missions. Today preserved as a state historic park, the authentically re-created buildings and pastoral **setting★** transport visitors back to the time of the mission's heyday in the early 19C.

Officially named Mission la Purísima Concepción de María Santísima ("Mission of the Immaculate Conception of the Most Holy Mary"), the 11th mission was first located in the foothills near present-day Lompoc in 1787. There it steadily flourished under the supervision of Padre Mariano Payeras until the early 18C, when the mission, which was unwittingly built over a fault line, was hit by a series of violent earthquakes in December 1812. A period of prolonged rains that followed the tremors demolished the church and other structures. When neophytes refused to return to the doomed site, Padre Payeras moved his mission 3mi to the northeast.

The second site of La Purísima lay in a wide plain of the Santa Ynez River Valley. With its fertile soil, ample water supply, and access to El Camino Réal *(p 23)*, the small Cañada de los Berros ("canyon of the watercress") proved an ideal spot. For reasons that remain unknown, La Purísima was the only mission whose structures were built in a straight line instead of framing a central quadrangle.

La Purísima

After nearly a decade of prosperity, Padre Payeras' death in 1823, coupled with a faltering economy, made the mission vulnerable to a Native revolt the next year. Secularization and a succession of owners had reduced the complex by 1883 to "one long, low adobe building . . . [that] has been so often used as a stable and sheepfold, that even the grasses are killed around it," as one traveler wrote. With a total of 507 acres of land donated to the state by the Union Oil Company (who purchased most of the site in 1903) and the Catholic Church, the Civilian Conservation Corps began restoring the mission in 1934, reviving construction methods used by the original builders. Seven years later, La Purísima was opened to the public as a state historic park.

VISIT *2hrs*

63mi northwest of Santa Barbara via US-101 and Hwy 246. 2295 Purisima Rd. Open Apr–Sept daily 8am–6pm, rest of the year 9am–5pm. Closed Jan 1, Thanksgiving Day, Dec 25. $5/car. Brochures ($.50) for self-guided tour available at visitor center and bookstore. ☎805-733-3713.

Main Complex – Designed without a formal facade, the long, narrow **church** (1818) was built with its main entrance on the side wall, to provide easy access to travelers on El Camino Réal. Padres added a cemetery and campanario in 1821. The existing bell wall is modeled after that of SANTA INÉS MISSION, since no descriptions of the original campanario exist. Some of the patterns stenciled on the back wall of the sanctuary were gleaned from those discovered during the restoration of the original church; additional designs were copied from other missions.

Next to the church, the **shops and quarters building** housed soldiers and contained workshops for weaving, candle-making, leather-working and carpentry operations. Rooms in this building have been furnished with period pieces to reflect their original appearance.

The mission's largest structure, the 318ft-long **residence building★** served as the padres' quarters. Erected so as to withstand earthquakes, this dwelling incorporated 4ft-thick adobe walls and unique, wide square pillars topped with fluted corbels. A stone buttress at the south end further shored up the structure, which also housed a library, office, wine cellar, guest quarters and the simple chapel.

Grounds – Plants raised by the padres for both food and medicinal purposes are cultivated in the restored **mission garden★**. A walk through this lovely area reveals the central fountain and two laundry basins that once formed part of the site's elaborate water system. Other buildings on the grounds include a blacksmith shop, spring house, barracks for Natives, and a girls' dormitory.

EXCURSION

Lompoc – Pop 37,649. *3mi. From La Purísima Mission, follow Hwy 246 west.* This former Chumash village is renowned today as one of the world's largest producers of flower seeds. In summer, a kaleidoscope of blossoms festoons fields nearby.

A glimpse of the town's ancient history is available in the **Lompoc Museum** *(200 S. H St)*, which houses an impressive collection of Chumash artifacts, including stone bowls, tools, arrowheads, jewelry and baskets *(open year-round Tue–Sun, closed major holidays; ☎805-736-3888)*.

★★ LAKE TAHOE High Sierras

Map p 73 Tourist Office ☎916-544-5050

A serene expanse of deep blue water completely enclosed in a valley amid snow-shrouded Sierra Nevada mountains, Lake Tahoe was hailed by Mark Twain as "the fairest picture the whole earth affords." Straddling the California-Nevada border at an altitude of 6,225ft, the lake is world-renowned for its lovely scenery, winter and summer sporting opportunities, glitzy casinos and live performances by celebrities of the entertainment industry.

"Water in a High Place" – Formed in a basin created by tectonic faulting some 24 million years ago, the lake was further sculpted and defined by glaciation, and today measures 22mi long and 12mi wide, with a total shoreline of almost 72mi and a surface area of 193sq mi. Its maximum depth of 1,645ft renders it the second deepest lake in the country, after Oregon's Crater Lake. Filtered through the decomposed granitic soils of the surrounding mountains, Lake Tahoe's waters are so clear that visibility is often possible to depths of 100ft, and so cold (averaging 60°F in summer) that wetsuits are usually necessary for swimming.

Signs of human occupation on the lakeshore date back 8,000 years. The Native Washoe summered here in more recent centuries and called the area *Da ow a ga* (thought to mean "water in a high place" although this interpretation is disputed), which was corrupted by non-Natives to "Tahoe." John C. Frémont *(p 24)* led the first party of Yankee explorers here in February 1844, but little attention was paid to the area until the 1859 silver rush on Nevada's nearby Comstock Lode, when trees on the lake shore were targeted as a source of lumber for the mines and their boomtowns. In the ensuing two decades, scattered resorts grew up around the lake, and steamboat traffic on its crystal waters increased.

Year-Round Playground – The number of elegant resorts and summer residences on Lake Tahoe grew in the ensuing decades, and, with the construction in 1915 of the first major road linking Tahoe to more populous areas, the area gradually acquired a reputation as a summer playground of affluent Californians. In 1931 the Nevada legislature voted to legalize gambling, and casinos were established along the Nevada side of the southern lakeshore. In 1960, the Winter Olympics were held in nearby Squaw Valley, further popularizing an already burgeoning ski industry. Today Lake Tahoe is a favored resort and recreation area for Californians and visitors alike; its many ski slopes, covered with both artificial and natural snow during the winter months, offer myriad opportunities for skiing and other snow sports, and entertainment lovers flock to the casinos and nightspots clustered on the south shore. The population around the lake often triples in the summer months, and traffic congestion is a worrisome issue and a threat to the pristine mountain environment.

CIRCUIT FROM TAHOE CITY *2 days. 70mi.*

Tahoe City – *Visitor center located at the junction of Hwys 89 and 28 on 560 N. Lake Tahoe Blvd.* This small village at the northern end of the Tahoe Basin is one of the oldest settlements on the lake and serves as a northern gateway to the area's many attractions.

Watson Cabin – *.5mi east of visitor center. Open mid-Jun–Labor Day daily. Contributions requested. ☎916-583-1762.* Nestled among the boutiques and restaurants that line North Lake Tahoe Boulevard (Highway 28) this charming log cabin (1909) is the oldest structure in Tahoe City. It was home to a local family for 40 years and operates today as a museum depicting life on Lake Tahoe during the early 20C.

Gatekeeper's Museum – *Follow Hwy 89 south to William B. Layton Park. Open mid-Jun–Labor Day daily. Contributions requested. ♿ ☎916-583-1762.* This building is a reproduction of the log cabin that served as home to the various "gatekeepers" who regulated the adjacent Lake Tahoe dam between 1910 and 1968. Built on the site of the original cabin, which burned in 1978, the museum displays Native American and early pioneer artifacts along with exhibits on the area's natural history. The simple concrete dam remains the lake's only outlet.

From Tahoe City, drive south on Hwy 89.

★ **Sugar Pine Point State Park** – *9mi. Western park entrance on right; access to Ehrman Mansion is .7mi farther, at eastern entrance. Open daily year-round. $5/car. ⛺ ♿ ☎916-525-7982. Facility information p 256.* The park encompasses part of the General Creek watershed west of the lake, as well as a lovely lakeside promontory topped by several historic buildings, including the Ehrman Mansion.

A Frontiersman and a Financier – One of the first settlers on the lake, Kentuckian "General" William Phipps chose this promontory to homestead in 1860. An irascible local character, he lived off the fish and game on his 160 acres, and built two cabins here before selling the land in 1888.

In 1897 San Francisco financier Isaias W. Hellman began quietly acquiring land along this part of the lake. Within three years, he owned almost two miles of lakefront and had hired San Francisco architect Walter Danforth Bliss to design the rustically elegant Pine Lodge for use as his summer residence. Upon Hellman's death in 1920, the estate passed to his youngest child, Florence Hellman Ehrman, who entertained lavishly at the house for decades. In 1965, her heirs sold the property to the state, and the house was renamed the Ehrman Mansion.

★ **Ehrman Mansion** – *Visit by guided tour (45min) only, Jul–Labor Day daily. ☎916-525-7232.* Built of dark wood and stone quarried from nearby Meeks Bay, the stately mansion (1903) is distinguished by its wide veranda and twin cupolas overlooking a gracefully sloping green lawn. The gracious living room features a large granite fireplace and ceiling richly paneled in oak. The elegant dining room is sheathed in mats of woven grass and of redwood strips. A circular staircase leads to a wide upstairs hallway and eight bedrooms. Furnishings in the house reflect mid-1930s decorative styles.

Surrounding the house are a number of outbuildings that formerly held servants' quarters and maintenance equipment. The turreted tank house, which originally sheltered an electrical generator, today serves as a park nature center, with exhibits on the natural history of the lake environs. Phipps Cabin, the simple log home built by General Phipps in 1872, stands on the lakeshore below the mansion.

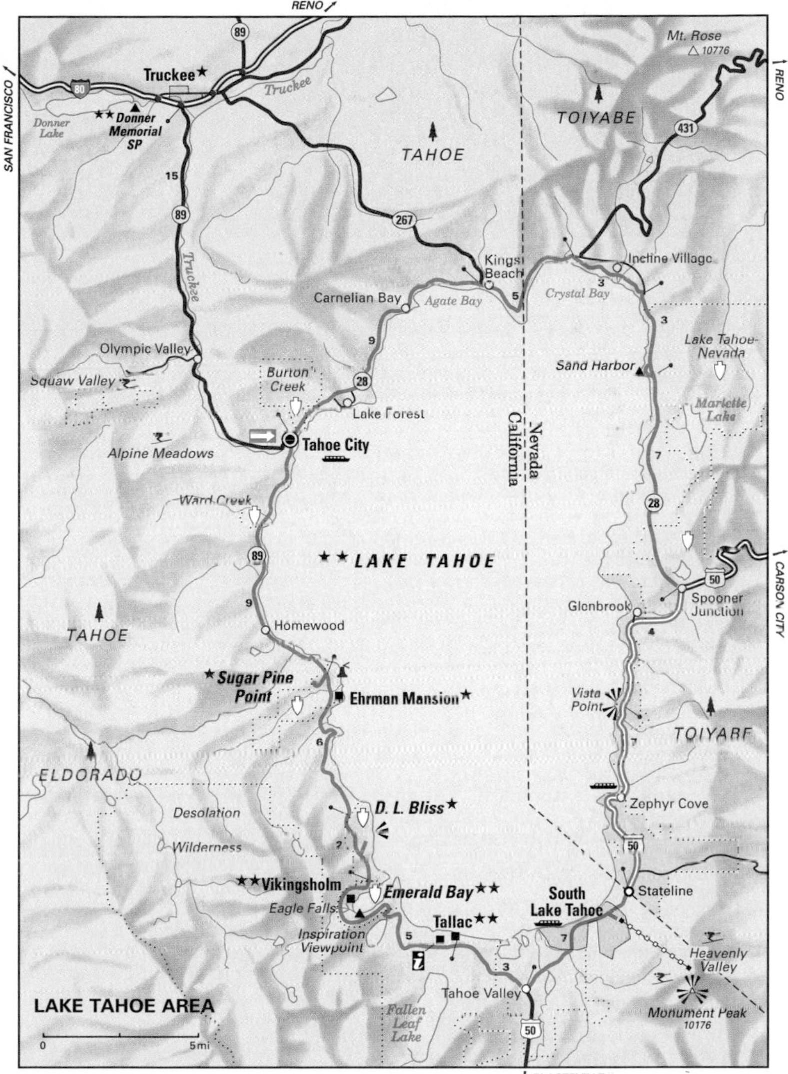

The interpretive **Dolder Trail** *(2mi round-trip)* winds through the forest north of the mansion, leading ultimately to the small wooden Sugar Pine Point Lighthouse. At an elevation of 6,235ft, the light ranks as the highest navigational aid in the US.

★ **D.L. Bliss State Park** – *6mi. Open mid-May–mid-Oct daily. $5/car.* △ ♿ ☎*916-525-7277. Facility information p 256.* This park stretching along the lake's southwestern shore is notable for two hiking trails. Balancing Rock Nature Trail *(.5mi loop; easy)* offers an interpretive look at the interaction between the region's plant and animal communities; the self-guided loop *(.5mi)* leads past **Balancing Rock**, a 130-ton granite boulder precariously perched on a granite base.

The **Rubicon Trail** *(4.5mi; moderate)* hugs the cliffs above the lake and offers both short- and long-distance hikers spectacular **views**★ along most of its length. Beginning at Rubicon Point, the trail reaches a turnoff *(.4mi)* for a small wooden lighthouse that functioned here from 1916 to 1919. *(A second, higher trail loops from the lighthouse back to the parking area, but the lower trail is recommended for its views.)* Continuing south from the lighthouse, the trail eventually ascends to Emerald Point and continues into adjacent Emerald Bay State Park *(p 74)*. It then follows the gentle contours of Emerald Bay's western shore before terminating at Eagle Falls.

Emerald Bay

★★ **Emerald Bay State Park** – *2mi. Open year-round daily.* △ ♿ ☎*916-525-7277. Facility information p 256.* Majestic alpine views, lovely hiking trails, and a distinctive, Scandinavian-style mansion highlight a visit to this popular state park surrounding scenic **Emerald Bay**★★, a small, glacially sculpted inlet celebrated for the deep blue-green color of its water.

★★ **Vikingsholm** – *Access by Vikingsholm Trail (2mi round-trip), which gradually descends from parking area. Interior accessible by guided tour (30min) only, mid-Jun–Labor Day daily 10am–4pm; Memorial Day–mid-Jun & Labor Day–Sept weekends only 10am–4pm. $2.* ☎*916-525-7277.* Set amid stately pine and cedar trees at the tip of Emerald Bay is an imposing mansion resembling a 9C Nordic castle. The structure was commissioned by philanthropist Lora J. Knight, who, inspired by the fjord-like appearance of the bay, hired Swedish-born architect Lennart Palme to create a 1920s version of a Viking residence. Before commencing, the two traveled throughout Norway, Denmark, Finland and Sweden collecting design ideas. Completed in 1929, Vikingsholm served as Mrs Knight's summer residence until her death in 1945; the property was purchased by the state in 1953.

Built of locally quarried granite around a central courtyard, the 48-room mansion incorporates such Scandinavian elements as dragons' heads, intricately hand-carved beams, sod roofing, hand-wrought door latches and light fixtures. The house is furnished in authentic antiques and reproductions of traditional pieces that were purchased or commissioned by Mrs Knight during her Scandinavian sojourn. The remains of a stone tea house built by Mrs Knight are visible just offshore on Fannette Island. A visitor kiosk located just south of the mansion contains displays on the construction of Vikingsholm.

Continue south on Hwy 89.

Ascending into open bluffs above the lake, the road passes Eagle Falls, visible as it courses beneath the road. Just beyond, **Inspiration Viewpoint** offers a striking **view**★ of jewel-like Emerald Bay and Vikingsholm. From here the road crosses a high narrow traverse with views of Emerald Bay to the left and Cascade Lake to the right. At the National Forest Service's Lake Tahoe Basin **visitor center**, exhibits detail the natural and human history of the area.

★★ **Tallac Historic Site** – *5mi. Buildings open Memorial Day–mid-Oct daily 10am-4pm. Grounds open year-round daily dawn–dusk.* ♿ ☎*916-541-5227.* One of the earliest resort areas on the lake, this site on the south shore recalls Tahoe's late-19C and early-20C "era of opulence." Several preserved summer estates, as well as the remains of an early hotel and casino, still grace the grounds.

"Yank" and "Lucky" – Realizing the lake's potential as a resort and tourism destination, stagecoach entrepreneur "Yank" Clement established a charming, yet rustic hostelry here in 1873. His Tallac Point House enjoyed almost immediate popularity, yet Clement experienced financial problems with the venture, and in 1880, San Francisco mining and real estate speculator **E.J. "Lucky" Baldwin** acquired the property through foreclosure. Under Baldwin's ownership, the hotel and grounds were improved, an elegant lakeside casino was added, and the Tallac Resort became fashionable among prominent Californians.

Upon Baldwin's death in 1909 the property passed to his daughter Anita, who continued operations until the early 1920s. In 1927 she had all Tallac buildings removed from the lakefront and the area returned to a more natural state. During the same period, several wealthy families established elaborate summer homes to the east of the resort; these graceful mansions still stand today and, along with the Tallac grounds, are owned and maintained by the National Forest Service.

A short trail leads west along the lakefront, past the foundations of the Tallac casino and the sites of the old Point House and hotel, then across the remains of a paved promenade that once connected the two.

★ **Baldwin-McGonagle House Museum** – The U-shaped, pitch-roofed log home was built in 1921 by Dextra Baldwin McGonagle, granddaughter of Lucky Baldwin and heiress through her mother to his Tahoe properties and much of his fortune. The interior was decorated with ornate mirrors and gilt work during the period when Mrs McGonagle summered here (1921-1967). Today, the gracious, 2-story living room is furnished in the rustic style popular with Lake Tahoe's early-20C summer residents, and adjoining rooms contain an excellent exhibit of **photographs**★ of the life and history of the area's Native Washoe people. Additional displays recount the history of the Baldwin family and early resort life at Lake Tahoe.
The **Washoe Demonstration Garden** beside the house features flora important to these hunter-gatherers and examples of their traditional shelters.

Pope-Tevis Estate – In 1894 George Tallant, a Bay Area banker, built a small cottage just east of the Tallac resort. Five years later Tallant sold his property to the wealthy Tevis family, who had garnered a fortune in railroads and real estate speculation. The Tevis' expanded the 1,000sq ft cottage into one of the most opulent mansions on the lake. In 1913 the family's United Property Corporation declared bankruptcy, and their Lake Tahoe estate was eventually acquired by George S. Pope, a wealthy Bay Area lumber and shipping executive. From 1923 to 1965, the Popes' lavish lifestyle at "Vatican Lodge," as the estate was known locally, became legendary.
The unimposing exterior of the hip-roofed, shingle-sided home belies the former extravagance of its interior. Coffered ceilings and wall paneling of California cedar adorn the downstairs entry hall, living room and dining room. The upstairs contains five bedrooms, while an unusual curved "whistleway" (breezeway) connects the main house to the kitchen and servants quarters. The estate also features a lovely pond garden and a small **arboretum** of various forest trees, including giant sequoias, eastern larch, western red cedar and Colorado blue spruce.

A short walk to the east lies **Valhalla**; built in 1924, the stately, shingle-sided mansion graced by wide verandas served as the summer home of San Francisco financier Walter Heller. At Heller's death in 1955, ownership passed through various hands until it was acquired by the forest service in 1971. Today the residence, graced by wide verandas, functions as a community events hall, and its interior is open only for performances.

South Lake Tahoe – Pop 21,586. *3mi. Chamber of Commerce and visitor center located 2.5mi east of the junction of Hwy 89 and Lake Tahoe Blvd (US-50). Visitor center located on US-50 just east of Hwy 89.* The lake's largest, and only incorporated town offers abundant opportunities for lodging, dining, shopping and recreation. Commercial paddle wheel, sailboat and glass-bottom boat excursions on Lake Tahoe's brilliant waters depart from landing areas on the south shore, and the Eldorado Recreation Area offers direct access to the lakefront. Stateline Avenue marks the California/Nevada border and the line of demarcation between South Lake Tahoe and the Nevada town of **Stateline**, where a handful of glittering, high-rise hotel/casinos offer round-the clock gambling and nightly musical and stand-up comedy performances by well-known entertainers.

Heavenly Aerial Tramway – *From US-50 turn south on Ski Run Blvd and follow signs to Heavenly Valley Ski Area. Open mid May–Sept & mid Nov–Apr daily. $12. ☎702-586-7000.* Enclosed, 50-passenger trams ascend the flanks of 10,167ft Monument Peak *(4.5min)*, the setting of one of the region's most popular ski resorts. The tram terminus is a well-appointed ski lodge, where broad decks and windows allow exceptional **views**★★ of the lake and the surrounding mountains. From the lodge, the **Tahoe Vista Trail**★ *(2.1mi, moderate)* edges the flanks of Monument Peak, offering further views of the lake.

Continue east and north on US-50.

From Stateline, the road skirts Lake Tahoe's undeveloped eastern shore; from Vista Point *(7mi)*, **views**★ extend across the lake to the western side. At Spooner Junction *(4mi)*, the lakeshore road becomes Nevada Route 28 and traverses a portion of Lake Tahoe-Nevada State Park. **Sand Harbor** *(7mi)* offers attractive picnic facilities, rounded granite outcroppings, and a sandy beach fringing a beautiful, sheltered cove where the shallow water tends to be warmer than in other parts of the lake.
Route 28 traverses the small residential communities of Incline Village and Crystal Bay before crossing the state line into California. The road then weaves along the northern shore through the well-developed resort community of Kings Beach, and on to Tahoe City.

Cruising Lake Tahoe

Several commercial operators offer boat excursions on Lake Tahoe's crystalline waters. Cruises generally last 1 1/2 to 3 1/3 hours and prices average $14-$34.

***Lake Tahoe Cruises** - Glass bottom boat, departs from Ski Run Marina in South Lake Tahoe ☎916-541-3364.*

***M.S. Dixie Cruises** - Historic paddlewheeler, departs from Zephyr Cove ☎702-588-3508.*

***North Tahoe Cruises** - Departs from Roundhouse Mall in Tahoe City ☎916-583-0141.*

EXCURSION

★ **Truckee** – *1/2 day. 15mi north of Tahoe City by Hwy 89. Description p 230.*

★★ LASSEN VOLCANIC NATIONAL PARK Shasta-Cascade

Map of Principal Sights p 3

Ragged craters, barren lava dunes and steaming thermal areas contrast with placid lakes and lush evergreen forests in this 106,000-acre national park, testifying to the awe-inspiring power of earth's destructive and healing forces. The park is dominated by looming Lassen Peak, a 10,457ft plug dome volcano renowned for a series of devastating eruptions that occurred between 1914 and 1917.

A Violent Landscape – The subduction of the Pacific Ocean floor beneath the North American plate, with the resultant creation of the Cascade Range *(p 13)*, has for some 3.5 million years engendered volcanic activity in the region today encompassed by the park. Roughly 600,000 years ago, a volcano now called Mt Tehama arose in the park's southwest corner, and continued building for 200,000 years, eventually topping 11,500ft and measuring 11mi in diameter. As volcanic activity at Mt Tehama declined, its summit began to wear away and several significant domes formed on its flanks. The largest of these was Lassen Peak *(p 77)*, which took shape about 25,000 years ago.

On May 30, 1914, Lassen Peak, long thought to be dead, started to spew steam and lava in the first of 298 eruptions that took place over several years. The most destructive activity occurred in May 1915, when hot lava and steam melted accumulated snow, causing an enormous mudflow that coursed down the peak's eastern slopes. Three days later, a searing blast of pyroclastic gas laid waste to everything in its path.

In 1916 this phenomenal volcanic terrain was declared a national park, and until the 1980 eruption of Mt St Helens, another Cascade volcano located in Washington State, the Lassen landscape remained the only example of recent volcanism in the 48 contiguous states. Though no eruption has been recorded for more than 70 years, the peak, one of the largest dome volcanoes in the world, still contains an active magma chamber and is considered very much alive.

Practical Information

Area Code: 916

Getting There – To **Southwest entrance** (Hwy 89): from **San Francisco** (237mi) I-80 east to I-505 north to I-5 north to Hwy 36 west to Hwy 89 north; from **Los Angeles** (569mi) I-5 north to Hwy 36 west to Hwy 89 north. To **Manzanita Lake entrance** (Hwy 44): from **San Francisco** (269mi) I-80 east to I-505 north to I-5 north to Hwy 44 east; from **Los Angeles** (601mi) I-5 north to Hwy 44 east. Visitor centers at both entrances. Closest airport (47mi): **Redding Municipal Airport** (RDD) ☏225-4121. Closest Greyhound (☏800-231-2222) and Amtrak station (☏800-872-7245): Redding (47mi). Rental car agency branches *(p 253)*.

Getting Around – Lassen is best visited by car. Southwest entrance to Lassen Winter Sports area open year-round, rest of the park closed Nov–May.

Visitor Information – **Lassen Volcanic National Park Visitor Center** open mid-Jun–Labor Day daily in Loomis Museum (near Manzanita Lake entrance) ☏335-7575. **Lassen Volcanic National Park Headquarters** (in Mineral, Hwy 36), open Jun–Sept daily, rest of the year Mon–Fri. $5/car entrance fee. Mailing address: Superintendent, Lassen Volcanic National Park, PO Box 100, Mineral CA 96063 ☏595-4444. **Lassen National Forest**, 55 South Sacramento St, Susanville CA 96130 ☏257-2151.

Accommodations – Accommodations available in the park at Drakesbad Guest Ranch (southern end of the park, $76/double) ☏529-1512. Accommodations also available in Red Bluff, Redding and Chester (27mi southeast). Advance reservations recommended. **Campsites** available by self-registration; no reservations accepted. Limited winter camping. **Backcountry camping** by permit only; permit (free) available at park headquarters. Campgrounds also located in Lassen National Forest.

★ LASSEN PARK ROAD *30mi. At least 1 day.*

Begin at Manzanita Lake entrance (Hwy 44).

★ **Manzanita Lake** – This sparkling lake was created approximately 1,000 years ago when an avalanche of rock from the collapse of one of the steep volcanic domes known as Chaos Crags *(below)* formed a natural dam across Manzanita Creek. Today, the lake's manzanita- and chaparral-covered shores provide habitat for a variety of small mammals and birds. A scenic **trail** *(1.7mi loop)* circles the lake.

Beyond Manzanita Lake, Highway 89 passes **Chaos Crags**, a series of 1,100-year-old dome volcanoes rising to the south. Landslides from the crags created the surrounding rock-strewn terrain known as **Chaos Jumbles**. Approximately 6mi farther, the road enters the **Devastated Area**, a bleak terrain that was once covered by lush evergreens. The forest was obliterated in the 1915 mudflow and hot blast. Aspen and pine trees are now slowly reclaiming the area.

After contouring the forested shore of **Summit Lake**, the road opens to vistas of the park's eastern expanse. Lake Alamanor is visible some 20mi to the southeast.

★ **Kings Creek Falls Trail** – *Trail 3mi round-trip; trailhead across the road from the Kings Creek parking area.* This pleasant trail leads through forests and meadowland to a series of cascades formed as Kings Creek plunges over polished stone ledges. Beyond the falls the trail continues another 6.1mi southeast into the Warner Valley *(p 77)*.

★ **Lassen Peak** – *Trailhead at Lassen Peak Trail parking area. Trail 5mi round-trip; strenuous, with 2,000ft elevation gain. Note: High altitude can cause altitude sickness (p 256). Check weather conditions before starting, as thunderstorms are frequent.* Southernmost volcano in the Cascade Range and centerpiece of the park, this barren gray volcanic dome, with its jagged pinnacles of dacite lava, towers ominously over the central part of the park. From the summit, a panoramic **view★** encompasses the many volcanic features that characterize the surrounding terrain.

★★★ **Bumpass Hell** – *Trail 3mi round-trip; interpretive brochure ($.35) available at trailhead.* This exceptional and intriguing example of hydrothermal activity was discovered in the mid-19C by Kendall Vanhook Bumpass, an early tourism promoter and guide. The trail winds along the eroded remains of Mt Tehama, offering views to the southwest of **Diamond Peak** (7,968ft) and **Brokeoff Mountain** (9,235ft), before descending into the steaming, odoriferous thermal area. A boardwalk leads past surface cracks that billow with sulfuric fumaroles (holes in the ground that emit steam and gas); boiling springs; and thick, bubbling mudpots fueled by a chamber of magma (molten igneous rock) far underground.

T. Bean/AllStock

Bumpass Hell

★ **Sulphur Works** Clouds of steam are emitted from this roadside hydrothermal area, believed to be part of the vent system that created Mt Tehama. Iron oxide gives the clays in the area a reddish tint, and hydrogen sulphide gas accounts for the distinctive odor.

SOUTHERN SECTION *At least 1/2 day*

Accessible from the town of Chester (31mi southeast of the park's Southwest entrance via Hwy 89 and Hwy 36).

★ **Warner Valley** – *17mi from Chester; follow signs north to the valley.* This beautiful valley marks the site of ancient Mt Dittmar, which appeared some 2 million years ago as the first center of volcanic activity within the park's present-day boundaries. After the volcano had quieted, glaciers moved through the area, carving a valley where the volcano once loomed. Located here is the picturesque Drakesbad Guest Ranch, a Western-style cabin resort founded in 1880s as a cattle ranch

★ **Boiling Springs Lake Trail** – *3mi round-trip.* Angling southwest to southeast from Hot Springs Creek, this popular trail ascends through fir, pine and cedar forests to a steaming lake, which may be the world's largest body of naturally heated water. Underground vents warm the water to about 125°F, causing vapor to rise from its surface on cool days. Several mudpots are located on the lakeshore.

★ **Juniper Lake** – *12mi north of Chester; follow signs north to lake; last 7mi on a rough, unpaved road.* Filling a depression left by Ice Age glaciers, this dark blue lake is the largest and deepest in the park. Its name derives from the juniper trees that grow near its eastern shore. A moderate trail *(1.6mi round-trip)* beside the parking area climbs to **Inspiration Point★**, from which extend views of Lassen Peak, Juniper Lake and Snag Lake.

EXCURSIONS

Subway Cave – *1hr. 12mi north of Manzanita Lake entrance via Hwy 89, 1mi south of Old Station. Note: Cave is completely dark; visitors should be equipped with at least two flashlights per party. Average cave temperature is 46°.* This 1,300ft lava tube *(p 78)* is thought to be the largest of several formed some 2,000 years ago during the Hat Creek lava flow, an outpouring of molten rock from a series of fissures in the earth's crust. A trail leads through the rounded tube, passing side tunnels, piles of rubble and the solidified drips of molten lava known as "lavacicles."

McArthur Burney Falls Memorial State Park – *1hr. 40mi north of Manzanita Lake entrance via Hwy 89. Description p 148.*

★★ LAVA BEDS NATIONAL MONUMENT Shasta-Cascade

Map of Principal Sights p 3

Occupying the heart of California's Modoc Plateau, a vast, volcanic tableland in the northeast corner of the state, is an eerie landscape paved with dark lava, pocked with volcanic craters and studded with cinder cones. This area, today encompassed in part by Lava Beds National Monument, reveals the indelible imprint of violence, both natural and human. Formed during the past 2 million years by spewing lava and rocks, the rugged terrain was the scene, in 1873, of a brief, but bloody war between displaced Modoc Natives and US Army forces.

The park is located on the broad northern flank of Medicine Lake Volcano, a low-lying shield volcano that last erupted about 1,000 years ago. The park's most distinctive feature is its vast network of more than 200 **lava tube caves**, several of which penetrate as much as 150ft below the lava beds' surface; others extend horizontally for thousands of feet. Such a cave is formed when the outer surface of a lava flow cools and hardens, insulating the interior mass of molten lava. This liquid rock thus continues to flow, leaving long tubular passages beneath the surface. Lava transported in such a way is commonly carried far from the eruption site and distributed over large areas, which accounts for the relatively flat profile of Medicine Lake Volcano.

The Modoc War – The area today known as the Modoc Plateau was traditional homeland of the Native Modoc and Klamath, neighboring peoples whose generally cordial relations were occasionally marked by periods of enmity. By the mid-1800s, tensions were mounting between the Natives and the many Easterners immigrating to the area; the influx of settlers disrupted the movements of game and polluted fishing streams, threatening the Modocs' hunter-gatherer way of life. The Natives reacted by attacking wagon trains and stealing livestock, and pressure began to mount on the US government to remove them from the area.

Under an 1864 treaty, the Paiute, Klamath and Modoc Natives were placed on a reservation in Oregon, on former Klamath land. Unable to tolerate political tensions among the Native factions there, a group of several hundred Modocs led by Kientpoos (known to the settlers as **Captain Jack**) returned to their homeland, thus reoccupying territory declared by the US government to be the property of American settlers. For several years the Natives and the settlers coexisted uneasily, but on November 29, 1872, a botched attempt by a small US Army platoon to force Captain Jack back to the reservation led to the killing of 14 settlers by vengeful Modocs; Army regiments quickly began to converge on the area, and various Modoc bands retreated to the lava beds, taking refuge in a series of natural fissures and crevices that became known as "Captain Jack's Stronghold." For nearly five months, the group of 53 warriors and their families held off a growing military force that eventually outnumbered them 20 times.

On April 11, 1873, Gen E.R.S. Canby was fatally shot by Captain Jack during talks intended to resolve the conflict peacefully. The Modocs fled again into the lava bed stronghold, but were eventually forced out and captured. The war ended as Captain Jack surrendered and was subsequently tried and hanged; the remnants of his band were exiled to an Oklahoma reservation.

VISIT *At least 1/2 day*

Park open daily year-round. $5/car. Visitor center open Jun–Aug 9am–6pm, rest of the year 8am–5pm. Closed Thanksgiving Day, Dec 25. ♿ *☎916-667-2282.*

Begin at the **visitor center**, where rangers and interactive displays interpret the lava beds' natural and human history. The center offers maps, books and hardhats for purchase; visitors may borrow flashlights at no charge for exploring the caves. Improved with lights, interpretive panels and a graded floor, **Mushpot Cave★** *(entrance near visitor center)* is a good place to begin exploring the park's many lava tubes. The tube was named for the unique formation *(left of the entrance)* created when a burst of lava penetrated its floor from a lava channel just below.

★ **Cave Loop Road** – *2mi. Begin at the visitor center.* The road *(2mi)* loops atop an area of hardened lava that flowed from Mammoth Crater, located just inside the monument's southern boundary. Winding beneath the lava carapace is the park's densest concentration of lava tubes, many of which are indicated and accessible by parking areas and improved stairways. Visitors can penetrate any or all of the caves to see various types of lava and lava formations, and to sample the eerie, chilly darkness of these mysterious underground spaces.

Not part of Cave Loop but well worth a visit are **Valentine Cave**, so named because it was discovered on Valentine's Day in 1933; and **Skull Cave**, which reveals a pool of ice at its bottom.

Schonchin Butte – *2.2mi from visitor center via main park road. Trail (1.5mi round-trip; moderate to difficult) from parking area.* The firetower atop this 500ft cinder cone offers a awe-inspiring **panorama★★** of the surrounding landscape. Best viewed from here is Gillem's Bluff, a massive fault scarp extending to the north; and several long crevices created where the roofs of lava tubes collapsed, forming ragged trenches through the volcanic plateau.

Modoc War Battle Sites – *9mi from the visitor center.* The main park road leads north through the park past sites where Modoc warriors clashed violently with Army forces and groups of armed and angry settlers. **Canby's Cross** marks the place where General Canby and Rev Eleasar Thomas, an accompanying negotiator, were killed by Captain Jack and his followers. At **Captain Jack's Stronghold★**, a self-guided trail *(interpretive pamphlet available at trailhead)* wanders through the trenches and caves that enabled the Modoc leader, 52 warriors and their families to keep the US Army forces at bay.

★ LONG BEACH Greater Los Angeles Area Pop 429,433

Map below Tourist Office ☎310-436-3645

Sprawling some 30mi south of LOS ANGELES on the shore of San Pedro Bay, Long Beach forms an important link in the coastal urban chain extending between Los Angeles and SAN DIEGO. Home to a major shipping port, the city balances large areas marked by heavy industry and transport activities with charming residential streets, beautifully landscaped and developed shoreline and beach areas, and such popular tourist attractions as the Queen Mary and Shoreline Village.

Oil and Water – Inhabited by Gabrieleño Natives prior to Spanish occupation, this area became part of the Los Cerritos and Los Alamitos ranches following Mexican independence. A seaside community developed here in concert with the growth of the region's cattle ranches; its capacious natural harbor served as principal port for the many goods transported to New England during the heyday of the hide and tallow trade. In 1906, the Pacific Electric Railway connected Long Beach with Los Angeles, and the Pike, a shoreline amusement park of piers, bathhouses, carnival rides and other amusements lured day trippers and seasonal visitors from all over the country.

By 1910 Long Beach's waterfront areas had attracted diverse industries; growth began in earnest with the 1921 discovery of oil at nearby Signal Hill. A powerful earthquake devastated the city in 1933, but further oil discoveries in the harbor fueled a quick recovery. World War II brought a naval port and shipbuilding facilities to Terminal Island, a man-made islet created at the mouth of Los Angeles harbor by channel dredging. Today the nearly 2,808-acre **Port of Long Beach**, the backbone of Long Beach's economy, ranks first in total tonnage among US Pacific Coast ports, and, together with the adjacent Worldport LA *(p 80)*, is the largest, busiest waterborne shipping center in the US.

Owing to early-20C conveyances stipulating that its tidelands be held in trust by the city for the benefit of all residents of California, Long Beach's portion of revenues generated by oil pumped offshore is automatically earmarked for waterfront development. These funds were instrumental in bringing the Queen Mary to the harbor as a tourist attraction in 1967, and in engendering construction of the world's largest municipal marina and waterfront convention center.

SIGHTS *1/2 day*

★★★ **Queen Mary** – *1126 Queens Hwy.* Dominating Long Beach Harbor at the mouth of the Los Angeles River, this 81,237-ton passenger ship measuring 1,019ft long was permanently docked here in 1967 after 31 years of service in Great Britain's Cunard White Star line. Built in the shipyards of Clyde Bank, Scotland, between 1930 and 1934, the *Queen Mary* made her maiden voyage in May 1936. Converted for military use, during World War II, she transported more than 750,000 troops a distance of over 550,000mi, earning the nickname "Gray Ghost" for her naval camouflage paint and zigzag ocean routes. In July, 1947, the ship returned to civilian use.

As the world's largest and reputedly most luxurious passenger vessel, the *Queen Mary* was a favorite of such international celebrities and socialites as Greta Garbo, Fred Astaire, Clark Gable, Elizabeth Taylor, Bob Hope, Beatrice Lillie and the Duke and Duchess of Windsor. But in the mid-20C, affordable air travel eclipsed the era of the great passenger ships, and the Queen Mary completed the last of her 1,001 transatlantic voyages on September 19, 1967. Sold to Long Beach for $3.5 million, she reigns today as the centerpiece of Queen Mary Seaport, the city's most prominent attraction.

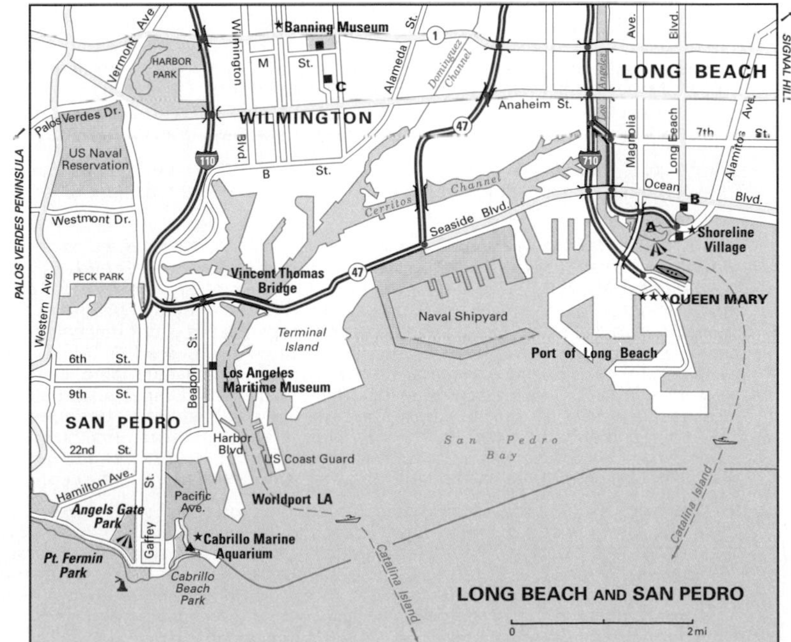

Visit – *Open mid-Jun–Labor Day daily 10am–6pm (Fri & Sat 9pm), rest of the year daily 10am–6pm. $5.* ✗ ♿ ☎*310-449-1696.* On board, visitors can explore the bridge, officers' quarters and other operational centers; passenger suites and dining rooms; the engine room, with its massive propeller box; and a display of model ships. Optional guided tours penetrate the ship's luxuriously furnished staterooms. Throughout, display cases and documentary photographs illustrate life aboard the *Queen Mary*, highlighting some of her notable passengers. Restaurants and snack and souvenir shops are scattered throughout the ship, and a hotel now occupies three of its twelve decks.

★ **Shoreline Park [A]** – *Shoreline Dr south of Ocean Blvd.* This lovely waterfront park serves as a visual link connecting the disparate elements of Long Beach's waterfront. Its rolling, grassy knolls and pleasant pedestrian paths offer splendid **views**★ of the Queen Mary at berth across Queensway Bay where the Los Angeles River empties into the Pacific. To the north, the office towers of downtown Long Beach rise behind the massive **Long Beach Convention and Entertainment Center [B]**; the outer wall of the center's circular Long Beach Arena displays *Whaling Wall XXXIII: Planet Ocean*, a 116,00sq ft mural (1992) by California-based muralist Wyland, that ranks among the world's largest murals.

The park's east end is fringed by **Shoreline Village**★, a tastefully ersatz seaport village of shops, restaurants and walkways highlighted by a marvelous, historic **carousel**★ of 62 camels, giraffes, horses and curly-horned rams, designed by Charles I.D. Looff in 1906.

EXCURSIONS

San Pedro – *2hrs.* Linked to Long Beach by the stately **Vincent Thomas Bridge**, the town of San Pedro was Southern California's predominant harbor community from the mission period until the 1920s. Although the town itself was eclipsed by Long Beach's oil-fueled growth, its vast **Worldport LA** outranks the neighboring Port of Long Beach in terms of size and tonnage. With its 75 cargo and cruise ship berths, the 7,500-acre complex is the nation's busiest container port and the West Coast's predominant cruise ship terminal.

In 1909, San Pedro was annexed to the City of Los Angeles via a "shoestring extension" of land, only .5mi wide in places, between downtown Los Angeles and the harbor areas. Yet areas of San Pedro, particularly Harbor Boulevard, reflect the ethnic flavor of its origins as a sea and fishing port. **Angels Gate Park** *(end of Gaffey St)* atop the crest of the Palos Verdes Peninsula, affords wonderful sea **views** that extend as far as CATALINA ISLAND on clear days. Just below lies **Point Fermin Park**, a 37-acre landscaped greensward offering in-season whale watching from coin-operated telescopes, and an 1847 wooden lighthouse *(not open to the public)*.

★ **Cabrillo Marine Aquarium** – *3720 Stephen White Dr off Pacific Ave. Parking in Cabrillo Beach Park. Open year-round Tue–Sun. Closed Thanksgiving, Dec 25.* ♿ ☎*310-548-7562.* Housed in an innovative gray structure (1981, Frank Gehry) bedecked with chain link and designed to evoke maritime images such as seashells, fish nets and billowing sails, this small aquarium and museum offers an excellent introduction to Southern California's marine life. More than 500 species of fish and other aquatic creatures are displayed in 34 aquariums organized to reflect the region's diverse environments, including rocky shores, sandy habitats, mud flats and the open ocean. A 800-gallon tank offers a look at dwellers of the kelp forest, and a touch tank allows hands-on interaction with various sea creatures.

Los Angeles Maritime Museum – *Foot of 6th St, Berth 84. Open year-round Tue–Sun. Closed major holidays. $1.* ♿ ☎*310-548-7618.* An impressive collection of nautical memorabilia is housed in San Pedro's historic Art Deco Municipal Ferry Building. Until 1968, the building welcomed ferries from neighboring Terminal Island. Centerpiece of the museum's holdings is its outstanding collection of **ship models**, highlighted by an 18ft cutaway version of the R.M.S. *Titanic.* The display of 64 seamen's knots challenges visitors to test their knot-tying skills on accompanying ropes, and an active ham radio station lets the curious eavesdrop on port traffic.

Wilmington – Founded in 1858 by Phineas Banning, the "Father of Los Angeles Transportation," this bustling suburb just west of Long Beach was named for the capital of Banning's native Delaware.

★ **General Phineas Banning Residence Museum** – *401 E. M St. Visit by guided tour (1hr 15min) only, year-round Tue–Thu, Sat & Sun. Closed major holidays. $2. Reservations required.* ☎*310-548-7777. From Harbor Fwy/US-110 exit Hwy 1 east and turn right on Avalon Blvd; turn left onto M St.* With its triangular pediment and squared columns, this elegant clapboard residence pioneered Greek Revival architecture in California at a time when adobe construction reigned as the state's predominant style. The 30-room mansion was built by Phineas Banning, who arrived in California in 1851 and became the driving force behind the development of Los Angeles Harbor, laying rail lines to the city and establishing stage routes to San Bernardino and Fort Yuma in Arizona. Today it is restored and furnished with period pieces, including a square Steinway grand piano. Historic photos *(lower level)* offer glimpses of the harbor's development through the turn of the century.

Drum Barracks [C] – *1052 Banning Blvd. Visit by guided tour (1hr) only, year-round Tue–Thu, Sat. Closed major holidays, Thanksgiving weekend, Christmas–New Years week. $2.50.* ♿ ☎*310-548-7509.* Officers' quarters are all that remain of the US Army headquarters for Southern California and Arizona during the Civil War and Native conflicts of the 1860s. The outpost, located here to be near the port, served to protect Union interests in the area. Today its period rooms house a museum of Civil War memorabilia and a collection of Civil War-era weapons.

★★★ LOS ANGELES Greater Los Angeles Area Pop 3,485,398

Map pp 82-83

Situated on a vast, coastal plain against a backdrop of towering mountains, this sprawling, sundrenched megalopolis is the largest metropolitan area in the US. Los Angeles is, in fact, not just one large city but a collection of smaller cities and towns that have grown together over time and through necessity. Its enviable location and climate, its role as a national and international entertainment center, and its remarkable ethnic and cultural diversity contribute to a heady, sometimes overwhelming mix of sights and experiences, and an ambience so casual that the city's inhabitants even refer to their home by its initials: L.A. "Los Angeles, like America, like freedom applied," penned political commentator George Will, "is strong medicine—an untidy jumble of human diversity and perversity." Although such diversity has inevitably led to clashes throughout the city's history, for the most part it continues to endow Los Angeles with its distinctive vitality and sense of possibility.

Geographical Notes – Greater Los Angeles lies within the Los Angeles basin, a mostly flat plain descending south and west to the Pacific Ocean and embraced by mountain ranges. Skirting the basin to the northwest are the Santa Monica Mountains, a modest range that rises from the sea at Oxnard, some 70mi west of downtown Los Angeles, and continues for 47mi to the Los Angeles River, passing en route through Beverly Hills, Hollywood and Griffith Park. The San Gabriel Mountains loom above the basin to the north. To the east, the San Gabriels meet the San Bernardino Mountains, the region's tallest range and a popular winter recreation area. The Santa Ana Range, to the southeast in Orange County, completes the basin's mountainous boundaries.

These mountains are reminders of geological stress (frequently manifested in earthquakes) present in the region and throughout the state. The Los Angeles basin itself was built and pushed up layer by layer from the Pacific Ocean floor by volcanic activity more than a million years ago. Remnants of ocean life in those geologic layers formed subterranean oil pools that are tapped today throughout the basin; congealed oil, or tar, also continues to bubble up in places, particularly in the **tar pits** of Rancho La Brea, near Wilshire Boulevard.

The mountains form a natural barrier for **smog**—fog driven inland by coastal air currents, trapped by the mountains and made heavier and darker by smoke and chemical fumes, notably automotive exhaust. Though strict local and federal regulations have decreased such pollution in recent years, Los Angeles smog can still be oppressive, particularly on hot summer days. But smog is not exclusively a product of the modern age. Spanish explorer Juan Rodríguez Cabrillo, sailing past Los Angeles in 1542, was moved by the dark haze from Native campfires hanging over the basin to name it "The Bay of Smokes."

Size and Population – The city of Los Angeles covers more than 464sq mi. But almost ten times that area is embraced by Los Angeles County, and the metropolitan area stretches beyond county boundaries to cover approximately 34,000sq mi. Because Los Angeles defines and dominates its greater metropolitan area, distinctions between city and county are sometimes hard to discern. Both are governed from Los Angeles City Hall, with the city headed by a mayor and city council, the county by a board of supervisors. Some 88 incorporated cities are contained within the county, many of them completely surrounded by the city of Los Angeles.

Today the city has a population in excess of 3.4 million, the county 8.8 million, and the metropolitan area more than 13.5 million. In 1990 the county's population was 40.8% Caucasian, 36% Latino, 11.2% African American and 10.4% Asian. Although these population groups are spread throughout the city, specific ethnic communities do exist, including Chinatown, Little Tokyo, Koreatown (south of Wilshire Boulevard), the Mexican-American enclave of East Los Angeles and the African-American neighborhoods of South Central Los Angeles.

HISTORICAL NOTES

The First Inhabitants – Before the arrival of the first European explorers, the region was inhabited by Native Gabrieleños who lived in small settlements, among them the village of Yang-Na near the present site of City Hall. Anthropologists have estimated that approximately 5,000 Gabrieleños lived in an area stretching roughly from present-day Orange County to MALIBU when, on August 2, 1769, a Spanish colonizing expedition led by Gaspar de Portolá arrived at Yang-Na. The Natives greeted the Europeans with gifts of grass baskets and shell beads. Juan Crespí, the Franciscan friar who served as the party's diarist, described the setting as "a very spacious valley, well grown with cottonwoods and alders, among which ran a beautiful river from the north-northwest." Having observed the jubilee of Our Lady of Los Angeles de Porciúncula the previous day, they named the river Porciúncula in her honor. Over the next week, areas such as the present-day La Brea Tar Pits and San Fernando Valley were explored by the party and duly described by Crespí.

Spanish and Mexican Pueblo – In 1781 **Felipe de Neve**, the Spanish governor of California, called for volunteers in Mexico to become *pobladores* ("settlers") of a new town on the Porciúncula River. After an arduous overland journey, 11 families finally reached the chosen site on September 4. Their new home was named El Pueblo de Nuestra Señora la Reina de Los Angeles de Porciúncula, meaning "The Town of Our Lady the Queen of the Angels by the Porciúncula." (By the mid-19C, the name had been shortened in common parlance to Los Angeles.)

The dusty town continued under Spanish rule until the founding of the Mexican Republic in 1825. By the time it was designated capital of Mexican California in 1845, it had become the commercial and social center for a region of vast cattle ranches and vineyards deeded by the Crown to such prominent families as the Picos and Sepúlvedas, whose memories are today preserved in the city's street names.

Americanization – Settlers from the eastern US began trickling into Los Angeles as early as 1826, gaining acceptance by adopting the language and lifestyle of the Latino majority. Although the city passed into American hands with the close of the Mexican War in 1848, it nevertheless remained for many years a bilingual city, with English playing the supporting role for some two decades.

Inexorably, Los Angeles was Americanized. Lt Edward O.C. Ord was hired by the city council in the summer of 1849 to survey and map the pueblo's initial Spanish land grant, comprising much of the present-day downtown, so that it could be sold as real estate to fill the city's coffers. His **Plan de la Ciudad de Los Angeles** set out an orderly rectangular street grid that is still evident today in older areas of downtown Los Angeles.

The Gold Rush of 1849 *(p 60)* brought a flood of fortune seekers to the city en route to and from northern California's gold fields. Their influx throughout the state raised demand for beef from Los Angeles' ranches, which enjoyed unparalleled prosperity. The combination of seemingly limitless money and a large transient population gave 1850s Los Angeles an unsavory reputation as a center of gambling, drinking, crime and violence.

Meanwhile, commissions set up by the US Congress to examine and certify Spanish and Mexican land grants froze the lands and money of Los Angeles' ranch owners in a legal mire. A 3-year drought in the early 1860s pushed many owners into bankruptcy, and their lands eventually passed into American hands.

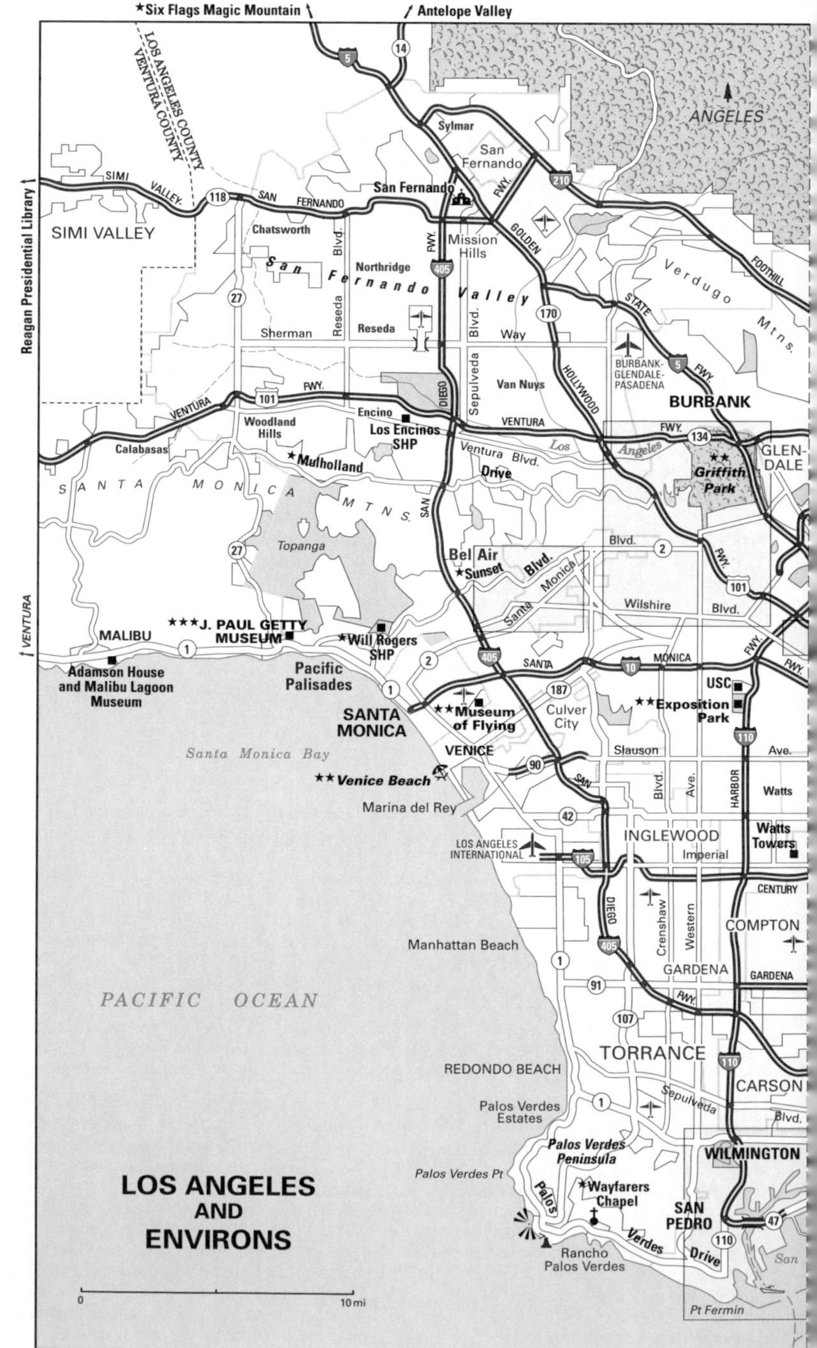

Late 19C: Growth of the City – By 1870 Los Angeles had a population of 5,000. That number more than doubled throughout the following decade, owing to the boosterism of railroad entrepreneur Henry E. Huntington, who paid journalist Charles Nordhoff in 1872 to write a book extolling the virtues of Southern California and its salubrious climate. In 1876 rail links to the east via SAN FRANCISCO were opened, and beginning in 1885, competition from the Santa Fe Railroad engendered fare reductions and a new influx of visitors and settlers.

Los Angeles' reputation as a latter-day Eden was further enhanced by the **citrus industry**. Oranges were first grown at SAN GABRIEL MISSION in 1804, and a 70-acre grove was planted near downtown in 1841. But the arrival in RIVERSIDE of seedless navel oranges from Brazil in 1873, coupled with refrigerated railroad cars that could ship them east in perfect condition, led to the establishment of vast orange groves to meet rising demand for the fruit nationwide. In 1877 a boxcar of California oranges sent from Los Angeles caused a sensation in St Louis and local fruit shipped by rail to a New Orleans fair in 1884 was judged better than Florida oranges. With wine grapes, wheat, and other fruits and vegetables also growing abundantly, agriculture became the new mainstay of Los Angeles' economy.

Such images of a sun-kissed good life produced an 1880s boom in local real estate, with new communities like H.H. Wilcox's Hollywood springing up in outlying areas. By 1890 the city's population had risen to more than 50,000, and by 1900, Los Angeles was home to more than 100,000 people.

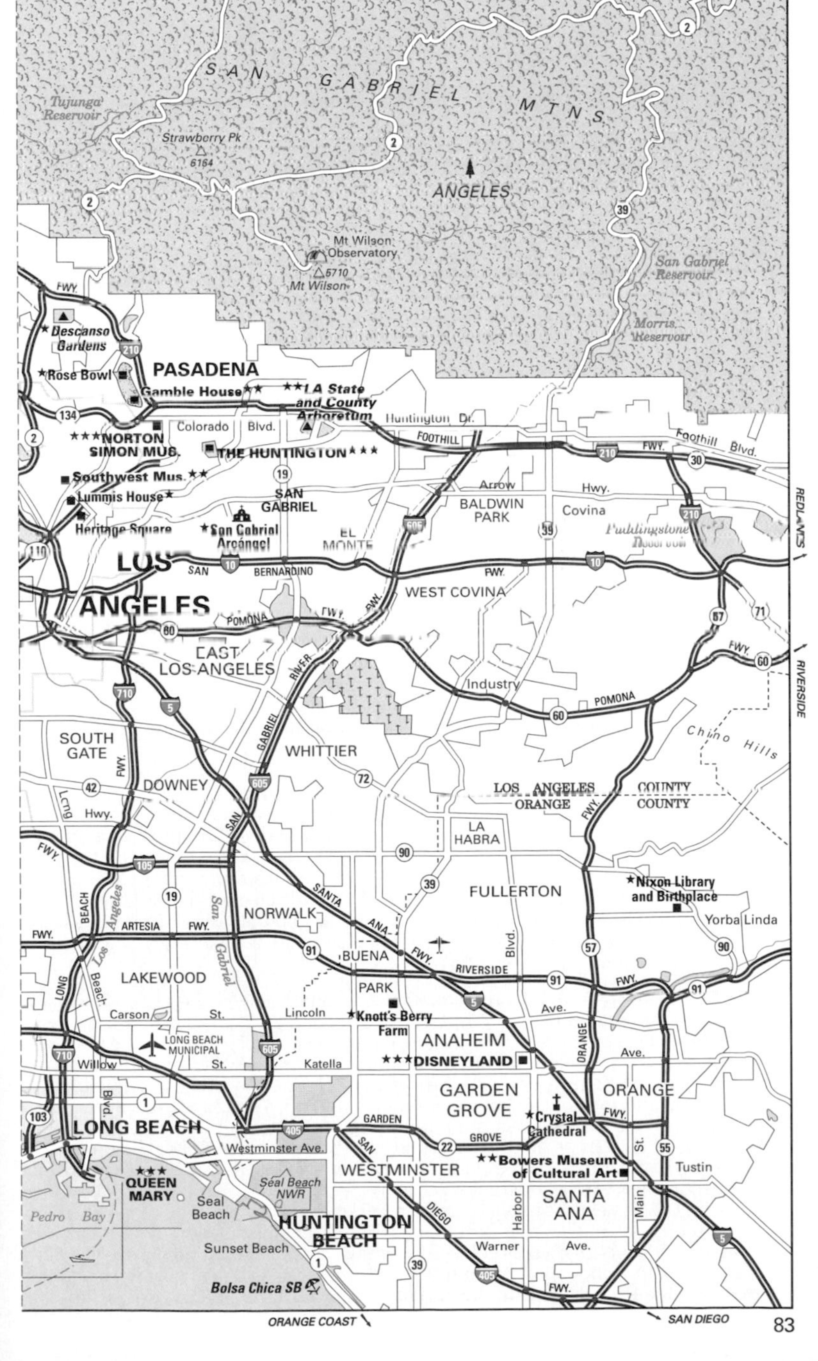

Located in a semi-desert region, Los Angeles' growth was severely limited by a lack of readily available water. But in 1904, county water superintendent William Mulholland initiated a $24.5 million project to bring Los Angeles water from the verdant OWENS VALLEY some 250mi to the north. The **Los Angeles Aqueduct** officially opened on November 15, 1913, its waters coursing along a concrete path, through 142 separate mountain tunnels and down a spillway at the northern end of the San Fernando Valley as Mulholland proclaimed simply, "There it is. Take it."

Although the controversial project laid waste to the Owens Valley and led to protracted legal battles with the farmers whose livelihoods it ruined, it enabled unprecedented growth for Los Angeles. The city expanded its boundaries, and by the 1920s, it had incorporated the neighboring cities of Beverly Hills, SANTA MONICA, LONG BEACH and PASADENA, all of which lacked adequate ground water.

Early 20C: Population Boom – The first decade of the 20C brought the fledgling **motion picture industry** from New York City and Chicago to the Los Angeles area in search of spacious and varied locations and the consistently gentle climate necessary for outdoor filming. Established largely in and around Hollywood, the studios soon made that town's and Los Angeles' names synonymous with movies: by 1920, 80 percent of the world's feature films were being produced in California, and by the middle of that decade, Hollywood's motion picture industry employed more than 20,000 people. Motion picture stars eagerly bought property in the hillside Hollywoodland development and in Beverly Hills, gradually bestowing upon these communities all the glittering fantasy aura of the movies themselves. Through the years, Los Angeles has provided the industry with an abundant supply of locations for popular films, making many parts of the city familiar even to those who have never visited.

In 1897, when the first automobile drove along the streets of Los Angeles, more than 500 oil wells were already pumping in the downtown area, contributing to California's ranking at that time as the third largest oil-producing state in the nation after Pennsylvania and New York. Local oil speculators, among them G. Allan Hancock, become millionaires almost overnight.

Turn-of-the-century Los Angeles enjoyed an outstanding public transportation system, the **Pacific Electric Railway Company**. But the automobile proved the perfect vehicle for the rapidly expanding city, and reasonably priced and readily available gasoline literally fueled the growth of automotive traffic, which finally rendered obsolete the last of Pacific Electric's "Big Red Cars" in 1949.

In the 1920s, pioneer aviators such as Glenn Martin, Donald W. Douglas, Allan and Malcolm Loughead (pronounced and later spelled "Lockheed") and John Northrup set up shop in the Los Angeles area, to be followed two decades later by Howard Hughes, establishing the city and its region as world center for the passenger and military aircraft industry.

By the start of World War II, Los Angeles had a population of some 1.5 million people. Following the war, the city's population boomed again as servicemen who had passed through Southern California en route to or from the Pacific decided to settle there, and the halcyon days of the Eisenhower era encouraged still more Americans to head west in search of their fortunes. Orange groves gave way to housing tracts as the city's boundaries expanded and its population grew. By 1960 the city's population had reached 2.5 million people; more than 6 million people lived in Los Angeles County.

LOS ANGELES TODAY

As it approaches the turn of the century, Los Angeles enjoys the benefits and faces the challenges of a major metropolis, though both the pros and cons of life in the city are magnified by its enormous size and its near-mythic reputation. Los Angeles' characteristic ethnic diversity endows it with rich cultural resources and can make a drive across town seem like a dizzying world tour. It can also, particularly in the face of social and economic adversity, lead to civic strife: devastating riots occurred in Watts in August 1965, and again in April and May of 1992 in other neighborhoods of South Central Los Angeles and beyond. The physical, spiritual and economic wounds of such unrest can take years, if not decades, to heal.

Yet Los Angeles continues to preserve, heal and renew itself, largely through the efforts of individuals and local and Federal organizations. Groups such as the **Los Angeles Conservancy** and **Project Restore** dedicate themselves to preserving the city's wealth of historic architecture, from the Art Deco masterpieces of the Business District and the Miracle Mile to residences by such architects as Frank Lloyd Wright, Rudolf Schindler and Richard Neutra. The city hosted the **Summer Olympic Games** of 1932 and 1984, and its unquenchable dynamism attracts a variety of international visitors and events.

The Performing Arts – Nonresidents have traditionally viewed Los Angeles—a city where movies are the predominant industry and art form—as a cultural wasteland. However, a plethora of fine cultural institutions and activities proves the cynics wrong. The Los Angeles County Museum of Art, the J. Paul Getty Museum, the Museum of Contemporary Art and other institutions now house outstanding collections and mount exhibits that tour the nation. The **Los Angeles Philharmonic Orchestra** rose to world-class status under conductors Zubin Mehta and André Previn, and continues to thrive under the baton of Esa-Pekka Salonen. The University of California, Los Angeles and the University of Southern California enjoy international esteem as institutions of higher education. The theaters of the Music Center of Los Angeles County and other local stages present a wide range of award-winning original and visiting productions of drama, music, opera and dance. And the city's widespread diversity and progressive character continually spark a spirit of creativity and innovation that attracts and embraces new talent, spawns and nurtures new ideas, and consistently welcomes new forms of artistic expression.

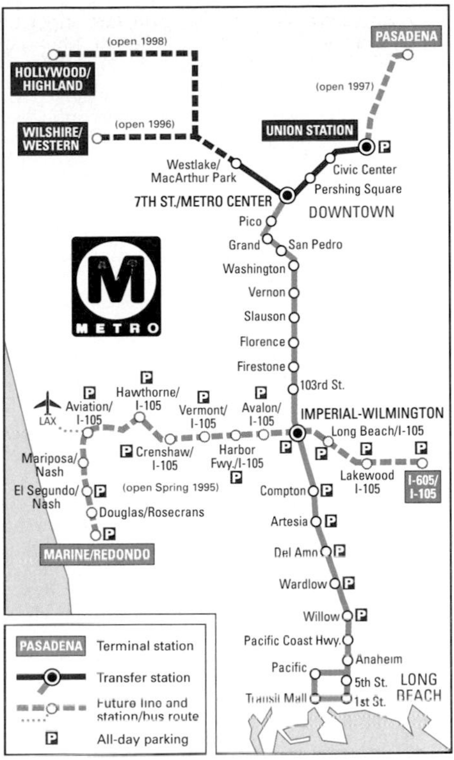

Metro Rail – Still in its infancy, Los Angeles' public rapid-transit system of underground and surface light-rail cars was inaugurated in July 1990 with opening of the Metro **Blue Line** between downtown's Union Station, and Long Beach; a future Blue Line link is planned between Union Station and Pasadena. The **Red Line**, connecting Union Station with MacArthur Park, opened in January 1993 and will eventually extend through Hollywood to Universal City and through East Los Angeles. The **Green Line**, slated to link the suburbs of Norwalk and El Segundo, is presently under construction. **Metro-link**, a network of high-speed commuter railroad trains connecting Los Angeles with outlying cities, is also being developed to further alleviate congestion on the area's freeways. Selected stations on the Metro Red Line are considered unique attractions in their own right, boasting high-caliber works of public art and design. Standouts include Civic Center, 7th Street/Metro Center, Pershing Square and Union Station. Metro tickets can be purchased from vending machines at each station; the distance traveled determines the ticket price. Ten-trip tickets and monthly passes are available. *For information ☎213-620-7245.*

Freeways – *Chart p 114.* Los Angeles' intricate but well-signed and easily navigable system of freeways began with the opening of the Arroyo Seco Parkway (now the Pasadena Freeway) in 1940. The Hollywood Freeway followed in 1947, and the 1950s were an era of extensive freeway construction. Following rights-of-way formerly traveled by the city's trolley cars, the freeways link Los Angeles' many centers with its myriad sprawling suburbs. Now measuring more than 528.3mi in total length, the network, like the city itself, continues to grow. When traveling via freeway, visitors are advised to check and review their route before departing, making special note of freeway on- and off-ramps and interchanges. All freeways are designated on maps with interstate or state highway numbers; but locals also refer to them by names that usually correspond to their destinations or the areas through which they pass. If possible, avoid traveling during the rush hours (6-10am and 3-7pm), when traffic can be heavily congested.

Visiting Los Angeles – Although public transportation continues to improve in Los Angeles, visitors staying for any length of time will find an automobile essential. Because it is so widespread and diverse, Los Angeles is easily visited as a collection of separate destinations to which whole days can be devoted: downtown, Griffith Park, Exposition Park, Hollywood, Beverly Hills and the Westside. Each of these areas, and others as well, merit exploration on foot, with the car parked and waiting to carry you to your next destination.

A city where cars are the most efficient means of travel, Los Angeles is well endowed with metered parking spaces. Parking availability is greater in the downtown area, where clearly indicated lots and garages provide abundant opportunities to park and explore the area on foot. Throughout the city, parking meters are strictly monitored and time limits enforced. Motorists in the city of Beverly Hills benefit from numerous free municipal parking lots.

Los Angeles' dry, subtropical climate is pleasant year-round, moderated both by gentle Pacific breezes and by the mountains that shield the Los Angeles basin from inland summer heat and winter cold. In summer, high temperatures average about 75°F and seldom exceed 90°F; in January, daytime highs average 63°F. Evenings, even during the warmest months, tend to be cool and breezy, requiring a light jacket or sweater. The rainy season usually lasts from November through March; but even at this time of year, days are more likely to be sunny than not.

L.A. Cuisine – Los Angeles restaurants enjoy the reputation of being among the best and most innovative in the country. Popular chefs, working for the most part in fashionable restaurants in Hollywood, Beverly Hills, the Westside and Santa Monica, enjoy celebrity status, their creations a lively amalgam of world cuisines featuring absolutely fresh ingredients and presented with painterly artistry.

The city's ethnic populations also provide the opportunity to sample a wide range of the world's cuisines. Restaurants featuring Mexican, Chinese, Thai, Vietnamese, Cajun and Indian cuisine, and cooking styles from soul food to Jewish deli, are found throughout the metropolis.

Practical Information

Getting There

By Air – **Los Angeles International Airport** (LAX): international and domestic flights, 10mi southwest of downtown; commercial shuttles to Greater Los Angeles area ($5-$20) ☎310-646-5252. Domestic flights: **Long Beach Municipal Airport** (LGB), 22mi south of downtown ☎310-421-8293; **Burbank-Glendale-Pasadena Airport** (BUR), 16mi north of downtown ☎818-840-8847; **Orange County/John Wayne Airport** (SNA), in Anaheim, 36mi southeast of downtown ☎714-252-5006. Rental car agency branches at all airports *(p 253)*. Call airports for shuttle information.

By Bus and Train – *p 253*. Greyhound: 6th and Los Angeles Sts ☎800-231-2222. Trailways: 6th and Main Sts ☎800-338-4014. Amtrak: Union Station, 800 North Alameda St ☎800-872-7245.

Getting Around

By Public Transportation – *p 85*.

By Car – *p 253*.

By Taxi – **Checker** ☎213-624-2227; **Independent** ☎213-385-8294; **L.A. Taxi** ☎213-627-7000; **United** ☎213-653-5050; **Yellow** ☎213-221-2331.

General Information

Visitor Information – **Los Angeles Convention & Visitor Bureau** information centers: **Downtown** 685 S. Figueroa St, Los Angeles CA 90017 ☎213-689-8822 (open Mon–Sat 8am–5pm); **Hollywood** The Janes House, 6541 Hollywood Blvd ☎213-461-4213 (open Mon–Sat 9am–5pm). **Beverly Hills Visitor and Convention Bureau**: 2339 S. Beverly Dr, Beverly Hills CA 90212 ☎310-271-8174 (open Mon–Fri 8:30am–5pm). Disabled visitor information: *Around the Town with Ease* guide ($2) available from The Junior League of Los Angeles, Farmers Market, Third and Fairfax, Los Angeles CA 90036 ☎213-937-5566. Architectural tours of the city: **Los Angeles Conservancy**, 727 W. Seventh St, Suite 955, Los Angeles CA 90017 ☎213-623-2489.

Accommodations – **Southern California Hotel Reservation Center** ☎818-708-7684. *Destination L.A.* lodging directory available (free) from the Los Angeles Visitor & Convention Bureau *(above)*. Accommodations range from elegant hotels ($200/day) to budget motels ($70/day). Most bed & breakfasts are in residential sections of the city ($80/day). *All rates quoted are average prices for a double room.*

Local Press – Daily news: *Los Angeles Times* (morning), *Calendar* entertainment section; *Herald Examiner* (afternoon). Weekly entertainment information: *L.A. Weekly* and *Los Angeles Reader*.

Entertainment – Consult the arts and entertainment sections of local newspapers for schedule of cultural events and addresses of principal theaters and concert halls. **Entertainment Hotline**: ☎213-689-2787. Tickets for local events: **Ticket Outlet** offers half-price tickets for selected events on the day of the performance (available by phone only Tue–Sat noon–5pm) ☎213-688-2787; or **Ticketmaster** ☎213-365-3500.

Currency Exchange Offices – *p 251*. Los Angeles International Airport currency exchange offices (Tom Bradley Terminal): **Los Angeles Currency Exchange**, daily 7am–11pm; **Bank of America**, Mon–Fri 9am–6pm, Sat 7pm, Sun 2pm.

Sports – Tickets for major sporting events can be purchased at the venue or through Ticketmaster outlets *(above)*.

Sport	*Team*	*Season*	*Venue*
Major League Baseball	Dodgers (NL)	Apr–Oct	Dodger Stadium
	Angels (AL)		Anaheim Stadium
Professional Football	Raiders (AFC west)	Sept–Dec	Memorial Coliseum
	Rams (NFC west)		Anaheim Stadium
Collegiate Football	USC Trojans		Memorial Coliseum
	UCLA Bruins		Rose Bowl, Pasadena
Professional Basketball	Lakers	Nov–May	The Forum
	Clippers		L.A. Sports Arena
Collegiate Basketball	USC Trojans		Memorial Sports Arena
	UCLA Bruins		Pauley Pavilion
Professional Hockey	Kings	Sept–Apr	The Forum
	Mighty Ducks of Anaheim		The Pond, Anaheim

Useful Numbers

Police/Ambulance/Fire (multilingual)	**911**
Police (non-emergency; multilingual)	213-485-3294
Medical Society Referrals (Mon–Fri 8:45am–4:45pm multilingual)	213-483-6122
Dental Society Referrals (24hrs; English only)	213-481-2133
Thrifty Drugstore 334 S. Vermont Ave (daily 8am–2am; English only)	213-666-5083
Main Post Office 5800 West Century Blvd (Mon–Fri 7:30am–midnight, weekends open at 8am; Spanish & English)	310-337-8885
Weather (English only)	213-554-1212

★ 1 DOWNTOWN

★ El Pueblo de Los Angeles Historic Monument *3hrs*

●*Union Station. Map below. Historic sites open year-round Tue–Sat (Sepulveda House open Mon-Sat).* ✗ ☎*213-628-1274.*

The city's historic heart is a 44-acre cluster of 27 buildings dating as far back as 1818, many of them restored or undergoing restoration. Popularly known as Olvera Street after the pedestrian thoroughfare leading off the central plaza, El Pueblo is a vibrant, multicolored showcase of the vestiges of early Los Angeles.

On September 4, 1781, a short distance to the southeast of El Pueblo's present site, 44 *pobladores* of Native, black, Spanish and *mestizo* ancestry founded the first Spanish farming settlement here *(p 81)*. In 1815 a severe flood of the nearby Río Porciúncula, now the Los Angeles River, forced the settlers to relocate their plaza to higher ground, and it was moved to its present location about 1825. By then, the town of adobe dwellings was the center of a thriving ranching community of more than 650 residents. The first official census recorded 2,228 inhabitants in 1836.

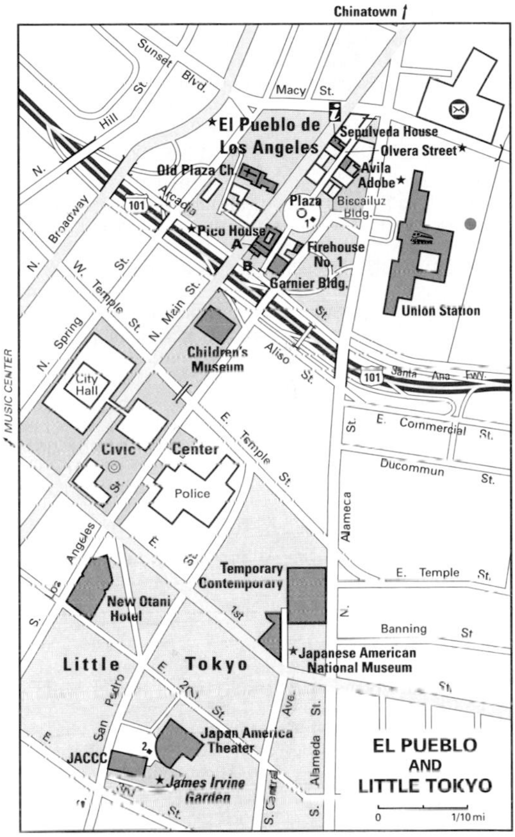

As Los Angeles grew, its centers of government and business gradually moved south to the current downtown. By the 1920s, Olvera Street was a dirty alleyway, and the buildings surrounding it were abandoned, condemned and decaying. Beginning in 1926, city resident **Christine Sterling** took an interest in the area and launched a one-woman campaign of lobbying and fund-raising that saw Olvera Street reopen on April 20, 1930, as a colorfully restored Mexican marketplace. Sterling's single-minded efforts on behalf of El Pueblo, which continued until her death in 1963, culminated in the area's designation as a state historic park in 1953.

Today a city historic monument, El Pueblo is a center of ethnic pride for Los Angeles' Latino community. Year round, it is the site of cultural celebrations, among them the Blessing of the Animals, a traditional ceremony for domestic pets (mid-Apr); City's Birthday Celebration and Mexican Independence Day (both early Sept); and Las Posadas, a candlelight procession depicting Mary and Joseph's search for lodging in Bethlehem (Dec 16-24).

Begin at the visitor center located in Sepulveda House.

★ **Olvera Street** – The brick-paved pedestrian street, originally called "Wine" or "Vine" Street, was renamed in 1877 for Agustín Olvera, the first county judge. Shops and wooden stalls sell a gaily jumbled assortment of crafts, clothing, souvenirs and food. A zigzag pattern of bricks in the pavement crosses the street diagonally, marking the path of the *zanja madre*, created in 1781 as the "mother ditch" of the city's first water system.

Sepulveda House – *W-12 Olvera St.* This 2-story Victorian structure (1887), blending Mexican and Anglo influences, was built by Eloisa Martinez de Sepúlveda as a commercial space and boarding house. Exhibits include a period kitchen and bedroom. The Main Street **facade** is an excellent example of the local Eastlake style. In the **visitor center**, a video *(18min; shown upon request)* presents the early history of Los Angeles and El Pueblo.

★ **Avila Adobe** – *E-11 Olvera Street.* The oldest existing house in Los Angeles, this one-story adobe (1818) was built by cattle rancher Don Francisco Avila. In January 1847, during the Mexican War, Commodore Robert F. Stockton briefly commandeered the house. The state purchased it in 1953, and Christine Sterling *(above)* resided here during her final years.

Today six rooms are furnished in the 1840s ranch style, and across the spacious courtyard, an **annex** features exhibits on the Los Angeles Aqueduct and the history of El Pueblo.

The Plaza – El Pueblo's central plaza has occupied this site since 1825, though its layout and landscaping date from the 1870s. Four Moreton Bay fig trees flank a wrought-iron bandstand (1962), and a plaque on the southern side lists the names and ethnic origins of the first 44 *pobladores*. On the eastern side, a bronze **statue [1]** of Felipe de Neve, erected in 1932, commemorates the man who drew up the plans for the city's settlement *(p 81)*.
Facing the plaza's northeast corner, on the first-floor facade of the Biscailuz Building (1926), home of the Mexican Cultural Center, a mural by Leo Politi depicts *The Blessing of the Animals* (1978).

Our Lady Queen of the Angels Catholic Church – *535 N. Main St, west side of the plaza.* Popularly known as **Old Plaza Church**, the city's oldest existing church (1822) has been restored and enlarged considerably over the years, though inside and out it retains the style of the early missions. On the exterior, facing the plaza, is a mosaic of *The Annunciation* (1981, Isabel Piczek), a replica of a mural panel in St Mary of the Angels Basilica near Assisi, Italy.

★ **Pico House** – *Southwest corner of the plaza.* At the time of its construction in 1870, this 3-story Italianate building (Ezra F. Kysor) was considered the finest hotel in Southern California. Its granite facade was restored in the 1960s.
Behind the Pico House along Main Street are the **Merced Theatre [A]** (1870, Ezra F. Kysor), Los Angeles' first theater *(not open to the public)*; and **Masonic Hall [B]** (1858), meeting place of the city's first Masonic Lodge and now the site of a small display on the early days of local Freemasonry.

Firehouse No. 1 – *Southeast corner of the plaza.* The 2-story brick building (1884) served as the city's first firehouse until 1897, when it became a saloon and boarding house. It now houses a museum of fire fighting memorabilia from the late 19C.
Behind the firehouse along Los Angeles Street, one bay of the 2-story brick-and-sandstone **Garnier Building** *(not open to the public)*, built in 1890 by Philippe Garnier as commercial and residential space for Chinese tenants, awaits conversion into a museum of Chinese-American history.

East of El Pueblo across Alameda St is **Union Station** (1939, Parkinson & Parkinson), a $13 million combined venture of the Southern Pacific, Union Pacific and Santa Fe railroads. Gracefully blending Mission Revival, Spanish Colonial, Moorish and Art Deco styles, the building is considered the last of the grand train stations built in the US during the heyday of rail travel. The **interior★**, featuring marble and tile floors and walls, elaborate walnut-beamed ceilings and Art Deco seats, has appeared in such Hollywood films as *Union Station* (1950), *The Way We Were* (1973) and *Bugsy* (1991). Union Station is a key hub in the city's Metrorail system *(p 85)*.

Chinatown *1/2 hr. ●Union Station.*

With roughly 15 square blocks bounded by Sunset Boulevard and Alameda, Bernard and Yale Streets, Los Angeles' Chinatown is a fairly small district compared to its sprawling San Francisco counterpart. Nevertheless, its collection of timeworn, chinoiserie-embellished buildings and modern shopping plazas serves as one of two main centers for the city's 170,000 residents of Chinese descent (the other being Monterey Park, 7mi to the east). Chinatown is also a noted dining destination, popular for its casual restaurants serving a variety of Chinese and other Asian cuisines.
In 1850, a census recorded two Chinese—both male house servants—among Los Angeles' 1,610 residents. But the growing city's need for laborers drew more to settle here, despite racial tensions that, in October 1871, led to the murder of 19 men and boys at the hands of a racist mob. By 1900, more than half of Los Angeles' 2,000 Chinese residents—most of them independent vegetable farmers and peddlers—lived in a cramped network of streets and alleys east of OLVERA STREET. Union Station's construction on that site, starting in the mid-1930s, led to the area's demolition and the opening in 1938 of the present, tourism-oriented Chinatown.

Visit – A pagoda-style **gateway** along the 900 block of North Broadway marks the entrance to Gin Ling Way, main street of Central Plaza, Chinatown's original pedestrian precinct. Just beyond the gate is a **statue** of Sun Yat-Sen, first president of the Chinese Republic. Chinatown's intriguing jumble of supermarkets, herbalists, curio and souvenir shops and discount stores attracts both local and visiting shoppers, and the area is the setting for the annual **Chinese New Year Parade** *(Jan-Feb)*.

Little Tokyo *3hrs. ●Union Station. Map p 87.*

The cultural, social, business and spiritual center of North America's largest Japanese-American community occupies an area of approximately seven square blocks southeast of El Pueblo. Although some charming touches of traditional Japanese style may be seen in architectural ornamentation and commercial signage, Little Tokyo is primarily a bustling, contemporary city environment of modern office buildings, shopping centers, residential apartments and cultural and religious institutions.
In 1885 Los Angeles' Japanese population totaled some two dozen *Issei*, or first-generation immigrants. Restricted from owning businesses or homes among Caucasian citizens, these early settlers and those who followed congregated in and around the area today preserved as the **Little Tokyo Historic District** *(1st St between San Pedro St and Central Ave)*. By 1905 the population of Little Tokyo, as it had come to be called, numbered 3,400. During World War II, its entire population of 6,000 was forcibly removed to government internment camps *(p 136)*; after the war, Japanese Americans returned to Little Tokyo.
The coming of age of second- and third-generation Japanese Americans *(Nisei and Sansei)* lent greater economic and social stability to Little Tokyo. Since the 1970s, both local and Japanese investments have resulted in substantial growth, with the 21-story **New Otani Hotel** serving as one the cornerstones of redevelopment.

Today, Little Tokyo thrives as a self-contained community in which small restaurants and retail shops tightly intermingle with apartment and office buildings, hotels, shopping plazas, cinemas and theaters, supermarkets and religious temples. The **Japanese American Cultural and Community Center (JACCC)** *(244 S. San Pedro St)* and adjoining **Japan America Theatre** are focal points for a rich variety of community programs and events, and numerous public sculptures in plazas and on street corners express a strong sense of civic pride.

★ **Japanese American National Museum** – *369 E. 1st St. Open year-round Tue–Sun. Closed Jan 1, Thanksgiving Day, Dec 25. $4. ♿ ☎ 213-625-0414.* Opened in 1992, America's first museum dedicated to the history of Japanese Americans occupies the former Nishi Hongwanji Buddhist Temple (1925), today greatly renovated and restored.
Its principal gallery, on the second floor, occupies the original temple's main hall, beneath an ornate gold-leafed, box-beamed ceiling. Changing exhibits are drawn from the largest collection of Japanese-American photographs, documents and artifacts in the US. On the building's lower level, a **Legacy Center** provides interactive displays emphasizing family heritage and Japanese crafts.

★ **James Irvine Garden** – *Adjacent to the JACCC, 244 S. San Pedro St. Open daily year-round. Closed major holidays. ♿ ☎213-628-2725.* Designed in the traditional Japanese style by Takeo Uesugi, the 8,500sq ft garden features a bamboo glen and a 170ft cascading stream symbolizing the Issei, Nisei and Sansei. A tranquil path meanders among more than 30 species of Asian and local semi-tropical plants.
Overlooking the garden is an expanse of red brick plaza anchored by a massive stone **sculpture [2]** entitled *To the Issei*. The plaza and the sculpture are the work of city native and internationally acclaimed artist **Isamu Noguchi** (1904-1988).

The Temporary Contemporary – *152 N. Central Ave. Open year-round Tue–Sun. Closed Jan 1, Thanksgiving Day, Dec 25. $4 (includes admission to MOCA). ♿ ☎213-626-6222. Closed for renovations, scheduled reopening autumn 1995.* Before the 1986 completion of the Museum of Contemporary Art (MOCA), the museum's first shows were held in this former warehouse complex with interiors redesigned for exhibition purposes by architect Frank Gehry. The structure remains part of MOCA and is used for presentation of self-contained, large-scale exhibits as well as works from the museum's permanent collection.

Civic Center Area *2hrs. ●Civic Center. Map p 90.*

The largest center for municipal administration in the US, this group of buildings and open plazas, planned and constructed between the 1920s and the 1960s, occupies approximately 13 blocks in the heart of Los Angeles.
Between 1900 and the 1920s, several master plans were drawn up for a homogeneous ensemble of monumental administrative buildings. No plan was ever formally adopted, however, and today Los Angeles' Civic Center is a random array of structures ranging widely in style from the monumental **Hall of Justice Building** (1925), with its neoclassical details *(northeast corner of S. Broadway and W. Temple St)*, to the 1960s structures of the Music Center. Several buildings of architectural merit and historic importance are interspersed with inviting, open, green spaces popular among downtown workers as a favorite place for al fresco lunches.

★★ **Los Angeles City Hall** – *200 N. Spring St. Open year-round Mon–Fri 7am–5pm. Closed major holidays. ✗ ♿ 🅿 ☎ 213-485-2891.* Standing apart from downtown's glittering skyscrapers to the southwest, City Hall's 28-story, pyramid-topped tower remains one of Los Angeles' most distinctive features and most widely recognized symbols.
Creation of the structure by a consortium of leading local architects, among them John C. Austin, John Parkinson and Albert C. Martin Sr, required passage of a special variance excluding the structure from height limits imposed by law in 1904. The 454ft building (1928) remained the city's tallest until the height limits were rescinded in 1957. A monument to civic pride, the building was designed to reflect the diversity of the city and state: the mortar used in construction included sand from every California county and water from each of the state's 21 missions.
The 135ft-wide **rotunda** reveals French limestone walls and a floor composed of 4,156 inlays cut from 46 varieties of marble. The tiled dome depicts the eight primary duties of municipal government: Public Service, Health, Trust, Art, Protection, Education, Law and Government.
The observation tower *(27th floor; closed until 1996)* affords, on clear days, sweeping **panoramas**★★ of the Los Angeles basin.

Los Angeles Times Building – *202 W. 1st St. Visit by guided tour (45min) only, year-round Mon–Fri. Closed major holidays. ♿ 🅿 ☎ 213-237-5000. An audiovisual presentation (5min) on the history of communication precedes guided tours, which depart from the 1st St lobby.* Located directly southwest of City Hall, the monumental complex occupying an entire block is the fourth home of Los Angeles' renowned newspaper, which enjoys one of the largest circulations in the nation (approximately 1.25 million copies daily; 1.5 million Sunday edition).
In 1882, when **Harrison Gray Otis** became a partner in the fledgling newspaper, it had a total circulation of less than 1,000 copies. But it prospered along with the city that it actively boosted, and the *Times* moved from its small original office to a large new 3-story building at the corner of 1st Street and Broadway; the structure was bombed by union terrorists in 1910.
The current facility stands as an architectural record of the newspaper's continued growth and prosperity. The central Art Deco structure (1935, Gordon B. Kaufmann) was expanded in 1948 with a 10-story addition, and again in 1973 with a sleek black-glass and steel 6-story extension (William Pereira & Assocs.).

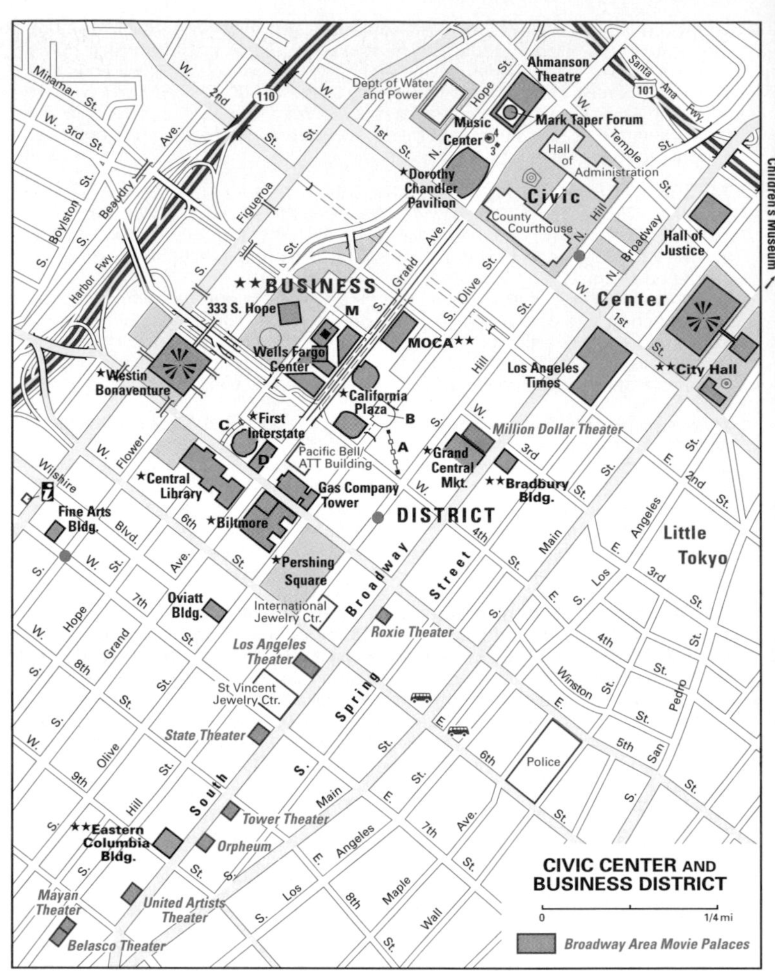

The **lobby★** features an original linotype machine, a large revolving world globe and a display of photographs and facsimile pages tracing the *Times*' first century. On the rotunda ceiling is *The Newspaper*, a double mural by Hugo Ballin.

Music Center of Los Angeles County – *North of 1st St between Hope and Grand Aves.* Los Angeles' hilltop mecca for the performing arts (1964, Welton Becket & Assocs.) is an elegant group of three white marble structures occupying a 7-acre elevated plaza. Home to the Los Angeles Philharmonic, the Los Angeles Master Chorale, the Los Angeles Music Center Opera, the Center Theatre Group and numerous visiting theater, music and dance companies, the complex hosts performances ranging from the traditional to the wildly experimental.

Until the Music Center opened on December 6, 1964, Los Angeles' performing companies appeared at a variety of private and public venues. In 1955, Dorothy Buffum Chandler, recognizing the county's need for a central performing arts complex, chaired a civic committee that eventually selected the site and raised $20 million in private donations towards the center's $34.5 million cost. The dynamic cooperation between public and private sectors is also evident in the plans for the proposed $200-million Walt Disney Concert Hall (Frank Gehry), due to open in 1996 on a site immediately across 1st Street.

The Buildings – An imposing composition of towering windows and columns, the **Dorothy Chandler Pavilion★** (1964), center for music, opera and dance productions and frequent site of the annual Academy Awards *(late March)*, is the largest and most opulent of the three buildings. Numerous artworks grace the palatial interior, and some 90 percent of its 3,197 seats are within 105ft of the stage, itself one of the nation's largest performance spaces. Innovative dramatic works are presented at the 752-seat **Mark Taper Forum** (1967), a low, cylindrical structure framed by a reflecting pool and a detached colonnade. The rectilinear 2,071-seat **Ahmanson Theatre** (1967), hosts plays, musicals, dance concerts and individual performing artists.

The Plaza – This favored pre-performance gathering place between the Chandler and the Taper theaters offers a sweeping view east to City Hall and features two sculptures: *Dance Door* **[3]** (1982) by Robert Graham and *Peace on Earth* **[4]** (1969) by Jacques Lipchitz. The latter is surrounded by an attractive fountain consisting of 280 dancing vertical jets of water.

Los Angeles Children's Museum – *Map p 87. 310 N. Main St. Open late Jun–Aug Tue–Sun, rest of the year weekends only. Closed mid–late Sept. $5.* ♿ 🅿 *☎213-687-8800.* More an indoor playground than an institution for learning, the multilevel maze of ramps, passageways and rooms includes an art workshop, audio and video studios, and such participatory theme-oriented areas as "City Streets" and "Club Eco." A small performance space presents theater, dance and puppet shows, often involving audience participation.

★★ **Business District** *1 day. Map 90.*
Bounded roughly by Figueroa, 2nd, Spring and 9th Sts. ●Pershing Square.

Los Angeles' business district has evolved into two distinct areas. The older one, anchored by Broadway and **Spring Street**, reveals many Beaux-Arts and Art Deco buildings dating primarily from the turn of the century through the 1920s; today it is the setting for a lively street scene dominated by the city's Latino community. Covering the area of Flower, Hope and Olive Streets north of 6th Street, the newer section's gleaming towers of commerce, built since the 1960s, rise to the west on Bunker Hill, overlooking their historic neighbors.

Following Edward Ord's survey in 1849 *(p 82)*, the city sold prime residential lots in its "lower district"—a rural area bordered by 2nd, 4th, Spring and Hill Streets—for as much as $200 each. After the turn of the century, successive population and financial booms saw magnificent hotels and commercial buildings encroaching on the residential neighborhoods below Bunker Hill. Banks occupied the Art Deco buildings along Spring Street, creating its early-20C reputation as the West Coast's premier financial center. From the Great Depression through the 1950s, the area entered a slow decline as the city's wealthy residents and leading businesses steadily relocated elsewhere, leaving downtown to poorer immigrant populations. Today, nonprofit organizations such as the Los Angeles Conservancy *(p 86)* actively campaign to save downtown's landmarks, joining with enterprising businesses to restore many buildings to their original architectural and ornamental glory and return them to use.

Described by local newspapers as a "howling coyote's wilderness," a large hilltop area just to the west of downtown was sold in 1867 for $500 to Prudent Beaudry, who developed it into Bunker Hill, a fashionable neighborhood of Victorian mansions accessed from the streets below by **Angel's Flight [A]**, a two-car funicular railway that opened in 1901. The area remained a popular residential enclave through the first half of the 20C, but subsequently declined along with old downtown; between 1959 and 1969, Bunker Hill's deteriorated residences were razed, and Angel's Flight was dismantled. Rejuvenation occurred during and after the 1960s: under the direction of the Community Redevelopment Agency, new office towers began to rise on Bunker Hill. Angel's Flight, which was put into storage, is currently being restored to again climb the slope between Hill Street and California Plaza *(scheduled completion 1995)*.

Beginning in 1910, **Broadway** became the site of nickelodeons and vaudeville houses, paving the way in 1918 for showman Sid Grauman *(p 102)* to open the Million Dollar Theater, the first of a dozen theaters that, by 1931, gave Broadway the world's highest concentration of ornate movie palaces. Today, many of the original dozen remain open in the stretch between 3rd and 10th Streets, catering to the area's Latino population.

★ **California Plaza** – *Grand Ave between 3rd and 4th Sts.* This striking, 11-acre complex comprises two curvilinear reflecting-glass office towers, an apartment building, a luxury hotel and the Museum of Contemporary Art *(below)*. Two plazas with fountains and outdoor stages, the Spiral Court and the **Watercourt [B]**, offer free weekday noon concerts *(late May–Oct, concert information ☎213-687-2159)*.

★★ **Museum of Contemporary Art (MOCA)** – *250 S. Grand Ave. Open year-round Tue–Sun 11am–5pm. Closed Jan 1, Thanksgiving Day, Dec 25. $4 (includes admission to The Temporary Contemporary). ✗ ♿ 🅿 ☎213-626-6222.* An intriguing assemblage of geometric forms clad in red Indian sandstone and green aluminum panels, this museum (1986), commonly referred to as MOCA, showcases visual art produced since the 1940s.

The museum was conceived in 1979 by a committee of local collectors and artists in conjunction with the Community Redevelopment Agency. A site was selected within the then-projected California Plaza commercial development on Bunker Hill, and prominent Japanese architect **Arata Isozaki** was commissioned in 1981 to design the structure. A protracted approval process led to the preparation of almost 30 different designs; Isozaki's final solution achieved an intimate, low-lying **complex**★ he described as "a village in a valley of skyscrapers." Cubes, a cylinder and 11 pyramidal skylights define MOCA's 2- and 3-story office, library and bookstore buildings; these above-ground buildings flank a sun well leading to 25,000sq ft of underground galleries. One wall of the sun well forms a sinuous line the architect originally traced from a nude photograph of Marilyn Monroe.

Visit – *1hr.* Changing selections from the growing permanent collection of more than 1,400 paintings, drawings, photographs, sculptures, videos, installations and works in other visual media are exhibited; highlights include works by Nevelson, Oldenburg, Pollock, Rothko, Johns, Rauschenberg, Stella, Ruscha and Borofsky. Most of the museum's display space, however, is devoted to important temporary shows, held here and in almost 45,000sq ft of additional space 10 blocks away at the Temporary Contemporary *(p 89)*.

Wells Fargo Center – *Grand Ave between 3rd and 4th Sts, across from California Plaza.* The trapezoidal twin towers of brown granite and tinted glass (1983, Skidmore, Owings & Merrill) sharply slice the Bunker Hill skyline. Between them, a 3-story atrium court features casual dining amid **sculptures** by Robert Graham, Joan Miró, Jean Dubuffet, Nancy Graves and Louise Nevelson. The adjoining plaza frequently hosts free mid-day concerts during the summer.

Wells Fargo History Museum [M] – *333 S. Grand Ave. Open year-round Mon–Fri. Closed major holidays. ✗ ♿ 🅿 ☎213-253-7160.* Tucked between the Wells Fargo Center towers, the museum traces the role played in the history of California by Wells

Fargo Company *(p 195)* from its founding in SAN FRANCISCO in 1852 as a banking and express shipping company to its current position as one of the state's foremost financial institutions.

The first-floor display area features a restored **Concord stagecoach** and the **Challenge Nugget**, a lump of nearly 77 percent pure gold weighing 26.4 troy ounces, found in 1975 near the town of Challenge, California.

333 South Hope Street – *Hope St between 3rd and 4th Sts.* Set at a 45-degree angle to the streets, the 55-story building (1974) is distinguished by the red Alexander Calder **stabile**, *Four Arches*, at its entrance. The adjoining concourse, with its tree-lined adobe paths, fountains and a central pool with a waterfall, provides a peaceful perspective on the business district's spires.

★ **Westin Bonaventure Hotel** – *404 S. Figueroa St.* Composed of five mirrored-glass cylindrical towers, the 35-story hotel (1976, John Portman) includes a 34th-floor revolving cocktail lounge reached by glass elevators that climb the building's exterior, offering **panoramas★** of downtown and the Los Angeles basin.

★ **First Interstate World Center Tower** – *639 W. 5th St.* At 1,017ft, the 73-story Italian-granite building (1992, I.M. Pei & Partners), topped by an illuminated crown, is the nation's tallest building west of Chicago. Flanking the building's west side, the **Bunker Hill Steps★ [C]**, inspired by the Spanish steps in Rome, descend gracefully from Hope to 5th Street, their four flights split by a cascade of water. On the steps' second level, a patio cafe offers a view of the Los Angeles Central Library *(below)*. Adjacent to the tower on the east sits **One Bunker Hill [D]** *(601 W. 5th St)*, a dignified Art Deco structure erected in 1931 as the headquarters of the Southern California Edison Company. The building's artwork and ornamentation reveal energy motifs, and the lobby incorporates 17 varieties of marble and *The Apotheosis of Power*, a mural by Hugo Ballin.

★ **Los Angeles Central Library** – *630 W. 5th St between Flower St and Grand Ave. Open daily year-round.* ♿ 🅿 *☎213-228-7000.* Its imposing tower crowned by a pyramid that echoes that of City Hall, this striking building (1926, Bertram Goodhue) was conceived as an allegory on "The Light of Learning," expressed through exterior and interior sculptures, murals, inscriptions and tilework. The **rotunda** is decorated with more than 9,000sq ft of murals by Dean Cornwell depicting California's eras of discovery, mission-building and Americanization, and the founding of Los Angeles. Seriously damaged by fire in 1986, the library reopened in October 1993 after extensive restoration and renovation of the original building and the addition of the East Wing (Hardy Holzman Pfeiffer Assocs.), an 8-story atrium structure, half underground, that doubled the facility's size to 540,000sq ft. A new 1.5-acre **garden** on the building's Flower Street side features contemporary sculptures on the themes of language and knowledge.

Gas Company Tower – *555 W. 5th St.* Crowned with a blue-glass ellipse, the 54-story tower (1991) features a water garden adjacent to the lobby. The lobby's glass wall showcases Frank Stella's *Dusk* (1992), one of the world's largest abstract murals, painted on the adjacent Pacific Bell/AT&T Building.

★ **Biltmore Hotel** – *506 S. Grand Ave.* Facing Pershing Square, the 11-story, 1,000-room hotel (1923, Schultze and Weaver) was built at a cost of $10 million. At that time the nation's largest hotel west of Chicago, the Biltmore, known as the "host of the coast," attracted a glittering clientele from the worlds of entertainment, business and politics. Extensively renovated since 1984, it still merits its reputation as one of Los Angeles' most distinguished hotels.

Although the main public entrance is now on Grand Avenue, the original Olive Street lobby, renamed the **Rendezvous Court★**, exemplifies the opulent detailing that won the hotel renown, with brickwork and terra-cotta in the 16C Italian style and towering hand-painted ceilings.

★ **Pershing Square** – *Bordered by S. Hill, S. Olive, W. 5th and W. 6th Sts.* The 5-acre square, the last remaining public parcel of the original Spanish land grant, was declared the city's first public park in 1866 and was named in 1918 for John J. Pershing, commander of the American Expeditionary Force during World War I. Once an oasis of birds-of-paradise and giant palm and banana trees enjoyed by area residents, the square was excavated in 1950 to make way for an underground parking garage, then landscaped with a severe geometric configuration of lawns, walkways, flower beds and trees. A 1993 renovation enhanced the site with a 125ft campanile, large shade trees, a fountain, amphitheater, cafe and kiosks.

Oviatt Building – *617 S. Olive St.* In 1925, clothing entrepreneur James Oviatt became enamored of the Art Deco style at the Paris Exposition Internationale des Arts Decoratifs *(p 27)*. He commissioned a local firm to design a 13-story office building and men's haberdashery (1928, Walker and Eisen) incorporating over 200 tons of French marble, glass and fittings—including René Lalique's largest commercial commission of Art Deco etched and frosted glass. Today, with much of the original glass replaced by replicas, the bulding houses an upscale restaurant.

Fine Arts Building – *811 W. 7th St.* A beautiful, 2-story Spanish Renaissance lobby of molded terra-cotta and colored tile incorporates an elaborately painted, beamed ceiling, sculpted figures and 17 bronze showcases.

★★ **Bradbury Building** – *304 S. Broadway. Open year-round Mon–Fri 9am–5pm; Sat 9am–4pm.* ♿ 🅿 *☎213-626-1893.* Mining magnate Louis Bradbury originally commissioned leading local architect Sumner P. Hunt to design his headquarters building. Dissatisfied with Hunt's initial plans, he offered the job to George H. Wyman, a draftsman in Hunt's firm. Completed in 1893, the 5-story building's modest brick exterior conceals a splendid **atrium** inspired by a description of an AD 2000 commercial building in Edward Bellamy's futuristic novel *Looking Backward*.

Bathed in diffused natural light from a skylight roof, the atrium features lacelike wrought-iron railings, stair frames and open-cage elevators; red-oak trim and paneling; stair treads of pink Belgian marble; and walls of glazed yellow brick and Mexican tile.

★ **Grand Central Market** – *315 S. Broadway. Open daily year-round. Closed Thanksgiving Day, Dec 25.* ✗ ♿ 🅿 *☎213-624-2378.* A cavernous hall open to both Broadway and Hill Street, the building (1897, John Parkinson) housed dry goods and department stores before being converted in 1917 as a public market catering to local European immigrants. Since the 1960s, it has cheerfully mirrored the neighborhood's bustling Latino atmosphere, with bright signs announcing a profusion of stalls selling everything from ready-to-eat Mexican food to fresh produce, meats and cheeses.

★★ **Eastern Columbia Building** – *849 S. Broadway.* The eye-catching **exterior** of the 13-story Art Deco building (1930, Claude Beelman) is faced in a pattern of turquoise and gold glazed terra-cotta rising to a 2-story clock tower *(illustration p 27)*.

Broadway Area Movie Palaces

Several of the Broadway theater district's original dozen movie palaces remain open today, catering largely to the area's Latino population. Others are closed or converted for other uses. *Interiors accessible by attending a movie, or by weekly walking tours offered by the Los Angeles Conservancy (p 86).*

Million Dollar Theater – *307 S. Broadway.* Spanish Baroque ceiling and decor in the auditorium (1918).

Roxie Theater – *518 S. Broadway.* Broadway's last theater; Art Deco exterior (1932).

Los Angeles Theater – *615 S. Broadway.* Opulent Louis XIV-style interior (1931).

State Theater – *703 S. Broadway.* Exotic interior with classical, medieval and Spanish detailing (1921).

Tower Theater – *802 S. Broadway.* Spanish Romanesque exterior with striking corner clock tower (1926).

Orpheum – *842 S. Broadway.* Lush interior neo-classical detailing (1926).

United Artists Theater – *933 S. Broadway.* Gothic and Spanish-style ornamentation (1926).

Mayan Theater – *1040 S Hill St.* Carved stone ornamentation in Mayan motifs (1927).

Belasco Theater – *1050 S. Hill St.* Elaborate Spanish Churrigueresque facade (1926).

Additional Sights near Downtown

★★ **Southwest Museum** – *Map p 83. 234 Museum Dr, off Ave 43 exit of the Pasadena Fwy (Hwy 110) approximately 3mi northeast of downtown L.A. Open year-round Tue–Sun 11am–5pm. Closed Jan 1, Jul 4, Thanksgiving Day, Dec 25. $5.* 🅿 *☎213-221-2164.* Towering castlelike above the freeway from a slope of Highland Park's Mt Washington, the Mission Revival building (1914) houses Los Angeles' oldest museum, dedicated to comprehensive collections and research facilities on Native American cultures.

In 1907 *Los Angeles Times* city editor and noted local historian, preservationist and archaeologist **Charles Fletcher Lummis** (1859-1928), in concert with fellow members of the Southwest Society, a local branch of the Archaeological Institute of America, established the museum in temporary quarters in a downtown department store. Since its move to the present site, the museum has amassed a collection of more than 500,000 items, less than 5 percent of which are on view at any one time.

Visit – Exhibits are organized by region in four cavernous halls on two levels; each hall is designed to evoke the cultures presented within. The **Plains Hall** features an outstanding collection of everyday and ceremonial garments and is dominated by an 18ft Southern Cheyenne **tipi**. The **Northwest Coast Hall**, concentrating on tribes of the Pacific Northwest and Canada, includes a pair of carved wooden Haida house posts (1860) resembling totem poles. In the **California Hall**, exhibits illustrating daily lives of the state's Native tribes are divided into four distinct geographical areas: Southern, Desert, Central and Northwest. Collections in the **Southwest Hall** include **clovis points** (10,000 BC), the earliest evidence of human life in the American Southwest. The adjoining **Basketry Study Room** presents rotating displays of fine examples from the museum's 12,000-piece collection, considered one of the largest in the United States.

Temporary exhibits and live programs are staged in two halls adjoining the main entrance *(upper level)*. A pre-Columbian-style tunnel entrance at the base of the museum property is decorated with dioramas of Native American life. Also below the museum lies the **Casa de Adobe** *(4605 N. Figueroa St; open for special events only)*, a fully furnished 1917 re-creation of an early-19C California hacienda.

★ **Lummis House** – *Map p 83. 200 E. Ave 43. Open year-round Fri–Sun. Closed end of Aug to mid-Sept. Contributions requested.* ♿ *☎213-222-0546.* Hand-built of local boulders between 1898 and 1910 by Southwest Museum founder Charles Lummis *(above)*, with input from architects Sumner Hunt and Theodore Eisen, this unique structure combines Mission, Pueblo and Craftsman styles. Lummis named it "El Alisal," Spanish for the sycamores shading its garden. The house today serves as headquarters of the Historical Society of Southern California.

Though few original furnishings remain, the **interior** preserves some of Lummis' personal collection of Native artifacts; a window glazed with positive photographic plates of Native American dances; doors and built-in furniture by Maynard Dixon; and an Art Nouveau fireplace executed by artist Walter Stetson.

Heritage Square Museum – *Map p 83. 3800 Homer St. Open year-round Fri–Sun. Closed Dec 24–first week of Jan. $5.* ♿ 🅿 ☎ *818-449-0193. Interiors accessible by guided tour (1hr) only.* Arrayed alongside the Pasadena Freeway is a rather forlorn collection of Victorian-era buildings. The structures are moved here from their original locations when they face demolition, and offer an opportunity to view a variety of Victorian styles. The collection currently includes eight structures in varying stages of restoration, most notably the **Hale House**, a fully restored and furnished exemplar of the Queen Anne and Eastlake styles *(p 26)*.

★★ 2 EXPOSITION PARK AREA

The city's showcase sports and cultural center, Exposition Park is an approximately 125-acre complex of event venues and museums located some 3mi southwest of downtown Los Angeles.

In 1872, the Southern District Agricultural Society established a 160-acre agricultural park on the site, dedicated to livestock shows, fairs and horse racing. Sections along the southern and western edges were sold off the following decade, and by the turn of the century, the park had become the scene of gambling, drinking and prostitution. Its decline inspired local attorney W.M. Bowen to head a campaign that resulted in the 1913 renaming and rededication of Exposition Park as a setting for public museums and exhibit halls, athletic facilities and gardens, all laid out in the grand Beaux-Arts tradition by landscape architect Wilber D. Cook Jr.

Today, Exposition Park again shows the signs of transition. Bordered on one side by the private University of Southern California and on three others by the strife-torn South Central area, its grounds and facilities appear somewhat worn by unfavorable social and economic conditions. Yet its institutions continue to grow and develop, reflecting an optimism about the area's future. A state-commissioned plan, currently seeking funding, aims to give the park a $350-million face lift, adding greenery, broad promenades and new community facilities.

Visit *1 day. Map p 82.*
Bounded by Flower St, Vermont Ave and Exposition and Martin Luther King Blvds.

★★ **Los Angeles Memorial Coliseum** – *Open year-round Mon–Fri 10am–6pm.* ♿ 🅿 ☎*213-748-6131.* Built at a cost of $1 million on the site of Agricultural Park's motor speedway, the oval 92,000-seat coliseum (1923, Parkinson & Parkinson) is Los Angeles' preeminent sports stadium, hosting college and professional football games as well as track and field competitions, rock concerts and a wide variety of other outdoor events. Adjoining it, the 16,000-seat turquoise **Sports Arena**, built in 1958, hosts basketball games and other indoor events.

With its original 75,000-seat capacity boosted to 105,000, the Coliseum became the world's largest arena of its day and gained international prominence as the site of the 1932 Summer Olympic Games. To mark its role as the principal venue of the 1984 Summer Games, an Olympic Arch was erected just outside the coliseum's eastern peristyle. A large bronze structure by sculptor Robert Graham, the arch depicts headless male and female nude figures atop a gateway of two piers.

★★ **Natural History Museum of Los Angeles County** – *900 Exposition Blvd. Open year-round Tue–Sun 10am–5pm. $5.* ✗ ♿ 🅿 ☎*213-744-3466.* This broad, varied collection of more than 16 million specimens and artifacts from the fields of life sciences, earth sciences and history ranks third in size in the US, after the American Museum of Natural History in New York City and the National Museum of Natural History in Washington DC. Opened to the public in 1913 as the Museum of History, Science and Art, the institution was housed in a dignified, Beaux-Arts structure featuring an elaborate marble rotunda at the eastern end. The building was expanded over the years, and in 1961 the institution was split into two separate entities: the Natural History Museum and the Los Angeles County Museum of Art *(p 100)*.

Main Level – To the west and east of the main foyer, which features skeletons of an Allosaur and a duckbilled dinosaur poised for battle, the **Halls of African and North American Mammals** present lifelike displays of animal specimens in their natural habitats *(halls under renovation)*. The **Hall of Gems and Minerals★** houses more than 2,000 specimens. At the eastern end, the **Discovery Center** allows hands-on experience of fossils, bones, historic costumes and other pieces from the collection; on a mezzanine overlooking the Discovery Center, the **Insect Zoo** includes terrariums crawling with such live specimens as scorpions, tarantulas and millipedes *(open Mon–Fri 10am–3pm, weekends 10am–4pm)*. The **Hall of Native American Cultures** features a floor-to-ceiling replica of a Pueblo cliff dwelling and a Craftsman-style bungalow displaying examples of Native American art.

Upper Level – The **Hall of Birds★**, opened in 1989, is a 17,000sq ft hall filled with ingenious and amusing interactive and animated displays, including three walk-through habitats: a Canadian prairie marsh, a tropical rain forest and the California condor's mountain home.

Lower Level – A permanent exhibit, "California and the Southwest 1540-1940," traces local history with replica dwellings, dioramas and historic artifacts including an architecturally detailed scale model of downtown Los Angeles constructed in the late 1930s by WPA artisans for use by city planners.

Along Exhibition Boulevard immediately east of the Natural History Museum's original entrance, the 7-acre sunken **Rose Garden★**, opened in 1911, has been dedicated exclusively to the cultivation of roses since 1928. With more than 19,000 specimens of over 190 rose varieties, it is a popular setting for local weddings. *Flowers bloom from late spring through autumn.*

★ **California Museum of Science and Industry** – *700 State Dr. Open daily year-round. Closed Jan 1, Thanksgiving Day, Dec 25.* ✗ ♿ 🅿 ☎*213-744-7400.* The largest and oldest institution of its kind in the western US, the museum opened in 1951 within the former State Exposition Building (1912). The adjoining Kinsey Hall of Health opened in 1967, and three new public facilities—the Aerospace Museum, the Mark Taper Hall of Economics and Finance and a giant-screen IMAX Theater—became part of the museum complex in 1984. *The Ahmanson Hall and the Hall of Economics will close in summer 1994 to accommodate construction of a new facility. Key exhibits will be displayed in temporary structures south of the main buildings. The Hall of Health, Aerospace Museum and IMAX Theater will remain open during construction.*

California Aerospace Museum – An F-104 Starfighter seems to be crashing out through the wall of the stark, angular building (1984, Frank Gehry). Inside the 3-story open space, stairs, landings and walkways provide close-up glimpses of replica aircraft ranging from a 1902 Wright glider to satellites and space capsules. The adjoining **IMAX Theater** presents documentary films on natural history, science and space flight, specially produced for projection onto a 5-story screen *($6).*

★ **California Afro-American Museum** – *600 State Dr. Open daily year-round. Closed major holidays.* ♿ 🅿 *☎213-744-7432.* Opened in 1981, the museum is dedicated to the presentation of African-American art, history and culture. Changing thematic exhibits of artworks and artifacts are displayed in three galleries surrounding a central sculpture court.

Additional Sights in Exposition Park Area

University of Southern California – *Immediately north of Exposition Park; main entrance on Exposition Blvd.* Founded in 1880, the university has grown from 53 students in one wooden building on donated land to its current 150-acre main campus with over 30,000 students and more than 2,000 full-time faculty members. Landscaped plazas, courtyards and walkways are punctuated by more than 100 major buildings, with contemporary structures abutting stately Romanesque Revival constructions. **Widney Alumni House**, a white-clapboard structure, is the oldest building on campus, dating from 1880 *(free 1hr guided walking tours depart from here Mon-Fri, 10am-2pm; by appointment ☎213-740-2300).* Romanesque-style **Mudd Hall** (1930), home of the Department of Philosophy, features an attractive cloister and a churchlike library. The **Fisher Gallery**, the university's main art gallery, includes a permanent collection of European works dating from the 15C, in addition to American art *(open Sept–Apr Tue–Sat, rest of the year by appointment only; closed major holidays;* ♿ *☎213-740-4561).* The geometric forms and cantilevered planes of the **Arnold Schoenberg Institute** (1974) seem to echo the atonal music of the Austrian-born composer (1874-1951); the building houses Schoenberg's archives and the study from his Brentwood Park home on Los Angeles' Westside, where he worked from the mid-1930s until his death.

★ **Hancock Memorial Museum** – *Visit by guided tour (30min) only, year-round Mon–Fri. Closed major holidays. Reservations required.* 🅿 *☎213-740-0433.* Located within the Hancock Building, headquarters of the Department of Marine Biology, this house museum consists of the grandly proportioned Palladian style reception hall, library, dining room and music salon preserved from the Hancock mansion built at the corner of Wilshire Boulevard and Vermont Avenue in 1907 and partly inspired by the Medici Palace in Florence, Italy. The museum and the Hancock Building were donated in 1930 by oil tycoon G. Allan Hancock.

★ **Skirball Museum** – *3077 University Ave at 32nd and Hoover Sts. Open year-round Tue–Fri, and 2 Sundays a month (call for schedule). Closed major and Jewish holidays.* ♿ 🅿 *☎213-749-3424.* Located within the Hebrew Union College, this museum presents selections from its 25,000-object collection of archaeological artifacts, ceremonial art, manuscripts, artworks and historical objects covering 4,000 years of Jewish life from ancient times to the present. The size and breadth of the collection place it among the top five such museums in the world. *In late 1995, the museum is scheduled to move to the new Hebrew Union College Skirball Cultural Center in West Los Angeles.*

★ **Automobile Club of Southern California** – *2601 S. Figueroa St.* With its octagonal tower and domed cupola, the building (1923, Hunt & Burns) is an outstanding example of the Spanish Colonial style. The **rotunda** features a fountain and imported Mexican terrazzo tilework; a collection of antique California road signs is displayed in the patio.

★★ 3 GRIFFITH PARK

One of the largest urban parks in the US, Griffith Park straddles some 4,103 acres of the Santa Monica Mountains approximately 5mi northwest of downtown Los Angeles and immediately northeast of Hollywood.

Griffith's Gift – In 1882, Col Griffith J. Griffith, a Welsh immigrant who made his fortune quarrying granite in the GOLD COUNTRY, bought 4,071 acres of Rancho Los Feliz, a 6,600-acre Spanish land grant originally deeded in 1795 to Vicente Feliz. On December 16, 1896, Griffith donated 3,015 of those acres to the city of Los Angeles for public use. The park reached its current size in the 1960s.

"Give Nature a chance to do her work," Griffith observed in 1912, "and Nature will give every person a greater opportunity in health, strength and mental power." Helping Nature along, he donated money for an observatory within the park as well as the **Greek Theatre**, an open-air summer concert venue; the Los Angeles Zoo, a merry-go-round, children's pony rides and two museums have subsequently joined those attractions. Three golf courses, tennis courts, a baseball field, an equestrian center and picnic grounds are also available for public use.

Nevertheless, Griffith Park remains largely a setting of untouched natural beauty inhabited by deer, opossum, cougars, quail, hawks and kestrels. Just north of Los Feliz Boulevard, near the park's southwestern corner, the cool glade known as

Ferndell offers a primeval setting of tall pines shading a fern-fringed brook. The **Bird Sanctuary**, at the head of Vermont Canyon .3mi north of the Greek Theatre, invites wandering along wooded pathways alive with birdsong. Allowing closer appreciation of the park are 53mi of hiking trails and 43mi of bridle trails.

Visit *1 day. Map p 97. Entrances to the park are located on Los Feliz Blvd; from the Ventura Fwy (Hwy 134); and from the Golden State Fwy (I-5).*

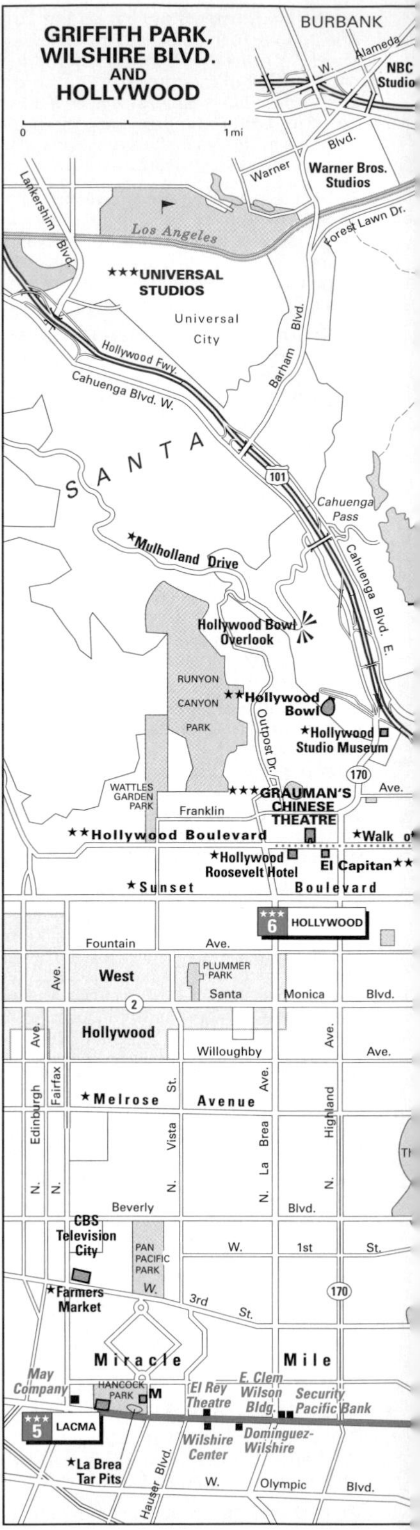

★★ **Griffith Observatory** – *2800 E. Observatory Rd. Open Jun–Aug daily 12:30–10pm, rest of the year Tue–Fri 2–10pm, weekends 12:30–10pm. Closed Thanksgiving Day, Dec 25.* 🅿 ☎*213-664-1191.* From a promontory on the south slope of 1,625ft Mt Hollywood, Griffith Park's hightest peak, this Art Deco observatory (1935) was donated by Colonel Griffith at a cost of $255,780. With its central 84ft copper planetarium dome and two smaller flanking domes, the observatory is one of Los Angeles' most distinctive landmarks. Facing the entrance, an obelisk pays tribute to six great astronomers.

A 240lb brass Foucault pendulum sways in the **main rotunda**, demonstrating the earth's rotation; murals by Hugo Ballin on the ceiling and eight panels depict astronomical symbols and the history of science. Halls extending from the sides of the rotunda present permanent and temporary science exhibits. The East Hall includes a 6ft-diameter globe of the moon, a camera obscura, and two working seismographs. Highlights in the West Hall include a working Tesla coil, a transformer that boosts household current to half a million volts, and a 6ft globe.

Beneath the main dome, the **Planetarium Theater** offers regular programs of astronomical and "Laserium" light shows choreographed to popular and classical music and projected onto the dome's 75ft-diameter interior from a massive 1-ton Zeiss projector built in West Germany in 1964 *(call above number for schedule, $4 ♿).*

Outside, stairs on either side of the building lead to the roof, where, on clear nights, a 12in Zeiss telescope, with an astronomer in attendance, is available to the public for viewing of the moon and planets *(same hours as above).* From the roof, as well as from the pathways and balustrades surrounding the observatory's ground floor, far-reaching panoramic **views**★★★ of Los Angeles sweep east to downtown, south and west to the coast and northwest to the nearby Hollywood Sign *(p 102).*

★★ **Gene Autry Western Heritage Museum** – *4700 Zoo Dr. Open year-round Tue–Sun 10am–5pm. $6.50.* ✗ 🅿 ☎*213-667-2000.* This contemporary Mission-Revival style building (1988) is dedicated to collecting, preserving and presenting the history of the American West, with a growing collection numbering more than 16,000 artifacts. Construction and the initial collection were financed and donated by the Autry Foundation, established by film star **Gene Autry** (b. 1907), affectionately known as "The Singing Cowboy." The main building houses exhibits designed by Walt Disney Imagineering that vividly combine artifacts and artworks with diora-

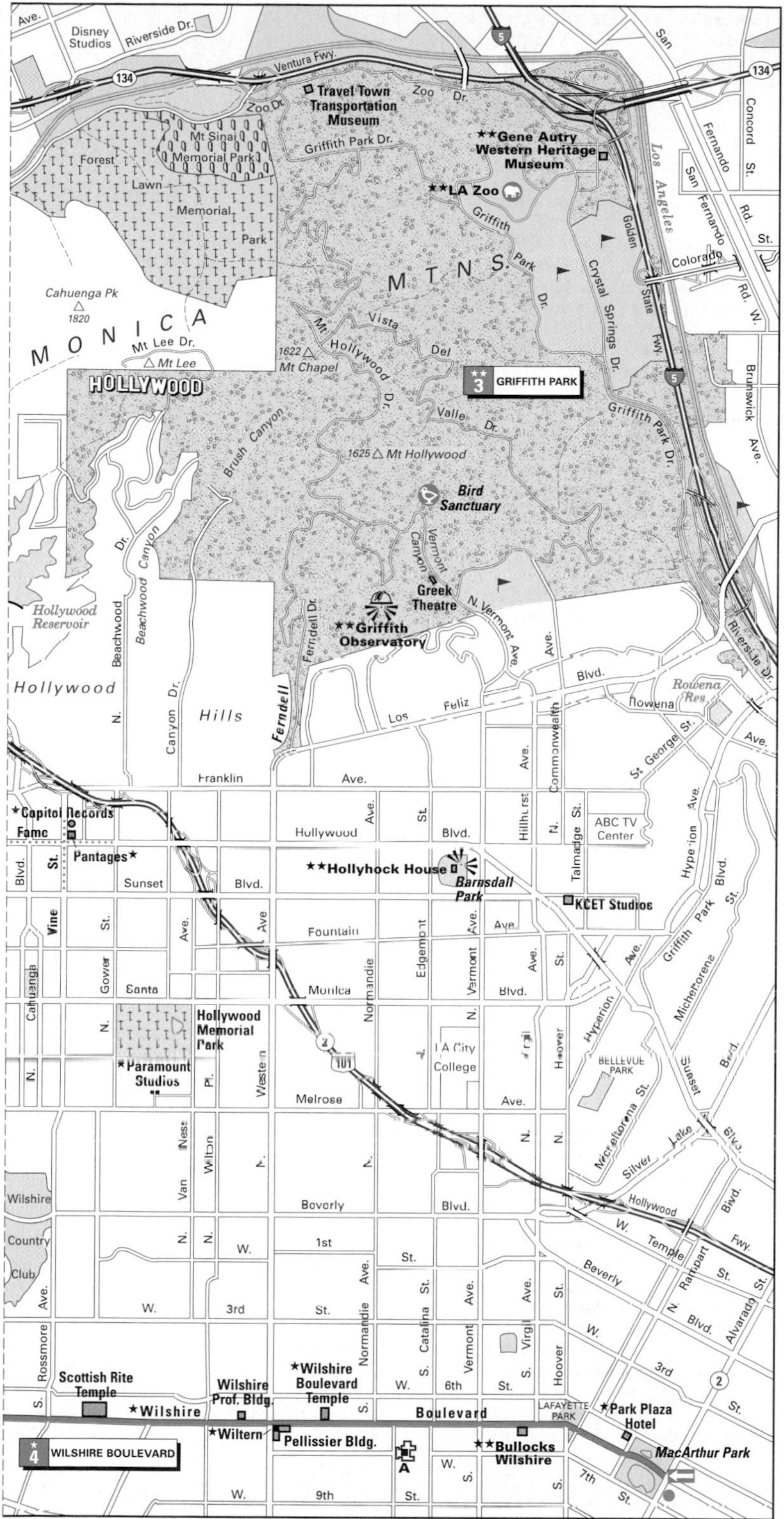

mas, lighting, sound, video and film. Also located here are a temporary exhibit gallery *(main level)*; a children's gallery *(lower level)*; the "Spirit of the West" mural, depicting 80 key people in the region's history and legend; and "Trail West," which compresses representative Western topographies into a small open-air courtyard. An adjoining 222-seat theater offers regular programs of films, documentaries and live performances.

Seven permanent galleries on the museum's main and lower levels present the collection thematically and in rough chronological order. Among these, the **Spirit of Discovery** highlights visitors and explorers from the continent's earliest nomadic hunters to the Spanish, Russian, French, English and Americans who came to the region starting in the mid-16C. **Spirit of Community★** depicts the formation of a social fabric among settlers through family, social organizations, business, politics and religion. On display are a diagram drawn by Wyatt Earp of the so-called 1881 "Gunfight at the OK Corral" in Tombstone, Arizona; personal firearms and other artifacts of such famous figures as Earp, Billy the Kid, Frank James, Black Bart *(p 63)* and Belle Starr; and the Colt Gallery display of more than 200 firearms. **Spirit of Romance** examines the 19C glamorization of the West through art, literature, advertising and Wild West shows; artifacts on display include William F. "Buffalo Bill" Cody's Burgess Rifle and Annie Oakley's L.C. Smith double-barrel shotgun. **Spirit of Imagination** traces the portrayal of the West in film, radio and television, concentrating on personal memorabilia of performers, the characters they played and the movies and programs in which they appeared.

★★ **Los Angeles Zoo** – *5333 Zoo Dr. Open year-round daily 10am–5pm. Closed Dec 25. $8.* ✗ ♿ 🅿 *☎213-666-4090.* The city's first zoological garden, Selig Zoo and Amusement Park, opened in the late 1890s some 2.5mi east of downtown. Owned by silent-film producer William N. Selig, the zoo rented out its animals for use in motion pictures; by 1915, with 700 species, it constituted one of the world's largest wild animal collections. Financial difficulties led Selig to donate the zoo to the city in the early 1920s; it was later relocated to Chavez Ravine, in the hills north of downtown, and then in 1966 to its present location on 80 acres in the northeastern sector of Griffith Park. Today the zoo is home to more than 1,600 mammals, birds, amphibians and reptiles representing some 400 species, including almost 70 endangered species.

Visit – From the entrance, a single walkway leads first to **Adventure Island**, a 3-acre children's zoo featuring five different animal environments of the American Southwest, along with interactive exhibits, a 250-seat amphitheater for animal shows and the zoo's nursery. The path branches into an intricate network of trails that follow the hilly terrain, leading to areas devoted to aquatic animals, Australia, North America, Africa, hillside animals, Eurasia, and South America. Not to be overlooked are the indoor **Koala House**, where nocturnal animals enjoy a natural twilight setting and the **China Pavilion**, home to endangered snow leopards. On the pathway below the aviary, a documentary display is devoted to the California condor and the zoo's successful program of breeding this endangered species and reintroducing it to the wild.

Travel Town Transportation Museum – *Zoo Dr at Forest Lawn Dr. Open daily year-round. Closed Dec 25.* ✗ ♿ 🅿 *☎213-662-5874.* The open-air museum of railroad cars and steam locomotives dating primarily from the 1880s to the 1930s was founded in 1952 by Charley Atkins, a Los Angeles Department of Recreation and Parks employee and lifelong railroad buff. From the entrance, a quarter-scale 4-cylinder propane locomotive takes visitors on a tour of the museum's perimeter *($1.25)*, and an indoor display presents antique firefighting equipment from the Los Angeles area.

★ 4 WILSHIRE BOULEVARD

Wilshire Boulevard is the city's grandest thoroughfare, reaching westward some 16mi from the heart of downtown through central Los Angeles, Beverly Hills, Westwood and Brentwood, and ending at the cliffs above the Pacific Coast Highway (Highway 1) in SANTA MONICA. As the main artery of the city's business and residential development in the early decades of the 20C, its architecture, particularly the stretch between downtown and Fairfax Avenue, chronicles the growth and change of modern Los Angeles.

Metropolis' Main Street – In the mid-18C, the boulevard was little more than a dirt road leading from the area around El Pueblo *(p 87)* toward the rural land tract of Rancho La Brea, present site of the La Brea Tar Pits *(p 99)*. For centuries local Native Americans and later, Spanish settlers, followed the trail to collect asphalt bubbling from the pits for use as a sealant. In the late 1880s, publisher H. Gaylord Wilshire, who held a monopoly over local billboard advertising, bought a tract of land between 6th and 7th Streets about 1mi west of downtown. He subdivided the land into residential plots and, in 1895, replaced the dirt trail with a wide boulevard bearing his name.

Wilshire Boulevard grew westward with the city, reaching La Brea Avenue by 1920, the year A.W. Ross began developing the Miracle Mile *(p 99)*. In recent decades, shifts in population and business have led to the neglect, decline and even demolition of some of the boulevard's most historic buildings. Others, however, have survived among newer office high-rises, and through restoration, the Miracle Mile is slowly regaining its former glory.

Driving Tour *1/2 day. 5mi. Map pp 96-97.*

Begin at MacArthur Park, approximately 1.3mi west of downtown.

Conceived with automobilists in mind, Wilshire Boulevard lends itself to a visit by driving tour. Distances between sights are great, and ample street parking is available for those who wish to enter the magnificent interior spaces of buildings along the boulevard.

MacArthur Park – When H. Gaylord Wilshire purchased the property, the park was "a large, rather stagnant mudhole," according to a 1934 *Los Angeles Times* article. He developed it in the 1890s into 32-acre Westlake Park. Wilshire Boulevard, which previously skirted its perimeter, was cut through its heart in 1934; in 1942, the park was renamed in honor of Gen Douglas MacArthur. Facing the park's northwest corner, the monumental Art Deco **Park Plaza Hotel**★ *(607 Park View St)* was originally built in 1925 as an Elks Lodge. The lobby features towering vaulted ceilings painted with mythological figures, part of Anthony Heinsbergen's somber, Romanesque-style interior design.

★★ **Bullocks Wilshire** – *3050 Wilshire Blvd. Not open to the public.* Recognizing the growing city's need for suburban shopping accessible by automobile, department store owner John G. Bullock and his partner P.G. Winnett decided to build a branch of Bullock's downtown headquarters on a barren stretch of Wilshire west of Lafayette Park. The store (1929, Parkinson & Parkinson) was not only one of the first ever conceived for the driving shopper, but also a masterpiece of Art Deco design. From the street, a 241ft tower calls attention to the terra-cotta-clad building, detailed in copper zigzag and snowflake patterns. The building itself occupies only one-third of the total property; the main entrance is actually at the rear, facing a parking lot that covers the remainder of the block.

Six blocks west, at 3400 Wilshire Boulevard, stands the now-defunct Ambassador Hotel. Formerly a celebrity haunt and home to the **Cocoanut Grove** nightclub, where Robert F. Kennedy was assassinated in 1968, the concrete structure ceased to function as a hotel in 1989 *(not open to the public)*.

★ **Wilshire Boulevard Temple** – *3663 Wilshire Blvd. Open Sept– May Mon–Fri, Sun; rest of the year Mon–Fri. Closed major and Jewish holidays.* ♿ 🅿 *☎213-388-2401.* At the time of its construction in 1929, this imposing, Byzantine-inspired synagogue was deliberately situated "beyond the car line" in anticipation of the westward movement of the city's Jewish community. The temple is home to the first Jewish congregation established in Los Angeles.
Lining the ground-floor hallways are exhibits on the history of Jews in Los Angeles and exhibits of ceremonial artifacts and Jewish holidays and events. An art gallery offers changing shows of Jewish interest.

★★ **Edgar F. Magnin Sanctuary** – Beneath a 125ft mosaic-inlaid dome, the principal place of worship is an octagonal auditorium paneled in rare woods with marble and wood inlays. A bronze screen encloses the Ark with Torah scrolls on the north wall. The **Warner Memorial Murals** by Hugo Ballin depicting 3,000 years of Jewish history form a frieze on the remaining seven walls, and a colorful rose window faces the Ark on the south wall.

★ **Wiltern Theatre** – *3790 Wilshire Blvd. Open to the public for performances only.* Centerpiece of the turquoise terra-cotta **Pellissier Building** (1931, Morgan, Walls and Clements), a 12-story Art Deco tower with two commercial wings, this theater was designed by G. Albert Landsburgh and features an elaborate sunburst on the ceiling beneath the corner marquee. Art Deco **interiors** were described by their designer, Anthony B. Heinsbergen, as a "steaming jungle" of pinks, purples and oranges. Originally a Warner cinema, the theater now hosts live performances and is open only to ticket holders.

Less than two blocks west stands the **Wilshire Professional Building** *(3875 Wilshire Blvd)*, a pale, terra-cotta-sheathed office tower (1929) revealing the chevrons and stylized ornamentation of the Art Deco phase known as Zigzag Moderne.

Scottish Rite Temple – *4357 Wilshire Blvd. Open daily year-round.* ♿ 🅿 *☎310-474-1549.* Completed in 1962, the imposing local headquarters for Scottish Rite Freemasonry is also an occasional venue for public performances. The exterior features 14ft statuary groups portraying key figures in the history of Freemasonry.

Miracle Mile – *Wilshire Blvd roughly bounded by La Brea and Fairfax Aves.* In 1920, real estate developer A.W. Ross paid $54,000 for 18 acres along Wilshire Boulevard between La Brea and Fairfax Avenues, within a 4mi radius of Hollywood, Beverly Hills, Westlake Park, Hancock Park and West Adams, then Los Angeles' wealthiest neighborhoods. His ambitious plan to transform the strip into a grand suburban shopping center geared to the driving shopper led friend and investor Foster Stewart in 1920 to name the area "The Miracle Mile."
Some of the city's most remarkable Art Deco buildings rose along the "mile" over the next three decades. Of the many that remain, some are in various stages of restoration while others are neglected or abandoned. Encompassed within the Miracle Mile are the La Brea Tar Pits *(below)* and the LOS ANGELES COUNTY MUSEUM OF ART.

Art Deco on the Miracle Mile

Security Pacific Bank – *5209 Wilshire Blvd (just east of La Brea).* Single-story structure (1929, Morgan, Walls and Clements) of glazed black and gold terra-cotta. Currently unoccupied.

E. Clem Wilson Building – *5217-5231 Wilshire Blvd (at La Brea).* Imposing 12-story stepped and terraced tower (1930, Meyer and Holler), its summit now obscured by a garish neon sign.

Dominguez-Wilshire Building – *5410 Wilshire Blvd.* Office tower above a 2-story retail block (1930, Morgan, Walls and Clements); interior features floral-patterned, acid-etched nickel elevator doors.

Wilshire Center Building – *5514 Wilshire Blvd.* Office tower (1928, Gilbert Stanley Underwood) rising 9 stories from a 2-story commercial block that housed, on its eastern side, Desmond's Men's Store; lobby displays flamboyant, Egyptian-inspired ornamentation.

El Rey Theatre – *5517 Wilshire Blvd.* Movie theater (1936, W. Clifford Balch) fronted by a multicolored terrazzo sidewalk.

May Company – *6067 Wilshire Blvd.* Department store (1939, Albert C. Martin and Samuel A. Marx) of 4 stories, with a rounded corner tower of gold leaf and black granite.

★ **La Brea Tar Pits** – *North side of Wilshire Blvd west of Curson Ave.* The square-block public park embracing the Los Angeles County Museum of Art and the Page Museum is the setting for the world's largest cache of Ice Age fossils.

A Hidden Trap of Asphalt – Some 38,000 years ago, during the Pleistocene era, now-extinct animals such as saber-tooth cats, imperial mammoths, ancient bison and giant sloths came to drink from streams here and were trapped in the thick, tar-like asphalt (*brea* in Spanish) lurking at the surface. In 1860, Maj Henry Hancock bought the land, then known as Rancho la Brea, and began an asphalt business; his son, **G. Allan Hancock** (1876-1965), established the Hancock fortune when he discovered oil on the site four decades later. As had previous discoverers, the Hancocks assumed that the site's fossilized bones came from stray farm animals. But in 1905, scientists from the University of California confirmed the bones' true age, and scientific excavations began that have to date unearthed over 100 tons of specimens. Hancock donated 23-acre Hancock Park to Los Angeles County in 1916.
Today, asphalt still bubbles up through the water in the **lake pit** beside Wilshire Boulevard; near the pit's edges, life-size statues portray Ice Age mammals struggling for their lives. On hot days, tar frequently seeps through the pavement and lawns of the park and surrounding streets. Visitors may view a dig in progress during two months each summer at Pit 91, located behind LACMA.

★★ **George C. Page Museum of La Brea Discoveries [M]** – *5801 Wilshire Blvd. Open year-round Tue–Sun 10am–5pm. Closed Jan 1, Dec 25. $5.* 🅿 ♿ *☎213-936-2230.* George C. Page, a Nebraska native who made his fortune shipping gift baskets of dried California fruit nationwide, funded the square-sided, single-story museum (1976) designed to appear as if on a burial mound and topped by cast-fiberglass friezes of Ice Age animals. The collection, administered by the Natural History Museum of Los Angeles County and originally housed there, features skeletons reconstructed from the more than 4.5 million bones of 390 animal species found at the site. Two display cases create the illusion that skeletons of a **saber-tooth cat** and 9,000-year-old **La Brea Woman** transform into flesh and blood, and in a glass-windowed **paleontology laboratory**, scientists and volunteers are visible at work, cleaning and examining bones.

★★★ **Los Angeles County Museum of Art (LACMA)** – *Description below*

★ **Farmers Market** – *6333 W. Third St at S. Fairfax Ave. Open daily year-round.* ✂ ♿ 🅿 *☎213-933-9211.* In the summer of 1934, farmers from the valleys surrounding Los Angeles gathered here to sell produce, engendering construction of a clapboard market complex that was largely completed by 1937. Though farmers' stalls have long since been replaced by more than 110 permanent businesses, the landmark open-air market retains a rustic charm. Greengrocers and butchers serve locals, while numerous international food and souvenir stands cater to visitors. Behind the market on S. Fairfax Avenue, the cube-shaped black-and-white **CBS Television City** (1952) is the national broadcasting network's local headquarters; a box office on the Fairfax side offers tickets for TV programs being taped there *(p 105)*.

★★★ 5 LOS ANGELES COUNTY MUSEUM OF ART (LACMA) *Map p 96*

This sprawling 5-building complex, frequently referred to by the acronym LACMA, is the nation's largest art museum west of Chicago. Housing a broad collection ranging from Egyptian and pre-Columbian art to contemporary works, LACMA is also the city's principal venue for major traveling exhibits, and offers regular programs of lectures, music and films.

From Exposition Park to Hancock Park – This prestigious institution began as part of the Museum of History, Science and Art *(p 94)*, which opened to the public in 1913 in Exposition Park. In 1961 the art collection was formally separated from the museum and reopened three years later in its present Wilshire Boulevard location as LACMA, occupying three imposing buildings by Pereira & Assocs. Continued growth of the collections led to the addition of the Robert O. Anderson Building (1986, Hardy Holzman Pfeiffer), a 4-level structure that presented a bold new face to Wilshire Boulevard; its monumental facade of limestone, glass blocks and green-glazed terra-cotta echoes the Art Deco traditions of the Miracle Mile, and its sweeping grand entry now leads to the complex's soaring, covered Central Court. The opening of the Pavilion for Japanese Art (1988, Bruce Goff and Bart Prince), a curvilinear Asian-inspired structure surrounded by Japanese gardens, added yet more architectural and artistic distinction to LACMA, underscoring the city's close ties to Pacific Rim culture.

The Collections – LACMA's holdings now comprise more than 250,000 works, their range evident in the museum's 10 curatorial divisions: American art; ancient and Islamic art; costumes and textiles; decorative arts; European painting and sculpture; Far Eastern art; Indian and Southeast Asian art; photography; prints and drawings; and 20C art. Though such a far-reaching curatorial approach sometimes leads to greater breadth than depth in the works on view, the museum's particular strengths include the Center for German Expressionist Studies, the largest and most comprehensive collection of its kind in the world; outstanding Japanese holdings; and one of the finest collections of decorative gold and silver in the US.

Visit *1 day*
5905 Wilshire Blvd. Open year-round Tue–Sun 11am–5pm. Closed Jan 1, Thanksgiving Day, Dec 25. $4. ✂ ♿ 🅿 *☎213-626-6222. Owing to budgetary constraints, the museum has instituted a policy of closing some galleries at certain times of day. The information booth in the Central Court provides daily schedules and museum floor plans. Schedules of gallery lectures as well as concerts and films held in the Bing Auditorium are also available.*

Ahmanson Building – One of the museum's original buildings, the 4-level structure houses the largest share of LACMA's permanent collections, displayed in galleries leading off a central atrium.

Plaza Level – The **pre-Columbian collection** *(galleries 101-102)* displays sculptures, pottery, textiles and gold from western Mexico. The **Gilbert Collections** feature approximately 200 gold and silver objects *(galleries 112, 113 & 116)* from Britain, Europe, America and India, dating from the 15C to the 19C, including extremely rare European silver from the 16C and early 17C; and European decorative mosaics *(galleries 111, 114 & 115)* from the 18C and 19C, the largest such collection in the world outside the Hermitage Museum in St Petersburg, Russia.

Second Level – A series of rooms *(galleries 201-206)* provides a sweeping survey of ancient Egyptian, Iranian, Greek and Roman art. The **Renaissance** and **Mannerist collections** *(galleries 210-211)* highlight works by Titian, Tintoretto, Vasari, Veronese and El Greco. Among 17C **Dutch** and **Flemish** works *(galleries 214-215)* are canvases by Rembrandt, Hals and Rubens. Gallery 221 features more than 24 small Rodin bronzes. A passageway *(gallery 218)* connects to the adjoining **Hammer Building** and its displays of **Impressionist** and **post-Impressionist** works *(gallery 209)* by such artists as Cézanne, Degas and Gauguin, as well as changing exhibits of photography and selections from the museum's extensive collection of German Expressionist prints and drawings by Kirchner, Schmidt-Rottluff, Bleyl and Heckel, among others.

Third Level – The galleries highlight works from the collection of Islamic, Indian, Tibetan and Nepalese art. Composed of approximately 3,500 paintings, sculptures, ceramics, textiles and works in silver, jade and crystal, the collection is considered one of the three finest in the Western world.
On the building's lower level, **Chinese** and **Korean** works, including bronzes, porcelains, polychrome-glazed pottery figures, and scroll paintings, share space with special exhibits.

Anderson Building – A small collection of 20C art *(levels 2 and 3)* encompasses representative works of Pablo Picasso's blue and Cubist periods; works by Rothko, Stella and Diebenkorn; and a lushly impressionistic rendering of the Hollywood Hills in *Mulholland Drive: The Road to the Studio* (1980) by Los Angeles-based English artist David Hockney *(illustration p 28)*. The plaza level is devoted to temporary exhibits.

Pavilion for Japanese Art – In 1982, Oklahoma oil millionaire Joe D. Price, and his Japanese-born wife, Etsuko, donated to LACMA their **Shin-enkan collection** of more than 300 scroll paintings and screens created during Japan's Edo period (1615-1868), considered the most outstanding collection of its kind in the Western world. One major stipulation of their donation was that it be housed in a building specifically designed by architect Bruce Goff to highlight the artworks as they were originally intended to be seen, in a setting of quiet contemplation. An elevator from the lobby brings visitors to the building's top level. In the west wing, changing exhibits of Japanese textiles and Buddhist sculptures, ceramics and lacquerware are displayed on the top floor. In the east wing, a ramp spirals downward past alcoves in which scrolls and screens from the collection are displayed, allowing them to be viewed individually; approximately 30 works are shown at one time, and the selection changes monthly. The structure's Lucite walls approximate the translucency of rice paper *shoji* screens, illuminating the artworks in soft natural light, and indoor waterfalls provide soothing background sounds.
Off the lobby, a small gallery presents a rotating display of **netsuke**—small, intricate carvings of wood, ivory or stag antler intended as toggles for attaching tobacco pouches or medicine boxes to the sash of the traditional Japanese kimono.

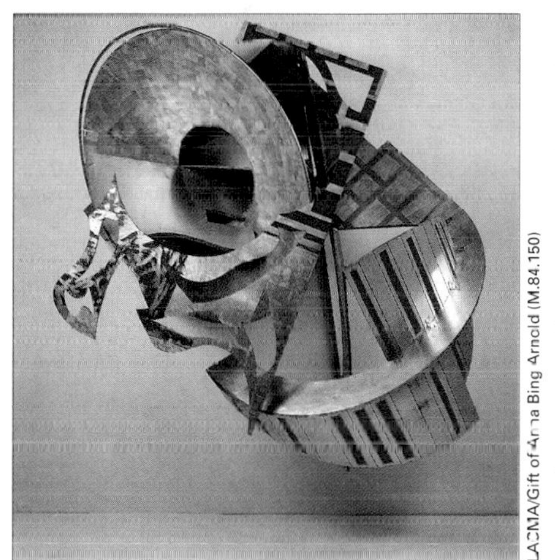

St. Michael's Counterguard (Malta Series)
by Frank Stella (1984)

Sculpture Gardens – Two open-air displays of large sculptures flank the Anderson Building on Wilshire Boulevard. The sculpture garden on the west side *(access via the Central Court)* is dominated by Rodin bronzes. On the eastern side *(access immediately to the right of the main entrance)* are nine contemporary works by such sculptors as Calder, Moore, Judd, Caro and Liberman.

★★★ 6 HOLLYWOOD *At least 1 day. Map pp 96-97.*

As much a state of mind as a geographic entity, Hollywood is the symbolic and real heart of the movie industry. Part of the city of Los Angeles, this renowned district of business, light industry, entertainment and residential areas is located approximately 8mi west of downtown and 12mi east of the Pacific coast, sweeping from an extension of the Santa Monica Mountains known as the Hollywood Hills south to the city below. Crossed east-west by major boulevards and avenues, Hollywood is a bustling part of Los Angeles; its main thoroughfares have an active street life, attracting a wide cross section of visitors and locals.

Historical Notes – Kansas Prohibitionist H.H. Wilcox founded the suburb in 1883, and by the turn of the century the quiet community of some 5,000 citizens was most notable for its lack of saloons. Named Hollywood by Mrs Wilcox, the town was incorporated in 1903, and seven years later was annexed by the city of Los Angeles in anticipation of water from the Los Angeles Aqueduct *(p 84)* and the growth that would ensue.

In 1911, Hollywood's first movie studio was opened by New York filmmaker David Horsely in an abandoned roadhouse at the corner of Sunset Boulevard and Gower Street. By 1912, five large East Coast film companies—Biograph, Bison, Kalem, Pathe and Selig—and many smaller producers had relocated to the vicinity of Hollywood, attracted by Southern California's year-round clement weather, open spaces and varied geography.

The community's growing reputation for glamour led a group of investors in the early 1920s to develop "Hollywoodland," a tract of elegant Spanish Mediterranean homes in the hills of Beachwood Canyon. To publicize the development, in 1923 the financiers erected, at a cost of about $21,000, what has come to be known as the **Hollywood Sign**★; composed of white-painted sheet metal letters measuring some 30ft wide and 50ft tall, the sign originally spelled "HOLLYWOODLAND." The sign fell into disrepair after 1939, and since the 1950s, with its last syllable removed, it has been repeatedly restored and maintained as Hollywood's most visible landmark. *The sign, located within Griffith Park's boundaries, is best viewed from the Observatory (p 96).*

Hollywood sign

Throughout the 1940s, Hollywood remained the center of the motion picture industry and community, although many major studios had relocated or established facilities in other areas: Warner Bros to Burbank *(p 110)*; Metro-Goldwyn-Mayer to Culver City; Twentieth-Century Fox to Century City *(p 108)*; and Universal Studios to Universal City. Since then, the town has experienced its share of modern urban woes, with some of its landmark buildings deteriorating and its major streets a haven for lost souls drawn by the mystique of the movie industry. But, since the 1980s, energetic efforts by private investors and local government have begun to remove some of the tarnish from Hollywood's glamour, visible most notably in many recently restored landmarks along Hollywood and Sunset Boulevards.

★★ Hollywood Boulevard

Hollywood's main thoroughfare is 4.5mi long, but the 1mi stretch through the center of town between Gower Street and Sycamore Avenue is easily navigable on foot. Here, along a sidewalk paved with stars, stand some of old Hollywood's grandest movie palaces, rubbing shoulders with souvenir stands and gaudy theme museums; the pavements are crowded with tourists and street people. Yet the boulevard continues to enthrall with the mystique of old Hollywood, which may be felt at its strongest at the intersection of **Hollywood and Vine**, immortalized as the hub of Hollywood in the 1930s and 1940s. Such leading restaurants as Sardi's and the Brown Derby were formerly located along two blocks of Vine Street at Hollywood Boulevard.

★ **Walk of Fame** – *Hollywood Blvd between Gower St and Sycamore Ave; Vine St between Sunset Blvd and Yucca St. For information on locations of individual stars, call the Hollywood Chamber of Commerce, ☎213-469-8311, or stop by the Hollywood Visitors Bureau, 6541 Hollywood Blvd ☎213-461-4213.* Embedded in the sidewalks are more than 2,500 bronze-trimmed coral-terrazzo stars conceived in 1958 by the Hollywood Chamber of Commerce as a tribute to major entertainment personalities. Approximately 2,000 stars (assigned by the Chamber) have been dedicated, at the approximate rate of twelve per year; names are inset in bronze along with circular plaques bearing symbols that indicate each honoree's field of achievement—motion pictures, radio, television, recording or live theater.

★★★ **Grauman's Chinese Theater** – *6925 Hollywood Blvd.* An ornate fantasy of chinoiserie, the theater (1926, Meyer & Holler) was commissioned by showman **Sid Grauman**; many locals still call it "Grauman's Chinese," though it is now owned by the Mann Theatres chain. Opened in 1927 with the industry's first gala premiere, for Cecil B. De Mille's *King of Kings*, "the Chinese" has hosted more premieres than any other Hollywood theater.

The monumental exterior is dominated by an eclectic, mansard-roofed pagoda topped by stylized flames and flanked by white-marble dogs; the ornate and cavernous interior took its inspiration from Chinese Chippendale furniture. The U-shaped cement **forecourt** features the footprints and signatures of more than 180 Hollywood celebrities, with new ones added almost every year. Various accounts exist of how the tradition began, most involving either Grauman, Mary Pickford, Douglas Fairbanks or Norma Talmadge accidentally stepping in wet cement during the theater's construction; Pickford and Fairbanks were the first to officially leave their prints, on April 30, 1927.

★ **Hollywood Roosevelt Hotel** – *7000 Hollywood Blvd.* Named in honor of Theodore Roosevelt, the 12-story hotel (1927) was a popular gathering spot for stars of the 1930s and 1940s. The first Academy Awards ceremony was held here on May 16, 1929. Restored and reopened in 1986, the hotel features a 2-story Spanish/Moorish lobby with a stenciled, beamed ceiling. On the walls of the lobby mezzanine, the **Hollywood Historical Review** presents a photographic history of the community from 1887 through the glittering 1940s. In 1987, the walls and bottom of the hotel's **swimming pool** *(behind main building)* were painted with blue swirls by English artist David Hockney.

★★ **El Capitan Theater** – *6834-38 Hollywood Blvd. Open year-round daily noon–midnight. $7.50. ♿ ☎310-855-8350.* Restored in 1991, the theater (1926, Morgan, Walls & Clements) features an ornate Churrigueresque facade. Originally presenting live shows, it was converted into a movie palace with the 1941 world premiere of Orson Welles' *Citizen Kane*. The East India-inspired **interior**, designed by G. Albert Lansburgh, sparkles with ornate grillwork and gold leaf.

★ **Capitol Records Tower** – *1750 Vine St.* Touted as the world's first circular office building (1954, Welton Becket & Assocs.), this 150ft complex of offices and studios resembles a stack of records surmounted by a phonograph needle. The beacon light on top blinks out H-O-L-L-Y-W-O-O-D in Morse code. Framed gold records won for best-selling recordings by Capitol Records artists are on display in the lobby.

★ **Pantages Theater** – *6233 Hollywood Blvd.* Vaudeville impresario Alexander Pantages opened the theater (1930, B. Marcus Priteca) as the first Art Deco movie palace in the US; from 1949 to 1959, it hosted the Academy Awards. In recent years, the theater has hosted touring stage musicals and dance companies.

The concrete-and-black-marble exterior is relatively understated in contrast to the **interior**, with its vaulted, extravagantly detailed lobby and the 2,812-seat auditorium. The latter was designed by Anthony Heinsbergen.

★ Sunset Boulevard

Stretching some 20mi from El Pueblo to the Pacific Ocean, Sunset Boulevard cuts through a dramatic cross section of life in Los Angeles: the Latino neighborhoods of Elysian Park; the studios and street-life of Hollywood; the mansions of Beverly Hills, immortalized in the Billy Wilder film classic *Sunset Boulevard* (1950); Bel Air; and the upscale neighborhoods of Westwood, Brentwood and Pacific Palisades.

The street's most famous stretch of all, however, is the 1.5mi **Sunset Strip★★** *(map p 107)*. Hugging the Santa Monica Mountains between Crescent Heights Boulevard and Doheny Drive, the street passes through an area that was once an unincorporated strip (hence its nickname) between Los Angeles and Beverly Hills; it is now part of the city of **West Hollywood**, one of Los Angeles' largest gay enclaves. Its former civic status and resulting lack of regulations gave rise to fashionable nightclubs and restaurants that attracted the entertainment industry and still define the Strip's character. Giant **billboards** erected above the low buildings tout the latest Hollywood productions, and major cross-streets provide dramatic vistas of the city below, particularly at night. Overlooking the easternmost end of the strip is the renowned **Chateau Marmont** *(8221 Sunset Blvd)*; the 7-story hotel—an amalgam of Norman and Moorish influences—has long been a favorite hideaway of actors, directors, producers, writers, musicians and artists.

★ **St James's Club and Hotel** – *8358 Sunset Blvd.* Originally known as the Sunset Towers Apartments (1931), the 15-story building was home to such stars as Errol Flynn, Jean Harlow, Clark Gable, Carole Landis, Paulette Goddard, John Wayne and Marilyn Monroe. The Art Deco exterior and interiors were restored in 1985, and the structure currently serves as the local branch of a London-based hotel group.

★ Melrose Avenue

Stretching in its entirety some 7mi from Hollywood's eastern edge to the Beverly Hills border, Melrose Avenue seems to distill all the creativity and craziness for which Los Angeles is known into the 16 short blocks between La Brea and Fairfax Avenues. Originally serving the surrounding residential neighborhoods, the shops in the low-lying buildings lining both sides of the avenue were taken over in the late 1970s and 1980s by hip boutiques, fashionable restaurants and shops specializing in bizarre collectibles and gifts. People-watching can be as entertaining as window-shopping.

★ **Paramount Studios** – *5555 Melrose Ave. Visit by guided tour only, year-round Mon–Fri. $10. ♿ 🅿 ☎213-956-5575.* Approximately 1.3mi east of Melrose Avenue's fashionable boutiques and restaurants, this complex of film and television production facilities is the only major studio remaining within the boundaries of Hollywood. Just north of Melrose Avenue, at Marathon Street, the wrought-iron Spanish Renaissance-style **studio gates**, surmounted by "Paramount Pictures" in script, endure as a well-known symbol of the studios. The walking tour *(2hrs; departs from the visitor center at 860 N. Gower St)* covers landmarks in the studio's history and offers glimpses of sound stages for movies and television shows currently in production on the lot.

Hollywood Memorial Park – *6000 Santa Monica Blvd, adjoining the Paramount Studios lot. Open daily year-round. Maps available at cemetery office next to entrance. ☎213-469-1181.* The 65-acre cemetery shelters the gravesites and crypts of such Hollywood legends as Rudolph Valentino, Douglas Fairbanks, Tyrone Power, Peter Lorre, Jesse Lasky and Cecil B. De Mille.

★★ **Pacific Design Center** – *Map p 107. 8687 Melrose Ave.* Anchoring the avenue's western end near Beverly Hills, the massive, 7-story, cobalt-blue glass building (1975, Cesar Pelli) quickly acquired the local nickname "The Blue Whale." In 1988, its hexagonal green glass annex, known as "The Green Turtle," expanded the center to its current 1.2 million sq ft of showrooms for the interior design trade.

Additional Sights in Hollywood

★★ **Hollywood Bowl** – *Map p 96. 2301 N. Highland Ave. Open year-round daily dawn–dusk.* ✗ ♿ 🅿 *☎213-850-2000.* Occupying a broad hollow of the Santa Monica Mountains and surrounded by 120 acres of greenery, the largest natural amphitheater in the world is a popular year-round concert site and summer home to the Los Angeles Philharmonic Orchestra.

Formerly known as "Daisy Dell," the site was acquired in 1919 for community sings, concerts and pageants. In 1921, the first Easter Sunrise Service (still an annual event) was held here. During the early Los Angeles Philharmonic summer concerts in 1922, the orchestra performed on a crude pine-and-canvas stage and the audience sat on blankets and wooden benches.

In 1926 a concrete stage was built, and the hillside was covered in concrete and steel to provide permanent seating for 17,619 people. The current band shell structure, a 100ft white quarter-sphere designed by Lloyd Wright (son of renowned architect Frank Lloyd Wright) was finalized in 1929. To compensate for acoustical changes and for ambient noise from the city and nearby freeway, a sound system was installed in 1945; the shell was acoustically modified by architect Frank Gehry in 1970 and 1980.

In the **Hollywood Bowl Museum**, photographs, artifacts and a video presentation *(20min)* recount the story of the amphitheater's evolution; the displays are complemented by changing exhibits on the performing arts *(adjacent to the restaurant; open year-round Tue–Sat; closed Dec).*

★ **Hollywood Studio Museum** – *2100 N. Highland Ave. Open late Jun–mid-Sept Thu–Sun, rest of the year weekends only. Call for schedule on major holidays. $4.* ♿ 🅿 *☎213-877-2276.* Originally a horse barn located at the corner of Vine Street and Selma Avenue, this rustic structure was rented in 1913 by Cecil B. De Mille to house offices, dressing rooms and set for *The Squaw Man*, the first feature Western shot in Hollywood. After joining producer Adolph Zukor, De Mille and producer Jesse Lasky transferred the barn to the Paramount Studios lot in 1926. In 1983 it was moved to its current site and transformed into a museum displaying artifacts from Hollywood's early years, including a reconstruction of De Mille's office, cameras and projectors, costumes, props and still photos. A video *(20min)* traces De Mille's role in Hollywood's growth during the early years of the motion picture industry.

★ **Mulholland Drive** – *Begins at Cahuenga Blvd, less than 1mi north of the Hollywood Bowl, and ends in Calabasas, almost 20mi to the west; continues as Mulholland Highway another 20mi to the Pacific Coast Highway (Hwy 1), near Los Angeles/Ventura county line.* Named for William Mulholland, engineer of the Los Angeles Aqueduct *(p 84)*, Mulholland Drive is one of Los Angeles' most spectacular roads, a series of sinuous curves following the crest of the Santa Monica Mountains. Along the way, it offers abundant **vistas**★★ of the Los Angeles basin and the SAN FERNANDO VALLEY, along with views of luxury homes dotting steep hillsides and ravines. From the **Hollywood Bowl Overlook** *(open daily;* 🅿 *☎213-463-3171)*, views extend to the Bowl *(above)*, the Hollywood Sign and the city. Laurel Canyon, Coldwater Canyon and Beverly Glen allow an easy return to the city below after a few miles' drive. Much of the road is unpaved between Interstate 405 and Topanga Canyon Road, toward Mulholland's western end.

★★★ **Universal Studios** – *Map p 96. 1 day. 100 Universal Plaza, Universal City. From Hollywood, take Highland Ave north to Cahuenga Blvd or US-101; continue north to Barham Blvd, Universal Center Dr or Lankershim Blvd, and follow the signs. Open Memorial Day–Labor Day daily 7am–11pm, rest of the year daily 9am–7pm. Hours may vary. $29.* ✗ ♿ 🅿 *☎818-508-9600. Upon admission, visitors are given boarding tickets with specified times for the Tram Ride, which departs from the Studio Center at the bottom of the hill. Make your way through the Entertainment Center to the Universal Starway, a .25mi escalator that carries visitors down to the Studio Center and tram boarding station.* Part fully functioning film and television studio, part live entertainment complex and amusement park, 420-acre Universal Studios sprawls across and down a hillside overlooking the San Fernando Valley, approximately 3mi northwest of Hollywood Boulevard. Adjoining it are the Universal Amphitheatre, a live concert venue; the Universal Cineplex Odeon, a 16-screen movie theater; Universal City Walk, a shopping, dining and entertainment complex; and several large restaurants.

"Quiet on the Set" – Silent film producer Carl Laemmle bought the land in 1915, converting a chicken ranch into his studio. He erected bleachers beside the sets and charged the public 25 cents to watch films being made. But the advent of motion picture sound in the late 1920s, with the need for "quiet on the set," put an end to such visits.

In 1964 Universal began to offer tram rides to boost lunchtime revenues at the studio commissary; visitors were shown makeup techniques, costumes, a push-button monster and a stunt demonstration. The popularity of the Universal Tour, as it was then called, led to the addition of new attractions almost yearly.
Today, Universal Studios is among the largest man-made tourist attractions in the US, annually welcoming some 5 million visitors, some of whom occasionally catch glimpses of actual films being made.

Studio Center – Situated in and around Universal's actual sound stages and back lot, the Studio Center offers a comprehensive behind-the-scenes look at the art and illusion of filmmaking. The narrated **Tram Tour**★★ *(45min)* winds through sets portraying the Wild West, small-town and suburban America, New York City, Mexico, Europe and other locales. En route, it passes the Bates house built for Alfred Hitchcock's *Psycho* (1960); is attacked by the shark from Steven Spielberg's *Jaws* (1975); encounters a rampaging 6.5ton, 30ft King Kong; and endures a collapsing bridge, a flash flood, the parting of the Red Sea, an avalanche and an earthquake measuring 8.3 on the Richter scale.
Film-related rides and attractions, among them "E.T. Adventure" and "Backdraft," are juxtaposed throughout the Studio Center; in **The World of Cinemagic**, visitors can participate in a special effects demonstration based on scenes from such popular films as *Back to the Future* and *Harry and the Hendersons*.

Entertainment Center – Arrayed on top of the hill and interspersed with souvenir and snack stands, the center's performance stages present regularly scheduled live shows *(15-30min)*, some inspired by popular films and television programs. Among them, the **Wild Wild Wild West Stunt Show** portrays Western fist- and gunfights, and **Animal Actors Stage** presents stunts performed by more than 60 trained animals.

Barnsdall Park – *Map p 97. 4800 Hollywood Blvd.* Located at the eastern edge of Hollywood, Barnsdall Park sits atop the former Olive Hill, so named for the trees that fringe it. In the late 1910s, oil heiress and arts patron Aline Barnsdall bought the 36-acre estate and, with Frank Lloyd Wright, developed plans for the site that included a house and guest quarters, and a theater and arts complex with studios and apartments. Only the main residence and two guest houses were ever built, and Barnsdall deeded them, along with 11 acres, to the city of Los Angeles in 1927. Built in 1971, a concrete **Municipal Art Gallery** shares the site, offering changing shows by local artists *(open year-round Tue–Sun, may be closed in between shows; $1; ♿ 🅿 ☎213-662-7272)*. The grounds provide good **views** of Griffith Observatory *(p 96)* and the downtown skyline.

★★ **Hollyhock House** – *4808 Hollywood Blvd. Visit by guided tour (50min) only, year-round Tue–Sun noon–4pm. Closed major holidays. $1.50. ♿ 🅿 ☎213-662-7272.* Hugging the top of the hill, the tile, wood and stucco house (1921) was the first Frank Lloyd Wright building in Los Angeles. Interior and exterior ornamentation was inspired by hollyhocks, Barnsdall's favorite flower.

KCET Studios – *4401 Sunset Blvd. Visit by guided tour (1hr 30min) only, year-round Tue & Thur. Closed major holidays. Reservations required. 🅿 ☎213-953-5242.* The square-block headquarters of Los Angeles' public television affiliate occupies a site previously owned by nine different film companies from 1912 until it became station property in 1971, making it the oldest continuously operating film studio in Hollywood. A guided tour highlights two historic sound stages, both still in use, and original 1920s brick bungalow offices.

Television Tickets. – Free television show tickets to tapings available by mail from addresses below. Include self-addressed stamped envelope; minimum 3-week advance reservation suggested (note that tickets do not guarantee admittance-admission on first come-first served basis). **Audiences Unlimited** (major networks), 100 Universal City Plaza, Bldg 153, Universal City CA 91608. **ABC Show Tickets**, 4151 Prospect Ave, Los Angeles CA 90027. **CBS Show Tickets**, 7800 Beverly Blvd, Los Angeles CA 90036. **NBC Show Tickets**, 3000 Alameda Ave, Burbank CA 91523.

★★ 7 BEVERLY HILLS (Pop 31,971)

Surrounded on three sides by Los Angeles and on the fourth by West Hollywood, Beverly Hills is an independent municipality covering almost 6sq mi of commercial and residential developments. The city's name is deservedly synonymous with wealth and elegance, qualities readily seen in its village-like shopping streets lined with international boutiques, its fashionable restaurants, and in the luxurious mansions that line its gracious, tree-shaded drives.

A Renowned Address – Beverly Hills was originally part of a Spanish land grant named *El Rancho Rodeo de las Aguas*, "the ranch of the gathering of the waters," referring to streams that ran from the narrow canyons in the Santa Monica Mountains north of the city and collected near the present site of the Beverly Hills Hotel *(p 106)*. During the 19C, most of the land was given over to lima bean farming, with some efforts at raising wheat, cattle and sheep.
Near the turn of the century, with oil prospecting going on several miles to the east in Rancho La Brea, three partners led by Burton E. Green unsuccessfully drilled 30 wells in El Rancho Rodeo. In 1907 they formed the **Rodeo Land & Water Co** to develop a new community that Green named Beverly Hills, reputedly after President William Howard Taft's Massachusetts vacation retreat, Beverly Farms. Architect Wilbur Cook laid out the city's grid, with parallel streets running at 45° angles north of Wilshire Boulevard through the commercial district, then gently curving through the residential section north of Santa Monica Boulevard. North of Sunset Boulevard, landscape architects John and Frederick Law Olmsted plotted sinuous drives winding through the foothills. Single-acre lots were offered for as little as $400.

After the 1912 opening of the Beverly Hills Hotel, Hollywood stars began to be attracted to the area. In 1920, Mary Pickford and Douglas Fairbanks built the city's first celebrity-owned mansion, Pickfair *(p 107)*, high on Summit Drive north of Sunset Boulevard.

Today Beverly Hills, as designated by the postal code 90210, ranks among the nation's highest in average household income and is home not only to many motion picture and television actors but also to moguls in the worlds of entertainment and business. Though Wilshire Boulevard, its main thoroughfare, is now dotted with high-rise office buildings, and the exclusive shopping district bordered by Wilshire and Santa Monica Boulevards and Cañon Drive merits its reputation as the "Golden Triangle," much of the area nevertheless guards a privacy and exclusivity that serve to enhance the city's aura of privilege.

Sights *1 day. Map p 107.*

★★ **Rodeo Drive** – The city's world-renowned luxury shopping street and heart of the "Golden Triangle" is a 3-block stretch of mostly 2- and 3-story buildings between Wilshire and Santa Monica Boulevards. Within that space, and to a somewhat lesser extent in the surrounding streets, are shoehorned dozens of fashionable boutiques and clothiers, jewelers, antique dealers and art galleries catering to a wide range of expensive tastes.

In the block between Dayton and Brighton Ways, **Anderton Court [A]** *(328 N. Rodeo Dr)*, an angular, 3-story white shopping complex with an open ramp winding around a central geometric spire, was built in 1954 from a design by Frank Lloyd Wright.

G. Wenger/Travel Image

Via Rodeo

Via Rodeo – *Two Rodeo Dr.* Occupying the northeast corner of Wilshire Boulevard and Rodeo Drive, the 4-story shopping complex (1990) lined with fashionable boutiques whimsically resembles the street of an Italian hillside town.

Beverly Hills Civic Center – *450 N. Crescent Dr. Open year-round Mon–Fri. Closed alternate Fridays. ♿ 🅿 ☎310-285-1014.* An elegant, 8-story Spanish Baroque tower crowned with a dome finished in multicolored tiles, the city hall (1932) sets the tone for a harmonious two-square-block contemporary addition (1990, Charles Moore/A.C. Martin & Assocs.) that arrays police and fire stations and a public library around landscaped courtyards.

Creative Artists Agency (C.A.A.) – *9830 Wilshire Blvd at Santa Monica Blvd.* Though not open to the public, this sleekly curving building of white marble, glass and steel (1989, Pei, Cobb, Freed), headquarters of one of Los Angeles' preeminent talent agencies, offers a glimpse from the street of the monumental Roy Lichtenstein mural inside its atrium foyer.

Beverly Gardens – Lining the northern edge of Santa Monica Boulevard, this narrow strip of gardens forms a verdant buffer between the commercial and residential sections of Beverly Hills. The section between Camden and Bedford Drives features an extensive assemblage of cacti and other succulents. Facing the gardens at 507 N. Rodeo Drive, the **O'Neill House [B]** (1989) is a private residence with swirling white walls and blue-tiled roof reminiscent of the fantastical Art Nouveau designs of Catalan architect Antonio Gaudi.

★ **Beverly Hills Hotel** – *9641 Sunset Blvd. Closed for renovation; projected reopening 1995.* The pink-stucco, Mission-style main building (1912) and its secluded bungalows are partly concealed by 12 acres of tropical gardens, bestowing an air of privacy that has long attracted Hollywood stars. Within, the casual restaurant known as the **Polo Lounge** is a legendary gathering spot for movie business deal-making.

★ **Virginia Robinson Gardens** – *1008 Elden Way. From Beverly Hills Hotel take Crescent Dr to Elden Way. Visit by guided tour only year-round Tue-Fri. $3. Reservations required ☎310-276-5367.* This lushly landscaped 6-acre estate crowning a hillside behind the Beverly Hills Hotel was a barren grassland when local department store heir Harry Robinson and his wife, Virginia, purchased it in 1911. It was the first residential lot sold in Beverly Hills. Inspired by a 4-year honeymoon in Europe, the Robinsons erected a Mediterranean-style villa and elegant pool house surrounded by formal English and terraced Mediterranean gardens, including 50 varieties of camellias. An additional 2-acre **palm forest** features the largest stand of king palms outside of Australia. Mrs Robinson left the estate to Los Angeles County in her will, and the gardens and house opened to the public in 1982.

★ **Greystone Park** – *905 Loma Vista Dr at Doheny Rd. Open daily year-round. ♿ P ☎310-285-1014.* Descending a terraced slope above Sunset Boulevard, this 18-acre formal garden surrounds **Greystone Mansion**, a 55-room English Tudor mansion (1928, Gordon B. Kaufmann) of brown-gray stone built by oil millionaire Edward L. Doheny for his son, Ned. The house, popular as a movie and television set, is closed to the public, though visitors can walk around its perimeter. The gardens afford panoramic **views** of the city.

Center for Motion Picture Study – *333 S. La Cienega Blvd. Library open for research only year-round Mon, Tue, Thu, Fri. Closed major holidays. ♿ P ☎310-247-3035.* A slender, ornate tower and graceful arches evoking the Spanish Colonial Revival style top the former La Cienega Water Treatment Plant (1928); the structure housed a pump system that provided Beverly Hills with a water supply other than the Los Angeles Aqueduct. Abandoned in 1976, the building was restored and reopened in 1991 by the Academy for Motion Picture Arts and Sciences.
Today the building is home to the **Margaret Herrick Library**, a research collection of more than 24,000 books, 6 million still photographs, 10,000 scripts, and clipping files on 82,000 films and 73,000 film personalities; and the **Academy Film Archive**, a comprehensive research collection devoted to early cinema works, Academy Award nominees and winners, and the personal film collections of Academy members and other important filmmakers.

Scenic Drives

Visitors can get a good taste of Beverly Hills' gracious and luxurious residential lifestyle by driving its streets. In the flatlands just north of Santa Monica Boulevard and Beverly Gardens, large, pricey homes are sited relatively close together and in view of the street, allowing appreciation of their lush landscaping and designs inspired by a wide variety of architectural styles, among them Tudor, Colonial, Georgian, Mediterranean, Ranch, Mission and Italian Renaissance. In the canyons and hills north of Sunset Boulevard, the richest of the rich reside behind walls and screens of greenery, though an automobile drive nonetheless reveals lush scenery and occasional tantalizing glimpses of mansions.

★ **Sunset Boulevard** – Four lanes wide and sinuously curving through the city's foothills, the boulevard offers some of the best views of large mansions surrounded by spacious grounds.

Beverly Drive – This quintessential Beverly Hills street is broad, gently curving and lined with towering palm trees. North of Sunset Boulevard, it becomes **Coldwater Canyon Drive**, and allows views of larger houses on the canyon's slopes and hilltops from its pine tree-lined curves.

Whittier Drive – In spring, jacaranda trees burst forth in blue blossoms.

★ **Summit Drive** – *Access via Benedict Canyon Drive.* The narrow, curving drive winds uphill past gated mansions to the renovated **Pickfair** *(1143 Summit Dr)*, a private residence originally built in 1920 by Mary Pickford and Douglas Fairbanks.

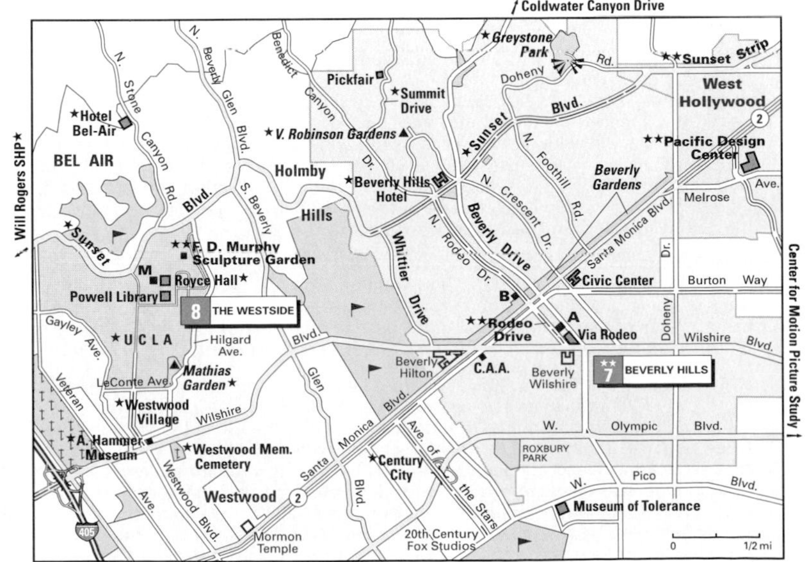

Additional Sights near Beverly Hills

Beit Hashoah Museum of Tolerance – *9786 W. Pico Blvd. Open year-round Mon–Fri, Sun. Closed major and Jewish holidays. $7.50.* ✗ ♿ 🅿 *☎310-553-8403.* Dedicated in 1993, this "museum of ideas" has two principal goals: raising awareness of racism and prejudice in American life, and exploring atrocities against humanity throughout history, with primary emphasis on the Holocaust. More a high-technology multimedia journey than a traditional museum experience, the visit begins with descent through the 8-level structure's domed atrium to the Tolerance Workshop *(45min)*, a tightly programmed series of interactive exhibits designed to provoke a powerful emotional response. Visitors then enter a stylized walk-through presentation of the events of the Holocaust *(1hr 15min)*. The third-floor Multimedia Learning Center offers access to a vast wealth of historical data on the Holocaust and World War II through 30 computer work stations. The **Archival Collections** feature concentration camp artifacts and some 10,000 documents, including original letters of Anne Frank.

★ **Century City** – *Bordered roughly by Santa Monica and W. Pico Blvds, Century Park East and Century Park West. Open daily year-round. Closed Thanksgiving Day, Dec 25.* ✗ ♿ 🅿 *☎310-277-3898.* Part of the city of Los Angeles, the 180-acre futuristic complex (1961) of hotels, office buildings, apartments and townhouses, live theaters, cinemas and shopping malls occupies a former ranch owned by Western film star Tom Mix. The site subsequently served as the back lot of the adjoining Twentieth Century-Fox Studios.

8 THE WESTSIDE *1/2 day. Map p 107.*

Although the "Westside" does not exist as an administrative entity, the term is commonly used throughout Los Angeles to refer to those parts of the city west of Hollywood and the Miracle Mile—a loose appellation generally delineating the neighborhoods of West Los Angeles, Westwood, Rancho Park, Cheviot Hills, Bel Air, Brentwood and Pacific Palisades, as well as the cities of Beverly Hills, SANTA MONICA and Culver City.

The Westside is primarily residential, with homes ranging from modest streetside bungalows in West Los Angeles to the secluded, multimillion-dollar mansions of Bel Air. The area also incorporates a business corridor of high-rise buildings along Wilshire Boulevard, as well as bustling Westwood Village adjoining the campus of the University of California, Los Angeles.

★ **Westwood Village** – *Bounded by Wilshire Blvd and LeConte, Glendon and Gayley Aves.* Covering roughly nine square blocks immediately south of the UCLA campus, Westwood Village is the closest thing Los Angeles has to a student quarter. Pedestrians outnumber automobiles, and a compact assortment of mostly 2-story Mediterranean-style buildings, largely developed by 1929, houses a varied assortment of casual clothing boutiques, book and record stores, stationery and gift shops, cafes and restaurants. Eight cinemas, many of which preview soon-to-be-released movies, and a small playhouse offering live performances, make the neighborhood even more popular as an evening and weekend haunt.

★ **Armand Hammer Museum of Art and Cultural Center** – *10899 Wilshire Blvd. Enter via the ground floor of the Occidental Petroleum building. Visit by guided tour (1hr) only, year-round Tue-Sun. Closed major holidays. $4.50.* ♿ 🅿 *☎310-443-7000.* This small museum presents selected works from the private collection of its billionaire founder, along with large-scale temporary art exhibits.

Armand Hammer (1898-1991) – Medical doctor, importer/exporter, art dealer, humanitarian and lifelong champion of business and cultural relations between the US and the former Soviet Union, Armand Hammer, while living in Moscow in the 1920s, began acquiring decorative arts sold off by the impoverished Russian aristocracy. His art collection was exhibited at museums worldwide starting in 1968; in 1990, it found a permanent home in an annex to the headquarters of Occidental Petroleum, where Hammer served as president, chairman and chief executive officer.

Visit – The collection of more than 100 works by Western European and American artists features paintings and drawings by Old Masters, French Impressionists and post-Impressionists. Its acknowledged highlight is Rembrandt's *Juno* (c.1662), a richly atmospheric portrait painted from memory of the artist's mistress, Hendrickje Stoffels. Gallery III displays the **Codex Hammer**, one of Leonardo da Vinci's celebrated 16C treatises, in which the artist/inventor detailed his studies of hydraulics. Displayed in Gallery II are selections from Hammer's collection of more than 4,000 lithographs and woodcuts by **Honoré Daumier** (1808-1879), in addition to other paintings, drawings and bronzes by the French caricaturist.

★ **Westwood Memorial Cemetery** – *1218 Glendon Ave. Open year-round Mon–Sat.* ♿ 🅿 *☎310-474-1579.* Hidden behind the AVCO Cinema and Wells Fargo Bank building on Wilshire Boulevard, the small, unassuming cemetery is the final resting place of many Hollywood stars, among them **Marilyn Monroe** *(left of the main entrance, in the Corridor of Memories)* and **Natalie Wood** *(center of the lawn)*.

★ **University of California, Los Angeles (UCLA)** – *Roughly bounded by Le Conte, Hilgard and Veteran Aves and Sunset Blvd. M Blue Line: UCLA.* Lodged on a 419-acre shield-shaped campus in the foothills between Westwood Village and Bel Air, UCLA began in 1882 as a state normal school in downtown Los Angeles. In 1919 the school became an accredited branch of the University of California and was moved to a 25-acre site on Vermont Avenue. The site for the Westwood campus was selected in 1925, when the university purchased 384 acres—then surrounded by barley fields—at below-market rates from the Janss Investment Co, the Letts estate and Bel Air developer Alphonso Bell. Inspired by the hillside setting and the

Southern California climate, early campus planners designed 40 cinnamon-colored brick and stone buildings in the Lombard Romanesque style of northern Italy, arranged on a system of axes to accommodate the sloping terrain.
Today UCLA is the largest member of the University of California's nine-campus system, with a total enrollment of more than 35,000 students and an academic staff of more than 5,000. The university has achieved prominence in several areas, including chemistry, biology, philosophy, linguistics, law, management and performing arts; its enormous medical school, located in the Center for the Health Sciences, is among the best in the country.

Royce Quadrangle – Crowning the highest point on the campus, this spacious plaza is bordered by the university's earliest structures. **Royce Hall★** (1929), inspired by the Basilica of San Ambrogio in Milan, houses classrooms and an 1,850-seat theater used for concerts and plays. **Powell Library** (1928) has an entrance modeled after the Church of San Zeno in Verona and an octagonal dome patterned after San Sepolcro in Bologna; the interior features terra-cotta-tiled staircases and ornate ceilings *(closed for renovation; scheduled reopening 1995)*. The **Janss Steps** sweep dramatically downhill from Royce Quadrangle to the student union and athletic facilities.

★ **Fowler Museum of Cultural History [M]** – *Open mid-Sept–Dec daily, rest of the year Wed–Sun. Closed Dec 25.* ♿ 🅿 *☎310-825-4361.* Adjacent to and downhill from Royce Hall, the 3-story brick building (1992) houses one of the four leading university-based museums of anthropology in the country. On view is the **Fowler Silver Collection**, a permanent display of 251 silver objects from England, Europe and America. Other galleries exhibit changing thematic displays of art and artifacts drawn from the museum's permanent collection of over 750,000 objects; the collection includes extensive holdings in textiles and Latin American art.

★ **Mildred E. Mathias Botanical Garden** – *Near the intersection of Le Conte and Hilgard Aves, at the campus' southeastern corner. Open daily year-round. Closed major holidays.* 🅿 *☎310-825-1260.* Established in 1930, the 7-acre garden features some 4,000 species in 225 families, emphasizing tropical and subtropical plants.

★★ **Franklin D. Murphy Sculpture Garden** – *Near the intersection of Hilgard Ave and Wyton Dr, at the campus' northeastern corner.* Named for the former UCLA chancellor who promoted the idea of an open-air space where students could come into contact with art in a natural setting, this tree-shaded, 7-acre garden (1967) showcases more than 70 works by such leading sculptors as Rodin, Matisse, Miró, Hepworth, Moore, Calder and Noguchi. Situated at the corner of the garden, the **Wight Art Gallery** presents changing exhibits on the visual arts.

★ **Hotel Bel-Air** – *701 Stone Canyon Rd. Open daily year-round.* 🍴 ♿ 🅿 *☎310-472-1211.* Secluded behind dense vegetation on a quiet residential street within the exclusive estate community of Bel Air, this 92-room luxury hotel complex (1946) comprises a gracious group of 1- and 2-story pink Mission-style buildings. Soon after its opening, the Bel-Air quickly established a devoted following among major Hollywood stars, who frequently retreated to its casual comfort and privacy. The 11-acre **gardens★★** surrounding the hotel are lushly landscaped with native sycamores and California live oaks, as well as floss silk trees, redwoods, Arizona cypresses, Japanese maples, palms, peaches, apricots, figs, ferns, bougainvillea, roses, camellias and azaleas—all carefully tended, yet left in a natural looking state to create the illusion of a subtropical paradise. Nearby Stone Canyon reservoir feeds a small stream, miniature falls and pond that is home to a family of swans.

★ **Will Rogers State Historic Park** – *1501 Will Rogers State Historic Park Rd in Pacific Palisades. Open daily year-round. $5.* 🅿 *☎310-454-8212.* Radio commentator, newspaper columnist, humorist and movie star Will Rogers (1879-1935) purchased this 186-acre ranch nestled in the foothills of the Santa Monica Mountains 1.5mi inland from the Pacific Ocean in 1922. Fondly dubbed the "Cowboy Philosopher" by his many admirers, Rogers moved here permanently with his family in 1928, and the ranch became a state park following Mrs Rogers' death in 1944.
The grounds feature a visitor center focusing on Rogers' life; the **ranch house**, filled with its original furnishings and Western memorabilia; stables; and riding and roping rings. Several moderate hiking trails lead up into the mountains, offering views of the ocean. On weekends, polo matches are held on the field below the house.

"[Los Angeles is] nineteen suburbs in search of a metropolis."

H.L. Mencken, 1925

ENVIRONS OF LOS ANGELES

Watts Towers – *Map p 82. 1765 E. 107th St, Watts; from downtown take Harbor Fwy (Hwy 110) south to Century Blvd exit; turn left; drive to Central Ave and turn right; at 103rd St turn left and continue to Graham Ave and turn right; continue to 107th St and turn left and proceed to the towers. Open year-round weekends only. $2.* ♿ 🅿 *☎213-569-8181. Note: Watts is subject to high incidence of crime and gang activity. Visitors should avoid exploring the area beyond the immediate vicinity of the towers.* Rising above a small, triangular plot of land in the predominantly African-American neighborhood of Watts is a celebrated work of folk art, recognized as a symbol of the human spirit. Simon Rodia, an Italian immigrant construction worker, erected the group of nine sculptures between 1921 and 1954, covering a complex steel framework with mortar and thickly studding it with bits of tile, shards of glass and pottery, and some 10,000 seashells. The tallest of the three slender spires surmounting the work measures 100ft. In the adjacent **Arts Center**, a small permanent collection of folk instruments is complemented by rotating exhibits of works by African-American artists.

San Gabriel (Pop 37,120) *1/2 day. Map p 83.*

San Gabriel lies at the center of the San Gabriel Valley, a former citrus-growing region immediately northeast of downtown Los Angeles.

★ **San Gabriel Arcángel Mission** – *537 W. Mission Dr. Open daily year-round. Closed Jan 1, Easter Sunday, Thanksgiving Day, Dec 25. $3. ♿ ☎818-282-5191.* Situated at the heart of a busy suburban intersection, this complex recalls the era when the mission was the heart of a prosperous Spanish settlement that predated Los Angeles.

Originally established in 1771 beside the San Gabriel River 5mi to the south, California's fourth mission was forced by flooding to relocate to its present site in 1775. The surrounding fertile lands, worked by laborers from the local Gabrieleño tribe, brought great prosperity. Between 1779 and 1805, a church unlike any other in the mission chain was built here, reputedly inspired by the Moorish cathedral in Cordova, Spain, birthplace of the church's designer, Padre Antonio Cruzado.

The mission passed through several owners following secularization, but was returned to use as a parish church in 1859. Since 1908, the old church has been cared for by the Claretian Fathers, but was severely damaged in the 1987 Whittier Narrows earthquake. Adjoining contemporary structures today serve an active community parish.

Visit – Bounded by the old and new churches and administrative buildings, the grounds present an overview of life in the mission's early days. Remnants of a water cistern, an aqueduct, soap and tallow vats, a kitchen and a winery share the spacious courtyard with olive trees dating from 1860, grapevines planted in 1910, cacti and other native plants. Beside the old mission church lies the **campo santo**; consecrated in 1778, it is the oldest cemetery in Los Angeles County and the resting place of some 6,000 Gabrieleño Natives.

The fortress-like exterior of the **church** is composed of 4ft-thick adobe walls pierced by narrow windows and supported by capped buttresses. The 6-bell tower near the sacristy replaced a tower at the opposite end that toppled in an 1812 earthquake.

Burbank (Pop 93,643) *3hrs*

Popular lore holds that this city located in the eastern end of suburban Los Angeles' SAN FERNANDO VALLEY honors horticulturist Luther Burbank *(p 224)*. In fact, it was named in 1887 for Dr David Burbank, one of its developers. Today the city is best known as the site of several major film and television studios.

Warner Bros. Studios – *Map p 96. 4000 Warner Blvd. Visit by guided tour (1hr 30min) only, Jul–Aug Mon–Sat, rest of the year Mon–Fri. Closed major holidays. $25. Reservations suggested.* ✗ ♿ *☎818-954-1744.* Since 1928 the 108-acre complex has been the headquarters of Warner Bros., the motion picture company founded in 1912 by Sam, Harry, Albert and Jack Warner. Today its 33 sound stages, along with office buildings and bungalows scattered throughout the lot, are in constant use for filming of movies, television programs and commercials, and sound recordings.

Guided tours begin in a small bungalow on the edge of the lot with the showing of a 12min film montage of clips from Warner Bros. movies. Visitors are then transported via golf cart to the back lot for a no-frills walk through outdoor and indoor sets, prop rooms, construction shops and other areas revealing the practical, working aspects of production.

NBC Studios – *Map p 96. 3000 W. Alameda St. Visit by guided tour (1hr) only, July 4–Labor Day Mon–Sat, rest of the year Mon–Fri. $6. ♿ ☎818-840-3537.* Housing the largest color television studio in the US, this expansive complex also serves as the West Coast headquarters of the National Broadcasting Company and home of its network-owned and -operated local station, KNBC. The tour offers a look at simple static and videotaped displays and demonstrations on special effects, sound effects, makeup, costumes and remote sports broadcasting. Visitors are also shown inside the 465-seat theater that serves as home to *The Tonight Show*.

San Fernando Valley (Pop 22,580) *1/2 day. Map p 82.*

Circumscribed by the Santa Monica, San Gabriel and Sierra Madre mountains, the 235sq mi suburb—known locally as "The Valley"—is Los Angeles' largest residential enclave, home to one third of its population. Most of its 22 contiguous towns are part of the city of Los Angeles, though Burbank, Glendale and San Fernando are independent municipalities.

San Fernando Rey de España Mission – *15151 San Fernando Rd, in Mission Hills. Open daily year-round. $4. ♿ ☎818-361-0186.* The 17th California mission was founded in 1797 by Padre Fermín Lasuén as a stepping stone between the SAN GABRIEL MISSION and the SAN BUENAVENTURA MISSION. Situated to take advantage of the valley's potential for agriculture and cattle-ranching, the mission thrived, grazing as many as 21,000 head of livestock by 1819, and was a popular hostelry for travelers en route to Los Angeles. During the period after secularization in 1834, the mission's buildings were neglected and fell into ruin.

Restoration, begun in 1916 and continuing today, is most notable in the **convento**, the original guest and missionary quarters completed in 1822 after 13 years of construction. Measuring 243ft long and 50ft wide, with 4ft-thick adobe walls and 21 Roman arches facing the street, the 2-story structure is the largest extant mission building in California. Its naturally cool interiors feature original furnishings and decorative wall paintings.

The mission church, destroyed in the 1971 Sylmar earthquake, was rebuilt in 1974 and is an exact replica of the original 1806 structure.

Los Encinos State Historic Park – *16756 Moorpark St in Encino. Open year-round Wed–Sun. Closed Jan 1, Thanksgiving Day, Dec 25. ♿ ☎818-784-4849.* The last remaining 5 acres of the original 4,460-acre Rancho del Encino (Oak Ranch) marks the site where the expedition party of Spanish explorer Gaspar de Portolá camped after discovering the San Fernando Valley on August 5, 1769. Most prominent among several 19C buildings on the grounds are the **De la Ossa Adobe**, an 8-room ranch house built in 1850 that includes 5 rooms restored with period furnishings, and the **Garnier Building**, a 2-story limestone Greek Revival farmhouse built in 1872, now restored to contain a visitor center and exhibits on local history. A rock-lined pond, home to migratory water fowl, is fed by hot springs that originally attracted Gabrieleño Natives to settle here.

Ronald Reagan Presidential Library – *40 Presidential Dr in Simi Valley. From Los Angeles take San Diego Fwy/I-405 north to Simi Valley Fwy/Hwy 118 west, exit south on Madera Dr; or take Ventura Fwy/US-101 north to Fillmore Fwy/Hwy 23 north, exit east on Olsen Rd. Open daily year-round. Closed Jan 1, Thanksgiving Day, Dec 25. $4. ♿ ☎805-522-8444.* Surveying lovely **vistas★** of the Simi Valley to the east and the Tehachapi Mountains and Pacific Ocean to the west from its 29-acre hilltop perch, this 153,000sq ft contemporary facility (1991) houses the archives of the 40th president of the US. The exterior incorporates Mission-style elements, and within, eye-catching audiovisual exhibits highlight Reagan's life from boyhood through his two presidential terms (1981-1989).

★ Venice *Map p 82*

A Los Angeles beachside community immediately south of SANTA MONICA, Venice is one of the city's liveliest melting pots, a tightly packed warren of beachside streets whose close proximity serves to highlight the diversity of people drawn to live beside its broad stretches of sand. In 1904, tobacco magnate Abbot Kinney began to develop the area as an artistic mecca modeled after Venice, Italy, draining its marshlands and dredging a 16mi network of canals. But Venice steadily declined into a gaudy, bawdy seaside town that welcomed those who were down on their luck or embraced alternative lifestyles. Sewage problems and lack of maintenance eventually led to the filling in of all but 3mi of Kinney's canals.

M. & T. Grimm/LACVB

Rolling in Venice Beach

In the 1960s, the community became a gathering place for local hippies, and today **Venice Beach★★** is among Southern California's most popular beaches, renowned not only for its beaches and good swimming, but also for its colorful street life—particularly along **Oceanfront Walk**, a 2.5mi pedestrian thoroughfare lined with cafes, boutiques and souvenir stalls facing the sand. On sunny days, and especially on weekends, the promenade is filled with folksingers and rappers, comic jugglers and swimsuit-clad skaters, musclebound weightlifters, vacationers and vagrants. In recent decades, Venice has also become a popular location for studios of leading local artists, fulfilling Abbot Kinney's vision of nearly a century ago.

★★ Pasadena *2 days. Description p 141.*

★ Malibu *1 day. Description p 114.*

★ Santa Monica *1/2 day. Description p 223.*

EXCURSIONS

★★ Bowers Museum of Cultural Art – *1/2 day. Map p 83. 35mi south of Los Angeles, in Santa Ana. Take I-5 south to Main St exit and proceed .5mi south on Main St. 2002 N. Main St. Open year-round Tue–Sun 10am–5pm. Closed Jan 1, Dec 25. $4.50. ✗ ♿ ☎714-567-3008.* Housed in a gracious structure considered to be one of the area's finest examples of the Mission style, Orange County's largest museum is dedicated to collecting and preserving the indigenous fine art of Oceania, the Americas, Africa and the Pacific Rim.

Endowed by local rancher and developer Charles Bowers (1842-1929), the museum opened in 1936 with collections devoted to local history. Its emphasis shifted to cultural art and natural history following expansion in 1974, and in the late 1980s the museum underwent a second, major expansion, this time with a view to hosting first-class international traveling exhibits of fine and cultural art. Today the permanent collection comprises 85,000 artworks and artifacts dating from 1500 BC to the mid-20C, and the museum mounts some 12 temporary exhibits annually.

Visit – Greatly augmented by the 1980s renovation, the original museum structure sports a scalloped belltower entrance and shady arcade. A haunting sculpture of a Native American figure by Apache artist Allen Houser graces the courtyard, opposite a statue of Spanish explorer Juan Rodríguez Cabrillo.
In the **Gallery of Oceanic Art**, bark paintings by Australian aborigines depict aspects of ancestral worship. Also on view are a magnificently carved Maori walking stick, an animated wooden puppet from Vanuatu employed to recount an ancient legend, and a Tahitian stone breadfruit pounder mysteriously discovered in the bed of the Santa Ana River. The **African collection** *(on permanent loan)* features some 100 ritual objects in wood, metal, textiles and ivory, representing most of the continent's significant tribal and regional styles.
Display cases incorporating photographic backgrounds set into context architectural elements and ceramics from the museum's extensive **pre-Columbian collection**. Particularly interesting are relics of *ulama*, the ancient ballgame played by Maya, Aztec and Toltec cultures. Dating from 1000 BC, the game is thought to symbolize the supernatural battles between forces of life and death.
The collection of **Native American art**, dating from 17C to the 1980s, reveals a wide variety of forms, among them baskets, beadwork and carved pipes. Stone sculptures from the arctic are particularly graceful. Among pieces from the Tlingit culture of British Columbia and Alaska is an intricately detailed rattle carved from cedar.
Religious and domestic artifacts from California's mission and rancho periods are housed in a gallery topped by an elaborate coffered ceiling, and collections representing Asia and early 20C California occupy the museum's upper level.

★ **Richard M. Nixon Library and Birthplace** – *2hrs. Map p 83. 32mi southeast of Los Angeles, in Yorba Linda. Take Golden State Fwy/I-5 south to Riverside Fwy/ Hwy 91 east to Orange Fwy/Hwy 57 north to Yorba Linda Blvd exit. Turn right and proceed 3.5mi. 18001 Yorba Linda Blvd. Open daily year-round. Closed Jan 1, Thanksgiving Day, Dec 25. $4.95. ♿ ☎714-993-3393.* This sleek, contemporary library combines letters, papers, memorabilia and interactive exhibits to illustrate and commemorate the life of Richard Milhous Nixon (1913-1994), 37th US President. The 9-acre complex, dedicated in 1990, incorporates the small house where Nixon was born; the graves of the former president and his wife, Thelma ("Pat"), are located on the site.
Nixon's personal artifacts appear in a timeline display detailing family history and early life, including his childhood dedication to the violin and his wartime poker prowess (his winnings helped to finance his first congressional campaign). Innovative exhibits chronicle Nixon's political career: his famed 1960 campaign debates with John F. Kennedy are shown on a period television. In a separate gallery devoted to the Watergate scandal, visitors can listen to excerpts from the renowned "smoking gun" tapes; and in the "Presidential Forum," touch screens are used to view taped responses by Nixon to some 300 questions.

★ **Knott's Berry Farm** – *At least 1/2 day. Map p 83. 20mi southeast of Los Angeles in Buena Park. Take San Diego Fwy/I-5 south to Beach Blvd exit and follow signs. 8039 Beach Blvd. Open daily year-round. Closed Dec 25. $26.95. ✗ ♿ ☎714-220-5200.* Situated on 150 acres of former farmland in northwestern Orange County, America's oldest independently owned theme park derives its particular flavor from old-fashioned charm and Old West atmosphere, rather than from the high-tech magic of later generations of theme parks.
In the 1920s, Walter Knott arrived in California with his family and established a berry farm and roadside stand here on 20 acres of rented land. The farm, known as Knott's Berry Place, specialized in cherry rhubarb and **boysenberries**, then a new strain developed locally by grafting together loganberry, blackberry and raspberry plants. By 1928 Knott had established the Berry Market and Tea Room, where, to supplement the family income during the Great Depression, his wife Cordelia began selling chicken dinners (served on her wedding china) for 60 cents. The tea room grew into an immensely popular restaurant, and in 1940 Knott constructed a replica Old West town to amuse the lines of hungry patrons waiting to get in. Other attractions and retail shops were added over the ensuing decades, and today Knott's Berry Farm comprises a wide variety of relocated or replicated historic structures, along with some 165 rides, shows and attractions. An updated version of Cordelia Knott's Chicken Dinner Restaurant today forms the core of the **California MarketPlace**, an extensive shopping and dining complex *(outside park gates, on Beach Blvd)*.

Visit – Begin with a ride on the Butterfield Stagecoach or the Denver & Rio Grande train to get your bearings in the park. Many of the structures in **Ghost Town** were brought from deserted mining towns, and here visitors with gold fever can pan for the real thing in a miner's trough. The park offers several areas designed especially for children, among them **Indian Trails**, with educational and interactive demonstrations of Native American crafts. In the **Roaring 20s**, old-fashioned rides, including a Coney Island-style parachute jump, recall the era when seaside amusement parks and boardwalks dotted the Southern California shoreline. In **Fiesta Village**, tiled arches, vine-laden trellises and terra-cotta fountains take the visitor back to the rancho period of Spanish California; adjacent lies the "Incredible Waterworks Show," in which musically choreographed jets of water leap and twirl in aquatic approximations of the Charleston, the tango and other popular dances. **Camp Snoopy**, where Charles Schulz' cartoon characters reside amid High Sierra-style waterfalls, bridges and streams, offers rides especially suited to the very young.

★ **Six Flags Magic Mountain** – *1 day. 30mi north of Los Angeles In Valencia. Take Golden State Fwy/I-5 north to Magic Mountain Pkwy exit. Open daily 2nd weekend in May–2nd weekend in Sept, rest of the year weekends & school holidays only. Closed Dec 25. $27.* ✗ ♿ ☎*805-367-5965.* Combining the attributes of an old-fashioned fun fair and a botanical garden, the family-oriented amusement park is set on 260 lushly landscaped acres in the western foothills of the Santa Clarita Valley. It features some three dozen rides, the most popular of which are such thrill rides as the traditional wood-framed roller coasters **Colossus** and **Psyclone**; tubular-steel roller-coasters like **Viper**, **Flashback** and **Revolution**; and such water rides as **Roaring Rapids**, **Log Jammer** and **Tidal Wave**.

Life-size Warner Bros. cartoon characters roam the grounds, and several theaters and pavilions present regularly scheduled live shows. Smaller children gravitate to **Bugs Bunny World**, with its gentler, fairground-style rides.

Palos Verdes Peninsula *1/2 day. Map p 82.*

This roughly square-shaped peninsula is almost entirely occupied by a 16,000-acre elite residential enclave planned and landscaped in the 1920s by John and Frederick Law Olmsted. For roughly 11mi, **Palos Verdes Drive** parallels the coast, allowing abundant vistas north to MALIBU, west to CATALINA ISLAND and south to SAN PEDRO.

★ **Wayfarers Chapel** – *5755 Palos Verdes Dr South. Open daily year-round.* ♿ ☎*310-377-2692.* Conceived as a hillside chapel where wayfarers could stop to meditate, and inspired by the teachings of 18C Swedish theologian Emanuel Swedenborg *(p 208)*, the chapel, completed in 1951, is the best-known work of architect Lloyd Wright, son of Frank Lloyd Wright. A popular setting for weddings, the angular structure of Palos Verdes stone, redwood beams and large glass panels is surrounded by redwood trees and 3.5 acres of lush gardens also designed by the architect, creating an illusion of communing with nature outdoors. The 50ft stone tower was added in 1954, and a carillon of bells was added in 1978.

Antelope Valley *1 day*

A vast, flat, dry expanse straddling the borders of Los Angeles and Kern counties approximately 100mi north of downtown Los Angeles, the 3,400sq mi Antelope Valley occupies the southwest corner of the **Mojave Desert** *(p 16)*.

Centered between Shoshonean, Yokut, Chumash and Gabrieleño cultural areas, the valley was originally home to several Native triblets. Members of pioneer families who arrived in the late 19C attest to the presence of antelopes in the valley, although great herds probably never roamed here. Ranchers and borax miners sought fortunes in the valley, and in the early 20C, the **California Aqueduct** *(p 16)* cut along its sparsely populated southern edge.

In the 1940s, Antelope Valley's perfectly flat, dry lake beds became home to several large aeronautics industries and US Air Force installations. Today a growing commuter suburb of greater Los Angeles, its population exceeds 300,000 and is largely centered in its two principal cities, Lancaster and Palmdale. The valley is famed as the location of the 1,745-acre **Antelope Valley California Poppy Reserve**, which presents annually in April and May one of the largest massed displays of the brilliant orange California poppy *(Eschscholzia californica)*, the official state flower *(open mid-Mar–mid-May daily. $5/car. ♿ ☎805-724-1180 for bloom schedule)*.

★ **Antelope Valley Indian Museum** – *1hr. 80mi north of Los Angeles in Lancaster. Take Antelope Valley Fwy/Hwy 14 to Avenue K exit and proceed east 15mi to 150th St. Turn right, proceed to Avenue M and turn left. 15701 E. Avenue M. Open Oct–mid-Jun weekends. Closed Dec 25 and preceding weekend. $2.* ♿ ☎*805-946-3055.* Housed in a Swiss-style chalet incongruously located on the side of rocky Piute Butte in the southeastern corner of Antelope Valley, the museum was originally built in the late 1920s as a private residence on the 160-acre homestead of self-taught painter and amateur anthropologist Howard Arden Edwards. In the early 1940s, Grace Oliver bought the property, added her own anthropological collections to Edwards' and opened the museum in 1940. The facility has been owned by the state since 1979.

The **interiors**★ feature rooms extravagantly painted in Native motifs; massive images of Kachina dolls adorn the ceiling of the great room. Some walls and floors are formed by the boulders of the butte itself. Exhibits focus on Native cultures of the Southwest, California and the western Great Basin. In a separate cottage, a **touch table** allows visitors to handle artifacts and try their hands at grinding corn or starting fires with bow drills. The museum grounds offer spectacular **vistas** of the northern faces of the San Gabriel and San Bernardino mountains.

★ **NASA Dryden Flight Research Facility** – *On Edwards Air Force Base. Take Hwy 14 to Rosamond exit and drive east about 2mi to base entrance; follow directions given at guardhouse. Advance reservations required to enter base and tour facility.* Set within the boundaries of 301,000-acre Edwards Air Force Base, located at the northern end of Antelope Valley, this is the principal center for military and civilian aeronautical flight research conducted by the National Aeronautics and Space Administration (NASA). The facility has access to seven runways laid out on the adjoining 44sq mi naturally smooth clay surface of Rogers Dry Lake, along with an additional 22sq mi of nearby Rosamond Dry Lake.

Testing began here in 1946 with the **X-1**, the first aircraft to fly faster than the speed of sound. Since then, significant aircraft flown at Dryden have included the **D-558-II**, the first aircraft to fly at twice the speed of sound; the rocket-powered **X-15**, which extended manned flight to speeds exceeding 4,500mph and altitudes of over 350,000ft; the **XB-70**, a prototype supersonic bomber, the largest experimental aircraft ever built; and the **SR-71**, also known as the "Blackbird," a high-altitude aircraft that flies at three times the speed of sound. The Rogers Dry Lake is also used for most landings of the **space shuttle**, NASA's celebrated reusable rocket-launched cargo and passenger vehicle. *Landings are usually open to public viewing; call for schedule ☎805-258-3520.*

Visit – *1.5hrs. Visit by guided tour only, year-round Mon–Fri. Reservations required.* ✗ ♿ *☎805-258-3446.* Facility tours begin with a 25min video presentation surveying experiments conducted here and highlighting the facility's achievements. The tour then proceeds through two of the facility's flight hangars, offering close-up looks at and commentary on test aircraft currently housed there. A separate **visitor center** displays models of aircraft tested at Dryden, along with a collection of aeronautical art.

★★★ **Disneyland** *1-3 days.* *Description p 50.*

★ **Catalina Island** *1 day.* *Description p 40.*

★ **Long Beach** *1 day.* *Description p 79.*

The Los Angeles Freeway

Number	Name(s)
Hwy 2	Glendale Freeway
I-5	Golden State Freeway *(north of downtown)* Santa Ana Freeway *(south of downtown)*
I-10	Santa Monica Freeway *(west of downtown)* San Bernardino Freeway *(east of downtown)*
Hwy 90	Marina Freeway
Hwy 91	Artesia Freeway Gardena Freeway
US-101 *(south of Hwy 134)* and **Hwy 170**	Hollywood Freeway *(north of downtown)*
US-101 *(west of Hwy 170)* and **Hwy 134**	Ventura Freeway
Hwy-110	Pasadena Freeway
I-110	Harbor Freeway
Hwy 118	Simi Valley-San Fernando Freeway
I-405	San Diego Freeway
I-710	Long Beach Freeway
Hwy 14	Antelope Valley Freeway
I-210	Foothill Freeway
I-105	Century Freeway

California State Highways ⬟ are indicated with a ◯ on maps in this guide.

"If you tilt the whole country sideways, Los Angeles is the place where everything loose will fall."

Frank Lloyd Wright

★ MALIBU Greater Los Angeles Area

Map p 82

Stretching along some 27mi of coastline where the Santa Monica Mountains abruptly meet the Pacific on the northern edge of Santa Monica Bay, the city of Malibu enjoys the widest renown and the loveliest setting of the beachside communities surrounding LOS ANGELES. Arrayed largely along State Highway 1, more commonly called the Pacific Coast Highway or "PCH," Malibu's restaurants, cafes and shops attract a casual crowd of beach goers, locals and resident glitterati.

From Humaliwo to Celebrity Hideaway – Chumash Natives originally inhabited this area, and the name Malibu is derived from the Native word *humaliwo*, thought to mean "the surf sounds loudly." In the early 19C, the area became part of a 13,300-acre Spanish land grant known as Rancho Topanga Malibu Sequit, which passed through several owners during the 19C. In 1892 millionaire businessman Frederick Hastings Rindge acquired it for a reputed $300,000, transforming the property into a country retreat, cattle ranch and wheat farm. Rindge's wife, May, retained ownership through the years following his death in 1905, and in 1926 she established Malibu Potteries, a beachside factory that for six years produced colorful Spanish-style ceramic tiles used in many homes and office buildings of the era, including the Los Angeles City Hall *(p 89)*.

May Rindge eventually sold most of the property. A parcel was purchased by developer Art Jones, who in 1928, established an exclusive residential enclave called the **Malibu Colony**; the beachside homesites leased for $1 per square foot per month and

and drew many celebrities of the day, among them Clara Bow, Ronald Colman, Delores del Rio, Barbara Stanwyck, Gary Cooper, John Gilbert and Gloria Swanson. Today, some of HOLLYWOOD's most glittering stars occupy multimillion-dollar homes in the security-gated colony; other famed personalities live in luxurious aeries clinging to the mountain foothills. Public beaches abound, and sparkling coastline views are accessible from turnouts along Malibu Canyon, Latigo Canyon and Kanan Dume roads, all of which lead north from Pacific Coast Highway (Highway 1); **Corral Canyon Road** ends 6mi inland at a parking area of Malibu Creek State Park that offers a sweeping **vista**★★ of Santa Monica Bay.

SIGHTS *1 day*

★★★ **J. Paul Getty Museum** – *17985 Pacific Coast Hwy, between Sunset and Topanga Canyon Blvds. Open year-round Tue–Sun 10am–5pm. Closed Jan 1, Jul 4, Thanksgiving Day, Dec 25. ✗ ♿ ☎310-459-7611. Parking prohibited on streets surrounding museum, parking at museum by reservation only (in season reserve a month in advance, off season two weeks) ☎310-458-2003. Visitors dropped off by bus or automobile not admitted without pass; obtain pass from driver if arriving by bus, or check in at guardhouse if arriving by automobile.* Hidden in a lushly landscaped 65-acre canyon overlooking the Pacific, a re-created ancient Roman villa provides a spectacular setting for an outstanding assemblage of antiquities and decorative arts, begun as the private collection of one of this century's wealthiest businessmen.

J. Paul Getty (1898-1976) – The only child of oil millionaire George F. Getty, who moved his family from Minneapolis to Southern California in 1906, Jean Paul Getty by the age of 23 had become a millionaire himself in Oklahoma's oil fields. Upon his father's death in 1930 he took over Pacific Western Oil, renaming it Getty Oil in 1956. Getty began collecting paintings in 1931, and in 1938, purchased an important collection of 18C French furniture. After World War II, he spent most of his time in Europe, developing his worldwide oil business while building a collection of antiquities and expanding his other art holdings.

The Villa dei Papiri – Having exhibited his collections since 1954 at his ranch house in the Santa Monica Mountains, Getty started planning a new museum there in 1968. The building, which opened in January 1974, recreates a 1C BC villa from the town of Herculaneum, on the Bay of Naples; completely buried during the eruption of Mt Vesuvius in AD 79 and excavated in the 18C, the structure was dubbed the "Villa dei Papiri" for its extensive library of papyrus scrolls.
Since Getty's death in 1976, the vast J. Paul Getty Trust has enabled the museum to continue expanding its holdings and educational and research activities. A new Getty Center, under construction in the hills above West Los Angeles *(scheduled completion 1996)*, is slated to house all collections but antiquities; the villa will remain the only US museum devoted exclusively to ancient Greek and Roman art.

Antiquities – *Main level.* Ranked among the most important of its kind in the US, the antiquities collection is especially strong in Attic and Italiote vases *(gallery 123)* and Greek and Roman sculpture *(galleries 107-124)*. Highlights include a marble *Head of Alexander* (4C BC); a bronze *Statue of a Victorious Athlete* (4-3C BC); a terra-cotta *Seated Musician Flanked by Two Sirens* (4C BC), and a limestone *Female Figure* (c.2500 BC). A small collection of Egyptian portrait paintings *(gallery 109)* highlights a tempera-on-wood *Personal Shrine* (mid-3C AD).

Decorative Arts – *Upper level.* Getty's superior assemblage of French decorative arts includes pieces dating from the mid-17C through the 19C. Four paneled period rooms *(galleries 211, 213, 218 & 220)* showcase objects from the 18C, including Beauvais tapestries depicting cartoon designs by François Boucher. A magnificent Gobelins cabinet *(gallery 210)* made in 1680, which displays intricate marquetry, was commissioned for Louis XIV, as indicated by its central Sun King medallion.

Superstock

Aerial view of the J. Paul Getty Museum

European Paintings (17-20C) – *Upper level.* Works in the collection encompass representative groups from major schools of European painting from the Early Renaissance through the early 20C. Holdings from the Dutch School *(galleries 202 & 203)* include such works as Rembrandt's *Saint Bartholomew* (1661) and canvases by Cuyp, Van Ruisdael, Steen and De Hooch. Among the Italian Renaissance and Baroque paintings *(galleries 205 & 206)* are works by Masaccio, Carpaccio, Canaletto and Veronese, including the latter's *Portrait of a Man* (c.1560). Impressionist paintings *(gallery 228)* feature Monet's *Still Life with Flowers* (1869) and Van Gogh's *Irises* (1889).

Drawings, Manuscripts and Photographs – *Upper Level.* Three adjoining rooms *(galleries 223-225)* highlight changing selections from the Getty's diverse collections of drawings by some of the most celebrated draftsmen of the late 15-19C, including Dürer, Raphael, Bernini, Rembrandt, Rubens, Watteau, Ingres and Millet; illuminated manuscripts from 11-16C Europe and Great Britain; and photographs dating from the early 1840s to the present.

Adamson House and Malibu Lagoon Museum – *23200 Pacific Coast Hwy. House accessible by guided tour (1hr) only, year-round Wed–Sat. $2 (museum & grounds free). ♿ ☎310-456-8432.* Overlooking Malibu Lagoon and the Pacific Ocean from a 26-acre garden setting, the 2-story Spanish Colonial Revival house (1929, Stiles Clements) was built for the daughter and son-in-law of Frederick and May Rindge *(p 114)*. An abundance of colorful **tilework★** from Malibu Potteries enlivens both the exterior and the furnished interior, and adorns a Moorish-style star fountain in the property's graceful **gardens**. Adjoining the house is a small museum devoted to local history from the Native period to the present.

★ MAMMOTH REGION High Sierras

Map of Principal Sights p 246 Tourist Office ☎619-934-8006

Situated roughly 40mi south of YOSEMITE NATIONAL PARK, and 318mi from LOS ANGELES, the region surrounding Mammoth Mountain offers year-round recreational opportunities and diverse natural phenomena, from lovely alpine lakes to unique geologic formations. Settled here in 1878 as the nucleus of a short-lived gold rush, the town of **Mammoth Lakes** declined through the late 19C and early 20C before its rebirth as a ski resort destination in the mid-1950s. Today it serves as a center of amenities for popular nearby Mammoth Mountain and June Mountain ski resorts, and is an excellent base from which to explore the region. Begin with a stop at the US Forest Service's Mammoth Ranger District **visitor center**, which offers tours, interpretive programs and recreational information *(Hwy 203, 3mi west of US-395; open Apr–Nov daily, rest of the year Mon–Sat; closed Jan 1, Thanksgiving Day, Dec 25; ♿ ☎619-924-5500).*

SIGHTS *At least 1 day*

★ **Mammoth Mountain** – Storms from the northwest drop some 335in of snow annually on this massive dormant volcano (11,053ft) because of its situation in a slight depression of the Sierra crest. Ski trails were established here as early as the 1940s, and today the mountain's flanks harbor one of California's most popular ski resorts. From the Mammoth Mountain Ski Center's Main Lodge *(4mi west of Mammoth lakes via Minaret Rd, ski information p 261; ☎619-934-2571)*, a gondola offers access to the summit, from which magnificent **views★★** extend as far as MONO LAKE *(daily year-round; closed Jun & Oct; $10; ♿ ☎619-934-2571).*
Stretching to the south in the mountain's shadow is the **Mammoth Lakes Basin★** *(3mi west of Mammoth Lakes via Lake Mary Rd)*, a high, glacially sculpted depression graced by six beautiful alpine lakes. The basin offers abundant opportunities for hiking and seasonal cross-country skiing on trails that wind through lush forests of evergreens.

Minaret Summit – *5mi northwest of Mammoth Lakes via Hwy 203 (Minaret Rd).* Situated on a granite outcropping atop the crest of the Sierra Nevada, this overlook offers a stunning panoramic **view★★** to the rugged peaks of the Ritter Range, and the crenelated tops of the Minarets—a thin, jagged ridge formed by two glaciers that flowed parallel to each other.

★ **Devil's Postpile National Monument** – *14mi from Mammoth Lakes via Hwy 203. Open Jun–Oct daily. ⛺ ☎619-934-2289. From late Jun–early Sept day visitors are required to visit the park by shuttle bus. Ticket sales and departures at Mammoth Mountain Inn.* Rising above the Middle Fork of the San Joaquin River is a 60ft gray wall of basalt columns that are nearly perfect geometrically. This "postpile" was formed some 100,000 years ago when a pool of molten lava was extruded from a nearby volcanic vent. The lava cooled, then cracked on the surface; as the interior cooled and hardened, the cracks extended to the interior of the flow, creating a mass of mostly pentagonal and hexagonal posts. About 10,000 years ago, a glacier flowing through the area exposed the wall of jointed columnar basalt.
Originally included within the boundaries of Yosemite National Park, the area was part of a 500-acre parcel deleted from the park in 1905. In 1911 the national monument was established to protect both the columns and nearby Rainbow Falls.

Visit – *1/2 day.* The trail *(.4mi)* from the monument headquarters to the postpile passes **Soda Springs**, a series of cold mineral springs situated on a gravel bar in the river. From the base of the postpile's basalt wall, a second trail leads to its top, where the jointed upper surfaces appear as clean and regular as a tiled floor.

The main trail continues south to **Rainbow Falls** *(1.5mi)*, where the river drops 101ft over a volcanic ledge and hovering mists refract the mid-day sun into colored arcs. A shorter trail to Rainbow Falls is accessible from the popular Reds Meadow area, and by shuttle bus from Mammoth Mountain Inn in summer. A months-long forest fire in 1992 devastated vegetation in this area.

★ **Convict Lake** – *From Mammoth Lakes drive 4mi south on US-395 to Convict Lake exit, then 2mi west.* Dramatic cliffs and peaks surround this lovely expanse of blue water, sparkling in a glacially sculpted basin. The alpine lake received its name in 1871, when posses pursued six escaped convicts into a nearby canyon and a fierce shoot-out ensued. Mt Morrison (12,268ft) offers a spectacular backdrop to the south of Convict Lake, today a popular hiking, picnicking and fishing destination.

★ **Hot Creek Geothermal Area** – *From Mammoth Lakes drive 2.5mi south on US-395, then 2mi east on Airport/Hot Creek Fish Hatchery Rd.* The picturesque creek traversing a volcanic basin that formed 700,000 years ago is one of numerous manifestations of geothermal activity present in the region. Hot springs and fumaroles feed into the creek, and roiling springs and mudpots steam beside it. *Swimming here is extremely hazardous owing to shifting ground and unexpected changes in temperature. The town of Mammoth Lakes maintains a public pool fed by natural hot springs at Whitmore, 3mi farther south off US-395.*

★ **June Lake Loop** – *Off US-395, 17mi north of Mammoth Lakes. Loop rejoins US-395.* Lying in the shadow of 10,909ft Carson Peak, this loop drive *(15mi)* leads past four lovely mountain lakes, offering spectacular high desert and alpine scenery. Mountains rise steeply above horseshoe-shaped valleys traversed by streams, and stands of aspen border the lakeshores. The quaint community of June Lake serves as the hub of activities and services, and June Mountain Ski Area attracts winter sports enthusiasts.

★★ MENDOCINO North Coast

Map p 127 Tourist Office ☎707-961-6300

Seated on a foggy headland where the Big River meets the ocean, this picturesque Victorian village, named for Antonio de Mendoza, the first viceroy of New Spain, appears little changed from its heyday as a lumber town in the late 19C. Today its tranquil atmosphere and idyllic setting draw artists and visitors alike.

An Auspicious Accident – In 1850 a ship bound for SAN FRANCISCO with a load of silks and tea from China ran aground several miles north of present-day Mendocino, and a group was dispatched from the logging camp at BODEGA BAY to recover the cargo. When the team reached the area of the shipwreck, instead of Oriental booty, they found virgin redwood forests. News of this fresh source of timber was quick to reach San Francisco lumberman Harry Meiggs, who hied to Mendocino and built a sawmill on the headland there in the summer of 1852. Unfortunately, the first mill lost its roof during a storm that winter, and Meiggs erected a second one on the sheltered Big River flat east of present Highway 1.

The town that sprang up around the mill resembled a New England seaside village, owing to the fact that Mendocino's founders hailed from the northeast and copied—as nearly as they could—the design of the homes they had left behind. Most of the present day architecture was constructed after 1870, the year a fire destroyed the majority of town's buildings. This disaster created a ready market for carpenter John D. Johnson, who arrived from England in the early 1870s. Johnson designed and built many of the town's finer structures, including the **MacCallum**

R. Lynn

Mendocino by the sea

House (1882) on Albion Street (now and bed & breakfast). With its steep, gabled roof and cut-out trim, this "pointed cottage" (as it was called at the time) typifies the houses constructed by Mendocino's affluent residents during the lumber boom. Wooden **water towers**, powered by windmills over 100 years ago, still store precious water that is pumped from the town's wells.

From Rags to Riches – Mendocino prospered until the 1920s, when loggers finally exhausted the local timber supply. After the mill closed forever in 1938, the town fell into an economic slump that was not relieved until the late 1950s. It was then that local newspaper editor Auggie Heeser donated his family's land to the State of California, under the condition that "the area will forever remain open to the public . . . " This land now forms part of Mendocino Headlands State Park *(below)*. In 1959, the opening of the **Mendocino Art Center** sparked a cultural revolution that brought an influx of artists to revive the sleepy village. Today the town's concentration of shops and galleries cater to a large tourist trade that generates the majority of Mendocino's revenues.
Over the years, Hollywood directors have also favored the town's quaint charm, using its quiet streets as the settings for a number of productions, including the films *Johnny Belinda (1947), The Russians Are Coming (1966)* and the TV series *Murder She Wrote.*

SIGHTS *1 day*

★ **Main Street** – Mendocino's principal commercial artery grew up across from Harry Meiggs' first mill, facing the turquoise waters of Mendocino Bay. Lumberman Jerome Ford built the cream-colored clapboard house (1854) on the headlands that now serves as the **Ford House Visitor Center** *(open daily year-round; $1; ☎707-937-5397)*. Along with information about Mendocino Headlands State Park, the center contains several exhibits related to the area's natural and cultural history, including a miniature model of the town as it looked in 1890.
On the upper part of the street, the Gothic Revival **Presbyterian Church** (1868), made of locally milled redwood, appears to be facing backward because it once fronted on the old coast highway. The false front of the **Mendocino Hotel** *(48050 Main St)* built by John D. Johnson *(p 117)* in 1878, is all that remains of the original hostelry.

★★ **Mendocino Headlands State Park** – *Open daily year-round. ☎707-937-5397.* Enveloping the town on three sides, these pristine headlands were saved from development in the 1970s by concerned residents. A stroll on the paths that lace the marine terrace reveals spectacular **views**★★ of the Mendocino coast with its fissure-riddled rocks and sea caves.

Kelley House Museum – *45007 Albion St. Open daily year-round. Closed Jan 1, 1st week Oct, Thanksgiving Day, Dec 25. $1. ☎707-937-5791.* Canadian entrepreneur William Kelley built this gabled redwood dwelling—one of the oldest in Mendocino—in 1861. Today the headquarters of Mendocino Historical Research, Inc, the museum owns a collection of over 4,000 historical photographs. Rooms are decorated with period furnishings and artifacts that belonged to the Kelleys and other founding families.

Masonic Hall Building – *10500 Lansing St.* Today owned by the Savings Bank of Mendocino County, whose offices occupy the first floor, this former Masonic temple (1872) is crowned with a sculpture carved from a single block of redwood by Erick Albertson, a Danish Mason who worked at the local mill. The figures atop the cupola, the Angel of Death and the Weeping Maiden, are symbolic to members of the Masonic Order.

Temple of Kwan Tia – *45160 Albion St. Visit by appointment only. ☎707-937-5123.* The single-room joss house (c.1880), or temple, once provided a place of worship for Chinese immigrants who came to Mendocino in the 1850s to seek their fortunes in the lumber industry. Preserved with its original furnishings, the temple honors Kwan Dai, the Chinese god of war.

★ MONO LAKE High Sierras

Map p 246 Tourist Office ☎619-647-6629

Cupped in a broad basin below YOSEMITE NATIONAL PARK, this pale blue body of water and the small islands at its center offer a surreal spectacle of white, mineral-encrusted shores, eerie tufa towers and squadrons of circling gulls. The small tourist town of Lee Vining sits above the lake's western shore, and US-395 contours its western edge.

The Lake of the Flies – One of the oldest lakes on the continent, Mono Lake appeared 700,000 years ago, when runoff from melting glaciers filled an extensive basin-like depression. Once five times larger than its present 60sq mi, the lake, which has no outlet, has slowly evaporated since the end of the last ice age (about 10,000 years ago), leaving behind a residue of minerals; its milky water is 3 times saltier than ocean water, 80 times more alkaline, and has a slippery feel. The distinctive **tufa towers** on the lakeshore were formed underwater when calcium deposits from submerged springs combined with lake water carbonates, creating gnarled limestone spires that were gradually exposed as the water level declined. Once dubbed by Mark Twain the "dead sea of California," Mono Lake is in fact far from dead, supporting a wealth of brine shrimp and alkali flies, which in turn attract migratory birds and year-round waterfowl.

C. Curran

Tufa towers at Mono Lake

Mono Lake's shores were inhabited by Natives as long as 5,500 years ago. Northern Paiutes harvested the alkali flies as food and traded them to the neighboring Yokuts people, whose word *mono*, meaning "fly-eaters," was attached to the lake itself.

A Conservation Battleground – Over past decades, Mono Lake has been the focus of a major legislative dispute that arose when four of its tributary streams were diverted into the Los Angeles Aqueduct *(p 84)*, causing the lake level to drop some 45ft between 1941 and 1981. By the 1970s, conservationists had launched a major campaign to preserve the lake, and in 1984, Congress designated a 116,000-acre region within Inyo National Forest as the Mono Basin National Forest Scenic Area, the first such designation of its kind. The Mono Lake Tufa State Reserve, established by the California Legislature in 1981, encompasses roughly 17,000 acres encircling the lake. In 1991 the El Dorado County superior court issued a preliminary injunction directing that the lake level be maintained at above 6,377ft. The diverted streams are currently feeding the lake under court order, but the legal battle over stream restoration continues; a final decision is expected in the fall of 1994.

VISIT *1/2 day*

15mi from Yosemite National Park (Tioga Pass entrance) by Hwy 120.

★ **Visitor Center** *North end of Lee Vining, off US 395. Open Jun–Oct daily, rest of the year weekends only. ♿ ☎619-647-3044.* Overlooking the lake is a handsome new forest service facility that serves as a museum of the region's natural and human history. Exhibits and a film *(20min)* detail the lake's formation and composition, the unusual food chain that it supports, its current ecological status and the Native presence here.

★★ **South Tufa Area** – *From Lee Vining drive 6mi south on US-395, then take Hwy 120 east for 4.5mi to gravel access road.* This area of the lakeshore is ornamented with towering tufa formations that range from 200 to 900 years old. An interpretive trail *(1mi)* leading through the tufa "forest" is edged with markers that trace the drop in the lake level over the past fifty years. **Navy Beach**, at the east side of the tufa area, is a place to stop for a swim, to experience the increased buoyancy that results from the water's high salt content.

Panum Crater – *Access via turnoff off Hwy 120, 1.5mi east of South Tufa turnoff.* This rimmed crater, formed 640 years ago, is the northernmost of a range of 21 volcanic cones extending south from Mono Lake. Considered the youngest "mountains" in North America, the Mono Craters began building 35,000 years ago through volcanic activity. A short trail leads up to the crater's rim; the obsidian dome in its center formed in a later eruption.

Situated on the west shore above the current water level, the Old Marina Site *(1mi north of visitor center on US-395; open daily year-round; $5/car; ♿)*, offers access to the lake, while at Mono Lake County Park *(4.2mi north of visitor center, then right on Cemetery Rd for .3mi; open daily year-round; $5/car)*, a trail winds from the park area to more tufa formations along the lake.

EXCURSION

★★ **Bodie State Historic Park** – *1/2 day. Map p 246. Follow US-395 north 18mi from Lee Vining, then east on Hwy 270 for 13mi. The last 3mi are unpaved. Road may be closed by snow in winter. Open June–August daily 9am–7pm, rest of the year 4pm. $5/car. ☎619-647-6445.* A poignant and photogenic piece of the "Wild West," this authentic, unrestored ghost town nestles in the silent hills of the high desert. Once a booming mining center of 10,000 souls, Bodie today is virtually deserted, though torn curtains still hang in windows and glasses gather dust in saloons.

"Badmen from Bodie" – In 1859 gold prospector Waterman S. Bodey discovered placer deposits *(p 61)* in these hills. Although he died the following year, others who searched the area after him gave a version of his name to the hills. A significant vein of ore was struck in 1874, and two years later the Standard Consolidated Company bought out a local mine, expanding operations and bringing an overwhelming wave of gold seekers into Bodie. By 1880 some 30 mines were operating here, and the town boasted 10,000 people, 2,000 buildings (among them 3 breweries and dozens of saloons), and a very bad reputation. Gunfights, robberies and other crimes were commonplace, leading wags to comment that Bodie suffered from the "worst climate out of doors." By 1882, however, Bodie's boom was over, and a decade later, fire destroyed much of its business district. A second fire in 1932 consumed 90 percent of the town's remaining structures.
The Standard Mine and Mill continued to function until World War II, when all gold mining was temporarily banned. In the early 1940s, the school and post office closed, and Bodie gradually became a ghost town. The state acquired it as a historic park in 1962, and now maintains the site in a condition of "arrested decay," meaning that while nothing is significantly changed or improved, the buildings are protected from further deterioration.

Visit – *2hrs. Self-guided tour booklet ($1) available at the entrance booth or the museum.* Some 150 buildings, most of them picturesquely weathered clapboard structures, still stand along the streets of Bodie, and visitors may peer through windows to view their abandoned, dilapidated interiors. Only the modest **Miller House** *(Green St)*, with its threadbare furnishings, is open to visitors, while the simple interior of the **Old Methodist Church** *(Green and Fuller Sts)* may be viewed through open doors. The **Miners Union Hall** on Main Street now functions as a park museum and visitor center, with cases displaying town photographs, clothing, utensils and other memorabilia *(open daily Jun–Sept)*. The processing buildings of the Standard Mine and Mill still loom over the northeastern edge of town. *Processing buildings accessible by guided tours only on summer weekends.*

★★ MONTEREY Central Coast — Pop 31,954

Map p 122

At the southern end of Monterey Bay, 115mi south of SAN FRANCISCO, California's longtime Spanish-Mexican capital retains its historic adobe charm, at the same time celebrating its 20C heritage as a fishing and cannery town.

El Puerto de Monterey – Ohlone Natives had been living in the area of present-day Monterey for more than a thousand years by the time the Spanish expedition under Juan Rodríguez Cabrillo sighted the bay from the sea in 1542 *(p 22)*. In 1602 Sebastián Vizcaíno rediscovered the area, made a landing near present-day Fisherman's Wharf and named the bay after his patron and the viceroy of New Spain, the Count of Monte Rey. Not until 1770, however, did the Spanish return. Based on Vizcaíno's glowing accounts of the area, Gaspar de Portolá was dispatched from Baja California with orders to establish Monterey as the first presidio in Alta California. Portolá was accompanied by Padre Junípero Serra, who was charged with founding a chain of missions along the coast. A historic marker commemorates the **landing site** of Vizcaíno and Portolá *(on Pacific St, at the southeast corner of the present-day Presidio)*.
Portolá built the original presidio near the southwest end of El Estero, and Serra quickly established a mission and began converting the local Natives to Catholicism. However, the padre found the soil there poor and the soldiers of the presidio a less than favorable influence on his converts, so a year later he relocated his CARMEL MISSION to its present site by the Carmel River. In 1775 Spain declared Monterey the capital of Alta and Baja California, and it became the Pacific coast's principal town. After Mexican independence in 1821, Monterey remained the provincial capital, and, with the repeal of old Spanish trading restrictions, it also became a thriving international port for the trade in cow hide and tallow.

View of Monterey in 1842

MAY WE SUGGEST FOUR MORE WAYS TO IMPROVE YOUR JOURNEY?

SET OUT ON A NEW SET

For the best the road has to offer, drive the best tires for the road. Michelin® makes them for whatever you drive.

PERFORMANCE TOURING CARS

Our MXV4™ brings out more performance and comfort in your performance touring car. You'll get a combination of responsive handling and ride only Michelins can provide, thanks to our exclusive Bead Tension Structure™. Plus all-season grip so superior, we call it Climate Control.

MXV4 offers the perfect blend of performance and comfort.

FAMILY CARS

With its breakthrough 80,000 Mile Treadwear Limited Warranty, our all-season XH4® may last as long as you own your family car. And the Michelin MX4® offers another reassurance families will value. Unequaled wet traction in an all-season tire that helps keep you going no matter what the weather brings.

The world's first 80,000-mile tires reflect Michelin's technological leadership.

The Michelin MX4 delivers unequaled wet traction with a proprietary rubber compound and three water channeling grooves.

OF MICHELIN® TI ES.

Michelin Higher Performance Tires are original equipment on some of the world's fastest cars.

HIGH PERFORMANCE CARS

With Michelin XGT® Series tires you'll boldly experience the outer performance limits engineered into your high performance car. Special belt technology delivers superb high-speed stability. And Bead Tension Structure ensures crisp steering response while it filters out road harshness. Our XGT Series tires deliver performance so outstanding we call them The Higher Performance Tires.™

LIGHT TRUCKS

If you drive a light truck – a pickup, van, or sport utility vehicle – Michelin can enhance its performance, too. Our LTX® Series tires set a new standard of durability. And blend traction with quiet comfort like no light truck tires before them.

Michelin LTX Series tires deliver rugged performance with no compromise in ride comfort.

You've got our Guide. Now, add our tires. And enjoy all the pleasures of the road.

MICHELIN®

BECAUSE SO MUCH IS RIDING ON YOUR TIRES.®

An increasing US interest in California culminated on July 7, 1846, when Commodore John Sloat landed in Monterey with 225 soldiers and proclaimed California part of America. Soon after the peaceful takeover, Monterey's fortunes turned. In 1849 the state capital was moved to SAN JOSE, and at the same time, gold fever swept California, taking with it many of Monterey's inhabitants. By 1850 the old capital had lapsed into oblivion.

Of Riches and Fishes – In 1880 Monterey regained prominence as a travel destination with the opening of its elegant **Hotel del Monte**, the brainchild of Southern Pacific Railroad moguls. One of the West's first resorts, the Del Monte (today home to the Naval Post-graduate School) offered its guests golfing, tennis, and carriage rides along the 17-Mile Drive *(p 124)*.

During the same period, Chinese and Italian fishermen had discovered the rich harvests afforded by the deep waters of Monterey Bay and **Monterey Canyon**, a 60mi-long submerged gorge whose cold, upwelling waters are rich in nutrients and support a wealth of marine life. In the early 1900s, a sardine canning operation opened in town, and Monterey was soon on its way to becoming the "Sardine Capital of the World." This lucrative industry lasted until the early 1950s, when the fish suddenly disappeared from the waters off Monterey.

Since 1958 the city has played host to the acclaimed annual **Monterey Jazz Festival** *(September)*, the oldest continuously operating event of its kind in the US. In recent decades, the Monterey Peninsula has again become a popular tourist destination and a favored weekend getaway for metropolites from the San Francisco Bay Area.

Practical Information

Area Code: 408

Getting There – From **San Francisco** (130mi): US-101 south to Hwy 15 west. From **Los Angeles** (347mi): US-101 north to Hwy 68 west. **Monterey Peninsula Airport** (MRY): domestic flights ☎373-3731; taxi service ($10) to downtown area and hotel courtesy shuttles. Major rental car agencies *(p 253)*. Amtrak **train** station: 11 Station Place, Salinas (20mi from Monterey), fare includes transfer ☎800-872-7245. Greyhound **bus** depot: 1042 Del Monte Ave (at Exxon gas station) ☎800-231-2222.

Getting Around – **Monterey-Salinas Transit** W.A.V.E. shuttle service to major attractions throughout the city (operates every 15min, Memorial Day–Labor Day daily, rest of the year weekends only, $.50/day) ☎899-2555. Parking garages & metered lots located throughout the city, parking regulations strictly enforced.

Visitor Information – **Monterey Peninsula Chamber of Commerce and Visitors & Convention Bureau Visitor Center**, 380 Alvarado St (open year-round Mon–Fri 8:30am–5pm); mailing address PO Box 1770, Monterey, CA 93942 ☎649-1770. **Monterey Visitors Center**, located on Lake El Estero at Camino El Estero & Franklin Sts (open year-round Mon–Sat 9am–5pm, Sun 10am–4pm).

Accommodations – *Monterey Peninsula Visitors Guide* lodging directory available (free) from the visitor center *(above)*. Accommodations range from elegant hotels & resorts ($120-$275/day), to moderate inns ($60-$135/day). Most bed & breakfasts are located in residential sections of the city ($80-$165/day). Reservation & referral services: **Bay Lodging Reservations** ☎655-1426, **Resort II Me** ☎646-9250. **Campsites** at Veterans Memorial Park ☎646-3865. *Rates quoted are average prices for a double room.*

** HISTORIC MONTEREY

Tours and information on historic buildings available at Stanton Center and Pacific House, both fronting Custom House Plaza. All sites open Wed, and Fri–Sun. Closed Jan 1, Thanksgiving Day, Dec 25. Combination ticket ($5) available for two days, 4 houses & walking tours; individual house museums $2. ☎408-649-7118.

Monterey's Spanish colonial past is still visible in the roughly two dozen mid-19C adobes scattered among the modern structures of downtown. The preservation of these adobes began in the early 1900s, with a grassroots effort to have the Custom House *(p 122)* designated a historic landmark. Throughout the 20C, local groups have contributed funds and manpower to the preservation of other historic buildings. With the creation of the California Park Service in the late 1920s, the state also became involved. Today, the Monterey State Historic Park encompasses 17 sites. An annual **Adobe Tour** is held in late April; **Christmas in the Adobes** is celebrated in mid-December. *Historic adobes are designated by plaques.*

Visit *At least 1 day*

A number of historic buildings are clustered around the waterfront near **Fisherman's Wharf**, once a working dock for the city's fishermen, today a commercial tourist spot lined with shops and eateries. **Pacific House**, a 2-story adobe built in 1847 by Thomas Larkin *(p 123)* to house US troops, now serves as the park information center and a museum of California history *(open daily year-round)*.

* **Maritime Museum of Monterey at Stanton Center** – *Custom House Plaza. Open Jun–Aug daily, rest of the year Tue–Sun. Closed Thanksgiving Day, Dec 25. $5.* ♿ 🅿 *☎408-373-2469.* Formerly the Allen Knight Maritime Museum, this collection devoted to the nautical history of the area is now housed in the sleek new Stanton Center (1992). Exhibits cover the history of Monterey from the 17C to the 20C; model ships and their creation; and navigational devices, including the 1,000-prism Fresnel lens (1887) from the Point Sur Light Station *(p 43)*.

Also located at Stanton Center is the Monterey State Historic Park visitor center, offering information, guided tours of selected historic buildings, and a film *(14min)* depicting Monterey's colorful past.

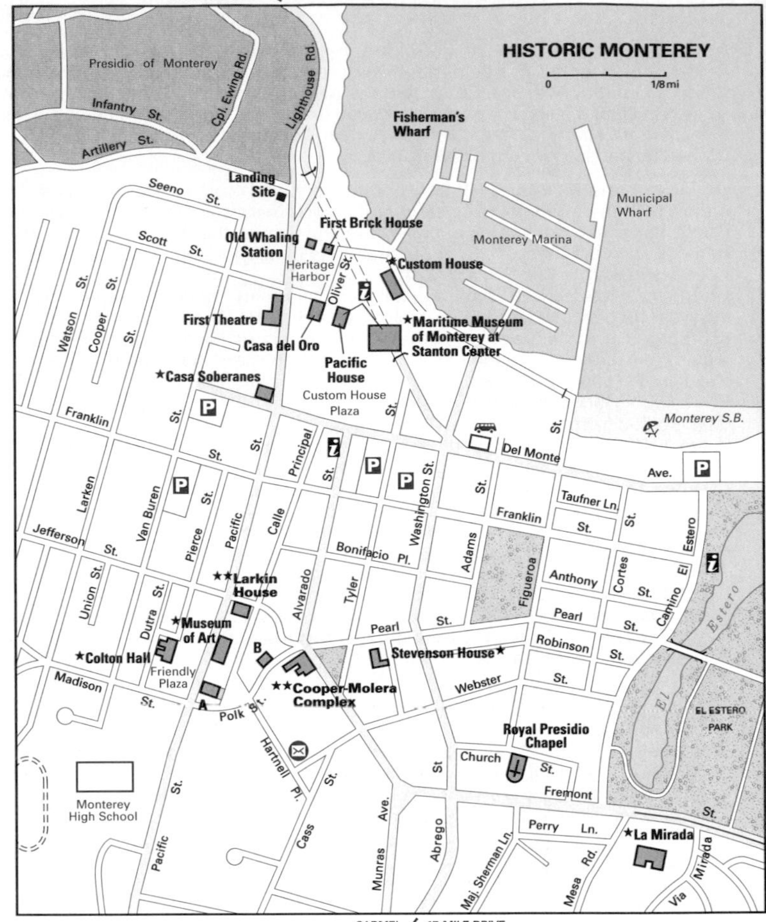

★ **Custom House** – *Custom House Plaza. Open daily year-round.* Reputedly the oldest government building west of the Rockies, the adobe Custom House bears the designation of California Landmark no. 1. Its 2-story north section was erected in 1827, and the building, with later additions, served continuously as a customhouse until 1867. The interior re-creates the building's appearance during the 1830s and 1840s, when it served as the hub of maritime commerce along the Pacific coast. The flagpole at the north end of the building marks the site where the American flag was raised in 1846 *(p 121)*.

At the far end of the nearby Heritage Harbor complex lies the **First Brick House**, begun in 1847 as the town's first home constructed of kiln-fired (rather than adobe) bricks. Recently restored, it now traces the lifestyles of past owners during the home's hundred-year occupancy. Beside it rises the **Old Whaling Station** (1847), a 2-story adobe modeled after the builder's ancestral home in Scotland. Used as an office and rooming house for Portuguese whalers in the mid-19C, the house is fronted by a walkway embedded with whale vertebrae.

A block south on Pacific Street, California's **First Theatre** (late 1840s) continues to feature 19C live-performance melodramas in its adobe wing, adjacent to the original redwood tavern. One block east on Scott Street, the 2-story **Casa del Oro**, built by Thomas Larkin *(p 123)* in the mid-1840s as a general store, has been restored and reopened as a gift shop.

★ **Casa Soberanes** – *336 Pacific St. Visit by guided tour (30min) only, year-round Mon, Wed, Fri–Sun.* A sloping garden bordered by a cypress hedge fronts this "house with the blue gate." Built in the 1840s, the adobe, with its 3ft-thick walls, is a charming example of Monterey Colonial architecture. A cantilevered balcony runs along the 2-story facade, while the rear of the house slants down to one story. The interior combines the furnishings of previous owners, including 19C New England pieces, China trade pieces and Mexican folk art.

★ **Colton Hall** – *Open daily year-round. Closed Thanksgiving Day, Dec 25. ☎408-646-5640.* Situated on a knoll above Friendly Plaza, this stately, porticoed building, constructed in 1849 of Monterey shale, was conceived as a public meeting hall and school by Monterey's first American administrator, Rev Walter Colton. In 1849 California's Constitutional Convention met here.The large meeting room *(2nd floor)* is furnished as it was during the convention; note the small pine table on which the constitution was signed on October 13, 1849.

At the north side of Colton Hall, the stone **Old Monterey Jail** reveals several restored cells tracing the jail's century-long history (1855-1959).

Across Pacific Street, the **Casa Gutierrez [A]**, one of the few extant examples of a simple Mexican-style adobe, now houses a restaurant.

★ **Monterey Peninsula Museum of Art** – *559 Pacific St. Open year-round Tue–Sun. Closed Jan 1, Thanksgiving Day, Dec 25. $2. ♿ ☎408-372-7591.* Founded in 1959, this museum is devoted to folk, tribal, ethnic and contemporary art. Its permanent collection, concentrating on regional and California art in addition to the arts of Asia and the Pacific Rim, also includes pieces by Man Ray, Picasso, Ansel Adams and Edward Weston.

★★ **Larkin House** – *Calle Principal and Pearl St; entrance through garden. Visit by guided tour (30min) only, Memorial Day–Labor Day Mon, Wed, Fri–Sun 10am–5pm, rest of the year 4pm.* This substantial adobe was built in 1834 by Thomas O. Larkin, a prosperous 19C merchant who served as US consul and secret agent before and during the American takeover of Alta California. A native of Massachusetts, Larkin designed a home that melded elements of New England architecture—including high ceilings, a hipped roof and central hallway—with the local adobe motif, giving rise to the architectural style today known as Monterey Colonial. The furnishings include family pieces and antiques collected worldwide by Larkin's granddaughter, Alice Larkin Toulmin, who lived here from 1922-57. The walled garden encompasses a 1-room stone structure that served as William Tecumseh Sherman's residence when he was stationed here as a young lieutenant in the mid-19C.

★★ **Cooper-Molera Complex** – *Pearl St at Munras Ave and Polk St. Visit by guided tour (45min) only, Memorial Day–Labor Day Tue–Sun 10am–1pm, rest of the year 10am–noon.* The 2-acre site features a lush period garden; a 19C carriage house; a visitor center, book and gift shop; and a large home whose separate wings reflect the quixotic fortunes of John Rogers Cooper, a half-brother of Thomas Larkin *(above).* Settling in Monterey in 1827, Cooper built a single-story adobe, the north end of which still stands and is furnished in simple period pieces. In the 1850s, when Cooper's fortunes took a lucrative turn, he appended a second story to the original adobe. The first floor of this structure now reflects the 1860s period, while the second floor is decorated with turn-of-the-century antiques.

Across Polk Street stands **Casa Amesti [B]**, another elegant example of the Monterey Colonial style. The 2-story adobe, begun in the 1830s, was home to interior decorator Francis Elkins from 1918-1953 and still contains many of her furnishings. Now owned by the National Trust for Historic Preservation, the building is leased by the Old Capitol Club, a men's organization.

★ **Stevenson House** – *530 Houston St. Visit by guided tour (30min) only, year-round Tue–Sun.* The original back wing of this adobe was built in the 1830s and served as the residence of Rafael Gonzales, the town's customs collector. After 1850, the building was expanded into a large adobe boarding house. Famed American author Robert Louis Stevenson resided here for several months in 1879 while courting Fanny Osborne. The interior now contains period furnishings along with Stevenson's furniture and memorabilia, much of it reflecting his last years on the island of Samoa.

Royal Presidio Chapel – *Church and Figueroa Sts.* The stone-and-adobe structure (1795), California's only extant presidio chapel, claims direct descent from the original Monterey mission founded by Padre Serra in 1770 *(p 120).* After Serra moved his mission in 1771 to its present location in CARMEL, Monterey's presidio chapel continued to serve the military. Its stonemasons, Manuel and Santiago Ruíz, also built the Carmel mission church. Though the bell tower is a later addition, the ornate facade, topped by a statue of the Virgin of Guadalupe, and the stations of the cross *(interior)* are original. The entry alcove displays a portion of the oak under which Serra said the first Mass in Monterey.

★ **La Mirada** – *720 Via Mirada. Open year-round Thu–Sun. Closed Jan 1, Thanksgiving Day, Dec 25. $5. ♿ 🅿 ☎408-372-3000.* Owned by the museum, this early-19C adobe crowns a wooded knoll southeast of downtown. Expanded in the early 20C, the home is now furnished with antiques and contemporary decorative arts, and surrounded by lovely gardens. A new wing was added to the structure in 1993; galleries display the museum's collection of *netsuke* (Japanese carved toggles); early Chinese ceramics and bronzes; and an extensive collection of works by San Francisco-born artist Armin Hansen, who has been called the "Winslow Homer of the West" for his oil paintings and etchings depicting themes of the sea.

★ CANNERY ROW *3hrs. Map p 40.*

"A poem, a stink, a grating noise . . . " author John Steinbeck called it in his 1945 literary classic, *Cannery Row,* set in the raucous old industrial area situated northwest of downtown. Sardine canneries first appeared here in the early 20C. By the advent of World War I, Monterey's sardines were in demand worldwide, and millions of cases were canned annually. In 1950 the fish abruptly disappeared from the bay—either from overharvesting or changes in ocean conditions—and most canneries shut down. Today, Cannery Row has been reborn as a popular tourist area, its old cannery buildings, bars and brothels now housing shops and restaurants. An untouched piece of the past still stands, however, at no. 800: the weather-beaten marine lab of "Doc" Ricketts, Steinbeck's friend and the main character in the novel.

★★ **Monterey Bay Aquarium** – *West end of Cannery Row. Open Jun–Aug daily 9:30am–6pm, rest of the year daily 10am–6pm. Closed Dec 25. $11.25. ✕ ♿ ☎408-648-4888.* Styled after the old Hovden Cannery that stood at this end of Cannery Row, the state-of-the-art aquarium houses a wide range of sea life in its enormous tanks. Built out over the water, it is devoted to presenting and conserving Monterey Bay's rich marine life.

In 1978 marine biologists working in nearby Pacific Grove conceived the idea of converting the old Hovden plant, largest of the canneries and the last one to cease operation (1972), into an aquarium. Fortuitously, two of the biologists were the daughter and son-in-law of philanthropist David Packard, a founder of Hewlett-Packard electronics. Packard and his family provided financial backing for the aquarium and were intimately involved in its conception and design. The San Francisco firm of Esherick, Homsey, Dodge and Davis designed the 216,000sq ft aquarium with decks and open spaces that incorporate the sea as an element of the architecture. The aquarium opened in 1984, and plans are underway for a new wing on the open ocean and deep sea *(scheduled opening 1996)*.

★ **Kelp Forest** – Centerpiece of the aquarium, this 335,000gal, 28ft-high tank—one of the world's tallest aquarium exhibits—contains giant kelp that can grow 4-6in a day. Leopard sharks, sardines, rockfish and a host of invertebrates including crabs, sea stars and sea cucumbers, cruise and creep among the swaying fronds. *Public feedings daily 11:30am, 4pm.*

Habitats Path – This route weaves through the west side of the aquarium's first floor, past re-creations of the various environments and creatures found both in the bay and along its shoreline, including octopuses, wolf-eels, and a touch pool for fast-gliding bat rays. The Sandy Shore, an open-air aviary, is home to shorebirds; and a final exhibit is devoted to Steinbeck's immortal Doc Ricketts.

Monterey Bay Habitats – Part of the Habitats Path, the 90ft-long tank re-creates four bay habitats and offers a spectacle of gliding sharks, bass, rays and rockfish. It was designed to give the sharks inhabiting it the kind of long straightaway they need to optimize their breathing and resting patterns.

★ **The Great Tide Pool** – Water from the bay courses into this man-made tide pool, bringing with it specimens of intertidal life, including sea stars, anemones, crabs, and even sea otters and harbor seals. Aquarium staff occasionally swim here with orphaned otter pups, preparing the animals for a return to the wild as part of the aquarium's Sea Otter Rescue and Care program. Also located here is the **Sea Otter** pool *(interior)*, one of the aquarium's most popular attractions. *Public feedings daily 10:30am, 1:30, 3:30pm.*

Major special exhibits are housed on the second floor, while the third floor is devoted to "Watching the Bay," a permanent exhibit celebrating the Monterey Bay National Marine Sanctuary. An exhibit detailing the operations of the old Hovden Cannery is located outside the aquarium entrance.

EXCURSIONS

Pacific Grove – Pop 16,117. Occupying the tip of the Monterey Peninsula, this pleasant, low-key community reflects its 1870s beginnings as a Methodist seaside resort. A number of early board-and-batten Victorian cottages still stand along Lighthouse Avenue, as do more elaborate Queen Annes, some of which now house inns and restaurants. Wild, windswept **Point Piños**, anchored by the oldest continuously operating lighthouse (1855) in the western US, juts into the Pacific on the west side of town.

Known as "Butterfly Town, USA," Pacific Grove is famous for the thousands of **monarch butterflies** that winter here from November to March. Butterflies can be sighted in Washington Park *(Pine Ave off 17-Mile Drive St)* and in the woods at Ridge Road and Short Street. The **Museum of Natural History [M]** *(165 Forest Ave)* features exhibits on monarch butterflies, as well as an extensive collection of taxidermied seabirds *(open year-round Tue–Sun; ♿ 🅿 ☎408-648-3119)*.

★★ **17-Mile Drive** – *Map p 40. Accessible via Pacific Grove Gate, off Sunset Dr; and Country Club Gate, off Congress Ave in Pacific Grove. Open daily year-round. $6/car. ✗ ☎408-649-8500.* Celebrated for its sylvan passages, glimpses of wildlife and exquisite views of the Pacific, this private toll road winds through the exclusive Pebble Beach residential enclave, past luxuriant oceanside golf greens, and into the 8,000-acre Del Monte Forest with its groves of gnarled Monterey cypress trees.

From the northernmost entrance gate at Pacific Grove, the drive passes its first golf resort, then bends west to join the coastline of Spanish Bay, so named because Gaspar de Portolá *(p 23)* camped here in 1769. Off rock-riven **Point Joe**, a favorite roosting place for seabirds, the turbulent surf is the result of two currents converging. Beyond the point lies the **Coastal Bluffs Walking Trail**, offering opportunities to explore the area's abundant tide pools.

Sea lions, harbor seals, sea otters and birds can be spotted at **Seal Rock** and **Bird Rock**. The **Cypress Point Lookout** affords **views**★ of the northern coastal bluffs and the sea stacks that stretch south. The **Lone Cypress**, classic landmark of the Monterey Peninsula, clings to its bald rock promontory above the Pacific. After bending around Pescadero Point, the drive winds through an enclave of wooded estates before reaching the renowned Pebble Beach resort. From the Carmel Gate, southernmost entryway to the drive, the road loops north through the residential neighborhoods nestled in the Del Monte Forest. At **Shepherd's Knoll Vista Point**, the **view**★ extends across Monterey Bay to the looming Gabilan Mountains.

★★ **Carmel** – *1/2 day. Description p 39.*

". . . over the green higher hills to the south, the evening fog rolled like herds of sheep coming to cote in the golden city."

John Steinbeck, 1962

★★ MT SHASTA Shasta-Cascade

Map of Principal Sights p 2 Tourist Office ☎916-926-4865

Described by poet Joaquin Miller as "lonely as God and white as the winter moon," this 14,162ft mountain is the second highest volcano in the **Cascade Range**, the majestic column of volcanic mountains traversing Washington, Oregon and northern California. Shorter than the Sierra Nevada's MT WHITNEY, Mt Shasta boasts a 17mi base and thus ranks as California's largest mountain mass. Towering above the surrounding landscape, its cloud-draped, snowclad, double-peaked summit is visible for miles in every direction, and has long been a source of inspiration to travelers, hikers, skiers and mystics.

A Mountain of Fire and Ice – Mt Shasta began forming about 400,000 years ago, but began to take its present shape roughly 10,000 years ago; its peak is composed of several volcanic masses. Research indicates that for the past few millennia, the mountain has erupted an average of every 500 years, and the most recent activity appears to have occurred some 200 years ago. Mt Shasta is now considered an active, though quiescent, volcano.

Seven glaciers, remnants of ice masses from the Little Ice Age (20C BC –18C AD), now drape Mt Shasta's summit, and are most noticeable on its north-facing slopes. The Whitney glacier, the largest in California, sprawls between the main summit and **Shastina**, the mountain's smaller western peak (12,433ft).

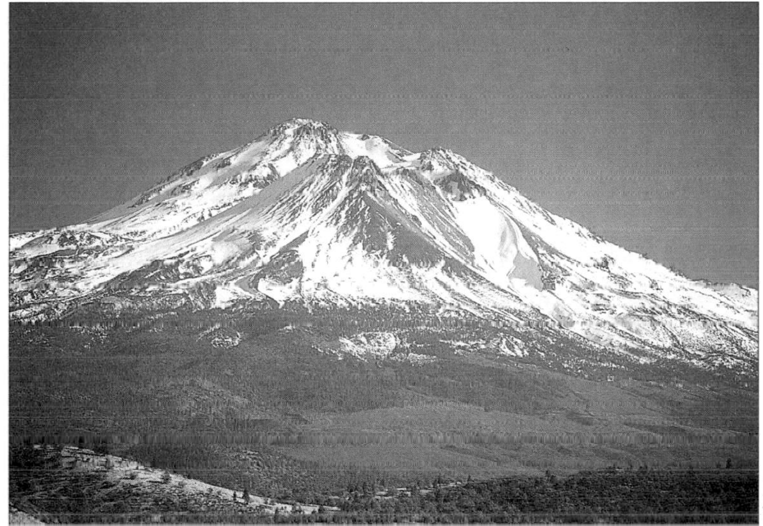

_niphoto

Mt Shasta

Long considered a place of special spiritual significance, Mt Shasta is believed by the Modoc, Wintu, Klamath and Shasta Natives of this region to be the first earthly place inhabited by the Chief of the Sky Spirits, and many New Age devotees regard it as sacred and worthy of pilgrimage. Owing to its porous composition, the mountain is water-permeable, and street-corner drinking fountains abound in nearby towns, offering passersby a chance to sample the pure, sweet, spring waters that seep from its base.

SIGHTS *1 day*

Mount Shasta – The small city located below the mountain's southwestern flank serves as a gateway to Mt Shasta and to the ski slopes at Mt Shasta Ski Park *(10mi east of Mount Shasta on Hwy 89; ski information p 260; ☎916-926-868)*. Hotels, campgrounds, restaurants, ski shops and other visitor facilities cater to those who come to partake of the mountain's outdoor recreational opportunities. Originally a stopping point on the route between the gold mining community of Yreka and the settlements of the northern Sacramento Valley, the city took the name of the looming mountain shortly after World War I.

The city's mix of shops reflects the mountain's diverse appeal: outfitter establishments serve a mountaineering and hiking clientele, while New Age shops carry occult literature and paraphernalia. The Sacramento River's northernmost source is located here, at **Big Spring** *(in City Park, off N. Mt Shasta Blvd)*. The US Forest Service **ranger station** *(204 W. Alma St; open May–Oct daily, rest of the year Mon–Fri; ☎916-626-4511)* offers information on hiking, skiing and other recreational opportunities on the mountain.

Sisson Museum and Mount Shasta Fish Hatchery – *1 N. Old Stage Rd at its junction with W. Lake St. Open year-round daily. Closed Jan 1, Easter Sunday, Thanksgiving Day, Dec 2 & mid-Jan–Feb. ♿ ☎916-926-5508.* This small museum features exhibits on pioneering, mountaineering, geology and Native American craftsmanship. Housed in a former fish hatchery building, the museum is adjacent to the hatching and rearing ponds of California's oldest trout hatchery; visitors can browse the hatching and rearing ponds to view fish in various stages of development.

Everitt Memorial Highway – *12mi. Begin at the east end of Alma St in Mount Shasta.* Threading the south slopes of Mt Shasta, this scenic highway offers extensive **views** of the surrounding terrain, including Lake Siskiyou and lesser mountain peaks to the south. Some 2mi north of Mount Shasta, the highway passes **Black Butte**, a distinctive 6,325ft conical plug dome composed of dark andesite lava that resulted from a series of eruptions over several thousand years.

Bunny Flat Scenic Trail – *10.8mi north of Mount Shasta. Trailhead at Bunny Flat parking area.* This popular trail climbs gently through meadows and scattered forests of Shasta red-fir trees to Horse Camp, a popular base for hikers planning to ascend the slopes of Mt Shasta. Dedicated in 1923, the stone **Sierra Club Lodge** *(open to the public)* sits below the southern summit, allowing exceptional **views**★★ of the mountain. The stone Olberman's Causeway, a traditional route for climbers continuing on to the summit, ascends above the tree line behind the lodge.

EXCURSIONS

Dunsmuir – Pop 2129. *1hr. 6mi south of Mount Shasta via I-5.* This picturesque town situated on the banks of the Sacramento River was an important railroad division point from the late 19C through the mid-20C. The town was originally named Pusher, because of the extra engines that were added here to push trains over the high elevations to the north. In 1886 a young Canadian named Alexander Dunsmuir offered to erect a water fountain for the townspeople if city fathers would rename the town for him. The fountain, burbling with pure Shasta drinking water, still stands in City Park. At the northern edge of town, on Frontage Road, a short trail leads to **Hedge Creek Falls**, a 30ft waterfall cutting through the remains of a river of basaltic lava that flowed through here from Mt Shasta thousands of years ago. The gazebo beside the trailhead offers a lovely **view**★ of the Sacramento River Canyon and the rail line running through it.

★ **Castle Crags** – *3hrs. 14mi south of Mount Shasta at the Castella exit.* These polished granite spires rise dramatically like sudden, unexpected sentinels along the northwest side of Interstate 5. Although created by the same tectonic instability that produced the Cascade Range, the crags are far more ancient, having formed between 170 and 225 million years ago. Today, their jagged surfaces polished by glacial action and weathering, the spires achieve heights of more than 6,000ft. The formations themselves are protected within the National Forest Service's 11,000-acre Castle Crags Wilderness, but are best viewed from **Castle Crags State Park**, a pleasant camping, hiking and recreational site bordering the south and east sides of the Wilderness *(open daily year-round; $4/car; ⛺ ♿ ☎916-235-2684)*. A narrow paved road winds 2mi through the park and up Kettelbelly Ridge to wooded **Vista Point**, which affords a spectacular **view**★ of the crags and the asymmetrical rise of Mt Shasta. The **Indian Creek Trail** *(1mi loop; trailhead across from park headquarters)* offers interpretive explanations of regional flora, fauna and history.

★★ NORTH COAST North Coast

Map p 127 Tourist Office ☎415-543-8334

Stretching 191mi from SAN FRANCISCO to north of Ft Bragg, where it joins US-101, Highway 1 snakes along the edge of the southern half of California's North Coast. On this route, spectacular views abound of steep, rocky cliffs pummeled by roiling Pacific surf. Sleepy seaside towns and state parks punctuate the wild shoreline, which nurtures a variety of birds and marine animals.

Marine Terraces – California's North Coast consists mainly of shale and sandstone Franciscan rocks that date back as far as 150 million years. Wave action has carved these relatively soft sediments into vertical benches backed by steep cliffs. When the Pacific plate slipped underneath the western edge of the North American plate *(p 12)*, it lifted these terraces above sea level. Continued tectonic activity, coupled with the fluctuating sea level caused by the advance and retreat of ice age glaciers, created the series of marine terraces visible along the coast. In Mendocino County, these terraces form a series of steps—the highest step being the oldest—each of which boasts a specialized ecosystem.

The same action that uplifted the marine terraces caused sea floor sediments along the North American plate to crumple and fold, forming the Coast Ranges with their ridges and valleys that parallel the continent's edge. North of Mendocino County, the terraces disappear, replaced by mountains that plunge sharply into the sea. These cliffs are composed of granitic rock, which is more resistant to erosion. Small pocket beaches characterize such coastal areas, whereas softer shale and sandstone cliffs to the south yield to longer stretches of beach.

Natives and Fur Traders – As early as 10,000 BC, Coast Miwok, Pomo and Yuki tribes hunted and fished along this part of the coast. The Natives met their first European in 1579, when English explorer Francis Drake *(p 145)* anchored his ship here for three weeks to make repairs. Although the Spanish explored and claimed this region of Alta California as early as the 16C, they never cemented their interests by establishing settlements. Thus, members of a Russian trading company met no resistance when they built the colony of Fort Ross *(p 128)* here in 1812.

With the exception of the Russians, this wilderness was inhabited only by Natives and fur traders until gold was discovered in the Smith and Klamath rivers in 1848. As the gold rush dissipated, the "red gold" of the area's virgin redwood forests brought an influx of loggers. Present-day residents continue to earn their livelihood by logging, commercial fishing and farming in the fertile valleys adjoining the coast; tourism, too, plays an ever-increasing role in the region's economy.

Visiting the North Coast – Temperatures along the coast remain moderate, with a year-round average high temperature of 65°F. Most of the region's rain falls in winter; summer months experience frequent fog. The best times to visit are in spring, when the otherwise-sere hillsides turn brilliant green and multicolored wildflowers festoon the meadows; and in fall, when the weather is apt to be fine. Amenities along Highway 1 from San Francisco to MacKerricher State Park are few. From south to north, Inverness, Bodega Bay, Gualala, Elk, Little River, Mendocino and Fort Bragg are good places to find lodging, restaurants and gas stations.

FROM SAN FRANCISCO TO FORT BRAGG *5 days. 159mi.*

★★ **Muir Woods National Monument** – *12mi north of the Golden Gate Bridge. Take US-101 to Hwy 1; continue 3mi and turn right on Panoramic Hwy and left on Muir Woods Rd. Open year-round daily 8am–sunset.* ✗ ♿ *☎415-388-2595.* This 560-acre plot of coast redwoods *(p 149)* remains the only virgin redwood forest in the Bay area. In 1905 Congressman William Kent purchased 295 acres of the redwood canyon, spared from loggers' saws owing to its inaccessibility. Muir Woods became a national monument in 1908 when Kent donated his land to the Federal Government, insisting that the park be named for conservationist John Muir *(p 241)*, who proclaimed it "the best tree-lover's monument that could possibly be found in all the forests of the world."

The level, paved Main Trail Loop *(1mi)* starts at the visitors center and continues to **Cathedral Grove**, where venerable trees—the oldest of which is 1,000 years of age—rise like spires toward the heavens. The return trail passes **Bohemian Grove**, the site of the park's tallest tree, measuring 252ft *(tree is unmarked)*.

Return to Hwy 1; after 3mi turn left at sign indicating scenic overlook.

The road leads to **Muir Beach Overlook**, where a wooden platform on the rock promontory affords sweeping **views**★ of the coast, including the GOLDEN GATE BRIDGE to the south. From the hooded concrete burrow behind the promontory, American forces calculated the position of Japanese ships during World War II.

Continue on Hwy 1; turn right on Panoramic Hwy and continue 8mi to the visitor center parking area.

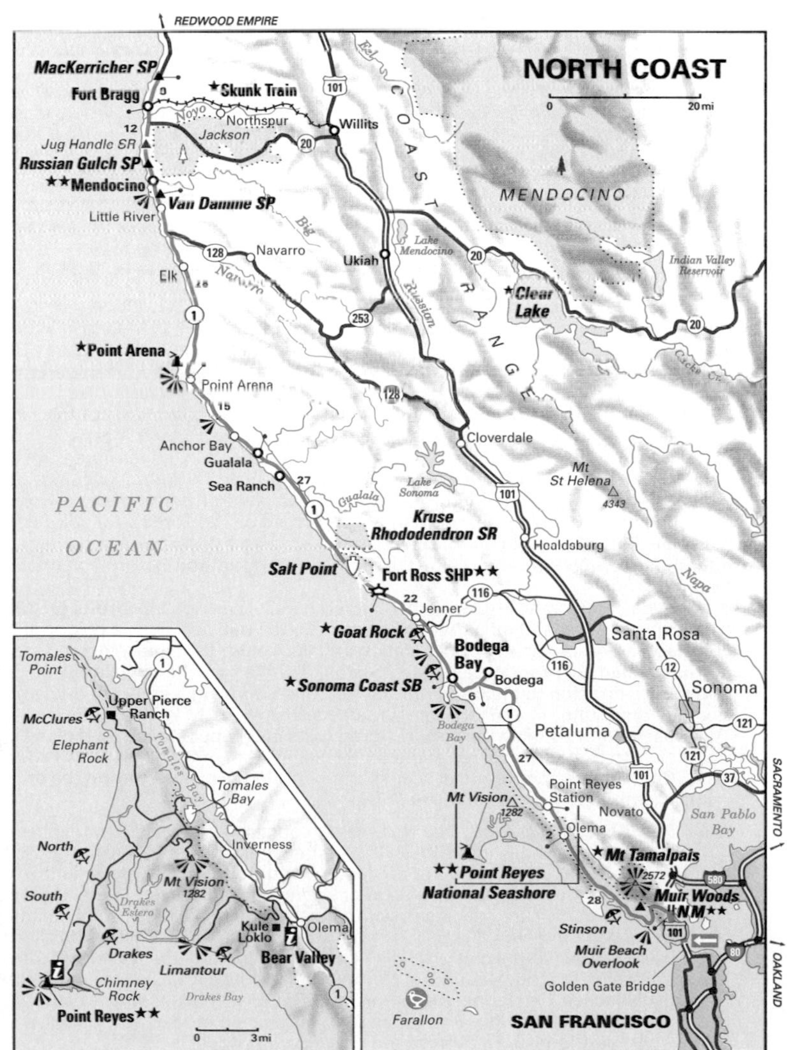

★ **Mt Tamalpais** – *Parking fee $5 at summit.* The serpentine ascent to the 2,572ft east peak of Mt Tamalpais (Tamal-PIE-us), known locally as "Mt Tam," is amply rewarded with sweeping **views★★★** embracing San Francisco and its bay to the southeast, and the Pacific coastline to the west. This lofty summit also provides an excellent vantage point for viewing the dramatic spectacle of fog banks enshrouding such landmarks as the Golden Gate Bridge.

Return to Hwy 1.

The road affords glimpses of expansive **Stinson Beach**, the area's most popular stretch of sandy shoreline.

Continue 19mi on Hwy 1 to Olema.

★★ **Point Reyes National Seashore** – *1 1/2 days. Description p 145.*

Follow Hwy 1 to Point Reyes Station (2mi). Continue north 27mi. Turn right at sign for Bodega; after almost 1mi, turn right on Bodega Lane.

In the town of **Bodega** you will find the building *(17110 Bodega Lane)* that served as the schoolhouse in Alfred Hitchcock's film *The Birds* (1962). Originally the Potter School (1873), the Italianate structure has been converted into a bed & breakfast.

Bodega Bay – Pop 1,127. *6mi north of Bodega.* The largest protected small boat anchorage between San Francisco and Noyo, just south of Fort Bragg *(p 130)*, bears the name of Spanish explorer Juan Francisco de la Bodega y Cuadra, who reached its sheltered waters in October 1775. Since the 1940s, when its commercial fishing industry began to thrive, Bodega Bay has grown into the second largest salmon port on the Pacific coast. Today its waterfront bustles with the comings and goings of some 300 commercial fishing boats.
On the far side of the bay rises **Bodega Head** *(take Hwy 1 north through Bodega Bay; turn left on Eastshore Rd, 3mi to the park).* From the bluffs atop this point stretch splendid **views★** of the coast from POINT REYES NATIONAL SEASHORE to Fort Ross *(below)*.

★ **Sonoma Coast State Beach** – *Beach listing p 258. Open daily year-round.* ⚠ *☎707-875-3483.* Rocky outcrops separate the 15 small, sandy crescents that punctuate this shoreline. Extending from Bodega Head to Russian Gulch just north of Jenner, this 12.5mi strip of coast affords striking oceanscapes and provides numerous opportunities for fishing, hiking, camping, sunbathing and beachcombing. Some of the most dramatic **views★** can be seen at **Duncan's Landing** *(5mi north of Bodega Dunes).*
One of the most accessible of the Sonoma Coast beaches is **Goat Rock Beach★** *(8mi north of Bodega Dunes)*, located at the mouth of the Russian River, where visitors can enjoy a unique **view** of river and ocean barely separated by a narrow spit of sand. From November to March, throngs of resident harbor seals vie with fishermen to catch the schools of salmon that return here each year to spawn.

Turnouts abound on this stretch of Highway 1, giving drivers ample chances to rest and drink in the rugged coastline. North of Jenner, the road becomes a series of switchbacks winding high above the ocean *(average speed 25mph).* Several miles south of Fort Ross, the road flattens out and wide terraces appear on the left.

★★ **Fort Ross State Historic Park** – *22mi north of Bodega Bay. Open year-round daily 10am–4:30 pm. Grounds open until sunset. Closed Jan 1, Thanksgiving Day, Dec 25. $5/car. ♿ ☎707-847-3437.* Built high on a desolate promontory above a sheltered azure cove and flanked by forested mountains to the east, Fort Ross reigned as Russia's easternmost outpost for nearly 40 years. This strategically located stronghold provided a base from which colonists hunted sea otters for their valuable pelts and supplied food to Russia's more remote outposts in Alaska.
Settlement Rossiia (Russia), as the colony was christened by its founders, was established in 1812 by members of the Russian-American Company, a commercial hunting and trading group authorized by the czarist government to manage Russian trade, exploration and settlement in North America. The fort's first colonists, a group of 25 Russians and 80 Alaskan Aleuts (recruited for their skill in hunting sea otters) negotiated with the resident Kashaya Pomo for land before constructing their garrison.
In its heyday, the fort housed several hundred people, who led a peaceful existence cultivating the land and its natural resources. By the mid-1830's, the colonists had depleted California's sea otter population and their attempts at farming and ranching had failed to produce expected yields. This led to the Russian-American Company's decision to abandon the colony. After surviving a series of owners, including John Sutter *(p 156)*, the site was deeded to the state in 1906.
The present fort has been partially restored to its early appearance, and plans currently exist to reconstruct three additional buildings that originally stood inside the walls. Costumed actors re-enact scenes from Fort Ross' history during the annual Living History Day *(last Saturday in July).*

Visit – *2hrs; site plan available.* The **visitor center** contains displays illustrating the history of the fort and the Pomo tribes who first occupied the site. From the visitor center, a short, paved loop trail *(.5mi)* leads through a cypress grove to the fort. Constructed of redwood and modeled after traditional edifices in Siberia, the stockade contains six structures designed with clean, simple lines. Most of the buildings on site have been restored; the only original edifice is the **Rotchev House** *(north wall);* the **officials quarters** *(southwest wall)* display artifacts evoking the fort's early days. The first Russian Orthodox church in North America outside Alaska, the small **chapel** boasts a distinctive, hexagonal tower and round cupola. This building is actually the third incarnation of the original structure that was erected in 1825 but collapsed during the 1906 earthquake. Fire destroyed the restored chapel in 1970.

V. Atkinson

Living History Day at Fort Ross

In two corners of the stockade, two-story **blockhouses**—one heptagonal and one octagonal—were once armed with as many as 40 cannon to ward off possible attack by the Spaniards. These weapons proved unnecessary since the fort was never threatened. From the southwest blockhouse there are good **views** of the coast. Visitors can return to the parking lot via the lower half of the trail that follows the bluffs overlooking the sea.

Salt Point State Park – *9mi. Open daily year-round. $5/car.* ☎*707-847-3221. Facility information p 257.* Named for the substance that Natives once collected from submarine crevices along its shores to use in preserving seafood, this 6,000-acre park runs along 4mi of the Sonoma Coast. Divers favor the site for its underwater sanctuary, the **Gerstle Cove Marine Reserve**. Off the shores of Gerstle Cove, seals sun themselves on glistening rocks; a short drive away at Fisk Mill Cove, a fern-lined path *(.25mi)* winds uphill to a platform overlooking Sentinel Rock and the frothy surf below.

Kruse Rhododendron State Reserve – *Entrance at right, 3mi north of Gerstle Cove. Open daily year-round.* ☎*707-847-3221.* Adjacent to Salt Point State Park, the reserve protects 317 acres studded with thickets of coast rhododendron that succeeded vegetation razed years ago by a forest fire. This site is best visited from April to June, when the towering rhododendrons' blossoms burst into bloom.

North of the reserve, Highway 1 skirts marine terraces that provide grazing land for local cattle. After some 7mi, the contemporary weathered-wood houses of **Sea Ranch**—a 5,000-acre, second-home community—appear on the left, tucked into the meadows sloping down to the sea. Designed in the 1960s by celebrated post-Modern architect Charles Moore (1925-1993) to "form an alliance of architecture and nature," these dwellings are considered the inspiration for beach houses and ranch-style homes common throughout the US today.

Commercial center for the area, the town of **Gualala** *(8mi north of Sea Ranch)* offers lodging and other amenities. Past Gualala, conifers replace the dry, brown brush that covers the hillsides farther south for three quarters of the year. About 5mi north of Anchor Bay, dramatic **views** unfold of open coast set against pale cliffs.

★ **Point Arena Lighthouse** – *15mi north of Gualala. Turn left on Lighthouse Rd and continue 2.3mi to parking lot. Open daily year-round. Thanksgiving Day–Dec 24 weekends only. Closed Thanksgiving Day, Dec 25. $2.* ☎*707-882-2777.* The approach to this lighthouse affords panoramic **views★** of high terraces carved by the Pacific. Built in 1870, the original brick lighthouse on Point Arena was damaged during the 1906 earthquake. Its replacement, made of reinforced concrete, contains the original Fresnel lens. Next to the beacon, the former Fog Signal Building (1869) displays defunct compressed-steam foghorns, as well as a series of photographs documenting the lighthouse's history.

Van Damme State Park – *28mi. North of Little River, turn right at sign for park. Open daily year-round. $5/car.* ☎*707-937-5804. Facility information p 257.* Although the boundaries of this park extend both east and west of Highway 1, the majority of its 2,160 acres falls on the inland side. Here, a short boardwalk loop *(10min)* threads through a **pygmy forest★**, a phenomenon unique to the upper marine terraces in Mendocino County. These areas were once bogs, where over centuries, acidic water leached precious nutrients from the soil, forming a hardpan layer just beneath the surface. The stunted plants that grow here—their roots unable to penetrate the hardpan to reach the water below—have adapted themselves to these impoverished conditions in order to survive. Several species found in this area exist nowhere else in the world.

About 2mi north of Little River, the quaint clapboard buildings of Mendocino slip into view.

★★ **Mendocino** – *1 day. Description p 117.*

Russian Gulch State Park – *2mi. Open daily year-round. $5/car.* ☎*707-937-5804. Facility information p 257.* Occupying the headland north of Mendocino, Russian Gulch treats visitors to a close-up look at some rock formations common to the Mendocino coast. The **Devil's Punch Bowl**★, located within a fenced area on the bluffs *(take first right after park gate)*, is actually a collapsed sea cave. Waves slosh inside this giant cauldron, ebbing and flowing through a tunnel leading to the original cave. A walk around the headland here reveals places where the surf has carved a variety of **sea caves** and **blowholes** (eruptions in a cave's roof caused by water pressure) into the bedrock below.

North of Russian Gulch State Park, Highway 1 winds past Jug Handle State Reserve, which occupies a series of five marine terraces uplifted from the sea over the past 500,000 years.

Fort Bragg – Pop 6,078. *8mi.* This workingman's town was established in 1857 as a US military post charged with overseeing the Mendocino Indian Reservation on the Noyo River. Named for Mexican War hero General Braxton Bragg (who later commanded Confederate troops during the Civil War), the city of Fort Bragg arose with the construction of the Union Lumber Company's mill on the site of the old army post in 1885. Today the smoky facilities of its successor, the Georgia Pacific Lumber Company, operate along the coast and, along with the fishing industry, support the local economy. The small clapboard Fort Building *(430 Franklin St)* survives as the only remnant of the original garrison.
Evidence of the town's artistic community, the Fort Bragg Center for the Arts exhibits work by local artists on the mezzanine of Dalys Department Store *(303 N. Main St).*

★ **Mendocino Coast Botanical Gardens** – *18220 N. Hwy 1. Open daily year-round. Closed 2nd Sat in Sept, Thanksgiving Day, Dec 25. $5.* ✕ ♿ ☎*707-964-4352.* Mild, rainy winters and cool, foggy summers of the Mendocino Coast nurture more than 20 collections of plants in the gardens that occupy this lovely 47-acre site. The gardens' principal arteries, the North and South trails, weave through beds of perennials and fuchsias, past rhododendrons, pine-forested landscapes and a lush, fern-blanketed **canyon** to the wind-swept headland. Here, the Coastal Bluff Trail offers exquisite **views** of the surf-washed cliffs reaching north.

Guest House Museum – *343 N. Main St. Open Apr–Oct Wed–Sun, rest of the year Sat only. Closed major holidays. $1.* ♿ ☎*707-961-2840.* Lumber baron T.L. Johnson once lived in this 3-story Victorian (1892), built entirely of redwood; it later provided lodging for his guests. Now it contains a collection of photographs and artifacts depicting the history of Fort Bragg and Mendocino coast logging.

★ **Skunk Train** – *Depart from Skunk Depot (Main St, near Guest House Museum) daily year-round. Closed Jan 1, Thanksgiving Day, Dec 25. Round-trip 3hrs to Northspur (Dec–Feb weekends only) $21; 7hrs to Willits $26.* ✕ *California Western Railroad* ☎*707-964-6371.* Originally a logging train, California Western Railroad's Skunk line carries passengers through old- and new-growth redwood forests as it snakes alongside the Noyo River on its 40mi route from Fort Bragg to **Willits**. When the company began using gasoline-powered engines in 1925, residents accustomed to coal fumes claimed that they could smell the train coming before they could see it. From this, arose the sobriquet "skunk train."
The train chugs slowly around a total of 381 curves, through two pitch-black mountain tunnels and across 30 trestle bridges, climbing over 1,700ft along the way. After the train crests the mountain's peak, the redwoods yield to pine forests.
For visitors who choose the day-long ride to Willits, the **Mendocino County Museum** *(400 E. Commercial, 2 blocks to the right of Willits depot; open year-round Wed–Sat; closed major holidays;* ♿ ☎*707-459-2736)* exhibits small collections of Pomo Native baskets, antique carriages and logging equipment.

MacKerricher State Park – *3mi. Open daily year-round.* ⚠ ☎*707-937-5804. Facility information p 257.* One of the most popular areas of this park is **Laguna Point**, where a boardwalk leads to an overlook providing the best view of the harbor seals that reside on the rocks offshore. Spanning 8mi of coast, MacKerricher also features trout-stocked Lake Cleone.

North of the park, the road cuts east across the Coast Range and joins US-101, thus avoiding the impenetrable wilderness known as the Lost Coast *(p 150).*

The fastest way to return to San Francisco is via Hwy 128 (11mi south of Mendocino) to US-101 south. To reach the REDWOOD EMPIRE, *continue north on Hwy 1 as it crosses the Coast Range to Leggett (this stretch of road is steep and tortuous; average speed 25mph). At Leggett, take US-101 north.*

"California is an Italy without its art. There are subjects for the artist, but it is universally true that the only scenery which inspires utterance is that which man feels himself the master of. The mountains of California are so gigantic that they are not favorable to art or poetry. There are good poets in England, but none in Switzerland. There the mountains are too high. Art cannot add to nature."

Oscar Wilde, 1882

★ OAKLAND San Francisco Bay Area Pop 372,242

Map p 132 Tourist Office ☎510-987-8200

Directly across the bay from SAN FRANCISCO, this East Bay city is compelling for its contrasts: an active port and manufacturing center, it also boasts a gleaming new high-rise downtown, museums, colleges and some 2,000 acres of parkland.

Historical Notes – With the founding of San Francisco's MISSION DOLORES, the Native lands of the East Bay became pasturage for mission cattle. In 1820 the area was ceded to Luís María Peralta, as part of an immense 46,800-acre land grant. For some 20 years, Peralta's Rancho San Antonio dominated the present-day East Bay, and at the family's boat landing, the Embarcadero de Temescal, cattle hides were shipped to markets in the eastern US.

By the 1850s, Americanization and the Gold Rush were spelling doom to the quiet ranchero life. In the early 1850s, failed gold seekers began settling in the lush *contra costa,* the "other coast," as the East Bay was called. By 1852 lawyers, squatters and land speculators had managed to dismantle the Peralta ranch, and a gritty new American boomtown had risen, named Oakland after the region's expansive stands of oak trees.

In 1868 Oakland became the western terminus of the transcontinental Southern Pacific Railroad, ensuring it decades of prosperity as a transportation hub. Though the city suffered economic decline and social unrest in the mid-20C, subsequent decades have brought a measure of recovery. The city has launched an aggressive campaign to attract new business, and it is now the corporate headquarters for several leading companies. Its downtown is undergoing a major rebuilding and revitalization, and the expanded, modernized **Port of Oakland,** operated by the Port Commission since 1927, now ranks as the fourth largest containerized cargo facility in the country. Predominantly involved in Pacific Basin trade, its 11 marine terminals and 28 shipping berths stretch 19mi along the San Francisco Bay and Oakland Estuary. *Cruises to San Francisco depart from Jack London Square daily year round. Closed Jan 1, Thanksgiving Day, Dec 25. Round-trip 90min. On-board commentary. Reservations required.* ✗ ♿ *Port of Oakland* ☎*510-272-1188.*

SIGHTS *1 day*

★★ **San Francisco-Oakland Bay Bridge** – *Toll $1 (westbound only).* Connecting San Francisco and Oakland, this 2-tiered bridge, measuring a total length of 5.2mi, is one of the longest high-level steel bridges in the world. Engineered by Charles Purcell and completed in 1936, the "Bay Bridge" actually comprises two distinct spans joined by a 500ft tunnel through Yerba Buena Island. The western portion is a twin-suspension design, supported by cables anchored at each end of the bridge and at a central pier. The eastern section, which was seriously damaged in the 1989 Loma Prieta earthquake, represents three design forms: a cantilevered span, suspended between two cantilevered arms extending off main piers; double-deck through trusses, in which the traffic actually travels on the bridge trusses, or supports; and double-deck trusses, in which bracing for the support comes from overhead cables. Westbound traffic on the entire bridgeway occupies the top tier, so that those approaching the city enjoy **views★** of the bay and the San Francisco skyline.

Downtown – *BART: City Center/12th St. Bounded by I-880, I-980, Grand Ave and Lake Merrit.* At the heart of Oakland's ongoing downtown rejuvenation lies **City Center★**, a multi-block high-rise "office park" set amid fountained plazas. The **Oakland Museum Sculpture Court**, featuring exhibits by Bay Area artists, occupies the west lobby of 1111 Broadway *(open daily year-round)*; a sculpture garden to the rear of the building features the works of California artist Richard Deutsch. Across 14th Street from City Center rises **City Hall★** (1914), an imposing granite Beaux Arts structure that suffered damage in the 1989 earthquake. The city's landmark skyscraper, the old **Oakland Tribune Building** (1923), with its distinctive lettering and clock tower, still stands at 13th and Franklin Streets but no longer houses the newspaper offices. A few blocks west of the core of downtown lies **Preservation Park** *(12th St and Martin Luther King, Jr. Way)*, a cluster of Victorian homes relocated to the site and now restored as an office park.

★★ **Paramount Theatre** – *BART: 19th St. 2025 Broadway. Open during performances and by guided tours 1st & 3rd Sat of each month.* ♿ ☎*510-465-6400.* This National Landmark structure is a resplendent example of Art Deco design in the spirit of great American movie palaces. Conceived by San Francisco architect Timothy Pflueger, the theater (1931) boasts a towering exterior tile mosaic and an interior lavish with gilded and sculpted plaster walls, filigreed grillwork ceilings and murals. The Paramount was authentically restored in 1973 and is now owned by the city as a movie theater and performing arts facility.

Lake Merritt – *BART: Lake Merritt. Northeast of downtown.* The shores of this 155-acre man-made saltwater lake rub shoulders with the bustle of downtown, offering a haven of green serenity. **Lakeside Park**, along the northwest shore, features Children's Fairyland, a small amusement park and petting zoo for young children. A serene walking path traces the lake's 3.5mi of shoreline.

Camron-Stanford House – *1418 Lakeside Dr. Open year-round Wed & Sun, rest of the week by appointment only. Closed Jan 1, Easter Sunday, Dec 25. $2.* 🅿 ☎*510-836-1976.* A landmark on the southwest shore of Lake Merritt, this sedate Italianate residence (1876) was home to a succession of prominent families, including Josiah Stanford, brother of railroad magnate Leland Stanford *(p 140).* From 1910 to 1967, the building housed collections of the Oakland Public Museum. The lower floor now re-creates early museum exhibits, while the main floor is restored to its original appearance and furnished with period antiques.

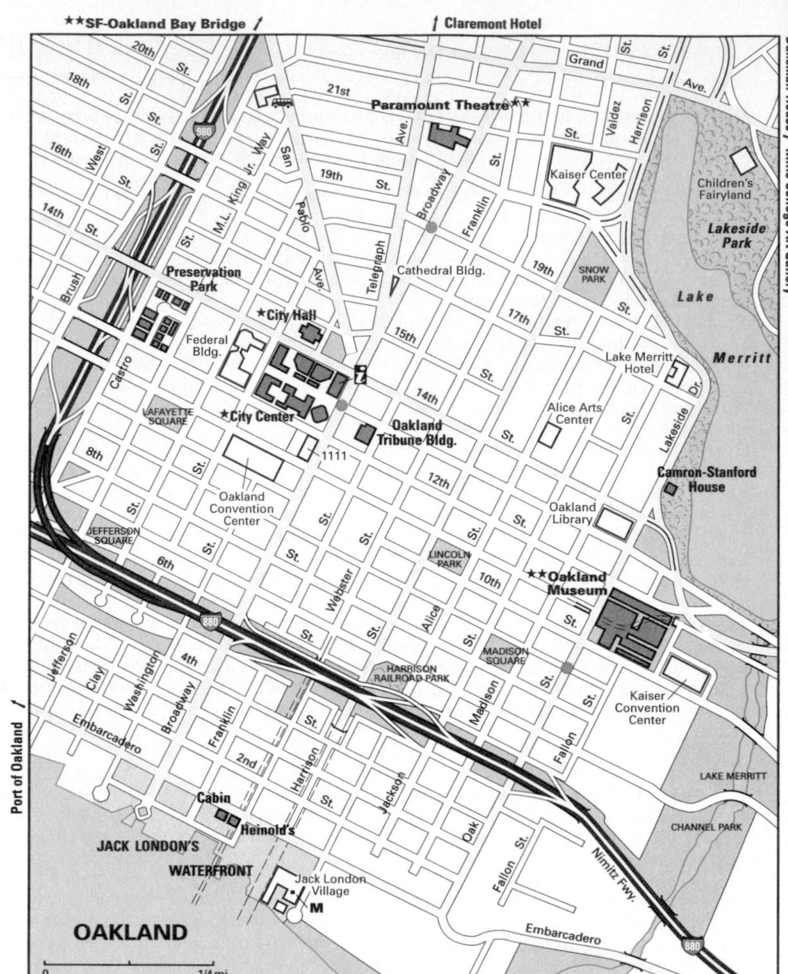

★★ **Oakland Museum** – *3hrs. 1000 Oak St, southwest side of Lake Merritt adjacent to the Kaiser Convention Center. Open year-round Wed–Sat 10am–5pm, Sun noon–7pm. Closed Jan 1, Jul 4, Thanksgiving Day, Dec 25.* ☎*510-238-3401.* The city's showpiece, this 6-acre cultural complex celebrates California's natural and human history and its art. The museum's innovative garden architecture invites visitor involvement and serves as a setting for "art, festivity, and noble events."

A "Park for the People" – In the early 1960s, city officials and private individuals launched a massive public campaign to build a grand new museum complex that would help heal some of the wounds of Oakland's social unrest and revive its decaying inner city. The facility consolidated three existing Oakland museums—the Snow Museum, focusing on natural history; the Oakland Public Museum, devoted to California Native American ethnological materials and the state's pioneer history; and the Oakland Art Museum.
Internationally acclaimed architect Eero Saarinen was the leading candidate to design the museum when he died unexpectedly in 1961. His colleague, Kevin Roche, was then chosen to undertake the project. Roche's "park for the people" is a series of tiered horizontal galleries overhung with roof gardens and fronting a central courtyard. Landscaped pools, patios and sweeping outdoor stairways are integral to the design. The museum opened in 1969 to rave reviews, with *New York Times* critic Ada Louise Huxtable calling it "one of the most thoughtfully revolutionary structures in the world."

Hall of California Ecology – *1st level.* Here, visitors can experience the astounding breadth and diversity of California's geology and plant and animal life. Prepared specimens of native flora and fauna in intriguing dioramas re-create the eight distinct biotic zones that stretch across California: the coastline, the coast mountains, the inner coast, the interior valley, the Sierran slope, the High Sierra, the Great Basin, and the desert. Located off the main hall are the Aquatic California Gallery, devoted to marine life, and the Natural Sciences Special Gallery, where temporary exhibits on ecology are mounted.

Cowell Hall of California History – *2nd level.* The hall's permanent exhibition, *California: A Place, A People, A Dream*, traces the state's human history through historical tableaux and displays of some 6,000 artifacts. Beginning with **First People**, the exhibition reveals the diversity of California's Native cultures through their rituals, basketry, stone tools and clothing. In **Explorers, Priests and Colonists** the hardships and successes of the Spanish-Mexican period are explored through church artifacts and the tools of the early colonists. **Adventurers and Goldseekers** re-creates the raucous boom times of the mid-19C, while **Founders, Organizers and Developers** details the more sedate lifestyles of the Victorian-era citizens who settled the state's fertile lands and established permanent communities. Finally, **Seekers, Innovators and Achievers** celebrates the 20C "California Dream" of a better life for all who come here, from Hollywood's star gazers and the surfing set to Silicon Valley's inventors. The hall's three computerized History Information Stations allow in-depth access to details. At the rear of the hall, the Breuner Gallery and the History Special Gallery feature changing exhibits on historical subjects.

Gallery of California Art – *3rd level.* Devoted to works by artists who have lived, worked or studied in California, this gallery covers the period from the early 19C to the present. The permanent collection—including sculptures, drawings, prints, photographs, installations and works in mixed media—features 19C landscapes, examples of Abstract Expressionism, works from the Bay Area Figurative movement, and photographs by such members of the group f.64 as Edward Weston, Ansel Adams and Imogen Cunningham. The museum also has the largest holdings of Dorothea Lange's photographs and negatives. The Oakes Gallery *(north end)* houses temporary exhibits of prints and photographs, and the Art Special Gallery *(rear of main gallery)* is also devoted to temporary exhibits.

The museum's **Great Hall High Bay** *(2nd and 3rd level)* and **Great Hall Low Bay** *(2nd level)* feature major traveling exhibitions, art shows and temporary exhibits organized from the museum's own collections.

Jack London's Waterfront – *BART: City Center/12th St. South end of Broadway, on the waterfront.* Stretching along the Oakland Estuary, this once-gritty dock area has been developed into an attractive commercial and tourist area named for writer Jack London *(p 239)*, who lived in Oakland as a boy and young man and unsuccessfully ran for city mayor twice on the Socialist ticket. In addition to **Jack London Square**, a marina pavilion (1990) containing hotels, shops and restaurants, the waterfront also contains the historic **Jack London Cabin**, a reconstruction, from original timbers, of the rustic, one-room log cabin London occupied in 1897 while prospecting for gold in the Klondike. (A similar cabin, also incorporating original timbers, is in Dawson City, Yukon Territory.) Beside the cabin is **Heinold's First and Last Chance Saloon** (1883), a picturesque 1-room structure built of the timbers of a whaling ship. Still a commercial bar, it was a favorite London watering hole, also visited by such literary figures as Robert Louis Stevenson, Ambrose Bierce and Joaquin Miller. The nearby **Jack London Museum [M]** *(in Jack London Village, east of the square)* traces the writer's life through his books, papers and memorabilia *(open year-round Tue–Sun; closed Jan 1, Dec 25; contribution requested; ♿ ☎510-451-8218).*

Mills College Art Gallery – *From downtown drive east on Grand Ave and take I-580 east; exit MacArthur Blvd. Open Sept–May Tue–Sun.* ✗ ♿ 🅿 *☎510-430-2164.* Housed in an elegant, Mission-style building (1925) ornamented with Spanish tiles and wrought iron, this skylit gallery features changing exhibits of contemporary art, as well as displays of the gallery's own 6,000-piece collection of European and American art (Renaissance to present), Japanese prints and pre-Columbian textiles and ceramics.

Dunsmuir House – *From downtown drive east on Grand Ave and take I-580 east; exit 106th Ave; left under freeway, then follow signs. Open Apr–Sept Tue–Fri, Sun. End of Nov–3rd weekend in Dec Thu–Sun. $4. ♿ ☎510-562-3232.* Built by Alexander Dunsmuir *(p 126)* at the turn of the century, this Colonial Revival country estate home sits amid 40 wooded acres at the southern edge of Oakland. The ornate interior contains original paneling and molding, and is furnished in period pieces.

Claremont Hotel – *Telegraph Ave north to Claremont Ave; turn right, continue to Ashby Ave and turn right. Open daily year-round.* ✗ ♿ 🅿 *☎510-843-3000.* Looming white in the hills between Berkeley and Oakland is a romantic old hotel, centerpiece of an upscale, 22-acre resort. Opened for the 1915 Panama-Pacific Exposition *(p 186)* and restored in the early 1980s, the glistening white, Mediterranean-style structure is notable for its **views** of the Bay and for its collection of contemporary Northwestern art, on display throughout public areas.

The 🅿 symbol indicates that on-site parking is available.

★ ORANGE COAST Orange County

Map of Principal Sights p 4

The waterfront communities of Huntington Beach, Newport Beach and Laguna Beach offer several variations on a beach town theme. These seaside cities were born in the first decade of the 20C when the Pacific Electric Railway (the "Red Cars") trolley line was extended from LOS ANGELES as far south as present-day Newport Beach. Development boomed during the 1920s when oil reserves were discovered in the area today encompassing Seal Beach and Huntington Beach; the southern communities concurrently grew as resorts and residential enclaves.

Today, coastal Orange County thrives on an economic base of commerce and light industry, as witnessed by the contemporary glass and concrete office towers rising inland from the seashore. Each city fringing the ocean is graced by a distinctive character and a charming waterfront where sun, sand and sea hold sway. Sun enthusiasts flock to the northern part of the county between Huntington Beach and Newport Beach, to loll on wide, sandy beaches; south of Newport Beach, the sandy stretches give way to the cliffs and promontories of the San Joaquin Hills.

SIGHTS *At least 1 day*

Huntington Beach – Pop 181,519. Considered the birthplace of the surfing craze in California, Huntington Beach epitomizes the contemporary California beach town. Miles of unspoiled sand embrace the community, and surf shops, some of which have existed for decades, dot Main Street near its intersection with the Pacific Coast Highway (Highway 1), rubbing shoulders with sleek new shopping and dining complexes. Surfers and sun enthusiasts stroll here, pausing at sidewalk cafes and popping into ice cream shops and clothing boutiques. Across from Main Street, a long concrete pier extends into the surf, marking the boundary between **Huntington State Beach** to the south and **Bolsa Chica State Beach** to the north.

★ **Newport Beach** – Pop 66,643. This upscale resort and residential community has in recent years rediscovered its maritime origins. In 1873, brothers James and Robert McFadden established a shipping port here at the mouth of the Santa Ana River. They later relocated their port further south to the long arm of Balboa Peninsula, a finger of land paralleling the shore, that was created when an 1825 flood deposited sediments from the Santa Ana River at the mouth of Upper Newport Bay. Today much of the city of Newport Beach extends over a gentle ridge that marks the northern boundary of the San Joaquin Hills. The slope overlooking the Balboa Peninsula is the site of Fashion Island *(Newport Center Dr, just off Hwy 1)*, a mammoth complex of department stores and boutiques that draws shoppers from throughout Southern California. The resort community of **Balboa** was established in 1905 on the eastern portion of the Balboa Peninsula; today it is a suburb of Newport Beach. The peninsula itself defines the boundaries of Newport Harbor, one of the largest pleasure craft anchorages on the West Coast.

Balboa Peninsula – *Exit Pacific Coast Hwy via Newport Blvd, which becomes Balboa Blvd.* The peninsula's ocean side invites swimmers and sunbathers to its miles of broad, sandy beaches. The **Newport Municipal Pier** (1888), originally a wharf on the site where the McFadden brothers established their "new port," served as an embarkation point for Orange County's agricultural bounty, as well as an offloading area for the lumber and supplies necessary to develop the area. Today a popular public fishing spot, the pier is accessed by charming Ocean Front Street, formerly the main street of Newport Beach. Since 1891 the fishermen of the **Dory Fishing Fleet** have nightly launched their small, colorful boats (dories) from here to fish up to 30mi offshore. Returning in the morning, they sell their catch of rock cod, sea trout, mackerel, shark and sand dabs from a piling-screened compound located near the foot of the pier.

Balboa Boulevard bisects the peninsula, leading to the **Balboa Pavilion**★ *(400 Main St)*. This charming wooden Victorian structure (1904), topped by a jaunty cupola, was a popular dance hall during the 1940s big-band era and served as the southern terminus of the Pacific Electric Railway line that engendered Newport Beach's development as a seaside playground. Extending along the bayfront east of the pavilion is the celebrated "Fun Zone," a midway-style stretch of game arcades, restaurants and amusement park rides, including a Ferris wheel and a carousel. Several private companies operate **harbor cruises** from here, offering opportunities for close-up glimpses of the magnificent yachts moored in Newport Harbor. Also from the Fun Zone, a small 3-car ferry runs a short distance across the bay to Balboa Island, the largest of three islets that were created when the marshy harbor was dredged in the early 20C. Some 1,500 charming vacation cottages of all styles crowd the island, and a plethora of shops and cafes line Marine Street, which crosses a bridge to the mainland and the Pacific Coast Highway.

★ **Newport Harbor Art Museum** – *850 San Clemente Dr. Open year-round Tue–Sun. Closed Jan 1, Dec 25. $4. ✗ ♿ ☎714-759-1122.* Situated on the slope overlooking the harbor, this small, yet respected museum is dedicated to the exhibition of modern and contemporary art. Selections from the permanent collection, which focuses on California art since World War II, are complemented by excellent traveling exhibits that highlight current trends in art around the world.

Sherman Library and Gardens – *2647 Pacific Coast Hwy, in Corona del Mar. Open daily year-round. Closed Jan 1, Thanksgiving Day, Dec 25. $2. ✗ (Sat–Mon) ♿ ☎714-673-2261.* Exquisitely planted and meticulously maintained botanical delights fill every nook and cranny of this 2-acre garden, established in 1966 by the Sherman Foundation as a setting for its research library of the Pacific Southwest. The lavish, colorful gardens specialize in tropical and sub-tropical plants and desert species from the Southwest. The tiny adobe (1940) on the grounds displays old photographs and other items from the Sherman Research Library's Southwestern History collection.

★ **Crystal Cove State Park** – *South of Corona del Mar. Open daily year-round. ♿ ☎714-494-3539. Facility information p 257.* Orange County's longest expanse of undeveloped coastline is preserved in this state park, which encompasses 2,791 acres of former Irvine Ranch holdings. Some 400 acres of coastal dunes, bluffs and hidden coves, disrupted by ranch and resort activities that occurred here from the late 19C to early 20C, are currently being restored and replanted with California buckwheat, sage, lemonade berry and other native plants.

★ **Laguna Beach** – Pop. 23,170. Backdropped by rocky cliffs and punctuated by deep canyons all within view of the sea along a gently curved coastline, Laguna Beach's magnificent natural **setting**★ has long attracted artists and poets, while limiting urban overdevelopment. A wide variety of residential architectural styles, ranging from Tudor to Mission to contemporary, enhances the city's gracious appearance and contributes to its popularity as a weekend getaway haven.

Unlike the neighboring coastal communities, Laguna Beach was not promoted as an oceanside resort. Professional artists began settling here permanently in 1903, and by the 1920s some 40 painters had established studios here, many of them landscapists attracted to the area's magnificent natural scenery and its isolation. The close proximity of these artists and their alliance as the **Laguna Beach Art Association** spawned several artistic movements, most notably the "Plein air" movement, a variant of American Impressionist painting characterized by representations of the region's distinctive light and dramatic landscapes. The association also lent credence to Laguna Beach's reputation as an art colony similar to that founded in CARMEL about 1904, and local residents began to hold art classes and organize studio tours for a growing number of tourists.

Although Laguna Beach's heyday as an art colony is past, more than 50 craft studios and galleries gracefully coexist with the trappings of a contemporary beach community. The annual **Festival of the Arts** *(July-August)* is the most popular of Laguna Beach's three annual art festivals, attracting some 200,000 visitors annually. A festival highlight is the renowned "Pageant of the Masters," in which models pose in living representation of well-known paintings.

B. Ross/AllStock

Coastline at Laguna Beach

★ **Laguna Beach Art Museum** – *307 Cliff Dr. Open year-round Tue–Sun. Closed Jan 1, Thanksgiving Day, Dec 25. $4. ♿ ☎714-494-6531.* Founded in 1918 as the Laguna Beach Art Association *(above)*, a cooperative of local artists who desired to show and sell their work, this well-endowed museum is a recognized center for the study and exhibition of American art, with particular emphasis on the development of modern art in California. Changing thematic exhibits of selections from the permanent collection of American Impressionist paintings, 20C photography and works of installation art are supplemented by frequent traveling shows. The striking, contemporary museum building was renovated in 1986.

Pleasant, palm-fringed **Heisler Park** *(north of the museum)* offers lovely **views** of the dramatic cliffs and bluffs that characterize Laguna Beach's coastline. A path leads from here to **Main Beach** *(foot of Broadway)*, the largest of the town's many beach areas. On the northern edge of town, **Crescent Bay Point Park** *(from Pacific Coast Hwy turn west on Crescent Dr)* offers a magnificent **view★★** across the bay and cliffs to the center of town.

★ OWENS VALLEY High Sierras

Map of Principal Sights p 5 Tourist Office ☎619-873-8405

Grand in its arid austerity, the Owens Valley sits at the geologic and climatic intersection of the Sierra Nevada Range, the Mojave Desert and the Great Basin. Flanked by two of the country's highest mountain ranges—the craggy granitic spires of the Sierra Nevada on the west and the barren White-Inyo Range on the east—the valley extends from the southern end of the Owens Dry Lake bed, south of Lone Pine, to the northern outskirts of Bishop.

Silver Booms and Water Busts – Lt Joseph Walker, leading a detachment of an 1833 Army reconnaissance expedition, was the first known white man to explore the Owens Valley and the eastern flank of the Sierra Nevadas. The valley is named for Richard Owens, who never came here, but did accompany John C. Frémont *(p 24)* on an 1845 expedition to locate overland routes into California.

By the 1860s, the area had become a thriving mining and ranching region. The Cerro Gordo mine, in the Inyo Mountains above Owens Lake, ranked as California's most productive silver mine in the 1860s, bringing prosperity to both Owens valley and the town of LOS ANGELES, where much of the silver was shipped. In the early 20C, the valley's ecology and economy were forever altered by the completion in 1913 of the Los Angeles Aqueduct *(p 84)*, which diverted water from the Owens River, directing it southwest to Los Angeles. With its construction, the valley's irrigation-based ranching was no longer lucrative, and large amounts of private land were sold to the Federal Government. Owens Lake, which covered 100sq mi in the 1860s, gradually dried up, as did the area's population. Today a smattering of small towns punctuates US-395, which traverses the valley from south to north, offering awe-inspiring vistas of the majestic eastern Sierra Nevada.

FROM OLANCHA TO BISHOP *1 day. 80mi (not including excursions).*

Leave Olancha by US-395 north

From the small crossroads community of **Olancha**, US-395 skirts the west edge of the Owens Lake, now a vast, arid playa fringed with the pinkish glow of halobacteria organisms that thrive in its alkaline environment. The **Eastern Sierra Interagency Visitor Center** *(north end of the lake at the junction of US-395 and Hwy 136; ☎619-876-6222)* offers information on the entire eastern Sierra corridor. The peak of Mt Whitney *(below)* is visible from the agency grounds.

Lone Pine – Pop 1,818. *23mi.* The primary tourist hub for the southern end of the valley, this pleasant little town serves as a gateway for hikers and climbers challenging Mt Whitney. Lone Pine's homespun simplicity belies its glamorous connections: from the 1920s to the present, the town was frequented by Hollywood stars, who came here to shoot films in the **Alabama Hills★**, an area of fabulous granitic boulder formations stretching like a ready-made movie set along the western side of town. Such celebrities as Errol Flynn, Gregory Peck, Cary Grant and Gene Autry have starred in the some 200 films made here, which include *The Lone Ranger* (1938), *Gunga Din* (1939), *The Gunfighter* (1950) and *Nevada Smith* (1966). **Movie Road** *(from Lone Pine, drive west 2.7mi on Whitney Portal Rd and turn right)* winds for several miles among the rocks backdropped by the Sierras; their red-brown tone is the result of iron oxidation.

★★ **Mt Whitney** – *Excursion: 26mi round-trip from Lone Pine via Whitney Portal Rd.* The highest peak (14,496ft) in the contiguous 48 states is ensconced amid other towering peaks of the Sierra crest. Like the rest of the granitic Sierra Nevada, Mt Whitney was formed through a combination of volcanism, tectonic movement and weathering. Its ranking as highest peak in the US was first recognized by members of the California State Geological Survey, who explored the area in 1864 and named the preeminent mountain for Josiah Whitney, California's first state geologist. The first ascent of the peak was made in 1873 by three fisherman setting out from Lone Pine to fish the Kern River.

Owing to its positioning among other high peaks, the stern visage of Mt Whitney is somewhat difficult to identify. However, views of it can be had from Lone Pine, as well as along the **Whitney Portal Road**. Constructed by the Civilian Conservation Corps in 1936, the road ascends the eastern flank of the Sierra, allowing **views★** down into the valley and up into the heart of the Sierra Nevada. The road ends at the **Mt Whitney Portal★**, a lovely mountain canyon (8,360ft) shaded by tall conifers and centered around a small trout pond *(license required for fishing, p 260)*. Lone Pine Creek cascades down the slopes behind the pond, and the Mt Whitney National Recreation Trail hugs the creek as it descends toward the valley. The rugged **Mt Whitney Trail** *(21.4mi round-trip; permit required, p 260)* ascends steeply into the backcountry, crossing into SEQUOIA NATIONAL PARK and leading eventually to the majestic mountain's summit.

Horseshoe Meadow Road – *Excursion: 48mi round-trip from Lone Pine. Take Whitney Portal Rd west 3.2mi and turn left.* Ascending from the valley floor to a vast meadowland lying at 10,000ft and laced with trails, this road offers striking **views★** of the Owens Dry Lake Bed, the Inyo Mountains and the Owens Valley floor. Roadside turnouts here are popular launching spots for hang gliders.

Continue north on US-395

On the northern outskirts of Lone Pine, US-395 passes the Tule (TOO-lee) Elk Refuge. Smallest of the elk subspecies, these mammals may be spotted anywhere from Lone Pine to Bishop.

★ **Manzanar** – *8mi.* Site of the first of ten relocation camps established to house interned Japanese-Americans during World War II, this bleak, 1sq mi stretch of scrub desert and the traces of its human occupation bear silent witness to the fear and racism that can arise in times of international conflict. Manzanar was established in 1942 following Franklin D. Roosevelt's signing of Executive Order 9066, which permitted the "evacuation" and internment of thousands of Japanese-Americans, many of whom were American citizens. During the camp's peak period, more than 10,000 people resided here amid the high winds, dust-filled air and other harsh desert conditions, under surveillance until the end of the war in 1945.

Today all that remain of the camp structures are two pagoda-style gatehouses, a cemetery, remains of stone garden walls, and an overgrown grid of unpaved streets. The camp's old auditorium, long used as a county maintenance facility, still stands, but Manzanar's many homes were dismantled after the war and sold to returning G.I.'s as inexpensive housing. The property was designated a national historic site in 1992, and the National Park Service is currently planning an interpretive program for the area.

Independence – *7mi.* The seat of government for Inyo County since 1866, the town boasts a Classical Revival courthouse (1923) and the picturesque, white clapboard **Commander's House** *(Main St and US 395).* Erected in 1872 on the grounds of a nearby military outpost called Camp Independence, it was moved to town in 1887 and now serves as a house museum, furnished in 19C style *(open Jun–Aug weekends; contribution requested; ☎619-878-0258).*

Eastern California Museum – *Three blocks west of US-395 on Center St. Open year-round Mon, Wed–Sun. Closed major holidays. Contribution requested. ♿ ☎619-878-0258.* Notable for its collection of documentation and photographs depicting life at Manzanar *(p 136)*, this regional history museum also displays basketry, artifacts and stone tools of various Native American cultures. The museum grounds feature Little Pine Village, a cluster of 1880s wooden buildings that have been relocated here to resemble a pioneer settlement.

Continue north on US-395 to Big Pine (28mi).

Palisade Glacier – *Excursion: 22mi round-trip from Big Pine via Glacier Lodge Rd.* The Glacier Lodge Road climbs the eastern face of the Sierra Nevada, terminating at Glacier Lodge. From here, the Palisade Glacier, southernmost active glacier in the US, can be seen tucked in the mountains high above. A steeply ascending trail *(21mi round-trip)* leads to the foot of the glacier.

★ **Ancient Bristlecone Pine Forest** – *Excursion: 46mi round-trip from Big Pine via Hwy 168. From US-395, follow Hwy 168 east 13mi to Cedar Flat, where the White Mountain Road leads north into the forest.* Pride of the Inyo National Forest, this 28,000-acre designated botanical area protects the oldest living things on earth—the ancient bristlecone pine trees *(Pinus longaeva).* Some of these small trees have survived on the high, barren slopes of the White Mountains for more than 4,000 years. The trees, which attain heights averaging just 25ft, grow extremely slowly, typically adding less than an inch a century to their diameter; this ability to adapt their growth to adverse climatic conditions helps account for their longevity. Though knobby and gnarled from years of wind and ice, the trees are, as naturalist John Muir wrote, "extravagantly picturesque." Pockets of bristlecone pines are also found at high elevations in Arizona and Utah.

Visit – *4hrs. Open Jun–Nov daily. ☎619-873-2300. Note: High elevations may cause altitude sickness (p 256).* From Cedar Flat the road climbs through a mixed forest of pinyon and juniper before reaching the turnout at **Sierra View Point** *(8mi).* Here **views**★★ extend over the snow-capped crest of the Sierra Nevada, which stretches in an unbroken line across the western horizon. A short trail *(.1mi)* leads out onto a roadside knoll offering further views.

The paved road ends at **Schulman Grove** (10,100ft), where a visitor center is located *(open Jun–mid-Sept daily ☎619-873-2500).* The grove is named for Dr Edmund Schulman, the dendroclimatologist who identified the world's oldest tree, the 4,600-year-old Methuselah Tree. Two self-guided nature trails ornamented with extensive stands of bristlecones cross the sere hills here. The Discovery Trail *(1mi)*, a self-guiding nature trail, loops above the road. The Methuselah Walk *(4.2mi)* winds over the arid mountain terrain, leading at its far end through the **Methuselah Grove**, a stand of 3,000 to 4,600-year-old bristlecones that includes the Methuselah Tree *(tree is unmarked).*

Beyond the Schulman Grove an unpaved road climbs through rolling alpine meadowland with fine **views**★★ of the distant Sierras, eventually arriving at **Patriarch Grove**★ *(11mi).* This beautiful stand of bristlecones occupies a level, alpine area at 11,000 feet. The dignified Patriarch, whose circumference measures nearly 37ft, ranks as the largest known bristlecone. A trail *(.25mi)* passes through the grove.

Bishop – Pop 3,475. *16mi.* The largest town in the Owens Valley, Bishop lies at the valley's northern end and serves as its commercial hub and as an outfitting center for pack trips into the Sierras. The town traces its origins to Samuel Bishop, a rancher who established himself in this part of the valley in 1861.

★ **Paiute Shoshone Indian Cultural Center** – *2300 West Line St. Open daily year-round. Closed Jan 1, Thanksgiving Day, Dec 25. Contribution requested. ♿ ☎619-873-4478.* Painted with bold geometric designs, this museum located on the grounds of one of four Native reservations in the Owens Valley interprets the history of the Paiute and Shoshone hunter-gatherers who occupied this region for 1,000 years. Their stone tools, basketry, beadwork and other artifacts are exhibited, as are several re-created traditional structures.

★ **Laws Railroad Museum and Historical Site** – *4.5mi northeast of Bishop via US-6. Open daily year-round. Closed Jan 1, Thanksgiving Day, Dec 25. Contribution requested. ♿ ☎619-873-5950.* Centered around the old Laws Depot, this small village depicts life in late 19C and early 20C Laws, a town that served as a major transportation center for the mining and agricultural communities in the Owens Valley. The narrow-gauge Carson & Colorado Railway, affectionately known to locals as the "Slim Princess," arrived in Laws in 1883, connecting the valley for the first time to the outside world. In 1900 the railroad was sold to the Southern Pacific, which continued to operate the line south from Laws to Keeler, on Owens Lake, until 1960.

Today the site consists of some 20 structures, including homes, shops and railroad-related buildings. Many have been moved here from surrounding areas, while several were built as parts of stage sets for westerns filmed in the area. Among the site's original structures are the Laws Depot and the pleasant board-and-batten Agent's House, furnished to reflect life in the late 19C and early 20C. On a portion of the original track stand boxcars and Old Engine No. 9, one of the last locomotives to make the run on the Slim Princess.

★★ PALM SPRINGS Deserts Pop 40,181

Map p 139 Tourist Office ☎619-778-8418

Palm Springs is the largest and most celebrated of a string of resort and retirement towns in the western end of the Coachella Valley, a broad basin between the San Jacinto and Little San Bernardino mountain ranges. Popularly known as the "golf capital of the world," the city annually welcomes some 2 million visitors and part-time residents, among them celebrities from the worlds of entertainment and politics, who come to play its extensive golf courses and browse its many upscale galleries and boutiques.

The Agua Caliente band of the Native Cahuilla were the area's first recorded residents, and much of present-day Palm Springs occupies land purchased or leased from them. The first white settler built an adobe house here in 1884, and by 1893 a hotel had opened. Both of these historic buildings have been relocated to the **Village Green Heritage Center** *(near the center of town at 221 S. Palm Canyon Dr)* and are operated as museums by the Palm Springs Historical Society *(open mid-Oct–May Wed–Sun; closed major holidays; $.50/museum; ♿ ☎619-323-8297).*

Natural hot springs and the dry climate made Palm Springs a little-known health resort in the early 20C, but much of its development did not occur until the 1930s, when Hollywood celebrities discovered the attractions of desert living. Wealthy business executives and successful professionals followed, and Palm Springs' reputation was established. Strict zoning maintains the city's elegant character: garish signs and tall buildings are prohibited, and new houses must be constructed so as to avoid casting shadows on existing houses.

Justine Hill

Desert Springs Resort in Palm Springs

Luxurious resorts and elegant homes are grouped in the surrounding affluent communities of Rancho Mirage and Indian Wells, and the town of **Palm Desert** is home to El Paseo, a 2mi boulevard lined with chic boutiques.

Golf, a game devised on the misty moors of Scotland, has reached its commercial pinnacle here in the California desert: some 80 golf courses dot the Coachella Valley, and the region annually hosts such major golf tournaments as the Bob Hope Desert Classic, the Dinah Shore LPGA Championship and the Frank Sinatra Celebrity Invitational. Most new residential developments are laid out around the links.

SIGHTS *At least 1 day*

★★★ **Palm Springs Aerial Tramway** – *Hwy 111 north to Tramway Rd, about 2mi from center of town, 3.8mi to parking lot. Open Apr–Oct Mon–Fri 10am–10:45pm, weekends 8am, rest of the year open Mon–Fri 10am–9:45pm, weekends 8am. Closed first two weeks in Aug. $15.95. ☎619-325-1391.* Bus-size gondolas with picture windows rise vertiginously up the face of the San Jacinto range (ha-SIN-tow) on cables suspended from five towers anchored in the rocky slope. The ascent *(14min)* from the bottom station, 2643ft above sea level, to the mountain station, 8516ft, carries the traveler from desert to mountain pine forests where snow lies deep through the winter. En route are spectacular **views**★★ down onto the crags below, and an ever-expanding vista across the Coachella Valley to the highlands of JOSHUA TREE NATIONAL MONUMENT and well beyond. The mountain station, housing a restaurant, a souvenir shop and video program on the construction of the tramway in the early 1960s, serves as a base for exploration of Mt San Jacinto State Park. Activities include hiking to the 10,804ft summit, cross-country skiing and showshoe trekking *(from Nov to Apr; rentals available at summit)*, and guided mule rides.

★★ **Palm Springs Desert Museum** – *101 Museum Dr, adjacent to the Desert Fashion Plaza at North Palm Canyon Dr and Tahquitz Way. Open mid-Sept–mid-Jun Tue–Thu 10am–4pm Fri 1–8pm. Closed major holidays. $5. ✗ ♿ ☎619-325-7186.* Housed in a sleek contemporary structure (1976), this museum offers an excellent overview of the natural history, culture history and art of the California deserts. The museum's size is striking in a city of such moderate size, until one remembers the revenue generated by Palm Springs' many visitors and seasonal residents.

The museum was established in 1938 as an anthropological and natural history museum of the Coachella Valley. As Palm Springs attracted more residents and retirees, among them art collectors from the East Coast and Middle West, the museum began to acquire works of contemporary American art by California and other western artists. The permanent fine arts collection now encompasses more than 4000 objects and the anthropological and natural history collections have grown as well. With the opening of the new complex and its 450-seat Annenberg Theater, the museum's offerings expanded to include the performing arts.

Visit – The **Natural Science Wing** *(right of the main entrance)* offers a fine introduction to desert geology, flora and fauna, and their interrelationships. Large dioramas of the California desert, relief displays and a group of terrariums housing such animals as scorpions, rodents and rattlesnakes, help to explain how the region was formed and how many desert creatures' behavioral and physiological adaptations have enabled them to survive in a hot, arid climate. A variety of high-quality **video presentations** presents desert ecology. The McCormick Gallery features temporary thematic exhibits drawn from the museum's permanent collection of artifacts.

The **Art Wing** *(left of the main entrance)* houses rotating exhibitions of contemporary California art from the permanent collection; long-term, high-quality visiting shows offer a balance of historical and modern art. Permanent exhibits include a large collection of Cahuilla basketry, American jewelry, a group of miniature rooms and a gallery of paintings of the American West. The sculpture court *(main level)* and sculpture garden *(lower level)* feature large pieces in outdoor settings by such sculptors as Henry Moore, Mark di Suvero and Jesus Morales. The Annenberg Theater *(lower level)* hosts a Sunday afternoon concert series as well as other music, theater and dance productions.

★ **Indian Canyons** – *End of S. Palm Canyon Dr about 4mi south of the town center. Open Sept–Jun daily. $5. ☎619-325-5673.* The Agua Caliente band retains ownership of three canyons in the lower slopes of the San Jacinto Mountains that contain extensive groves of **fan palms** *(Washingtonia filifera)*, California's only native species of palm. The trees flourish in the desert heat as long as their roots reach a reliable supply of water, provided here by runoff through these canyons. From the entrance gate, a paved road leads to a parking lot overlooking **Palm Canyon**★★, which shelters California's largest fan palm grove, comprising some 3,000 trees. The main grove extends 2mi back into the canyon and smaller groves flourish at intervals farther upstream. An easy trail traverses the sandy area in the shade of the trees, becoming more challenging as it ascends the narrow, upper reaches of the canyon.

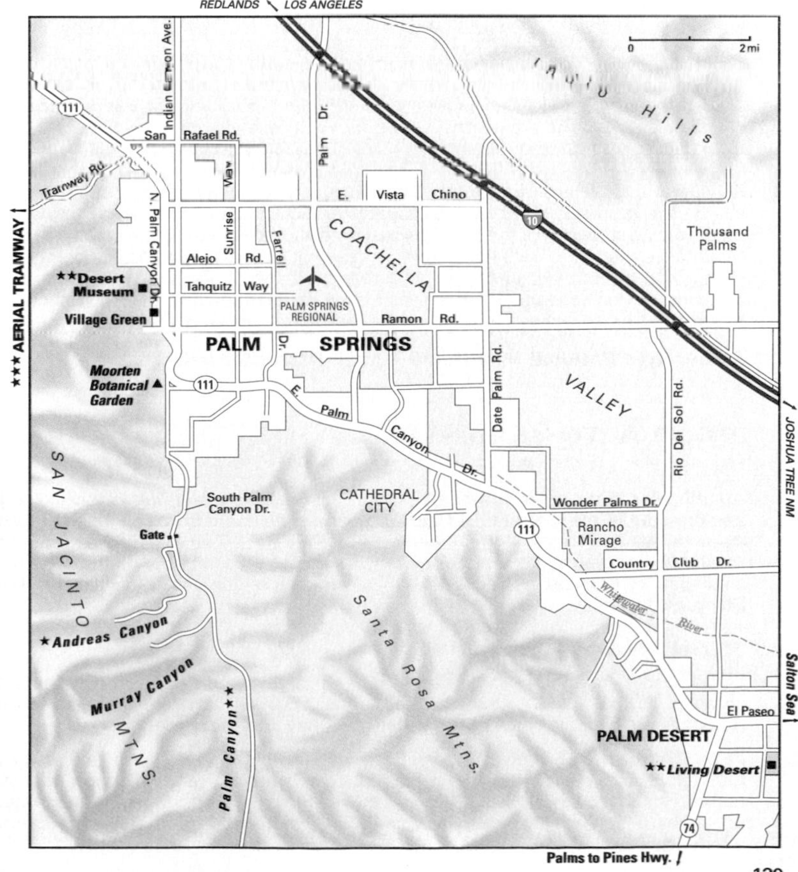

The path leading to smaller, but equally lush **Andreas Canyon**★ *(turn right 100yds past entrance gate and continue .8mi)* requires clambering over boulders that have rolled down from the canyon wall above. The trail through more remote **Murray Canyon** *(trail leads from parking lot at Andreas Canyon)* covers approximately 1mi of unshaded, low vegetation until it suddenly comes upon a dense stand of palms growing in a rocky stream bed.

Moorten Botanical Garden – *1701 South Palm Canyon Dr, about 2mi south of the center of Palm Springs. Open daily year-round. $2. ☎619-327-6555.* In a whimsically designed alternative to the formal and scientific presentations of national and state park botanical displays, a profusion of strange and curious plants from the world's deserts flourishes here in a dense diversity usually associated with tropical rain forests—3000 species in the garden's 2 acres. While some are for sale, many are for display only.

★★ **Living Desert** – *In Palm Desert, 15mi east of Palm Springs, 1.3mi south of Hwy 111 on Portola Ave. Open Sept–mid-Jun daily 9am–5pm. Closed Dec 25. $8.* ✗ ♿ *☎619-346-5694.* This botanical garden and zoo offers a comprehensive view of North American desert plant communities, and animals from arid lands.
Still being developed, the spacious grounds harbor 1500 varieties of plants and 75 species of animals. A central path connects a series of gardens representing each of the main subdivisions of the North American deserts, including the Upper Colorado Desert, the Yuman Desert and the arid territory of the Baja Peninsula. Interspersed with these gardens are enclosures for such small desert creatures as coyotes and desert tortoises. Bird aviaries are distributed about the grounds, and a reconstructed Cahuilla dwelling stands in a garden of plants used by these Native Americans for food and medicines. Bighorn sheep, Arabian oryx, gazelles and zebras graze within larger enclosures on the reserve's perimeter. Many of the animals are endangered or extinct in the wild, and the Living Desert plays a significant role in worldwide captive breeding and conservation efforts.

EXCURSIONS

Salton Sea – *About 50mi southeast of Palm Springs via Hwy 111.* A recent addition to the California landscape, this approximately 525sq mi sea was created in 1905 when the Colorado River broke through the levees of an irrigation project into a dry desert depression that lay some 250ft below sea level. (This area, including the Imperial and Coachella valleys, would be the north end of the Gulf of California had it not been separated from the sea by the delta of the Colorado River.) For almost two years the entire flow of the Colorado poured into the basin, until engineers were finally able to return the river to its former channel. The lake would soon evaporate in the desert heat if drainage from irrigated agriculture did not replenish it. The brownish-green water is now saltier than the Pacific Ocean (and getting more so each year), but still supports a large number of migratory birds. The **Salton Sea State Recreation Area** *(Hwy 111, 22mi south of Indio)* offers campgrounds, beaches, and fishing *(open daily year-round; $5/car;* ⚠ ♿ *☎619-393-3052).*

★ **Palms to Pines Highway** – *42mi from Palm Desert to Idyllwild; begin at intersection of Hwys 111 and 74 in Palm Desert.* Designated a National Scenic Byway in 1993, this mountain highway offers a beautiful and intriguing look at the incredibly diverse desert and alpine environments. As it ascends numerous switchbacks from the desert floor, the route offers **vistas** down into the Coachella Valley, across the Santa Rosa Mountains National Scenic Area and up into the peaks of the Santa Rosa and San Jacinto Mountains. Desert vegetation, including joshua trees and cholla cacti, gradually gives way to chaparral, which at higher elevations is replaced by the alpine splendor of the San Bernardino National Forest. At the small town of Mountain Center, the route turns north, traversing alpine mountainsides before arriving in charming **Idyllwild**★, a rustic resort village of shops, restaurants and lodgings nestled beneath tall pine trees. Home to the renowned Idyllwild School of Music and Arts, the village enjoys a reputation as an artistic retreat.

★★ **Joshua Tree National Monument** – *1 day. Description p 68.*

PALO ALTO San Francisco Bay Area — Pop 55,900

Map p 183 — Tourist Office ☎415-324-3121

An affluent college town situated between the marshlands of San Francisco Bay and the Santa Cruz Mountains, Palo Alto derives its name from the twin-trunked coast redwood under which Gaspar de Portolá camped on his 1769 expedition *(p 23)*. Now single-trunked and timeworn, **El Palo Alto**, "the tall tree," still stands in a small park by the railroad tracks off Alma Avenue. It remains the official symbol of Stanford University.

★★ STANFORD UNIVERSITY

Established by railroad magnate Leland Stanford, this world-renowned institution sprawls across 8,180 acres, its gracious Spanish-flavored Richardsonian Romanesque buildings shaded by eucalyptus, bay and palm trees.

"The Children of California..." – Born on a farm in New York, the university's founder, **Leland Stanford** (1824-1893), was a lawyer by training and an opportunist by nature. He moved to California during the Gold Rush, became state governor, then president of the Central Pacific Railroad *(p 24)*, a high-risk venture that earned him a fortune.

In 1884 Stanford and his wife, Jane, lost their only child, 15-year-old Leland Jr to typhoid fever. The bereaved couple, declaring that "the children of California shall be our children," set out to establish a university on the grounds of their Palo Alto ranch. Landscape architect Frederick Law Olmsted conceived the low, arcaded buildings that would house the university, which opened in 1891. Two years later, Stanford died at age 69, and his wife was left to shoulder the 1890s financial depression that threatened the existence of the university. By the early 20C, with the economic crisis resolved, Stanford University was on its way to becoming a solid academic institution.
Though the campus suffered severe earthquake damage in 1906 and 1989, it has remained a leading academic and research center, with a current enrollment of 13,893 students. Among its 1,408 faculty members are nine Nobel laureates, six Pulitzer Prize winners, and 19 winners of the National Medal of Science. The **Stanford Linear Accelerator Center**, devoted to research in particle physics, opened here in 1961.

Visit *3hrs*
Visitor information booth located at the entrance to the Quadrangle. Student-led campus tours depart from here Mondays year-round. ♿ ☎415-723-2560.

★ **Main Quadrangle** – The historic heart of the campus, this expansive, tiled courtyard is bordered by the university's 12 original colonnaded buildings and anchored by the impressive **Memorial Church★**. Built in 1903 by Mrs Stanford to commemorate her husband, the church features elaborate Byzantine-style mosaics, stained glass, and a renowned 7,777-pipe organ equipped to play Renaissance and Baroque music.

★ **Hoover Tower** – *Open daily year-round. Closed between academic quarters. $1. ♿ ☎415-723-2053.* The landmark 285ft campanile houses part of the Hoover Institution on War, Revolution and Peace, a public policy research center inspired by university alumnus Herbert Hoover. A small museum *(right of entrance hall)* is devoted to the accomplishments of Hoover and his wife, Lou Henry Hoover. The top of the tower features a 35-bell carillon and an observation deck offering panoramic **views** of the campus and of SAN FRANCISCO and the Bay Area to the north.

★ **Rodin Sculpture Garden** – Located on the southwest side of the university's Museum of Art *(closed until 1996 for structural repairs)*, this 1-acre, cypress-lined garden displays 20 large-scale bronze casts by French sculptor Auguste Rodin, including his famed *The Gates of Hell* (1880-1900).

Figures from Rodin's series, *The Burghers of Calais*, are also displayed throughout campus, as are sculptures by such prominent artists as Joan Miró, Alexander Calder, and Henry Moore. A free *Guide to Outdoor Sculpture* is available at the visitor information booth *(above)*.

★★ PASADENA Greater Los Angeles Area — Pop 131,591

Map p 83 Tourist Office ☎818-795-9311

Located less than 10mi from downtown LOS ANGELES, Pasadena seems a world away from the bustle and sprawl of its neighbor to the southwest. Bordered to the west by the Arroyo Seco, a "dry gulch" of the San Gabriel Mountains, the city moves at a more leisurely pace, and boasts architecture, cultural attractions and civic events worthy of a much larger city.

Rose City – Pasadena (the name was derived from a Native word meaning "crown of the valley") was born in 1874 when a small settlement of Indiana farmers was induced to try growing citrus here by the San Gabriel Orange Grove Association. Their efforts failed, but within the following decade, the Southern Pacific and Santa Fe railroads connected Pasadena to Chicago and the East, and the agricultural community became a winter resort for the wealthy. Eastern and Midwestern socialites built lavish mansions here, many of which survive today, and the city's early-20C prosperity is reflected in the Spanish Baroque and Renaissance buildings of the **Civic Center**, erected in the 1920s.
In 1889 Pasadena's elite Valley Hunt Club voted to mark New Year's Day with an annual parade of flower-decked coaches; in subsequent years the parade preceded a variety of sporting events, including footraces, tug-of-wars and other friendly competitions. Over the years, the carriages evolved into elaborate floats covered with flowers; and in 1916 the sports events were replaced by a championship college football match. Today the **Rose Parade** and the **Rose Bowl Game**, pitting the winners of the Pacific Coast and Big Ten conferences, are nationally televised.

SIGHTS *At least 1 day*

★★★ **Norton Simon Museum** – *411 W. Colorado Blvd. Open year-round Thu–Sun noon–6pm. Closed Jan 1, Dec 25. $4. ♿ ☎818-449-6840.* Elegantly displayed in a stark contemporary building overlooking Pasadena's main thoroughfare is a selection of approximately 1,000 works from one of the world's choicest private art collections, spanning seven centuries of European painting and sculpture as well as 2,000 years of Asian sculpture.

A Personal Vision – Through the mid-19C, entrepreneur Norton Simon (1907-1993) built a multinational corporation that included Hunt-Wesson Foods, McCalls Corporation and Canada Dry Corporation. Guided by a personal vision of art "in which the human presence is always seen or presumed," Simon began collecting paintings in 1954, beginning with canvases by Gauguin, Bonnard and Pissarro. A visit to New Delhi in 1971 inspired him to begin collecting Asian art. By the time of his death, Simon had amassed a collection of more than 11,000 pieces, with particular strengths in 14-18C European art, French Impressionist paintings, the works of Edgar Degas, and Indian and Southeast Asian sculpture.

Starting in the late 1960s, Simon loaned works to major museums in the US and Europe, including two exhibits of 19C and 20C sculpture to the financially troubled Pasadena Art Museum. In 1974, the Norton Simon Foundation and the Norton Simon Art Foundation took over that museum, re-establishing it as a permanent home for his collections and renaming it for its benefactor.

14C-18C European Paintings – *To the right of the main entrance.* Outstanding among the collection's earliest works are *Madonna and Child with a Book* (c.1502) by Raphael; *The Coronation of the Virgin* (1344), an altarpiece by Arpo, who introduced the Gothic style into Venetian painting; and two lovely, life-size depictions of *Adam* and *Eve* (c.1530) by Cranach the Elder. Lining a passageway, six giant **tapestry cartoons** (c.1630) by Romanelli depict the story of Dido and Aeneas. Baroque canvases from the 17C include works by Jan Steen, Zurburán and Rubens. Paintings in the Rococo style of the 18C include works by Goya; an additional gallery displays monumental paintings from that period, including *The Piazzetta, Venice, Looking North* (before 1755) by Canaletto; and Tiepolo's *The Triumph of Virtue and Nobility Over Ignorance* (1740-1750), which was originally a ceiling painting.

The Mulberry Tree (1889)
by Vincent van Gogh

19C-20C European paintings – *To the left of the main entrance.* Holdings are particularly strong in paintings by renowned French Impressionists, including Monet, Renoir and Pissarro. Also well represented here are Picasso, Cézanne, Klee, Van Gogh, Feininger, Matisse, Jawlensky and Kandinsky.

Degas Collection – Occupying the stairwell rotunda and adjoining spaces on the lower level, the permanent exhibit of over 100 works by French Impressionist Edgar Degas (1834-1917) includes drawings and pastels of ballet dancers and such well-known paintings as *The Ironers* (c.1884).Highlighting the collection is a group of 71 bronze sculptures or *modeles*, cast directly from Degas' wax originals for use as foundry models.

Indian and Southeast Asian Sculpture – On display are selections from the museum's extensive holdings of Jain, Buddhist and Hindu sculptures from India; and Buddhist and Hindu sculptures from the Himalayas, Thailand, Cambodia and Vietnam. Also included are Nepalese watercolors and a monumental 18C silk-appliqué festival hanging from Tibet.

Displayed in the museum's forecourt, throughout its galleries and in the **sculpture garden** are outstanding works by 19C and 20C sculptors, most notably Rodin, Maillol and Moore.

★★★ **Huntington Library, Art Collections and Botanical Gardens** – *1151 Oxford Rd, San Marino. Open year-round Tue–Fri 1–4:30pm, weekends 10:30am–4:30pm. Closed major holidays. $5.* ✗♿ *☎818-405-2141.* One of the Los Angeles area's most distinguished cultural institutions, "The Huntington" comprises one of the world's finest research libraries of rare books and manuscripts; a world-class collection of 18C and 19C British art, along with French and American works; and internationally renowned botanical gardens. Secluded in the upscale Pasadena suburb of San Marino, the Huntington occupies 207 idyllic acres remaining from the former 600-acre ranch of turn-of-the-century tycoon Henry E. Huntington and his wife Arabella.

From Railroads to Rarities – Born in 1850 in Oneonta, New York, **Henry E. Huntington** began his career in the employ of his uncle, Collis P. Huntington *(p 24)*, an owner of the Central Pacific Railroad. In 1892, Henry moved to SAN FRANCISCO to help run the Southern Pacific Railroad. His uncle died in 1900, and two years later Henry left the company and settled in Los Angeles. There he made his own fortune by expanding and consolidating the city's electric railway system, the so-called "Big Red Cars," into a network that helped fuel the region's growth.

In 1902 Huntington bought a rugged working ranch known as San Marino, and in 1904 hired landscape gardener William Hertrich to begin developing the estate's grounds, a task Hertrich continued until his retirement in 1949 at the age of 70. Huntington also commissioned a residence and a library in the Beaux-Arts style.

In 1903 Huntington retired at the age of 60 to devote his life to collecting books and art and to landscaping his estate. Joining him in these pursuits was Arabella Duvall Huntington, the widow of his uncle and herself one of America's most notable collectors. The same age as Henry, she became his second wife in 1913. They continued avidly buying art and antiques until Arabella's death in 1924; Henry died three years later.

In 1919 the Huntingtons had transferred their estate and collections to a nonprofit trust that continues to administer the Huntington, providing 60 percent of the annual budget; the remainder comes from public and private donations. First opened to the public in 1928, the Huntington now draws more than 500,000 visitors each year. Over 1,800 scholars are granted access to the research library, and the estate's holdings continue to grow through purchases and donations.

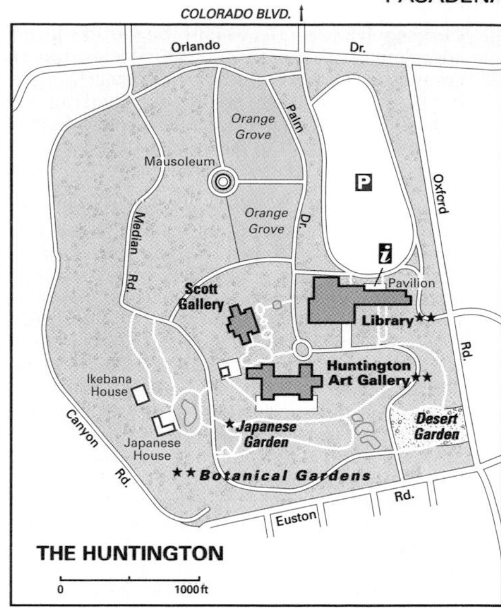

★★ **Library** – The stately Beaux-Arts building (1920, Myron Hunt) houses approximately 3.1 million manuscripts, 357,000 rare books and 321,000 reference works, with an emphasis on British and American history, literature, and art from the 11C to the present. While most of the library's space is devoted to closed stacks and research facilities, the exhibition hall displays approximately 200 outstanding pieces from the collection. Highlights include the **Ellesmere Chaucer**, an exquisitely illustrated manuscript (c.1410) of *The Canterbury Tales*; a **Gutenberg Bible** (c.1450), one of only three vellum copies in the United States; selections from the world's leading collection of early Shakespeare editions, including a **First Folio**, or first edition of his plays, four massive volumes (known as a "double-elephant folio") of *Birds of America* (1827-1828) by **John James Audubon**; and handwritten letters and manuscripts by famous Americans including Benjamin Franklin, George Washington, Thomas Jefferson, Abraham Lincoln, Mark Twain and Henry David Thoreau.

The library's west wing features a collection of Renaissance paintings and 18C French decorative arts.

★★ **Huntington Art Gallery** – Works housed in the former Huntington residence (1910, Myron Hunt) focus on 18-19C British art and 18C French art. The collection of **British art**★★★ is considered among the finest outside of London, particularly for its grouping of twenty late-18C life-size, full-length portraits by Joshua Reynolds, Thomas Gainsborough, George Romney and Sir Thomas Lawrence *(main gallery)*. Most notable among these are Gainsborough's *Jonathan Buttall: "The Blue Boy"* (c.1770); Lawrence's *Sarah Barrett Moulton: "Pinkie"* (1794); and Reynolds' *Sarah Siddons as the Tragic Muse* (1784). The adjoining passage displays a collection of English miniature portraits (late 16C to early 19C), along with early-16C English silver pieces. The remainder of the 2-story building displays paintings, drawings and sculpture in rooms richly appointed with English and French 18C furnishings.

Virginia Steele Scott Gallery – Opened in 1984, this small gallery features works of American art from the 18C to the early 20C, including representative pieces by Gilbert Stuart, John Singleton Copley, Charles Wilson Peale, George Caleb Bingham, Frederic Edwin Church, Robert Henri, Thomas Moran, Mary Cassatt, John Sloan and Edward Hopper. A separate room presents early 20C decorative pieces and room settings by Arts and Crafts architects/designers Charles and Henry Greene, who worked in Pasadena and executed most of their major commissions here, including the Gamble House *(p 114)*.

★★ **Botanical Gardens** – Covering 150 acres, the gardens include approximately 14,000 different species and cultivars, all labeled and presented in 15 thematic groupings. Crisscrossed by pathways, the gently rolling terrain of the 12-acre

The Huntington

Sarah Barrett Moulton: "Pinkie" (1794) by Sir Thomas Lawrence

desert garden presents one of the world's largest collections of mature cacti and succulents, with more than 2,500 species. The tranquil, terraced **Japanese garden★** encompasses a koi pond and gracefully arching moon bridge, a traditional Japanese house, a Zen garden of raked gravel and rocks, and a collection of miniature bonsai trees. Both the rose and camellia gardens feature more than 1,400 different cultivars of their species. Other gardens feature palms, lily ponds, Australian plants, jungle and subtropical species, herbs and English plants from Shakespeare's time.

★★ **Gamble House** – *4 Westmoreland Pl, paralleling the 300 block of N. Orange Grove Blvd. Visit by guided tour (1hr) only, year-round Thu–Sun noon–3pm. Closed major holidays. $4. Ticket office in gift shop adjacent to house. ☎818-793-3334.* Considered a masterpiece of the Arts and Crafts movement and the finest surviving home designed by renowned Pasadena-based architects Charles and Henry Greene, this 8,800sq ft house was built in 1908 as the winter family residence of David B. Gamble, heir of the Procter & Gamble soap company. Construction lasted just ten months and cost $54,000. Since 1966 the house has been jointly maintained and administered by the City of Pasadena and the USC School of Architecture.
Covered in redwood shingles, the sprawling, 2-story gabled "bungalow" and its contents exemplify the Greene brothers' dedication to fine craftsmanship and totally integrated design. Wide overhanging eaves shelter broad verandas and upstairs open-air sleeping porches, while 15 exterior doors and numerous interior windows ensure excellent cross-ventilation. The **interior** abounds with decorative masterworks conceived for the house by the Greene brothers, including furnishings and intricate woodwork incorporating some 20 types of wood. A fine assemblage of stained-glass windows was executed by Emile Lange of the Tiffany Studios.
Westmoreland Place and nearby **Arroyo Terrace** and **Grand Avenue** feature eight more examples of Greene and Greene bungalows in varying states of preservation.

★ **Rose Bowl** – *991 Rosemont Blvd.* Set on the floor of the Arroyo Seco with views of the surrounding San Gabriel Mountains, this famed oval stadium (1922, Myron Hunt), measuring 880ft by 695ft, was originally horseshoe-shaped. Its south end was enclosed in 1932, and later modifications enlarged it to its current capacity of 103,553. Annual New Year's Day site of the Rose Bowl Game *(p 141)*, it is also home stadium for UCLA football and hosts a wide variety of other sporting events.

Pacific Asia Museum – *46 N. Los Robles Ave. Open year-round Wed–Sun. Closed major holidays. $3. ✗ ☎818-449-2742.* With its upturned roof, ornate ornamentation and central courtyard, the 2-story building (1924) mimics the Chinese Imperial Palace style. Its **courtyard garden★**, completed in 1979, is one of only two authentic Chinese gardens in the US; the other is located at New York's Metropolitan Museum of Art.

★★ **Los Angeles State and County Arboretum** – *301 N. Baldwin Ave, Arcadia. Open year-round daily 9am-4:30pm. Closed Dec 25. $5. Tram tours (45min) depart adjacent to gift shop. ✗ ♿ ☎818-821-3222.* Set against the majestic backdrop of the San Gabriel Mountains, these gardens display extensive international plant collections and offer vivid glimpses of local architectural history.
The land originally lay at the heart of the 13,319-acre Rancho Santa Anita, deeded in 1841 to Hugo Reid, a Scottish-born immigrant and naturalized Mexican citizen. Mining millionaire E. J. "Lucky" Baldwin *(p 74)* purchased them in 1875 as the cornerstone of San Gabriel Valley holdings that eventually totaled 46,000 acres.
In 1936 Baldwin's daughter, Anita, sold the last remaining 1,300 acres to a real estate syndicate headed by *Los Angeles Times* owner Harry Chandler. The lake on the property became a location for Hollywood films, including *Road to Singapore* (1939) and *Tarzan and the Huntress* (1947). Chandler sold 111 acres to the county in 1947 for development as an arboretum; later purchases brought it to its present size, and the grounds opened in 1955.
Today the 127-acre arboretum features some 30,000 plants representing over 7,000 species, largely arranged by continent of origin. Highlights include 150 of the 500 known species of eucalyptus, one of the largest collections outside of Australia; and 2,299 different species of orchids, one of the largest collections in the US.
The centerpiece of the grounds is the spring-fed lake, a serene body of water bordered on the north by a collection of plants representing the diversity found in tropical environments. South of the lake are historic buildings furnished in period style: reconstructed Gabrieleño wickiups; the rustic, 3-room **Hugo Reid Adobe**, built in 1840; and the ornately decorated white and red Victorian **Lucky Baldwin Cottage** (1885), built as a guest house by the mining entrepreneur.

★ **Descanso Gardens** – *1418 Descanso Dr, La Cañada-Flintridge. Open daily year-round. Closed Dec 25. $5. ✗ ♿ ☎818-952-4401.* Nestled in a hollow of the San Rafael hills and facing the nearby San Gabriel Mountains is a 165-acre botanical haven that provides an Eden-like respite from downtown Los Angeles.
In 1937 E. Manchester Boddy, publisher of the *Los Angeles Daily News*, purchased the land (originally part of a ranch deeded to the Verdugo family) and built a 22-room mansion on a hill overlooking the site. An avid horticulturalist, he recognized the setting's 25-acre grove of gnarled California live oaks as an ideal environment for growing camellias, and developed there a successful wholesale camellia nursery, eventually expanding his gardens to include roses, lilacs, and other flowering plants. In 1953, Boddy sold the estate to the County of Los Angeles.
Descanso Gardens—the name is derived from the Spanish word for "rest"—today feature more than 100,000 plants from some 600 different species. The **camellia forest★** *(in bloom Jan-Mar)*, includes specimens as tall as 20ft or more, forming dense, cool groves of towering greenery crossed by footpaths; in one corner, a Japanese **tea house** is surrounded by traditional gardens and a koi fish pond.

★ PETALUMA North Coast Pop 43,184

Map p 236 Tourist Office ☎707-762-2785

Set astride the Petaluma River in a fertile valley 40mi north of SAN FRANCISCO, this small agricultural town grew from a hunters' camp to a grain-shipping port in 1852. The Great Petaluma Mill *(Petaluma Blvd & B St; restored as a shopping complex)*, once the region's largest feed mill, survives as a testimony to the city's early industry. In 1879 Lyman Byce put Petaluma on the map when he invented a new incubator for the mass production of poultry. Dubbed the "World's Egg Basket," Petaluma shipped as many as 600 million eggs per year until high labor and feed costs caused the decline of the poultry industry after World War II. The city today remains a dairy center; the **Creamery Store** offers local products for sale *(711 Western Ave; open year-round; visit by guided tour only; ♿ ☎707-778-1234)*.

VISIT *1/2 day*

★ **Historic Downtown** – *Walking tour maps available at Chamber of Commerce, 215 Howard St.* River commerce and poultry generated the revenue used to construct the city's grandest cast-iron buildings at the turn of the century. Widely used in the construction of commercial buildings in the mid- to late-18C, cast iron was molded and sold in prefabricated parts. It thus provided an inexpensive way to reproduce the ornately carved cornices and columns that distinguished the architectural styles of the day. In addition to its low cost and ease of use, cast iron was thought to protect buildings from fire, a notion which later proved false.

Petaluma's finest row of ironfront architecture *(Western Ave between Kentucky St & Petaluma Blvd)* is bounded on the north corner by the Italianate **Mutual Relief Building** (1885) and on the south by the **Masonic Hall** (1882), topped by a landmark clock tower. Nearby, the **McNear Building** *(15-23 Petaluma Blvd)*, with its elegant row of second-story arches, actually incorporates two structures; the original (1886) and the addition (1911) were owned by one of Petaluma's first families. Garlands, wreaths and marbled columns constitute some of the rich detail that distinguishes the facade of the **Old Opera House**★ *(149 Kentucky St)*, built in 1870 to host minstrel shows and theater productions.

Completed in 1906, the sandstone Classical Revival **Petaluma Historical Museum and Library** houses a small collection of artifacts related to local history *(20 Fourth St; open daily year-round; closed Jan 1, Easter Sunday, Dec 25; ♿ ☎707-778-4398)*. The building's free-standing, stained-glass dome is the largest in California.

★★ **Petaluma Adobe State Historic Park** – *3325 Adobe Rd. Take E. Washington St; turn right on Adobe Rd, 1.9mi to park entrance on left. Open year-round daily 10am–5pm. Closed Jan 1, Thanksgiving Day, Dec 25. $2. ☎707-762-4871.* Mexican commander Mariano Vallejo *(p 229)* chose this hilltop overlooking the rolling Sonoma County countryside as the site of his headquarters in 1834. Here he established a 100sq mi ranch on land granted to him by the Mexican governor. Rancho Petaluma thrived, raising cattle, horses, sheep and bountiful crops of grain until Vallejo leased the property in September, 1850. Over the next 100 years, the adobe saw a number of different owners until the state took it over in 1951.

Originally, the dwelling surrounded the courtyard on four sides. Today the restored 2-story structure, which is one-half its initial size, recreates the atmosphere of a prosperous ranch. Authentic period pieces decorate Vallejo's personal chambers and other rooms upstairs; ground-floor rooms are outfitted with looms, kitchen tools and candle-making equipment. In the courtyard stand hive-shaped ovens once used to prepare meals for the adobe's residents.

Marin French Cheese Company – *7500 Red Hill Rd; 9mi south of Petaluma via D St extension. Open daily year-round. Closed Jan 1, Thanksgiving Day, Dec 25. ✗ ♿ ☎ 707-762-6001.* Nestled among tranquil hills next to a tree-shaded pond, the factory offers a behind-the-scenes glimpse of the cheese-making process, from separating the curd to aging the cheese and packaging the final product. A sales room carries a full line of the company's products.

★★ POINT REYES NATIONAL SEASHORE North Coast

Map p127

White sand beaches, rocky headlands, windswept moors, salt marshes and densely forested hillsides can all be found within this 102sq mi park. These diverse ecosystems, created by centuries of the earth's shifting, harbor a wide variety of plant and animal life, including tule elk, sea lions and 338 species of birds.

Lying along the San Andreas fault, Point Reyes Peninsula was thrust to its present position some 20ft northwest of the mainland when an earthquake jarred the area in 1906 *(p 185)*. Inverness Ridge now parallels the fault's submerged rift valley and constitutes the high ground of the seashore, which slopes to the ocean across a landscape of rolling pasture land and saltwater estuaries.

Drake's Debated Anchorage – Purportedly the first European to set foot on Point Reyes Peninsula, English explorer Francis Drake set out from England in 1577 to reconnoiter Spanish defenses in the New World. Many historians believe that the "convenient and fit harborough" where Drake anchored his ship, the *Golden Hind*, for repairs two years later was the bay that now bears his name. Supporting this claim is the fact that Drake called his landfall "New Albion" for "the white bancks and cliffes" (resembling the blanched palisades along England's Dover coast) that still stand sentinel over Drakes Beach. Opponents claim Drake landed in BODEGA BAY; still others argue for San Francisco Bay. Since the *Golden Hind's* log has long since disappeared, historians may never know for certain.

Drake's claim to New Albion was never upheld by further English activity, and the area became a distant colony of Spain. After the Mexicans shrugged off the mantle of Spanish rule in 1822, they introduced cattle ranching to the Point Reyes Peninsula; eventually Americans leased the land for dairy farming. Today beef and dairy cattle still graze on the peninsula's brushy pasturelands. Threat of suburban development in the 1950s led to the creation of the Point Reyes National Seashore in 1962.

VISIT *1 1/2 days*
Open daily year-round. ♿ ✗ ☎415-663-8522. Main park roads: Sir Francis Drake Hwy (Bear Valley to Point Reyes Lighthouse), Pierce Point Rd (Tomales Bay State Park north to McClures Beach) and Hwy 1 (north to south, eastern end of park). Southwestern portion of park primarily accessible by hiking trails. Swimming allowed at Limantour & Drakes beaches only, no lifeguards on duty.

Take Hwy 1 north to Olema. Just past main intersection, turn left on Bear Valley Rd and left again at sign for Visitor Information.

Bear Valley Visitor Center – *Open daily year-round. Closed Dec 25. Site and trail maps available. ♿ ☎415-663-1092.* This attractive wood structure contains exhibits that recount the area's cultural and natural history. A film *(20min)* introduces visitors to the park.
Near the visitor center, the **Earthquake Trail** *(.4mi loop)* traces the San Andreas fault. Another trail *(1mi round-trip)* leads to **Kule Loklo** (Miwok for "Bear Valley"), a charmingly re-created Miwok village.
Limantour Beach *(9mi from visitor center on Limantour Rd)*, sheltered to the north by the Point Reyes headland, offers a **view** along Drake's Bay that extends from Double Point to Chimney Rock.

Point Reyes Peninsula – *From the visitor center, turn left on Bear Valley Rd. Bear left on Sir Francis Drake Hwy.* From Inverness Park, the road runs along Tomales Bay for 4.5mi, passing through the charming town of **Inverness**, with its quaint houses and bright gardens set back on the hills overlooking the bay. It then cuts west across the treeless moors of the peninsula that terminates at Point Reyes. The fog that often rolls over this landscape from the coast creates an eerie atmosphere. Narrow Mt. Vision Road *(turn left 1mi after Sir Francis Drake Hwy turns west)* winds 2.3mi to an **overlook** that commands a striking **view★** across tranquil Drakes and Limantour esteros to the Pacific. The road continues *(1.5mi)* to the summit of **Mt Vision** (1,282ft), where hikers can connect to several different trails.

Beaches – The splendid 12mi strip comprising **North Beach** and **South Beach** *(follow Drake Highway southwest for 4.7mi; turn right at sign)* faces northwest—directly into the strongest winds and roughest surf of the open ocean. Framed by high, chalk-white cliffs, **Drakes Beach** *(2mi west of North Beach)* nestles in the southern crook of precipitous Point Reyes headland.

★★ **Point Reyes Lighthouse** – *Continue to the end of Sir Francis Drake Hwy. Turn right and follow signs to lighthouse parking lot. A short walk (.25mi) leads to a small visitor center and viewing platform. Open year-round Mon, Thu–Sun 10am–5pm. Closed Dec 25. ♿ ☎415-669-1534.* Subject to some of the highest winds and thickest fogs on the Pacific coast, this beacon perches halfway down the 600ft precipice of Point Reyes. A flight of some 300 steps *(closed when wind speed exceeds 40mph)* descends to the lighthouse, where visitors can see the original Fresnel lens imported from France to light the rocky coast in 1870.
On a clear day, this dramatic setting offers sweeping **views★★** of the Farallon Islands to the southwest and of distant San Francisco. Whale-watchers flock here to glimpse hundreds of gray whales that pass close to the point on their annual migrations *(Dec–Apr).*

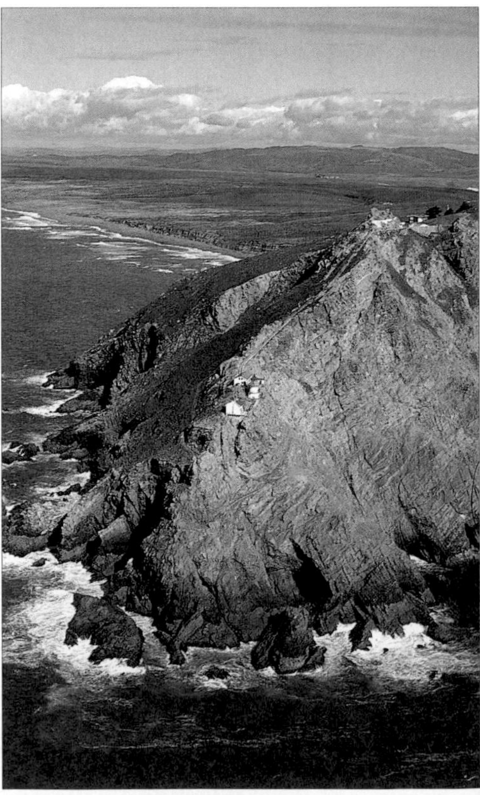

Point Reyes Lighthouse

Tomales Point Area – *From the Bear Valley visitor center, take Sir Francis Drake Hwy north 7.5mi. Turn right on Pierce Ranch Rd.* The spit of land extending north from Inverness borders Tomales Bay on the east and the Pacific on the west. Along Pierce Ranch Road, ranch houses and herds of cattle punctuate barren rolling moors. At the road's end lies **Upper Pierce Ranch**, a former dairy farm that offers a self-guided tour of whitewashed buildings dating back to 1858 *(under restoration; open year-round daily; ♿ ☎415-663-1092).* From the trailhead here, the road *(10mi round-trip)* that once linked the Pierce family's two ranches leads out to Tomales Point. A herd of tule elk, recently reintroduced into this wilderness, roams the range surrounding the road.

The wild, mile-long stretch of **McClures Beach** *(turn left at the end of Pierce Point Rd; beach accessible by a steep .5mi dirt path)* is bounded on each end by granite outcrops. At the south end of the beach, a narrow passageway through the rocks *(accessible only at low tide)* opens onto a pocket beach where bird-watchers can observe cormorants nesting on Elephant Rock.

REDDING Shasta-Cascade — Pop 66,462

Map of Principal Sights p 2 Tourist Office ☎916-243-2643

This sprawling city in the rolling foothills that separate the Cascade Range from the Central Valley serves as a regional commercial center and the seat of Shasta County. Positioned at the hub of several major highways, Redding affords travelers a good selection of amenities and is thus a convenient base for exploring interior northern California's myriad recreational opportunities and natural wonders, including MT SHASTA, LASSEN VOLCANIC NATIONAL PARK and LAVA BEDS NATIONAL MONUMENT. Redding also boasts several noteworthy attractions of its own.

The Wintu and Yana Natives, who hunted and fished in the areas surrounding the Sacramento River, disappeared from the vicinity around the mid-1800s. The first Anglo settler here was Pierson B. Reading, who in 1848 discovered gold in nearby Clear Creek and established the community of Reading Springs 5mi west of present-day Redding. Copper strikes bolstered mining activity in the region through the turn of the century. The present city was founded in 1872 by B.B. Redding, a land agent of the Central Pacific Railroad, and developed as a shipping center for the region's bountiful agricultural and mineral output.

The collapse of the copper boom in 1920 brought about a severe depression, but construction of Shasta Dam, beginning in 1938, had a tonic effect on Redding's economy. Today the city enjoys an enviable location between the eastern and western sections of Shasta-Trinity National Forest and within easy reach of the three segments of the **Whiskeytown-Shasta-Trinity National Recreation Area**, established in 1965 to prevent development of the unspoiled lands surrounding Whiskeytown, Shasta and Clair-Engle lakes. Outdoor enthusiasts flock to this area for its abundant opportunities for hiking, camping, hunting and water sports.

SIGHTS *1 day*

★ **Shasta State Historic Park** – *4mi west of Redding via Hwy 299. Open Mar–Oct Mon, Thur–Sun, rest of the year Fri–Sun. Closed Jan 1, Thanksgiving Day, Dec 25. $2. ♿ ☎916-243-8194.* Empty, roofless brick walls, black iron shutters and silence are all that remain of once-booming Shasta City, formerly known as the "Queen City of the Northern Mines." Founded in 1848 as a mining camp called Reading Springs, the community grew quickly as gold seekers flocked here to prospect the tributaries of the Sacramento River. By 1850 the camp had taken on the appearance of a permanent settlement, and its name was changed to Shasta City; several months later it was designated the seat of Shasta County. Severe fires consumed most of the town in 1852 and 1853, but the wooden commercial buildings were rapidly replaced by structures of brick and iron.

Expansion of road systems in the surrounding area decreased Shasta City's importance in the late 1850s, and the Central Pacific Railroad's decision to locate its terminus 5mi to the east sounded the town's death knell. Residents and businesses slowly relocated to Redding, and by the turn of the century, Shasta City had been virtually abandoned.

Restoration and preservation began in the 1920s, and today visitors can wander among the brick walls and other traces of the town. The former **courthouse** has been refurbished as a museum displaying artifacts and photos from the disappeared town; and interpretive displays in the visitor center recount the story of Shasta City and the surrounding region.

★ **Shasta Dam** – *14mi north of Redding via I-5; exit Shasta Dam Blvd.* Completed in 1945, this massive concrete barrier is the keystone structure of the **Central Valley Project** *(p 16)*, a vast network of dams, canals and pumping stations designed to control flooding and supply irrigation water to the farmlands of the Sacramento and San Joaquin valleys. Measuring 602ft high and 3,460ft long, the dam is taller than the Washington Monument in the nation's capital, and its central spillway is three times as high as Niagara Falls in Ontario, Canada. The Sacramento, McCloud and Pit rivers, and Squaw Creek are impounded behind the dam to create beautiful **Shasta Lake★**, the state's largest reservoir and one of the area's most popular recreation sites. When full, the lake boasts 365mi of shoreline and 29,500 acres of water surface. Houseboating is popular here, and the lake boasts the state's largest fleet of houseboats for rent.

An overlook on the road approaching the dam allows a stunning **view★** of the dam and lake; Mt Shasta looms in the background. Historical displays in the visitor center recount the fascinating story of the dam's construction and of the Central Valley Project *(open daily year-round; ♿ ☎916-275-4463).*

★ **Lake Shasta Caverns** – *20mi north of Redding via I-5; exit Shasta Caverns Rd. Visit by guided tour (2hrs) only, daily year-round. Closed Thanksgiving Day, Dec 25. $12.* ✗ ♿ ☎*916-238-2341.* Secreted within the eastern bank of Shasta Lake's McCloud River arm is a series of subterranean chambers created by dissolution of water-soluble limestone beneath the earth's surface. A private concessionaire operates guided tours through the caverns, introducing visitors to a variety of beautifully colored and formed mineral features, including flowstone, draperies and fluted columns. Tours begin with a boat ride across Shasta Lake and a bus ride up to the cavern entrance.

EXCURSIONS

Weaverville – *2hrs. 48mi west of Redding via Hwy 299. Description p 232.*

McArthur-Burney Falls Memorial State Park – *65mi northeast of Redding via Hwys 229 and 89. Facility information p 257. Open daily year-round. $5/car.* ⛺ ✗ ♿ ☎*916-335-2777.* Perhaps the loveliest phenomenon in a region endowed with an abundance of natural phenomena is 129ft **Burney Falls★★**, once dubbed by Theodore Roosevelt as the "eighth wonder of the world." Though not exceptionally tall, the falls owe their uniqueness to the presence of an underground stream flowing just beneath the surface of spring-fed Burney Creek, which cascades over a basalt cliff in a thundering shower. Water from the underground stream emerges from the fern-covered face of the cliff in myriad wispy falls, creating stunning aquatic effects. The mist-filled air above the falls provides a blank canvas for the light filtering through the foliage above, presenting an ever-changing play of shadows and frequent rainbows.

A nature trail *(1.6mi loop)* leads in a circuit along the gorge beneath the falls and across Burney Creek; panels and an interpretive brochure explain the geological features and flora visible in the immediate area.

REDLANDS Inland Empire — Pop 60,394

Map of Principal Sights p 4 — Tourist Office ☎909-793-2546

Named for the color of the local soil, tinged red by iron oxide, this small city at the base of the San Bernardino Mountains about 65mi east of LOS ANGELES thrived, like neighboring RIVERSIDE, as an agricultural center and winter resort destination. Residents made wealthy by the flourishing navel orange industry erected large, luxurious homes that came to be known as the "Marmalade Mansions." Over 300 of these survive today, along with numerous well-preserved examples of Victorian architecture. Agriculture continues to support the local economy, which also benefits from the University of Redlands.

SIGHTS *1/2 day*

San Bernardino County Museum – *2024 Orange Tree Lane; exit I-10 at California St and drive north 1mi. Open year-round Tue–Sun. Closed Jan 1, Thanksgiving Day, Dec 25. $3.* ♿ ☎*909-798-8570.* Housed in a large, buff-colored building set amid fields of orange trees, this museum celebrates local anthropology, agricultural and mining heritage. The **Hall of Anthropology** *(lower level)* offers an introduction to the prehistoric Natives of Southern California; of particular note are items excavated from Pleistocene Lake Manix in the Mojave Desert, today the setting for archaeological explorations at the CALICO EARLY MAN SITE. In the adjacent hall, a Conestoga wagon (called a "prairie schooner") and other relics of the Great Westward Migration illustrate the arrival of Anglo settlers to the area. The upper floor is devoted to ornithological collections, highlighted by the Wilson Hanna Collection of 30,000 bird eggs gathered from all over the world.

The museum mounts long-term temporary exhibitions in the adjacent **Discovery Hall**, which also contains hands-on science displays designed for children.

Directly behind the museum is the striking, Italianate **Edwards Mansion** *(not open to the public)*, erected in 1890 and worth a look for its ornate, beautifully restored exterior.

Lincoln Memorial Shrine – *125 W. Vine St. Open year-round Tue–Sat (open Lincoln's Birthday). Closed major holidays. Contribution requested.* ♿ *(with notice)* ☎*909-798-7632.* The only memorial to Abraham Lincoln west of the Mississippi River, this small, octagonal structure displays elements of one of the largest collections of Lincoln memorabilia outside Washington DC and Springfield, Illinois. Among the artifacts on display are a Ford's Theatre playbill dated April 14, 1865 (the night of Lincoln's assassination there), and letters of Confederate generals Stonewall Jackson and Robert E. Lee. The shrine's exterior is inscribed with quotations from Lincoln's speeches, and interior lunette paintings interpret the events in the life of the 16th President through allegorical symbols.

★ **Kimberly Crest House and Gardens** – *1325 Prospect Dr. Gardens open daily year-round. House by guided tour (1hr 30min) only, year-round Thur–Sun. Closed Aug & major holidays. $3.* ♿ ☎*909-792-2111.* Built in 1897, this elegant residence resembling a French chateau was purchased in 1905 by Kimberly-Clark Corporation founder J. Alfred Kimberly, who moved here with his family to spend his retirement years. Upon the Kimberlys' deaths, ownership passed to their daughter Mary Shirk, who promised to will the 6-acre estate to the people of Redlands, on the condition that the community raise funds to purchase the adjacent property (today known as Prospect Park) and preserve it from development.

The house crowns a gentle hill landscaped in the Italian Renaissance style, with cascading fountains, stairways, balustrades and terraced gardens replete with more than 53 species of plants. The luxurious interior, renovated between 1905 and 1910 by Mrs Kimberly, offers an excellent look at early-20C decorative elements, including rich woodwork, elegant wall coverings (rose damask, painted silver glaze), stained-glass windows and Tiffany lamps; all of the furnishings are original to the house.

San Bernardino Asistencia Mission – *26930 Barton Rd. Open year-round Wed–Sun. Contribution requested. ♿ ☎909-793-5402.* Established in 1830, this branch of the SAN GABRIEL ARCÁNGEL MISSION was to serve as a link in a secondary, inland mission chain that was planned by the Franciscan padres before secularization brought an end to mission activities. The structures were never completed, and were mostly disintegrated by the 1930s, when they were meticulously restored as a project of the Works Progress Administration (WPA). Today the small chapel is a popular location for weddings, and dioramas in the small museum recount the outpost's brief history.

EXCURSION

★ **Rim of the World Drive** – *103mi round-trip. From downtown Redlands drive west on I-10 to Hwy 38 and drive north to Lugonia Ave. Turn right and continue on Hwy 38 as it becomes Mill Creek Rd and climbs into the mountains. At Big Bear Lake, follow Hwy 38 around the lake's north shore and continue west on Hwy 18 26mi to Crestline. Turn south on Hwy 18 to return to Redlands. Note: Winter weather conditions can cause difficulty. Chains may be required, and roads may be closed. Information ☎909-383-5588.* Designated in 1915, this spectacular drive traces a portion of the Rim of the World National Scenic Byway. From Redlands, the route winds up to traverse the crest of the San Bernardino Mountains, passing sparkling mountain lakes, conifer forests and some of the region's most popular recreation areas. Turnouts along the way offer opportunities to rest and view the changing landscape and stunning vistas. From the tiny Mentone, the road ascends along the Mill Creek Canyon, crossing two branches of the San Andreas fault. The chaparral vegetation characteristic of lower elevations gives way to big-cone Douglas fir and canyon live oak as the road begins its steady climb around the western and northern boundaries of the wilderness area surrounding Mt San Gorgonio, Southern California's highest peak at 11,499ft. Black oaks, white fir and incense cedar are among the trees that grow in these higher elevations. The route peaks at Onyx Summit (8,443ft); from here views extend west down into the desert valleys north of JOSHUA TREE NATIONAL MONUMENT.

From Onyx summit, the route descends through canyons on the south flank of Sugarloaf Mountain to **Big Bear Lake**, a resort community popular for skiing and other sports *(ski information p 261)*. The route traverses the mostly undeveloped north shore before joining Highway 18 and continuing west. Just east of Skyforest, signs point to Heap's Peak Arboretum, where a nature trail *(guidebook available)* enables visitors to acquaint themselves with native and non-native trees including Jeffrey pines and dogwoods. Just west of here, Highway 173 detours to Lake Arrowhead, formerly a lumbering area, and today developed as a resort. Highway 18 continues to the community of Crestline, allowing spectacular views southwest to the Santa Ana Mountains, southeast to the San Jacinto Mountains, and, on clear days, along the vast valley to the ocean *(views frequently obscured by smog in summer)*. Near Crestline, Highway 18 turns south to return to San Bernardino and Redlands; the route of the National Scenic Byway continues west on Highway 138.

★★ REDWOOD EMPIRE North Coast

Map p 152 — Tourist Office ☎415-543-8334

Majestic spires of coast redwoods tower along a 173mi band extending between Leggett *(184mi north of San Francisco)* and Crescent City *(p 154)*. In this remote, rugged land, trees thrive in the moderate temperatures and abundant rainfall that characterize the north coastal fog belt. The greatest concentration of redwoods lies astride US-101, which cuts through a series of parks containing awe-inspiring groves.

Primeval Relics – In the Miocene epoch, these lofty titans covered much of the Northern Hemisphere. Cool, dry weather conditions brought about by the southward movement of ice age glaciers some 18,000 years ago caused the demise of all but three redwood species: *Sequoia sempervirens*, commonly known as the **coast redwood**, *Sequoiadendron giganteum (p 226)*, found in California's Sierra Nevada, and *Metasequoia glyptostrobiodes*, unique to Central China *(illustration p 226)*.

When Spanish explorers first sighted the *palo colorado* ("red trees") along the California coast in 1769, these trees blanketed over 2 million acres. By the early 1900s, however, loggers had stripped countless acres of virgin forests, causing alarmed environmentalists to create the Save-the-Redwoods League in 1918. The formation of California's State Park System nine years later ensured the preservation of these treasures for future generations. Today 68,000 acres of virgin, or old-growth redwoods—some of which are over 2,000 years old—are protected in California parks.

Found only along a narrow, 500mi strip of the Pacific coast ranging from Oregon to Big Sur, the world's tallest trees can attain heights equal to that of a 36-story building. When given ideal growing conditions in fertile stream flood plains or protected river valleys, coast redwoods—the fastest-growing softwood tree in the US—can shoot up as much as 2ft to 3ft per year.

Redwoods, with their short, narrow evergreen needles, are one of the few conifers that can sprout from knotty outgrowths called burls, as well as reproduce by seeds. The absence of resin in the trees' 6- to 12-inch-thick bark, coupled with the high tannin content of the wood renders them impervious to fire, insect damage and disease. High winds remain the most persistent natural nemesis of these venerable giants, which have root systems that delve only 3ft to 6ft into the ground. However, roots can extend horizontally for hundreds of feet, forming a net with roots of nearby trees to help anchor them in place.

Visiting the Redwood Empire – The presence of the Pacific Ocean to the west ensures moderate temperatures year-round in this cool, foggy region; the warmest months, September and October, are ideal times to visit; after October, many restaurants and shops close for the winter season.
Amenities are scarce along this part of the remote redwood coast. From south to north, principal service centers include the cities of Garberville, Ferndale, Eureka and Arcata. Within Redwood National Park, campsites abound, but motels are few. Trinidad and Crescent City, at either end of the park, provide the widest selection of accommodations and other amenities in this area.

FROM LEGGETT TO ORICK *3 1/2 days. 133mi. Map p 152.*

Chandelier Drive-Thru Tree Park – *Drive-Thru Tree Rd in Leggett, just south of the junction of Hwy 1 and US-101; follow signs. Open daily year-round. $3/car. ☏707-925-6363.* Commercial sites like this one, boasting a redwood carved so that a car can pass through its massive trunk, are considered a popular tourist attraction in redwood country.

Smithe Redwoods State Reserve – *4mi north of Leggett. Open daily year-round. ♿ ☏707-925-6482. Facility information p 257.* Bordering the highway, the highlight of this 620-acre park is the small Frank and Bess Smithe Grove, which was the site of a private resort from the 1920s to the 1960s.

Richardson Grove State Park – *11mi. Open daily year-round. $4. ⛺ ✕ ♿ ☏707-247-3318. Facility information p 257.* This stately stand of redwoods honors William Friend Richardson, governor of California in the early 1920s. Opportunities for fishing and swimming abound in the South Fork of the Eel River, which cuts through the park.

North of Richardson Grove State Park, US-101 passes through the commercial strip of Garberville *(8mi)*. From Garberville, a detour *(25mi)* west on Shelter Cove Road crosses the King Range and emerges at the planned beach community of **Shelter Cove**. This is the only paved access to the isolated Lost Coast, which stretches for 23mi below the Mattole River through the King Range, an area explorable only by hiking trails through the King Range National Conservation Area and Sinkyone Wilderness State Park.

★★ **Humboldt Redwoods State Park** – *South entrance 6mi north of Garberville. Open daily year-round. $4. ⛺ ♿ ☏707-946-2409. Auto tour brochures available at either end of the Avenue of the Giants. Facility information p 257.* Once inhabited by the Native Sinkyone people, this 51,000-acre park lies along both sides of the Eel River between Phillipsville and Pepperwood and contains one of the world's finest reserves of coast redwoods. The first redwood park on the north coast, it was established in 1921 by the Save-the-Redwoods League.

★★★ **Avenue of the Giants** – *Entrance off US-101, 6mi north of Garberville.* Few experiences can equal the feeling of driving through the silent, breathtaking groves that line the scenic 32mi parkway running parallel to US-101. Along the way, numerous parking areas afford nature-lovers the opportunity to explore ancient forests.

Rockefeller Forest at Humboldt Redwoods State Park

At Weott *(17mi from south entrance)*, the **visitor center** offers maps, information and a small natural history exhibit. One of the park's highlights is the **Founder's Grove★★** *(3mi north of Weott)*, where a self-guided nature trail *(20min)* begins at the Founder's Tree, once considered the world's tallest (364ft before the top 17ft broke off). Farther along the trail lies the mammoth **Dyerville Giant★** (362ft), which toppled in a storm in 1991. This redwood presents visitors with a close-up look at the expansive shallow root system characteristic of its species.

Avenue of the Giants rejoins US-101 5mi north of Pepperwood.

★★ **Rockefeller Forest** – *Turn left on Mattole Rd, 2.5mi north of Weott.* Comprising 10,000 acres, the world's largest remaining virgin redwood forest grows here on the Bull Creek Flats. A 2-lane road threads through the Bull Creek watershed, where two parking areas and numerous hiking trails offer access to the sublime depths of these venerable groves. Superlatives here include Giant Tree, Tall Tree and Flatiron Tree *(access from Bull Creek Flats parking lot)*.

From the Rockefeller Forest, **Mattole Road** provides an alternate route *(62mi; 3hrs)* to Ferndale *(below)*. This two-lane road climbs 2,000ft over the mountains and affords panoramic **views★** of the King Range and Cape Mendocino before reaching Ferndale. *The only gas station along this route is located at Petrolia (32mi from Rockefeller Forest).*

Scotia – *7mi north of Pepperwood.* Owned by the Pacific Lumber Company since 1887, this mill town is home to some 270 families. Note the two distinctive redwood buildings (both built in 1920): the **Scotia Museum** *(Main St; open Jun–Sept Mon–Fri; closed major holidays; ☎707-764-2222)*, which resembles a Greek temple and contains local history exhibits; and the nearby **Winema Theatre** *(not open to the public)*, that now serves as a meeting hall.

★ **Pacific Lumber Company Mill Tour** – *South end of Main St. Open year-round Mon–Fri. Closed major holidays. Passes available at the Scotia Museum Memorial Day–Labor Day, rest of the year at the Pacific Lumber Company headquarters, 125 Main St ☎707-764-2222.* A self-guided tour *(1hr)* through the company's redwood sawmill allows a rare view of modern lumber-industry technology. From a catwalk high above the floor, visitors can watch massive redwood logs being stripped of their bark by high-pressure water spray and hewn into smooth, uniform-size boards by a series of mechanized saws. At each point of interest, a plaque describes the process.

★ **Ferndale** – Pop 1,331. *17mi. Turn left on Hwy 211 at Fernbridge.* Fertile farmland of the Eel River delta first attracted Danish and other European immigrants who began a thriving dairy industry here in 1852. While dairying remains the principal industry, increasing numbers of visitors come each year to see this Victorian village, which was transformed into a State Historic Landmark in the early 1960s by the preservation efforts of residents who restored the wealth of Victorian architecture along **Main Street**. Characteristic of the "butterfat palaces" constructed by prosperous citizens at the turn of the century, the much-photographed **Gingerbread Mansion★** *(400 Berding St; now a bed & breakfast)*, was built in 1899 by a local doctor.

Ferndale Museum – *Corner of Shaw & Third Sts. Open year-round Tue–Sun. Closed Jan & major holidays. $1.* ♿ *☎707-786-4466.* A working Bosch-Omori seismograph donated to the city by a scientist at University of California, Berkeley, highlights the collection of this small local history museum. Other features include 19C period rooms and an annex full of antique logging, dairy and farming equipment.

US-101 rejoins the coast north of Ferndale.

★ **Eureka** – *20mi. Description p 58.*

Arcata – Pop 15,197. *6mi.* Originally known as Uniontown, for the Union land company whose members established a settlement here in 1850, the town's name was later changed to the appellation first given it by the local Wiyot Natives. Founded on a sheltered bay as a coastal supply center for mining operations in the nearby Trinity Mountains, Arcata bustled in its early days with the comings and goings of pack trains that hauled goods to the mining camps. With the advent of the lumber industry on the North Coast, EUREKA and its superior harbor supplanted Arcata as the county seat. Although lumbering remains an important industry, much of the town's commerce now centers around tourism, light manufacturing and the large student population of Humboldt State University.
The only coastal access in the city is through the **Arcata Marsh and Wildlife Sanctuary** *(at the end of South I St; open daily year-round; ☎707-822-8184)*, created in 1979 as part of a project to restore the bay's marshland using treated waste water.

★ **Humboldt State University Natural History Museum** – *1315 G St. Open year-round Tue–Sat. Closed Jan 1, Jul 4, Dec 25. Contribution requested.* ♿ *☎707-826-4479.* The size of this small museum, which opened in 1989, belies the scope of its holdings. Housed in Wells Fargo Hall, the museum contains a fine **fossil collection** comprising nearly 2,000 specimens ranging in age from 10,000 to 1.9 billion years old. Temporary exhibits depict Northern California's natural history.

Arcata Community Forest – *Accessible through Redwood Park at the east end of 14th St. Open daily year-round.* ♿ *☎707-822-8184.* Encompassing 600 acres of second-growth redwoods, which replaced those cut by loggers in the late 19C, this was California's first municipally owned forest. A nature trail *(.5mi loop; access from west side of parking lot at the end of Redwood Park Rd)*, formerly a logging route, threads through a fern glade in this lovely redwood forest. Markers along the path detail early logging practices. More than 10mi of trails crisscross the forest.

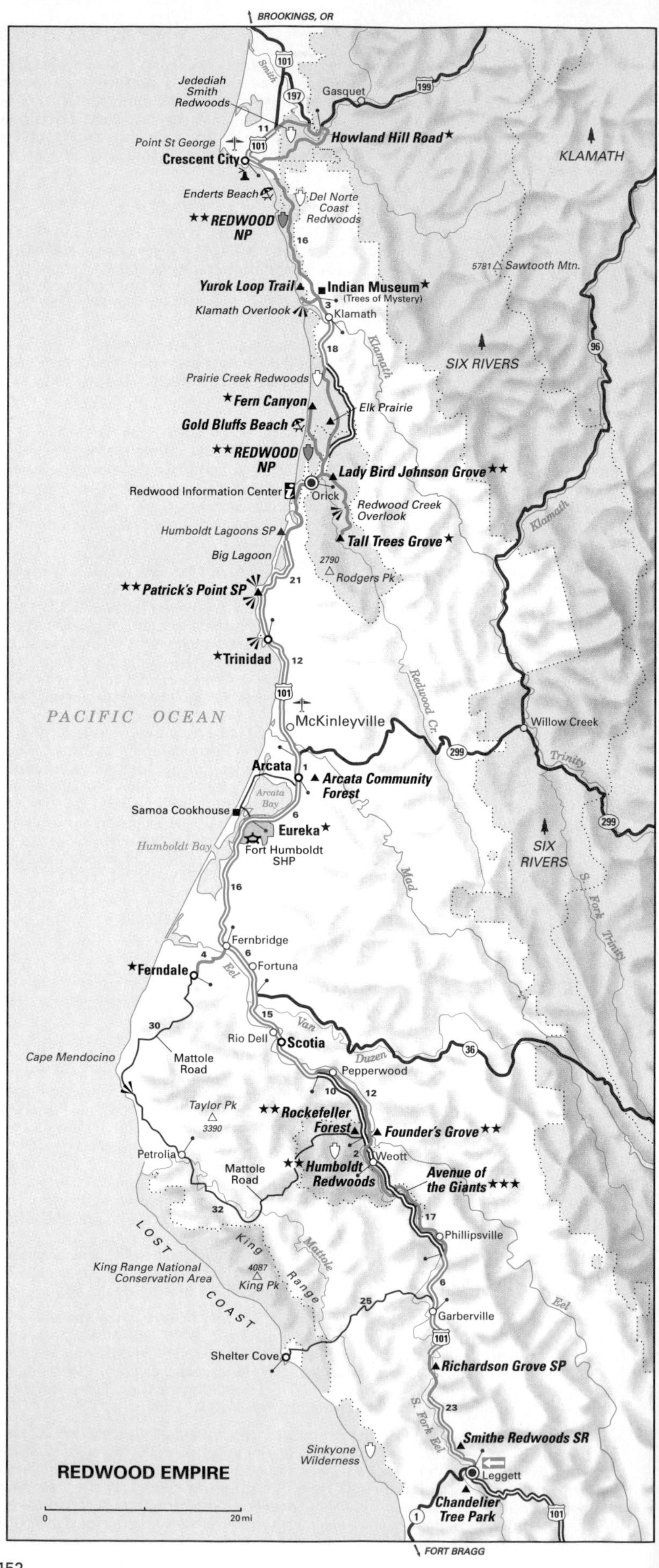

BROOKINGS, OR
Jedediah Smith Redwoods
Gasquet
Howland Hill Road★
Point St George
Crescent City
KLAMATH
Enderts Beach
Del Norte Coast Redwoods
★★REDWOOD NP
5781 Sawtooth Mtn.
Yurok Loop Trail
Indian Museum★
(Trees of Mystery)
Klamath Overlook
Klamath
SIX RIVERS
Prairie Creek Redwoods
★Fern Canyon
Elk Prairie
Gold Bluffs Beach
★★REDWOOD NP
Lady Bird Johnson Grove★★
Redwood Information Center
Orick
Redwood Creek Overlook
Humboldt Lagoons SP
Tall Trees Grove★
Big Lagoon
2790 Rodgers Pk
★★Patrick's Point SP
★Trinidad
PACIFIC OCEAN
McKinleyville
Willow Creek
Redwood Cr.
Trinity
Arcata
Arcata Community Forest
Arcata Bay
Samoa Cookhouse
Eureka★
Humboldt Bay
Fort Humboldt SHP
SIX RIVERS
Mad
S. Fork Trinity
Fernbridge
★Ferndale
Fortuna
Eel
Van Duzen
Rio Dell
Scotia
Cape Mendocino
Mattole Road
Pepperwood
Taylor Pk 3390
★★Rockefeller Forest
Founder's Grove★★
Petrolia
Weott
★★Humboldt Redwoods
Mattole Road
Avenue of the Giants★★★
LOST COAST
King Range
Mattole
Phillipsville
King Range National Conservation Area
4087 King Pk
Eel
Garberville
Shelter Cove
Richardson Grove SP
S. Fork Eel
Smithe Redwoods SR
Sinkyone Wilderness
REDWOOD EMPIRE
Leggett
Chandelier Tree Park
0
20 mi
FORT BRAGG

★ **Trinidad** – Pop 362. *13mi.* This sleepy resort town overlooking a turquoise harbor was first the site of Tsurai, the largest permanent Yurok settlement; a plaque at the south end of Ocean Street indicates the spot where Natives established their village 5,000 years ago. Like Arcata, Trinidad began as a coastal gateway for hopeful gold prospectors. As the flush of gold fever faded, settlers turned their attention to fishing, whaling and logging for their livelihood. Today revenues garnered from commercial and sport fishing, as well as tourism, support the local economy.

Trinidad is also home to the **Fred Telonicher Marine Laboratory** *(Edwards St)*, a marine research lab affiliated with Humboldt State University. Displays relating to coastal marine life can be viewed in the laboratory's entrance hall *(open year-round Mon–Fri; closed major holidays & mid-Dec–mid-Jan; contribution requested; ♿☎707-677-3671).*

Just west of town *(turn left at the end of Edwards St to parking lot adjacent to pier)*, a 400ft promontory known as Trinidad Head protects the harbor from damaging northwest winds. For a striking birds-eye **view**★ of the town and miles of Pacific coast, follow the **trail** *(1.4mi)* that loops up around the headland. The granite monument near the top of the headland commemorates the wooden cross planted here by Spanish explorers in 1775.

★★ **Patrick's Point State Park** – *5mi. Open daily year-round. $5. ⛺♿ ☎707-677-3570. Facility information p 257.* Named for 1851 homesteader Patrick Beegan, the park comprises 632 acres of dense forests, agate-strewn beaches and sweeping clifftop vistas. **Wedding Rock** and **Patrick's Point** overlooks provide some of the site's best **views**★★ of wave-lashed shoreline. Running along the headlands, the Rim Trail *(2mi)* links all the overlook points.

A re-created **Yurok Village** *(off Patrick's Point Dr, .3mi north of park entrance)*, including living quarters, a dance pit and a sweat house, recalls the days when the Yurok people erected seasonal encampments in the area.

As US-101 continues north, notice **Big Lagoon** on the left *(4mi north of Patrick's Point State Park; entrance on Big Lagoon Park Rd).* Together, Big Lagoon, Stone Lagoon and Freshwater Lagoon *(also visible from the road traveling north)* form Humboldt Lagoons State Park *(☎707-488-2127; facility information p 257)*, which preserves 1,036 acres of marshland used by birds traversing the Pacific Flyway.

Continue north on US-101 to Orick.

★★ REDWOOD NATIONAL PARK – Orick to Crescent City

2 1/2 days. 61mi. Map p 152.

With its majestic redwood groves and 33mi of beaches, this 110,000-acre site encompasses three state parks: Prairie Creek Redwoods, Del Norte Coast Redwoods and Jedediah Smith Redwoods. In 1968 Congress set aside 58,000 acres of land to be preserved as Redwood National Park; another 48,000 acres were added ten years later. This park, which contains some of the world's tallest trees, has been designated by UNESCO as a World Heritage Site.

In general, the three state parks within the national park boundaries are open daily year-round. $5/car day fee to visit sights within the parks. Day-use fee transferable to other state parks. No charge for driving through.

Redwood Information Center – *1mi south of Orick on US-101. Open daily year-round. Closed Jan 1, Dec 25. Area state park camping availability, and facility information available. Park headquarters located in Crescent City.⛺♿ ☎707-464-6101.* Park information and trail maps are available at this contemporary wooden structure near the beach. Exhibits detail the park's natural history.

★★ **Lady Bird Johnson Grove** – *5.7mi from information center via US-101 and Bald Hills Rd.* A level nature trail *(1mi)* loops around the stately old-growth forest named for the former First Lady. A brochure *($.35)* available on-site describes the flora encountered along the way.

Turn right on Bald Hills Rd.

Coastal fog often settles in the forested valleys below **Redwood Creek Overlook** *(3mi from Lady Bird Johnson Grove)*, where the **view** spans acres of redwoods and firs to the ocean.

★ **Tall Trees Grove** – *Turn right on gravel Tall Trees Access Rd (4mi from Lady Bird Johnson Grove); follow 6.5mi to trailhead; loop trail (3.2mi; steep) to grove. Shuttle service to trailhead from Redwood Information Center (4hrs 30min round-trip including visit) mid-Jun–Labor Day daily; end of May–early Jun & after Labor Day–mid Sept weekends only; shuttle seating limited to 7, first come, first served basis, $7.* Set on the fern-carpeted flats surrounding Redwood Creek, the grove contains the world's tallest known **tree**★ (367.8ft high), discovered by a National Geographic Society scientist in 1963. The massive trunk on this 600-year-old giant measures 14ft in diameter.

Return to US-101 north and continue 1.5mi. Turn left on Davison Rd (unpaved) and follow it 4mi to beach.

Gold Bluffs Beach – When flakes of gold were found in its sands in 1851, this beach experienced a flurry of mining activity. However, the site never yielded a significant amount of the precious element, and operations soon ceased. A herd of Roosevelt elk now roams the beach where prospectors once gathered.

★ **Fern Canyon** – *8mi from US-101 via Davison Rd.* Home Creek cleaves the bluffs here, creating a steep, narrow canyon walled with a variety of lush ferns, including five-fingered ferns, lady ferns and giant horsetails. A short loop trail *(.7mi)* crisscrosses the creek.

Return to US-101 north.

A short distance *(2.3mi)* past Davison Road, **Elk Prairie** appears on the left as US-101 enters Prairie Creek Redwoods State Park. This area is home to a herd of Roosevelt elk that can often be seen from the road.
As US-101 continues north, it crosses the Klamath River and passes through the fishing resort town of Klamath. Just north *(2mi)*, **Klamath Overlook** *(turn left on Requa Rd)* commands a striking **view★** of the point where the river meets the Pacific.

★ **End of the Trail Indian Museum** – *5mi north of Klamath. Located within the gift shop of the Trees of Mystery commercial park (note: it is not necessary to enter the park to visit the museum). Open daily year-round. Closed Thanksgiving Day, Dec 25. ✗ ♿ ☎707-482-2251.* This museum houses a remarkable collection of artifacts from Native peoples west of Missouri. Five rooms, divided by geographic area, display fine examples of clothing, jewelry, baskets, pottery and other items.

Yurok Loop Trail – *1mi. Turn left to Lagoon Creek parking lot.* This path leads up over the bluffs past a driftwood-littered beach. A pamphlet *(available on site)* explains the early ways of the Yurok who once inhabited the region.

North of Lagoon Creek, lofty trees line the road as US-101 cuts through Del Norte Coast Redwoods State Park. The sandy stretch of **Enderts Beach** lies at the base of steep bluffs *(3mi south of Crescent City, left on Enderts Beach Rd; access to beach via steep, .5mi dirt trail).*

★ **Howland Hill Road** – *27mi. Follow US-101 through Crescent City; turn right on Hwy 199. Turn right on South Fork Rd, then right again on Douglas Park Rd, which connects to Howland Hill Rd.* This one-lane unpaved road weaves through the southern end of **Jedediah Smith Redwoods State Park**, named for the first white man to travel overland to California in 1827 *(open daily year-round; $5/car; ⛺ ♿ ☎707-458-3310).* On its 5mi course, Howland Hill Road passes lovely **Stout Grove★** *(entrance on right)*, then parallels Mill Creek as it winds through solemn redwood forests.

Crescent City – Pop 4,380. *61mi from Orick.* Built around the crescent-shaped harbor from which it takes its name, the largest city in Del Norte County was settled in 1852. The area's rich veins of gold and timber ensured Crescent City's position as the principal shipping and supply center for Northern California and Southern Oregon during the city's early years. In 1964 a tidal wave resulting from an earthquake in Alaska destroyed 29 blocks of the downtown area including the waterfront, which was never completely rebuilt. Lumbering continues to be a major industry, along with dairy farming, commercial fishing and the cultivation of lily bulbs.

Battery Point Lighthouse – *Parking lot is located at the foot of A St. Accessible only at low tide. Open Apr–Sept Wed–Sun (if tides permit). $2. ☎707-464-3089.* A short walk across a sandy spit leads to Battery Point, once the site of three brass cannons salvaged from an 1855 shipwreck. Established here the following year, this stone and masonry lighthouse warned ships away from the dangerous rocks at the harbor's mouth. In 1892 another beacon *(no longer operational)* was built 9.5mi to the north to keep vessels from running aground on the reef lying off Point St George. The lighthouse building contains a small collection of artifacts, photographs and a Fresnel lens.

Del Norte County Historical Museum – *577 H St. Open May–Sept Mon–Sat. $1.50. ☎707-464-3922.* This large historical museum occupies a former courthouse building—complete with old jail cells upstairs. The highlight of the collection, which includes Tolowa and Yurok artifacts and antique mining equipment, is the 5,000lb First Order Fresnel lens from the Point St George Reef Lighthouse *(above).*

"The attraction and superiority of California are in its days.
It has better days, and more of them, than any other country."
R.W. Emerson, 1871

RIVERSIDE Inland Empire — Pop 226,505

Map of Principal Sights p 4 Tourist Office ☎909-787-7950

Situated on the banks of the Santa Ana River in the northwest corner of Riverside County approximately 55mi east of LOS ANGELES, this sprawling city is heralded as the birthplace of California's citrus industry.
Until the mid-18C, the area was home to the Native Cahuilla, who occupied a village named Jurupa near the Santa Ana River. Following Mexican independence, the land encompassed within the present-day downtown became part of Rancho Jurupa, a 32,000-acre parcel granted to Don Juan Bandini. In 1870 several investors from the eastern US formed a partnership to acquire part of the rancho, on which they laid out a 1sq mi townsite.

Birthplace of the Orange Industry – Riverside had grown into a thriving agricultural center in 1873 when Eliza Tibbets, wife of one of the town's original investors, received two seedling orange trees from a friend at the US Department of Agriculture. The trees, which had been propagated in Bahia, Brazil, thrived in Riverside's fertile soil and mild climate, producing abundant seedless navel oranges that surpassed in quality any oranges previously raised in the area. By 1895 Southern California's orange-growing industry was well established, and the citizens of Riverside boasted the highest per capita income in the country. In 1907 the University of California dedicated its Citrus Experiment Station here; in 1954 a branch campus known as the **University of California, Riverside** was established at the site. The **Parent Navel Orange Tree**, one of the two originally sent to Eliza Tibbets, is a

city landmark and still bears fruit *(Magnolia Ave at Arlington St)*.
By the early 20C, Riverside had become known as a winter resort for wealthy Easterners, and elegant homes and hostelries graced its wide, tree-lined avenues. Buildings in the downtown area adopted a turn-of-the-century Southern Californian trend towards Hispanic themes in architecture; examples include the **First Church of Christ, Scientist** *(3606 Lemon St)* and the Riverside Municipal Auditorium *(corner of Lemon and 7th Sts)*, both Mission Revival; the Spanish Renaissance **First Congregational Church** *(3755 Lemon St)* and the Spanish Colonial Revival **Fox Riverside Theater** *(3801 7th St)*.
Today downtown Riverside is undergoing extensive revitalization, exemplified by the restoration of the Mission Inn *(below)*. Four blocks of Main Street have been converted as a pedestrian mall with retail stores, benches, fountains and public works of art. Just south of the pedestrian mall lies the ornate **Riverside County Courthouse** (1904, Franklin Pierce Burnham); its exterior is inspired by that of the 1900 Paris Exposition's Palace of Fine Arts. The **Riverside Municipal Museum** *(3720 7th St)*, housed in the Italian Renaissance Revival former post office (1912), chronicles the region's development with artifacts from Riverside's Native, agricultural and industrial periods.

SIGHTS *1/2 day*

★★ **Mission Inn** – *3649 7th St. Visit by guided tour (1hr 15min) only, year-round Tue–Sun 11am–4pm. Closed Jan 1, Jul 4, Thanksgiving Day, Dec 25. Contribution requested. ♿ ☎919-788-9556.* Riverside's most celebrated landmark is an eclectic fantasy of art and architecture that looms like a regal Spanish palace amid the bustle of downtown. With domes, towers, buttresses, and arcades incorporated into facades copied from many of California's missions, the gracious hostelry offers multifaceted homage to Hispanic architectural styles.
The inn was founded in 1876 by Christopher Columbus Miller, a local engineer who erected a 2-story adobe structure to serve as his family home and as a guest house. His son, Frank Augustus Miller, a budding entrepreneur who had already ventured into the worlds of citrus-growing and real estate, recognized Riverside's potential as a winter resort and purchased the property in 1880. In 1902, with financing from railroad baron Henry E. Huntington *(p 142)*, Miller began expanding the hotel, adding a succession of new wings that eventually resulted in a 240-room pastiche of architectural styles, among them Oriental, Mission and Spanish Renaissance Revival. An equally eclectic assortment of art and decorative objects acquired by Miller on his world travels adorned the hotel interiors, and the Mission Inn's growing reputation attracted leading national and international figures, among them Theodore Roosevelt and Andrew Carnegie.
The hotel declined in the 1950s following its sale by Miller's heirs, and was poorly maintained during the subsequent two decades. It was taken over by the City of Riverside in 1976 and purchased in 1985 by private investors, who closed it for an extended program of restoration and seismic retrofitting. The refurbished hotel reopened in 1993.

Visit – The U-shaped Mission Wing (1902), designed by Mission Revival proponent Arthur B. Benton, surrounds a lush courtyard known as the "Court of the Birds" for the parrots and macaws that formerly flew about it. The Cloister Wing (1910) features catacombs *(now closed)* and facades inspired by those at the CARMEL MISSION and SAN GABRIEL ARCÁNGEL MISSION. Above the patio in the Spanish Wing (1914, Myron Hunt) is a replica of a 1707 Nuremberg clock with five revolving figures: Junipero Serra, Juan Bautista de Anza, St Francis, a California Native and a California grizzly bear. The clock's original face is displayed in the museum *(below)*. The International Rotunda Wing (1931, G. Stanley Wilson) houses offices, shops and the **St Francis Chapel**★, created to highlight Miller's prized possessions: an 18C Mexican altar encrusted with gold leaf; seven Tiffany windows; and choir stalls from a Belgian convent.
Guided tours terminate at the **Mission Inn Museum** *(corner of 7th & Main Sts)*, where artifacts and photographs tell the story of the hotel and of its impact on developing Riverside. Also on display are art and memorabilia from the Miller family collections, including 36 paintings of California missions by Henry Chapman Ford, and a 7ft lacquered wood statue of Buddha dating from Japan's Edo period.

California Museum of Photography – *3824 Main St, on the mall. Open year-round Wed–Sun. Closed Jan 1, Dec 25, Jan 31. $2. ♿ ☎909-784-3686.* Founded in 1973, this museum of photographic art and technology is housed in a former Kress dimestore (1929) that was remodeled in 1990 to house UC Riverside's collection of photographs and photo equipment. Today the building embodies a large camera: its entrance reveals a spacious interior resembling a camera's dark chamber, and the Art Deco facade incorporates the aperture of a room-size camera obscura.
A highlight of the museum's holdings is the Keystone-Mast Collection of stereographs, reputedly the largest extant collection of this early form of photography; examples from the collection are available for public viewing. In addition to changing exhibits of contemporary and historical photography, a permanent exhibition traces the artistic and technological development of photography from its invention in 1837 to the present. Particularly suited to children is the Interactive Gallery *(upper level)*, where hands-on displays demonstrate color, light, perception and other aspects of the visual sense.

UC Riverside Botanic Garden – *On the campus of University of California. From downtown Riverside drive east on University Ave to campus entrance; follow signs to garden. Open daily year-round. Closed Jan 1, Jul 4, Thanksgiving Day, Dec 25. ♿ ☎909-787-4650. Self-guided tour booklets available at garden entrance gate.* Glimpses of the San Gabriel and San Bernardino mountains highlight a stroll through this lovely botanic garden set in two shallow canyons on the eastern edge of campus. Collections feature species native to California, Australia and Southern Africa, and a geodesic lathhouse shades rare trees.

★ **Heritage House** – *8193 Magnolia St; from downtown drive south on Market St, which becomes Magnolia St. Visit by guided tour (45min) only, Sept–Jun Tue, Thu, Sun. $1. ♿ ☎909-689-1333.* This beautifully preserved Victorian residence (1891, John Walls) sports exceptional craftsmanship typical of the prosperous houses that lined Magnolia Avenue during the late 19C. The structure was commissioned by Catherine Bettner, then recently widowed, as a showplace to entice and welcome afternoon callers. Elaborate ornamentation displays the many traditions typically incorporated into the Queen Anne style *(p 26)*, with exterior embellishments revealing Moorish, Palladian and Chinese influences. A mill was installed in the adjacent carriage house during construction to provide woods for the interior carved oak wainscoting, fireplace grilles, and frames for 9ft pocket doors. Some of the furnishings are original to the house, and all are authentic to the period. The interior also features many examples of Victorian "hobby art," simple, inexpensive craft projects such as handmade picture frames.

EXCURSIONS

Planes of Fame Air Museum – *2 hrs. 15mi west of Riverside via Hwy 60, exit Euclid Rd (Hwy 83) and drive south 3.4mi; turn left on Merrill Ave and continue 1mi to Chino Airport. 7000 Merrill Ave. Open daily year-round. Closed Thanksgiving Day, Dec 25. $4.95. ☎909-597-3722.* Aircraft enthusiasts will delight in the celebration of aviation history found at this museum of flying. Located at the former site of the Cal Aero Academy, a pilot training ground during World War II, the collection of more than 100 restored historical aircraft includes some 30 planes in flying condition, with ongoing restoration of more recent acquisitions.

Outside the museum, visitors may climb through a B17 "Flying Fortress" used in filming "Twelve O'Clock High" (1950) *(open weekends only; $1)*. Hangar 2 features the largest known collection of Japanese warplanes, including the only known Mitsubishi Zero in flying condition. Highlights in the Fighter Jets Museum *(hangar 4, additional fee $4.95)* include an ME-262 "Schwalbe," the first combat jet fighter, developed in Germany during World War II.

Orange Empire Railway Museum – *2201 South A St, Perris. 20mi south of Riverside via Hwy 215. Open year-round daily. $5 (weekends & holidays only). Closed Thanksgiving Day, Dec 25. ☎909-657-2605. Weekend visit recommended, when most carbarns are open and train rides are available.* Located in the former depot community of Pinacate, this museum of railroad history was founded in the mid-1950s to preserve relics of the era when steam, diesel and electric trains served as an important mode of transport. The earliest artifact in the collection of some 200 vehicles (many currently being restored by members of a volunteer organization) dates from the 1870s; highlights include "Red Cars" from the Pacific Electric Railway, the interurban system that during the first half of the 20C connected Los Angeles to outlying suburbs. Also on view are a 1924 Santa Fe Railway Post Office car, the last rolling sorting station used by the US Postal Service; and the "Descanso," a funeral car in use in Los Angeles from 1909 to 1929. Recent acquisitions include the "Grizzly Flats Railroad," assembled during the 1950s by Disney animator Ward Kimball.

★★ SACRAMENTO Central Valley — Pop 369,365

Map p 157 — Tourist Office ☎916-264-7777

Although sometimes hastily dismissed as an overgrown valley town, California's capital possesses a rich historical heritage and an appealing all-American gentility. This flat site at the confluence of the Sacramento and the American rivers was urbanized with a grid of long, straight, tree-lined streets that remind many visitors of the Midwest. The residents, who seem indifferent to most of the fads of California's trendy hotspots, reinforce this impression. Yet this capital city has almost despite itself developed the aura of a modern metropolis, with many contemporary cultural attractions to complement the vestiges of its pioneer-day past.

From New Helvetia to State Capital – Sacramento began as Sutter's Fort, built in 1839 by the Swiss-German adventurer **John Sutter**, who dreamed of establishing his own commercial empire in the wild interior of Alta California. This intrepid entrepreneur had persuaded the government at MONTEREY that it would greatly benefit from the settlement of the long-ignored Central Valley, and received a grant of 47,827 acres. Within a few years, hundreds of Natives were working on this "New Helvetia," and trained craftsmen were recruited from as far away as Europe. The adobe fort attracted wagon trains traveling overland to California in the decade before the Gold Rush. Sutter expected to benefit from this influx, which could provide him with employees and purchasers of family farms. For some years his ventures prospered; in 1844, the Mexican governor granted Sutter another 96,800 acres, as a reward for the help of his small private army in putting down a Native revolt.

In 1848 an employee, John Marshall, discovered gold in the tail race of a new lumber mill that Sutter had commissioned him to build in COLOMA. Marshall had unwittingly set in motion the California Gold Rush that within a year lured away most of Sutter's employees and flooded his land with hordes of squatters. The new American administration in California belatedly, and only partially, recognized

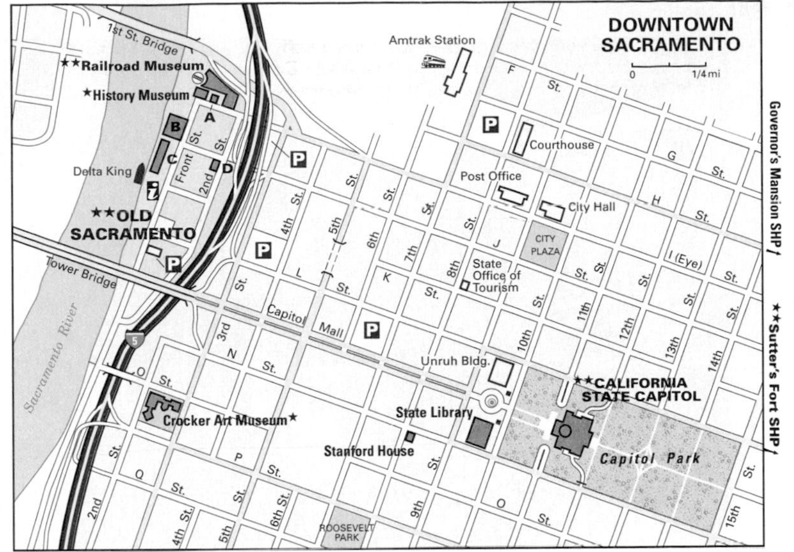

Sutter's land holdings. His own son betrayed him, in his view, by assisting in the founding of Sacramento about 2mi west of the fort, on the banks of the Sacramento River, thus undermining the elder's efforts to create "Sutterville" 2mi south of Sutter's Fort.

But it was almost inevitable that any settlement in this area would have grown up along the riverbank. Ships from San Francisco Bay landed here, full of men in transit to the gold camps. Proprietors of hotels, blacksmith shops, saloons, hardware stores, stagecoach stations and all other businesses involved in outfitting the mining enterprise found it advantageous to locate near the docks. After devastating floods and fires in the early 1850s, the town was put on a more permanent footing thanks to a protective levee and the use of brick as the primary building material. Old Sacramento is a remnant of this period. (Sutter went to Washington DC to press his claims, unsuccessfully, and never returned to California. He settled in Pennsylvania, and died in 1880 in a Washington hotel.)

Sacramento remained an important inland port and jumping-off place to the gold diggings into the 1860s. In 1856 California's first railroad was built from Sacramento to Folsom, now an outlying suburb. In the 1860s, a consortium of Sacramento businessmen—the "Big Four"—inspired by a visionary young engineer named Theodore Judah, began to build a railroad across the Sierra Nevada, and Sacramento thus became the terminus of the first transcontinental railroad *(p 24)*. Later it became the intersection of the most important highways crossing the Sierras and those traversing the Central Valley lengthwise. The processing and shipping of agricultural products in particular, and transportation and distribution in general, have long been mainstays of the local economy.

In 1854 Sacramento became the capital of California. The present Capitol building, begun in 1860, housed the Legislature and Governor's office. The Supreme Court met above a stage coach and express station in Old Sacramento until 1869. (It was then moved to SAN FRANCISCO where it has remained.) State government was relatively small until the 1930s, but since then has grown in numbers of buildings and employees. This growth, along with the presence of regional offices of many Federal agencies, has made government a major Sacramento industry.

SIGHTS *2 days*

★★ **Old Sacramento** – *Extending from I to L Sts between the Sacramento River & I-5. Parking garages on I St under I-5 and on Front St at L St. Self-guided walking tour brochure is available at the visitor center on Front St at K St.* Sacramento's original downtown constitutes the nation's largest ensemble of Gold-Rush era buildings and is the city's premier tourist attraction. Old Sacramento sprung up in the early 1850s around the embarcadero that serviced Sutter's Fort *(p 159)*, located 2mi to the east, and for several decades, this district flourished as Sacramento's commercial heart. The area's decline began later in the century as business activity shifted east to the vicinity of the Capitol, and the long-neglected quarter barely escaped the wrecker's ball during the construction of Interstate 5 in the 1960s. Subsequently, an ambitious restoration project transformed much of the original downtown into a 24.5-acre state historic park, noteworthy for its judicious integration of new structures into the existing historic urban fabric. The 2- and 3-story buildings fronted by covered wooden sidewalks lining the 3-block stretch of **Second** and **Front Streets** evoke the ambience of a prosperous 19C frontier town despite the multitude of eateries and souvenir shops that occupy many of the storefronts today.

★★ **California State Railroad Museum** – *2nd & I Sts. Open year-round daily 10am–5pm. Closed Jan 1, Thanksgiving Day, Dec 25. $5. ♿ ☎916-445-7387. Introductory film (30min) shown hourly.* Appropriately situated in the city that served as the terminus of the first transcontinental railroad, this distinctive 2-story brick museum (1981) celebrates railroading and its determinant role in the development of the West. A

D. Henry/Sacramento Convention & Visitors Bureau

Old Town Sacramento

passage leading to the main floor documents the great challenges of surveying and building the Central Pacific Railroad over the Sierra Nevada in the 1860s. In the large, open exhibit hall, designed partly in the manner of a 19C roundhouse, are a dozen meticulously restored locomotives, including the Central Pacific's **Engine No. 1** from the mid-1860s and a cab-forward behemoth from the final years of the steam engine in the 1940s and 1950s. Mingling with the locomotives are numerous railroad cars, including a railway post office, a luxurious private car, and a sleeping car with realistic rocking motions and sound effects. Smaller displays include a railroad telegraph office and a country railroad station. The second-floor galleries feature a delightful collection of toy trains.

Adjacent to the museum is a row of brick storefronts that include the museum's bookstore—a treasure trove for rail buffs—and the **Huntington, Hopkins & Co. Hardware Store [A]**, a reconstruction of the 1850s business formerly located just blocks away on a site overrun by I-5. The original store was the financial base of Collis Huntington and Mark Hopkins, two members of the "Big Four" *(p 24)*, the Sacramento businessmen who organized and directed the Central Pacific.

★ **Sacramento History Museum** – *101 I St. Open year-round Wed–Fri. Closed Thanksgiving Day & Fri after, Dec 25. $3.50. ♿ ☎916-264-7057.* An architectural complement to the nearby railroad museum, this brick building presents the history of Sacramento and its environs. The main exhibit space is organized in a chronological sequence of densely packed displays of items of everyday life from the Native American period to the present day. An adjoining gallery documents the agriculture and food processing industries that thrive in Sacramento County. The museum also mounts changing special exhibits on subjects of local interest.

Along nearby Front Street, extends a replica of the Central Pacific **passenger station [B]** as it existed in 1876. Outfitted with a "sound stick" providing narration and sound effects, visitors experience the bustling atmosphere of a working train station replete with antique trains waiting at the platform.

At the adjacent Central Pacific **freight depot [C]**, steam trains take passengers aboard for a 7mi excursion along the river *(departures weekends year-round; round-trip 45min; commentary; $4; Sacramento History Museum ☎916-445-7387)*. The 1930s riverboat *Delta King*, permanently docked behind the depot, now functions as a floating hotel.

B. F. Hastings and Co. Building [D] – *2nd St at J St.* This handsome building (1850s) housed important express companies like Wells Fargo and served as the western terminus of both the Pony Express and the first transcontinental telegraph line. Its ground floor now features a small museum illustrating the importance of communication and transportation services to the isolated new state of California *(open daily year-round ☎916-445-7387)*. The state's Supreme Court convened in the upper floor during much of the 1850s and 1860s. Courtroom and offices have been restored to period appearance.

★★ **California State Capitol** – *10th St between L & N Sts. Open daily year-round. Closed Jan 1, Thanksgiving Day, Dec 25. ✂ ♿ ☎916-324-0333.* Unmistakable with its 237ft dome, Sacramento's most prominent landmark echoes the neoclassical style of its Federal counterpart in Washington DC. Granite was employed on the ground floor, while lighter white-painted bricks face the two upper floors. The pediment over the main entrance on the west side, supported by Corinthian columns, shows Minerva surrounded by Justice, Mining, Education and Industry. (Minerva is the central figure in the state seal, which appears at several places in the Capitol. As Minerva is said to have sprung full-grown from the forehead of her father Jupiter, California attained statehood without going through the normal gestation period as a territory.)

Begun in 1860, the Capitol underwent many alterations over the years, and had become somewhat decrepit by the 1970s, when a proposal to move government activities to office towers nearby threatened its existence. The approaching US Bicentennial, however, galvanized local interest in preserving this historic building, and over the next few years it was renovated to its original splendor. Several first-floor rooms, including the offices of the Governor and the Treasurer, have been restored to their early 20C appearance. The grand **rotunda** is dominated by the finely decorated dome soaring 120ft overhead. Visitors may observe proceedings of the senate and assembly in their chambers on the third floor.

The grounds, encompassing 40 acres, are known as **Capitol Park**. The park is actually an arboretum containing 341 labeled species of trees *(tree list with map available at visitor center in basement)*. West of the Capitol *(914 Capitol Mall)* stands the **California State Library** (1926), a neoclassical granite building with interior halls and reading rooms featuring Art Deco motifs and allegorical murals. The California Room on the third floor is a major archive of California history, with changing exhibitions from its special collections of documents such as photographs, restaurant menus and political posters *(open year-round Mon–Fri; closed major holidays; ♿ ☎916-654-0261)*.

Around the corner from the library stands the **Stanford House** *(8th & N Sts)*, an elegant Italianate mansion. Statesman, railroad magnate and Stanford University founder Leland Stanford *(p 140)* purchased the house in 1861, and it served as his gubernatorial residence until 1863. *(Restoration in progress; call ☎916-324-0575 for tour information)*.

★ **Crocker Art Museum** – *Entrance on corner of 2nd & O Sts. Open year-round Wed–Sun. Closed Jan 1, Jul 4, Thanksgiving Day, Dec 25. $3.50. ♿ ☎916-264-4523.* Housed in a handsome Italianate mansion just south of Old Sacramento, this venerable Sacramento institution opened its doors in 1872, making it the West's first public art museum. The original 2-story structure at 2nd and O Sts was commissioned by Judge Edwin Bryant Crocker to serve as a showcase for his collection of some 700 paintings largely by popular 19C German and American artists. In his lifetime, Crocker also amassed a fine collection of over 1,200 European Master drawings, selections of which are occasionally displayed. To accommodate the growing collection, the museum expanded into the adjoining Crocker residence (1850s) in the late 19C. Since the 1960s, modern glass and concrete wings, which contrast sharply with the elegant lines of the 19C buildings, were added to display temporary exhibits.

The mansion's splendidly restored **interior★★**—note in particular the entrance hall and adjoining ballroom—features decorative woodwork, ornate ceilings, stencil-work and tile floors. The California Gallery *(2nd floor)* is devoted to 19C California landscape painters and late-20C artists from the state. The museum's most famous single work, Charles Nahl's often-reproduced *Sunday Morning in the Mines* (1872), hangs in the adjoining foyer.

★★ **Sutter's Fort State Historic Park** – *27th & L Sts. Open year-round daily 10am–5pm. Closed Jan 1, Thanksgiving Day, Dec 25. $2. ♿ ☎916-445-4422.* This important landmark was the "castle" of John Sutter's domain *(p 156)*, a walled compound with a variety of workrooms and living quarters built against the interior of the thick adobe brick wall. In the center of the spacious grounds stands Sutter's administration building, the only structure that is mostly original, and thus the oldest building in Sacramento. The rest of the complex was in ruins in the 1890s, when restoration began in belated recognition of Sutter's adventurous career and his many contributions to early California.

Visitors tour the compound accompanied by "sound sticks" *(available at the ticket booth)*, which provides interpretive talks on the history and activities of the fort. A series of rooms near the entrance feature insightful panel displays outlining the vicissitudes of John Sutter's extraordinary life. The materials and tools of daily life in Sutter's agricultural empire have been assembled in the various rooms and buildings of the compound, both as fixed exhibits and as material for "living history" reenactments.

★ **California State Indian Museum** – *2618 K St, adjacent to Sutter's Fort. Open daily year-round. Closed Jan 1, Thanksgiving Day, Dec 25. $2. ♿ ☎916-324-0971.* This rich collection of dance regalia, baskets, hunting and fishing equipment, and other artifacts—including a Yurok boat hewn from a single redwood trunk— accompanied by many photographs, both historical and contemporary, emphasizes the continuity of Native American culture from before the Spanish conquest to the present day.

Governor's Mansion State Historic Park – *16th & H Sts. Visit by guided tour (40min) only, daily year-round. Closed Jan 1, Thanksgiving Day, Dec 25. $2. ♿ ☎916-323-3047.* This landmark Second Empire Italianate pile was built in 1877 by Sacramento hardware tycoon Albert Gallatin and acquired by the state in 1903 as the official residence for the state's chief executive. The interior contains a motley assemblage of furnishings and artifacts—including First Ladies' gowns—left by the families of the 13 governors who set up household here. The last governor to inhabit the mansion was Ronald Reagan in the 1960s. His successor, Jerry Brown, preferred an apartment across from the Capitol, and subsequent governors took up lodgings in a modern house elsewhere in Sacramento.

★ **Towe Ford Museum** – *2200 Front St, about 1mi south of Old Sacramento. Open daily year-round. Closed Jan 1, Thanksgiving Day, Dec 25. $5. ♿ ☎916-442-6802.* Housed in a former warehouse, this vintage vehicle museum salutes "America's most popular car": the Ford. The core collection of 120 Fords was donated by Montana businessman and rancher, Edward Towe, and the holdings have grown to include over 200 cars, trucks and tractors, primarily Fords, which are arranged in chronological order from the early 20C to recent years.

Sacramento Zoo – *3mi south of downtown. Take I-5 south to Sutterville Rd exit and follow the signs. Open daily year-round. Closed Dec 25. $4.50. ✗ ♿ ☎916-264-5885.* Located within a large recreational park that also features a popular theme playground, this small zoo is home to some 340 specimens including such exotic felines as Siberian tigers, jaguars and margay cats.

SALINAS VALLEY Central Coast

Map p 43

Broad, rolling and fertile, the Salinas Valley embraces the Salinas River as it snakes north 150mi from its source in the Sierra Madre Mountains east of SAN LUIS OBISPO to Monterey Bay. The Franciscan padres founded missions here to convert the area's Costanoan and Salinan Natives; later, Anglo farmers cultivated the rich soil to grow barley, sugar beets, lettuce, carrots and other crops. The valley also yielded a rich harvest of characters and settings for the stories of Nobel Laureate and Salinas native John Steinbeck.

SIGHTS *1 day*

Salinas – Pop 108,777. *111mi south of San Francisco via US-101.* In a region still known for the richness of its soil and the quality and abundance of its crops, this town has served as a nexus for the prosperous farms of the Salinas Valley for more than a century. Settled in the late 19C in a swampy area ridden by mosquitoes and subject to thick fog, the unassuming little town grew into a farming center as the surrounding marshes were drained to reveal fertile, nutrient-rich soil. In 1898 San Francisco "Sugar King" Claus Spreckels established a sugar refinery in the region, and farmers converted their acreage to the cultivation of sugar beets. Lettuce and other crops also thrived, and the town and its residents prospered.

Salinas was the birthplace and boyhood home of **John Steinbeck** (1902-1968), renowned author of novels and short stories, who set many of his best-known works in the Salinas Valley and Monterey County. Steinbeck's characters populated the town of Salinas in *East of Eden* (1952), camped along the riverbed near Soledad in *Of Mice and Men* (1937), and journeyed from the Oklahoma dust bowl to work on Salinas Valley farms in his most celebrated work, *The Grapes of Wrath* (1939), for which he won a Pulitzer prize. Steinbeck's family resided in a large, Victorian home near the center of town; today the structure is a luncheon restaurant known as the **Steinbeck House** *(132 Central Ave)*. Visitors can also browse the **John Steinbeck Library** *(110 W. San Luis St)*, the main branch of the public library, which displays letters, photographs and items from its extensive Steinbeck archives, including original manuscripts and signed first editions *(open year-round Mon–Sat; closed major holidays ♿ ☎408-758-7311)*. The author's remains lie in the Garden of Memories *(768 Abbott St)*.

Nuestra Señora Dolorosísima de la Soledad Mission – *29mi south of Salinas; exit US-101 at Arroyo Seco Rd; drive 1.2mi west to Fort Romie Rd and turn right; continue 1.5mi north to mission. Open daily year-round. Closed major holidays. Contribution requested. ♿ ☎408-678-2586.* Perhaps none of the California missions was as bleakly situated as this lonely outpost in the middle of the Salinas Valley. Founded in 1791 by Padre Fermín Lasuén to bridge the gap between the San Antonio Mission *(p 161)* and the CARMEL MISSION, the 13th mission was named for Our Most Sorrowful Lady of Solitude. Plagued by hot dry summers, cold wet winters, and a lack of ready converts, Soledad nevertheless grew to modest prosperity. Sheep, cattle and horses grazed the grasslands; wine, olive oil and flour were produced nearer the mission complex.

An 1824 flood destroyed the original church, and subsequent chapels were washed away in 1828 and 1832. Following secularization in 1835, the mission's roof tiles were sold to pay a debt to the Mexican government, leaving the adobe walls exposed to the elements. Bare traces remained when restoration began in 1954.

Visit – *1/2 hr.* Only the simple, whitewashed chapel and the 7-room convento have been rebuilt; the remainder of the quadrangle lies in ruins. The mission's original bell hangs from a low beam outside the church, while the original stations of the cross adorn the interior. Mounds of melted adobe brick indicate the workshops of the north and east wings; the south side is marked by the tile remnants of the original church floor. Beneath this floor lies the grave of José Joaquin Arrillaga, Alta California's first Spanish governor, who died while visiting the mission in 1814.

★ **Pinnacles National Monument** – *14mi east of Soledad. West entrance: exit US-101 at Hwy 146 east, and follow signs to the monument. East entrance: drive south on US-101 19.5mi to King City (Broadway exit) and continue east 14.5mi on Hwy G13. Turn left on Hwy 25 and continue north 14mi to Hwy 146; follow signs to monument. Open daily year-round. $4/car. ⛺ ♿ ☎408-389-4526.* Rising from the granite bedrock of the Gabilan Range east of Soledad is a fortress of towering spires and ramparts that bear witness to the massive power of earth's natural forces. The eerily beautiful Pinnacles, marked by the artistry of natural erosion, tell a complicated story of continental drift, ancient oceans and a vanished volcano.

The park's distinctive ridgetop rock formations are the remnants of an unnamed volcano, formed 23 million years ago as the Pacific plate slid north past the North American plate along the fault now known as the San Andreas rift zone. This movement opened a deep crack through which molten lava erupted, forming an 8,000ft volcanic cone that straddled the fault itself. Over the subsequent millenia, the Pacific plate continued its northward journey, carrying with it the western portion of the mountain; the remnants of the eastern half today lie some 195mi to the south. During this same period, erosive forces such as wind and water washed away the mountain's surface, exposing pinkish-gray ancient lava known as rhyolite. Tiny cracks in the lava's hardened surface were enlarged and deepened until all that remained were the striking stone towers that today punctuate the surrounding landscape of smooth, rounded hills.

Visit –*1/2 hr (not including trails).* The 25sq mi park is accessible from either east or west, although the two sides are linked only by some 45mi of hiking trails. The more scenic west entrance provides access to a small ranger station and vantage points offering stunning views of the pinnacles. The east entrance provides access to the Bear Gulch **visitor center**, which features exhibits on aspects of California geology. Both sections offer picnic areas and trails leading into the heart of the park. Several trails, particularly the **Juniper Canyon Trail** *(2.4mi round-trip; trailhead at west entrance)* and the **High Peaks Trail** *(5.4mi loop; trailhead at east entrance)*, climb steeply up to the pinnacles themselves, while more moderate footpaths offer pleasant hiking to the caves and other peaks throughout the park.

★ **San Antonio de Padua Mission** – *26mi southwest of King City. Exit US-101 at Hwy G14 (Jolon Rd) and continue south 23mi to Jolon Store. Turn right to enter Ft Hunter Liggett. Sentries will direct visitors 6mi through the military base to the mission. Open daily year-round. Museum closed major holidays. Contribution requested.* ♿ *☎408-385-4478.* California's third mission is situated in an eastern valley of the coastal Santa Lucia Range, separated from the Salinas Valley by one mountainous ridge. Although the mission grounds are encompassed within the boundaries of Ft Hunter Liggett, a US Army reservation, the landscape immediately surrounding the restored structures appears little changed since the late 18C.

Founded by Padre Junípero Serra in 1771, the mission was originally located on the banks of a river that Serra named in honor of St Anthony of Padua. About two years later, it was moved 1.5mi north to its present location. During its peak years, the mission was home to some 1,300 neophytes, and boasted wheat fields and a substantial infrastructure of workshops, padres' quarters, neophyte dwellings and an elaborate irrigation system that included a dam, reservoirs and an aqueduct to operate a gristmill. The main church was completed in 1813.

J. Randklev/Allstock

Mission window

Following secularization in 1834, the mission lands occupied by the neophytes were taken over by an appointed administrator and sold. Despitethe return of 33 acres of mission lands by President Lincoln to the Catholic Church in 1863, the mission was mostly abandoned for some 46 years, during which time the buildings collapsed into disrepair. In 1903 it was singled out for preservation by the Historical Landmarks League, and restoration was begun on the roof of the church. Franciscan friars returned in 1928, and in 1948 embarked on extensive renovations. The US Army purchased much of the land surrounding the missionin 1940 and established Ft Hunter Liggett. One wing of the quadrangle and the church, which today serves a local parish, are open to the public; the remaining two wings house a Franciscan retreat center.

Visit – *1hr.* Signs along the approach to the mission point out the many visible remnants of San Antonio's infrastructure, including a tannery, gristmill and aqueduct. An elegant colonnade fronts the restored quadrangle, and a large, barrel-vaulted passageway, erected in 1821, connects the scalloped campanario to the church entrance. The front wing of the mission, originally the convento, now houses exhibits of mission life, including a collection of herbs used by the neophytes for medicinal purposes. Particularly noteworthy is the music room, where the walls reveal authentically replicated drawings of methods specifically developed by the padres to teach the neophytes to sing.

★ **San Miguel Arcángel Mission** – *Exit US-101 in San Miguel. Open daily year-round. Closed Jan 1, Easter Sunday, Thanksgiving Day, Dec 25. Contribution requested. ♿ ☎805-467-3256.* A well-kept garden, patched stucco and faded red tiles lend California's 16th mission an air of tranquillity despite the proximity of busy US-101. In the care of Franciscan padres since 1928, the mission is noteworthy for its fine church interior.

Named for St Michael the Archangel, the mission was founded in 1797 by Padre Fermín Lasuén to link the San Antonio Mission *(above)* and the SAN LUIS OBISPO MISSION. The padres were well received by the local Salinan Natives, many of whom moved from the already existing missions to the north and south to reside here. Under the padres' direction, the neophytes erected a series of dams and canals that brought water from the Salinas River to irrigate wheatfields and orchards. Masses were offered in a large, mud-roofed church until 1806, when the church succumbed to a devastating fire that consumed nearly all of the mission buildings. The catastrophe prompted the padres to design a new, tile-roofed church better equipped to withstand such disasters.

San Miguel was the last of the missions to be secularized, and in the ensuing years, the structures variously housed a saloon, dance hall, retail stores and private residences; several structures were neglected and collapsed. However, priests who remained in residence at the mission throughout the 19C kept the church and its interior in good repair.

In 1859 the property was returned to the Catholic Church, but a resident priest was not assigned here until 1878. In 1928 it was granted to the Franciscan order, which maintains and operates it today as a monastery.

Visit – *1hr. Enter through the convento gift shop.* The mission's gracious appearance is enhanced by a peaceful front garden planted with 34 varieties of cactus. The garden fountain, copied from that of the Santa Bárbara Mission, was added during restoration. The facade of the convento is unique among California's mission structures in that its arches are of unequal size and shape; six rooms within display statues and artifacts of the mission period, including an expressive statue of St Michael the Archangel triumphing over Satan, and the church's original crucifix. The church's beautifully preserved **interior★** is adorned with frescoes executed in 1820 by Native artisans under the direction of Don Estéban Munras, a native of Barcelona who settled in Monterey in 1812. The original trompe l'œil **murals**, depicting arches, draperies and balustrades, have never been altered. Colored in rich pigments of ochre, charcoal, cinnabar and cobalt, they are considered the California missions' finest examples of interior decoration.

★★★ SAN DIEGO San Diego County Pop 1,110,549

Map p 164

With its gleaming high-rises overlooking the bustling waters of a vast bay, San Diego at first glance appears the very image of its ranking as the second largest city in California (after LOS ANGELES) and the sixth largest in the US. The Balboa Park cultural institutions that share the verdant mesas and canyons north of downtown with affluent neighborhoods of mostly Spanish-style mansions only underscore the city's cosmopolitan nature.

San Diego's appeal to residents and visitors alike runs counter to that of most big cities. Charming and well-defined residential communities and business districts contribute to its welcoming character. Streets are clean and generally free of traffic jams. Public transportation runs efficiently and cheaply, connecting downtown with outlying areas. Though its population is large, the 319.6sq mi city feels as if it has room to spare; San Diego County's 4,255sq miles encompass more than double the city's residents. Just a short drive east of town are sparsely inhabited farmlands, deserts and mountains whose small settlements harken back to a century or more ago.

San Diego also enjoys a year-round mild climate, with a preponderance of sunny days, and annual temperatures averaging 70°F. Breezes off the bay keep the air relatively pollution-free. With such world-class tourist attractions as the San Diego Zoo and Sea World, as well as the enticing proximity of the Mexican border less than 20mi away, San Diego well merits its self-proclaimed reputation as one of the most livable cities in the nation.

HISTORICAL NOTES

Centuries before the arrival of European explorers and settlers, the coastal plain, surrounding bluffs and hills and the nearby Cuyamaca Mountains were inhabited by the Kumeyaay tribe. Migrant hunter-gatherers, they found ample sustenance in fish from Pacific waters and game and plant life of the region.

On September 28, 1542, this peaceful people greeted the area's first visitors, as Spanish ships under the command of Juan Rodríguez Cabrillo sailed into the bay. Cabrillo named the place San Miguel to mark the feast of Saint Michael the Arch angel. After seven days, his expedition continued northward. Sixty years later, on November 10, 1602, three ships commanded by Sebastián Vizcaíno arrived in search of safe harbors for Spain's Manila galleons. On the 12th, Vizcaíno rechristened the harbor and surrounding lands San Diego, honoring the feast day of Saint Didacus of Alcalá, Spain; he and his men left two days later.

Spaniards did not return for more than a century and a half, until 1769, when the various land and sea columns of the Sacred Expedition *(p 22)* to colonize Alta California joined forces at the bay marked in the previous explorers' charts. The group, led by the expedition's captain, Gaspar de Portolá, included Padre Junípero Serra, head of the mission chain. On July 22, 1769, Serra raised a cross beside a hastily built brushwood chapel on present-day Presidio Hill *(p 167)*, celebrated High Mass, and with a band of 22 settlers thus established the first mission and first Spanish garrison in California.

Early Challenges and Growth – Exhausted and ill from the rigors of its expedition, harassed by the Natives, and short of food, water and medicine, the tiny settlement struggled to survive the winter of 1769-1770. Supplies from Baja California eventually arrived to help the settlers get through their first year, and on January 1, 1774, the Spanish crown declared San Diego a Royal Presidio. But the proximity of the garrison hindered the mission's work, as the soldiers intimidated and sometimes molested potential Native converts. In August 1774, the mission re located 6mi inland from Presidio Hill to a new complex of thatch-roofed log buildings beside the San Diego River.

Despite severe attacks from Natives the following year, the mission began to stabilize and prosper. To the west, the walled presidio, further fortified against the threat of British and Russian incursions into California, grew into a hardscrabble community of farmers and cattle ranchers.

Following Mexican independence in 1821, San Diego began to prosper, particularly with ships from Boston docking in the harbor to pick up cattle hides from local ranches. On flat land below the garrison, a pueblo, known today as Old Town, slowly developed, complete with a rectangular plaza, gardens and a schoolhouse. The first *alcalde* or mayor, Juan María Osuna, was elected in December 1834; laws were passed levying taxes and prohibiting cattle, weapons, gambling, drunkards and indigents within city limits.

During the Mexican War, the 22-gun corvette USS *Cyane* sailed into San Diego on July 30, 1846, and the US flag was raised over the pueblo; but fierce fighting continued in the San Diego area into December, most notably in the bloody Battle of San Pasqual *(p 181)*. San Diego's first census was taken at the time of California's statehood in 1850: the city numbered 2,287 inhabitants—1,550 of whom were designated as "wild Indians."

Davis' Folly and Horton's Vision – Beneath the shadow of Presidio Hill, San Diego thrived with businesses and residential construction. But its potential for development as a seaport was limited by its distance from the harbor. With that in mind, in March 1850 a group of citizens led by San Francisco financier **William Heath Davis** bought 160 acres of bayfront land some 5mi south of the town for $2,304 and formulated ambitious plans to develop the area. But their scheme received little support from the local citizenry or the Federal Government, and the few buildings they erected soon stood deserted, ridiculed as "Davis' Folly."

That same vision of a prosperous new city also struck **Alonzo Horton**, a San Francisco businessman who, upon first setting foot in San Diego in 1867, regarded its bayfront as "the best spot for building a city I ever saw." That year, he bought 960 acres at

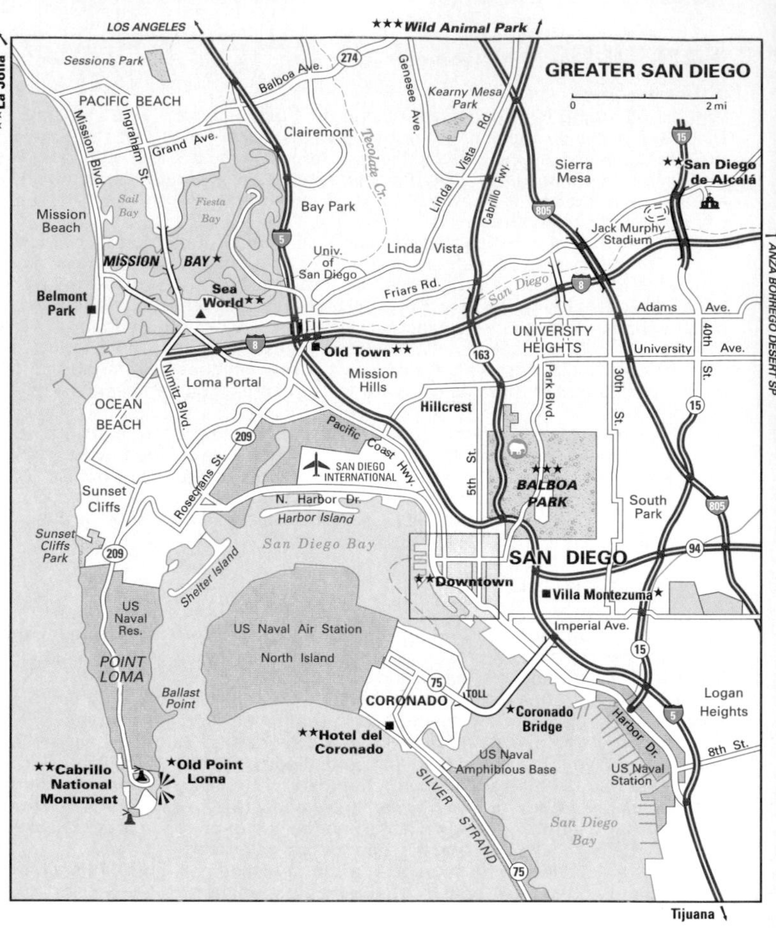

auction for $26,400 and began to promote their sale back in his hometown. Just over a year later, buildings rose on almost every block of "New Town" San Diego, and Horton himself returned to settle and build there, opening the Horton House Hotel on the present site of the U.S. Grant Hotel *(p 174)*.

San Diego stood poised for economic growth, but prosperity came in fits and starts. The whaling industry flourished for a time in the early 1870s, profiting from the gray whales' annual arrival to calve in the bay. But the whales began bypassing the bay, heading farther south to Baja California to calve. Likewise, gold fever briefly rushed through the area with the discovery of deposits 40mi inland near the town of JULIAN in the winter of 1870. The local geology, however, made the ore difficult to locate and extract, and this short-lived gold rush had fizzled by 1880.

Despite these setbacks, the city continued to grow. Anticipation of the arrival of the Santa Fe Railroad in 1885 helped fuel a real estate boom, and that same year, across the bay, Elisha Babcock began developing the elite enclave of Coronado and its elegant hostelry, Hotel Del Coronado. By the 1890s, upscale residential neighborhoods had formed in the hills and mesas north of Horton's downtown business district.

During this period, commercial agriculture burgeoned in the city's outlying areas. Groves of oranges, lemons, apples, pears, olives and figs were planted in the early and mid-1870s, and some 6,000 acres of wheat were grown in the El Cajon Valley in 1876. By 1877 most flat, arable land in San Diego County was under cultivation. Though the agricultural boom went bust before the turn of the century, farming continued to be an important part of the region's economy.

Sea and Air – In 1900 San Diego County was home to more than 35,000 people; the city's population of approximately 17,000 went on to more than double in the next ten years. Stimulating both the population and the economy was a growing military presence, as the US Government came to recognize the strategic importance of San Diego Bay. Forts Rosecrans and Pico were built to safeguard a harbor increasingly filled with navy warships. Both world wars underscored the harbor's strategic importance, as it became headquarters of the 11th Naval District and the Pacific Fleet. San Diego continues as an important naval center to this day.

The naval presence, combined with San Diego's mild sunny climate, also made the city an ideal setting for advances in aviation. In the years before World War I, naval aviators trained at North Island on the bay under the direction of **Glenn H. Curtiss**. In 1925, T. Claude Ryan began offering regularly scheduled flights between San Diego and Los Angeles; his service, known as Ryan Airlines, was the nation's first commercial passenger airline. Two years later, the company was commissioned by Charles Lindbergh to modify a plane capable of making a solo transatlantic flight. Lindbergh's historic aircraft, the *Spirit of St. Louis,* was completed in only two months. A decade later, with another war looming in only Europe, Reuben H. Fleet moved his Consolidated Aircraft Company to the city from Buffalo, New York, becoming a major local employer.

Practical Information

Area Code: 619

Getting There

By Air – **San Diego International Airport** (SAN): international and domestic flights; 3mi northwest of downtown ☎231-5220. Taxi service to downtown ($7-$10); commercial shuttles ($6); rental car agency branches *(p 253)*.

By Bus or Train – *p 253.* Greyhound: 120 West Broadway ☎800-231-2222. Amtrak: Santa Fe Depot, 1050 Kettner Blvd ☎800-872-7245.

Getting Around

By Public Transportation – The **San Diego Transit** system offers broad coverage of San Diego County. Day Tripper passes offer unlimited rides on system buses, trolleys and the Bay Ferry to Coronado; good for 1 ($4) and 4 ($12) days; available at the Transit Store, 449 Broadway, ☎234-1060. Trolley lines travel between the Convention Center and Central City (C & B Sts), also to the Mexican border *(p 180)*. System route information ☎233-3004. **Old Town Trolley Tours** (daily year-round, $15) offer 2hr narrated tours of the city; visitors can board at major attractions along the route ☎298-8687.

By Car – *p 253.* Parking garages average $1.75/hr or $5/day.

By Taxi – **American** ☎292-1111; **Co-op Silver** ☎280-5555; **Orange** ☎291-3337; **Yellow** ☎234-6161.

General Information

Visitor Information – **San Diego Convention & Visitors Bureau** information center: 11 Horton Plaza ☎236-1212 (open Mon–Sat 8:30am–5pm; closed Jan 1, Thanksgiving Day, Dec 25). Mailing address: 1200 Third Ave, Suite 824, San Diego CA 92101-4190. Handicapped visitor information: **Accessible San Diego**, 2466 Bartel St, San Diego CA 92123 ☎279-0704.

Accommodations – *San Diego Accommodations* directory available (free) from the San Diego Convention & Visitors Bureau *(above)*. **San Diego Budget Accommodations** ☎800-225-9610. Accommodations range from elegant hotels ($150/day) to budget motels ($65/day). **Bed & Breakfast Directory for San Diego,** PO Box 3292, San Diego CA 92163 ☎297-3130. Most bed & breakfasts are located in residential sections of the city ($70-$130/day). *All rates quoted are average prices for a double room.*

Local Press – Daily news: *San Diego Union-Tribune*, Thursday entertainment section. Weekly entertainment information: *San Diego Reader, San Diego This Week.*

Entertainment – Consult the arts and entertainment sections of local newspapers for schedule of cultural events and addresses of principal theaters and concert halls. **Entertainment Hotline**: 560-4094. Tickets for local events: **Times Arts Tix** offers full price advance sale tickets and half-price tickets for selected events on the day of the performance, cash sales only at Horton Square location (Broadway at Broadway Circle) ☎238-3810; or **Ticketmaster** ☎278-8497.

Currency Exchange Offices – *p 25.*

Sports – Tickets for major sporting events can be purchased at venue or through Ticketmaster outlets *(above)*.

Sport	*Team*	*Season*	*Venue*
Major League Baseball	Padres (NL)	Apr–Oct	Jack Murphy Stadium
Professional Football	Chargers (AFC)	Sept–Dec	Jack Murphy Stadium
Professional Hockey	Gulls	Sept–Apr	San Diego Sports Arena
Horse Racing		Jul–Sept	San Diego Sports Arena
Bull Fighting		May–Sept	Toreo de Tijuana

Useful Numbers

Police/Ambulance/Fire (multilingual)	**911**
Police (non-emergency; multilingual)	531-2000
Weather	289-1212
Main Post Office 2535 Midway Dr (Mon–Fri 7am–1am)	221-3125
House Call Physicians (24hrs; multilingual)	800-362-5511
Dental Emergencies (Mon–Thu 6am–8pm, Fri 6am–6pm, Sat 8am–2pm; Spanish and English)	800-336-8478
24-hour pharmacy Kaiser Permanente Medical Center, 4647 Zion Ave (English only)	528-7770

Shopping in San Diego and Environs

In this area...	*You will find...*
Downtown *(p 173)*	Horton Plaza (over 140 stores) Paladion (designer boutiques)
Mission Valley *(p 168)*	Fashion Valley Center (over 140 stores) Mission Valley Center (over 150 stores)
Gallery District (G St)	Art galleries, cafes
Old Town *(p 166)*	Bazaar del Mundo (boutiques, craft shops, galleries) Old Town Esplanade (specialty shops)
LaJolla *(p 69)*	Designer boutiques, art galleries, trendy shops

All the while, San Diego continued to attract military personnel who had been stationed here and settled in the area after decommissioning. Two successful expositions in 1915 and 1935 transformed Balboa Park into an enduring civic landmark and impressed hundred of thousands of visitors with the city's beauty. By the end of World War II, San Diego County's population had reached half a million; that number doubled before 1960.

San Diego Today – As it approaches the 21C, San Diego can and does acknowledge some of the problems besetting modern cities. Political battles wage between citizens who favor continued development of commercial and residential properties, and those who wish to safeguard the city's charms with slow-growth or no-growth policies. Faced with competition from abroad, important industries have closed down—most notably the Van Camp Sea Food cannery in 1984. Parts of downtown show signs of urban decay. The need for water rationing occasionally looms in this semidesert region.

Yet San Diego seems to face even its toughest challenges with a freshness and resolve other cities sometimes lack, as evidenced by the preservation of the Victorian-era residences in the **Hillcrest** neighborhood north of Balboa Park, and the revitalization of Old Town and the Gaslamp Quarter. New businesses in the field of biomedical research burgeon in the Golden Triangle northeast of LA JOLLA, spurred on by the groundbreaking work of the Salk Institute *(p 70)* and the Scripps Clinic and Research Foundation. New and ever-growing developments such as Mission Bay, Seaport Village, Horton Plaza and the San Diego Convention Center continually increase the role of tourism as an economic mainstay, while providing fresh delights for area residents. And such local treasures as the San Diego Zoo, the Old Globe Theatre and the Museum of Contemporary Art endure as exemplars of the city's rich, cultural tradition.

★★★ OLD SAN DIEGO *1 day. Map below.*

Sights preserving and commemorating the birth of San Diego and the beginnings of European presence in Alta California lie in the vicinity of Interstate 8 as it stretches from east to west, roughly following the course of the San Diego River.

★★ Old Town San Diego State Historic Park

From downtown San Diego take I-5 north; exit at Old Town Ave and follow signs.

A broad plaza surrounded by restored adobe and wood structures marks the original heart of San Diego. Situated at the foot of Presidio Hill *(p 167)*, the area became known as Old Town when it was eclipsed by the development of Alonzo Horton's waterfront New Town in the 1860s *(p 163)*. Today the festive group of restored historic buildings, colorful shops and eateries recreates San Diego from the Mexican and early American periods.

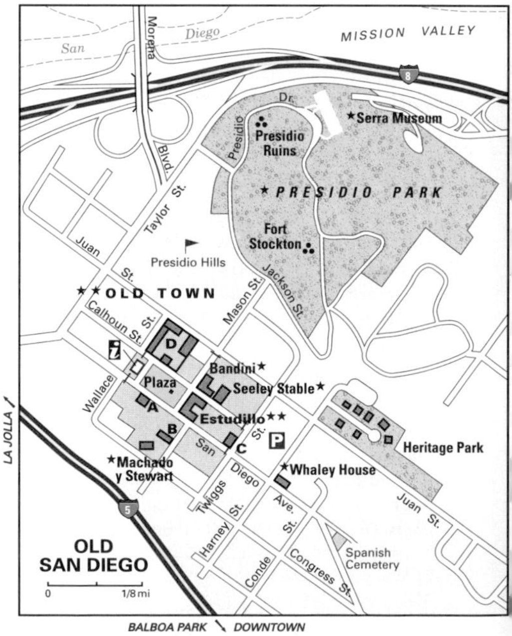

Following Mexico's independence from Spain in 1821, the hub of settlement in San Diego shifted from the presidio and mission areas to the flat plain below the presidio. A pueblo was laid out, focusing on a central plaza in keeping with Spanish and Mexican urbanistic traditions. Through the entire Mexican period, the pueblo remained little more than a cluster of single-story, crudely thatched or mud huts with dirt floors; only a few major land-owning families—most notably the Estudillos, Bandinis and Picos—built more substantial structures. Trade in cattle hides and tallow dominated the local economy.

In the summer of 1846, during the Mexican War, a detachment from the USS *Cyane* marched on the town and raised the American flag over the plaza, signaling the beginning of American occupation. The city was incorporated in 1850, two years after California passed into American control, and Yankee influences became increasingly evident, particularly through the introduction of New England-style architecture. The area's role as the city's center faded in 1867 with Horton's plans for a new town oriented toward the harbor; a major fire in 1872 that destroyed many buildings sealed Old Town's fate.

In 1968, a 13-acre section of Old Town was designated a state historic park, and work began to restore and stabilize its seven surviving buildings; others were reconstructed according to archaeological and archival records. Many historic structures, in addition to newly built shops and eateries, surround the 2-acre **plaza**, site of fiestas during the Mexican period, and of seasonal festivals and art shows today.

Begin at the visitor center located in the Robinson-Rose House at the west end of the plaza. Open year-round daily 10am–5pm. Closed Jan 1, Thanksgiving Day, Dec 25. $2 (to visit La Casa de Estudillo & Seeley Stable). ℜ ♿ 🅿 ☎619-220-5422.

Casa de Machado y Silvas [A] – This modest, single-story adobe, built by José Nicasio Silvas between 1830 and 1843, was owned by the same family for more than a century; it then served the community variously as a boarding house, brothel and church. Restored today to resemble a period restaurant, it also houses a museum featuring an audio-visual presentation *(20 min)* of Old Town history.

Mason Street School [B] – This wood-frame one-room structure (1865) was San Diego's first public schoolhouse; its first teacher received a monthly salary of $65. Today it features artifacts representing the history of education in San Diego; and replicas of the 15 flags that have flown at various times over California.

★ **Casa de Machado y Stewart** – Considered an outstanding example of adobe restoration, this simple, single-story residence (1833) was still occupied by descendants of the Machado family when it was purchased by the state in 1966. Some 70 percent of the structure is original; materials for the restored sections were made from surrounding soil. The kitchen garden has been replanted with vegetables, herbs and spices commonly used in the 19C.

San Diego Union Museum [C] – Prefabricated in Maine and shipped around Cape Horn in 1851, one of Old Town's first wood-frame structures served originally as a store, but in 1868 became home of the *San Diego Union*, which, as the *San Diego Union-Tribune*, remains the city's principal newspaper. Restored to its 1868 appearance, the interior replicates the newspaper's first offices; on view is a Washington handpress used to publish early editions.

★ **Seeley Stable** – Until the Southern Pacific Railroad was extended to San Diego in 1887, the stagecoaches of Albert Seeley traversed the 130mi route between San Diego and Los Angeles in as little as 24 hours. The reconstructed barns and stable now contain an extensive **collection** of horse-drawn vehicles, including covered wagons, carriages, buggies and stagecoaches, as well as Native artifacts and other memorabilia. A slide show *(18min)* traces early California transportation history.

★ **La Casa de Bandini** – Peruvian-born Juan Bandini, one of Old Town's most influential residents, built the first floor of this lovely hacienda in 1829. Albert Seeley *(above)* purchased the home in 1869, added an upper floor and converted it into the Cosmopolitan Hotel. In later years, it housed a store and apartments; today a popular Mexican restaurant occupies its refurbished rooms and beautiful garden.

★★ **La Casa de Estudillo** – The largest and most impressive of the park's original adobes was constructed in 1829 by retired presidio commander Capt José María Estudillo and offers an excellent glimpse of the lifestyle of an upper-class family during the pueblo's peak years. The elegant home, occupied by the Estudillo family for 60 years, was the social and political hub of Mexican and early American San Diego. Its 13 rooms connected by an inner veranda wrap around a central patio, with a larger garden in the rear. During the time of the family's residence, the main room, or **la sala**, was filled with the very best purchases from ships bringing goods from Europe, North and South America and Asia. The house was restored in 1910.

Skirting the north side of the plaza are new and rebuilt structures housing gift shops and eateries. In **Bazaar del Mundo [D]**, a festive shopping and dining complex arranged around a central patio, shops specialize in Latin American arts, crafts and apparel, and strolling mariachis add to the lively ambience.

★ **Whaley House** – *Open daily year-round. Closed major holidays. $5. ☎619-298-2482.* Considered to be the city's first 2-story brick building (1856), this dignified residence illustrates the influence of the East Coast on San Diego's architectural history. The north room functioned briefly as the county courthouse between 1869 and 1871, but forcible removal of county records by an armed mob from New Town marked the end of the pueblo's prospects as a city center. Now restored and appointed with local period furnishings, the house features one of six life masks of Abraham Lincoln. Whaley House is one of only two California houses certified (by the US Department of Commerce) as being haunted.

Heritage Park – *Off Juan St adjacent to Old Town.* Gathered around a picturesque cobblestone cul-de-sac are seven Victorian buildings, all originally erected during the 1880s in Horton's Addition, an elite neighborhood on the edge of downtown. The rapid growth of San Diego during the 1960s threatened destruction of many of the city's fine Victorians, and preservationists, unable to convince the city to maintain them on-site, created Heritage Park. The charming, stately buildings reflect a variety of Victorian substyles *(p 26)*, among them Eastlake, Queen Anne, Stick and Italianate. Today they house offices, shops and a bed & breakfast.

★ Presidio Park

From Old Town take Mason St toward Presidio Hill to Jackson St and turn left, following signs to the park. Open year-round Tue–Sun.

The foundations of Spanish colonial history in Alta California lie atop this prominent knoll, from which sweeping views extend over the city of San Diego. The beautifully landscaped park features a fine historical museum and archaeological remains of the first European settlement on the West Coast.

The Fortress on the Hill – In 1769, the twin columns of the Sacred Expedition led by Gaspar de Portolá and Padre Junípero Serra arrived by land and sea, and designated the hill overlooking the bay as the site for both mission and presidio. Soldiers built log stockades while Serra courted Kumeyaay Natives at the nearby village of Cosoy. Although the mission was relocated in 1774, the Royal Presidio, as it was named that year, remained an active military installation throughout the Spanish period, and a colonial settlement was established in the area immediately around the fortress. With Mexican independence in 1821, funding to maintain the presidio ceased; the fortress was abandoned and subsequently fell into ruin as its occupants moved downhill to establish Old Town as a civilian settlement.

During the first decades of the 20C, San Diego department store owner George White Marston systematically acquired much of Presidio Hill, landscaping the property with some 10,000 shrubs and trees, and commissioning the Serra Museum. A renowned philanthropist, Marston presented the park and the museum to the city as a gift in 1929.

★ **Serra Museum** – *Open year-round Tue–Sun. $3.* 🅿 *☎619-297-3258.* Looming over the western end of Mission Valley, this stately, white museum building (1929, William Templeton Johnson) is a San Diego landmark. Capped by a commanding tower, the Mission Revival structure features characteristic Spanish Colonial elements, including red-tile roofs, arches and clerestory-type windows. Within, five galleries contain exhibits concentrating on the region's early history; highlights include a remarkable collection of Spanish Renaissance furniture and a display devoted to Native populations of San Diego County that describes the effects of colonization during the mission and Mexican periods.

Presidio Ruins – *Downhill from the museum.* A modern wall marks the perimeter of the original presidio complex, today a group of grass-covered mounds. Archaeological excavations conducted here since 1965 have revealed the outlines of various structures, among them the presidio chapel and the commandant's residence; excavations are ongoing.

A flagpole at the summit of Presidio Hill marks the site of **Fort Stockton**, erected by Mexican soldiers in 1838 and commandeered by American forces during the Mexican War. Monuments commemorate members of the Mormon Battalion, which marched 2,000mi from Iowa to San Diego in 1847 to assist in the war effort.

★★ San Diego de Alcalá Mission

From Old Town take I-8 east 7mi to Mission Gorge Rd and follow signs. Open year-round daily 9am–5pm. Closed Jan 1, Thanksgiving Day, Dec 25 (open for Mass only). $2. ♿ 🅿 *☎619-283-7319.*

California's first mission occupies a secluded site on the north slope of the San Diego River valley, today known as **Mission Valley** and flooded with the thoroughfares, shopping centers and urban sprawl of a 20C megalopolis. The "Mother of the Missions" was named for St Didacus of Alcalá, a 15C Spanish Franciscan friar credited with miraculous cures.

The First Link in the Chain – Originally established atop Presidio Hill in 1769 by Padre Junípero Serra, the mission was relocated in 1774 by Padre Luis Jayme to its present site some 6mi inland. The new location offered several advantages: it was farther from the corrupting influences of presidio soldiers, had better soil, and offered a larger population of Natives as prospective converts. In 1775 the mission was burned and looted in a violent Kumeyaay uprising; Padre Jayme and two workmen were killed in the attack, which drove the remaining padres temporarily back to the presidio.

A larger complex, surrounded by high adobe walls, was completed in 1776, and subsequent years were marked by economic and ecclesiastic prosperity. An aqueduct system developed between 1813 and 1815 provided a steady water supply despite periodic droughts. Sheep and cattle grazed on the surrounding hillsides, and in 1813 a new larger adobe church was completed. The mission's population reached its peak in 1824 when some 1,829 neophytes resided here.

Following secularization, mission lands were passed to a wealthy Californio who allowed the

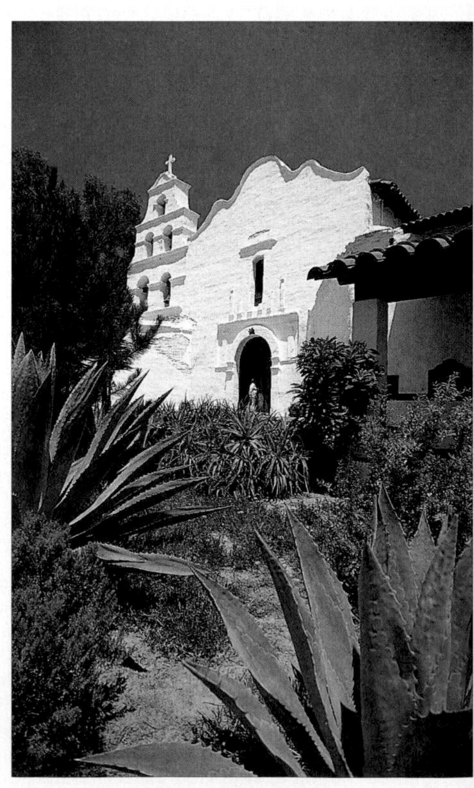

San Diego de Alcalá Mission

abandoned buildings to fall into disrepair. Between 1846 and 1862, the US Cavalry occupied the property, and by the time ownership was returned to the Catholic Church in 1862, little of the original structures remained. The present restoration occurred between 1895 and 1931, and the mission was designated a Minor Basilica in 1976 by Pope Paul VI.

Visit – *Enter through the gift shop.* The church's original buttressed facade of gleaming white stucco and distinctive 5-bell campanario herald the entrance to the mission complex. The sparsely furnished **casa del Padre Serra**, where the friar resided during his frequent visits to the mission, is the only remaining fragment of the original monastery. The church **interior**, restored to its 1813 appearance, measures 139ft by 34ft, its width kept narrow by the lack of tall trees for use as ceiling beams. The beams, adobe bricks in the baptistry arch, and darker floor tiles were salvaged from the 1813 church. In the sanctuary, note the 18C painting of St Agnes, rescued from the fire of 1775, and the hand-carved wooden statues, which survive from the early mission period. The grave of the slain Padre Jayme lies beneath the sanctuary floor.
In the small **garden** *(adjacent to the church)*, crosses fashioned from adobe and burnt tile pay homage to hundreds of Natives buried during the mission period. The tranquil enclosure is profuse with local vegetation including palms, pepper trees, roses, succulents and bougainvillea.
The mission **museum** *(behind the church)* houses artifacts of the Native, mission, Mexican and American periods of regional history, including artifacts recovered from the site by archaeological excavations. Especially noteworthy is the original baptismal font used at the mission during Padre Serra's time.

*** BALBOA PARK

San Diego's cultural focal point is a 1,200-acre park rising immediately to the north of downtown. Velvet lawns, lush gardens and century-old shade trees surround a world renowned zoo, outdoor and indoor performance spaces, and a wealth of diverse museums housed in buildings lovingly cherished and restored from two great world expositions.

A Civic Dumping Ground – In 1868 San Diego's Board of Trustees, urged on by Alonzo Horton *(p 163)*, designated a 1,400-acre tract on the city's northern outskirts as City Park. But the sandy expanse, covered in cactus and chaparral and infested with rattlesnakes, languished unused for more than 20 years, save for the refuse dumped there by the citizenry.
The park's image began to change in 1892, when horticulturist Kate Sessions leased 30 acres of it for her nursery business. As her rent, she promised to plant 100 trees per year throughout the park and to donate 300 more trees for planting in other parts of the city. Over the next decade, Sessions also cleared brush, planted lawns and flower beds, and laid out nature trails. A Park Improvement Committee, founded in 1902, hired Samuel V. Parsons, consulting architect for greater New York City, to oversee the planning and development. Roads were graded and oiled, irrigation installed and, as in San Francisco's Golden Gate Park, street sweepings and manure from city stables improved the soil. John McLaren, superintendent of Golden Gate Park, sent plants as a gift. By 1910 the landscape resembled its present-day form, and a contest was held to rename City Park. The winner suggested that it honor Spanish explorer Vasco Nuñez de Balboa, the first European to sight the Pacific Ocean in 1513.

Two Great Expositions – Burgeoning enthusiasm for Balboa Park led to its designation as the setting for the **1915 Panama-California Exposition**, a year-long world fair that aimed to promote San Diego as the US's first West Coast port of call from the newly opened Panama Canal. A team of architects led by Bertram Goodhue erected a stylized Spanish city of exhibit pavilions around two central plazas, called Plaza de Balboa and Plaza de Panama. The plazas were linked by El Prado, a broad thoroughfare. As a dominant style, the architects selected Spanish Colonial, which combined Spanish Renaissance architecture with Native American influences from Mexico, resulting in a rich hybrid of Moorish, baroque and rococo ornamentation contrasted with colorful tiles and flat, unadorned walls. Many facades were richly encrusted with stonework as ornately crafted as silverplate, in a style known as Plateresque (from the Spanish word *plata*, meaning "silver").
The exposition was so successful that it was extended another year, and many of its buildings were preserved and later restored or rebuilt to house cultural institutions. Two decades later, as America wallowed in the depths of the Great Depression, enterprising San Diegans once again looked to Balboa Park as they planned another fair, the **1935 California Pacific International Exposition**, to lift spirits and boost commerce. Surrounding Pan-American Plaza, architect Richard Requa designed new pavilions in a mixture of Art Deco, Mayan and American Southwestern styles; these too have survived to serve the city.

A Park for All People – Today Balboa Park endures as an idyllic sylvan retreat and a cultural haven, fulfilling the vision of those who contributed to its development. Year-round, people from all walks of life—locals and visitors alike—flock to this urban park to enjoy its myriad attractions. Schoolchildren scamper, artists sketch and poor souls seek refuge along the arcaded sidewalks of El Prado, which links the park's major museums. Joggers and cyclists navigate its trails, and enamoured couples court in its isolated glades. Come nightfall, concert enthusiasts and theatergoers throng live performances at the **Starlight Bowl** *(open Jun–Sept daily; ♿ 🅿 ☎619-696-6920)* and the Simon Edison Center for the Performing Arts, built around a 1935 replica of Shakespearean London's **Old Globe Theatre** *(open daily year-round; ♿ 🅿 ☎619-239-2255)*.

Sights *2 days. Map p 171.*

The park information center located in the House of Hospitality (open year-round daily 9am–4pm, closed Jan 1, Easter Sunday, Thanksgiving Day, Dec 25; ☐ ♿ ☎619-239-0512) offers books and maps, as well as a listing of museums with free admission on Tuesdays. Ample free parking located throughout the park. Tram to sights within the park (free) operates Apr–Oct daily 9:30am–5:30pm, every 8-12 minutes; rest of the year daily 11am–5pm, every 12-24 minutes.

★★★ **San Diego Zoo** – *Park Blvd & Zoo Place. Open year-round daily 9am–4pm (closing times may be later during summer and school vacations). $13.* ✗ ♿ ☐ *☎619-234-3153.* One of the largest, most diverse and most celebrated zoological parks in the world, the San Diego Zoo occupies 100 acres of lushly landscaped hillsides and ravines at the northern end of Balboa Park. Some 3.3 million visitors each year come to see its 4,000 animals representing 800 different species, in a setting cooled and shaded by plants representing more than 6,500 botanical species, many of them subtropical.

An Inspirational Roar – During the Panama-California Exposition, a small menagerie of wild animals was assembled near the eastern edge of Balboa Park, just southeast of the zoo's present location. The roar of a caged lion there inspired local surgeon Dr Harry Wegeforth, who had a lifelong passion for circus animals, to found the Zoological Society of San Diego, which began its collection with specimens gathered from the various exhibits at the time of the fair's close. In 1922 the city granted the society its permanent home, a hilly, chaparral-covered tract of 100 acres.

Under Wegeforth's direction until his death in 1941, the zoo increased its holdings, landscaping the enclosures to resemble the animals' natural environments. Moats rather than cages were employed to confine the animals, resulting in habitats that were not only naturalistic but also gave visitors a closer view of the animals than cages allowed. That spirit continues today, both in recently completed state-of-the-art walk-through habitats, part of a 20-year plan to redesign the zoo into 10 bioclimatic zones, and at the zoo's sister institution, the San Diego Wild Animal Park *(p 180)*.

As worldwide awareness has grown of mankind's role in preserving the planet, the San Diego Zoo has increasingly played a major role in conservation. In 1966 it hosted the first international conference on the role of zoos in conservation. Most notably, it launched the Center for Reproduction of Endangered Species in 1975, dedicated to increasing animals' chances of reproduction and survival both in zoos and the wild.

The zoo's vast and undulating terrain may seem daunting at first; the best way to learn the lay of the land is to begin the visit with the guided **bus tour** *(departs just inside zoo entrance; 30min; $3 ♿)*. The double-decker buses cover approximately 70 percent of the zoo's total area, including the outer reaches that are less accessible on foot. Thus oriented, you can spend a pleasant day idly wandering the intricate network of pathways in roughly clockwise order, aided when necessary by several moving sidewalks that climb steep hills; **Skyfari**, an aerial tram that traverses the zoo's western end, yields easy access to the displays of horned and hoofed mammals along the zoo's northern edge. Allow time, as well, for animal shows presented regularly in the Wegeforth Bowl in the zoo's southwestern corner and the Hunte Amphitheater on its northeastern side *(20-25min; check daily program for schedule)*. Everything is small-scale in the **Children's Zoo**, where young visitors are drawn to a baby animal nursery, small walk-through aviaries and a petting paddock with barnyard animals.

Tiger River – A winding trail descends through a misty tropical rain forest, passing crocodiles, Chinese water dragons, fishing cats, a dozen species of birds, tapirs, pythons and mouse deer. The walk concludes at three viewing stations overlooking an extensive habitat for Sumatran tigers.

Gorilla Tropics – The 2.5-acre simulation of an African rain forest includes an 8,000sq ft enclosure for a troop of western lowland gorillas. Below the gorilla habitat are: the **Scripps Aviary**, a walk-through multilevel enclosure housing more than 200 African bird species, surrounded by waterfalls and tropical foliage; and a 6,000sq ft naturalistic environment for lively bonobos *Pan paniscus*, or **pygmy chimps.**

Bear Canyon – This example of the early zoo-without-cages philosophy presents various bear species in individual open-air enclosures. At the bottom of Bear Canyon is **Sun Bear Forest**, a 1.5-acre habitat featuring playful Malaysian sun bears in an environment of rocks, waterfalls and lush greenery.

Koalas – A small separate enclosure is home to the zoo's Australian koalas. Nearby is **Elephant Mesa**, its large open paddocks home to elephants and rhinoceroses.

African Rock Kopje – Pronounced "copy," the volcanic-rock outcropping reflects the terrain typical of the African plains and features soft-shelled pancake tortoises and klipspringers, a small species of antelope. The canyon below features habitats for dogs and cats of the wild.

★ **San Diego Natural History Museum** – *Open daily year-round. Closed Jan 1, Thanksgiving Day, Dec 25. $6.* ☐ ♿ *☎619-232-3821.* Founded in 1874, the San Diego Society of Natural History opened its first museum in 1920 in Casa de Balboa *(p 171)*. Ellen Browning Scripps funded the current, imposing 2-story building (1933, William Templeton Johnson) fronting Plaza de Balboa. Beyond the foyer's Foucault pendulum and allosaur skeleton, the main level features a 3,000sq ft **Hall of Mineralogy**, entered via a recreation of a San Diego County mine tunnel. The lower level presents exhibits on local ocean, shore and desert ecologies while the main floor features traveling exhibits.

Adjoining the museum is the **Casa del Prado**. Modeled after the chapels of the Metropolitan Cathedral in Mexico City, this structure (1915, Carleton Winslow) was among the largest and most ornate of those erected for the Panama-California

Exposition. Originally known as the Food and Beverage Building, it was completely rebuilt and renamed in 1971, and now includes a 1,500-seat civic theater. Beyond a 140-year-old Moreton Bay fig tree *(behind the museum)* lies the **Spanish Village Art Center**, a gathering of some 40 artists' studios and galleries designed to appear as a small Spanish town. The village was constructed for the California Pacific Exposition *(open daily year-round; ♿ 🅿 ☎619-233-9050).*

Reuben H. Fleet Space Theater and Science Center – *Open daily year-round. $6. ✂ ♿ 🅿 ☎619-238-1233.* A planetarium theater and museum of physical sciences share this Spanish Colonial structure built in 1973. Named for Reuben H. Fleet, founder of San Diego's Consolidated Aircraft Corporation, the theater features tiered seating facing a 75ft domed screen on which planetarium and laser shows and large-format films are projected *($7.50).* The adjoining Science Center houses more than 60 interactive physical science exhibits.

★ **Casa de Balboa** – ✂ 🅿. This richly ornamented 2-story structure was originally designed in 1914 by Bertram Goodhue after the Federal Government Palace in Queretaro, Mexico. In 1978 the building was destroyed by arson; a slightly larger reconstruction opened two years later and is now home to four museums. The **Museum of San Diego History** presents permanent and changing exhibits on the city's history since 1850 *(open year-round Wed–Sun; closed Jan 1, Thanksgiving Day, Dec 25; $3; ♿ ☎619-232-6203).* The **Museum of Photographic Arts** hosts visiting shows as well as changing exhibits drawn from the museum's permanent collection of approximately 2,800 images *(open daily year-round; closed major holidays; $3; ♿ ☎619-239-5262).* The **San Diego Hall of Champions Sports Museum** exhibits memorabilia, photographs and videos devoted to more than a century of local amateur and professional athletes in over 40 different sports *(open daily year-round; closed Jan 1, Thanksgiving Day, Dec 25; $3; ♿ ☎619-234-2544).* The **San Diego Model Railroad Museum** pays tribute to actual and imagined Southern California railroads with four working scale-model train exhibits *(open year-round first Tue of month, Wed–Sun; closed Martin Luther King's Birthday, Thanksgiving Day, Dec 25; $2.25; ♿ ☎619-696-0199).*

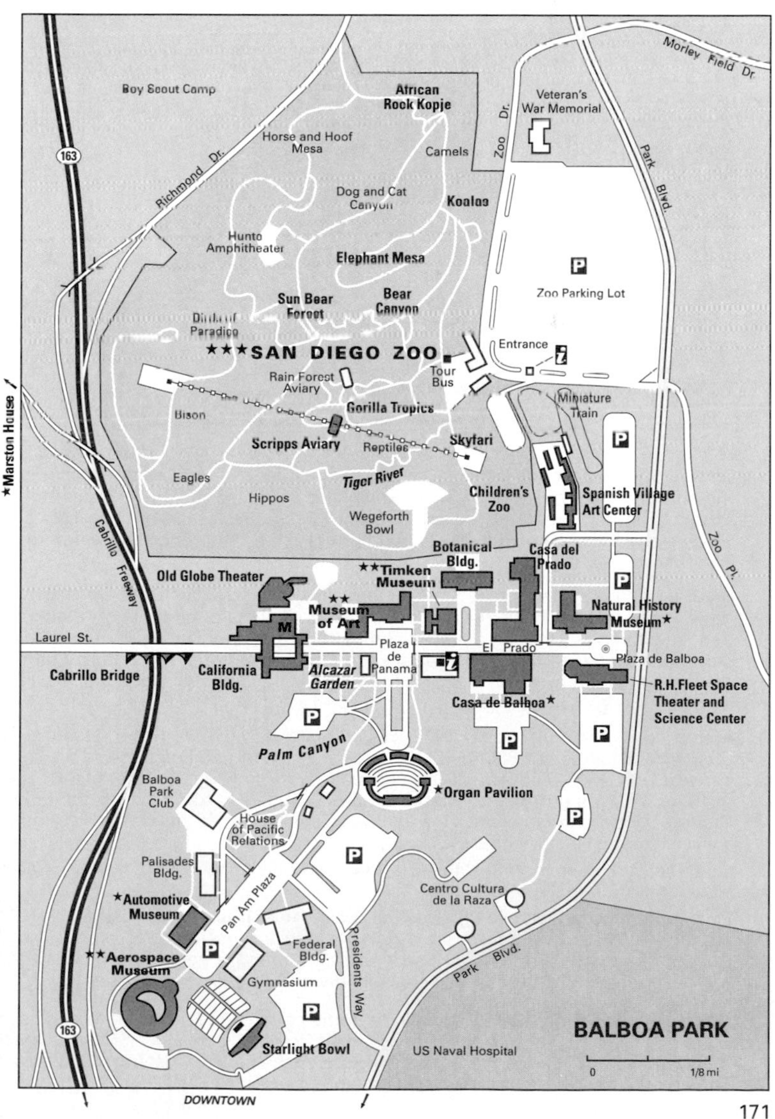

★★ **Timken Museum of Art** – *Open Oct–Aug Tue–Sat 10am–4:30pm Sun 1:30–4:30pm.* ♿ 🅿 ☎*619-239-5548.* Sleekly clad in Italian travertine marble, the compact, single-story museum (1965) displays in its six galleries and rotunda a collection begun in 1950 by local art benefactors Anne and Amy Putnam. Funds for the building were largely provided by H.H. Timken Jr, brother of San Diego Museum of Art founder Amelia Bridges *(below).*

The Putnam sisters' passion for **European Masters** is evident in such works as *Portrait of a Man* (1634) by Frans Hals, *Portrait of a Young Captain* (c.1625) by Rubens and Rembrandt's *Saint Bartholomew* (1657). Highlights of the outstanding holdings in **American Paintings** include *Cho-looke, The Yosemite Fall* (1864) by Bierstadt and *Mrs. Thomas Gage* (1771) by Copley. Miss Amy Putnam's private collection of **Russian icons** dating from the 14C to the 19C is displayed in a separate room on walls covered in velvet custom-woven in Florence for the museum.

Behind the museum, a 257ft-long **Lily Pond** extends from El Prado to the **Botanical Building** (1915, Carleton Winslow), a graceful Victorian-style pavilion built from 70,000 feet of redwood laths.

★★ **San Diego Museum of Art** – *Open year-round Tue–Sun 10am–4:30pm. Closed Jan 1, last Wed in Apr, Thanksgiving Day, Dec 25. $5.* ✗ ♿ 🅿 ☎*619-232-7931.* After the Panama-Pacific Exposition, a local exhibition of modern masters inspired benefactors Amelia and Appleton S. Bridges to donate $400,000 for construction of the Fine Arts Gallery of San Diego. The city's first and still preeminent art museum opened on February 28, 1926; the name was changed in 1978 to the San Diego Museum of Art. Today the collection totals some 10,500 objects, with particular strengths in Renaissance, Asian and contemporary California art.

San Diego Museum of Art in Balboa Park

Dominating the Plaza de Panama, the elaborate Plateresque **facade** was inspired by the entry to the University of Salamanca, and depicts Spanish Baroque masters Murillo, Ribera, Velázquez, Zurbarán and El Greco; replicas of Donatello's *Saint George* and Michelangelo's *David*; and heraldry of Spain, America, California and San Diego.

First Floor – The region's largest collection of **contemporary California art** *(gallery 4)*, donated by benefactor Frederick R. Weisman, includes major works by Albuquerque, Bengston, Francis, Hockney, Ruscha, Smith and Thiebaud. The **Japanese** and **Chinese Collections** *(galleries 7 & 8)* include a sculpted pair of early-16C Shinto guardian deities, a suit of armor (1578) by Myochin Morisuke, and two statues of the divinity Kwan Yin from the Sung dynasty (AD 960-1279).

Second Floor – The collections of **17C-18C European Art** *(galleries 16 & 17)* feature *The Penitent Saint Peter* (c.1600) by El Greco and two works by Francisco de Zurbarán: *Agnus Dei* (c. 1635-1640) and *Madonna and Child with Infant Saint John the Baptist* (c.1658). A highlight of the **15C-16C European Art** collections *(gallery 18)* is Luca Signorelli's *Coronation of the Virgin* (1508). Gallery 19 presents works by Bonnard, Vuillard, Braque and Modigliani.

Adjoining the main building, the **sculpture court** displays works by Moore, Calder, Nevelson and Miró.

Facing the museum across Plaza de Panama is the **Spreckels Organ Pavilion**★ (1914), housing a 72-rank, 4,445-pipe instrument, the largest outdoor pipe organ in the world. Concerts in the 4,800-seat amphitheater are held Sunday afternoons *(2pm–3pm)*, and on Monday evenings in July and August *(8pm–9:30pm)*.

California Building – With its massive dome covered in Moorish tiles and its imposing 3-belfry, 180ft campanile, the Spanish Colonial structure (1915) was one of the few buildings intended to be preserved from the Panama-California Exposition. The ornate facade is adorned with important figures from San Diego's early history.

The campanile, called the **California Tower**, is considered an outstanding example of the Spanish Colonial Revival style; it houses a 100-bell carillon, which chimes the quarter-hour. Diagonally across El Prado is the **Alcazar Garden**, a Moorish courtyard inspired by the gardens of Seville's Alcazar palace; beyond lies **Palm Canyon**, a small trail-crossed ravine lushly planted with over 50 palm species.

★★ **San Diego Museum of Man [M]** – *Open year-round daily 10am-4:30pm. Closed Jan 1, Thanksgiving Day, Dec 25. $4.* ♿ 🅿 *☎619-239-2001.* Exhibits on human evolution, anthropology and ethnology were first gathered in the California Building by the Smithsonian Institution for exhibition at the Panama-California Exposition. The exhibits formed the core of the San Diego Museum, renamed the Museum of Man in 1942, which now boasts a permanent collection of more than 70,000 objects. Beneath the building's dome *(1st floor)*, **The Ancient Maya** displays life-size replicas of stelae and other massive stone monuments from the Mayan city of Quirigua in Guatemala, dating from AD 780 to 805.

On the second floor, human evolution is the focus of **Early Man**; the exhibit includes a rare cast of the 3 million-year-old fossil skeleton of **Lucy**, a 3.5ft-tall female *Australopithecus*, the oldest known skeleton of an upright-walking human ancestor. **Life and Death on the Nile** presents artifacts from ancient Egypt, including mummies and a collection of *ushabtis,* magical tomb figurines dating from 1250 to 300 BC. A separate display of **mummies** includes bodies unearthed in Peru, Mexico and Egypt. In **Life Cycles and Ceremonies**, human rites of puberty, marriage, sexual union and birth are explored in audio-visual exhibits and artifacts from cultures worldwide.

Cabrillo Bridge – Immediately west of the California Building, the 405ft-long, 125ft-high structure (1914) was the first multiple-arched cantilever bridge built in California. The main entrance to the Panama-California Exposition, it was officially opened on April 12, 1914, by then-Assistant Secretary of the Navy Franklin D. Roosevelt. The bridge once spanned an idyllic lagoon; today, the Cabrillo Freeway (Highway 163) rushes beneath it.

★★ **San Diego Aerospace Museum** – *Open year-round daily 10am–4pm. Closed Jan 1, Thanksgiving Day, Dec 25. $4.* ♿ 🅿 *☎619-234-8291.* The white and blue ring-shaped Art Deco structure (1935), formerly called the Ford Building, housed a demonstration automobile assembly line for the California Pacific Exposition. The Aerospace Museum, founded in 1963, reopened here in 1979 after its quarters in Casa de Balboa were razed by fire.

Dedicated to chronicling the history of flight, the ever-growing collection today encompasses some 66 full-size vintage aircraft, from biplanes to space capsules, 42 of which are original; 14,000 scale model aircraft; and some 10,000 aviation-related items. Just inside the entrance, in the **International Aerospace Hall of Fame**, oil portraits and biographical displays salute notable inventors, industrialists and pilots. Encircling the interior wall is artist Juan Larinaga's 468ft by 18ft **mural**, *The March of Transportation* (1935).

Adjacent to the Aerospace Museum is the **San Diego Automotive Museum★**, which presents changing thematic displays of classic, exotic and special-interest automobiles and motorcycles *(open daily year-round; closed Jan 1, Thanksgiving Day, Dec 24 & 25; $4;* ♿ 🅿 *☎619-231-2886).*

★ **Marston House** – *3525 7th Ave, near the northwestern entrance to Balboa Park. Visit by guided tour (45min) only, weekends year-round. Closed Jan 1, Thanksgiving Day & Fri after, Dec 24 & 25. $3.* 🅿 *☎619-298-3142.* The 8,500sq ft Arts and Crafts mansion (1905, Irving Gill) was built as the home of local department store owner George White Marston, benefactor of Presidio Park, and his wife Anna Gunn Marston. Currently undergoing restoration to its original condition by the San Diego Historical Society and the city of San Diego, the house displays a collection of authentic Craftsman furnishings, few of which are original to the house. The 4.5-acre grounds reflect the work of several noted landscape designers, among them Kate Sessions *(p 169)*.

"Southern California . . . which however the real C, I believe much repudiates, has completely bowled me over—such a delicious difference from the rest of the US do I find in it. . . . The days have been mostly here of heavenly beauty, and the flowers, the wild flowers just now in particular, which fairly rage, with radiance, over the land, are worthy of some purer planet than this."

Henry James, 1905

★★ DOWNTOWN *1/2 day. Map p 175.*

Its modern spires and historic buildings stretching between Balboa Park and San Diego Bay, downtown San Diego serves as the city's center for business, commerce and government.

Until recent years, this urban center showed signs of decline as the city grew to the north, south and east, ignoring its historic heart. Civic leaders and enterprising developers began to stem that tide in the 1970s and 1980s, saving and restoring the Victorian treasures of the Gaslamp Quarter, spurring new shopping and office developments of cutting-edge architectural distinction along Broadway, and creating a waterfront renaissance with Seaport Village, the San Diego Convention Center and its attendant luxury hotels.

★ Gaslamp Quarter

With its wealth of restored and reused Victorian-era buildings, the 16 square blocks bounded by Broadway and Harbor Drive, 4th and 5th Avenues preserve the aura of late-19C and early-20C San Diego in a district now popular for its trendy restaurants, boutiques and offices.

From New Town to Stingaree – In the early 1850s, San Franciscan William Heath Davis failed in his attempt to establish a New Town north of San Diego's waterfront. Alonzo Horton succeeded in 1869 after building a commercial wharf at the end of 5th Avenue. But the boom years of the 1880s attracted unsavory types—including famed lawman Wyatt Earp, who ran three gambling halls—and respectable commerce moved north of Market Street. New Town became a red-light district known as the Stingaree, reputedly because unwary souls could get as badly stung there as by the stingrays in San Diego Bay.
Prostitution died down following police raids in 1912, and a portion of the Stingaree thrived as a Chinese and Asian quarter; the rest fell into decline. When buildings were threatened with razing in 1974, area owners and merchants formed the Gaslamp Quarter Association, and active restoration and redevelopment began in 1982. Work continues today, with parts of the quarter still downtrodden and forbidding, others—particularly large stretches of 5th Avenue—beautiful and welcoming.
Almost 100 historic buildings may be found in the Gaslamp Quarter today; a selection appears below. **Walking tours** of the historic quarter, conducted by the Gaslamp Quarter Foundation, depart from the William Heath Davis house *(2 hrs; year-round Sat; $5; ☎619-233-4691).*

William Heath Davis House – *410 Island Ave. Open year-round Mon-Sat. $1. ♿ ☎619-233-4691.* The district's oldest surviving structure, a 2-story saltbox built on the East Coast in 1850 and shipped around Cape Horn, is an exact duplicate of one lived in briefly by Davis; Alonzo Horton lived in this house for a brief period in 1867. The main floor serves as a visitor center and house museum, with five rooms decorated in period style.

★ **Horton Grand Hotel** – *311 Island Ave.* Regal bay windows front San Diego's oldest Victorian-era hotel (1886). Restored in 1981, the structure combines two hotels that were dismantled from their original sites in the downtown area and relocated here: the original Horton Grand, and the Brooklyn Hotel, formerly a saddle and harness shop. A lovely atrium connects the two structures, which feature original bay windows, balconies and wrought-iron work.

The narrow, elegant 3-story **Yuma Building** *(631 5th Ave)* was one of downtown's first brick structures (1888); it variously housed offices, a Japanese bazaar and a brothel before restoration began in 1982. Twin gabled towers top the 4-story, ornately embellished **Louis Bank of Commerce** *(835 5th Ave)*, San Diego's first granite building (1888). The interior of the 1907 **Ingle Building** *(801 4th Ave; open during office hours)* reveals a magnificent, 25ft stained-glass dome, constructed in 1906 and installed here in 1982. The building formerly housed the Golden Lion Tavern, that served lunches to men only.

★ Broadway

★ **Horton Plaza** – *Bordered by Broadway & G St, 1st & 4th Aves. Open year-round daily. Closed Easter Sunday, Thanksgiving Day, Dec 25. ✗ ♿ 🅿 ☎619-238-1596.* With its twisting and turning passageways, multiple ramps and stairways, crazy quilt of architectural styles and dazzling palette of 49 pastel colors, the open-air, multilevel, post-Modern shopping center (1985, Jon Jerde) is deliberately designed to disorient visitors, thus encouraging delightful browsing. The 11.5-acre complex includes four department stores, more than 150 specialty shops and restaurants, a 7-screen cinema and two live-performance theaters. Street entertainers perform in its courtyards and plazas. Fronting the entrance on Broadway is the original Horton Plaza, a small park established by Alonzo Horton in 1871; its electric fountain, designed by Irving Gill, was dedicated in 1910.

★ **U.S. Grant Hotel** – *326 Broadway.* Downtown's stateliest hotel is an 11-story Italian Renaissance Revival structure (1910) facing Horton Plaza. In 1895 Fannie Grant, daughter-in-law of 18th President Ulysses S. Grant, bought the Horton House Hotel that had occupied the site since 1870. The new hotel she and her husband built in its place, named to honor the former president, was considered one of the grandest of its day. Restored in the early 1980s, its **interior** boasts such lavish decorations as 107 chandeliers, 150 tons of marble in more than two dozen colors and eight different kinds of wood including Carpathian elm burl, mahogany, birdseye maple and American black walnut.

Spreckels Theater – *121 Broadway. Auditorium open for performances only. ☎619-235-9500.* Sugar magnate John D. Spreckels commissioned the imposing and elegant Baroque theater (1912) to celebrate the opening of both the Panama Canal and San Diego's 1915 Panama-California Exposition in Balboa Park. The lobby's walls and ceiling gleam with Predora onyx. Allegorical paintings decorate the proscenium and ceiling of the 1,456-seat auditorium, considered acoustically perfect and still in use for a wide variety of music, theater and dance performances.

★ **Emerald-Shapery Center** – *402 W. Broadway. Open daily year-round. ♿ ☎619-239-7000.* This 30-story cluster of eight hexagonal glass office towers (1990) lights the downtown skyline by night with the glow of emerald-green neon. The complex includes the Pan Pacific Hotel, whose 100ft-high **atrium** is dominated by a hanging green glass sculpture, *Flying Emeralds* (1990), by Richard Lippold, who also created the baldachin that hangs in St Mary's Cathedral *(p 209)* in San Francisco.

America Plaza – *1001 Kettner Blvd at Broadway. Open year-round Mon–Fri.* ♿ ☎*619-595-1128.* San Diego's tallest building, this tapered, 34-story office tower (1991) rises to a star-shaped pinnacle above walls of glass and white granite. The 4-story atrium **lobby**, clad in black granite and white and gray marble, features a 40ft waterfall. Adjoining, a crescent-shaped glass-and-steel canopy shelters a trolley station and connects the tower to the 10,000sq ft downtown branch of the **Museum of Contemporary Art, San Diego** *(open year-round Tue–Sun; $2, free Thu evening;* ♿ 🅿 ☎*619-234-1001)* which mounts traveling exhibits and changing exhibits of works from the permanent collection of its La Jolla-based counterpart *(p 69)*.

Santa Fe Depot – *1050 Kettner Blvd at Broadway. Open daily year-round.* ♿ ☎*619-232-6203.* Distinguished by two elegant towers facing Broadway, the Spanish Colonial-style train station (1915) was built to handle the increased traffic of visitors arriving for the Panama-California Exposition in Balboa Park, replacing a smaller station originally constructed for the arrival of the Santa Fe Railroad in 1885. Ornate yellow-and-blue tilework graces the cavernous **interior**.

★ Waterfront

★ **Maritime Museum of San Diego** – *1306 N. Harbor Dr. Open daily year-round. $6.* ☎*619-234-9153.* Currently docked harborside opposite the eye-catching Spanish Colonial **San Diego County Administration Building** (1938), three historic ships and their on-board exhibits form the core of a museum dedicated to the city's maritime history. Plans are underway to move the museum permanently to the Broadway Pier, just to the south, before the turn of the century.

The Berkeley [A] – Serving as museum headquarters, the second propeller-driven ferry on the Pacific coast was constructed at the Union Iron Works in San Francisco and launched on October 17, 1898. Measuring 289ft in length and displacing 1,945 tons, this historic vessel carried passengers between San Francisco's Ferry Building *(p 195)* and OAKLAND, and she evacuated thousands of people to the East Bay following the 1906 earthquake.
Moored alongside and boarded from *The Berkeley* is **The Medea [B]**. Built in 1904, the luxurious, 140ft iron-hulled steam yacht first carried hunting parties on the lochs and coastal waters of Scotland. She saw military action during both world wars and served as a pleasure ship in the Mediterranean and Baltic seas.

★★ **Star of India [C]** – Launched as the British full-rigged ship *Euterpe* on November 14, 1863, at Ramsey, Isle of Man, the vessel is the oldest iron merchant ship afloat and is considered among the oldest of all seaworthy ships. Between 1871 and 1897, she circumnavigated the globe 21 times, carrying British emigrants to Australia and New Zealand. Sold in October 1901 to the Alaska Packers of San Francisco, the ship was rerigged as a bark and in 1906 was rechristened the *Star of India*. With the rise of steam shipping in the 1920s, she was moored and neglected in the Oakland Estuary, until the founders of the Maritime Museum purchased her and brought her to San Diego in 1927. Not until 30 years later, however, was the vessel fully restored. The *Star of India* sets sail off the shore of San Diego on special occasions.

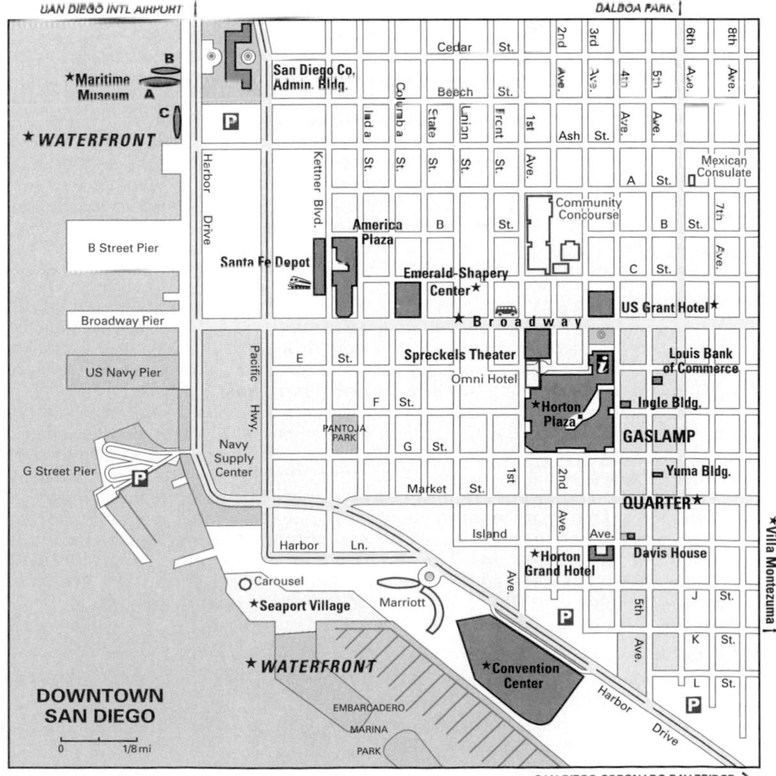

C. Curran

San Diego skyline

★ **Seaport Village** – *West Harbor Dr at Kettner Blvd. Open daily year-round.* ♿ ☎*619-235-4014.* Hugging the harbor within sight of the downtown skyline, this popular, 14-acre complex of 1- and 2-story New England- and Mediterranean-style buildings connected by cobblestone pathways includes gift shops, restaurants and a waterside boardwalk. The historic **carousel**, moved here in 1980, was originally built in 1890 by Charles I.D. Looff, who also created carousels in SANTA MONICA and LONG BEACH.

★ **San Diego Convention Center** – *111 West Harbor Dr.* With its open-air rooftop plaza surmounted by a giant white tent, the 760,000sq ft convention center, inaugurated in 1990, resembles a futuristic sailing ship docked on its 11-acre site beside San Diego Bay.

★ MISSION BAY *Map p 164*

Once a swampy landscape of marshes and tidal basins known as False Bay, this 4,600-acre seaside playground was first developed in the 1930s to stimulate San Diego's tourism industry. Today, with abundant green lawns, concrete foot and bike paths snaking along the shores of dredged coves and man-made islands, and some 44mi of sandy beach, Mission Bay is known as a recreational headquarters for both visitors and residents of San Diego and the surrounding communities.

Prior to the 19C, frequent and severe floods caused the unpredictable San Diego River to alternate its course between False Bay and San Diego Bay. As shipping traffic and a new harbor increased the latter's importance during the 1850s, dikes directing the river toward False Bay were constructed to prevent silt deposits from choking the harbor entrance. Over subsequent decades, a beach began to emerge at the entrance to the bay, and in 1921 the Spreckels Company developed **Belmont Park** there as an amusement center to boost the number of riders on its streetcar line. In the 1930s, city planners masterminded a plan to develop the bay as an aquatic park, and its growth continued through the 1960s.

Today, with its area evenly divided between land and water, Mission Bay Park offers a multitude of opportunities for land and water recreation.

★★ **Sea World** – *1 day. From downtown San Diego, drive north on I-5, exit at Sea World Dr and follow signs. Open daily year-round. $27.95.* ✕ ♿ 🅿 ☎*619-226-3901.* Billed as a marine zoological park, this waterfront attraction mixes entertainment and education in a commercial venue designed to heighten awareness of conservation issues while raising funds for research programs.

The park boasted just 4 attractions when it opened in 1964 on a 22-acre site on the south shore of Mission Bay. Since then its entertainment and research facilities have expanded to cover 150 acres, featuring 5 live-performance animal shows, 25 marine life exhibits and 4 aquariums. More than 200,000 people participate each year in its education programs emphasizing awareness of environmental concerns. Sea World's research, conservation and education departments are nationally recognized, and the park has pioneered breeding programs for killer whales, emperor penguins and other species. The park also operates a trauma center for beached marine mammals, rescuing an average of one animal per day. Sea World sister parks were opened in Ohio (1970); in Florida (1973); and in Texas (1988).

Sea World Facts

Water for Sea World's aquariums and research facilities is taken from Mission Bay and filtered every three hours.

The resident animal population eats nearly 2.5 tons of fish, shellfish and squid daily (over 2 million pounds a year).

Guided Tour – *90min. Tickets and schedules available at park entrance; tours depart from Tour Booth, adjacent to entrance.* This informative, behind-the-scenes tour offers access to the park's animal rescue facility, training and medical facilities, and other areas not open to the public.

Animal shows – *Each show approx. 25min; daily schedule available at park entrance.* Highlight of the entertainment offerings is **Shamu New Visions★**, featuring the park's beloved family of killer (orca) whales and their trainers in something of an aquatic ballet. The effect is enhanced by a 300ft video screen displaying live close-ups and views of the action under water. *Note: Spectators who like getting splashed are advised to sit in the front 14 rows.*
Pilot whales, dolphins and false killer whales (pseudorcas) take to the air in a display of skyward twists and leaps in **One World**, while **Marooned with Clyde and Seamore** presents the foibles of a duo of sea lions and other sea creatures. **Wings of the World** features the skills and antics of more than 30 trained birds.

Interactive Exhibits – Opened in 1993 as the world's largest interactive dolphin display, **Rocky Point Preserve★** invites visitors to touch, feed and play with bottlenose dolphins in a sculpted habitat resembling a rocky shoreline; Alaskan sea otters occupy a separate section of the exhibit. In the **California Tide Pool**, visitors can touch starfish, eels and other examples of intertidal zone life, while bat rays swim close to the edge at the **Forbidden Reef** *(upper level)*, allowing visitors a hands-on experience.

Exhibits and Aquariums – One of the park's top attractions, **Shark Encounter★** offers an intriguing close-up look at these often-feared predators of the deep. Visitors in search of a thrill can pass through a 57ft underwater viewing tube that tunnels through the bottom of the tank, offering good views of the bellies and mouths of Pacific blacktip and sandtiger sharks as they swim about in the company of rays and other exotic fishes. Coral reef sharks cruise in an outdoor tropical lagoon. Underground viewing tunnels also offer a look at fearsome California moray eels and graceful bat rays in Forbidden Reef.
Penguin Encounter recreates the icy 28° conditions of Antarctica, natural habitat of Sea World's resident population of nearly 400 penguins, many of which can be seen cavorting on an ice shelf or swimming gracefully under water. The exhibit also features such northern Arctic birds as puffins and auklets.
Sea World's more than 50 freshwater and saltwater aquariums house hundreds of exotic fishes from oceans and freshwater habitats throughout the world. Other displays include rare birds, seals, sea lions, walruses and a group of magnificent Clydesdale horses, symbol of the park's owner, Anheuser-Busch Companies, Inc.

Skytower – Bird's-eye **views★★** of the park complex, the surrounding Mission Bay area and the San Diego skyline in the distance can be enjoyed from this revolving chamber as it ascends to its 265ft observation point.

Addresses, telephone numbers, opening hours and prices published in this guide are accurate at press time. We apologize for any inconveniences resulting from outdated information, and we welcome corrections and suggestions that may assist us in preparing the next edition. Send us your comments:

Michelin Travel Publications
Editorial Department
P.O. Box 19001
Greenville, SC 29602-9001

ADDITIONAL SIGHTS

★ **Villa Montezuma** – *Map p 164. 1925 K St between 19th and 20th Sts. Visit by guided tour (45min) only, weekends year-round. $3. ☎619-239-2211. Note: Owing to incidence of street crime in the vicinity, it is advisable to arrive by car or taxi.* Erected in 1887, this elaborate mansion was commissioned by wealthy city residents for Jesse Shepard, a popular musician, spiritualist and author who was persuaded to remain in San Diego by the promise of an elaborate mansion in which to perform and hold salons. The villa's exterior exemplifies the Queen Anne substyle of Victorian architecture *(p 26)*, with its corner and side towers, windows of various shapes and sizes, and walls covered with a variety of shingle patterns. The interior boasts luxurious woodwork in redwood and walnut, fine stained-glass windows, and ceilings covered in Lincrusta-Walton patterned linoleum. Shepard occupied the mansion for two years; it then passed through several owners before being transferred to the City of San Diego. Today beautifully restored, it is operated as a house museum by the San Diego Historical Society.

★★ **Cabrillo National Monument** – *Map p 164. End of Catalina Blvd, Pt Loma. From downtown drive north about 7mi on Harbor Dr. Turn left on Rosecrans St and right on Canon St, then left on Catalina Blvd to the gate of Ft Rosecrans. Continue 3mi south on Cabrillo Memorial Dr to the visitor center. Open year-round daily 9am–5:15pm. $4/car.* 🅿 ♿ *☎619-557-5450.* Located on the crest of a sandstone ridge 400ft above the sea, this 144-acre park at the southern tip of Point Loma commemorates the European discovery of North America's Pacific coast in 1542 and preserves one of the oldest lighthouses on the West Coast.

Historic Point Loma – Once a separate island, the 6mi-long sandstone formation joined with the shifting sandbars in the delta of the San Diego River millions of years ago to form the northwest boundary of San Diego Bay. Juan Rodríguez Cabrillo *(p 22)* anchored his caravels here and stepped ashore on September 28, 1542, the first European to set foot on California soil. During the 19C, ships calling at Old Town anchored at Ballast Point, a finger of land jutting into the bay on the east side of Point Loma, rather than risking the shallower waters closer to the fledgling settlement. Ballast Point became the site, in 1797, of Fort Guijarros, a 10-gun port battery erected by the Spanish to defend against potential incursions by the British. Point Loma remained a coastal artillery fort until 1947.

Sea traffic along the coast greatly increased during the first half of the 19C, and in 1851 the US Congress ordered eight lighthouses erected on the West Coast. Activated in 1855, the light at Point Loma stood at a height of 462ft above sea level, making it both the southwesternmost and highest lighthouse in the US. However coastal fog and low clouds frequently obscured the beam, and in 1891 a new lighthouse was erected at the southwest tip of the point, well beneath the cloud ceiling. The old lighthouse and surrounding half-acre were designated in 1913 as a national monument, although the building was not restored until 1935. During World War II, it served as a harbor control entrance post. Today the monument encompasses 144 acres and is among the state's most visited national historic monuments.

Visit – Offering sweeping **views★★★** that extend over San Diego and its bay as far south as Mexico, the patio behind the visitor center is an ideal vantage point to observe the passage of Navy ships, planes and the occasional submarine. Displays in the center include exhibits on Spanish exploration and the area's natural and cultural history.

The parlor, kitchen and two upstairs bedrooms of the **Old Point Loma Lighthouse★** *(uphill from the visitor center)* have been restored to their 1880s appearance and offer glimpses of a lightkeeper's lonely life on the isolated peninsula. From the lighthouse, the scenic **Bayside Trail** *(4mi round-trip; brochure available at visitor center)* descends the point's eastern slope, offering a look at the plants of the coastal chaparral community. A short walk south of the lighthouse, the sheltered Whale Overlook is an ideal vantage point for seasonal whale watching *(p 261)*. On Point Loma's rocky western shore, a **tidepool area★** offers a chance to explore a protected tidal zone.

★ Coronado (Pop 26,540) *3hrs. Map p 164.*

Take I-5 south to Hwy 75; $1 toll at bridge exit.

Directly across the bay from downtown San Diego, the Coronado peninsula is San Diego County's landmark resort community. The affluent enclave of houses, condominiums, boutiques, restaurants and hotels seems serenely sheltered from the bustling urban center visible less than .5mi away.

A Wasteland Transformed – In 1884, ill health forced 36-year-old Indiana railroad executive Elisha Babcock Jr to retire to San Diego with his family. Reinvigorated, he joined his friend Hampton Story on hunting expeditions to Coronado, at the time a flat, brush-covered wasteland inhabited by rabbits and quail. The two men hatched a plan to transform the peninsula into a resort that would capitalize on increased tourism expected in the wake of the opening of San Diego's link to the transcontinental railroad scheduled for the following year. For $110,000, they bought the entire 4,100-acre peninsula in 1885.

With streets laid out and landscaped, their Coronado Beach Company welcomed 6,000 potential investors to a picnic and land auction on November 13, 1886. Having recouped the initial investment on that day's sales alone, planning and construction began on the Hotel del Coronado *(below)*, a hotel Babcock hoped would become "the talk of the Western world."

Energized by that vision, Coronado grew into an elite town, now home to some 27,000 residents. For many years, it could only be reached by ferry or the Silver Strand, a spit connecting it to the bay's southern end. Coronado finally became more accessible in 1969 with the opening of the 11,179ft **San Diego-Coronado Bay Bridge★**, the West's longest non-suspension bridge, which forms a graceful 90° arc between the peninsula and downtown San Diego.

★★ **Hotel del Coronado** – *1500 Orange Ave.* California's last surviving Victorian-era seaside resort is a landmark structure of white wood and red shingles, sweeping balconies and graceful spires, rising beside Coronado's southern shore. Filled with memories of elite guests and immortalized in books and film, "The Del," as it is affectionately known, preserves an aura of turn-of-the-century grandeur.

Coronado founders Babcock and Story hired Indiana railroad architects James, Merrit and Watson Reid to design the hotel. Ground was broken in January, 1887 and, with teams of mostly Chinese laborers working round-the-clock and an iron works, brick kiln and glass factory erected on-site, the hotel was miraculously opened after just 11 months. Thomas Edison supervised the installation of the electrical lighting system.

Over the years, the hotel has hosted 14 US presidents and numerous celebrities. Its most famous foreign guest was Edward, Prince of Wales; while staying in 1920, he reputedly first met Wallis Simpson, 16 years before he abdicated Britain's throne to marry her. The Del reputedly inspired Coronado resident L. Frank Baum's vision of the Emerald City in *The Wizard of Oz,* and was long a favored location for Hollywood filmmakers, appearing most notably in Billy Wilder's 1958 comedy *Some Like It Hot*, starring Jack Lemmon, Tony Curtis and Marilyn Monroe.

Visit – *Self-guided audio tour available year-round daily during daylight hours from the Signature Shop. No tours during inclement weather. $5.* ✗♿ ☎*619-435-6611.* The opulent, English-style, 2-story **grand lobby** is richly finished in Illinois oak; during the hotel's heyday as a first-class resort, men would stroll in from a day of hunting and fishing and dump their catch on the lobby's then-marble floor. The vast main dining room, the **Crown Room**, boasts walls and ceiling of Oregon sugar pine held together with wooden pegs; the whimsical, crown-shaped chandeliers were designed by L. Frank Baum. From the end of the palm-shaded **Garden Patio**, the History Gallery, a hallway lined with historical exhibits, leads to ocean-view public terraces and decks.

EXCURSIONS

Cuyamaca Rancho State Park – *4hrs. 43mi northeast of San Diego via I-8 east and Hwy 79 north. Open daily year-round. $5. ♿ ☏619-765-0755. Facility information p 257.* Situated amid forests of oak trees and conifers peppered with outcrops of granite and sandstone, this 25,000-acre park preserves the legacies of local Native culture and of the late-19C gold rush that brought renown to this relatively remote region of San Diego County.

Local Kumeyaay Natives camped in this region to gather acorns during summers until 1857, when a portion of their lands was purchased by James Lassitor for the purpose of establishing a ranch to supply hay to stations along the Butterfield stage route. Southern California's largest gold rush occurred in the region between 1869 and 1880; one of the area's wealthiest sources, the **Stonewall Mine**, was located within the ranch's boundaries and gave rise to a bustling company town on the banks of Lake Cuyamaca.

In 1923 retired Detroit businessman Ralph Dyar purchased Rancho Cuyamaca, dismantled the mine and the town structures, and built the rustic stone cabin that now houses the park headquarters. Ownership of the ranch was transferred to the state in 1933.

Visit – Exhibits in the **Cuyamaca Indian Museum** *(in the park headquarters)* recount local history from the perspective of a young Native woman; a short trail continues the narrative, explaining uses of local plants as it leads to a Kumeyaay village site. Near the entrance to the Stonewall Mine ruins *(3.5mi north of park headquarters)*, a re-created miner's shack interprets the history of the late-19C gold rush. Over 110mi of foot and equestrian trails lace the park's meadows, forests, streams and diverse plant communities.

★ **Julian** – Pop 1,284. *2hrs. 57mi northeast of San Diego via I-8 east and Hwy 79 north. Map p 5.* This charming mountain village situated at 4,200ft on the flank of Volcan Mountain is popular as a weekend getaway destination. Julian developed in the wake of the discoveries that set off a gold rush in Southern California between 1870 and 1880 *(above)*; during its heyday, the town boasted eight saloons and numerous other businesses. Today the town lies amid an agricultural region known for its abundant production of apples, peaches and pears, and its broad Main Street, lined with 19C-style storefronts, evokes an atmosphere of history preserved that attracts artists and writers. Artifacts dating from 1869 are on view at the **Julian Pioneer Museum** *(2811 Washington St; open Apr–Nov Tue–Sun, rest of the year weekends only; $1; ☏619-765-0227).*

Julian is a good base for exploring San Diego County's back roads and small communities. To the south, the 24mi **Sunrise National Scenic Byway** *(Hwy 51 between I-8 and Hwy 79)* traverses the Cleveland National Forest, offering stunning views to the east of ANZA-BORREGO DESERT STATE PARK.

Santa Ysabel Asistencia Mission – *1/2 hr. 8mi northwest of Julian via Hwy 79. Open daily year-round. ☏619-765-0810.* Situated in a pleasant valley surrounded by rolling hills, the only surviving outpost of the SAN DIEGO DE ALCALÁ MISSION was established in 1818, and by 1822 boasted several adobe structures and an active population of some 450 neophytes. The present stucco chapel (1924), located just north of the original church site, serves as a parish church and houses a small museum of original mission photographs and Native artifacts. Excavations in the 1960s uncovered cobblestone flooring from the original church (visible downhill near a windmill).

Palomar Observatory – *1hr. 55mi northeast of San Diego via Hwy 163 north, I-15 north and Hwy 56 east. Open daily year-round. Closed Dec 24 & 25. ☏619-742-2119.* Located near the peak of Palomar Mountain (6,126ft), the observatory operated by the California Institute of Technology in PASADENA has played a significant role in furthering our understanding of the universe beyond the solar system. The observatory boasts the largest optical telescope in the US: the celebrated **Hale Telescope★**, with its 200in Pyrex lens, has a range surpassing 1 billion light-years. Adjacent to the observatory building, a gallery explains the development and use of the telescope, as demonstrated by stunning photographs of Milky Way stars, distant galaxies, quasars, nebulae and other celestial features. In the domed observatory structure, an observation level allows glimpses of the scope itself—a huge tube-like truss with the mirrored lens at one end and an astronomer's viewing cage at the other. Sweeping terrestrial **panoramas** may be seen from the access road leading to the observatory.

Sights described in this guide are rated:

★★★ ***Worth the trip***

★★ ***Worth a detour***

★ ***Interesting***

Tijuana *At least 1/2 day. 16mi from downtown San Diego. Map p 4.*

The bustling home to some 750,000 people, Tijuana is the most visited Mexican city along the US border, offering Southern California residents and tourists the opportunity to spend a day in a foreign country. San Diego's growth as a naval port and the relative proximity of fast-living Hollywood contributed to Tijuana's reputation as a bawdy town of inexpensive pleasures. But tourist dollars, in turn, have begun to transform the city—sometimes affectionately called "TJ" by Americans—into a commercial center where high-rises and luxury hotels have replaced some of the meaner streets of decades past. With its shopping areas, bars and discos, two bull rings and jai alai arena, Tijuana continues to attract visitors in search of excitement, as well as serving as a gateway to the beaches and rugged inland wilderness of Baja California.

Practical Information

Area Code: 619

General Information – **Tijuana Tourism & Convention Bureau**, PO Box 434523, San Diego CA 92143-4523, ☎299-8518. Currency exchange offices located on both sides of the border; in general it is not necessary to exchange currency as most Tijuana shops and restaurants accept American dollars.

Entry – American or Canadian citizens must show proof of identification (such as driver's license or birth certificate) to enter Mexico; citizens of other countries must show citizenship papers. Entry regulations may differ for destinations other than Tijuana and the Baja Peninsula, or if stay is to exceed 72 hours; for information contact the **Mexican Consulate**, 610 A St, San Diego CA 92101, ☎231-8414.

Getting There and Getting Around – Sights described below are within walking distance of the San Ysidro border crossing. Visitors can enter on foot by driving to San Ysidro and parking in one of the many lots on the American side, or by taking the **San Diego Trolley** *(p 165)* to its terminus at San Ysidro. For those who elect to drive across the border, Mexican auto insurance ($14-$17/day) is strongly advised, and can be purchased on the American side of the border. Note that US auto insurance is not recognized within Mexico. Driving is extremely hazardous within Tijuana, and drivers at fault in accidents are considered guilty of felony. Authorities expect all drivers to show proof of financial responsibility (cash or a Mexican auto insurance policy).

Avenida Revolución – *Between Calles 1 & 9.* Tijuana's main street for shopping, dining and drinking is crowded with shopping arcades, their merchants persistently importuning tourists and ready to bargain over the prices of jewelry, leather goods, clothing and folk crafts. A distinctive statue of a leaping player atop a mosaic globe announces the elaborately tiled Moorish **Palacio Frontón** *(at Calle 7)*, erected in 1947 as a *frontón*, or playing court, for the high-speed, two-player ball game of jai alai.

★ **Mexitlán** – *Avenida Ocampo at Calle 2. Open year-round Tue–Sun. Closed major holidays. $3.35.* The open-air rooftop attraction presents 150 precise 1:25 scale models of Mexico's architectural landmarks, from the Pyramid of the Soothsayer in the Mayan city of Uxmal (7-10C AD) to Mexico City's Olympic Stadium (1968).

Centro Cultural – *Paseo de los Héroes at Avenida Mina. Open daily year-round. ✂ ♿ ☎011-52-66-84-1132.* Dominating the Zona Río, the city's upscale development along the Tijuana River, this starkly geometric complex of buildings (1982) includes a **Museum of Mexican Cultures** *($1)*, surveying the country's pre-Columbian era, its customs, and the history of Tijuana and Baja California. Also within the complex are a spherical OMNIMAX Theater *($4.50, one show in English daily)*, temporary exhibit halls, and indoor and outdoor venues for live performances.

★★★ San Diego Wild Animal Park *6hrs. Map p 4.*

30mi northeast of San Diego, in Escondido. Take I-15 to Via Rancho Parkway exit and follow signs. Open year-round daily 9am–4pm (closing times may be later during summer and school vacations). $17.45. ✂ ♿ ☎619-234-6541.

Exotic and endangered animals from around the globe find safe haven in this 2,200-acre park of rolling grasslands in the heart of San Diego County. Operated by the San Diego Zoo *(p 170)* primarily as a facility to ensure survival of endangered species, the park also serves to educate the public about conservation issues, and annually attracts some 1.2 million visitors

A "Backcountry Zoo" – In 1953 San Diego Zoo officials conceived the idea of creating an open-air captive breeding center for endangered species as an adjunct facility of the zoo; it was later decided to open the facility as a "backcountry zoo" to increase public awareness about conservation. The foothills surrounding the undeveloped San Pasqual Valley in central San Diego County were found to be similar to a variety of biogeographic regions in Asia and Africa, and proved an ideal environment for many endangered species. Special landscaping incorporated such elements as tree stumps for rhinoceroses to rub their hides on, and trees tall enough that giraffes could feed from their branches without stooping, so that the animals would feel comfortable enough in captivity to breed. Such careful measures were successful: the first southern white rhinoceros male brought to the park sired 59 calves over 13 years, contributing to the animal's removal from the endangered species list, and almost half of the severely endangered California condors *(p 17)* now alive were hatched at the park.

Today as many as 600 animals are born or hatched at the park each year, with five times the survival rate of newborn creatures in the wild. Since the park's opening in 1972, more than 30 endangered species have reproduced successfully. The total

R. Garrison/Zoological Society of San Diego

San Diego Wild Animal Park

collection of about 2,500 mammals and birds represents some 260 species, including 90 species of **ungulates**, or hooved animals, the largest assemblage of these animals in captivity.

Nairobi Village – *Inside the main entrance.* In this 17-acre theme area recreating the atmosphere of a Congo fishing village, visitors pass through aviaries filled with exotic birds and vegetation and view small animal exhibits. **Animal shows** designed as much for education as entertainment spotlight natural behaviors and abilities of birds of prey, exotic North American animals and Asian elephants. A **petting Kraal** allows visitors to interact with hand-raised animals of several exotic species. Opened in 1993, the **Hidden Jungle** features 2,500 animals representing 140 species in a tropical glass house alive with as may as 2,000 butterflies and such unusual forest creatures as Emperor scorpions, poison-arrow frogs and two-toed sloths.

★★ **Habitats** – *50min monorail tour departs from Nairobi Village.* The **Wgasa Bush Line** monorail *(5mi)* traverses the park's five principal biogeographical areas, where herds of animals roam free, engaging in routines and behaviors demonstrated in the wild. Habitats represent east and south African savannah, north African desert, and Asian plains and waterholes.

The 125-acre **Eastern Africa** enclosure is home to 15 different species including Ugandan giraffes, white-bearded wildebeest and the northern white rhinoceros. A family of Indian rhinoceroses shares the **Asian Plain** habitat with Persian goitered gazelles, Indian gaur and blackbuck antelope. Hooved animals, including addra gazelles and African oryx, graze peacefully in **Northern Africa**, while **Southern Africa** features the park's prized collection of 20 southern white rhinoceroses, the largest group in the US. The **Asian Waterhole** is home to several species of deer, among them the Formosan sika deer (extinct in the wild). Other, smaller habitats feature successes from the zoo's breeding programs, including Sumatran tigers, Przewalski's wild horses, okapi and pygmy chimpanzees.

★ San Pasqual Battlefield State Historic Park *1hr*

30mi northeast of San Diego. 8mi east of Escondido on Hwy 78. Open year-round Fri–Sun. Closed Jan 1, Thanksgiving Day, Dec 25. Contribution requested. ♿ ☎619-220-5430.

Situated on a northern slope of the hills surrounding the broad San Pasqual Valley, a highly informative visitor center tells the story of the bloodiest California battle of the Mexican War.

In the summer of 1846, under orders to establish an American government in California, Brig Gen Stephen W. Kearny and a detachment of the Army of the West set out toward Los Angeles from Fort Leavenworth. En route in New Mexico, they encountered Kit Carson riding eastward with the news that California was already in American hands. Kearny dispatched all but 100 of his troops to a garrison in Santa Fe and continued west, the remaining men suffering from hunger and cold. Near the San Pasqual Valley, within a day's march of San Diego, they learned that the Mexican settlers, called "Californios," had revolted and re-taken all of the southern part of the state except San Diego.

On the foggy morning of December 6, Kearny's troops engaged a Mexican troop commanded by Andrés Pico. Their rifles disabled by wet powder, the Americans were severely routed by the Californio lancers: 22 Americans and 1 Californio were killed. Pressing on toward San Diego the following day, they were again halted by the Mexicans atop a nearby hill. Five days later, American reinforcements arrived from San Diego, enabling Kearny's troops at last to enter the city.

Museum – An observation area with explanatory diagrams overlooks the scene of the battle, while interpretive displays and a video *(10min)* relate the history of the area and of the Mexican war. Traversing the slopes surrounding the visitor center is a self-guided nature trail *(.5mi)* offering a good introduction to the plants of the chaparral community. A plaque .4mi west marks the site where the Americans camped the night after the battle.

San Diego County Coast *3hrs. 28mi. Map p 4.*
Leave La Jolla by N. Torrey Pines Rd, which becomes Hwy 21.

North of LA JOLLA, the coast of San Diego County is lined with a string of residential towns and scenic beaches where sun, sand and sea prevail alongside the every-day suburban bustle. North of Torrey Pines State Reserve *(p 70)*, the road passes through **Del Mar**, an upper-class enclave famed among devotees of thoroughbred racing as the home of the Del Mar Racetrack. North of the town of Solana Beach, the road skirts lovely Cardiff State Beach and San Elijo State Beach, both part of the city of **Encinitas**, which is known as the "Flower Capital of the World" for its production of poinsettias. The **Quail Botanical Gardens★**, known for the diversity of their plant collections, are a lovely haven of native, exotic and drought-resistant species *(from Hwy 21 turn right on Encinitas Blvd, pass under I-5 and turn left on Quail Gardens Dr; open daily year-round; closed major holidays; $2 ♿ ☎619-436-3036)*. Moonlight State Beach and Leucadia State Beach fringe the coastline several blocks to the east of Highway 21 as it traverses northern Encinitas. Beyond the Batiquitos Lagoon ecological reserve lies the charming town of **Carlsbad**, named in 1887 when local mineral waters were found to be chemically identical to those of Karlsbad, the famed German spa. Today pleasantly shaded State Street *(from Hwy 21 turn right on Elm Ave and left on State St)* is lined with shops and sidewalk cafes, and surrounding streets reveal several restored 19C buildings. The visitor center *(400 Carlsbad Village Dr)*, housed in a refurbished Santa Fe Railroad Depot (1887), offers brochures and self-guided tours of the town.

North of Carlsbad, Highway 21 passes through Oceanside, San Diego County's third largest city and home to the popular **Oceanside Pier** and beach. Originally measuring 1,600ft, the pier was touted as the longest pleasure pier on the West Coast before storms reduced it to its present length of 910ft.

North of Oceanside, Highway 21 joins Interstate 5, which traverses the vast territory of Camp Pendleton Marine Corps Base, occupying the northwestern corner of San Diego County.

★★ **La Jolla** – *1 day. Description p 69.*

★★ **San Luis Rey de Francia Mission** – *2hrs. Description p 216.*

★ **Anza-Borrego Desert State Park** – *1 day. Description p 34.*

J. Stein Grove/Profiles West

Wind generators

★★★ SAN FRANCISCO San Francisco Bay Area Pop 723,959

Map below

Lying at the tip of a peninsula forming the western boundary of a 496sq mi bay, vibrant and sophisticated San Francisco attracts more visitors than any other US city. The sea is a presence here, creating an exhilarating climate of bracingly cool summers, bright sunshine, brisk ocean breezes and sudden invasions of fog. San Francisco's splendid natural setting lends it renown as a city of views: vistas extend from hilltops, street corners, balconies and park benches. A broad mix of architectural styles graces both business and residential areas, and inviting neighborhoods lend a welcoming air to many areas of the city.

The City by the Bay – The cliff-lined entrance to the bay was dubbed the **Golden Gate** by John C. Frémont in 1846, in evocation of the Golden Horn of Byzantium. Mid-18C accounts describe the city as a treeless jumble of sand hills barely covered with coarse grasses and low shrubs; its naturally rugged topography—a manifestation of the region's intense seismic activity—has since been softened by more than a century of dedicated landscaping. The city's archivist lists 43 named hills, including such renowned peaks as Nob (376ft), Russian (294ft) and Telegraph (274ft) hills; Mt Davidson, San Francisco's highest point, exceeds 936ft.
The city's remarkably equable climate, with modest annual rainfall and few temperature extremes, is a boon to residents and visitors alike. The California current *(p 16)*, flowing south along the coast, moderates winter chill and affords San Francisco the lowest summer temperatures of any American city outside Alaska. The most remarkable local weather phenomenon is **advection fog**, resulting from the evening arrival of moisture-laden west winds from the Pacific Ocean. As this air is chilled by contact with cold water offshore, the moisture condenses into a low, dense, but shallow fog layer that hugs the ground, cascading over hills and flowing through the Golden Gate like a cinematic special effect.

Size and Population – The city of San Francisco itself is not large, ranking 4th in the state and 14th among US cities, with an area of 46sq mi. Unlike other major American cities such as New York, Chicago and LOS ANGELES, San Francisco has never annexed its surrounding communities. OAKLAND and BERKELEY remain administratively distinct, as do the smaller Bay Area municipalities.

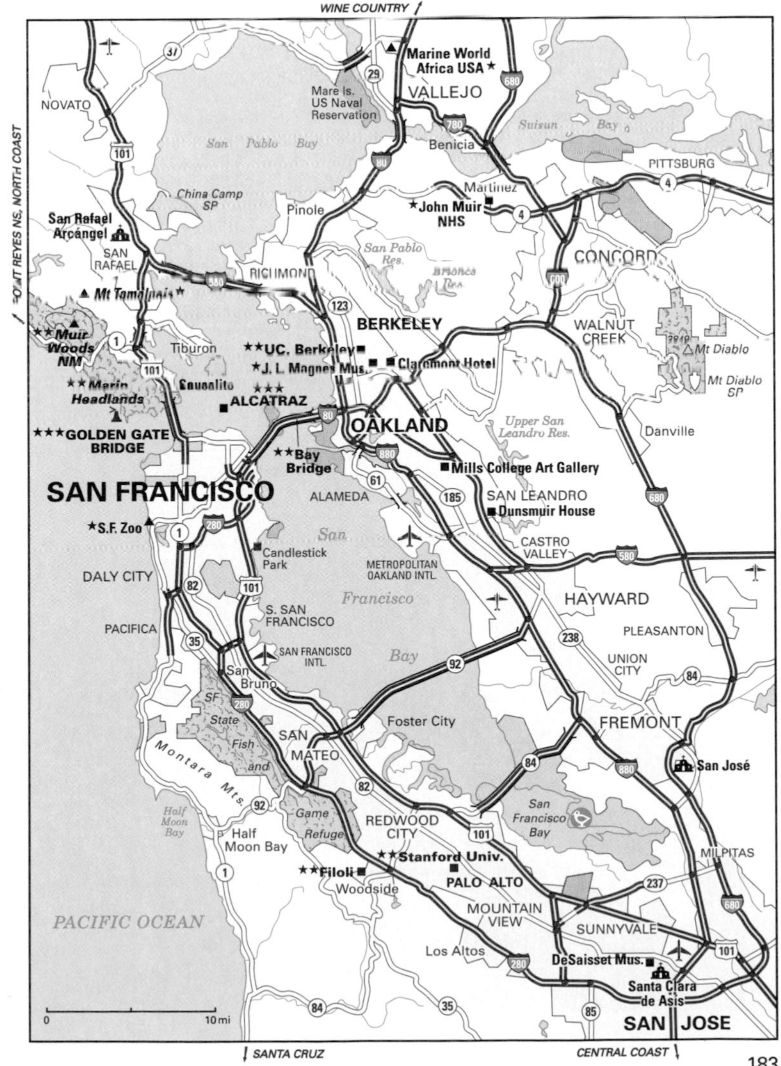

French, German, Irish, Italian and Jewish immigrants played prominent roles in the city's early history, and during the 1870s, fully one-fifth of its residents were Chinese immigrants. The city's Japanese population was removed to internment camps at the beginning of World War II and became dispersed over the Bay Area after the war.

San Francisco's African-American population remained small until World War II, when large numbers arrived from the South to work in war industries. In recent years, the number of African Americans has decreased in San Francisco proper and increased in the Bay Area municipalities, particularly in Oakland and Richmond. The Latino population was reduced to a tiny fraction of the total after the American takeover of Mexican California in 1846 and did not really recover until well into the 20C. At present, Latinos constitute between 10 and 15 percent of the city's population, with an increasing proportion coming from Central America.

HISTORICAL NOTES

San Francisco Bay remained unknown to European explorers long after Juan Rodríguez Cabrillo reconnoitered the California coast in 1542 *(p 22)*. Unmarked and frequently obscured by fog, the entrance to the bay was inconspicuous against the background of surrounding hills. In 1769 an exploring party under the command of Gaspar de Portolá marched north from newly founded SAN DIEGO to occupy Monterey Bay in defense against Russian colonizers *(p 128)*. As ocean explorers had never described Monterey Bay from an inland perspective, Portolá and his men failed to recognize it, and marched on northward along the coast. On November 4, 1769, a scouting detachment of Portolá's party, led by **Sgt José Ortega**, climbed the coastal hills, saw a large body of water to the north and east, and incorrectly assumed it was the bay today known as Drake's Bay, located farther to the north at present-day Point Reyes *(p 145)*. Initially discovered in 1579 by Francis Drake, the bay had been renamed in honor of Saint Francis of Assisi in 1595 by a Spanish exploring party, and the huge inlet discovered by Ortega was thereafter referred to as Puerto de San Francisco—the Port of San Francisco.

Spanish and Mexican Rule – Growing realization of the strategic and economic value of the bay led Spanish authorities in distant Mexico City to establish the Presidio and SAN FRANCISCO DE ASÍS MISSION in 1776, on sites chosen by Juan Bautista de Anza. When Mexico achieved independence from Spain in 1821 *(p 23)*, these were still small frontier settlements. In 1835 William A. Richardson, an Englishman, and Jacob P. Leese, an American, built houses near present-day downtown and others followed, creating a third settlement known as *Yerba Buena*, or "good herb," for the wild mint that grew in the area. The shore of the bay, called Yerba Buena Cove, at that time extended as far west as the present location of Montgomery Street.

The primary economic activity during the first half of the 19C was the beef hide and tallow trade between local cattle ranchers and merchants who brought in a variety of manufactured and fancy goods by sailing ship from New England. In 1845 Yerba Buena was home to some 300 people, about half of whom carried some degree of Spanish ancestry and a third of whom were Natives and Hawaiians; the remainder were Americans and Europeans who had arrived from the eastern US.

By the mid-19C, the hide and tallow trade had brought greater awareness of California's economic riches to the colonizing forces of England, France and Russia, and the US Government moved quickly to wrest the territory from the weak grasp of Mexico. On July 9, 1846, during the Mexican War, **Capt John Montgomery** sailed in on the USS *Portsmouth* and raised the Stars and Stripes over Yerba Buena's central plaza, renaming it Portsmouth Square *(p 193)*. On January 30, 1847, Yerba Buena was renamed San Francisco by Washington Bartlett, the village's first American *alcalde*, or mayor.

Historic Urban Plans

View of San Francisco in 1868

The Gold Rush – In 1847 Jasper O'Farrell, an Irish surveyor, laid out the first street grid, anchored by Portsmouth Square, but the village changed little during the first year and a half of American administration. San Francisco's destiny was determined in January 1848, with the discovery of gold at COLOMA. Many residents set out immediately for the GOLD COUNTRY but others remained, aware that fortunes were to be made by supplying miners. The little settlement was perfectly situated to benefit from the Gold Rush. Mining camps flourished and declined with remarkable volatility, and a stable center was necessary for providing goods and services to the whole mining region. San Francisco's port made it the center of trade and transportation between interior California and the rest of the world. As ships unloaded men and equipment, the shores of Yerba Buena Cove sprouted storehouses, banks, offices, saloons and brothels.

As San Francisco boomed and grew, the streets of O'Farrell's plan were extended up the hills to the west, and east toward the shore, continuing as long wharves reaching out to deeper water. These wharves later became streets, as landfill extended the shoreline east from Montgomery Street. Up the hillsides stretched acres of tents, which were replaced by wooden houses as a lumber industry developed. Devastating fires frequently swept the crowded, flimsy neighborhoods, but the town continued to grow.

A half-mile to the south of Portsmouth Square, streets were surveyed on a different pattern. A wide boulevard was projected to mark the transition from one grid to another, and **Market Street** remains today a grand, if awkward, suture in San Francisco's street pattern.

Business Center of the West – California's geographic isolation worked to San Francisco's advantage during the first two decades after the Gold Rush. Cut off from the nation's major manufacturing centers, the city developed its own diversified economy of goods and services. The Gold Rush had attracted an influx of skilled craftsmen and experienced business entrepreneurs—professionals who founded and enlarged the economic structure of the city. Heavy equipment for mining gold was produced to supply the needs of mining concerns to the east, and by the 1860s, local industrial capabilities encompassed shipbuilding and the manufacture of farm implements and railroad equipment.

Gold, carried from the mining districts to San Francisco by express companies like Wells Fargo, formed a tremendous pool of capital under control of San Francisco financiers. In the 1860s, gold production stabilized and dwindled, but Nevada's 1862 Comstock Lode silver boom brought in another flood of wealth. Much of the late 19C economic development of the entire western half of the US in mining, timber, agriculture, ranching, oil and electric power generation was financed from San Francisco.

By 1860 San Francisco boasted 56,000 inhabitants and had ceased to be a jumble of tents and shacks. The expanding city faithfully adhered to O'Farrell's street grid despite hills that were too steep for horse-drawn vehicles. The potential value of real estate on undeveloped hills stimulated efforts in transportation innovation that gave rise to the cable car, today one of the city's trademarks.

Cable Cars – Scottish immigrant **Andrew Hallidie** arrived in the Gold Country in 1852 and established a reputation as a builder of wire suspension bridges and cable tramways for transporting ore. San Francisco's hills inspired Hallidie to modify this technology to accommodate the needs of urban areas. The concept involved a loop of wire cable running at a constant speed through an underground slot along the middle of the street. The cable was gripped by a device extending from the bottom of the car into the slot; the car ran on rails placed on either side of the slot, pulled by the continually moving cable. This mechanism, designed by Hallidie in 1872, remains essentially unchanged and in use today.

The cable car did much to mold the residential pattern of San Francisco through the 1870s and 1880s. The California Street line, still in service, brought development to Nob Hill, and other cable car lines opened up the Western Addition and Pacific Heights for the middle and upper classes. It was in these neighborhoods during the last decades of the 19C that many of the city's distinctive Victorians were built *(p 26)*. By the turn of the century, electric streetcars had replaced the cable cars, and the present 4.5mi network and 28-car fleet, a remnant of the system at its heyday, are a national historic landmark.

The Great Earthquake and Fire of 1906 – On April 18, 1906, at 5:13am, an earthquake estimated at 8.3 on the (not then invented) Richter scale, shook the California coast. The main tremor, lasting 48 seconds and emanating from an epicenter on the San Andreas fault in Olema *(p 145)*, toppled structures from FORT BRAGG to MONTEREY. Because of the early hour, most city residents were at home; the resultant death toll of more than 3,000 people was considered low.

The temblor destroyed water mains leading from reservoirs south of town, and with no water to extinguish them, small fires caused by broken gas mains and toppled chimneys soon coalesced into a conflagration that raged unchecked for three days. Desperate to prevent the fire from spreading west, military personnel dynamited some of the houses along Van Ness Avenue to create a firebreak, but by the time the fire burned itself out, flames had consumed 28,000 buildings in 514 city blocks (4.11sq mi), about 80 percent of the property value of San Francisco. The devastated area comprised the Financial District, Union Square, Chinatown, North Beach, and a large area south of Market Street and into the fringes of the Mission District. Some two-thirds of the city's residents were left homeless.

Recovery and reconstruction efforts began almost immediately, with displaced residents living in makeshift shacks and tent cities, or in such neighboring counties and cities as Oakland, which had escaped severe damage. By 1910 the downtown area had been largely completed, and spotting an opportunity to show off the rebuilt city, business and political leaders entered a winning bid to host a world's fair celebrating the completion of the Panama Canal in 1914. On landfill in the present-day

Marina District *(p 207)* rose elaborate Beaux-Arts-style pavilions representing countries around the world, and the **Panama-Pacific International Exposition** attracted some 19 million visitors between February and December of 1915. After the fair's close, the elaborate plaster structures were destroyed; only the Palace of Fine Arts *(p 207)* was left standing and eventually replicated in concrete.

Early 20C Growth – Along with the rest of the country, San Francisco prospered in the years after World War I. Newer and larger buildings went up in the Financial District before the Great Depression halted skyscraper construction: the 31-story Russ Building *(p 194)*, built in 1927, remained the city's tallest structure until 1964. However, the 1930s saw completion of two celebrated landmarks: the Bay Bridge *(p 131)* and the Golden Gate Bridge *(p 205)*.
During World War II, the San Francisco Bay Area became a major shipbuilding center and the main port of embarkation for the Pacific theater. The war also stimulated the high technology sector when the nascent electronics and aircraft industries turned to military production. San Francisco's population burgeoned anew as workers came and stayed; soldiers and sailors who passed through noticed the attractions of the area and returned at the end of the war.

SAN FRANCISCO TODAY

San Francisco's economy has changed enormously in the last half century. As recently as World War II, San Francisco was a hard-working port and industrial town, with a large and strongly unionized blue-collar work force. With increased use of containers for transporting goods by truck, shipping activities relocated across the bay to the Port of Oakland, and much industry has moved out of the densely packed city to suburbs, where modern plants have room to sprawl.
The city is now a Pacific Rim center of finance, trade and high technology, its attractive downtown office towers serving as the factories of this new economy. Waterfront warehouses and port structures are being transformed into offices, shopping centers, cafes and apartment complexes. The prominence of professional and high-tech employment in the city's economy does not entirely account for the large number of restaurants, hotels and shops. Many of them are supported by tourism, now San Francisco's premier industry.

Aerial view of San Francisco

Cultural Center – San Francisco has been an important performing arts center since the mid-19C, when actors and singers discovered that gold miners and shop keepers alike would pay well for an evening's entertainment. San Francisco's symphony, opera and ballet are internationally recognized, and a host of smaller performing arts organizations mount productions each week. The city boasts an active theatrical community, four large art museums and a lively experimental art scene in the South of Market area.

Dining Out – Said to have more restaurants per capita than any other American city, San Francisco is strewn with intriguing, reasonably priced eateries, particularly in the areas of Chinatown and North Beach. Visitors should not overlook the Mission District for Mexican and Central American fare, or Clement Street in the Richmond District for a tantalizing array of Asian cuisine, including Burmese, Indonesian and Vietnamese. San Francisco proclaims itself an American capital of such delicacies as **cioppino**, a rich seafood stew similar to the French *bouillabaisse*; Irish coffee; and crusty, tangy sourdough bread.

Cable car and MUNI bus lines are indicated by 🚋 and 🚌 in sight descriptions.

Practical Information

Area Code: 415

Getting There

By Air – **San Francisco International Airport** (SFO): international and domestic flights, 11mi south of downtown ☎761-0800. **Metropolitan Oakland International Airport** (OAK): primarily domestic flights, 22mi from downtown San Francisco ☎510-577-4015. From both airports: taxi service to downtown ($30); commercial shuttles ($5-$11); rental car agency branches *(p 253)*.

By Bus and Train – *p 253*. Greyhound: 101 7th St ☎800-231-2222. Trailways: Transbay Bus Terminal, 425 Mission St ☎800-231-2222. Amtrak: 1707 Wood St, Oakland (fare includes transfer to Transbay Bus Terminal) ☎800-872-7245. Commuter trains (from San Jose and the Central Valley): 700 4th St ☎495-4546.

Getting Around

By Public Transportation – Most public transportation in San Francisco is operated by San Francisco Municipal Railway (MUNI). All lines (except cable cars) operate daily 6am–1am, limited service available 1am–6am. Fare $1 for **buses** and **streetcars**; transfers free, exact fare required. **Cable cars** operate daily 6am–midnight ($2). Ticket machines located at end of lines, and at California and Powell transfer point (Nob Hill). MUNI Passports are good for 1 ($6), 3 ($10) or 7 ($15) days; MUNI maps ($1.50) sold at retail outlets throughout the city ☎673-6864. **BART** (Bay Area Rapid Transit) is convenient for trips to Berkeley and Oakland ☎788-2278. **Commuter Ferries** generally run daily 7am–7pm, no service on legal holidays. Departures from Fisherman's Wharf *(p 190)* and Ferry Building *(p 195)*.

By Car – *p 253*. Use of public transportation is strongly encouraged within the city as streets are often congested and street parking may be difficult. Parking garages average $1.25/hr or $11.75/day. Drivers must yield to cable cars. When parking on a hill, drivers must block front wheels against the curb (facing downhill turn wheels *toward* the curb, facing uphill turn wheels *away* from the curb); use of parking brake is mandatory. Restricted parking indicated by the color of the curb: **red** (no standing or parking), **yellow** or **black** (truck or car loading zone), **white** (limited to 5 minutes), **green** (limited to 10-30 minutes), **blue** (reserved for the disabled).

Taxis – **De Soto** ☎673-1414; **Luxor** ☎282-4141; **Yellow** ☎626-2345.

General Information

Visitor Information – **San Francisco Convention & Visitors Bureau** Information Center: lower level of Hallidie Plaza, 900 Market St ☎391 2000. Mailing address: PO Box 6977, San Francisco CA 94101 ☎974-6900.

Accommodations – *San Francisco Lodging Guide* available (free) from the San Francisco Convention & Visitors Bureau *(above)*. Accommodations range from elegant downtown hotels ($160/day) to budget motels ($60/day). **San Francisco Reservations** ☎800-333-8996. **Bed and Breakfast San Francisco** reservation service ☎479-1913. Most B&B's are located in residential sections of the city ($85/day). *All rates quoted are average prices for a double room.*

Local Press – Daily news: *San Francisco Chronicle* (morning), *San Francisco Examiner* (afternoon); Sunday joint edition entertainment section. Weekly entertainment information: *San Francisco Bay Guardian* and the *Key*.

Entertainment – Consult the arts and entertainment sections of local newspapers (particularly *Bay Guardian)* for schedule of cultural events and addresses of principal theaters and concert halls. **Entertainment Hotline:** 391-2001. Tickets for local events: **STBS** offers half-price tickets for selected events on the day of the performance, tickets and event listing at Union Square location (Stockton St between Post and Geary), cash sales only ☎433-7827 (recording); or **BASS** ☎510-762-2277.

Currency Exchange Offices – *p 251*. **Citibank** and **Bank of America** currency exchange offices located in the International Terminal, San Francisco International Airport (daily 7am–11pm).

Sports – Tickets for major sporting events can be purchased at the venue or through **BASS** outlets *(above)*.

Sport	*Team*	*Season*	*Venue*
Major League Baseball	Giants (NL)	Apr–Oct	Candlestick Park
Professional Football	49ers (NFC)	Sept–Dec	Candlestick Park
Professional Basketball	Golden State Warriors	Nov–May	Oakland Coliseum
Horse Racing		year-round	Bay Meadows

Useful Numbers

Police/Ambulance/Fire (24hrs)	**911**
Police (non-emergency, 24hrs)	553-0123
Medical Society Referrals (Mon–Fri 9am-5pm)	561-0850
Dental Society Referrals (24hrs)	421-1435
24-hour pharmacy Walgreens, 3201 Divisadero	931-6415
Main Post Office 7th & Mission Sts (Mon–Fri 8:30am–5:30pm)	621-8646
Weather	936-1212

★★★ 1 NORTHERN WATERFRONT

Relics of San Francisco's maritime past occupy the city's shoreline, particularly along the Northern Waterfront between Telegraph Hill and the Marina District. The visitor can board historic sailing ships, explore a submarine, watch the antics of sea lions and shop for souvenirs. From the waterfront's splendid **setting★** the view encompasses passing freighters, the Golden Gate Bridge, the prison island of Alcatraz, and the rugged shoreline of Marin County.

Sights *1 day. Map below.*
Powell-Hyde line. 30 Stockton, 19 Polk, or 42 Downtown Loop.

★★ **Fisherman's Wharf** – *Waterfront between Hyde and Taylor Sts.* One of San Francisco's most popular tourist attractions, Fisherman's Wharf is a colorful array of piers, docks for the fishing fleet, and multitudinous seafood eateries ranging from outdoor food stands to formal restaurants.

When the fishing fleet moved here in 1900 from the foot of Union Street east of Telegraph Hill, the wharf area was already dominated by Italian immigrants whose family names appear on many restaurants and small businesses. The number of working fishing boats based at the wharf has declined greatly in recent decades, however, and much of the seafood is now brought in by truck. But early in the morning, fishermen can still be seen returning with the day's catch. The south side of Jefferson Street unites a great variety of souvenir stands, novelty museums and sidewalk performers; shoppers gravitate to **Pier 39** *(across the Embarcadero from Jefferson St intersection)*, a complex of shops and restaurants erected in 1978 on a turn-of-the-century fishing pier.

★★ **Hyde Street Pier** – *Foot of Hyde St. Open mid-May–mid-Sept daily 10am–6pm, rest of the year 9:30am–5pm. $3.* ♿ *☎415-556-3002.* This historic wood pier served automobile ferries to SAUSALITO and BERKELEY before the Golden Gate Bridge and the Bay Bridge were erected. Today, the pier is home to five historic ships, three of which can be boarded and explored.

★ **Balclutha** – *End of pier on the left.* This 3-masted merchant ship, launched in 1886, made 18 trips around Cape Horn between Europe and California. From 1903 to 1930, the *Balclutha* worked the salmon trade between Alaska and California. Visitors can inspect the comfortable, wood-paneled living quarters of the captain and his wife in the stern, as well as the crew's cramped quarters in the bow. On the lower deck are exhibits of such nautical gear as anchors, rudders, a Lyle gun (used for firing ropes to ships in distress), and the large metal ball whose descent down a pole atop Telegraph Hill used to mark the moment of noon in pre-radio days. The hold contains a detailed model of an Alaskan salmon cannery.

★ **Eureka** – *East side of the pier.* This passenger and car ferry, in its day the world's largest, plied the waters between San Francisco and Sausalito from 1922 to 1939, and remained in service between OAKLAND and San Francisco until 1957.

★ **C. A. Thayer** – *Across from the Eureka.* This historic timber schooner (1895) was designed to carry lumber to San Francisco from North Coast "doghole ports," wave-pounded coves where the crew had to hold the ship steady as logs were loaded from the bluffs above.

Two other vessels, the sidewheel steam tug *Eppleton Hall* and the shallow draft Bay and Delta schooner *Alma*, are moored at the pier but not open to visitors. On the

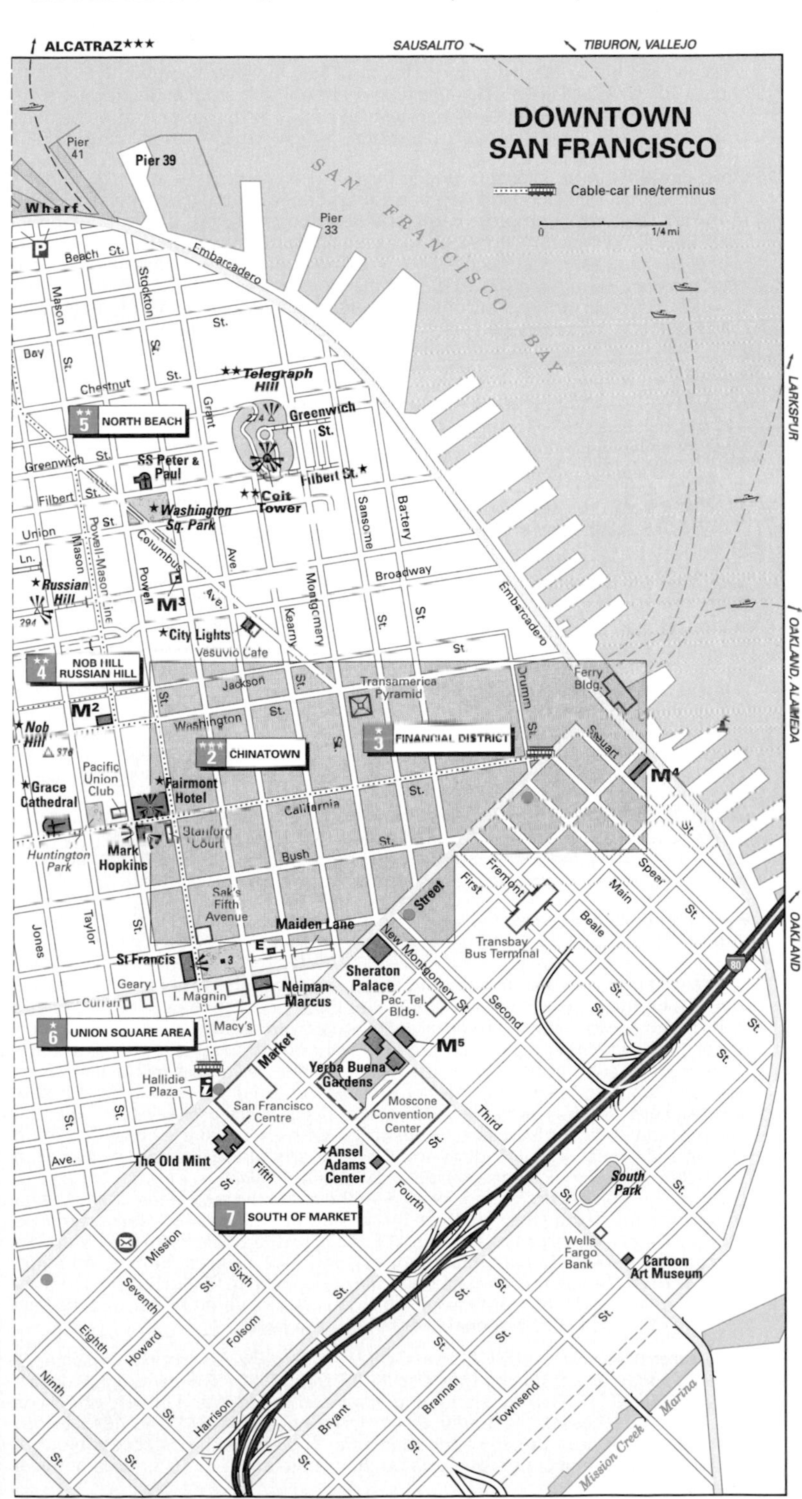

pier itself is a Sausalito houseboat and the **Small Boat Shop**, offering demonstrations and courses in boat building. At the entrance to the pier is the museum bookstore, specializing in maritime subjects.

★ **USS Pampanito** – *East side of Pier 45 near the foot of Taylor St. Open daily year-round. $5. ☎415-441-5819.* Built in 1943, this World War II submarine made six patrols through the Pacific and sank six Japanese ships. In 1944 the *Pampanito* and two Allied subs successfully executed a mission to attack a convoy of Japanese ships carrying war matériel, ignorant of the fact that the ships carried British and Australian prisoners of war. Returning to the scene three days later, the *Pampanito* discovered survivors clinging to pieces of wreckage, and rescued 73 Allied POWs. A self-guided audio tour of the 311ft sub begins in the rear torpedo room and goes through the engine rooms, crews' quarters, command centers and the fully functional galley before ending at the forward torpedo room.

★ **The Cannery** – *Corner of Leavenworth and Jefferson Sts.* Formerly a fruit cannery, this brick structure (1907), with its light-filled interior courtyard and contemporary boutiques, is today one of San Francisco's most attractive shopping complexes. Most of the interior is entirely new, built in 1968 within the original walls. In the **Museum of the City of San Francisco** *(3rd floor)*, changing historical displays and city-related memorabilia present glimpses into San Francisco's colorful, often-turbulent past *(open year-round Wed–Sun; contribution requested; ♿ ☎415-928-0289).*

★★ **Ghirardelli Square** – *Block bounded by Polk, Larkin, Beach and North Point Sts.* This famous group of industrial brick buildings has been renovated and landscaped to form a multilevel complex of shops and restaurants. The oldest building is a woolen mill built in 1864. In 1893 Domingo Ghirardelli bought the mill and surrounding land and built a chocolate factory. Additional buildings appeared over the next 25 years, culminating in 1916 with the clock tower at North Point and Larkin Streets. Chocolate production continued here until 1962, when the company transferred operations to a new factory across the bay in San Leandro.

Cruising on the Bay

Scenic ferry trips on the San Francisco Bay offer some of the finest opportunities to view the Golden Gate Bridge, the wharf areas and city's celebrated skyline. Ferry trips generally last 1-3 hrs, and prices average $15.

- ***Blue & Gold Fleet** - departs from Pier 39 ☎415-781-7877.*
- ***Red & White Fleet** - departs from Pier 41 and Pier 43 1/2 ☎415-546-2628.*
- ***Hornblower Dining Yachts** - departs from Pier 33 ☎415-394-8900.*

★ **Maritime Museum [M[1]]** – *Beach St at Polk St. Open daily year-round. ♿ ☎415-556-3002.* A fine example of the Art Deco style, the museum **building** (1939) resembles a luxury ocean liner, complete with decks, railings and portholes. A project of the WPA, the structure originally served as the Aquatic Park Casino restaurant and features 37 interior murals by Hilaire Hiler and unusual intaglio carvings on slate by Sargent Johnson around the front door. The museum houses an extensive collection of model ships, figurines, historic photographs and other artifacts of ocean and inland water transport.
The building's architectural lines are continued in the Art Deco bleachers and lifeguard towers of **Aquatic Park**, with its small swimming beach and grassy picnic area.

Coast Walk – A paved pedestrian path connects Fort Mason Center with the Maritime Museum over the hill on which the older part of the fort stands. Lined with Monterey cypress, the path overlooks San Francisco's last surviving remnant of undeveloped, natural bay shoreline and offers views across to the Marin Headlands.

★ **Fort Mason Center** – *Parking lot entrance at Marina Blvd and Buchanan St. 🚌 28 19th Avenue. Main office in Building A provides information and monthly calendar of events. Open year-round Mon–Sat. ✕ ♿ 🅿 ☎415-979-3010.* This bayside complex of barracks, warehouses and docks was the embarkation point for 1.5 million GI's bound for the Pacific in World War II. Embodying the concept of beating swords into plowshares, the fort presently houses numerous cultural organizations, performance spaces and galleries, providing a good introduction to San Francisco's contemporary cultural life. Among the highlights are the **Craft and Folk Art Museum** and the San Francisco Museum of Modern Art Rental Gallery *(Building A)*; the **Museo Italo-American** and the **San Francisco African American Cultural Society** *(Building C);* and the intriguing **Mexican Museum**★ *(Building D)*, with a permanent collection of pre-Hispanic, Colonial, Folk, Modern and Chicano arts of Mexico *(open year-round Wed–Sun; closed major holidays; $3; ♿ ☎415-441-0404).*
The older section of Fort Mason, located on the hill to the east of the Center, served as the western headquarters of the US Army during the late 19C Native American conflicts. A vast lawn, site of the annual San Francisco Blues Festival, is graced by a striking representation of the Madonna **[1]** by Italian sculptor Beniamino Bufano (1898-1970) and a statue of the late Bay Area congressman Phillip Burton **[2]**. Former officers' quarters, dating from the 1850s, today house a youth hostel, and the headquarters of Golden Gate National Recreation Area *(p 191)*.

★ **SS Jeremiah O'Brien** – *Pier 3, Ft. Mason Center. Open daily year-round. Closed Jan 1, Easter Sunday, Thanksgiving Day, Dec 24-25, Dec 31. $2 ($3 Steaming Weekends). 🅿 ☎415-441-3101.* This last remaining unaltered World War II Liberty Ship is one of 2,751 cargo vessels hurriedly constructed between 1941 and 1945 to ferry supplies to battles in Europe and the Pacific. The entire ship is accessible, from the wheel house and crew's quarters on the bridge down to the bowels of the engine room.

Golden Gate National Recreation Area

Embracing San Francisco's northern and western boundaries as well as Angel Island, Alcatraz and a significant portion of coastal Marin County, the Golden Gate National Recreation Area (GGNRA) was established by Act of Congress in 1972. The 26,000-acre system, encompassing historic landmarks, military sites, redwood forests, beaches and undeveloped coastal lands, came about largely through the efforts of US Congressman Phillip Burton, who championed the movement to preserve the area's unused military lands as parks for nature conservation and recreation. Today the GGNRA attracts more than 25 million visitors annually and enjoys a reputation as one of America's most popular national parks.

GGNRA sites described in this guide include:

San Francisco Maritime National Historical Park
- Hyde Street Pier *(p 188)*
- Maritime Museum and Aquatic Park *(p 190)*
- SS Jeremiah O'Brien *(p 190)*

Fort Mason Center *(p 190)*
Marina Green *(p 207)*
The Presidio (beginning 1994) *(p 206)*
Fort Point *(p 206)*
Golden Gate Bridge *(p 205)*
Cliff House *(p 207)*
Ocean Beach *(p 204)*
Alcatraz *(below)*
Marin Headlands *(p 206)*
Muir Woods *(p 127)*
Mt Tamalpais *(p 128)*
Muir Beach *(p 127)*
Stinson Beach *(p 128)*

★★★ Alcatraz *Access by ferry from Pier 41*

Situated just inside the Golden Gate, this renowned 12-acre island, with its sheer cliffs and crumbling buildings, is aptly characterized by its nickname – "the Rock." Today transformed as a national park and museum, the US Federal Penitentiary here housed many of America's most hardened criminals from 1934 to 1963.

Military Stronghold and Military Prison – Alcatraz was a island of bare rock inhabited only by birds when the bay was first sighted by Spanish explorers in 1769. As the story goes, the island was initially named Yerba Buena Island, and in 1775 the name *Isla de Alcatraces*, meaning "pelicans island" in Spanish, was given to the jut of land that today anchors the Bay Bridge's west pier. The names were reversed by mistake on an 1826 map, and the error was never corrected.

Because its location at the mouth of the bay made it a natural fortress against naval invasion, President Millard Fillmore in 1850 designated Alcatraz a military reservation, and a series of brick and stone fortifications was constructed on the island. In 1861 Confederate sympathizers and Native Americans were incarcerated on Alcatraz, and for 30 years the island served simultaneously as a defense installation and military prison. Its fortifications were gradually rendered obsolete by newer, more powerful batteries around the Golden Gate, while the prison was expanded to accommodate an influx of prisoners from the Spanish American War. In 1907 the island was degarrisoned as a military fortress and became the US military prison.

Federal Prison – By the early 1930s Alcatraz had become too expensive for the army to maintain, and in 1934 the island was acquired by the Federal Bureau of Prisons. Redesignated as the Federal Penitentiary at Alcatraz, it served for 30 years as an isolated, maximum-security installation to house "public enemies": members of large, organized crime gangs whose connections made them a menace even behind bars. With a strictly enforced "no talking" rule, one guard for every three prisoners, and a roster of infamous inmates—among them Al "Scarface" Capone, George "Machine Gun" Kelly and Robert "Birdman" Stroud—Alcatraz quickly gained a reputation as the toughest prison in America.

The high cost of maintenance, deteriorating facilities and a number of near-successful escape attempts led to the 1963 decision to close the prison. A group of Native Americans took over Alcatraz in 1969 in an ultimately unsuccessful attempt to establish a Native American Center there. On October 12, 1972, Alcatraz was incorporated into the Golden Gate National Recreation Area *(above)*.

Visit – *3hrs. Alcatraz open daily year-round. Closed Jan 1, Dec 25. $5.75. Reservations recommended. ♿ ☎415-556-0560. Ferries depart from Pier 41 every 30min Memorial Day–Labor Day daily 9:30am–4:15pm, rest of the year daily 9:45am–2:15pm. 15min. $8.50. ✕ ♿ 🅿 Red & White Fleet ☎415-546-2628. Caution: The boat launch and the island are subject to chill winds and sea spray year-round. Protective clothing is advised.* The boat trip to and from the island offers splendid **views★★** of the waterfront and the Golden Gate on fogless days. After debarking, visitors are free to wander around the island on their own or join the scheduled ranger talks and ranger-led strolls to various parts of the island *(topics vary seasonally)*. An orientation show *(10min)* is presented in the barracks museum located at the base of the footpath to the cellhouse.

★★ **Cellhouse** – *At the top of the island, accessible by footpath (steep ascent). Self-guided audio cassette tour (highly recommended) available at prison entrance.* Now partially in ruins, the long, foreboding cellhouse structure (1911) of reinforced concrete offers a vivid, if chilling look at the daily life of Alcatraz inmates. Visitors may wander at will through the cavernous interiors, down the main cell block (nicknamed "Broadway"), past diminutive, steel-barred cells. The mess hall offers tantalizing views of San Francisco's skyline. Also worth inspecting are the inmates' library, to which access was a privilege rewarded for good behavior; and the "dark holes," or solitary confinement cells, where prisoners were punished for infractions of the will-breaking rules enforced at Alcatraz.

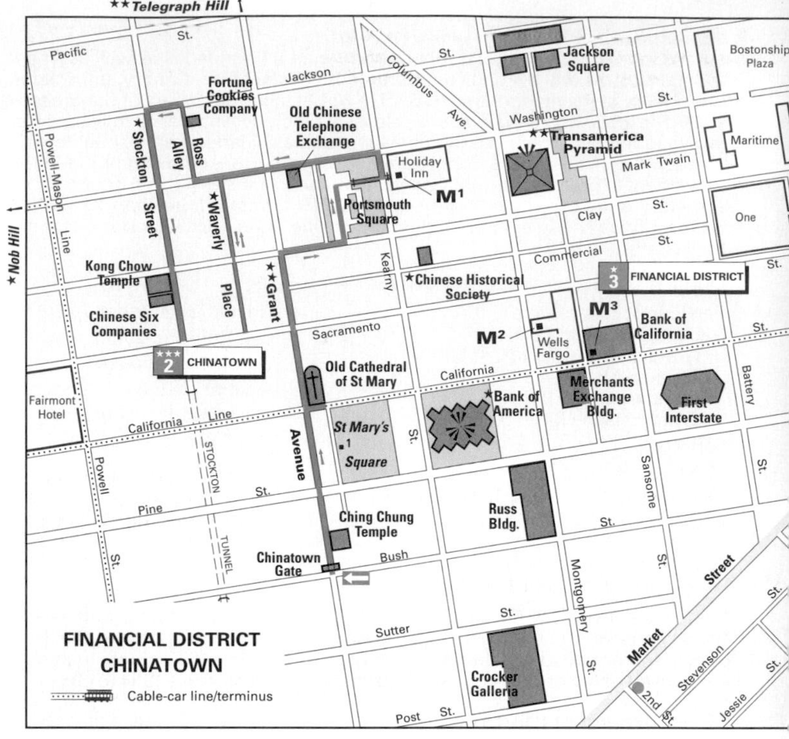

★★★ 2 CHINATOWN

On the lower slope of Nob Hill just west of the Financial District, Chinatown remains today what it has been since it first formed in the 1870s: a city within a city. Some 75 percent of Chinatown's 20,000 residents are first-generation immigrants, and a steady flow of newcomers keeps the area energetically and vividly Chinese.

The Chinese in California – At the time of the 1849 Gold Rush, political conditions in many areas of China were chaotic, and economic conditions desperate. By 1852 some 10,000 Chinese, many of them young men of peasant stock from the vicinities of Guandong (Canton) and Hong Kong, had made their way to California, the "Golden Mountain," in search of a better life. Many of the immigrants paid for their passage by the "credit-ticket" system: the prospective employer paid for the ticket in exchange for the immigrant's promise to work for a specified period at reduced wages. Under this system, many Chinese remained in debt-bondage for years after their arrival in California.

From 1863 to 1869, some 10,000 Chinese workers were employed on construction of the Central Pacific Railroad *(p 24)*. Upon its completion, they turned to jobs in canneries, lumber mills, agriculture and construction, exacerbating a rampant discrimination born of the resentment of American and European immigrant workers forced to compete with cheap Chinese labor. Race riots in many Western towns, including San Francisco, led to the Federal **Chinese Exclusion Act** of 1882, which banned further Chinese immigration.

The Birth of Chinatown – In response to persecution, the Chinese left the countryside and smaller towns during the 1870s, congregating in more defensible enclaves within the cities. In San Francisco they settled in the area around present-day Portsmouth Square, the heart of Chinatown.

The community's relatively complex social structure is based on a variety of organizations. Businesses were controlled by "companies" or family associations, organizations of immigrants from the same districts in China. Family and benevolent associations today provide mutual assistance and promote Chinese culture. Several "tongs," guilds based for the most part on legitimate economic activities, specialized during the early 20C in the prostitution and opium popular with single Chinese men, many of whom had arrived with the intention of earning a fortune and returning to China. Most remained indefinitely. To this day, Chinatown has a large population of elderly bachelors, who congregate for games and socializing in Portsmouth Square.

The 1943 repeal of the Chinese Exclusion Act, and later immigration reforms, opened the door to new waves of immigration, and Chinese-Americans began relocating from Chinatown to other city neighborhoods and suburbs. This ongoing process serves to renew Chinatown as a community of first-generation immigrants.

Chinatown Today – Today the most densely populated area of San Francisco, Chinatown is home to approximately 20,000 people. Importing, retailing, manufacturing and tourism are the mainstays of its economy. In addition to residents, many of the Bay Area's 200,000 Chinese-Americans throng Chinatown's streets on weekends to shop amid the profusion of herbal medicines, food items, embroidered linens, religious art, gold jewelry and printed material. Garment factories, tucked away in alleys and side streets, employ many local residents, and restaurants

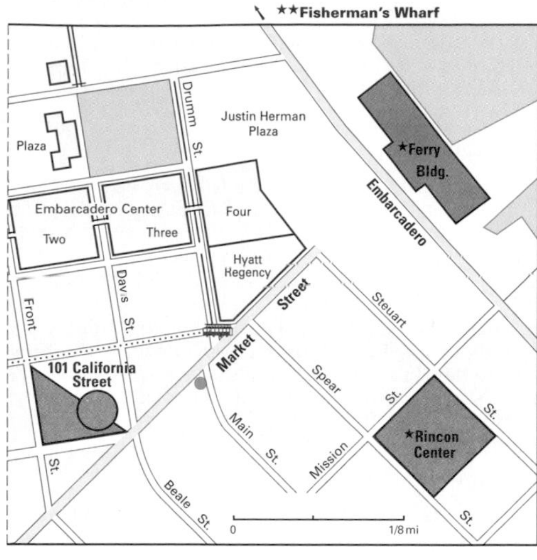

abound, reflecting the area's reputation as one of San Francisco's most popular places for eating out. Tourists gravitate to crowded, colorful Grant Avenue, especially during the celebration in late winter of **Chinese New Year**.

Religious life – Chinatown's active spiritual life revolves around its numerous Taoist, Buddhist and Confucian temples, commonly located on the upper floors of commercial buildings. Several welcome visitors to enter, view the elaborate altars and decorations, and absorb the atmosphere of prayer and tradition *(it is customary to leave a small donation)*. Ongoing devotions often incorporate elements from all three religious traditions; prayers for specific personal requests, such as recovery from illness or success in business, are accompanied by offerings of money, food, whisky and incense.

Walking Tour *1/2 day*

Powell-Mason or Powell-Hyde lines (descend at Washington St), or California St. 30 Stockton, 1 California or 15 Third.

Begin at the Chinatown Gate, at the intersection of Bush St and Grant Ave.

★★ **Grant Avenue** – Chinatown's principal touristic avenue is entered through the elaborate **Chinatown Gate** (1971), with its green tile roof and sculpted dragon and serpent figures. The eight blocks between Bush Street and Broadway bustle with shoppers in search of food, jewelry, cameras, electronic goods, T-shirts, Chinese art objects, curios and gifts. Visitors may wish to enter the **Ching Chung Temple** *(532 Grant Ave; open daily year-round; contribution requested ☎415-433-2623)* to view an authentic Taoist center of worship; a plethora of Chinese restaurants are located on Grant Avenue's side streets.

Continue to California St.

Old Cathedral of St Mary – *Open daily year-round.* Predating the surrounding neighborhood, this brick edifice was dedicated in 1854 as San Francisco's first cathedral seat for a Roman Catholic diocese. Across California Street is **St Mary's Square**, a patch of green amid tall buildings, anchored by a statue of **Sun Yat-sen [1]** by sculptor Beniamino Bufano. Sun spent two years in Chinatown organizing revolutionary movements that eventually overthrew the Manchu Dynasty in China and established the Chinese Republic in 1911.

Turn right on Clay St, walk 1/2 block to Portsmouth Sq.

Portsmouth Square – Formerly the plaza of the Mexican settlement of Yerba Buena, and renamed for the ship carrying troops to claim the village for the US in 1846, Portsmouth Square is now a social gathering point for local residents. From

Uniphoto

Grant Avenue in Chinatown

the square's east side, a pedestrian bridge leads across Kearny Street to the **Chinese Culture Center and Foundation [M[1]]** *(Holiday Inn 3rd floor, open year-round Tue–Sat; closed major holidays ♿ ☎415-986-1822)*, featuring temporary exhibitions of Chinese and Chinese-American art.

Leave the square via Washington St.

Old Chinese Telephone Exchange – *743 Washington St.* Formerly headquarters of an extensive and intricate Chinese-language telephone exchange, the building today houses a branch bank. The 1-story, pagoda-like structure (1909) represents the epitome of early 20C efforts to make Chinatown look Chinese.

Cross Grant St. and continue west on Washington.

★ **Waverly Place** – This 2-block alley offers good examples of the *chinoiserie* (Chinese-style ornamentation) added to the fundamentally plain brick 3- and 4-story office and apartment buildings erected after the 1906 earthquake and fire. The colors are symbolic: red stands for happiness; green for longevity; black for money; and yellow for fortune beyond money. Look for signs for family associations on or near many doors along Waverly Place.

Return to Washington St and turn right into Ross Alley.

Ross Alley – Much of Chinatown's hustle and bustle takes place in small alleys connecting the main thoroughfares. Worth a visit is this short, narrow passage, humming with the noise of garment factories and redolent with fragrances emanating from the **Golden Gate Fortune Cookies Company** *(no. 56)*, where visitors can sample the merchandise hot off the press while viewing the making of these well-known Chinese treats.

Turn left on Jackson St. Walk up the hill and turn left on Stockton St.

★ **Stockton Street** – Chinatown residents and Bay Area Chinese-Americans alike frequent the many specialty food stores, tea shops and pharmacies of this principal commercial thoroughfare. With fewer gift shops, restaurants and tourists than its counterpart Grant Avenue, Stockton Street offers an in-depth look at tradition and commerce in residential Chinatown. Well worth a stop is the **Kong Chow Temple** *(above post office, southwest corner of Stockton and Clay Sts; elevator to top floor; open daily year-round)*. Just south of the temple is the elaborately embellished building housing the **Chinese Six Companies** *(no. 843)*, a powerful benevolent association consolidated in 1882 from several smaller organizations. The colorful facade is a fine example of chinoiserie.

Additional Sight

★ **Chinese Historical Society of America** – *650 Commercial St. Open year-round Tue–Sat. Closed Chinese New Year and major holidays. ☎415-391-1188.* Historical photographs and artifacts document the role played by newly arrived immigrants and Chinese-Americans in such important national ventures as the transcontinental railroad, the wine industry, and the commercial fishing industry.

★ 3 FINANCIAL DISTRICT

Glittering canyons formed by the glass, marble and steel facades of bank towers and office skyscrapers converge on the corner of California and Montgomery Streets, reflecting the latter's historic role as financial center of the West.

In the 1850s, the area experienced many construction booms, punctuated by severe fires, as the wealth of the Gold Country poured into the city. By the end of the decade, sturdy brick buildings had replaced wood and canvas structures. The district was extended by landfill into Yerba Buena Cove from the original shoreline at Montgomery Street until it was eventually bounded in the 1880s by the **Embarcadero**, a broad waterfront street linking the city's piers.

Devastated by the 1906 earthquake and fire, the Financial District was quickly rebuilt following the same street pattern. Seismic engineering became a part of architectural design. Foundations were designed to absorb shocks, so that buildings swing with earthquake tremors rather than buckling against them.

For many years, the **Russ Building** *(235 Montgomery St)* punctuated the skyline as San Francisco's tallest structure; a building boom from the early 1960s through the mid-1980s produced some of today's landmarks. Some prominent newcomers, including **First Interstate Center** (1986), **Crocker Galleria** (1982) and Rincon Center *(p 195)* show marked respect for their architectural predecessors, but this has not eliminated a powerful movement against further high-rise development. In 1984 the city government approved the **Downtown Plan**, a system of regulations to establish controls on height and bulk, with setback requirements for upper stories, in an effort to encourage designs of a more sculpted profile rather than the boxy, flat-topped structures of the 1970s.

Sights *1/2 day. Map pp 192-193.*

California Street line. 15 Third or 42 Downtown Loop.

Jackson Square – *Jackson St between Montgomery and Sansome Sts.* Among the very few downtown survivors of the 1906 earthquake and fire, the buildings along this block of Jackson Street and adjacent alleys are the last vestige of mid-19C commercial San Francisco. Designated as the city's first historic district in 1971, the buildings, with their cast-iron facades and elaborate cornices, now house the offices and studios of antique dealers and interior designers.

★★ **Transamerica Pyramid** – *600 Montgomery St.* The elegant, 48-story office tower (1972) gracing the Financial District skyline is a recognized symbol of the city. Conceived by William Pereira & Assocs., the 853ft pyramid was designed to absorb earthquake shocks by swaying with the motion of the earth: its crowning 212ft spire can move as much as a foot during severe tremors.

A public observation area on the 27th floor *(open during business hours)* offers **views** of North Beach, the northern waterfront and the bay beyond. The small park at the eastern base of the building, with its tranquil benches set amid some 80 transplanted redwood trees, is a popular lunchtime retreat.

★ **Wells Fargo History Museum** [M²] – *420 Montgomery St. Open year-round Mon–Fri. Closed major holidays. ♿ ☎415-396-2619.* Located in the corporate headquarters of Wells Fargo Bank, long one of California's foremost financial institutions, this display area presents the colorful history of the company that figured so prominently in California's early development. The Concord coaches of the **Wells Fargo Express Company** began transporting freight and passengers in 1852, initially throughout California and later across the continent. During the course of the Gold Rush, assay and express offices had been established in the mining camps, and Wells Fargo's trade in the shipment of gold and the issuance of receipts led naturally to the establishment of a banking enterprise.

After perusing the numerous photographs, gold specimens and other artifacts on display, visitors can climb aboard a restored **Concord coach**, immersing themselves in stories of harrowing coach trips, marauding bandits such as Black Bart *(p 63)*, and the valiant riders of the Pony Express.

★ **Bank of America** – *555 California St.* California's premier financial institution is housed in a massive 52-story office tower, sheathed in dark red carnelian granite, that dominates the Financial District skyline (1971, Wurster, Bernardi & Emmons; Skidmore, Owings & Merrill). In 1904 Italian entrepreneur A.P. Giannini founded the Bank of Italy to serve the banking needs of Italian and other immigrants. Giannini's vision of ways that branch banking could benefit customers led to the company's rapid growth, and it was renamed the Bank of America in 1930. Panoramic **views**★★ from the Carnelian Room cocktail lounge on the top floor are among the best in the city.

Merchants Exchange Building – *465 California St. Open year-round Mon–Fri. ✗ ♿ ☎415-421-7730.* Formerly the nerve center of the Pacific coast shipping activities, this building (1903, Willis Polk) today houses a First Interstate Bank branch. In the former **Grain Exchange Hall** are six massive oil paintings of maritime subjects, five of them the work of Irish painter William A. Coulter. The entrance hall features an exemplary display of model ships.

Bank of California – *400 California St.* This stately Corinthian temple (1908, Bliss & Faville) is home to the first West Coast bank, founded in 1864 by the protean financier **William Ralston**. The interior **banking hall**★ is among the city's grandest, with an opulent coffered ceiling and walls of pale marble.

Museum of Money of the American West [M³] – *Basement level; entrance through banking hall. Open year-round Mon–Fri. ✗ ♿ ☎415-765-0400.* A series of displays incorporates stamped ingots and "necessity coinage" struck by assaying firms in the early 1850s before the San Francisco Mint was established. Particularly noteworthy is a beautiful $20 double-eagle gold coin designed by sculptor Augustus Saint-Gaudens.

101 California St – This roughly cylindrical glass office tower (1982, Johnson & Burgee) is a striking newcomer to the downtown skyline. Its low-rise base runs through the block on the diagonal, bounding a large plaza.

★ **Ferry Building** – *Embarcadero at Market St. Ferry information p 187.* Crowned by a distinctive 240ft clock tower, this 3-story arcaded ferry terminal (1898) was, for four decades before construction of the Bay Bridge, the debarkation point for passengers arriving by ferry from the East Bay. Today home to the offices of the Port of San Francisco and the World Trade Center, the building welcomes ferries from Marin, Solano and Alameda Counties.

★ **Rincon Center** – *Mission between Spear and Steuart Sts.* The former Rincon Annex Post Office (1939) was transformed in 1989 into an office and shopping complex and today stands as a symbol of the rebirth of the South of Market/Waterfront area. The restoration preserved the original Art Deco exterior and **lobby**, which features 27 WPA murals by Anton Refregier depicting California's history.

★★ 4 NOB HILL AND RUSSIAN HILL *1/2 day. Map pp 188-189.*

San Francisco's renowned hills, actually summits of a ridge of high ground immediately west of the downtown area, served as barriers to urban growth during the city's early years. As today, the peaks offered splendid views, but their sloping sides proved too steep for horse-drawn carriages. The advent of the cable car in the 1870s *(p 185)* opened the hills for development, engendering Nob and Russian Hills' past and present reputation as desirable residential addresses.

★ Nob Hill *California St line. 1 California.*

Initially home to railroad magnates and silver barons, Nob Hill developed as a chic hotel and apartment district extending northwest onto Russian Hill. Its name is a contraction of "nabob," a Hindu moniker for wealthy Europeans living in India.

The Central Pacific Railroad's wealthy "Big Four" *(p 24)*, seduced by the sweeping city views and the prestige of the address, erected palatial wooden residences at the summit of Nob Hill during the late 19C. All four of the renowned mansions were destroyed in the 1906 earthquake and fire; three live on symbolically in the names of structures crowning the hill today. The **Mark Hopkins Hotel** *(southeast corner of*

Mason and California Sts), was the site of the Hopkins mansion; its rooftop bar, the Top of the Mark, features outstanding city **views**★★ and has been the classic aerie for a big date since World War II. The hotel stands just west of the Stanford Court Hotel, site of Leland Stanford's mansion. Huntington Park, across Taylor Street from Grace Cathedral, marks the site of Collis Huntington's residence, and Charles Crocker's home occupied the present site of Grace Cathedral *(below)*. The landmark **Fairmont Hotel**★ *(northeast corner of Mason and California Sts)* memorializes James Fair, who made his fortune in the silver mines of the Comstock Lode. Its exterior elevator offers an expanding view of Chinatown, North Beach, and eventually much of the bay as it rises 24 stories to the Crown Room restaurant, renowned for its panoramic **views**★★★ of the entire city. The Fairmont was completed just before the 1906 fire; its interior was gutted and rebuilt. Another partial survivor of the 1906 conflagration was the stone-walled mansion of Fair's partner James Flood *(across Mason St from the Fairmont)*; the building now houses San Francisco's exclusive Pacific Union Club.

★ **Grace Cathedral** – *1051 Taylor St. Open daily year-round.* ♿ *☎415-776-6611.* Constructed in the French Gothic style, this San Francisco landmark is the third largest Episcopal cathedral in the US. Although construction began in 1929, financial and technical obstacles delayed consecration until 1964, and some of the interior work is not yet complete. The front, facing east rather than the traditional west, features the **Doors of Paradise,** bronze replicas of Lorenzo Ghiberti's doors to the baptistry of the Duomo in Florence, depicting ten scenes from the Old Testament. The somewhat severe interior is enlivened by many stained-glass windows and murals, some of which depict such illustrious 20C figures as Luther Burbank and Albert Einstein. An abundance of sculptures, tapestries and furnishings includes an altar of California granite and redwood, and a magnificent oak reredos carved in Flanders about 1490.

Uniphoto

Cable cars on Hyde Street

★ **Cable Car Museum** **[M²]** – *1201 Mason St at Washington St. Open daily year-round. Closed major holidays.* ♿ *☎415-474-1887.* Sheltering the central powerhouse of San Francisco's unique urban transport system, this 2-story brick structure also houses a museum presenting the 120-year history of the cable car. From the mezzanine level overlooking the humming machinery, visitors are treated to a close-up view of the sheaves, giant wheels that loop the continuous cables from the Powell-Mason, Powell-Hyde and California Street lines. The mezzanine level itself features historical displays, public transportation memorabilia and several historic cable cars, among them car no. 8 from the Clay Street Hill Railroad, San Francisco's first cable line. Hallidie himself operated the car on its inaugural run in 1873. Cable ports, through which the cables leave the barn to run under the street, are visible on the basement level.

★ Russian Hill *Powell-Hyde line. 45 Union-Stockton.*

Best explored on foot or glimpsed from the Hyde Street cable car, Russian Hill is primarily residential. Vallejo Street is interrupted just east of Jones Street above the impassably steep east face of the hill, providing a splendid **view**★ of downtown and the distant East Bay hills. Two blocks north is Macondray Lane, an unpaved wooded pedestrian path lined with charming homes.

★★ **Lombard Street** – *Between Hyde and Leavenworth Sts.* Affectionately dubbed "The World's Crookedest Street," the 1000 block of Lombard Street is undeniably one of San Francisco's most renowned (and most photographed) passageways. Originally an all-but-impassable grade of 27 percent, the hill in 1922 was landscaped to a 16 percent grade, and a one-lane cobbled street of eight hairpin turns was built onto the slope. Nestled within the curves are terraces profusely bedecked with flowers and shrubs; from the top of the hill, a celebrated **view**★ extends north to Alcatraz and east to Coit Tower and beyond.

San Francisco Art Institute – *800 Chestnut St. Open daily year-round. Closed major holidays & Dec 24–Jan 2.* ✗ ♿ ☏*415-749-4588.* This renowned school of fine arts is housed in a Spanish Colonial style building (1926, Bakewell & Brown); its simple, unadorned concrete annex was added in 1969. From the expansive terrace, a broad **view★** encompasses the waterfront areas and Telegraph Hill. The Diego Rivera Gallery, one of the institute's two exhibition galleries devoted to changing shows, features *The Making of a Fresco Showing the Building of a City*, a 1931 mural by the celebrated Mexican artist.

★★ 5 NORTH BEACH

San Francisco's premier Italian neighborhood since the late 19C occupies the area north of Broadway and east of Russian Hill, and was named for an actual sandy beach obliterated more than century ago by landfill dredged from the bay. North Beach is unlike most Italian-American urban enclaves in that its population emigrated from northern Italy rather than from Sicily or the southern regions of the peninsula.

Italian-Americans began settling here during the late 1870s, displacing the immigrants from South America and southern Europe who had nicknamed the area the "Latin Quarter." By the early 20C, many of the neighborhood's immigrant residents had begun relocating to rich farmlands north of the city such as the WINE COUNTRY and Marin County.

Despite this trend, which continues today, and the encroaching northward spread of Chinatown *(p 192)*, the neighborhood's traditional Italian flavor remains very much in evidence in its restaurants, cafes and shops. At the **Museum of North Beach [M³]** *(1435 Stockton St, on the mezzanine of Eureka Bank; open year-round Mon–Fri; closed major holidays ☏415-391-6210)*, changing displays of historical photographs and artifacts document the history of North Beach during the late 18C and early 19C. Among the memorabilia of the Italian and Chinese communities that occupied the neighborhood are numerous photographs of North Beach, Fisherman's Wharf and Telegraph Hill in the years before and during the earthquake and fire of 1906.

The Beat Generation – As the Italian-American population began vacating North Beach, low-rent housing became available and was occupied by the poets, artists, musicians and assorted hangers-on who became known as the "Beat Generation." Poet Lawrence Ferlinghetti founded the **City Lights Booksellers and Publishers★** *(261 Columbus Ave; open daily year-round; closed Thanksgiving Day, Dec 25)*, where other renowned literati Allen Ginsberg, Jack Kerouac and Gregory Corso congregated, nurtured by the red wine and espresso ambience of North Beach during the 1950s. Today the bookstore, along with the adjacent Vesuvio Cafe, is one of the principal surviving landmarks of that period.

Sights *3hrs. Map p 189. 🚌 39 Coit, 30 Stockton, or 15 Third.*

★ **Washington Square Park** – This grassy, open space, attractively dotted with trees and benches, lies on the western slope of Telegraph Hill in the heart of North Beach. The airiness and greenery attract local residents of all ages and types: young mothers with their children at the playground, groups of retirees chatting in the sunshine, and vagabonds seeking the sense of belonging that prevails in this long-established gathering place.

Church of SS Peter and Paul – *North side of the square. Open daily year-round.* ♿ ☏*415-421-0842.* The 191ft spires of San Francisco's "Italian Cathedral" (1924) loom over Washington Square. A verse from Dante's *Paradiso* ("The glory of Him who moves all things penetrates and glows throughout the Universe") adorns the facade, and impressive marble graces the interior. Reflecting North Beach's increasingly multi-ethnic character, the church offers Mass in Cantonese and English as well as Italian.

★★ **Telegraph Hill** – This 274ft hill is one of San Francisco's prominent topographical landmarks. At its summit, presided over by a bronze statue of Christopher Columbus, visitors can take in some of the city's most remarkable **views★★** over the downtown area, the waterfront and the distant shores of the East Bay and Marin County. The hill was named for the semaphore constructed at the summit in 1849 to announce the approach of ships entering the Golden Gate.

Owing to its steep slopes and proximity to the port and wharf areas, Telegraph Hill remained a working class neighborhood through the 19C. The advent of the automobile opened the hill to more aggressive development, and moneyed residents began purchasing and remodeling homes formerly occupied by fishermen and dock workers. Present-day land values in the area are among the city's highest.

Descending Telegraph Hill's precipitous east slope, **Greenwich Street** and **Filbert Street★** are less city thoroughfares than staircased pedestrian paths *(access to Greenwich St indicated at east side of summit parking lot; to Filbert St at uppermost curve leading to summit)*. From the lushly landscaped Filbert Steps, Darrell Place and Napier Lane lead beneath leafy canopies past charming wooden houses, some of which date from the 1860s. Sections of the east and northeast sides of the hill were quarried for construction stone and ship's ballast in the mid-19C, and the resulting steep cliffs remain undeveloped today.

★★ **Coit Tower** – *Summit of Telegraph Hill. Access on foot from Washington Sq: north on Stockton St, then east on Lombard St; or by the 39 Coit bus from Washington Square. Parking at the top very limited.* One of San Francisco's best-known landmarks, this 210ft fluted concrete shaft (1934) commemorates **Lillie Hitchcock Coit** (1843-1929), who spent her childhood in San Francisco in the years before the Civil War and willed $100,000 to the city for beautification projects.

The lobby in the tower's rectangular base features 3,691sq ft of celebrated fresco **murals★** painted by 26 local artists and 19 assistants as part of the Public Works of

Art Project, an initiative of the New Deal whereby artists were hired as civil servants by the Federal Government to decorate public buildings. The murals, depicting vignettes of everyday life in California during the period of the Great Depression, incorporated both subtle and blatant expressions of social criticism that contradicted the conservative values of San Francisco's business elite, and consequently sparked a heated political controversy between the artists and the San Francisco Art Commission. Complicating matters was the concurrent Pacific Maritime Strike of West Coast longshoremen; the murals were viewed by the media and the public as sympathetic to the workers' position, and conservative groups threatened to alter or remove the offending images. In the heat of the debate, the Park Commission delayed opening Coit Tower for four months. When the doors finally opened to the public in October 1934, only the no. 4 mural by Clifford Wight had been altered.
From the tower's observation deck, sweeping **views★★★** encompass the hills and streets of San Francisco.

★ 6 UNION SQUARE AREA

San Francisco's leading upscale shopping district is anchored at pleasant **Union Square**, named for the mass meetings held here by Union sympathizers to demonstrate their loyalty during the Civil War. Among the buildings surrounding the square are the city's luxury department stores, including Sak's Fifth Avenue, Macy's, and I. Magnin. The post-Modern **Neiman-Marcus** store (1982, Philip Johnson) features a stunning interior **rotunda** topped by an elaborate art glass dome removed from the City of Paris store that previously occupied the site. Smaller specialty shops and boutiques line Sutter, Post and Geary Streets leading east to the Financial District. By day, a broad mix of street performers, homeless persons, flower vendors and members of the area's working population frequent Union Square. At its center is the 97ft **Dewey Monument [3]**, surmounted by "Victory," a bronze sculpture commemorating Admiral Dewey's 1898 defeat of Spanish naval forces. Beneath the square is a parking garage, the first in the city to be located under a public park. Glass elevators zooming up the tower annex of the **St Francis Hotel** (1904, Bliss & Faville), which dominates the square's west side, offer a superb **view** of the Financial District and the bay.

Sights *2hrs. Map p 189.*

Powell-Mason or Powell-Hyde lines. 30 Stockton or 38 Geary.

Maiden Lane – *East of Union Sq between Post and Geary Sts.* This two-block passage is lined with specialty shops, art galleries, and boutiques for upscale shoppers and all kinds of browsers. The intriguing **Circle Gallery★ [E]** *(no. 140)* is the only San Francisco building designed by Frank Lloyd Wright (1949); a private gallery of contemporary art, it sports an interior reminiscent of the Guggenheim Museum in New York City *(open daily year-round; closed Jul 4, Thanksgiving Day, Dec 25; ♿ ☎415-989-2100).*

Theaters – San Francisco's theater district is small but active, with several distinguished old structures located near Union Square. Among them are the Geary Theater (1909, Bliss & Faville), adorned with fanciful columns of polychrome terracotta and home of American Conservatory Theater *(415 Geary St)*; and the Curran Theater (1922, Alfred Henry Jacobs), with a mansard roof and a grand marquee *(445 Geary St).*

7 SOUTH OF MARKET

Long a flat landscape of wide thoroughfares and narrow residential streets, small factories and long blocks of warehouses, the district south of Market Street, where the streets run diagonally to the prevailing city pattern, is fermenting with new activity. Trendily nicknamed "SoMa" (for South of Market), the area is the new heart of San Francisco's contemporary art scene.

Elite Rincon Hill – Very early in the city's history, an elite residential neighborhood grew up on Rincon Hill, now obscured by the west anchor of the Bay Bridge. When the cable car was introduced in the 1870s, society abandoned Rincon Hill for the hills west of downtown. The only remnant is **South Park**, a green island deep within the block formed by Second, Third, Bryant and Brannan Streets, created in 1852 in imitation of a London square. The novelist Jack London *(p 239)* was born nearby in 1876, at a site marked by a plaque on the Wells Fargo Bank *(601 3rd St).*
Attempts to expand San Francisco's financial district into the relatively cheap land south of Market Street began in the early 1870s when financier William Ralston erected his Palace Hotel, the grandest on the West Coast at that time. Gutted by fire in 1906, the Palace was rebuilt in 1909 with a stunning, glass-roofed **Garden Court★★**; today renamed the **Sheraton Palace Hotel** *(639 Market St)*, it was reopened in 1991 after being sumptuously refurbished. Despite Ralston's enthusiastic promotion of the area, his glowing dreams for the area south of Market Street failed to take root, and the terra-cotta-clad Pacific Telephone Building (1925, Miller & Pflueger) remained for many years an isolated landmark on New Montgomery Street.
Construction of the Moscone Convention Center (1981, Hellmuth, Obata & Kassabaum) and the 1991 demolition of the stifling Embarcadero Freeway have inspired new development. Established in 1984, the **Jewish Museum San Francisco [M[4]]** offers changing exhibits of contemporary Jewish art and culture *(121 Steuart St. Open year-round Mon–Thu, Sun; $3; ♿ ☎415-543-8880).* Remodeled factories and new apartment buildings enliven the blocks near the waterfront, and a proliferation of galleries, nightclubs, performance spaces and cafes in the area of Folsom Street between 7th and 12th Streets attracts those in search of the daring, the progressive and the experimental. *For a current listing of venues and events, consult the San Francisco Bay Guardian.*

Sights *1/2 day. Map p 189.*

Yerba Buena Gardens – *3rd St between Mission and Howard Sts. Open daily year-round.* ✂ ♿ ☎*415-541-0312.* Embodying the renaissance of South of Market is this new cultural complex dedicated to showcasing works of local visual and performing artists from a multicultural perspective. The complex melds landscaped gardens, outdoor sculptures, a man-made waterfall and a memorial to Dr Martin Luther King Jr, with a performing arts center and exhibit hall. In 1995 the Museum of Modern Art is slated to occupy its new building (designed by an international team of architects) across 3rd Street; new office and retail spaces are planned for 1996; and the Mexican Museum *(p 190)* will relocate here in 1998.

★★ **Museum of Modern Art [M⁵]** – *151 3rd St. Scheduled opening: Jan 1995* ☎*415-357-4000.* The museum's permanent collection of 17,000 pieces features works by German Expressionist, Fauvist, Abstract Expressionist and Latin American painters. The museum also frequently hosts traveling shows.

The Old Mint – *5th and Mission Sts.* 🚌 *14 Mission or 27 Bryant.* This imposing neoclassical edifice (1874), nicknamed "the Granite Lady," served as the principal western US Mint from 1874 to 1937. One of downtown's few public buildings to survive the 1906 earthquake and fire, the bastion-like structure was briefly the the city's only financial institution for disaster relief. Today the building houses Treasury Department offices.

★ **Ansel Adams Center for Photography** – *250 4th St.* 🚌 *30 Stockton, 45 Union-Stockton or 12 Folsom. Open year-round Tue–Sun. Closed Jan 1, Thanksgiving Day, Dec 25, Monday holidays. $4.* ♿ ☎*415-495-7000.* The city's only museum devoted solely to photography is named for the San Francisco-born photographer (1902-84), renowned for his landscapes and wilderness portraits of such places as YOSEMITE NATIONAL PARK. One of the five galleries is reserved for continuing displays of Adams' works; the remaining four annually present some 20 thematic exhibits each year on topics related to photography.

Cartoon Art Museum – *665 3rd St. Open year-round Wed–Sun. Closed major holidays. $3.* ♿ ☎*415-546-9481.* This museum takes seriously the idea that cartoons, comic strips and animation art provide a commentary on our social and cultural history. With a permanent collection of more than 6,000 pieces dating from 1738 to the present, the museum also hosts frequent temporary exhibits of individual artists and works on loan from private collections.

Shopping in San Francisco

In this area...	*You will find...*
Union Square *(p 198)*	Designer boutiques, department stores, art galleries,
Union St *(p 207)*	Trendy shops and boutiques, art galleries
Fisherman's Wharf *(p 188)*	Pier 39 (100 stores), Ghiradelli Square (over 70 stores), The Cannery
Fillmore St (between Jackson and Bush)	Apparel, antiques, specialty stores
Mission District *(p 208)*	Ethnic food shops
Chinatown *(p 192)*	Gift shops, Asian food shops
South of Market *(p 198)*	San Francisco Centre (over 90 stores), outlet stores, art galleries
The Haight *(p 204)*	New Age items, hip and hippie apparel

★ 8 CIVIC CENTER

This complex of public buildings is San Francisco's center of government and its principal venue for music and dance performances .

Sights *2hrs. Map p 188.*
BART all lines. 🚋*Powell-Mason or Powell-Hyde lines.* 🚌*30 Stockton or 38 Geary.*

★ **City Hall** – *Polk St between McAllister and Grove Sts. Open year-round Mon–Fri. Closed major holidays.* ✂ ♿ ☎*415-554-6120.* This splendid Renaissance Revival domed building (1915, Bakewell & Brown) sits on the western edge of a large public square, scene of many historic political demonstrations. The stately dome soars 308ft above the ground, and the grand staircase in the rotunda has served as a location for several movies.

San Francisco Public Library – *Larkin and McAllister Sts. Open year-round Mon–Sat.* ♿ ☎*415-558-3949.* Echoing the architectural style of City Hall across the square is the city's elegant Renaissance Revival library (1916, George Kelham). It has long been overcrowded, and a new building is scheduled to open in early 1996 immediately to the south. The present library will eventually be remodeled to house the Asian Art Museum, now in Golden Gate Park *(p 202).*

Davies Symphony Hall – *Van Ness Ave and Grove St. Concert information p 187.* With its distinctive rounded facade, this hall (1981, Skidmore, Owings & Merrill), seating 2,743, is the home of the San Francisco Symphony. The facade echoes that of the **New State Office Building** *(two blocks to the north)* by the same architects.

Veteran's War Memorial Building [F] – *Van Ness Ave between Grove and McAllister Sts.* This imposing structure in the Renaissance Revival style and the nearby **War Memorial Opera House [G]** were constructed as a matched pair in 1932 by Brown & Lansburgh. The Opera House is home to the San Francisco Opera and the San Francisco Ballet. On the first floor of the War Memorial Building is the **Herbst Theater**, home to a number of smaller performing arts groups and several lecture series.The building's third and fourth floors housed the San Francisco Museum of Modern Art until September 1994 *(description p 199).*

Visitors should resist the temptation to walk west from Civic Center to Alamo Square, the Haight and Golden Gate Park. Distances are not great, but the intervening areas are subject to a high level of street crime.

★★★ 9 GOLDEN GATE PARK *Map below*

Reclaimed from an expanse of windswept sand dunes, this 1,017-acre rectangular greensward, sloping to the sea from the middle of densely developed San Francisco, is home to a celebrated complex of art and science museums, in addition to a wealth of recreational opportunities. An urban oasis of meadows, gardens, lakes and woodlands, the park is the result of careful planning by two inspired landscape architects and the labors of an army of gardeners.

"Uncle John" – Following the establishment of the park's boundaries in 1870, superintendent William Hammond Hall surveyed the unpromising tract west of the city and established the basic landscaping plan and road pattern. Resisting political pressure to grade the site flat, he determined to stabilize the dunes into hills and valleys by anchoring the shifting sand with vegetation. In 1887 **John McLaren**, a Scottish estate gardener, took over as superintendent, with a Park Commission mandate to make the park "one of the beauty spots of the world." During his 56-year tenure, McLaren experimented extensively with sand-holding grasses and plants from all over the world, built up the sandy soil with clay and manure swept from the city's streets, and transformed a "white elephant" into one of the nation's loveliest urban green spaces.

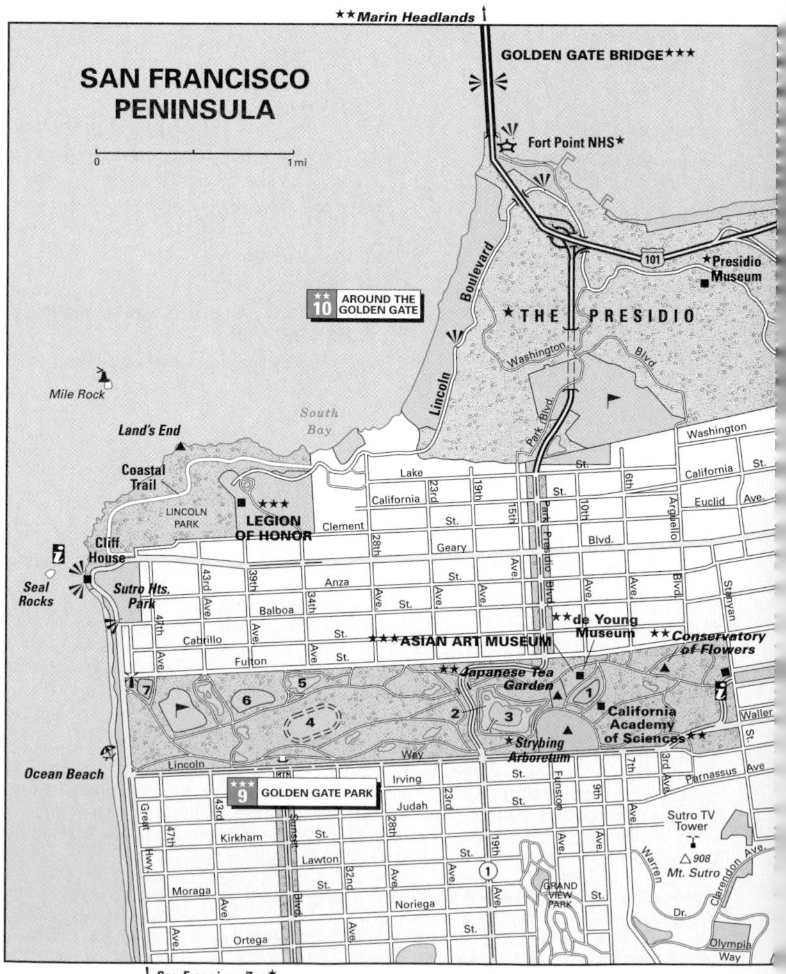

Golden Gate Park was permanently transformed when it hosted San Francisco's **Midwinter Fair of 1894**, conceived by Michael H. de Young *(below)* to jolt the city into economic recovery following a nationwide depression in 1893. Between January and July of that year some 2.5 million people had entered the park to peruse elaborate exhibits and pavilions representing 37 nations. Crowds thronged the Japanese Tea Garden built especially for the fair, and the Conservatory of Flowers, both of which remain among the park's most popular attractions today.

Visiting the Park – Golden Gate Park is 3.5mi long and .5mi wide, laced with curving drives that emerge to connect with the city's street grid at some 20 points along the park perimeter. The museums and principal attractions are situated in the park's eastern half, with sports and recreation areas spreading to the west. The visitor center at **McLaren Lodge** *(Fell and Stanyan Sts, just inside park entrance)* offers park maps and schedule information. *Note: Some roads in the park's eastern section are closed to automobile traffic on Sundays.*

The Museums

38 Geary to 6th Ave, transfer to 44 O'Shaughnessy (south).

San Francisco's principal museums of the arts and sciences are situated around a formal **Music Concourse [1]** created for the Midwinter Fair of 1894; the band shell at its western end was erected in 1899. To the north, the buff-colored stucco structure housing the M.H. de Young Museum and the Asian Art Museum is dominated by its monumental entry tower; to the south, the California Academy of Sciences occupies a more modern building.

★★ **M. H. de Young Memorial Museum** – *2hrs. Enter collections through the Hearst Court, opposite the main entrance. Specific location of artworks is subject to change. Open year-round Wed–Sun 10am–5pm. Closed Thanksgiving Day, Dec 25. $5.* ☎*415-863-3330.* Home to one of the nation's most comprehensive collections of American art, the "de Young" also features noteworthy collections of Ancient art and the traditional arts of Africa, Oceania and the Americas. The museum building was designed by Christian Mullgardt, one of the architects who designed the structures of the Panama-Pacific International Exposition *(p 186)*.
Established by Michael H. de Young, co-founder and publisher in 1865 of the *San Francisco Chronicle*, the museum began as the Arts Museum of the Midwinter Fair. At the close of the fair, de Young housed there his personal assemblage of arts and curiosities, a collection that remained notably eclectic through most of the 20C. In 1972 the de Young organization was merged with that of the California Palace of the Legion of Honor *(p 206)* into a single administrative entity known as the Fine Arts

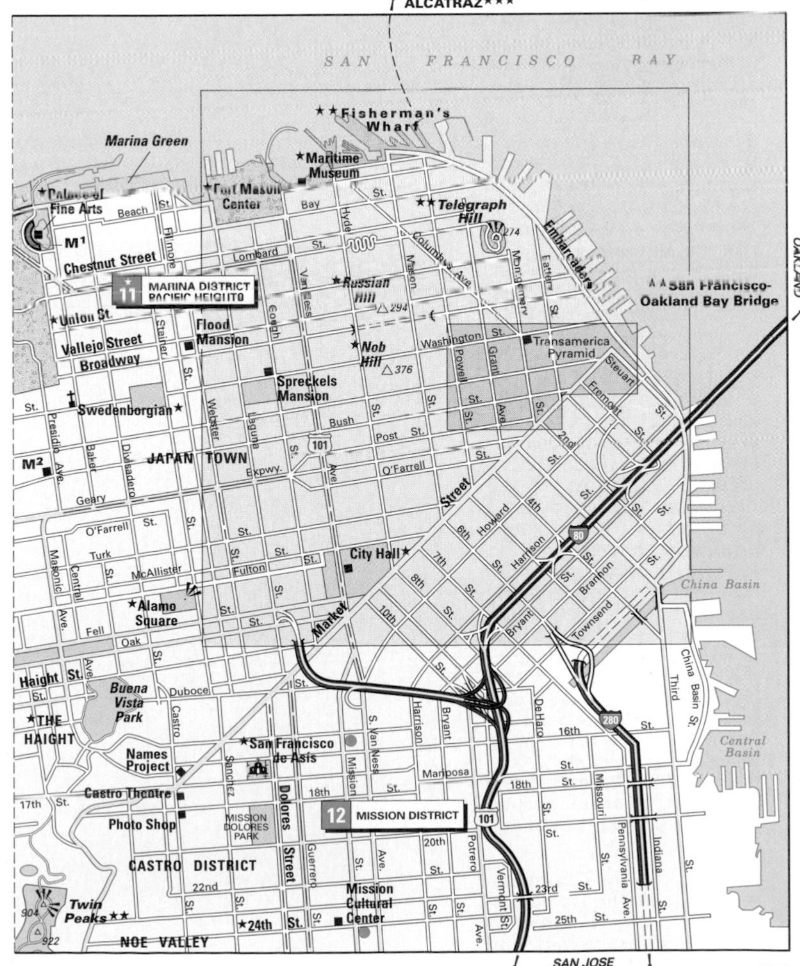

Museums of San Francisco. The collections of these two venerable institutions underwent a major reorganization in 1989, and today the de Young is primarily devoted to the collection and presentation of American Art.

★★ **American Collection** – Works trace the development of American painting from its beginnings in the late 17C to the early 20C. Arranged chronologically in 21 galleries, paintings are displayed with works of sculpture and the decorative arts from their respective periods, an integration that offers a broader understanding of artistic norms and trends throughout American history.

Highlights of the **17-18C** *(galleries A-B)* include works by John Smibert and John Singleton Copley, America's greatest 18C portraitist. Silverware by Paul Revere is also displayed here. The **early-19C** section *(galleries C-K)* incorporates a Federal period room from a 1805 Massachusetts home; landscapes by Albert Bierstadt and Frederick E. Church; and genre paintings by Eastman Johnson and artist/politician George Caleb Bingham. Also noteworthy is a collection of Shaker furniture and 19C folk art.

Works by George Inness, Thomas Eakins and Winslow Homer represent the **late 19C** *(galleries L-O)*; particularly interesting here are trompe-l'oeil paintings by contemporaries William Harnett and John Frederick Peto, and several fine portraits by renowned portraitist John Singer Sargent.

Completing the American collection *(galleries P-V)* are paintings and sculptures on Western themes by George Catlin and Frederic Remington, furniture from the Arts and Crafts movement, paintings by Robert Henri and his students in the "The Eight," and 20C paintings by members of the Ash Can school.

African Art and Art of the Americas – *Galleries 42-43.* Traditional artworks, among them masks and figurines of natural materials from the African continent, headdresses, costumes, and furniture from Oceania, carved stone figures, effigies, and jewelry from Meso-America and the Central Andes reveal the importance of spirituality and ritual in the everyday lives of indigenous peoples. A wide variety of Native North American art includes a Tlingit totem pole, Eskimo ivory, wood carvings and fabrics from the Northwest Coast, Plains beadwork, California baskets, Pueblo pottery and kachina dolls.

Ancient Art – *Gallery 1.* The museum's small but varied collection of works from the ancient Mediterranean and Middle East includes Egyptian figurines and Iranian plates and bowls; amphorae and other containers from Greece and Greek colonies in southern Italy; and Roman mosaics.

Six galleries are devoted to special and traveling exhibits, for which the de Young is one of the leading venues on the West Coast.

★★★ **Asian Art Museum** – *2hrs. Entrance from the west side of the de Young lobby. Open year-round Wed–Sun 10am–5pm. Closed major holidays. $5.* ✗ ♿ 🅿 ☎*415-668-7855.* Possessing what is today considered the finest collection of Asian art in the nation, this museum was born of the efforts of Avery Brundage (1887-1975), a Chicago engineering executive and longtime president of the International Olympic Committee.

An Interest in Asia – Though Brundage's first and abiding interests, fostered during extensive travels in Asia, were Japanese *netsuke (p 101)* and 3,000-year-old Chinese bronzes, he later broadened his collecting efforts to include objects from Korea, Southeast Asia, India and its neighbors, and the Middle East. His early acquisitions included numerous objects that, owing to laws since passed restricting the export of art objects from their countries of origin, could not today be legally removed to the US. Thus, such a comprehensive collection will almost certainly never be assembled again.

In the 1950s, anticipating a growing awareness of the need for closer relations with Pacific Rim nations, Brundage endeavored to found a museum that would be a "bridge of understanding" across the Pacific. San Francisco, with its growing reputation as a "gateway to the Pacific Rim," in 1960 passed a bond measure earmarking funds to build an addition to the de Young Museum as a home for the Brundage collection. The Asian Art Museum opened here, as a separate institution, in 1966.

First Floor – *Enter from the west end of the de Young museum lobby and begin at the first gallery to the right.*

Asian Art Museum of San Francisco

Kaliya Krishna (bronze, 15C)

Constituting over half of the museum's holdings, the **Chinese collection**★★ comprises ceramics, jade, paintings, ritual bronzes, sculptures and decorative arts dating from prehistory to the present. Organized chronologically and thematically, the works on display exemplify the beauty and diversity of Chinese art.
Scroll paintings from the Qing, Ming and Yuan dynasties depict monumental landscape scenes. The extensive collection of **ceramics** offers a comprehensive look at the development of this important art form. Included are some beautiful examples of the technique of celadon glazing. Blue-and-white vessels from the late Ming and Qing dynasties reveal the influence of Western tastes as the demand for export ware in Europe gave rise to the China trade.
One of the largest assemblages of ritual bronzes on public display outside China is highlighted by a Shang dynasty ritual bowl shaped like a rhinoceros (11C BC). The **sculpture** collection features the oldest known dated Chinese Buddha (AD 338), a gilt bronze seated figure. Selections from the museum's collection of more than 1,200 **jades** produced over a period of 5,000 years are dispersed chronologically throughout the Chinese galleries.
The **Korean** collection, comprising some 350 objects, features hanging painted scrolls and stoneware ceramics from the 5-9C AD. Two slate daggers (c.600 BC) are the oldest items.

Second Floor – Galleries present works of art from Japan and India, including the development of the Indian art tradition in Southeast Asia and Tibet. The **Japanese** galleries feature screens and scroll paintings from AD 1168 to 1185; examples from the collection of more than 1,800 *netsuke* miniatures in horn and ivory; ceramic ware spanning the period from 20C BC–20C AD; archaeological bronzes and decorative art objects. Highlights include a lacquer palanquin and a set of iron armor.
Examples of **Indian Art** include stone sculptures from central India, south Indian bronzes and Mughal miniatures. The **Southeast Asian** gallery shows Hindu and Buddhist sculptural motifs as they were reinterpreted in Burma, Thailand, Cambodia, Vietnam and Indonesia. The colorful **Himalayan** gallery features Tibetan scroll paintings and a variety of Tibetan and Nepali ritual implements, jewelry, and bronze statues of gods and bodhisattvas.
The museum hosts frequent traveling shows in the galleries to the left of the entrance court.

★★ **California Academy of Sciences** – *2hrs. Information on planetarium shows, dolphin feedings and any special programs is available at the entrance desk. Open Jul 4–Labor Day daily 10am–7pm, rest of the year 5pm. $7.* ✗ ♿ 🅿 ☎*415-750-7142.*
Founded in 1853, the California Academy of Sciences is the oldest scientific institution in the West. Housed in Golden Gate Park since 1915, the Academy comprises a natural history museum, planetarium and aquarium. The institution also sponsors research and expeditions devoted primarily to the study of natural history.

★ **Museum of Natural History** – The **Wild California** hall features dioramas of wildlife from different regions of this exceedingly varied state. Video screens provide additional information. One diorama shows a teaspoon of sea water at a magnification of 200, and at the far end of the hall, a salt water surge tank recreates the surf zone on the rugged Farallon Islands, which lie some 32mi offshore.
The **Gems and Minerals Hall** holds a sparkling display of stones and minerals organized according to chemical composition and crystal structure.
The **African Safari** hall displays dioramas of African wildlife in their native habitats. A highlight of this exhibit is "The Water Hole," an assemblage of animals of the African savanna, accentuated with light and sound effects. The adjacent African Annex features additional large animal dioramas.
Earth and Space elucidates the solar system and deeper space, and explains continental drift and plate tectonics along with such related phenomena as volcanoes and earthquakes. Visitors can stand on a **shake table** that simulates earthquakes, observe the swinging Foucault pendulum as it demonstrates the earth's rotation, and view a fragment of moon rock retrieved by the astronauts of Apollo 11.
The **Hall of Human Cultures** incorporates lifelike human figures with artifacts in settings representing daily life of 11 distinct societies, among them Inuit ice hunters, Australian aborigines and Native Americans of the northwest California coast. **Life Through Time** illustrates evolution with fossils and reconstructed models of extinct life forms. Don't miss the skull of *Tyrannosaurus Rex*, or the 15 million-year-old fossil shark teeth. The exhibit is organized into four major divisions: Early Life in the Sea, Transition to Land, Age of Dinosaurs and Age of Mammals.

The **Morrison Planetarium** offers changing programs presenting a wide variety of astronomical and atmospheric phenomena. Laserium shows are also offered. *Check schedule outside planetarium for titles and show times. $2.50.*
Adjacent to the planetarium, a humorous take on human and animal cultures is presented in the **Far Side of Science**, a gallery featuring the creations of satirical cartoonist Gary Larson.

★ **Steinhart Aquarium** – *Entrance across the Fountain Courtyard from the Academy's main entrance. Same hours as the Academy.* Founded in 1923, the Steinhart Aquarium houses 189 separate displays of freshwater and saltwater species of fish, marine mammals, amphibian and reptiles for a comprehensive look at life under and around the water. The entrance hall features an imitation tropical swamp where alligators and turtles roam; surrounding the swamp are glass cases containing an amazing variety of amphibians and reptiles, including snakes, toads, newts, frogs, Gila monsters and a 30ft reticulated python.
From the entrance hall, corridors lined with large tanks display some 6,000 aquatic creatures of 610 species, including toxic and electric fish piranhas and other natives of the Amazon River, chambered nautilus, flashlight fish and a giant octopus. The main hall's west end features a habitat for black-footed penguins and a glass-walled

swimming pool for seals and dolphins. From the main hall, a passage lined with small tanks leads to the **Fish Roundabout**, a 100,000-gallon doughnut-shaped tank surrounding a central observation area.

The Park

🚌5 Fulton (north perimeter park entrances); or streetcar N-Judah (1 block south of south perimeter entrances).

★★ **Japanese Tea Garden** – *Northwest corner of Music Concourse, immediately west of Asian Art Museum. Open Mar–Sept daily 9am–6:30pm, rest of the year 8:30am–5:30pm. Closed Thanksgiving Day, Dec 25. $2.* One of the park's most beloved attractions, the 5-acre garden unites Japanese-style landscaping and architecture for an atmosphere of serenity and tranquillity. Points of special interest include a pagoda, a Zen gravel garden, a hillside of bonsai trees with a miniature waterfall, a bronze Buddha dating from 1790, and an open-air Japanese tea shop offering cookies and green tea.

★★ **Conservatory of Flowers** – *North side of JFK Dr, .5mi west of Stanyan St. Open year-round daily 9am–5pm. $1.50. ☎415-641-7978.* Set like a white bubble amid a sea of flowering parterres, this glass and wood greenhouse composed of two wings flanking an octagonal rotunda is Golden Gate Park's oldest structure. Originally purchased by James Lick for installation on his estate in SAN JOSE, the greenhouse was shipped in prefabricated parts from Dublin, but arrived after Lick's death in 1876. A consortium of San Francisco businessmen then purchased the building and donated it to Golden Gate Park. Following a fire in 1883, the central dome was enlarged and several of its panels were set with panes of colored glass.
Today the conservatory's holdings constitute less a scientific study than a celebration of the beauties of the plant world. A walk through the verdant, humid paths of the central rotunda offers an introduction to a miniature rain forest. The east wing features smaller tropical plants and a lily pond, while the west wing is devoted to rotating seasonal displays of flowers.

★ **Strybing Arboretum and Botanical Gardens** – *Main gate near park entrance at 9th Avenue and Lincoln Way. North gate near Japanese Tea Garden. Open daily year-round. ♿ ☎415-661-1316.* Covering some 70 acres of rolling terrain, this outstanding botanic collection comprises 7,500 species of plants from all over the world. The primary emphasis is on regions of Mediterranean climate, with significant collections from California, the Cape Province of South Africa, southwestern Australia and Chile.
Among other attractions are the Garden of Fragrances, where plants are labeled in Braille; a hillside garden of succulents; the New World Cloud Forest, where special mist emitters supplement the San Francisco fog; and a Redwood Trail planted with coast redwoods dating from 1898.

Stow Lake [2] – *Immediately west of Strybing Arboretum.* Serving as the park's main irrigation reservoir, this moat surrounding **Strawberry Hill [3]** is the largest of the 15 man-made lakes and ponds that dot Golden Gate Park. The 428ft summit of Strawberry Hill, accessed by a spiral footpath, is the highest point in the park and was famed for its panoramas of the city before trees grew to block the view. From the summit, water is released from an outlet to cascade down a man-made waterfall donated in the 1890s by railroad magnate Collis P. Huntington.
The western section of Golden Gate Park, from Stow Lake to the ocean, abounds with great stretches of meadows and woods, with a scattering of attractions and facilities for various sports.
Half way to the ocean from Stow Lake is the immense **Polo Field [4]**, often busy with a half dozen simultaneous football, soccer and softball games, and surrounded by three concentric tracks used by a variety of runners, bicyclists, roller skaters and horseback riders. At **Spreckels Lake [5]**, model boat enthusiasts launch their radio-controlled vessels. A bit farther west along JFK Drive is the **Buffalo Paddock [6]**, where a small herd of the shaggy beasts graze under the eucalyptus trees.
In the northwest corner of the park, the **Queen Wilhelmina Tulip Garden [7]**, a small, but beautifully cultivated formal garden *(blooms early spring)*, provides a setting for the **Dutch Windmill**, which pumped water for irrigation during the early years of the park. The windmill was restored for decorative purposes in 1981.
Golden Gate Park's western boundary is delineated by **Ocean Beach**, now administered by the GGNRA *(p 191)*. Though few brave the chill waters without wetsuits, Ocean Beach is a haven for joggers, beachcombers and pensive strollers.

★ The Haight *Map p 201. 🚌7 Haight, 37 Corbett or 43 Masonic.*

Famous worldwide in the late 1960s as Haight-Ashbury, this neighborhood was a center, perhaps *the* center, of the "counterculture," a mishmash of music, mysticism, drugs, clothing, hair styles and alternative lifestyles, much of which was later absorbed into mainstream popular culture.
Since its glory days, "the Haight" has seen many changes. At the end of the 1960s, the peace, love and good vibes culture of marijuana gave way to the harsher realities of heroin, and Haight Street became shabby and depressed. By the end of the 1970s, a wave of gentrification had set in. Storefronts reclaimed from headshops and other purveyors to the hippie subculture were transformed as boutiques and upscale cafes.
Today **Haight Street** between Stanyan Street and Central Avenue is a pleasant, diverse thoroughfare. Facades and marquees are colorfully painted, public art abounds, and residents browse for secondhand records, books and clothing. Victorian-era residences are being reclaimed and rehabilitated on the surrounding streets, and just to the east, **Buena Vista Park** offers shaded strolls on hilly paths, and pleasing views from its summit.

★★ [10] AROUND THE GOLDEN GATE

The narrow, windy and fog-haunted passage connecting San Francisco Bay to the open ocean is the only sea-level entryway to California's interior. Though the precipitous rocky headlands on both the San Francisco and Marin County sides remain free of overwhelming urban development, works of human engineering have for more than two centuries guarded, defended and spanned the Golden Gate's swift waters and the lands at the entrance to San Francisco Bay.

Sights *1 day. Map p 200.*

★★★ **Golden Gate Bridge** – San Francisco's most widely recognized symbol is this graceful Art Deco suspension bridge, spanning the Golden Gate via twin 746ft towers and an intricate tracery of cables supporting a roadway (1.6mi excluding approaches). With its graceful form painted in vibrant "international orange," the bridge attracts the eye irresistibly from any point along the city's northern shore.

Uniphoto

Golden Gate Bridge and Fort Point

Superspan – A bridge across the Golden Gate was proposed as early as 1873, but not until after World War I were design proposals and bids solicited. **Joseph Strauss** of Chicago, a renowned bridge engineer, won with a bid of $17 million. The projected bridge met with opposition from the Southern Pacific Railroad, worried about competition with its Marin County ferry service; and from the military, concerned about obstructed navigation through the Golden Gate. By the time bonds to finance the bridge were issued, the Depression had begun and funding was in short supply. The majority of the bonds were ultimately purchased by the Bank of America *(p 195)*, and construction began in January 1933.

Work on the bridge was difficult and often treacherous. Divers anchoring the immense concrete pier for the south tower in bedrock 100ft under water could operate only during the brief periods between tidal flows surging swiftly in and out of the bay. Those erecting the steel towers faced winds sweeping through the Golden Gate at 40mph and bone-chilling fog alternating rapidly with blinding sunlight. Tragedy struck just three months before completion when a scaffold broke loose and tore through the safety net beneath the bridge, carrying twelve men into the outgoing tide. Only two survived.

On opening day, May 27, 1937, the span was occupied all day by pedestrians as some 200,000 people surged across the bridge on foot. Vehicular traffic was introduced the following day by a formal motorcade, and inaugural celebrations lasted a full week.

Viewing area – *Access from US-101 northbound, or take Lincoln Blvd through the Presidio.* *🚌29 Sunset.* Today the bridge is crossed daily by approximately 100,000 vehicles (both directions). The visitor's viewing area on the San Francisco side offers picture postcard views and interesting historical displays, as well as pedestrian access for those who want to walk across (*about 2.5mi round trip; warm clothing advisable*).

Keeping the Bridge Golden

The job of maintaining the Golden Gate Bridge in its traditional "international orange" is continual: a 31-member crew works full time to sandblast and repaint the entire structure. The process takes a year and requires some 5,000 gallons of paint.

★★ **Marin Headlands** – *Take Alexander Ave exit on US-101; from ramp, turn left, then bear right onto Barry Rd instead of merging into bridge traffic. 🚌76 Marin Headlands (Sunday only).* This windswept landscape of coastal cliffs and hills anchoring the northern end of the Golden Gate Bridge forms a quasi-wilderness adjacent to urban San Francisco. Owing to its strategic importance at the mouth of the bay, the area long remained under the ownership of the US Army and thus was spared commercial development. Today a unit of the GGNRA *(p 191)*, the headlands are accessed by a scenic road offering astounding **views**★★★ of urban San Francisco and the Golden Gate Bridge. The road terminates at Point Bonita Lighthouse. Hiking trails thread the grassy slopes, connecting with other trails leading to the top of MT TAMALPAIS and north to POINT REYES NATIONAL SEASHORE.

★ **The Presidio** – *Entrances at Lombard St (east) or Presidio Ave (south). 🚌29 Sunset or 43 Masonic. Open daily year-round. ♿ 🅿 ☎415-561-3660.* Overlooking the Golden Gate from the San Francisco peninsula's northwest tip, this 1,540-acre military reservation enjoys a **setting**★★ acknowledged to be one of the loveliest in the Bay Area. San Francisco's Presidio combines natural forests with designed landscaping, attractive historic architecture with utilitarian military buildings, and a long and fascinating history with an uncertain future.

Established by the government of New Spain in 1776 as the third and northernmost of California's four garrisons, the complex served the dual function of protecting the Franciscan friars in their quest to convert local Natives, and defending Spain's colonial interests in Alta California against possible invasion from the north by such nations as Russia and Great Britain. After Mexico gained independence from Spain in 1822, the Ppresidio was largely abandoned as the new government turned its attention toward the increasing threat of American incursion from the east. With the American takeover of California and the end of the Mexican War, the threat of invasion was considered diminished and the Presidio was largely abandoned until the advent of the Civil War, when it was rebuilt and regarrisoned to defend California against Confederate takeover.

Having served throughout the 20C as a US Army post, the Presidio was declared surplus to the military's needs in 1988. Late 1994 was the date set for its transfer to the National Park Service as part of the GGNRA, and plans for its future remain indefinite. Today many of its spacious, forested acres are open to the public, laced with some 75mi of scenic byways. **Lincoln Boulevard**, tracing the perimeter of the complex, offers stunning **views** of the Golden Gate Bridge and the Marin Headlands, in addition to glimpses of architecture in styles revealing Mission, Spanish, Georgian and Victorian influences. The Presidio shelters a trove of horticultural treasures as well, including lush forests of cypress, pine and eucalyptus; thickets of vine and ivy; and several rare and endangered plant species.

★ **Presidio Museum** – *Corner of Funston Ave and Lincoln Blvd. Open year-round Wed–Sun. Closed Jan 1, Thanksgiving Day, Dec 25. ☎415-556-0856.* Originally constructed as an army hospital, this white brick and clapboard building (1862), the Presidio's oldest, today presents military and San Francisco history through models, artifacts and photographs. Highlights include dioramas of the original Spanish Presidio, downtown San Francisco as it appeared during the 1906 earthquake and fire, and the 1915 Panama-Pacific International Exposition. Particularly noteworthy is the museum's extensive collection of photographs and memorabilia of the 1906 disaster. The holdings include two of the thousands of earthquake shacks the Army erected for those who had lost their homes. The Presidio itself served as a temporary refuge for some 70,000 displaced residents.

★ **Fort Point National Historic Site** – *Take Lincoln Blvd in the Presidio to Long Ave. Open year-round Wed–Sun. 🅿 ☎415-556-1373. Illustration p 205.* Nestled beneath a giant arch of the Golden Gate Bridge, this imposing bastion (1861) guarded the Golden Gate during the Civil War against the threat of Confederate raids. Fort Point never saw combat, however, and shortly after its construction, the invention of more powerful armaments made its brick ramparts obsolete. The abandoned fort would have been demolished in the early 20C to make way for the Golden Gate Bridge, but for the intervention of Joseph Strauss, the bridge's architect. Establishing his construction headquarters there, he designed an arch to carry the bridge over Fort Point. Today administered by the GGNRA *(p 191)*, the fort welcomes visitors to inspect the three tiers of arched casemates, to note the thickness of the brick walls and to peruse displays and rooms restored to their 19C appearance. The terrace reveals an astounding **view**★★ of the Golden Gate Bridge's massive piers.

★★★ **California Palace of the Legion of Honor** – *Entrance at 34th Ave. 🚌18 46th Ave. Closed for renovation. Scheduled reopening: summer 1995. ☎415-863-3330.* From its commanding hilltop site in the center of Lincoln Park, this stately structure has served as San Francisco's leading repository for works of European, particularly French, artists since the merging and regrouping of the collections of the Fine Arts Museums of San Francisco *(p 201)*. The building is a replica of the Palais de la Légion d'Honneur in Paris (built in 1788 as the Hôtel de Salm) and served as the French pavilion for the 1915 Panama-Pacific International Exposition. Alma Spreckels, wife of San Francisco sugar magnate Adolph Spreckels, was so impressed with the structure and its exhibition of Rodin sculptures that she determined to have a permanent version erected in San Francisco to house a museum of European art. Mrs Spreckels succeeded in drawing the city and wealthy benefactors into her project, and the museum opened in 1924.

The permanent collection includes an outstanding group of cast bronze Rodin **sculptures**, medieval stained glass, 15C Flemish tapestries, 16C German woodcarving and French Impressionist paintings of the early 20C. Works by El Greco, Rembrandt, Rubens and Cézanne are among the collection's highlights.

The museum also presents changing exhibits of works on paper from the Achenbach Foundation for Graphic Arts.

Cliff House – *Take Geary Blvd west to 39th Ave, bear right on Point Lobos Ave to its end.* 🚌 *18 46th Ave or 38 Geary. Open daily year-round.* ✕ ♿ 🅿 ☎*415-556-8642.* One of San Francisco's most venerable tourist attractions, Cliff House has undergone four reincarnations since the first version was erected here in 1858. The most renowned Cliff House was undoubtedly the 7-story, 1896 rendition of a French chateau, commissioned by Adolph Sutro *(below)* but consumed by fire in 1907. The present structure is surpassed by its extraordinary setting: from the craggy cliffs overlooking **Seal Rocks**, the **view**★ of the coast sweeps from the prominent headland of Point Reyes some 30mi to the northwest, to Point San Pedro 15mi to the south. On clear days the **Farallon Islands**, some 32mi offshore, are visible on the horizon. The exterior lower deck features a camera obscura, a giant reflector that projects images of the surrounding view onto an 8ft parabolic screen; and the Musée Mécanique, housing coin-operated player pianos, games and animated displays. The GGNRA **Visitor Center** *(base of Cliff House)* offers detailed maps and information about the entire GGNRA *(p 191; open year-round Mon–Fri; closed major holidays;* ♿ 🅿 ☎*415-556-0560).*

Sutro Heights Park – *On the bluff above the Cliff House. Open daily year-round.* 🅿. Former site of Adolph Sutro's luxurious estate, this grassy bluff offers yet more extensive **views**★★ of the coast and the horizon. In addition to his elegant mansion, Sutro, a German native who garnered a fortune as a mining engineer on the Comstock silver lode, also erected on the property an extensive public baths capable of accommodating upwards of 20,000 people daily. Today, the **Coastal Trail** *(1mi; departs from Cliff House parking lot)* traverses the ruins of Sutro Baths and skirts the bluffs above surf-battered **Land's End**, emerging in the Seacliff neighborhood.

★ 11 MARINA DISTRICT AND PACIFIC HEIGHTS *1/2 day. Map p 201.*

★ Marina District and Cow Hollow

In the mid-19C the sloped valley between Russian Hill and the hills of the Presidio was a lush grassland of dairy farms, popularly known as Cow Hollow. Real estate entrepreneurs purchased the land around 1890, developing the area as a comfortable residential district. By the 1960s Cow Hollow had become a fashionable neighborhood, home to trendy galleries, boutiques, antique stores, upscale restaurants and cafes. Today **Union Street**★ between Van Ness Avenue and Fillmore Street is the district's bustling commercial thoroughfare. *Free parking (2hr limit) on nearby residential streets.*

Following the 1906 earthquake and fire, shallow water off the shore of Cow Hollow was filled in to create new land for the buildings of the 1915 Panama-Pacific International Exposition. When the fair closed, the structures (with the exception of the Palace of Fine Arts) were demolished, to be replaced by a new, middle class residential housing area that became known as the Marina District; its prevailing architectural style echoed the Spanish and Italian Baroque theme of the exposition. Unfortunately, the early-20C landfill was hurriedly executed, a fact not revealed until the 1989 Loma Prieta earthquake, when the ground under some buildings liquefied, causing them to collapse. The neighborhood survived, however, and continues to be regarded as one of the city's more desirable residential locations. **Chestnut Street** *(parallel to Union St, four blocks north)* is pleasant for strolling in the blocks between Divisadero and Fillmore and projects a more settled, stable atmosphere. **Marina Green**, a 10-acre shoreline greensward maintained by the GGNRA *(p 191)*, is popular with joggers, bikers, kite flyers and neighborhood residents in search of a good ball game. Views from the green extend across the bay to the Golden Gate Bridge, and from here, paths traverse the shore as far west as Fort Point *(p 206)*, east through upper Ft Mason to Fisherman's Wharf *(p 188)*.

★ **Palace of Fine Arts** – *Baker and Beach Sts.* 🚌 *28 Sunset.* A historical anomaly amid the contemporary dwellings of the adjacent Marina District, this grandiose rotunda and colonnade were designed by renowned architect Bernard Maybeck to

M. Ueda/Travel Image

Palace of Fine Arts

house art exhibits for the 1915 Panama-Pacific International Exposition. On calm days, the small lagoon spreading from the foot of the rotunda offers charming mirror views. The original structure, built of wood and plaster, was to be torn down at the end of the Exposition, but became so popular that it was spared. By the early 1960s, the elements were taking their toll, and the Palace was replicated in concrete. Note the draped maidens along the colonnade; facing in rather than out, they pose in lamentation of the decline of culture.

★★ **Exploratorium** **[M[1]]** – *Open Memorial Day–Labor Day daily 10am–5pm (Wed 9:30pm), rest of the year Tue–Sun 10am–5pm (Wed 9:30pm). Closed Dec 25. $8.* ✗ ♿ 🅿 *☎415-561-0360.* Located in the annex structure of the Palace of Fine Arts, this innovative museum of science, art and human perception features some 650 exhibits, many of them requiring active participation. Visitors are encouraged to push buttons, activate objects, crank handles and emit sounds to achieve a "hands-on" learning experience. Instructions and explanations accompany each exhibit, and staff members are available to answer questions. The Exploratorium has become a model for science museums nationwide, and new exhibits are continually under development in the extensive workshops along the west wall, visible from the mezzanine level.

★ Pacific Heights

Rivaled only by Nob Hill in the years before the 1906 disaster, Pacific Heights has been San Francisco's most fashionable residential district for more than a century. Topographically, Pacific Heights is the ridge running east-west along Broadway, Pacific and Washington Streets between Van Ness Avenue and the Presidio. Residents on the north side of the crest look down along precipitous streets to the Marina District and the bay beyond. The south side descends more gradually towards Japan Town and the Western Addition. California Street is usually considered to be the southern edge of Pacific Heights.

The grandest Pacific Heights residences line **Broadway** and **Vallejo Street** west of Steiner Street. Highlights include the **Spreckels Mansion** *(2080 Washington)*, commissioned in 1913 by Adolph and Alma Spreckels; and the former **Flood Mansion** *(2222 Broadway)*, built in 1916 for James Leary Flood and presently housing a convent school.

★ **Swedenborgian Church** – *2107 Lyon St. Open daily year-round. Closed major holidays. ☎415-346-6466.* This rustic church (1895) is one of the earliest examples of the Arts and Crafts movement in the West. With ivy-covered brick walls, wooden wainscoting and roof supports of bark-covered madrone trunks, the building reflects the naturalist tenets of Swedenborgianism, a Christian denomination with beliefs rooted in the mystical Biblical interpretations of Swedish philosopher Emanuel Swedenborg. The church was designed by A. Page Brown and Bernard Maybeck; works by American landscape painter William Keith adorn the walls.

12 MISSION DISTRICT

San Francisco's teeming Latino section consists of noisy streets, crowded sidewalks and colorful storefronts occupied by a variety of small businesses, many with signs in Spanish.

Beginning as a village surrounding the Mission Dolores *(below)*, the district was absorbed into the expanding city of San Francisco in the late 19C. The area lost much of its Latino character during that period, as waves of European immigrants, mostly German and Irish, settled in the neighborhood. After World War II, Mexicans and Mexican-Americans returned to the area.

Today new arrivals from Central America reinforce the Mission District's Latino ambience, particularly along **Twenty-Fourth Street**★, where a great variety of small shops, produce markets, restaurants and street murals form the heart of Latino San Francisco. The **Mission Cultural Center** *(2868 Mission St, near corner of 24th St; open year-round Wed–Sun ☎415-821-1155)* houses an art gallery, with changing exhibits on Latino themes, as well as music and dance events. **Dolores Street** is one of the city's most attractive thoroughfares; its median strip was planted in 1910 with five different species of palms by city parks superintendent John McLaren *(p 200)*.

Sights *2hrs. Map p 201.*
BART 16th or 24th St stations. Streetcar J-Church. 🚌 14 Mission.

★ **San Francisco de Asís Mission** – *16th and Dolores Streets. Services held in the adjacent basilica. Open daily year-round. Closed Dec 25. $1.* ♿ 🅿 *☎415-621-8203.* California's sixth mission serves as a distinct reminder of the city's Spanish origins amid the urban development of more recent decades.

Originally located some two blocks to the east on a site selected by Juan Bautista de Anza, the mission was dedicated by Padre Francisco Palóu at a Mass on June 29, 1776, marking the official founding of the city of San Francisco. The mission quickly acquired its nickname, **Mission Dolores**, after a nearby stream which, discovered on the Friday of Sorrows, had been named "Laguna de los Dolores." In 1791 a new chapel was erected on the present site.

Following secularization in 1834, the building served various purposes, but in 1859 was renovated and reconsecrated as a parish church for a congregation composed predominantly of Irish immigrants.

Chapel – Today San Francisco's oldest surviving building, the chapel appears as it did in 1791; its walls were reinforced in the early 20C. The tile roof and bells are original, but the interior was completely re-created in 1859, with a ceiling design based on basket patterns of the local Natives. The ornate altar and statues are of late-18C Mexican origin. Adjacent to the chapel is a larger basilica (1918), which today serves as the parish church. Artifacts in the small **museum** include the mission's baptismal registry (with an entry in Padre Serra's hand), and an ornate tabernacle from the Philippines. Also within the compound is a **cemetery**, where lie the remains of, among others, Luís Antonio Arguello (1784-1830), first native-born governor during the Mexican period; Francisco de Haro (1803-1848), first Mexican *alcalde* (mayor) of Yerba Buena; and José Noé, the last Mexican *alcalde*.

ADDITIONAL SIGHTS

★★ **Twin Peaks** – *Map p 201. 🚌36 Terracita. Bus stop at the base of the hills; steep climb on foot to the summit. Exposed summits can be quite cold, even during the summer months.*
These two high points dominate the western skyline as seen from downtown. Most visitors content themselves with the grand **view**★★★ of the entire eastern side of the city from the parking lot at Christmas Tree Point, though it is possible to climb up the grassy slopes of the north peak (904ft) or the south (922ft), for the panorama to the west as well. Mt Davidson to the south is the city's highest point at 928ft, but a eucalyptus forest obscures the view on the west side.

★ **Haas-Lilienthal House** – *Map p 188. 2007 Franklin Street. 🚌49 Van Ness, 1 California, 45 Union-Stockton. Entrance from passageway along north side of house. Open year-round Wed & Sun. $4. ☎415-441-3004.* One of San Francisco's few Victorian-era residences open to the public, this imposing gray edifice is a historical grace note amid the area's more recent constructions. Unlike the grandiose mansions of the great railroad and mining magnates on Nob Hill, the elegant residence typifies the architectural aspirations of San Francisco's upper-middle class during the 19C. Constructed for William Haas, a prominent San Francisco retailer, the house was donated in 1974 by his descendants to the Foundation for San Francisco's Architectural Heritage. The foundation currently maintains the property as a house museum and headquarters.
The exterior embellishments are exemplary of the Queen Anne style, replete with multi-patterned siding, numerous gables and a deceptive corner tower with windows 10ft above the floor. Rooms on the first and second floors reflect decorative styles ranging from the 1880s to the 1920s and feature rich wainscoting, embossed wallpaper and a sitting-room hearth faced with red Numidian marble.

★ **St Mary's Cathedral** – *Map p 188. Geary and Gough Sts. 🚌38 Geary. ☎415-567-2020, ext 207.* Differing considerably from traditional cathedrals, this enormous concrete edifice (1971, Pietro Belluschi and Pier Luigi Nervi) is square rather than cruciform in floor plan, its four gently curved walls converging to a 190ft peak. Executed by artist Richard Lippold, a contemporary baldachin of shimmering anodized aluminum highlights the breathtaking sanctuary, and ribbons of stained-glass windows traverse the walls to form a cross. *Organ recitals held Sunday afternoons; call for schedule.*

★ **San Francisco Zoo** – *Map p 183. The Great Highway and Sloat Blvd. 🚌18 46th Ave. Open daily year-round. $6.50. ✗ ♿ ☎415-753-7083.* Set on 65 park-like acres near the ocean in the southwest corner of the city, the zoo harbors approximately 300 species, of which 38 are endangered, including Asian elephant, black rhinoceros, Siberian tiger and spectacled bear. The **Primate Discovery Center** features an innovative Nocturnal Gallery recreating the environment of primates active at night, and an extended family of gorillas in a large wooded enclosure. The zoo also exhibits a number of rare snow leopards and an aviary of tropical birds. The Children's Zoo *($1)* is notable for its insect zoo and petting barnyard.

Castro District – *Map p 201. Bounded by Dolores, 23rd, Douglass and 17th Sts.* Centered on the first two blocks of Castro Street south of Market Street, the Castro District lies at the geographical center of San Francisco and is the heart of the city's vibrant gay community.
Formerly a blue-collar and lower middle-class neighborhood, the area experienced a marked change in character in the early 1970s when its residents began putting their property up for sale and relocating to the suburbs. Previously, gay men had created community enclaves in such areas as Haight Ashbury and Polk Street, but their presence had always been somewhat covert. The Castro District, resulting from the 1960s social liberalization as well as from unusual real estate opportunities, was more overt about its new identity, and it was here that gays acquired some of the characteristics of a large and politically powerful group, while creating a prosperous permanent enclave of restored Victorian homes, churches, professional offices and community service organizations.
By 1977 the gay residents of the Castro District were instrumental in electing Harvey Milk, one of their own, to the Board of Supervisors. Milk's life and career were cut short one year later when he and then-mayor **George Moscone** were gunned down in City Hall by City Supervisor Dan White.

Visit – The Castro District is best experienced by strolling along its main thoroughfare, the two blocks of Castro Street south of Harvey Milk Plaza *(intersection of Castro and Market Sts)* where the neighborhood lives its life. The street (and subsequently the district) was named for the **Castro Theater** *(429 Castro St)*; this ornate Spanish Renaissance Revival movie palace (1922, Timothy Pflueger) is a popular neighborhood institution and one of the venues of the San Francisco International Film Festival *(p 248)*.
Harvey Milk's **photo shop** *(573 Castro St)* served during the mid-1970s as the headquarters of the movement that launched Milk's political career. **The Names Project**, founded to commemorate those who have died of AIDS, is the home of the AIDS Memorial Quilt, panels of which are continually exhibited around the country *(2362 Market St, open year-round Tue–Sun; closed Jan 1, Thanksgiving Day, Dec 25; ♿ ☎415-882-5500)*.

Castro Street continues south into **Noe Valley**, a prosperous district of lovingly restored Victorians and intriguing shops along 24th Street between Dolores and Diamond Streets.

★ **Alamo Square** – *Map p 201. Bounded by Fulton, Scott, Hayes and Steiner Sts.* This pleasant, green-lawned square situated amid a somewhat rundown area of the Western Addition, is famous for its **view★★** of the Financial District skyscrapers rising above the row of virtually identical, and impeccably restored Victorians lining its east side. The square forms the core of the Alamo Square Historic District, an area boasting a high concentration of 19C Victorians.

Japantown – *Map p 201. Vicinity of Post and Buchanan Sts.* This district of Japanese restaurants and specialty shops was initially settled by Japanese-Americans prior to their exile to internment camps during World War II *(p 136)*. Few returned to the neighborhood during the postwar period, and in the 1960s the area underwent urban renewal, during which whole blocks of Victorian-era buildings were destroyed.
North of Japan Center, with its Peace Pagoda, a block of Buchanan Street has become a pedestrian mall with a Japanese village architectural theme. The street boasts Japanese art galleries and restaurants, but lacks the historical continuity and immigrant vitality of Chinatown.

San Francisco Fire Department Museum [M[2]] – *Map p 201. 655 Presidio Ave, between Pine and Bush Sts. Open year-round Thu–Sun. Closed major holidays.* ♿ *☎415-861-8000.* This converted firehouse garage (adjacent to present-day Firehouse no. 10) houses a wonderful collection of historic fire engines, including early hand-drawn pump carts. Memorabilia, photos and historical displays tell the stories of several of the city's devastating fires—among them the conflagration of 1906—and heroic figures from San Francisco's firefighting past.

Steepest Streets of San Francisco:

- ***Filbert St between Leavenworth and Hyde Sts (31.5% grade)***
- ***Jones St between Union and Filbert Sts (29% grade)***
- ***Duboce St between Buena Vista and Alpine Sts (27.9% grade)***

EXCURSIONS

★★ **Filoli** – *1/2 day. Map p 183. 30mi south of San Francisco in Woodside. Take I-280 south to Edgewood Road exit and turn right; turn right on Cañada Rd and continue 1.3mi to gate. Visit by guided tour (2hrs) only, Tue–Thu, Sat 10am–3pm (reservations required). Self-guided tours Fri 10am–3pm. Closed major holidays. $8.* ♿ *☎415-366-4640.*
Nestled into the inland side of the Coast Range's heavily wooded foothills is an elegant, 654-acre estate that exemplifies the gracious, cultured lifestyle made possible during the turn of the century by fortunes derived from California's great economic forces: real estate speculation, mining and agriculture.
The property's formal gardens and U-shaped, Georgian Revival mansion (1907, Willis Polk) framed by stately oak trees were commissioned by William Bourn (1857-1936), owner of the vast Empire Gold Mine in GRASS VALLEY. Bourn selected this site for his country home because of its similarity to Muckross House, his family's estate around the Irish Lakes of Killarney. The name of the property derives from a credo Bourn admired: *Fight for a just cause; Love your fellow man; Live a good life.* After the deaths of Mr Bourn and his wife in the 1930s, Filoli passed into the possession of its only other owner, William Roth, who died in 1963. His widow donated the estate in 1975 to the National Trust for Historic Preservation.

Mansion – The ground floor is appointed with furniture and art from the Bourn and Roth families as well as gifts and pieces loaned from various museums. House tours commence in the reception room, where a 17ft by 28ft Persian carpet (19C), woven over three generations, covers the floor. The kitchen features an impressive stove taken from an ocean liner of the Matson Navigation Company, owned by Mrs Roth's father. A 16C Flemish tapestry hangs in the dining room, and the grand ballroom reveals French crystal chandeliers and large murals of the Bourn estate in Ireland.

Gardens – Designed according to Italian and French styles by Bruce Porter with assistance from Isabella Worn, this 16-acre botanical wonder successfully combines the formal with the natural. The gardens comprise several distinct areas, each offering an individual menu of horticultural delights to appreciate. Some 30 species of flowering plants bloom seasonally, beginning in spring with rhododendrons, wisteria, magnolias and azaleas. Summer sports clematis, hydrangeas, cyclamens and more than 500 roses, and autumn brings chrysanthemums, Japanese maples and gingko trees. More than 200 sculpted Irish yews are a striking visual component of the gardens, and six varieties of fruit trees flourish on the grounds. The cutting garden and greenhouse are the source of all floral arrangements displayed in the mansion.

★ **Marine World Africa USA** – *1 day. Map p 183. 35mi northeast of San Francisco in Vallejo. Take I-80 east across the Bay Bridge and continue east and north to Vallejo. Exit Hwy 37 west (Marine World Parkway) and continue 1mi to park. High-speed catamaran ferry service departs from Pier 41 at Fisherman's Wharf ☎800-229-2784 or ☎415-546-2896. Open Memorial Day–Labor Day daily, rest of the year Wed–Sun. Closed Thanksgiving Day, Dec 25. $23.95.* ✂ ♿ *☎707-643-6722.* This 160-acre, pleasantly landscaped wildlife park and oceanarium is part impressive zoo, part informative, outdoor museum. Operated by the nonprofit Marine World Foundation, the park offers shows and exhibits to entertain as well as educate visitors about conservation issues.

Marine World began as a modest theme park in 1968 in Redwood City, 25mi south of San Francisco. In 1972 the park merged with Southern California-based Africa USA, and animals from that park were moved to the Redwood City location. Further growth necessitated relocation in 1986 to the present site in Vallejo, and today Marine World Africa USA annually welcomes nearly 2 million people.

Visit – A day at Marine World Africa USA is best structured around the nine live performance shows presented up to three times daily in various outdoor amphitheaters *(shows last 20-30min; guidebook with map and daily schedule available at entrance)*. Prominent among the live performance offerings are the **Killer Whale and Dolphin Show**, in which two killer (orca) whales (10,000lbs and 6,000lbs) and several dolphins perform a variety of natural-behavior stunts; **Wildlife Theater**, where exotic animals from around the world are presented in a manner that furthers appreciation for endangered species; and the **Water Ski Show**, showcasing the park's ski team in a myriad of waterborne stunts *(Apr-Oct)*. Visitors can pass through a transparent viewing tunnel as sharks swim overhead in **Shark Experience**★; hand-feed giraffes at the **Giraffe Feeding Dock**; and team up in a game of tug-of-war with pachyderms at **Elephant Encounter**. Also worth visiting is the innovative children's playground, where young visitors can play amid balls that fill a life-size replica of a blue whale.

San Rafael Arcángel Mission – *30min. Map p 183. 15mi north of San Francisco in San Rafael. Take US-101 north to Central San Rafael exit. Mission located at 5th Ave and A St. Open daily year-round. ♿ ☎415-454-8141.* The 20th and penultimate mission of the California chain was founded in 1817 in the hills north of San Francisco Bay as an *asistencia* to Mission Dolores in San Francisco. Owing to the location's warmer, drier climate, the branch mission was used as a sanatorium for those Natives in San Francisco who were in failing health, and was named for the patron saint of bodily healing. The establishment of a mission here was also intended to solidify the Spanish claim to the territory against incursion by the Russians, who had by then settled FORT ROSS on the Sonoma coast.
In 1833, San Rafael was the first of the California missions to be secularized; the buildings were razed in 1870. The current replica on the site dates from 1949; a recorded narration in the church provides brief historical details, and fragments of the original church are on display in the adjacent gift shop.

★★ **Wine Country** – *1-3 days. Description p 233.*

★★ **Point Reyes National Seashore** – *1 1/2 days. Description p 145.*

★★ **North Coast** – *5 days. Description p 126.*

★ **Berkeley** – *1/2 day. Description p 35.*

★ **Oakland** – *1 day. Description p 131.*

★ **Sausalito** – *1 day. Description p 225.*

★ **San Jose** – *1 day. Description below.*

Palo Alto – *2 hrs. Description p 140.*

★ SAN JOSE San Francisco Bay Area Pop 782,248

Map of Principal Sights p 2 Tourist Office ☎408-283 8833

Now California's third largest city and the self-proclaimed "capital of Silicon Valley," San Jose bustles with high-tech prosperity. In its revitalized downtown, stately old buildings mix with modern high-rises in a park-like setting of palm-lined plazas and avenues. Spread through the city are a number of unusual museums, from innovative new ones to "mysterious" older ones.

From Crops to Computers – This site in the fertile Santa Clara Valley was chosen in 1777 by Spanish administrators for the founding of El Pueblo San José de Guadalupe, the first civilian settlement in Alta California. The new farming community, on the banks of the Guadalupe River, supplied food to the soldiers quartered in the presidios in SAN FRANCISCO and MONTEREY. Twenty years later, the San José Mission *(p 213)* was founded some 13mi to the north. In 1849, three years after the American takeover of California, members of the state's Constitutional Convention chose San Jose as the state capital, an honor it held for several months before the capital was moved to Vallejo.
From the mid-19C to the mid-20C, agriculture remained San Jose's chief industry. The abundant flowering orchards attracted weekend tourists who came from throughout the Bay Area to enjoy "the Garden City in the Valley of Heart's Delight." In the postwar period, the character of Santa Clara County changed dramatically as structures housing electronics industries began to sprout in place of the orchards, and by the late 1960s, "Silicon Valley" had encompassed San Jose. Such computer giants as IBM, Hewlett-Packard and Apple developed facilities in the city and in neighboring communities. San Jose today ranks as the 11th largest city in the US.

SIGHTS *1 day*

★ **San Jose Museum of Art** – *110 S. Market St. Open year-round Wed–Sun. Closed Jan 1, Thanksgiving Day, Dec 25. $5. ✗ ♿ ☎408-294-2787.* Established in 1933 in the city's old sandstone Richardsonian Romanesque post office (1892) and expanded in 1991 with a modern wing of glass and concrete, the museum features nationally significant traveling shows and changing exhibits highlighting the art of the 20C. Until the turn of the century, the museum will have on view rotating **exhibits** of masterworks on loan from the collection of the Whitney Museum of American Art in New York City.

★ **The Tech Museum of Innovation** – *145 W. San Carlos St. Open year-round Tue–Sun. Closed Jan 1, Thanksgiving Day, Dec 25. $6.* ✗ ♿ ☎*408-279-7150.* Formerly known as "The Garage" and now simply as "The Tech," this state-of-the art, interactive exhibit hall is designed to encourage the spirit of innovative curiosity characteristic of the original techno-tinkerers of Silicon Valley. Aimed at the "information generation"—a loose designation for persons in 4th grade and up—the museum, which opened in 1990, takes a playful, participatory approach to fields such as microelectronics, space exploration, robotics and biotechnology. *Presently housed in a wing of the former convention center, the museum is scheduled to move to a new building at the corner of Park Ave and Market St in 1998.*

★ **Children's Discovery Museum** – *180 Woz Way. Open year-round Tue–Sun. Closed major holidays and first week of September. $6.* ✗ ♿ ☎*408-298-5437.* The whimsical, building-block-like lavender museum opened in 1990 in Guadalupe River Park. Its hands-on exhibits for families and school-age children explore the themes of "community, connections and creativity." Highlights include **Streets**, an intersecting corridor where kids can explore fire trucks, culverts and the ways in which communities work; interactive arts and nature exhibits; and activity areas designed to teach cultural diversity. A variety of performers are featured in the museum's theater.

Peralta Adobe – *184 W. St. John St. Visit by guided tour (1hr) only, year-round Wed–Sun. $5.* ♿ ☎*408-993-8182.* Ensconced amid the modern structures of downtown, this early-19C adobe represents the last vestige of San Jose's Spanish Colonial past. Surrounded by a walled yard and fronted by a verandah, the modest single-story house, now unfurnished, was the residence of Luís María Peralta, whose vast Rancho San Antonio covered much of the East Bay *(p 131)*.

★ **San Jose Historical Museum** – *1600 Senter St, in Kelley Park, 2mi southeast of downtown. Open daily year-round. Closed Jan 1, Thanksgiving Day, Dec 25. $4.* ♿ ☎*408-287-2290.* This 25-acre complex is intended to re-create turn-of-the century life in San Jose, when the town was the hub of a prosperous farming region. The museum currently comprises some 20 historical homes and shops, a third of which are re-creations; the remainder were relocated from their original sites. Restoration is ongoing.

Centered around a grassy shaded plaza, the complex is notable for its 115ft reproduction of the famous **San Jose Electric Tower**, a fanciful metal-beamed pyramid of street lights; and the **H.H. Warburton Doctors Office**, with its medical and dental paraphernalia. Other highlights include the **Print Shop**, where traditional typesetting and printing techniques are demonstrated; and a brick reproduction of the city's **Chinese Temple**, featuring an elaborately carved Cantonese wooden altar from the original 1880s temple.

★ **Japanese Friendship Garden** – *Adjacent to the Historical Museum in Kelley Park. Open daily year-round.* ♿ ☎*408-277-5254.* The meticulously landscaped 6.5 acres is modeled after the Korakuen Garden in Okayama, Japan, San Jose's sister city. Winding paths lead past waterfalls, ornamental rock formations and a variety of flora, including flowering trees and shrubs and carefully placed conifers. The centerpiece of the serene gardens, a large pool where brightly colored koi flash by, is spanned by a lovely Moon Bridge.

Winchester Mystery House – 525 S*outh Winchester Blvd. Visit by guided tour (2hrs 30min) only, daily year-round. $12.50.* ✗ ♿ ☎*408-247-2101.* This strange, rambling 160-room Victorian hodgepodge is the creation of Sarah Winchester, widow of rifle magnate William Wirt Winchester. After purchasing an 8-room San Jose farmhouse in 1884, she added to it compulsively until her death in 1922. Local legend avers that Mrs Winchester was guided in her architectural excesses by the ghosts of those who had lost their lives to Winchester firearms. Now largely unfurnished, the house is notable for its collection of Tiffany and European **art glass**. The **Historic Firearms Museum** on the grounds displays an international collection of pistols and rifles.

Rosicrucian Park – *1324 Naglee Ave, at the intersection with Park Ave.* Filling a 5-acre city block, this complex of Egyptian- and Moorish-style buildings, statues, and gardens serves as headquarters for the English Grand Lodge of the Rosicrucian Order, AMORC (Ancient and Mystical Order Rosae Crucis). First gaining widespread recognition in 17C Europe, the non-sectarian organization now has a worldwide membership devoted to individual spiritual development through the combined study of "the ancient mysteries and the modern sciences."

Rosicrucian Park was established in 1927, when the order's Imperator, H. Spencer Lewis, established the organization's headquarters in San Jose, drawn by the city's pleasant, semi-rural character, its climate, and its proximity to the facilities of OAKLAND and San Francisco. The grounds now house university, research and administrative buildings; an auditorium; a planetarium; and a public museum.

★★ **Egyptian Museum and Planetarium** – *Open year-round daily 9am–5pm. Closed Jan 1, Thanksgiving Day, Dec 25. $6.* ✗ ☎*408-947-3636.* Modeled after the Temple of Amon at Karnak, the exterior is dominated by a columned entryway and gold-paneled doors incised with hieroglyphs. The interior features one of the most extensive displays of Egyptian and Mesopotamian artifacts on the West Coast, numbering some 5,000 pieces. Note in particular the display on mummification *(gallery A)*, with

painted coffins; **sarcophagi**; human and animal remains, including an unsheathed, mummified body; and a full-scale reproduction of a Middle Kingdom **Rock Tomb** *(accessible by guided tour only).*
Displays of Egyptian pottery, jewelry, glass, funerary objects, writing implements, and statues of deities *(galleries B, C, & D)* range from the pre-Dynastic period (4800 BC) to the Coptic period (late 2C–mid-7C AD) and include Babylonian, Sumerian and Assyrian cylinder seals and cuneiform tablets.
The planetarium presents shows ranging from the mythologies and star lore of ancient peoples to recent astronomical discoveries.

EXCURSIONS *Map p 183*

San José de Guadalupe Mission – *13mi north of San Jose in Fremont. Take I-680 to second Mission Blvd exit and turn right on Mission Blvd. Open year-round daily. Closed Jan 1, Easter Sunday, Thanksgiving Day, Dec 25. $1. ♿ ☎510-657-1797.* Set in the rural outskirts of Fremont, this 14th mission in the California chain was founded by Padre Fermín Lasuén in 1797 and named for St Joseph. The mission's first permanent adobe church was completed in 1809. Before secularization in 1834, San José was one of the most prosperous missions in California. During the Gold Rush, the mission served as a rooming house and general store for gold seekers on their way to the southern mother lode mines. In 1858 the mission complex was returned to the Catholic Church, but a massive earthquake ten years later destroyed the old adobe church, and a wooden Gothic-style structure was erected in its place. In the early 1980s, work began on the careful reconstruction of the original adobe church that occupies the site today.

Visit – Within the simple, unadorned exterior walls, the church interior reflects the 1833-1840 period, featuring an ornate gold-leaf replica of the reredos and historic **statuary**. Note the statue of St Joseph (c.1600) from Spain and that of the Virgin (18C) from Mexico; rear side altars display statues of Christ (early 19C) and of St Bonaventure (1808). The hammered copper baptismal font (1830s) was painted by Augustín Davila, painter of the interior of the original church.
A small garden separates the church from the original adobe **padres' quarters**, now housing a museum of mission history featuring Native and church artifacts.

Santa Clara de Asís Mission – *2.5mi northwest of San Jose, on the grounds of Santa Clara University. From San Jose, follow The Alameda to university entrance. Open daily year-round. ♿ ☎408-554-4023.* Established on the banks of the Guadalupe River in 1777, the eighth mission was founded as an additional outpost in the vicinity of San Francisco Bay, but was moved in 1781 to its present site on higher ground. Padre Junípero Serra officiated at the laying of the cornerstone for an impressive adobe church that was completed in 1784. Surrounded by fertile lands, the mission prospered until an earthquake destroyed the complex in 1812. A new church, completed in 1814, served as a mission, then parish chapel until it was destroyed by fire in 1926. The current building resembles the original 1784 adobe.

Visit – Offset by a campanile, the **church** exterior features statues of saints and a roof covered in clay tiles gleaned from the ruins of earlier mission structures. Today encased in redwood, the wooden cross standing in front of the church dates to the 1777 founding of the mission. The painted ceiling of the Victorian-style interior replicates the original design of Mexican artist Augustín Davila.
The simple **St Francis Chapel** *(behind the main sanctuary)* still contains an original wall, ceiling and flooring, and to the left of the church lies a landscaped **quadrangle**, where a number of plants survive from the mission days (olive trees, roses and wisteria).

De Saisset Museum – *On the grounds of Santa Clara University, across from entrance to Santa Clara Mission (above). Open year-round Tue–Sun. Closed major holidays, and between exhibits. ♿ ☎408-554-4528.* Since 1955, this Mission-style building, named for its benefactor Isabel de Saisset, has functioned as a university museum devoted to art and history. The main level features temporary exhibits of selections from the museum's permanent collection of European and American art from the 16C to the 20C, and Asian and African art. Notable among the holdings are works by Dürer, Turner and Chase, as well as contemporary photographs by Ansel Adams, Imogen Cunningham, Edward Weston and Annie Liebovitz. The **California History Collection** *(lower level)* covers the period before European arrival through the mid-19C. Spanish coins and crucifixes from the mission's 1781 cornerstone are displayed here.

★ SAN JUAN BAUTISTA Central Coast Pop 1,570

Map of Principal Sights p 2 Tourist Office ☎408-623-2454

Nestled in the foothills of the Gabilan Mountains, this pleasant historic mission village is dominated by two incongruous elements: a serene mission complex and the San Andreas Fault, which runs along its northeastern edge. With its simple adobe and board-and-batten architecture, San Juan Bautista retains the flavor of a 19C farming community. The town lies north of the SALINAS VALLEY, amid a rich agricultural region dotted with small towns.

Historical Notes – In May 1797, a small contingent of Spanish soldiers arrived in this area to erect a chapel and other buildings, in preparation for the establishment of a new mission. Located here because of the region's large Native population, the mission proved highly successful, and by 1814 a town had begun to grow up around it. With the 1834 secularization of the mission, the town briefly became known as San Juan de Castro, after its civil administrator, José Tiburcio Castro. In the 1850s and 1860s, the town burgeoned with new settlers from the East and as a critical way station and supply center at the intersection of major north-south and east-west stage routes. However, the Southern Pacific Railroad passed San Juan by in 1876, and the town's boom abruptly ended.

The original plaza and surrounding historic buildings now form the San Juan Bautista State Historic Park, though the mission complex remains in Church hands and continues to function as a parish. In recent decades, the mission and park have attracted increasing numbers of tourists and the town itself, again a popular travel stop, offers shops and amenities.

SIGHTS *2hrs*

★★ **San Juan Bautista Mission** – Arriving here in June of 1797, Padre Fermín Lasuén dedicated this site as California's 15th mission, naming it for St John the Baptist. The Native population in the area responded positively to the padres, and the mission's growth was rapid: by 1800 some 500 Natives were living here, and numerous structures had been built, among them a church, monastery and barracks. Unfortunately, the mission site bordered the San Andreas fault, and the buildings were thus extremely vulnerable to earthquakes. A series of temblors in 1800 damaged buildings, including the church, and in 1803, construction began on a grand new adobe church that was completed in 1812.

Following secularization, the mission continued to offer Mass, and in 1859 was returned to the Catholic diocese. The church suffered severe earthquake damage in 1906, but was repaired, and remains today the largest church on the mission chain. The structure underwent a major restoration in 1976.

Visit – *Open daily year-round 9:30am-5pm.♿ ☎408-623-24330.* A series of arches graces the facade of the single-story adobe **padres' quarters**, which fronts a walled garden and today houses a small museum of mission artifacts and a re-created mission kitchen, dining room and parlor.

The L-shaped adobe **church** is offset by a bell tower added in 1976. The church interior is distinctive for its three naves, separated by frescoed arches. The ornate designs painted on the interior walls and the reredos were executed in 1820 by an American sailor, Thomas Doak, who jumped ship in MONTEREY and undertook the commission in exchange for room and board. Doak is believed to be the first US citizen to settle in California.

The cemetery contains the graves of some 4,000 neophytes. The steep slope rising behind the cemetery wall actually marks the San Andreas fault line. A small portion of the original pavement of the El Camino Réal, the King's Highway that traversed this part of California *(p 23)*, lies to the north of the cemetery.

★ **San Juan Bautista State Historic Park** – *Entrance tickets available at Plaza Hotel.* The grassy **plaza** fronting the mission is bordered on the south and east by the state park complex of mid-19C buildings. The large **Plaza Hotel**, originally a single-story adobe structure, was built in 1814 as a mission barracks and converted to a hotel in the 1850s by Angelo Zanetta, who topped it with a wooden second story. It contains re-created period rooms, including a **saloon** with the original carved wood bar.

The lovely adobe **Castro House** retains its 1814 appearance on the exterior, but the interior reflects the 1870s period, when the structure was home to the Breen family, survivors of the ill-fated Donner Party *(p 230)*. **Plaza Hall**, built as a single-story barracks, was also expanded in 1868 by Zanetta, who hoped it would be chosen as the new county courthouse. When this did not occur, the structure became the Zanetta home and now reflects the period of the family's occupancy. The stables, blacksmith shop and washhouse display additional 19C artifacts.

EXCURSIONS

Gilroy – Pop 31,487. *14mi northwest of San Juan Bautista via US-101. Map p 2.* The "Garlic Capital of the World," Gilroy anchors the southern end of the fertile Santa Clara Valley. Beyond its residential streets stretch garlic fields whose bounty the town celebrates each summer with the popular annual **Gilroy Garlic Festival**.

Castroville – Pop 5,272. *15mi west of San Juan Bautista via Hwy 156.* Set amid a sea of artichoke fields, this small wayside community bills itself as the "Artichoke Center of the World"; surrounding fields produce 90 percent of the nation's 'choke crop. Castroville's annual festival honoring the thistle delicacy occurs the third week in September.

★★ SAN JUAN CAPISTRANO MISSION Orange County

Map of Principal Sights p 4 Tourist Office ☎714-493-4700

Ruins of a large stone church lend a mysterious and romantic air to California's seventh mission, anchoring the quiet town of San Juan Capistrano in the southwest corner of Orange County. Nicknamed the "Jewel of the Missions" for its beautiful site and for its impressive church, San Juan Capistrano ranked among the most prosperous of California's missions and was home to 1,361 neophytes during its peak years. Both town and mission are renowned for the **swallows** that arrive here each year on March 19 from their winter nesting grounds in Argentina; their annual return is celebrated by a popular festival.

Historical Notes – Founded by Padre Serra *(p 22)* in 1776, San Juan Capistrano prospered, owing to the surrounding valley's favorable soil and climate and to the thriving hide-and-tallow trade that furnished a market for mission-raised cattle. By 1796 work was begun on a magnificent stone edifice to accommodate the mission's burgeoning neophyte population. Completed in 1806, the **Great Stone Church** stood only six years before being toppled by an earthquake in 1812.
Following secularization the mission population gradually declined from a peak of 1400 neophytes, and in 1845 the buildings passed into private ownership. Deeded back to the Church by Abraham Lincoln in 1865 *(p 23)*, the mission underwent numerous unsuccessful restoration attempts, but work begun in 1920 is largely responsible for its present appearance. Today operated by the Church as a historic site, the mission is also the focus of continuing archaeological research; excavation pits are visible about the property.

Visit *2hrs*

Intersection of Ortega Hwy and Camino Capistrano in downtown San Juan Capistrano. Open daily year-round 8:30am-5pm. Closed Good Friday, Thanksgiving Day, Dec 25. $4. ♿ ☎714-248-2049.

Main Complex – *Entrance on Ortega Hwy.* Dominating the mission's entrance courtyard, the **ruins** of the Great Stone Church reveal the size and splendor that made the cross-shaped edifice the grandest in the mission chain. Its 65ft-high roof was topped by seven domes and a bell tower that could be seen from 10mi away. Only the sanctuary was left intact after the 1812 earthquake that collapsed the ceiling onto the congregation, killing 40 neophytes. The church's original four bells now hang in a low wall adjacent to the ruins, and the nearby garden shows remnants of original Romanesque arches, door frames and lintels. *Church ruins currently undergoing restoration; scheduled completion 1999.*
Three rooms in the west wing of the central courtyard today display items from the San Juan Capistrano's Native, mission and rancho periods. Behind the west wing lies the factory area where workers pressed olives and grapes, tanned leather, forged metal and made soap from tallow.
Occupying the courtyard's east wing is the mission's original chapel (1777). Today known as the **Serra Church**, it is thought to be the only remaining building in California in which Serra offered Mass. The Baroque reredos from Barcelona, dating from the 17C, was added in 1924.

Surrounding Streets – The streets extending north and west of the mission reveal several historically and architecturally noteworthy structures. The **Garcia Adobe** *(31861 Camino Capistrano)* is Orange County's only surviving Monterey Colonial Style structure (1840s). The lovely **San Juan Capistrano Regional Library** (1983), designed by prominent architect Michael Graves, offers a post-Modern interpretation of the mission style, with its earth toned colors, thick walls and arched metal canopy above the main entrance staircase.

SAN LUIS OBISPO Central Coast Pop 41,958

Map p 43 Tourist Office ☎805-781-2777

Nestled at the southern foot of the Santa Lucia range halfway between LOS ANGELES and SAN FRANCISCO, this small bustling city grew up around the mission that Padre Junípero Serra founded overlooking La Cañada de los Osos ("Valley of the Bears") in 1772. A rich agricultural area in its early years, San Luis Obispo burgeoned into a regional merchandising and market center with the 1894 arrival of the Southern Pacific Railroad. Artifacts and historic photographs that trace the area's history can be seen in the **San Luis Obispo County Historical Museum** *(696 Monterey St; open year-round Wed–Sun; closed major holidays ☎805-543-0638).* The county seat since 1850, San Luis Obispo today derives its revenues from government, tourism, retailing, agriculture, and from the presence of California Polytechnic State University.

SIGHTS *1/2 day*

San Luis Obispo de Tolosa Mission – *782 Monterey St. Open daily year-round. $1. ♿ ☎805-543-6850.* Padre Serra chose a fertile spot between two creeks on which to construct the fifth mission, which he named for St Louis, Bishop of Toulouse, France in the 13C. Ravaged by three fires in ten years, the first buildings, constructed of tule, adobe and tar, were rebuilt with fireproof tile roofs by 1794.
The mission became self-sufficient in the late 18C, raising herds of livestock and producing ample farm crops. A 40-year period of decline began with a severe earthquake in 1830, and was exacerbated by the secularization of mission lands in 1834. As the mission's centennial year approached, a renovation effort, influenced by the New England style of Victorian architecture that was popular at the time,

drastically altered the appearance of the buildings. In the late 19C, an L-shaped brick wing was added to the side of the church to accommodate the swelling number of parishioners. The site's present restoration began in 1933.

Visit – The mission **church** (1793) features a unique vestibule-belfry; Peruvian bells, cast in 1820, hang in the three openings cut into its front wall. In the sanctuary, a carved wooden reredos painted with turkey feathers to resemble green marble adorns the area behind the altar. The statue of St Louis in the center niche and hand-hewn oak rafters represent some of the building's remaining original elements. Adjacent to the church building, the **museum** exhibits a well-presented collection of religious and historical objects, featuring vestments, altar pieces, statuary, tools and clothing that belonged to the area's early settlers. Several rooms are devoted to a fine group of **Chumash artifacts**★, which includes early pottery, stone tools, jewelry and baskets.

Downtown – *Maps available at Chamber of Commerce, 1039 Chorro St.* A road once ran through what is now **Mission Plaza**, the area along San Luis Creek that was built in 1961. Centered around the plaza, the downtown area boasts a variety of architecture, from mid-19C adobes to the Art Deco **Fremont Theater** *(1035 Monterey St)*. The 110-year-old **Ah Louis Store** *(800 Palm St)*, built of hand-fashioned bricks by Chinese merchant Ah Louis, once functioned as market, bank and post office for the Chinese laborers who dug railroad tunnels through Cuesta Pass.

A local landmark off US-101, the **Madonna Inn** *(100 Madonna Rd)* embodies owner Alex Madonna's idea of eclectic excess in its remarkable decor.

★ **Cuesta Ridge** – *Take US-101 north 5mi; turn left on unmarked road at the top of Cuesta Grade.* This one-lane, pot-holed road climbs for 5mi along the ridge overlooking the Atascadero hills *(north)* and the Santa Lucia Wilderness *(east)*. A dirt turnout *(1.6mi)* along the road commands a stunning **view**★★ of the 21-million-year-old "Seven Sisters" peaks *(p 44)*, ending in a silhouette of Morro Rock against the blue Pacific.

★★ SAN LUIS REY DE FRANCIA MISSION San Diego County

Map of Principal Sights p 4 Tourist Office ☎619-721-1101

Occupying a sheltered valley some 5mi from the coast in northern San Diego County, the 18th mission was a vast, architecturally impressive complex which at its height ranked among the largest of the Catholic outposts in the New World. Established to bridge the long distance between the missions at SAN DIEGO and SAN JUAN CAPISTRANO, the "King of the Missions" was named for 13C King Louis IX of France, who was canonized for his crusades to the Holy Land.

Historical Notes – Founded on June 13, 1798, by Padre Fermín Lasuén, the mission prospered from the start, owing to the compliance of the local Luiseño Natives, and to the able direction of Padre Antonio Peyri, an effective pastor who possessed exceptional architectural talent. Throughout his 34-year tenure, expansion and construction were almost continuous; by the time of his departure for Spain in 1832, Mission San Luis Rey boasted one of the loveliest churches on the mission chain and a quadrangle that sprawled over six acres, with fields and pastures extending in a 15mi radius. By the time of secularization, some 2,800 neophytes were in residence here, raising livestock and grain, and producing butter, candles, soap, leather, wine, oil and cloth.

Following secularization, local Californios rapidly tricked the resident neophytes into selling the mission lands for extremely low prices. US soldiers were quartered here during the 1850s, but in 1865 ownership was restored to the Catholic Church by Abraham Lincoln, and the mission housed a Franciscan monastery in the late 19C. Today it serves an active parish community.

VISIT *1hr*

40mi north of San Diego via I-5 and Hwy 76 (Mission Ave). 4050 Mission Ave, San Luis Rey. Open year-round Mon–Sat 10am–4:30pm, Sun noon–4:30pm. Closed Jan 1, Thanksgiving Day, Dec 25. $3. ✗ ♿ *☎619-757-3651.*

Complex and Grounds – The peaked, scalloped white facade of Peyri's noble structure rises above the roof line, and pilasters flank the door. A domed bell tower crowns the right front corner; early drawings suggest that Peyri may have intended to eventually balance it with a second tower.

The church anchors a 2-story cloister that once extended 500ft on each side; 12 arches remain of the 32 that formerly graced the front wall. In the **museum**, displays recounting local and mission history are arranged thematically throughout the cloister's eastern section. The mission boasts one of the largest collections of old Spanish **vestments**★ in the US, and the only surviving walking staff and padre's hat from the mission era. Upon exiting the museum, step into the small cloister *(left)* to view a model showing the appearance of the original complex.

The restored **church**★★, the second of two cruciform churches on the mission chain (the other was at SAN JUAN CAPISTRANO MISSION), was designed to accommodate 1,000 neophytes and measures 180ft long, 28ft wide and 30ft high. The crossing is topped by a wooden dome unique among the California missions; its 8-sided lantern incorporates 144 panes of glass. In the vaulted and brightly painted baptistry, the original baptismal font designed for the mission is still in use.

Across the street from the mission is a large and beautifully restored **lavanderia** (laundry), formerly fed by two springs that spouted through the side gargoyles.

Excursion

San Antonio de Pala Asistencia Mission – *20mi east of San Luis Rey Mission via Hwy 76. Open year-round Tue–Sun. Closed major holidays. $2.* ♿ *☎619-742-3317.* The only remaining mission still true to its original purpose of serving the local Native population, this small outpost on the grounds of the Pala Indian Reservation was founded in 1815 as a branch of San Luis Rey Mission, and at its peak was home to some 1,300 neophytes. Pala's isolated location spared it some of the scavenging that stripped other mission buildings in the years following secularization, and ownership was returned to the Catholic Church in 1903. The dark, narrow chapel interior reveals drawings of Native motifs, restored after an overzealous pastor whitewashed them in 1903.

★★ SANTA BARBARA Central Coast — Pop 85,571

Map p 218

Red-tile roofs, whitewashed stucco buildings and palm-fringed beaches create a distinctly Mediterranean atmosphere in this chic, yet easygoing Southern California city. Arrayed along a coastal ledge and extending up into the hills between the Pacific Ocean and the Santa Ynez Mountains some 90mi northwest of LOS ANGELES, Santa Barbara relishes the reputation it has enjoyed since the 19C as a fashionable vacation spot.

Spanish Beginnings – Sixty years after Juan Rodríguez Cabrillo entered the waters now known as the Santa Barbara Channel, King Philip III of Spain dispatched Sebastián Vizcaíno with a fleet of three ships in search of a good harbor off the California coast *(p 22)*. Vizcaíno arrived here on the feast of Saint Barbara (December 4, 1602), prompting the ship's friar to name the channel for the 4C martyr from Asia Minor.

Following Vizcaíno's voyage, the Spanish did not return to Alta California for some 150 years. In 1782 Padre Junípero Serra, accompanied by a regiment of Spanish soldiers, sailed some nine leagues (roughly 31mi) north from SAN BUENAVENTURA MISSION and consecrated an oak grove overlooking the ocean as the site of the fourth and last Spanish military fortress on the coast. El Presidio de Santa Bárbara *(p 219)* formed the core of the small community, originally composed of soldiers and members of the Chumash tribe that had inhabited the area for some 10,000 years.

From Settlement to City – An increasing number of colonists poured into Santa Barbara during the turbulent years of Mexican rule. After California finally fell to the Americans in 1846, Yankee settlers looking for gold and cheap ranch land added to their ranks. Soon 1- and 2-story wood-frame structures outnumbered the adobes surrounding the presidio, creating the appearance of a New England coastal town. By the late 19C, the construction of Stearns Wharf *(p 218)* and the addition of a new branch of the Southern Pacific Railroad brought wealthy Easterners to Santa Barbara for its mild climate and health-promoting mineral springs.

The city began its architectural transformation from New England Victorian to Spanish Colonial Revival in the 1920s, when a group of citizens took an interest in reclaiming their Spanish heritage. **El Paseo** *(814 State St)*, a downtown shopping arcade designed after a rural Andalusian village, became the first major development to be built in the new style. When a severe earthquake leveled much of the business district in 1925, residents seized the opportunity to reconstruct the city in a style reminiscent of its Spanish roots; the showpiece of this effort is the stately Santa Barbara County Courthouse *(p 219)*, which resembles a Moorish castle.

Today this vibrant city thrives mainly on tourism and agriculture. Local educational institutions, including the University of California, Santa Barbara; Santa Barbara City College; and the prestigious Brooks Institute of Photography, also impact the area's economy.

Practical Information — Area Code: 805

Getting There – From **Los Angeles** (95mi): I-110 east to US-101 north. From **San Francisco** (316mi): US-101 south. **Santa Barbara Municipal Airport** (SBA): domestic flights ☎683-4011. Taxi service ($22 to downtown area) and hotel courtesy shuttles. Major rental car agencies *(p 253)*. Amtrak **train** station: 209 State St ☎800-872-7245. Greyhound **bus** station: 34 Carrillo St ☎800-231-2222.

Getting Around – Public parking lots located throughout the city, first 90min free. **Downtown-Waterfront Shuttle** offers free transportation around downtown and waterfront (year-round daily, every 10–30min depending on location) ☎683-3702. **Santa Barbara Trolley** offers narrated transport to major attractions throughout the city (year-round daily, every 90min; no service Jan 1, Thanksgiving Day, Dec 25; $4) ☎965-0353.

Visitor Information – **Santa Barbara Chamber of Commerce** visitor information centers: **Beachfront Information Center,** 1 Santa Barbara St (open Memorial Day–Labor Day daily 9am–6pm, rest of the year 5pm closing) ☎965-3021; **Downtown Visitor Information Center,** 504 State St (open year-round Mon–Fri 9am–5pm) ☎965-5334. Mailing address: **Santa Barbara Conference and Visitors Bureau,** 510 State St, Suite A, Santa Barbara CA 93101 ☎966-9222.

Accommodations – Reservation services: **Accommodations Santa Barbara** ☎687-9191; **Hot Spot** ☎564-1637. Accommodations range from elegant hotels ($173/day), to moderate inns ($81/day). Most bed & breakfasts are located in residential sections of the city ($75–$125/day). **Campsites** available at Santa Barbara County Parks ☎564-5410. *Rates quoted are average prices for a double room.*

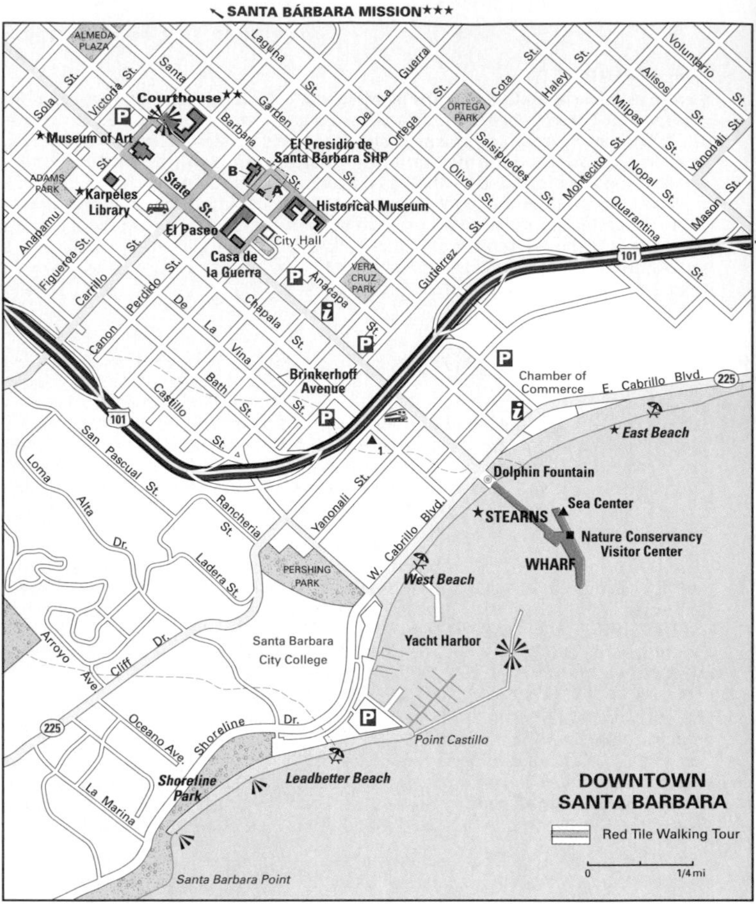

SIGHTS *2 1/2 days*

Waterfront

The coastline curves sharply inward at Point Conception, making Santa Barbara one of California's south-facing coastal cities. Its attractive shoreline consists of a wide expanse of white-sand beach edged with stately palm trees. Stearns Wharf and Santa Barbara Harbor define the mile-long waterfront area, bordered by popular **East Beach★**, **West Beach**, and **Leadbetter Beach**. On Sundays, visitors can view the work of local artists displayed east of the wharf along Cabrillo Boulevard, which runs the length of the waterfront. Overlooking Leadbetter Beach, clifftop **Shoreline Park** provides a grassy vantage point from which to watch whales during the migrating season *(Nov-Apr)*. On clear days, **views** stretch to the CHANNEL ISLANDS of Anacapa and Santa Cruz.

★ **Stearns Wharf** – *Foot of State St. Parking available on wharf.* Built in 1872 by local lumberman John P. Stearns, this 2,640ft pier, lined with small shops and restaurants, is the oldest working wooden wharf in the state. The playful **Dolphin Fountain**, commemorating the city's bicentennial, graces the State Street entrance. Located next to the Sea Center *(below)*, the **Nature Conservancy Visitor Center** features displays relating to the Channel Islands and other preservation projects *(open daily year-round; closed major holidays ☎805-962-9111)*.

Sea Center – *211 Stearns Wharf. Open daily year-round. Closed Jan 1, Thanksgiving Day, Dec 25. $2. ♿ ☎805-962-0885.* This small aquarium, devoted to educating visitors about coastal marine life and geology, is a joint project of the Santa Barbara Museum of Natural History and the Channel Islands National Marine Sanctuary. A touch tank outside the building allows the curious a hands-on experience of local sea creatures.

Santa Barbara Yacht Harbor – *West Cabrillo Blvd, .5mi west of wharf.* Catering to the city's commercial fishing fleet, the harbor area contains bait shops, boat supply stores, gift shops and restaurants. A walk out along the flag-lined, man-made breakwater affords excellent **views** of the Santa Barbara Channel, as well as the city and surrounding mountains.

★ **Santa Barbara Zoo** – *500 Niños Dr, 1.5mi east of wharf. Open daily year-round. Closed Thanksgiving Day, Dec 25. $5. ✕ ♿ ☎805-962-6310.* Set amid 40 lush acres of cacti and palm gardens overlooking the ocean, the zoo contains some 700 animals displayed in environments that approximate their native habitats. Discovery and play areas are popular features with youngsters.

Adjacent to the zoo, the 40-acre **Andree Clark Bird Refuge** *(1400 Cabrillo Blvd)* surrounds a placid lagoon that harbors some 200 species of birds *(open daily year-round; ♿)*.

Downtown

A map of the Red Tile Walking Tour of Santa Barbara's historic core is available from the Chamber of Commerce (corner of Santa Barbara St and Cabrillo Blvd).

This area of the city grew from a cluster of adobes scattered around the presidio to an orderly grid of streets laid out in the 1850s. Once the hub of the city's political and social life, **Casa De la Guerra** *(15 E. De la Guerra St. Closed for renovation; scheduled reopening winter 1995)* exemplifies the early adobes. Built in 1827, the dwelling was home to José De la Guerra, fifth comandante of the presidio. Today the heart of Santa Barbara's business and shopping district beats along a portion of **State Street** bounded by Ortega and Victoria Streets. Evidence of Spanish influence remains in the terra-cotta sidewalks and in the tilework details that decorate even mundane objects like mailboxes and trash receptacles.

Remnants of the city's 19C period of New England-style architecture survive on **Brinkerhoff Avenue** *(2 blocks southwest of State St between Cota and Haley Sts).* Nearby stands the **Moreton Bay fig tree [1]** *(Chapala and Montecito Sts),* reportedly the largest such tree in the US. Planted in 1877, this local landmark boasts a branch-spread of nearly 200ft.

★ **Santa Barbara Museum of Art** – *1130 State St. Open year-round Tue–Sun. Closed major holidays. $3. ♿ ☎805-963-4364.* Housed in an elegant Italian Renaissance-style structure, the museum reigns as one of the country's outstanding regional art museums. It was founded in 1941 through a collaborative effort between private citizens and the city government.

Main Level – One of the remarkable features of the permanent holdings, the collection of **antiquities** comprises a group of Greek and Roman sculptures dating from the 4C BC, including the famed Lansdowne Hermes (2C AD), in the airy atrium. Surrounding galleries contain a fine collection of **Asian art**. To the right of the State Street entrance lie two galleries of 18-19C **American art**, including works by Albert Bierstadt, Georgia O'Keefe, William Merrit Chase and John Singer Sargent.

Upper Level – Portions of the permanent collection, featuring **French** and **British art** of the 19C-early 20C, line the walls of the upper floor around the central atrium. Works by Marc Chagall, Henri Matisse, and three paintings by Claude Monet are among the highlights. Changing shows of graphics and photography occupy adjacent galleries. Permanently rotating exhibits, often showcasing contemporary art, are complemented by a series of temporary exhibits.

★ **Karpeles Manuscript Library** – *21 W. Anapamu St. Open daily year-round. Closed Jan 1, Dec 25. ♿ ☎805-962-5322.* Original historical documents, including the Treaty of Ghent and the Constitution of the Confederate States of America, as well as the writings of renowned authors, scientists and statesmen, are preserved in this gracefully designed house setting. Small changing exhibits, drawn from the permanent collection of over one million manuscripts, rotate among the library's six locations across the US.

★★ **Santa Barbara County Courthouse** – *1100 block, Anacapa St. Open year-round Mon–Fri 8am–5pm, weekends 9am–5pm. Closed Dec 25. ♿ ☎805-962-6464.* Shining star of Santa Barbara's architectural renaissance, the L-shaped Moorish courthouse (1929) surrounds a verdant sunken courtyard and garden. Above the cornice of the facade's Anacapa Arch is chiseled the city's motto: "God gave us the country. The skill of man hath built the town." Arched doorways, open-air galleries and graceful curving staircases distinguish the interior of the steel-frame building. Intricate Tunisian tile mosaics and metal work abound; even elements such as telephone booths are cached in carved wood frames. The Board of Supervisors' Assembly Room *(2nd floor)* features a series of **murals** by artist Dan Sayre Groesbeck illustrating the area's history.

From the observation deck atop the 85ft clock tower extends an excellent **panorama**★★ of the city.

El Presidio de Santa Bárbara State Historic Park – *123 E. Canon Perdido St. Open daily year-round. Closed Easter Sunday, Thanksgiving Day, Dec 25. ✗ ☎805-965-0093.* Enveloped by the bustle of modern Santa Barbara, this reconstructed Spanish fortress, which once covered an area equivalent to a square city block, formed the earliest nucleus of the city. Completed by 1788, the presidio served as the region's military and government headquarters. Today the only original structures are the soldiers' residences (c.1788), known as **El Cuartel [A]** *(122 E. Canon Perdido St; closed for renovation),* and Cañedo Adobe (c.1782), now housing a visitor center and displays relating to the site's history. Flanked by the padres' and the comandantes' quarters, the **chapel [B]** was rebuilt according to existing records. Work is in progress to restore half of the quadrangle to its original appearance.

Santa Barbara Historical Museum – *136 E. De la Guerra St. Open year-round Tue–Sun. Closed major holidays. Contribution requested. ♿ ☎805-966-1601.* Administered by the Santa Barbara Historical Society, the museum presents a well-organized collection of artifacts that chronicle the region's colorful past. Highlights include a Chinese joss house **altar** from the city's 19C Chinatown, Victorian costumes, and a group of saddles from the rancho period.

Consult the Practical Information section (pp 248-261) for travel tips, useful addresses and phone numbers, and details on planning your trip, sports and recreation, and annual events.

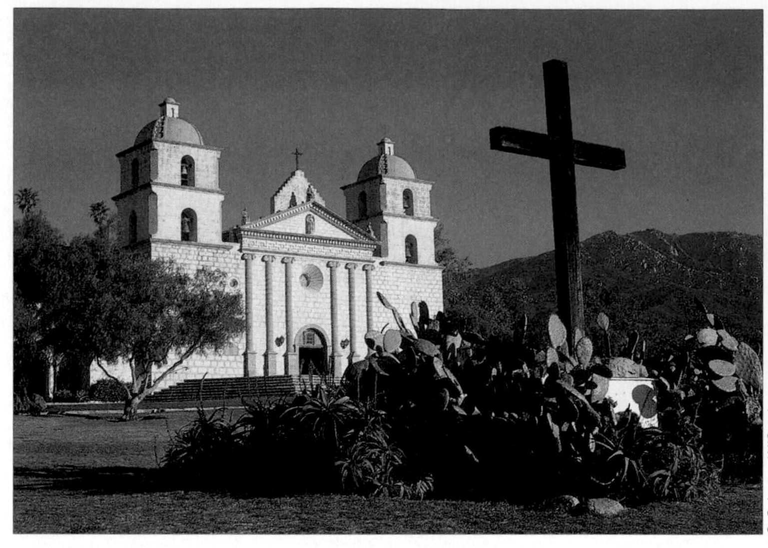

The Queen of the Missions

Mission Canyon

★★★ **Santa Bárbara Mission** – *Upper Laguna St. From downtown proceed northwest on Laguna St. Open year-round daily 9am–5pm. Closed Easter Sunday, Thanksgiving Day, Dec 25. $2. ☎805-682-4149.* Its twin towers rising majestically against the foothills surrounding Mission Canyon, the church of California's tenth mission dominates the city both physically and spiritually. Santa Bárbara has never ceased to serve as a parish church throughout its 200-year history.

Although Padre Serra wished to establish the mission in concert with the construction of the nearby presidio *(p 219)*, permission to proceed was delayed for four years by Spanish governor Felipe de Neve, who, distrustful of the mission chain's increasing economic power, insisted that the presidio be built first. The mission was dedicated by Padre Fermín Lasuén in 1786 (two years after Serra's death); the first church, erected in 1787, was replaced three times by larger structures. A short distance from the main quadrangle stood 250 single-room adobe dwellings for the neophytes, who constructed the most sophisticated water system in the mission chain; Mission Dam is still visible at the nearby Botanic Garden *(below)*.

In 1812 a severe earthquake wreaked havoc on the existing structures, and the entire complex had to be rebuilt. Completion of the present church in 1820 signaled the heyday of Santa Bárbara Mission, which quickly surpassed the presidio in size, wealth and political influence. Today the mission serves not only as a parish church, but also as a research library and archive for the entire chain.

Visit – Designers of the church **facade** borrowed freely from *De architectura*, an encyclopedic work by the 1C BC Roman architect Vitruvius. The regal facade—with its central pediment and six Ionic engaged columns crowned by twin pink-domed towers—accounts for the site's sobriquet, "Queen of the Missions."

Thick-walled, heavily beamed rooms of the **padres' quarters** contain a collection of mission artifacts from the late 18C to early 19C, including crafts, vestments and musical instruments. Note in particular the large **psalter** (book of psalms), dated 1792, of 75 hand-lettered sheepskin pages. The lovely **sacred garden** *(behind the padres' quarters)* once contained numerous neophyte workshops.

Little changed from its original appearance, the **interior** of the long, narrow church is adorned with bright motifs; the painted canvas reredos (1806), of which only fragments remain, formed the basis for the detailed design scheme. Imported from Peru in 1789, two large oil paintings, *The Assumption and Coronation of the Virgin* and *The Crucifixion*, hang on either side of the altar. *Before exiting the church, note that you cannot re-enter the church building from the cemetery.*

A skull and crossbones over the side door of the church mark the shady **cemetery**, where some 4,000 neophytes lie buried.

★ **Santa Barbara Museum of Natural History** – *2559 Puesta del Sol. From the mission (above) turn right on Los Olivos St; follow signs. Open daily year-round. Closed Jan 1, Thanksgiving Day, Dec 25. $3. ♿ ☎805-682-4711.* Exhibits in this complex of Spanish-style stucco buildings, which sits on 11 acres in a wooded canyon, display the flora, fauna, geology and ethnography of the West Coast. The **Chumash Indian Hall** contains one of the state's largest collections of artifacts from this tribe. In other galleries, dioramas depict the natural habitats of a variety of local wildlife from sharks to seagulls. Visitors can explore the relationship between water, plants and insects via a combination of live specimens, videos and computer terminals. Weekend shows in the Gladwin Planetarium present seasonal celestial phenomena *(Wed, Sat & Sun, check for show times)*.

Santa Barbara Botanic Garden – *1212 Mission Canyon Rd. From the mission (above) turn right on Los Olivos St and right on Foothill Rd; follow signs. Open daily year-round. Closed Jan 1, Dec 25. $3. ☎805-682-4726.* Some 5mi of trails meander across 65 acres of wooded canyons, open meadows and high ridges in this pleasant site. Over 1,000 species of native California plants, including redwoods, cacti and rare Channel Island species grow here. In the north section, visitors can see the original **Mission Dam**, built by Chumash neophytes in 1807 to provide water for the mission's growing population.

EXCURSION

Chumash Painted Cave State Historic Park – *10mi northwest of Santa Barbara. Take US-101 north to Hwy 154 north; turn right on Painted Cave Rd and continue 2mi to cave on left. Open daily year-round. ☎805-682-4711.* Hidden amid the rocks off a 1-lane road high in the San Marcos Pass, this small cave *(closed off by a metal gate)* allows visitors a glimpse of rare **Chumash pictographs**. Although the secret to the meaning of the symbols—executed some 400 years ago—died with the last member of the 'antap cult, it is thought that they were painted by Chumash shamans during sacred rituals. Primitive motifs representing the supernatural world, including a black disc that may depict a solar eclipse, were created using animal-tail brushes and red, black and white mineral pigments.

★ SANTA CRUZ San Francisco Bay Area — Pop 49,040

Map of Principal Sights p 2 — Tourist Office ☎408-425-1234

Curving around the northern end of Monterey Bay, this archetypal California beach community is celebrated for its turn-of-the-century amusement park, its surfing beaches, arts community, casual atmosphere and diverse culture.
The city traces its origins to the 1791 establishment of Mission Exaltación de la Santa Cruz *(below)*. By the 1860s, the town had grown from a small, only moderately prosperous mission site to a bustling American business hub for a wide variety of industries, including lumbering, fishing, limestone quarrying, tanning and agriculture. In the late 19C, the Southern Pacific Railroad came to town and soon thereafter, Santa Cruz became a thriving seaside resort. In 1904 one of the West Coast's first boardwalk amusement parks was built here and remains today a popular attraction. With the establishment of a University of California campus in the Santa Cruz hills in the mid-1960s, the resort milieu was overlaid with a college atmosphere that attracted artists and craftspeople to the area. In 1989 the Loma Prieta earthquake devastated the city's **Pacific Garden Mall**, a gathering of vintage Art Deco structures. Now emerging from the process of reconstruction, the area benefits from its lively cafe scene, live music venues and a number of book, arts, and curio shops.

SIGHTS *1/2 day*

★★ **Santa Cruz Beach Boardwalk** – The oldest amusement park in California, this official state historic landmark preserves the appeal of an early 20C seaside amusement park. Its renovated boardwalk features a series of turreted and brightly painted buildings and rides fronting a wide bay beach. The **Giant Dipper**, a .5mi-long wooden roller coaster, has been the boardwalk's most distinctive feature since 1924. The **Looff carousel** (1911) is the work of the respected Danish woodcarver Charles I.D. Looff. Both enjoy the status of national historic landmarks.
The adjacent **Cocoanut Grove Banquet and Conference Center** (1907) is famous for its now-renovated Grand Ballroom, where such Big Band celebrities as Artie Shaw, Benny Goodman and Xavier Cugat often performed. A few blocks west, the broad **municipal wharf** stretches into the bay and is lined with tackle shops and eateries. North of the waterfront, Ocean View Avenue (200-400 block) is a neighborhood of Victorian homes built in the 1880s and 1890s. The **Santa Cruz City Museum** *(1305 E. Cliff Dr)*, on a cliff above the bay, covers the natural history of the area and includes an exhibit detailing the Loma Prieta earthquake *(open year-round Tue–Sun; closed major holidays; contribution requested; ♿ ☎408-429-3773)*.

Santa Cruz Mission State Historic Park – *Off Mission Plaza on School St. Open daily year-round. ♿ ☎408-426-5686.* Founded in 1791 under promising circumstances, the 12th mission, named in honor of the Holy Cross, suffered severe hardships brought about mainly by the ruffianesque settlers in the nearby pueblo of Branciforte. After achieving a peak population of 531 neophytes (the smallest of all the missions), Santa Cruz declined slowly; following secularization, its structures were destroyed by earthquakes, fires and floods. In 1931 a small replica of the adobe church was erected some 200ft from the original site; a 7-room barracks is the only remaining structure from the original mission complex. Built in 1824 to house Native converts, it was later occupied by Mexican, Irish and American citizens and is today maintained by the state park system.

★ **University of California, Santa Cruz** – *Follow Bay St northwest to campus main entrance. Maps of the campus and of Cowell Ranch are available at main entrance kiosk.* Renowned for its distinctive architecture and spectacular setting in the lush hills above Santa Cruz amid groves of redwood trees, the university campus actually comprises a loop of eight architecturally and academically distinct college campuses surrounding an academic and administrative core.
In 1965 the state established this branch of its extensive university system by purchasing 2,000 acres of ranchland from the Cowell family and carefully integrating the original ranch structures into the new campus. Today the university claims a total enrollment of some 10,000 students.

Visit – Occupying the hillsides on either side of Coolidge Drive are 14 structures from the **Cowell Ranch** established in the 1860s by Henry Cowell, a wealthy county landowner and entrepreneur *(open daily year-round; ♿).* A number of these buildings, including the simple old ranch house, carriage house, and barns, now house university-related services. The picturesque remains of Cowell's prosperous limekiln are prominent features on the old ranch site.
The **Mary Porter-Sesnon Gallery** *(open year-round Tue–Sun; closed major holidays; ✂ ♿ ☎408-459-2314)* and the **Eloise Pickard Smith Gallery** *(same hours as Mary Porter-Sesnon Gallery; ☎408-459-2953)* mount changing exhibits of contemporary art; the **arboretum** is devoted to exotic flora, particularly from Africa, South America and New Zealand *(Empire Grade, .25mi west of main entrance; open daily year-round; closed major holidays; ♿ ☎408-427-2998).*

EXCURSIONS

★ **Año Nuevo State Reserve** – *22mi north of Santa Cruz on Hwy 1. Visit by guided tour (2hr 30min) only, Dec–Mar daily; rest of the year daily, self-guided. $2. ☎415-879-0227 or MISTIX 1-800-444-PARK (guided tour reservations).* This 4,000-acre coastal reserve encompasses a rocky offshore island *(not open to the public)* and a wildly beautiful Pacific promontory of bluffs and beaches which is the only mainland rookery between Baja and Northern California for **northern elephant seals**. From December through March, the seals gradually congregate here, the females giving birth to single pups and joining harems dominated by massive 2.5-ton alpha bulls. Bloody clashes between males over harem control are common. In spring and summer, Año Nuevo is again visited by the seals, who come ashore to molt.

★ **Henry Cowell Redwoods State Park** – *6mi north of Santa Cruz on Hwy 9. Open daily year-round. $5/car. ♿ ☎408-335-4598. Facility information p 257.* Trails weave through the woodlands of this biotically diverse 1,760-acre tract, bisected by the San Lorenzo River and notable for its fine stands of coast redwoods. The site is named for Henry Cowell *(above),* whose heirs deeded over the land for the park. The **Redwood Grove Trail** *(.8mi; begin south of parking lot)* loops past the park's largest trees, some towering 300ft.

Roaring Camp & Big Trees Narrow-Gauge Railroad – *Ticket office east of parking lot. Departs daily year-round. Commentary. $12. ✂ ♿ ☎408-335-4484.* Departing from the site of a former logging camp named for its rambunctious inhabitants, this commercial steam train tour *(6mi, 1hr 15min)* penetrates deep into the forest of ancient redwoods, snaking around hairpin turns and negotiating a series of steep switchbacks before arriving near the summit of Bear Mountain.

★ SANTA INÉS MISSION Central Coast

Map of Principal Sights p 4 Tourist Office ☎805-688-6144

Founded in 1804, the stately mission sits at the east end of the town of Solvang *(p 223)* in the pastoral Santa Ynez Valley, an increasingly important wine-producing region. Today the church, part of the convento and the gardens are all that remain of the original quadrangle. Members of this active parish, named for 4C martyr St Agnes, plan to restore the site to its original appearance.
California's 19th mission formed the final link in the southern chain extending from San Francisco to San Diego, and bridged the distance between LA PURÍSIMA MISSION and SANTA BARBARA MISSION. Known for its large herds of cattle and fine leather and silver craft work, isolated Santa Inés mission prospered until 1824, despite the 1812 earthquake that felled most of the church. It took neophytes five years to repair the damaged structures and to erect a new church.
When a guard at Santa Inés flogged a neophyte in 1824, Native converts reacted by setting fire to the mission. Order was quickly restored, but not before the sacristy had been burned to the ground. After the revolt, the mission never again thrived as it had in its early days; following secularization, the property remained in a state of disrepair until the turn of the century, when a 20-year restoration project created the present complex.

VISIT *1hr*

1760 Mission Dr, 1 block east of downtown Solvang. Open daily year-round. Closed Easter Sunday, Thanksgiving Day, Dec 25. $2. Self-guided tour starts at the gift shop. ♿ ☎805-688-4815.

Museum – *Enter through the gift shop.* An informative recorded narrative *(30min)* summarizes the mission's history and describes the highlights of the museum's artifacts. A well-restored collection of handmade **vestments**★ dates from as far back as the 4C AD.

★ **Church** – An engraving of a Roman theater stage may have inspired the trompe l'œil painting on the wall in back of the sanctuary, with its seemingly recessed marbleized panels divided by Ionic columns. In the niche above the altar stands the original wood polychromed statue of Santa Inés, carved in Mexico in the early 17C. Side walls are adorned by *Ecce Homo*, the work of a 17C Peruvian painter, and Stations of the Cross (18C), modeled after Italian woodcuts. The gilt-trimmed Madonna Chapel contains a 17C painted wood carving of the Mother of Sorrows. Behind the church lies a lovely garden, and a cemetery harboring the graves of 1,700 neophytes.

ADDITIONAL SIGHT

Solvang – Pop 4,741. With its mild climate and rich soil, the Santa Ynez Valley provided the perfect site for Danish settlers from the Midwest who were seeking to start a colony on the West Coast in 1911. Life in the farming village christened Solvang ("sunny field") centered around the Danish folk school. Ferd Sorensen built the first Danish provincial dwelling in 1945, and soon thereafter the style caught on throughout the town. Soon hordes of visitors flocked here, attracted by a description of the Danish town that ran in the *Saturday Evening Post*. Today Solvang, with its 20C interpretations of windmills and timbered houses, still caters to the tourist trade.
Danish culture is preserved in the **Elverhøj Museum** *(1624 Elverhoy Way)*, the former residence (1950) of artist Viggo Brandt-Erichsen. Named after a popular Danish folk play, the title of which means "Elves on a hill," the gracefully designed dwelling resembles an 18C Jutland (northern Denmark) farmhouse *(open year-round Wed–Sun; closed Dec 25; ♿ ☎805-686-1211)*.

★ SANTA MONICA **Greater Los Angeles Area** Pop 86,905

Map p 82 Tourist Office ☎310-393-7593

Situated on the Pacific Ocean some 13mi west of downtown LOS ANGELES, Santa Monica, dubbed in the 1870s the "Zenith City of the Sunset Seas," is a thriving urban center that hosts a wide array of cultural and commercial activities, yet still maintains a seaside ambience and casual lifestyle.
Legend has it that the city's name was coined in the 18C by Spanish missionaries, who likened the trickling water of the natural springs they discovered here to the tears of the 4C St Monica as she mourned her heretical son, Augustine. In 1872 Col Robert S. Baker, a former Rhode Island businessman, joined forces with Sen John P. Jones, a multimillionaire from Nevada, to purchase and subdivide the lands of the present-day city. The pair developed a town center, wharves and rail lines, and registered Santa Monica as a townsite in 1875.
In the late 18C, the city came under consideration as a potential site for the Port of Los Angeles. After hotly contested debates, the port was located in SAN PEDRO, and Santa Monica developed as a beachfront community, widely known for its grand hotels, summer estates, beach clubs and amusement parks. Land values skyrocketed with the completion of the Santa Monica Freeway in 1966; efforts to halt gentrification and promote rent control became subjects of great political debate that continue today.
Since the late 1980s Santa Monica has become one of Southern California's leading arts and entertainment centers, replete with high-caliber art galleries, first-run movie complexes, abundant performance spaces and fashionable cafes and boutiques. Evenings and weekends, both visitors and denizens of the area throng Santa Monica's **Third Street Promenade**, a welcoming outdoor pedestrian mall *(3rd St between Wilshire Blvd and Colorado Ave)* and **Santa Monica Place** (1979), an innovatively designed shopping center by prominent architect Frank Gehry.

SIGHTS *1 day*

★ **Santa Monica Pier** – *Western end of Colorado Ave.* Jutting some 1,000ft over the ocean, this wooden pier has been a landmark and gathering place since the turn of the century. Its 9.5-acre expanse features an antique **carousel★**, bumper cars, arcades, curio shops, food stands and fishing decks, all evoking the carnival spirit

Justine Hill

View of Malibu coastline from Ocean Avenue in Santa Monica

of a festive, albeit somewhat frayed, past. The pier also affords sweeping **views★** of the dramatic coastline of MALIBU to the north, and of the PALOS VERDES PENINSULA to the south.

The present structure consists of the Municipal Pier (1909) and the adjacent Pleasure Pier (1916), the latter designed by Coney Island creator Charles I.D. Looff. During its 1920s heyday, attractions such as the carousel (also designed by Looff), the La Monica ballroom and other amusement rides made the pier a hub of constant activity. The fabled strand declined after World War II and by the 1970s was in danger of demolition. Extensive restoration plans began in the early 1980s; the Hippodrome and the carousel were the first projects to be completed. New restaurants have been added, and two music clubs are under way *(scheduled to open by 1994 and 1995)*. On weekends the pier is frequented by a colorful crowd of sightseers, fishermen and street performers.

Santa Monica's renowned sunset **vistas★★** are best taken in from **Palisades Park** *(adjacent to the pier)*, a lovely stretch of green grass, palm trees and seaward-facing benches. Featured in the Senior Citizens building at the park's southern end is a 19C **camera obscura**, which projects images of the surrounding area through a series of lenses onto a white circular viewing surface *(inquire at Senior Citizens building for access)*.

Edgemar Plaza – *2435 Main St.* This mixed-use cultural and commercial development (1989, Frank Gehry) combines tony shops and restaurants with a museum, galleries and offices. Like a European piazza with a post-Modern flair, the open-air courtyard is ringed by a 2-story architectural assemblage of skewed geometric forms and dramatically contrasting materials, from galvanized steel sheets to chain-link fences to stucco.

In the corner of the plaza is the **Santa Monica Museum of Art**, a gallery-size renovated warehouse with 25ft ceilings and clerestory windows. The nonprofit museum does not have a permanent collection, but uses its raw, open spaces for changing installations of multimedia work and performance art *(open year-round Wed–Sun; closed Jan 1, Jul 4, Thanksgiving Day, Dec 25; $4; ☎310-399-0433)*.

Santa Monica Heritage Museum – *2612 Main St. Open year-round Wed–Sun. Closed major holidays. $2. ♿ ☎310-392-8537.* This stately Queen Anne home (1894, Sumner P. Hunt) was built for Roy Jones, son of city founder John P. Jones *(p 223)*. Originally located on Ocean Avenue, the structure, abandoned and deteriorated, was moved to its present site in 1977. Today completely restored, it functions as a museum of life in Santa Monica at the turn-of-the-century; the living room and dining room are outfitted with furniture and other accoutrements of the period. Upper-level gallery spaces host temporary shows of historical and contemporary California arts and crafts.

★★ **Santa Monica Museum of Flying** – *2772 Donald Douglas Loop North. Open year-round Wed–Sun. Closed Dec 25. $5. ✗ ♿ ☎310-392-8822.* Housed in a contemporary steel and glass structure on the grounds of the Santa Monica Airport, this museum is dedicated to the preservation, restoration and exhibition of historically significant passenger and military aircraft. The airport itself is the former site of Douglas Aircraft Company, founded here by aviation pioneer Donald Douglas.

The main interior exhibit space, extending the full height of the building, displays planes from a collection of 45 vintage aircraft, many of which are in flight-ready condition. Several craft are suspended from the ceiling, including the "New Orleans," a Douglas World Cruiser that was one of the first planes to fly around the world in 1924. World War II-era planes include a Curtiss P-40 Warhawk, a JN-4 Jenny and a North American P-51 Racing Mustang "Dago Red." Visitor-activated video kiosks *(lower level)*; collections of military memorabilia; and an extensive collection of models *(second level)* enlighten visitors about airplane construction and aviation history. Changing films documenting important events in aviation history and military technology are screened continuously in the theater *(third level)*, and additional craft are displayed on the outdoor ramp adjoining the airport's runway.

SANTA ROSA North Coast — Pop 113,313

Map p 240 — Tourist Office ☎707-575-1191

This sprawling city of the southern RUSSIAN RIVER REGION is the commercial hub and seat of Sonoma County. Incorporated in 1858, Santa Rosa experienced a significant population and development boom in the period following the opening of the Golden Gate Bridge and World War II. Northeast of the downtown area are lovely residential streets lined with well-preserved late 19C Victorian homes. One of the finest, located at 1015 McDonald Avenue, was featured in Walt Disney Studios' 1960 movie *Pollyanna.*

SIGHTS 1/2 day

★ **Luther Burbank Home and Gardens** – *Corner of Sonoma and Santa Rosa Aves. Open daily year-round. $2 (gardens free). ♿ ☎707-524-5445.* Located at the intersection of two bustling thoroughfares, this attractive residence was home to renowned horticulturist **Luther Burbank** (1849-1926), who moved to Santa Rosa from Massachusetts in 1875. Burbank's extensive experiments in plant hybridization—resulting in such now-commonplace strains as the Russet Burbank potato, the Shasta daisy and the Santa Rosa plum—produced over 800 new varieties of fruits and vegetables and earned him a reputation as magician of the botanical world.

Visit – In the renovated Carriage House, displays tell the story of Burbank's life and work, and the simple furnishings of his charming Greek Revival home *(accessible by guided tour only)* bear witness to the horticulturalist's modest lifestyle. Before he acquired a larger property outside Santa Rosa, the grounds surrounding the home served as his laboratory; the gardens were redesigned as a memorial park in 1960, and today have been reconstructed to feature many of his experimental hybrids. Burbank is buried in an unmarked grave on the property.

Church of One Tree Ripley Museum – *In Juilliard Park, across Santa Rosa Ave from Luther Burbank Home and Gardens. Open Apr–Oct Wed–Sun. $1.50. ♿ ☎707-524-5233.* Constructed of boards from a single 275ft redwood tree, this Gothic Revival church now houses a small museum dedicated to the life and discoveries of Santa Rosa native **Robert Ripley** (1893-1949). Ripley's passion for adventure and personal credo "Truth is stranger than fiction" took him to 198 countries and led him to create his famed "Believe It Or Not!" cartoon. His collection of "oddities"—bizarre facts and artifacts of humans, animals and objects—is contained in 20 "Believe It or Not!" novelty museums throughout the world.

★ **Sonoma County Museum** – *425 7th St. Open year-round Wed–Sun. Closed major holidays. $2. ♿ ☎707-579-1500.* Santa Rosa's former post office (1909), designed in the Classical Revival style, today serves as a repository for the county's assemblage of artistic, cultural and historical artifacts.

Selections from the collection of 19C landscape paintings are displayed on a rotating basis, along with a small interactive science exhibit. Historical exhibits cover the period from the early 18C, when the area was occupied by Native Miwok, Pomo and Wapo peoples, through the growth of the wine industry and population explosions of recent decades.

Railroad Square – *Bounded by Third, Davis and Sixth Sts and the railroad tracks. Open daily year-round.* ✕ ♿. Santa Rosa's historic district comprises a charming cluster of restored brick and stone buildings constructed in 1870 to serve the Santa Rosa and North Pacific railroad. Today the square has been transformed into an attractive group of offices, specialty shops, boutiques, eateries and a visitor center.

Snoopy's Gallery and Gift Shop – *From US-101 north exit at Steele Lane and turn left; continue straight on W. Steele Lane as Guerneville Rd bears to the left. Gallery is adjacent to ice arena. Open daily year-round. Closed Easter Sunday, Thanksgiving Day, Dec 25, Dec 30–Jan 5.* ✕ ♿ ☎ *707-546-3385.* A fascinating assortment of memorabilia, cartoons and original drawings by **Charles Schulz** (b. 1922), famed creator of the beloved *Peanuts* comic strip, occupies the mezzanine level of this large gift shop. Schulz lives and works in Santa Rosa.

Adjacent to the gallery building is the **Redwood Empire Ice Arena**, whimsically designed to resemble a Swiss Chalet. Its icy skating surface can be converted to a wooden floor, and the building serves as a venue for numerous local and national sporting events.

★ SAUSALITO San Francisco Bay Area — Pop 7,152

Map p 183 Tourist Office ☎415-332-0505

Nestled among the steep bluffs across the Golden Gate from SAN FRANCISCO, this friendly, upscale residential community retains the air of a Mediterranean hill town. Its winding streets, secluded alleys and attractive homes and gardens perched on steep slopes create an atmosphere distinctly more relaxed and mellow than that of the bustling city across the bay, and its setting affords some of the finest possible views of San Francisco and the Golden Gate Bridge.

In 1775 Juan Manuel de Ayala, the first known Spanish explorer of San Francisco Bay, moored his ship near a thicket of willow trees (*sauces* in Spanish) flourishing on the bluffs that form the northern boundary of the Golden Gate. The area later became part of the 19,572-acre Rancho Saucelito that was granted to William A. Richardson, an English born pilot and shipbuilder who served as captain of the Port of San Francisco. Richardson sold water from the ranch's numerous hillside springs to the citizens of San Francisco, and developed the property's shoreline areas as an anchorage and supply station for whaling ships and other vessels. By 1870 a portion of the ranch had been acquired by the Sausalito Land and Ferry Company, which built wharves, laid out plots of land, initiated passenger ferry service to San Francisco, and promoted the area as a desirable resort and residential community.

By 1885 the town had become an important transport hub as trains carrying lumber from the redwood forests to the north halted here to unload their cargo onto vessels bound for booming San Francisco. Saloons and gambling dens lent the village an unsavory reputation, but by the turn of the century it had quieted into a pleasant community of commuters, fishermen and small-craft builders.

Serene Sausalito burst into activity during World War II when a shipyard was established to build tankers and other cargo vessels. Toward the close of the war in 1945 the shipbuilders departed and the area, now known as Marinship *(p 226)*, was taken over by eccentric squatters who constructed ramshackle houseboats out of shipyard scraps. Residents of this colony of **floating homes** claim status as Sausalito's bohemian element.

Sausalito today is known as a pleasant weekend getaway destination for out-of-state travelers and San Francisco residents alike. Among its historic hostelries are the **Casa Madrona** *(801 Bridgeway)*, a restored Victorian villa (1885) nestled in the wooded hillside overlooking the Yacht Harbor; and the **Alta Mira** *(125 Bulkley Ave; take Excelsior stairs from Viña del Mar Plaza)*, a Spanish-style inn renowned for the **vistas** that extend from its terrace.

SIGHTS *1 day*

★ **Bridgeway** – Snaking along the base of the hills overlooking the waterfront, Sausalito's attractive main thoroughfare was originally called Water Street. The name was changed in 1937 when highway engineers anticipated routing traffic to and from the Golden Gate Bridge directly through Sausalito. A route across the ridge above the village was selected, however, and Bridgeway became the center of a charming commercial district that stretches several blocks in both directions from the ferry landing. Many of the small, colorful buildings date from the turn of the century and house restaurants, cafes, galleries and retail shops; the street itself affords delightful **views**★★ of San Francisco, the bay and its islands. Situated just above the ferry landing is **Viña del Mar Plaza** *(Bridgeway and El Portal)*, an airy, triangular park; its lovely fountain and unique, elephant-shaped light standards were designed for the 1915 Panama-Pacific International Exposition.

From Bridgeway, Princess Street *(first street south of Viña del Mar Plaza)*, leads up into the hills that backdrop Sausalito's waterfront. Secluded here are both older and more contemporary homes, tucked beneath pine, oak, acacia and eucalyptus trees. Visitors can stroll along shaded Bulkley Avenue *(turn right from Princess St)* past several excellent examples of Shingle style architecture, including **St John's Presbyterian Church** (1905), before returning to Bridgeway via the Excelsior stairs.

North of the Viña del Mar Plaza, Bridgeway fronts **Yacht Harbor**, where visitors can stroll out among the masts of Sausalito's resident flotilla of yachts.

Marinship – *1mi north on Bridgeway to Marinship Way.* Some 75,000 workers built 93 ships, mostly tankers, invasion barges and Liberty ships on this site between 1942 and 1945. Artists, manufacturers and other businesses occupy part of the site today. Marinship is home to the **Bay Model Visitor Center of the US Army Corps of Engineers**★, a 2-acre hydraulic scale model of the San Francisco Bay and Delta. When filled with water, the model simulates tidal flow through this estuary system, thus providing data for researchers studying tidal conditions. Visitors view the model from raised walkways augmented by slide presentations and other exhibits, including one recounting the history of Marinship *(open Memorial Day–Labor Day Tue–Sun, rest of the year Tue–Sat; ♿ ☎415-332-3871)*.

★★ SEQUOIA AND KINGS CANYON NATIONAL PARKS High Sierras

Map of Principal Sights pp 4-5

These two adjacent and jointly administered parks encompass the mighty granitic peaks of the southern Sierra Nevada, including 14,495ft MT WHITNEY, the highest point in the US south of Alaska. They also harbor the planet's finest stands of **giant sequoias** *(Sequoiadendron giganteum)*, the largest living things on earth. Less developed and far less crowded than YOSEMITE NATIONAL PARK, Sequoa and Kings Canyon contain vast acres of wilderness accessible only on foot.

The Big Trees – Naturalist John Muir called the giant sequoia "nature's forest masterpiece . . . the greatest of all living things." These leviathans, which can live as long as 3,200 years, normally attain heights of more than 200ft. Though coast redwoods *(p 149)* grow taller, and there is a known Montezuma cypress in the state of Oaxaca, Mexico, with a larger girth, giant sequoias, with a volume exceeding 20,000cu ft, are considered the largest living things on earth. They grow naturally only in scattered pockets along the western flanks of California's Sierra Nevada, at elevations of 5,000-7,000ft. About 68 percent of the existing groves are now protected within national and state parks, while 21 percent are within national forests.

The giant trees sprout from tiny seeds lodged in cones the size of a chicken's egg. While a mature tree produces millions of cones annually, only one seed in a billion will become a mature sequoia. Once mature, however (after centuries of growth), the trees are seemingly invincible. The high tannin content of the bark thwarts insect damage and heartrot, and the bark itself grows up to 18in thick, serving as a shield against fire. Forest fires actually perpetuate sequoia groves, in part because intense heat is needed for the cones to release their seeds and also because fires clear competing underbrush and leave behind a nutrient-rich soil for seed germination.

Giant sequoias grow extremely fast, adding as much as 500 board feet annually (equivalent to a sapling growing 50ft in height and a foot in diameter). Their roots penetrate a mere 3ft to 5ft beneath the soil's surface, thus rendering the trees vulnerable to toppling from high winds or heavy loads of snow. Excessive foot or auto traffic around their bases can further weaken the root systems of the venerable monarchs.

Practical Information Area Code: 209

Getting There – To Sequoia National Park **Ash Mountain entrance** (Hwy 198): from **Los Angeles** (221mi) I-5 north to Hwy 99 north to Hwy 198 east; from **San Francisco** (275mi) I-80 east to I-580 east to I-5 south to Hwy 198 east. To Kings Canyon National Park **Big Stump entrance** (Hwy 180): from **Los Angeles** (265mi) I-5 north to Hwy 99 east to Hwy 180 east; from **San Francisco** (240mi) I-80 east to I-589 east to I-205 (toward Manteca) to Hwy 120 east to Hwy 99 south to Hwy 180 east. **Cedar Grove entrance** (closed in winter) 32mi past Big Stump entrance on Hwy 180. Ranger stations at all entrances ($5/car entrance fee). Closest airport (84mi): Fresno (FAT) ☎498-4700. Closest Greyhound **bus** (☎800-231-2222) and Amtrak **train** (☎800-872-7245) stations: Fresno, or Visalia (51mi west). Major rental car agency branches *(p 253)*.

Getting Around – Kings Canyon and Sequoia National Parks are best visited by car, although some sights are easily accessible on foot. Many park roads are closed in the winter; check at visitor centers or ☎565-3351. Summer motor tours of Giant Forest and Kings Canyon ☎565-3381. Gas available at Lodgepole, Grant Grove and Cedar Grove. Use caution when driving; many park roads are narrow or rough.

Visitor Information – **Foothills Visitor Center** (near Ash Mountain entrance); **Lodgepole Visitor Center** (near Giant Forest); **Grant Grove Visitor Center; Cedar Grove Ranger Station; Mineral King Ranger Station**; visitor centers open Memorial Day–Labor Day daily 8am–6pm; rest of the year hours depend on weather conditions. Mailing address: Superintendent, Sequoia and Kings Canyon National Parks, Three Rivers CA 93271 ☎565-3134.

Accommodations – Reservations for rooms recommended. Accommodations in the parks include rustic and deluxe cabins, and motel units ($35-$88/day). Reservations and information: Sequoia Guest Services, PO Box 789, Three Rivers CA 93271 ☎561-3314. Rooms also available in Three Rivers (5mi west), Fresno and Visalia. **Campsites** available by self registration; no reservations accepted (except for Lodgepole Campground from mid-May–mid-Oct, reservations available through MISTIX ☎800-365-2267). Limited winter camping. **Backcountry camping** by permit only; permit (free) available at nearest ranger station. Campgrounds also located in Sequoia National Forest ☎784-1500, Sierra National Forest ☎487-5155 and Inyo National Forest ☎619-873-5841.

Preserving the Wilderness – In the late 1880s, logging concerns had penetrated the western Sierra Nevada and were laying plans to fell massive stands of giant sequoias. Recognizing the unique natural beauty of both the sequoias and the landforms of this area, the US Congress acted to protect the area. In 1890 a small parcel encompassing giant sequoia groves and watersheds that provided moisture to the San Joaquin Valley was designated Sequoia National Park. A week later, legislation was introduced to expand the parcel and to create General Grant National Park and YOSEMITE NATIONAL PARK. The three were the first national parks in the country to be created, after Yellowstone National Park in Wyoming. Sequoia National Park was doubled in size to include Mt Whitney in 1926, and in 1940 Kings Canyon National Park was formed, encompassing General Grant National Park and a massive portion of wilderness backcountry. Spectacular Kings Canyon, excluded from preservation owing to its hydroelectric potential, was not incorporated into the park until 1965.

★★ SEQUOIA NATIONAL PARK *1 day*

★★★ **Giant Forest** – *30mi from the Big Stump entrance, 16mi from Ash Mountain entrance.* Four of the largest known giant sequoias are found in this grove at the heart of Sequoia National Park. Numerous popular trails penetrate the forest, allowing serene acquaintance with the more than 8,000 well-established sequoias that flourish here, and Giant Forest Village offers traveler facilities and amenities.

★ **General Sherman Tree** – *1.5mi north of Giant Forest Village on Hwy 198 (Generals Hwy).* Largest sequoia on earth, this behemoth rises 274.9ft, measures 102.6ft in circumference, weighs almost 1,400 tons, and is between 2,300 and 2,700 years old. Its lowest major branch, hangs 130ft above the ground. It was named by a local cattleman in 1879 for Gen William Tecumseh Sherman, a hero of the Union Army during the Civil War.

Congress Trail – *500ft north of the General Sherman Tree on Hwy 198 (Generals Hwy). Pamphlet ($.50) available at trailhead.* This paved loop trail *(2mi)* winds through a forest of sequoias almost mythic in their majesty and proportion. Many of the park's most impressive trees stand at the far end of the trail, including the **President**, fourth largest tree in the world; the **House** and **Senate**, both tightly clustered groupings of sequoias; and **Chief Sequoyah**, a beautifully shaped sequoia named for the 19C Cherokee chieftain who created a phonetic alphabet for his people. The botanical designation for the genus *Sequoiadendron* is also thought to derive from the chief's name.

Crescent Meadow Road – *South from Giant Forest Village.* This scenic road accesses several attractions in the Giant Forest's southern portion. The **Auto Log** *(1mi)* is a felled and flattened sequoia trunk onto which cars may be driven. A short walk from a parking area *(1mi)* provides access to **Moro Rock**★; the impressive granite dome jutting into the sky offers, from its summit, inspiring views of the peaks of the Great Western Divide to the east and of the serpentine south park road and the Kaweah

River canyon to the south. Leading up to the rock is a 400-step stairway, built in 1931 by the Civilian Conservation Corps and designated a national historic structure in 1978, in recognition of its harmonious integration into the natural setting.

South of Moro Rock, the road loops past the **Triple Tree**, an unusual three-trunked sequoia, then continues east to **Crescent Meadow** *(1.5mi)* where an easy loop trail offers views of the rich green bog's serene beauty and of the majestic trees surrounding it.

Crystal Cave – *1hr 30min. 8mi south of Giant Forest.; 2mi on General's Hwy to turnoff on twisting access road. Visit by guided tour (45min) only, Memorial Day–Sept. $4 (tickets sold at Lodgepole or Foothills visitor centers).* One of a hundred caves inside the park, this subterranean wonderland reveals intriguing marble formations, including stalactites, stalagmites, draperies and flowstone. Within the cavernous interior are spaces variously dubbed "Organ Room," "Dome Room" and "Marble Hall."

★ KINGS CANYON NATIONAL PARK *1 day*

Big Stump Basin Trail – *Access .5mi from Big Stump Entrance. Trail pamphlet ($.50) available at trailhead.* The trail *(1mi loop)* leading through this picturesque basin reveals scattered stumps, felled sequoias and other reminders of late 19C logging operations. Many of the trees and stumps bear witness to the cavalier attitudes toward conservation that held sway during the late 19C; the Mark Twain Stump, measuring 24ft across, is all that remains of a giant sequoia felled in 1891 so that a section of it could be exhibited at the American Museum of Natural History in New York City.

★★ **Grant Grove** – *1mi west of Grant Grove Village. Pamphlet ($1) available at trailhead.* A short loop trail *(.5mi)* passes among several noteworthy giants, among them the **General Grant Tree**, ranked as the world's third largest sequoia. Towering 267ft with a circumference of 107ft, the tree was officially named the Nation's Christmas Tree in 1926, and 30 years later it was designated a living shrine to all American war dead. The **Gamlin Cabin** *(behind General Grant Tree)*, a reconstruction of a log cabin built in 1872 by the pioneering Gamlin brothers, contains some of the original structure's hand-hewn sugar pine timbers.

★ **Panorama Point** – *2.5mi northeast of Grant Grove Village; follow road to village cabins, then turn right.* A trail *(.4mi round-trip)* leads up to this overlook, offering spectacular **views** into the heart of the austere, 14,000ft Sierra peaks that rise to the east. Picturesque Lake Hume is visible below the point to the north. From the overlook, the **Park Ridge Trail** *(4.7mi round-trip)* offers vistas not only of the high country to the east, but out over the descending ranges to the west into the Central Valley.

★★ **Kings Canyon** – *From Grant Grove Village, drive north and east on Hwy 180.* Highway 180 winds 30mi east to Cedar Grove, hugging the walls of this spectacular canyon along the way. From rim to base, the gorge measures 4,000ft to 8,000ft deep, making it one of the deepest canyons on the continent. Actually, it comprises two distinct gorges: the western section is a broad U-shaped canyon gouged by glaciation; the eastern portion is a narrow, steep-sided V-shaped gorge cut by the South Fork of the Kings River.

Secreted in the cliffs of the lower canyon lies **Boyden Cavern**, a commercially managed marble cavern hung with luminous cave formations, including draperies, stalactites and stalagmites *(45min; open May–Oct daily; ☎209-736-2708)*.

From Boyden Cavern, Highway 180 follows the South Fork of the Kings River to **Cedar Grove Village**, a cluster of park facilities and a small visitor center nestled below peaks that loom more than 3,000ft above. The small village is named for the stands of incense cedars that grow in the vicinity. At Road's End *(5mi beyond Cedar Grove Village)*, several popular trails lead into the backcountry; the Mist Falls Trail *(8mi)* follows the Kings River in a moderate ascent to **Mist Falls**★, where the river washes down a sheer granite face.

★ SONOMA North Coast — Pop 8,121

Map p 236 — Tourist Office ☎707-996-1090

Site of the northernmost and final mission established in the California mission chain, this charming community set amid the sun-soaked orchards and vineyards of the Sonoma Valley is the WINE COUNTRY's most historically significant town.

The Bear Flag Revolt – Sonoma was born as the site of the San Francisco Solano Mission, established in 1823 as an initial outpost against the threat of Russian invasion from FORT ROSS, located on the coast about 30mi to the north. After secularization in 1834, a young Mexican general named Mariano Vallejo *(p 229)* was assigned to oversee distribution of the mission property and to establish a pueblo and presidio at Sonoma. Although the Russian threat never materialized, Sonoma's central plaza was the scene, on June 14, 1846, of the Bear Flag Revolt, an uprising of American settlers disgruntled with the Mexican control of California. The town was formally incorporated in 1850 and served as a supply and trade center for the area's nascent winemaking industry.

Today Sonoma's historic adobe buildings, occupied by shops, restaurants and inns, rub shoulders with contemporary structures. Several noteworthy examples of 19C architecture grace the town's residential streets south and west of the plaza, where attractive dwellings display elements of the Mission, Bungalow and Monterey Colonial styles.

SIGHTS *1 day*

★ **Plaza** – *Bounded by Spain St, 1st St West, Napa St, and 1st St East. Open daily year-round.* Laid out by Vallejo in 1835, Sonoma's 8-acre plaza is the largest of its kind in California. Anchored by the centerpiece **City Hall** (1906), an eye-catching Mission Revival structure of roughly hewn basalt stone, the plaza today is an attractively landscaped public park laced with walkways and dotted with duckponds, benches and play areas. Near the northeast corner, a dramatic bronze statue of a soldier raising the Bear Flag commemorates the 1846 revolt. Plentiful yew bushes and sycamore trees enhance the plaza's peaceful atmosphere amid the bustle of surrounding streets. At the **Sonoma Jack Cheese Factory** *(2 Spain St, north of the plaza)* visitors can observe, through a large window, the production of the area's famed version of Monterey Jack cheese. Located in the vicinity of the plaza are several buildings of the **Sonoma State Historic Park**.

★ **San Francisco Solano Mission** – *Open daily year-round. Closed Jan 1, Thanksgiving Day, Dec 25. $2. ♿ ☎707-938-1519.* Founded in 1823, California's 21st and final mission was established by Padre José Altamira as Mexican governor José Figueroa's preliminary step in solidifying Mexican holdings against potential invasion. Harsh conditions at the mission led to an 1826 Native uprising, during which the original wooden church and mission structures were burned. Reconstructed of adobe, the mission continued operation until 1834 when, following Mexican independence, General Vallejo dismantled the property and erected a parish chapel on the site of the original church.
Fully restored in 1913 and today part of the Sonoma State Historic Park, the simple, unadorned mission building now features period furnishings and artifacts displayed in the former padres' quarters, and a collection of watercolor paintings depicting the California missions, executed by turn-of-the-century artist Chris Jorgensen. In the restored chapel (now desanctified), the stations of the cross and framed paintings are authentic to the mission period.

Across Spain Street *(no. 217)* is the **Blue Wing Inn** (1840), an attractive, symmetrical adobe structure that formerly served as a saloon and hotel. Now housing an antique shop, the building is graced by an enormous wisteria vine winding along the second-story loggia. Adjacent to the inn is the **Ray-Adler Adobe** *(205 East Spain St)*, a dignified, Monterey Colonial structure with a hipped roof, second-story veranda and thick adobe walls.

Sonoma Barracks – *Open daily year-round. Closed Jan 1, Thanksgiving Day, Dec 25. $2. ☎707-938-1519.* This spacious, 2-story adobe structure (1841), its wide balcony overlooking the plaza, was erected to house Mexican troops stationed in Sonoma to guard the new pueblo against possible attack. Following US occupation of California, the barracks served various American regiments during the Mexican War. Now a museum of the Sonoma State Historic Park, the barracks features displays illustrating aspects of Sonoma's history, including artifacts from the various periods of Mexican and American settlement. The upper-level sleeping quarters are arranged as they might have appeared during military occupation, with cots and bunks in neat rows.
Adjacent to the barracks is the now-defunct **Toscano Hotel**, frequented during the 1890s mainly by Italian immigrants. Today the wood-frame structure is refurbished to its original appearance, and passersby can view a portion of the interior through its iron entrance gate.

★ **Lachryma Montis (Vallejo Home)** – *.5mi from the plaza. Leave the plaza by Spain St and turn right on 3rd St West; continue to its end. Same hours as Sonoma Barracks.* The elegant Victorian Gothic Revival residence set amid attractively landscaped grounds was named "tear of the mountain" in Latin, for the mountain spring on the property.
Born in MONTEREY, **Mariano Vallejo** (1807-1890) was commander of the Presidio at SAN FRANCISCO when he was called by Mexican governor Figueroa to administer the secularization of the Sonoma mission and the founding of a pueblo and defense outpost. In return, Vallejo received 44,000 acres of land near PETALUMA, which he developed as a private ranch. Appointed commander of all Mexican troops in California in 1835, Vallejo increased his land holdings and became a powerful figure in Mexican California.
Resigned to American takeover of the state and jailed briefly during the Bear Flag Revolt, Vallejo was elected to California's first state senate in 1850, and served as mayor of Sonoma (1852-1860) before retiring at Lachryma Montis.
The home's airy, spacious interior is furnished to reflect the period when Vallejo lived here, and provides a delightful picture of the lifestyle of Sonoma's renowned citizen. Also on the property is brick storehouse containing a small interpretive center and collection of artifacts from the 19C.

★★ **Buena Vista Winery** – *18000 Old Winery Rd. From downtown drive east on Napa St, turn left on 7th St and right on Lovall Valley Rd. Follow signs to the winery. Open Jul-Sept daily 10:30am–5pm, rest the year 4:30pm. Closed Jan 1, Thanksgiving Day, Dec 25. ♿ ☎707-252-7117.* Set on a pleasantly rolling site amid eucalyptus, oak and bay laurel trees is Sonoma County's oldest premium winery, founded in 1857 by Agoston Haraszthy, who bought the land from Mariano Vallejo *(above)*. Winemaking operations at the historic cellars ceased in 1979.
Of particular note are Haraszthy's renowned **wine cellars** *(closed to the public)*, dug into the limestone hill behind the winery by Chinese laborers in 1863 and visible through an iron gate. The lovely stone **Press House**, reputed to be California's oldest remaining winery structure, today reveals a refurbished interior; the wooden beams are original. The second-floor gallery hosts an artist-in-residence program featuring works by local artists and craftspeople.

★ **Sebastiani Winery** – *From downtown drive east on Spain St and turn left on 4th St East. Winery is on the right. Visit by guided tour (25min) only, daily year-round. Closed Jan 1, Good Friday, Easter Sunday, Thanksgiving Day, Dec 25. ♿ ☎707-938-5532.* This sprawling winery incorporates sections of a 1903 livery stable purchased by Italian immigrant Samuele Sebastiani in 1904. Sebastiani transformed the stone structure into a wine cellar, and construction of more recent buildings progressed throughout the first half of the 20C. The winery's reception room displays rudimentary casks, crushers and other equipment from the early part of the century. Sebastiani's two 60,000-gallon oak fermentation tanks are reputed to be the largest in the world outside of Heidelberg, Germany, and scattered throughout the winery are over 300 wooden cask heads and doors embellished with whimsical **carvings**, executed from 1967 to 1984 by local artist Earle Brown.

STOCKTON Central Valley — Pop 210,943

Map of Principal Sights p 2 — Tourist Office ☎209-943-1987

Stockton was founded just before the Gold Rush by German immigrant Charles Weber, who arrived in California in 1841 as a member of the Bidwell party *(p 20)*. Situated on the banks of the San Joaquin River, the town boomed during the mid-18C as a transportation hub for men and equipment bound for the southern mines of the GOLD COUNTRY. As gold declined and agriculture increased in importance, the city became a leading producer of the oversize farm machinery used to work the vast wheat farms that replaced cattle ranches in much of the Central Valley during the 1860s and 1870s. By the end of the 19C, production had shifted to steam tractors and the first caterpillar-tracked vehicles. Shipbuilding and agricultural processing were important early industries as well, and in the late 19C and early 20C, Stockton ranked second to SAN FRANCISCO in industrial importance.

Downtown Stockton has been in decline for several decades, much of its retail trade having relocated to malls on the north side of town. The city still boasts large areas of attractive, older neighborhoods, several situated in the vicinity of the **University of the Pacific**, California's first university.

SIGHT *1 hr*

★ **Haggin Museum** – *1.5mi from downtown. Take I-5 N, exit at Pershing Ave and continue to Victory Park. Open year-round Tue–Sun. Closed Jan 1, Thanksgiving Day, Dec 25. ♿ ☎209-462-4116.* This brick neoclassical structure standing amidst a large city park houses an **art collection**★★ *(1st floor)* rich in 19C American landscapes (*Looking Up the Yosemite Valley* by Bierstadt) and French academic and genre paintings (*The Nymphaeum* by Bouguereau). Additional highlights include works by Renoir, Gauguin and Inness. Other permanent exhibits focus on Native cultures and Stockton's history.

★ TRUCKEE High Sierras — Pop 3,484

Map p 73 — Tourist Office ☎916-587-2757

Sitting just north of LAKE TAHOE near the eastern edge of the state, along the former California Trail, this robust little town named for a 19C Paiute chief cultivates its Old West atmosphere. A bawdy railroad and logging center in the late 1800s, Truckee is also associated with the earlier 1840s tragedy of the **Donner Party** *(below)*. Its main street, **Commercial Row**, features quaint brick buildings dating from the 1870s and 1880s and today refurbished as restaurants and shops. A visitor center is located within the Southern Pacific Depot (1896), which still serves bus and rail passengers.

SIGHTS *1/2 day*

★★ **Donner Memorial State Park** – *1hr. From Commercial Row, follow Donner Pass Rd 2.3mi west. Or take park exit off US-80 west. Open year-round daily dawn–dusk. ⛺ ♿ ☎916-582-7892. Facility information p 257.* Commemorating one of the most dramatic episodes in American pioneer history, this park is situated on the site where members of the westward-emigrating Donner Party spent the fateful winter of 1846-1847.

A Shortcut West – Among the torrent of pioneering families who joined the Great Westward Migration of the mid-1840s was a group of three prosperous Illinois families headed by George and Jacob Donner and James Reed. After traveling to Independence, Missouri, the group started west on the Oregon Trail as part of the 300-member Russell Party. Along the way, they learned of Hastings' Cutoff, a newly touted, but untried route that left the established Oregon Trail just south of the Continental Divide, crossed the Wasatch Mountains and passed south of the Great Salt Lake to rejoin the California Trail at the Humboldt River. The "shortcut" was advertised as saving some 350mi. George Donner decided to try it and was joined by the Reed family and others.

In late July, the party of 89 people left the established wagon trail. Passing through the trading post of Fort Bridger, they set out on the new route, which they anticipated would bring them to California in ample time to cross the Sierra Nevada before the first snowfall. However, the Hastings' Cutoff proved more treacherous than they had imagined: after spending a month hacking a road through the Wasatch mountains, they had to struggle 80mi across the burning Great Salt Desert, which was twice as wide as they had been led to believe. By the time they joined the California Trail, crossed Nevada and arrived at the foot of the Sierras in late October, the party had lost most of its livestock and provisions, its good morale, and three crucially important weeks.

After resting for a week, the party started the trek over the Sierras, but they began too late. Early snows trapped them on the east side of the pass, and the group dispersed around Truckee (now Donner) Lake, constructing makeshift shelters. As the tortuous winter wore on, starvation took its toll. Desperate with hunger, survivors were forced to cannibalize the dead in order not to perish. It was not until mid-February that the first relief expedition was able to reach the snowbound "Starvation Camp." Though other relief parties followed, only 47 of the 89 pioneers survived the ordeal.

State Historical Society of Wisconsin

Pioneers on the Great Westward Migration

Pioneer Monument – Dedicated in 1918, this impressive, cast-bronze monument immortalizes the hardships and courage of early pioneer families. Sculpted by John McQuarrie, the figures of a man, woman and two children stand atop a 22ft pedestal, which marks the depth of the snow during the fateful winter of 1846-1847. The monument occupies the site of the cabin where the Breen family waited out the winter.

★★ **Emigrant Trail Museum** – *Open Memorial Day–Labor Day daily 10am–5pm, rest of the year 4pm. Closed Jan 1, Thanksgiving Day, Dec 25. $2. ♿.* Displays and a film *(25min)* recount the history of the Donner Party. In the museum's exhibit area, dioramas and artifacts detail the area's natural and human history, from early Native American life to the Great Westward Migration and the construction of the transcontinental railroad.

A nature trail *(.5mi loop)* leads along Donner Creek and past the large granite boulder that formed the back wall part of the Murphy family cabin. The boulder is now inset with a plaque listing the names of the survivors and of those who perished in the Donner Party.

Old Truckee Jail – *Spring and Jibboom Sts. Open Memorial Day–Labor Day weekends. $1. ☎916-582-0893.* This facility was constructed in 1875, when the town's rowdy population and red-light district necessitated a local lock-up. Originally a single-story, cavern-like stone structure with 30in-thick walls, the jail was modified in the early 1900s. Downstairs rooms were lined with steel plates, and an upper floor of brick, now used to display local history exhibits, was added to house female and juvenile offenders. The jail remained in use until 1964.

VENTURA Central Coast

Map of Principal Sights p 4 Tourist Office ☎805-648-2075

This low-key coastal city grew up around San Buenaventura Mission, which was built on the northwest edge of the Oxnard Plain in 1782. Spanish padres quickly discovered that the basins of the Santa Clara and Ventura rivers yielded voluminous crops of grain, fruits and vegetables, but not until Yankee and European settlers started buying up the area's ranches in the latter half of the 19C did agriculture surpass cattle-raising as the major industry.

Incorporated in 1866 as San Buenaventura, the city saw its first Europeans in 1542 when Juan Rodríguez Cabrillo *(p 22)* claimed the area for the King of Spain. Two major land booms in the last half of the 19C both corresponded with the coming of railroad lines from the East Coast. During this era, new settlers replaced the downtown's modest adobe dwellings with 2-story brick buildings. **Ortega Adobe** *(215 W. Main St)*, built in 1857, remains the only example of the early adobe structures *(open daily year-round; closed Jan 1, Easter Sunday, Labor Day, Dec 25 ♿ ☎805-644-4346).*

Between 1920 and 1930, the city's population nearly tripled when oil fields were developed along Ventura Avenue. The completion of the Ventura Freeway some 20 years later opened the area to still more growth. In contrast to the historic sites preserved along Main Street, the city's modern commerce has blossomed at busy **Ventura Harbor** *(access via Spinnaker Dr)*, replete with shops, restaurants and a fleet of 1,500 pleasure boats.

SIGHTS *1/2 day*

San Buenaventura Mission – *225 E. Main St. Open daily year-round. $1. ♿ ☎805-648-4496.* Padre Junípero Serra set the ninth mission (the last one he established before his death in 1784) at the foot of Sulphur Mountain overlooking the Pacific, a site halfway between SAN DIEGO and CARMEL. The mission, named for Saint Bonaventure, was scheduled to be the third established in the chain, but political power struggles delayed its founding for a dozen years.
When the first church burned down 10 years after it was built, laborers spent 15 years constructing its replacement, the large stone structure (1809) that still serves as the parish church. Over 1,300 neophytes lived at the mission during its peak years, and it became renowned for its horticulture, especially of such exotic crops as bananas, coconuts and figs. Some 60 years after secularization, an overzealous pastor whitewashed the beautiful Native American paintings that once adorned the interior walls (vestiges of these paintings remain in the Serra Chapel), but a restoration effort begun in 1956 corrected this and other so-called improvements.

Visit – *Enter through gift shop at 225 E. Main St.* A single-room **museum** displays a variety of religious relics, including vestments, the original side doors of the church, and the only wooden bells used in any of the 21 missions.
Now returned to a close approximation of its original appearance (buttresses on the facade were added after the 1812 earthquake), the **church** is distinguished by its stone-and-brick construction, arched side entry and tiered bell tower topped by a striped dome. A Moorish decoration crowns the side doors, which are reproductions carved with the river-of-life motif. Inside, the Romanesque reredos, painted to resemble marble, was made in Mexico City and shipped to the mission for the church's dedication in 1809.
Confined to a small courtyard adjoining the church, San Buenaventura's renowned gardens once stretched for many acres around the mission.

★ **Olivas Adobe Historical Park** – *4200 Olivas Park Dr. Open daily year-round. Closed major holidays. ♿ ☎805-644-4346.* Set on a bluff near the Santa Clara River, this well-preserved Monterey Colonial-style hacienda (1847) once belonged to wealthy cattle rancher Raymundo Olivas. The land on which he built his residence formed part of Rancho San Miguel, a 4,692-acre grant awarded Olivas and his partner in 1841. Don Raymundo, his wife, and their 21 children lived in the house for 50 years before the family sold the ranch in 1899. The site was donated to the city of Ventura in 1963.
Surrounded by a walled courtyard, the 2-story house is authentically furnished with period pieces. A small visitor center contains artifacts and historical photographs from the rancho era.

EXCURSIONS

Channel Islands National Park – *1 day per island. Park headquarters located at 1901 Spinnaker Dr in Ventura Harbor.* *Description p 44.*

Oxnard – Pop 142,216. *Follow Harbor Blvd south 10mi.* In 1898 brothers Harry, Robert, Benjamin and James Oxnard opened a sugar beet factory on a flat stretch of land south of the Santa Clara River to process the crop that grew abundantly in the region. The fledgling factory spurred the growth of the city that reigns today as Ventura County's manufacturing center.
Dredged from dunes and wetlands by the US Army Corps of Engineers in 1960, **Channel Islands Harbor** *(access via Channel Islands Blvd)* abounds with recreational activities such as boating, fishing and windsurfing.

CEC/Seabee Museum – *Naval Construction Battalion Center, Port Hueneme. From Channel Islands Blvd, turn right on Ventura Rd. Enter through Sunkist gate and obtain pass from guard. Open daily year-round. Closed major holidays. Contributions requested. ☎805-982-5191.* The museum honors members of the US Navy Construction Battalions (Seabees), who have served as military construction forces in combat zones since 1942.

WEAVERVILLE Shasta-Cascade — Pop 3,370

Map of Principal Sights p 2 — Tourist Office ☎916-243-2643

The passage of nearly a century appears to have had minimal effect on historic Weaverville, picturesquely set amid Weaver Bally, Oregon and Browns mountains. The town's 20C residents and visitors enjoy surroundings charmingly tinged with the flavor of the 19C; storefronts line sloping Main Street, and many commercial and residential structures survive from the late 1800s.
Gold strikes in the Trinity Mountains during the 1840s and 1850s spawned numerous mining camps; Weaverville is one of the few that prospered and survived to the present. Thousands of miners, many of them Chinese, settled here during the late 18C, and the town was designated the seat of Trinity County in 1850. Colorful exhibits detailing the history and geology of Weaverville and of gold mining in the

area are mounted at the **Jake Jackson Museum** *(south end of historic district)*, where collections include a fine assortment of antique firearms, Native arts and jewelry, historic photographs, and artifacts from Weaverville's Chinese residents, who constituted one-third of the town's population in the early 1870s. A restored, fully operable 2-stamp mill is located on the museum grounds *(open Apr–Nov daily, rest of the year Tue only; closed Easter Sunday, Thanksgiving Day; contribution requested; ☎916-623-5211)*.

SIGHT *1hr*

★ **Joss House State Historic Park** – *Adjacent to Jake Jackson Museum. Visit by guided tour (30min) only, Mar–Oct Mon, Thu–Sun; rest of the year Fri–Sun. $2. ♿ ☎916-623-5284.* This beautifully preserved Taoist temple (1874) is California's only authentic mid-19C joss house remaining in its original location (other joss houses have been relocated to NEVADA CITY and MENDOCINO). Temples of worship such as this were erected in California during the Gold Rush period by Chinese miners, in an effort to maintain their ancient religious traditions in the new, foreign land. Although Weaverville's Chinese population had greatly declined by the turn of the century, a temple keeper remained in residence until 1956, when the property was deeded to the state. Since its construction, the building has been continuously maintained as a house of worship, and even today the devout frequently pray here.

The temple is set back from the street on a peaceful knoll; its facade is distinguished by an ornamented wooden gate and panels brightly painted in bold Oriental characters. Elaborate canopies, symbolic hangings and figures of Chinese deities enliven the dark interior; offerings of food may be seen on the table before the carved altar. Displays in the **visitor center** *(adjacent to the temple)* offer glimpses into the history of the Chinese in California.

★★ WINE COUNTRY North Coast

Map of Principal Sights p 2

Lying just inland some 50mi northeast of SAN FRANCISCO, the Wine Country, defined here as the Napa Valley, the Sonoma Valley and the Russian River Region, thrives on natural gifts of abundant sunshine and fertile soil. A temperate climate, verdant farmlands and varied natural beauty have attracted and inspired writers such as Mark Twain, Robert Louis Stevenson and Jack London. Today the region, celebrated as the producer of North America's finest wines, is one of California's foremost tourist destinations.

HISTORICAL NOTES

Wine grapes first appeared on the peninsula of Baja California in 1697, planted by Padre Juan Ugarte at San Francisco Xavier Mission. Cuttings of these Criolla, or "Mission" vines, traveled north with the Franciscan padres as they established the Alta California mission chain, and the making of altar wine was the extent of California wine production until secularization in 1833. In the early 1830s, a French immigrant, propitiously named Jean-Louis Vignes (*vigne* is French for "vine"), established a large vineyard near LOS ANGELES, and by the mid-19C winemaking had became one of Southern California's principal industries. Vignes was the first in California to experiment with cuttings of European vines *(Vitis vinifera)* imported from his native France.

Father of California Viticulture – In 1849 **Agoston Haraszthy** (1812-1869), a Hungarian immigrant, arrived in California, having first worked at various occupations throughout the US. An experienced winemaker, in 1857 he purchased a 400-acre estate in Sonoma County from Mariano Vallejo *(p 229)* and cultivated Tokay vine cuttings imported from his homeland. The grapes flourished in the Sonoma County soil and **Buena Vista** *(p 229)*, Haraszthy's estate, became California's first winery dedicated to the production of premium wines.

In 1861, with promises of state funding from Governor William Downey, Haraszthy traveled to Europe to gather assorted *vinifera* cuttings for experimentation in California soil. But by the time he returned, Downey had been voted out of office, and the new administration refused to uphold its predecessor's commitment. Undeterred, Haraszthy persisted in selling or distributing at his own expense some 100,000 cuttings, training the area grape growers (many of whom were also recent immigrants), and experimenting with varieties and soil types. The quality of California wines steadily improved, and areas around San Francisco surpassed Southern California as the state's principal viticultural region.

Wine Country Boom... – Successful application of Haraszthy's discoveries resulted in a veritable boom of the wine industry throughout the Napa and Sonoma valleys in the last decades of the 19C. Among the wineries established during this period were **Gundlach-Bundschu [1]** (1858), founded by Bavarian immigrant Jacob Gundlach; **Charles Krug [2]** (1861), Napa Valley's first winery, established on land acquired by Krug, a native of Prussia, as part of his wife's dowry; and **Schramsberg Cellars** (1862), the wine country's first mountainside winery, with storage caves hewn out of the rock. Other renowned names of the present-day wine industry, including Inglenook, Beringer, Beaulieu and Trefethen (then known as Eschol), were established at this time.

...and Bust – As the 19C drew to a close, California grapevines fell prey to **phylloxera**, a root louse that attacks the susceptible *vinifera* plants. Entire vineyards were decimated. Researchers at the University of California, in concert with French grape growers who had experienced similar devastation in the 1850s, discovered that they could only combat the treacherous louse by uprooting the rotting vines, and replanting vineyards with disease-resistant wild grape rootstocks from the midwestern US, onto which *vinifera* cuttings had been grafted. The rebuilding process was slow, however, and the wine industry, having finally achieved a modicum of recovery by the early 20C, found itself faced with reduced demand and growing opposition from the American temperance movement. On January 29, 1919, the US Congress ratified the 18th Amendment, which expressly prohibited the manufacture, sale, importation and transportation of intoxicating liquors in the US.

N. Kerby

Pinot grapes

Prohibition and the Early 20C – Prohibition brought California's winemaking industry to a near standstill. Grape growers converted their vineyards to the cultivation of other crops, and industry-related artisans, such as barrel makers (coopers) and cork makers, turned to other pursuits. The vineyards did not disappear entirely, however; licenses were granted to seven California wineries (among them Christian Brothers, Beringer Vineyards, Sebastiani Winery and Beaulieu Vineyards) to produce wines for sacramental and medicinal purposes. Home production of "non-intoxicating" grape juice for private consumption was also permitted, although limited to 200 gallons per family annually. Passage of the 21st Amendment in 1933 repealed Prohibition, leaving grape growers and winemakers again faced with the prospect of rebuilding the industry. Reclamation of vineyards and organization of related trades and distribution systems were hampered by the Great Depression, and it was not until the early 1970s that the demand for fine wines increased, and California's wine industry was fully reestablished.

Wine Country Today – In recent decades the Wine Country has experienced tremendous development, despite the ever-present threat of phylloxera. The 1970s witnessed an explosion of small-scale operations, some of them housed in old wineries updated with state-of-the-art equipment, and significant increases in acreage devoted to grape production. A new generation of researchers and winemakers from the renowned Department of Enology at the University of California, Davis introduced advanced methods of cultivation and processing. Advisory boards began to oversee quality control of the region's output, and trade associations have dedicated themselves to the promotion of California wines throughout the world.
Today the Wine Country, moving beyond its traditional role, has become a renowned center for fine art and gastronomy. Trendy restaurants evince a growing awareness of the joys of pairing food and wine, and the past decade has given rise to a new generation of showplace operations, among them **Opus**, Clos Pegase *(p 238)* and the Hess Collection Winery *(p 235)*, combining wine production with the display of fine art and architecture.

Visiting the Wine Country – The best time to visit the Wine Country is in the spring, before the summer's heat sets in; and in fall when days are unfailingly sunny and winemakers are preparing for the harvest and "crush" (pressing of grapes). Visitors attempting to rush through the Wine Country, sampling an overabundance of wines and taking too many tours, may miss the chance to experience the region's relaxed pace and easygoing character. We recommend that visitors select no more that four wineries per day for tasting, and limit guided tours to one per day. Many wineries offer self-guided process tours. Visitors can also select from the region's more than 250 wineries by choosing to visit those of favorite labels, in addition to historic or famous wineries. In sum, the selection of wineries to visit should be informed, but personalized.
Travelers on tight schedules should bear in mind that despite the Wine Country's lush vegetation, inspiring vistas and enviable climate, its formal tourist attractions are secondary to its vineyards and wineries. Visitors for whom wines and winemaking hold limited appeal should plan less time to visit the region.
Picnicking is one of the joys of a visit to the Wine Country. Delis and roadside markets offer abundant, often elegant, takeout fare and nonalcoholic beverages, and many wineries feature picnic areas in attractive settings.

Wineries described below have been selected and rated based on their historic, architectural or touristic merit, not on the quality of their products. A comprehensive, updated listing of wineries with accompanying maps is available in the Wine Country Guide, *published annually by* Wine Spectator Magazine *and available at bookstores, newsstands and visitor centers.*

★★★ NAPA VALLEY *At least 1 day. Map p 236.*

Cradled between two shallow mountain ranges and extending roughly 29mi from San Pablo Bay northwest to Mt St Helena, the renowned Napa Valley is home to some of California's most prestigious wineries. Although the flat valley floor and surrounding slopes are planted with some 29,000 acres of vineyards, Napa Valley wines account for less than 4 percent of California's total wine production. Celebrated wineries are thickly clustered along Highway 29, the valley's principal thoroughfare, and are scattered along the Silverado Trail *(p 238)*.

Sights in Napa Valley are described from south to north.

Napa – Pop 61,842. Originally settled in 1832, this sprawling city on the banks of the Napa River experienced its first significant population boom during the post-Gold Rush period, when weary miners and vacationing San Franciscans made their way upriver from San Francisco Bay to the then-peaceful little resort town. Riverboat captains and bankers established businesses and elegant Victorian residences here throughout the mid-19C, transforming Napa into an active shipping and administrative center. Napa County's largest city, it still serves as a gateway for the abundance of wines and agricultural goods produced in the verdant Napa Valley. The name was derived from a Native American word meaning "plenty."

Downtown – *First and Second Sts between Main and Randolph Sts.* At the bustling heart of downtown Napa, the venerable **Goodman Building** (1901) with its gray stone facade *(1219 First St)*, is now home to the research library and museum of the Napa County Historical Society. Just across the street, an enormous contemporary **Clock Tower** overlooks the site where the first Magnavox speaker was invented in 1915 (a plaque commemorates the achievement). Other noteworthy buildings include the Italianate **Napa Opera House** *(1018 Main St)*, constructed in 1879, closed in 1914, and currently undergoing renovation for use as a performance space; and the stately, ornate **Winship-Smernes Building** *(948 Main St)*.

Victorian Neighborhoods – *South and west of downtown. Walking tour brochures available at the Chamber of Commerce, 1556 First St.* Napa's residential neighborhoods hold a wealth of elegant houses from the late 19C and early 20C. A stroll or a slow drive in the vicinity of **Jefferson, First, Third** or **Randolph** Streets reveals numerous well-restored homes built in the Italianate, Queen Anne, Eastlake and Shingle styles characteristic of Victorian architecture around the turn of the century.

★ **Codorniu Napa** – *1345 Henry Rd. From downtown Napa take Hwy 29 south to Hwy 121. Turn right and drive west 4mi, turning right on Old Sonoma Rd. After one block turn left on Dealy Lane and continue until it intersects with Henry Rd. Veer left and continue 1/2mi to driveway. Open daily year-round. $4 (tasting fee). ♿ ☎707-224-1668.* In 1872 the Codorniu family of Barcelona became Spain's first producers of sparkling wine made in the *méthode champenoise* tradition. Their Napa Valley operation is housed in this sleek contemporary structure (1991, Domingo Triay) at the foot of Miliken Peak. Sloping, grass-covered earth berms cover the winery walls, maintaining consistently cool temperatures in the storage and production areas within. From the entrance plaza, a peaceful view extends eastward over the lower Napa Valley. Prism-like window walls bring the view to the interior, which features a serene courtyard and displays of 16-17C European winemaking equipment.

★★ **The Hess Collection Winery** – *4411 Redwood Rd. From Hwy 29 north of Napa take the Redwood Rd/Trancas exit and drive west on Redwood Rd 6mi to winery entrance. Open year-round daily 10am–4pm. $2.50 (tasting fee). ✗ ♿ ☎707-255-1144.* Nestled in a remote corner of the Napa Valley on the slope of Mt Veeder, this renovated winery exemplifies the Napa Valley's growing trend of combining the production of wine with the display of fine art and contemporary architecture. Upon arriving at Mt Veeder in the early 1930s, the Christian Brothers *(p 237)* acquired the original stone structure (1903) from a local vintner and established their Mont LaSalle winery. In 1983 Swiss mineral water magnate Donald Hess leased the winery building, transforming the lower floors into a state-of-the-art winemaking operation and the upper portion into galleries to house his outstanding collection of works by 20C American and European artists. Francis Bacon, Robert Motherwell and Frank Stella are among those represented, and the collection also includes the work of such lesser-known artists as Rolf Iseli and Magdalena Abakanowicz.

The property adjacent to the Hess Collection Winery is graced by the **Christian Brothers Retreat and Conference Center [3]** *(4405 Redwood Rd)*, an attractive, Mission Revival-style complex (1932) of residential, religious and school buildings interspersed with lush, serene courtyards.

Yountville – Pop. 3259. *9mi north of Napa on Hwy 29.* This small, attractive community ranged along the east side of Highway 29 began in 1835 as a 6sq mi tract of land granted by Mariano Vallejo to George C. Yount (1794-1865), a frontiersman from North Carolina. Yount planted extensive vineyards and farmlands on the tract, and a community of Natives and workers developed on the fringe of the property. Two years after Yount's death, the community was named Yountville in his honor. Today the town is a good base for visiting the southern Napa Valley, with numerous hotels, bed-and-breakfast inns and trendy eateries. Of particular note is the historic brick Groezinger winery, today restored as **Vintage 1870**, a charming group of specialty shops and boutiques.

★★ **Domaine Chandon** – *1 California Dr. From the Yountville exit of Hwy 29 drive west toward the Veterans Home. Entrance on the right. Open May–Oct daily 11am–6pm, rest of the year Wed–Sun 11am–6pm. Closed Dec 25. ✗ ♿ ☎707-944-2280.* Visitors to this innovative complex (1973) are introduced to French

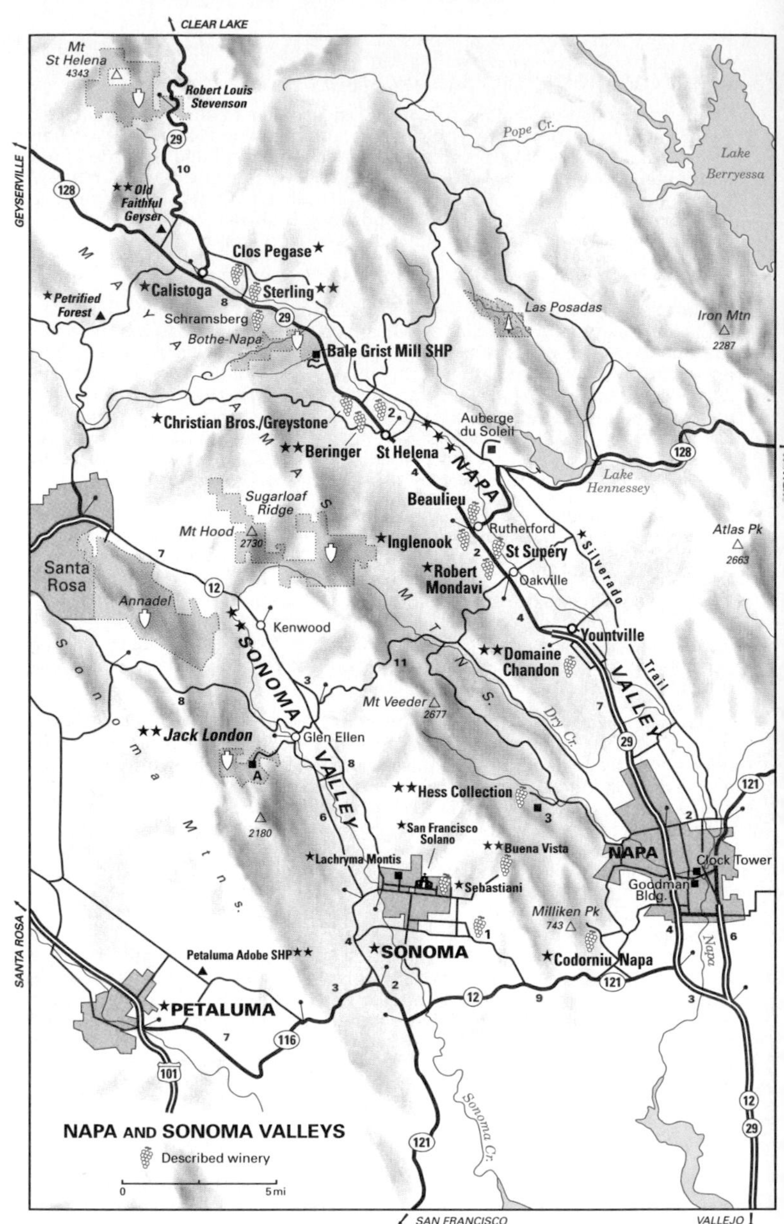

winemaking tradition with a dash of California style and appeal. Commissioned by Moët-Hennessy, an offshoot of France's famed Moët et Chandon, the modern structures of gray concrete harmonize with the sweeps and curves of the surrounding terrain; the arched ceilings are reminiscent of traditional wine caves in France's Champagne region.

In the entrance hall, an attractive gallery highlights skills and trades related to winemaking; an informative guided tour explains the principal stages of sparkling wine production according to the traditional *méthode champenoise*. An upscale restaurant is located within the visitor center; its outdoor terrace allows picturesque glimpses of the beautifully landscaped winery grounds, old oak trees and vineyards.

★ **Robert Mondavi Winery** – *7801 St Helena Hwy (Hwy 29), Oakville. Open daily year-round. Closed Jan 1, Easter Sunday, Thanksgiving Day, Dec 25. ♿ ☎707-226-1395.* Constructed in 1966, this striking building heralded a new generation of modern wineries designed to showcase art and architecture as well as wine. Sculptor Beniamino Bufano's figure of St Francis with outstretched arms greets visitors beneath the monumental arched entry to the complex, and temporary exhibits of works by local artists are regularly mounted here. In addition, Robert Mondavi Winery hosts an annual Summer Music Festival and a winter concert series.

St Supéry – *8440 St Helena Hwy (Hwy 29), Rutherford. Open daily year-round. Closed major holidays. $2.50 (tasting fee). ♿ ☎707-963-4507.* The modern winery structure houses a comprehensive **Wine Discovery Center**★ *(2nd floor)*, featuring in-depth displays explaining soil types, seasonal viticulture and the winemaking process. A unique, interactive display allows visitors to whiff and identify various wine-related aromas. Adjacent to the winery is the charming Victorian home built by Joseph Atkinson, the first vintner to own the property. The house *(accessible by guided tour only)* has been restored to reflect the lifestyle of an 1880s winemaker.

★ **Inglenook** – *1991 St Helena Hwy (Hwy 29), Rutherford. Open daily year-round.* ♿ *☎707-967-3300.* A tranquil drive through the vineyards leads to this stately, historic winery structure (1879) designed in an Americanized Gothic style. Constructed by Gustave Niebaum, an immigrant Finnish fur trader, the massive ivy-covered stone building contains one of the area's first "gravity-flow" wineries, designed to take advantage of the earth's natural forces in moving the liquid through the winemaking process, from the crushing of the grapes on the upper level to aging and storage in the cellar.
Guided tours of the building present the aging cellars, containing Inglenook reserves dating from 1882; and the **sampling room**, richly embellished with oak paneling and stained-glass windows. In the lobby, displays of photographs and memorabilia chronicle the history of Inglenook and of the Napa Valley. Inglenook wines are now produced at facilities in Oakville and Madera, California.

Beaulieu Vineyards – *1960 St Helena Hwy (Hwy 29), Rutherford. Open daily year-round. Closed Jan 1, Thanksgiving Day, Dec 25.* ♿ *☎707-967-5231.* Founded in 1900 by Georges de Latour, an entrepreneurial immigrant from France's Périgord region, Beaulieu ("beautiful place" in French) has become renowned for its California Cabernet Sauvignon. The visitor center features displays of corkscrews and coopering instruments dating from the 18C.

St Helena – Pop 4,990. A picturesque main street distinguishes this charming town at the heart of the Napa Valley. Owing to its varied and plentiful accommodations, numerous renowned restaurants and central location within striking distance of many celebrated wineries, St Helena is an excellent base for visitors exploring the entire Napa Valley.

Silverado Museum – *From Main St north turn right on Adams St, cross the railroad tracks and turn left on Library Lane. Open year-round Tue–Sun. Closed major holidays.* ♿ *☎707-963-3757.* Located in a contemporary structure adjacent to the town library, this small, densely packed museum is devoted to the life and works of **Robert Louis Stevenson** (1850-1894), author of such popular 19C stories as *Treasure Island* and *Kidnapped*. Stevenson, who honeymooned in a cabin on the slopes of Mt St Helena *(p 38)* during the summer of 1880, based his story *The Silverado Squatters* on his Napa Valley experiences. The museum's holdings comprise photographs, books, manuscripts and the author's personal belongings.

★★ **Beringer** – *2000 Main St (Hwy 29), north of downtown St Helena. Open May–Oct daily 9:30am–6pm (rest of the year 5pm). Closed Easter Sunday, Thanksgiving Day, Dec 25.* ♿ *☎707-963-7115.* Napa Valley's oldest continuously operating winery was established in 1876 by brothers Jacob and Frederick Beringer, German immigrants who arrived in the US in the 1860s. The winery operated throughout Prohibition, escaping the legislative strictures of the period by acquiring a license to produce wine for religious and medicinal purposes. Extending into the sloping hillside at the rear of the complex are some 1000ft of tunnels where the temperature remains a constant 58°F, an ideal environment for the aging of wine.
The centerpiece of the property is the stately **Rhine House** (1883), constructed by Frederick Beringer as his residence. Modeled after the Beringer ancestral home in Germany, the 17-room mansion features elegant woodwork, inlaid floors and an exceptional collection of **stained-glass windows**★. The oleander trees about the property were planted around the turn of the century by Jacob Beringer.

★ **Christian Brothers/Greystone Cellars** – *2555 Main St (Hwy 29), north of downtown St Helena.* The massive stone structure looming over Highway 29 was erected in 1889 as a cooperative effort by Napa Valley vintners in need of aging and storage facilities. The building changed hands several times before being purchased by the **Christian Brothers** in 1950s. This Catholic teaching order arrived in Martinez, California, in 1868, and began making wine for sacramental use during the early 1880s. In 1930 the winemaking operation was moved to the slopes of Mt Veeder in the Napa Valley, where the brothers established the Mont LaSalle winery (named for St John Baptist de la Salle, founder of the order). Profits from the sale of Christian Brothers wines were used to finance the order's network of schools for poor children, and the winery was licensed to continue production of wine during Prohibition for sacramental and medicinal use. The structure is planned as a future branch of the Culinary Instituteof America *(under renovation: scheduled opening 1995).*

Bale Grist Mill State Historic Park – *3369 St Helena Hwy (Hwy 29), 3mi north of downtown St Helena. Open daily year-round. Closed Jan 1, Thanksgiving Day, Dec 25. $2.* ♿ *☎707-963-2236.* From the parking area, a pleasant, sylvan path leads to this charming historic **grist mill**★, powered by a 36ft waterwheel. Established in 1846 by Edward T. Bale, an English physician who married a niece of Mariano Vallejo, the mill ground into flour the grain harvested by area farmers. The wooden mill building and waterwheel, which was replaced by a turbine in 1879, have been completely restored.
Docent tours and an audiovisual presentation provide a good introduction to the milling process, and periodic demonstrations allow a look at the mill in action *(call for mill demonstration schedule).*

★★ **Sterling Vineyards** – *1111 Dunaweal Lane. From downtown St Helena drive north 6.8mi on Hwy 29 to Dunaweal Lane and turn right. Entrance is on the right. Open year-round daily 10am–4:30pm. Closed Dec 25. $6.* ♿ *☎707-942-3300.* Perched like a secluded monastery atop a 300ft knoll rising abruptly from the valley floor, this contemporary complex of pristine white buildings (1969, Martin Waterfield) is one of the Wine Country's architectural grace notes. Conceived as an escape from the bustle and traffic of Highway 29, Sterling offers a unique twist on the traditional winery visits of the Napa Valley.

Visitors ascend to the winery from the parking area by a hushed ride *(5min)* on the vineyard's **aerial tramway**, from which tranquil views extend over the surrounding area. At the summit, visitors can follow informative panels on a self-guided tour through the winery, past colorful examples of tile work, across terraces with **views★** of the northern Napa Valley, and under campaniles that are a contemporary take on traditional mission-style bell towers. Sterling's collection of eight bells, dating from the early 18C, was acquired for the winery in 1972 from London's church of St Dunstan-in-the-East.

★ **Clos Pegase** – *1060 Dunaweal Lane. From downtown St Helena drive north 6.8mi on Hwy 29 to Dunaweal Lane and turn right. Entrance is on the left. Open daily year-round. $3 (tasting fee).* ✗ ♿ ☎*707-942-4981.* Housed in a harmonious sprawl of terra-cotta and earth-toned structures at the base of a volcanic knoll, Clos Pegase is a striking counterpoint to Napa Valley's numerous architectural styles. Founded by Jan Shrem, art collector and publishing magnate, the winery is named for Pegasus, the celebrated winged horse of Greek mythology, who is said to have given birth to wine when he struck his hooves to the ground of Mt Helicon, unleashing the Spring of the Muses and irrigating a vineyard below.

Clos Pegase Winery

Conceived as a temple to wine and art, the monumental winery **buildings★★**, designed in 1987 by Michael Graves, embody a contemporary view of themes from classical antiquity, reflected in oversize columns, triangular pediments and an open atrium at the heart of the complex. Selections from the owner's private art collection appear throughout the winery, from the tasting room walls to niches in the 28000sq ft of storage caves hewn into the backdrop knoll of volcanic tufa *(caves open to the public by guided tour only)*. Shrem's residence *(not open to the public)*, also designed by Graves, crowns the knoll, and is best viewed from the terrace at Sterling Vineyards *(above)*.

★ **Calistoga** – *1/2 day. Description p 38.*

★ **Silverado Trail** – Ranging parallel to Highway 29 between Napa and Calistoga, this scenic road offers a refreshingly slow pace and relaxed atmosphere that are a psychological as well as physical departure from the valley's main thoroughfare. Numerous crossroads link the pastoral Silverado Trail with the often traffic-choked Highway 29, allowing visitors ample opportunity to sample both aspects of the Wine Country as they proceed through the Napa Valley.

The road's many dips and curves accommodate the rolling terrain at the base of the ridges bordering the valley to the east, and acres of serene vineyards separate numerous wineries. Horseback riders and bikers are a common sight. A superb view of the Napa Valley can be had from the terrace of Auberge du Soleil, a fashionable upscale inn renowned for its fine restaurant.

★★ SONOMA VALLEY *1 day. Map p 236.*

Agriculturally more diversified than Napa Valley, Sonoma Valley's vineyards and wineries rub shoulders with orchards and pastures. The area's rolling hills and low, partitioning ranges inspired author Jack London to create the sobriquet "Valley of the Moon," in reference to the luminous orb's capricious disappearance behind mountain peaks during the author's nocturnal horseback rides through the valley.

★ **Sonoma** – *1/2 day. Description p 228.*

★★ **Jack London State Historic Park** – *From Sonoma, drive 5mi north on Hwy 12, turn left on Madrone Rd and drive to its end. Turn right on Arnold Dr, continue into Glen Ellen and turn left on London Ranch Rd. Open Apr–Sept daily 9:30am–7pm, rest of the year daily 9:30am–5pm. Closed Jan 1, Thanksgiving Day, Dec 25. $5/car.*

☏*707-938-5216.* Sprawling among the peaceful hills of the Valley of the Moon in the shadow of Sonoma Mountain is the 800-acre "Beauty Ranch," home of writer Jack London (1876-1916) throughout the last years of his life. Today the ranch is a state park dedicated to the memory of the author of such classic adventure stories as *Call of the Wild* and *White Fang*.

Sailor on Horseback – Raised among the factories and warehouses of OAKLAND, young Jack London felt early the stirrings of his adventurous spirit: at age 13 he had earned enough to buy his own skiff; at age 14 he pirated oysters from his own sloop, and at age 17 set off as a seaman on a 7-month voyage to Siberia aboard a seal hunting schooner. London also adventured all over North America; served as an overseas corespondent; and journeyed to Canada in the late 1890s to participate in the Klondike Gold Rush.

In 1905 London, then renowned as an author, socialist lecturer and champion of the underdog, purchased a run-down, 130-acre ranch in the hills near Glen Ellen, and settled there with his second wife, Charmian. In 1911 the Londons began construction of Wolf House, a massive 4-story mansion of hewn red boulders and redwood logs. On the night of August 22, 1913, just a few days before the couple was to move in, a fire roared through the house, leaving only the stone shell. Devastated by the loss, the Londons never rebuilt Wolf House, but continued to live in a small cottage on the ranch. Jack London died there, of uremia, at the age of 40.

Visit – *2hrs. Site plan available at park entrance.* Erected by Charmian London in 1919 as her residence and eventually a museum commemorating her husband, the rustic stone **House of Happy Walls★[A]** today serves as the park visitor center. Appointed with some of the custom-made furniture originally intended for Wolf House, the massive building contains memorabilia of both Londons, including artifacts from the author's life and work, letters, photographs, clothing, and objects amassed during the couple's world travels. Charmian London resided here from 1934 to 1945. A trail *(1.2mi round-trip; trailhead at House of Happy Walls)* winds through rolling meadows and forests to the ruins of **Wolf House★**, overlooking a peaceful valley in silent testimony to the Londons' dream. A short detour from the Wolf House trail leads to the **gravesite**, where the Londons' remains lie beneath a boulder atop a peaceful hill.

An additional **ranch trail** *(.5mi loop; accessible from the upper parking lot)* wanders about the ranch past stables, silos, piggery and the modest cottage where the author lived and worked *(not open to the public)*. More extensive hiking trails lead throughout the park and up the steep slope of Sonoma Mountain *(summit located on private property)*.

★ RUSSIAN RIVER REGION *2 days. Map p 240.*

The Russian River Region comprises three principal viticultural areas: the **Russian River Valley**, the **Dry Creek Valley★** and the **Alexander Valley**. Secondary viticultural areas of the region include Knight's Valley, Green Valley and Chalk Hill.

Santa Rosa – *1/2 day. Description p 224.*

★ **Healdsburg** – Pop 9,469. Founded in 1857 by Harmon Heald, a migrant farmer turned merchant, tranquil Healdsburg (HEELDS-burg) surrounds a picturesque central **plaza**, scene of numerous civic festivals and events. The community's location at the confluence of the Alexander, Dry Creek and Russian River valleys makes it an ideal starting point for forays into these areas.

Healdsburg Museum – *221 Matheson St, 2 blocks east of the plaza. Open year-round Wed–Sun. Closed major holidays.* ♿ ☏*707-431-3325.* Housed in a former Carnegie library (1911), this small museum houses a collection of artifacts from indigenous peoples and from California's Mexican period. Highlights include photographs, Native Pomo basketry, grinding rocks and weapons; extensive explanatory text illustrates the history of northern Sonoma County. Rotating displays highlight local arts, crafts and history relating to Healdsburg and the neighboring communities *(displays change three times a year)*.

★ **Hop Kiln Winery** – *6050 Westside Rd. From Healdsburg Ave in Healdsburg, drive west on Mill Ave and bear left on Westside Rd. Open daily year-round. Closed Jan 1, Easter Sunday, Thanksgiving Day, Dec 25.* ☏*707-433-6491.* This historic **hop barn** (1905), one of the finest existing examples of its type, functioned as part of California's North Coast hop-growing industry. Hops were dried in the three huge wooden kilns resembling giant inverted funnels, before being pressed and baled for shipment to area breweries. The kiln was renovated as a winery in 1974.

★ **Korbel Champagne Cellars** – *13250 River Rd. Open daily year-round. Closed Jan 1, Thanksgiving Day, Dec 25.* ♿ ☏*707-887-2294.* In the early 1870s, Anton, Francis and Joseph Korbel, recently immigrated from Bohemia, acquired a lumber mill at this site on the sloping banks of the Russian River and established a cigar-box factory. By the late 1870s, the surrounding hillsides had been largely denuded of their redwoods, and the Korbels planted grapevines among the stumps they couldn't remove. Construction of a large, handmade-brick winery building was completed in 1886 for the production of brandy and sparkling wine.

Highlights of a visit to Korbel include an informative guided tour covering both historical and contemporary versions of *méthode champenoise* sparkling wine production; and a wander through the lush rose garden on the slope below the Korbel mansion *(in bloom May-Sept)*. Visitors can also stroll through the old train depot, formerly the terminus of the Fulton-Guerneville branch of the Northwest Pacific Railroad.

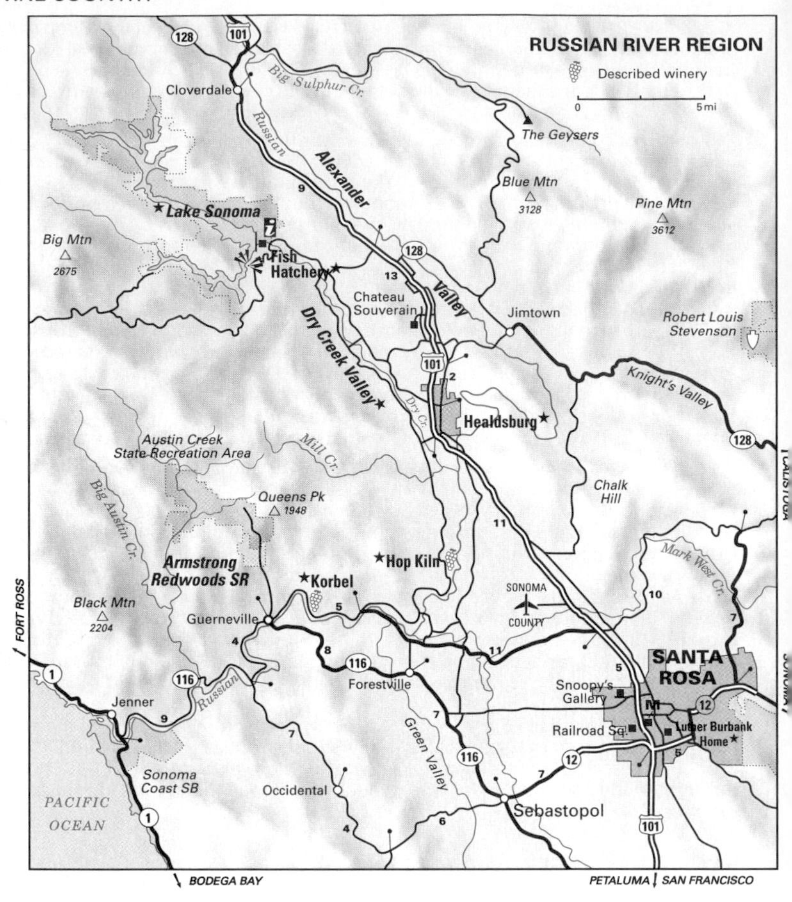

Armstrong Redwoods State Reserve – *2mi north of Guerneville on Armstrong Woods Rd. Open daily year-round. $5/car.* ♿ ☎*707-869-2015.* Lush, dense forests of varied species of trees surround a 500-acre grove of ancient redwoods that survived 19C logging operations owing to the conservationist efforts of Col James Armstrong. Today the grove forms the heart of an 800-acre state park that boasts some of Sonoma County's loveliest surviving redwood trees. A self-guided nature trail *(.5mi)* passes through cool, fern-laced glades to two enormous redwood trees.

★ **Lake Sonoma** – *21mi from Healdsburg by Dry Creek Rd. Visitor center at entrance to park.* Nestled in the coastal foothills of northern Sonoma County, this elongated reservoir was created in 1983 when the Warm Springs Dam was constructed at the confluence of the Dry and Warm Springs Creeks. Now a popular recreation area, Lake Sonoma offers a plethora of activities including boating, swimming, fishing, picnicking, hiking and camping in and around its sapphire waters.

★ **Visitor Center and Fish Hatchery** – *Open year-round Mon, Thu–Sun. Closed Jan 1, Thanksgiving Day, Dec 25.* ♿ ☎*707-433-9483.* Displays of craftwork and artifacts highlight the traditions and beliefs of the region's indigenous Pomo peoples, and the effects of the arrival of Hispanic and Caucasian settlers. Informative panels illustrate geographical formations and thermal activity in the area. The adjacent hatchery building, created by the Army Corps of Engineers to mitigate the environmental disruption of the Dry Creek engendered by construction of the dam, offers a unique opportunity to observe the spawning and hatching activities of steelhead trout and silver salmon. Fish climb an inclined channel or "ladder" into the hatchery where they are held, sorted and spawned, activities all visible from a mezzanine-level interpretive center. *Viewing times: Thursdays 10am, Jan 15–Mar 7 for steelhead trout; early Oct–Dec for salmon. Call ahead to verify.*

Overlook – *2.5mi from visitor center; follow signs.* Designed in harmony with the natural surroundings, the pergola-like belvedere offers soaring **views**★★ of Lake Sonoma, the dam and the surrounding mountains, including Mt St Helena in neighboring Napa Valley.

EXCURSION

Ukiah – Pop 14,599. *45mi north of Healdsburg on US-101. Map p 127.* Named for the fertile Yokaya Valley in which it lies (*yokaya* is Pomo for "deep valley between high hills"), Ukiah was first settled by farmers in 1856. Lumber is the leading industry today, followed by agriculture and tourism. Nearby, Lake Mendocino *(take North State St to right turn at Lake Mendocino Dr)* and **Clear Lake**★ *(24mi southeast on Hwy 20)*, California's largest natural lake, provide a host of recreational activities.

★ **Grace Hudson Museum and Sun House** – *431 S. Main St. Open Jul–Aug Tue–Sun, rest of the year Wed–Sun. Closed major holidays. Contribution requested. ♿ ☎707-462-3370.* Portraits of Pomo Natives by famed Ukiah artist Grace Carpenter Hudson (1865-1937) and the collections of her husband, ethnologist John Hudson (1857-1936), form the core of the art, history and anthropology exhibits in this museum. The adjacent 6-room redwood bungalow (1911), where the Hudsons lived for 25 years, was designed in the Craftsman style by San Francisco architect George Wilcox. Called the Sun House in honor of the Hopi sun deity whose image crowns the front door, the dwelling contains pieces from the couple's eclectic collection of furnishings.

★★★ YOSEMITE NATIONAL PARK High Sierras

Map p 246

One of the crowning jewels of America's national park system, this 1,200sq mi parcel in the Sierra Nevada mountains encompasses alpine lakes and meadowlands, awe-inspiring granitic peaks, waterfalls and groves of giant sequoia trees. The rare natural beauty of Yosemite Valley and the high country attract millions of visitors annually, who come to hike, camp, ski or simply drink in the magnificent scenery.

Human History – This area may have been populated as long as 4,000 years ago. In more recent centuries, it has been home to Miwok-speaking Natives who called themselves Ahwahneechee, "people of the place of a gaping mouth," presumably in reference to the shape of Yosemite Valley. The first recorded European incursion into the valley was in 1851, when 200 volunteers of the **Mariposa Battalion** set out to apprehend Tenaya, an Ahwahneechee chieftain accused of raiding nearby trading posts. Descending into the valley, the battalion named it Yo-sem-i-ty, apparently a corruption of a Miwok phrase they had misunderstood.

By 1853 the Ahwahneechee had been permanently forced out of the valley. Throughout the ensuing decade, Yosemite's beauty came to widespread attention through the works of artists such as Albert Bierstadt and journalists such as Horace Greeley and James Hutchings, publisher of *Hutchings' California Magazine* and the owner of an early hotel in Yosemite.

Fearing that commercial developers and homesteaders would destroy Yosemite's pristine character, concerned citizens, including respected landscape architect Frederick Law Olmsted, encouraged Congress to pass a law to protect it. In 1864 the Yosemite Park Act (later known as the Yosemite Grant) was passed, putting 39,200 acres of the valley and the Mariposa Grove of Big Trees *(p 246)* under the stewardship of the State of California. For decades the California legislature was torn between preserving Yosemite and developing its potential for further tourism, ranching and farming.

A Voice in the Wilderness – In 1868 a young wanderer named **John Muir** (1838-1914) found his way into the valley. Born in Scotland, Muir grew up on a Wisconsin farm and at the age of 29 set off on a botanizing expedition that took him a thousand miles on foot, from Kentucky to Florida. A year later he settled as a sawyer in Yosemite, building himself a small cabin near Yosemite Falls *(p 244)*. He spent the next five years in Yosemite, reveling in its natural beauty and gaining a reputation as an eccentric but intriguing local character. In the 1870s, he began publishing articles on Yosemite in prominent Eastern establishment magazines.

Muir left Yosemite in 1875 but continued his love affair with nature. Increasingly concerned with unchecked development in the West, particularly Yosemite, he wrote a series of articles for influential *Century* magazine, proposing that Yosemite be declared a national park. His efforts on Yosemite's behalf began a long career as the nation's foremost spokesman for conservation: Muir is credited with the 1892 founding of the **Sierra Club**, the nation's preeminent organization dedicated to preservation and expansion of wildlife and wilderness areas.

In 1890 Congress passed the Yosemite National Park bill, which set aside the wilderness surrounding Yosemite Valley and Mariposa Grove. It was not until 1905, however, after lobbying from Muir and others, that California receded the valley and Mariposa Grove back to the Federal Government, to be incorporated in the park.

National Park Service

John Muir in Yosemite, 1907

Testimony of the Rocks – The granite that characterizes Yosemite's landscape began as underground magma, forming from 200 million to 50 million years ago. As the sedimentary rock overlaying it eroded away, the granite was gradually exposed. Roughly 10 million years ago, movement along the San Andreas fault caused the Sierra Nevada range to dramatically uplift and tilt toward the west. Owing to its higher elevations, river courses became steeper, cutting into the granite and forming canyons. With the coming of the Ice Age, glaciers began to flow through the river courses, gouging out large U-shaped valleys and chiseling dramatic landforms. When the last glaciers receded 10,000 years ago, lakes formed in the depressions left behind. These in turn filled with sediment, becoming the meadowlands scattered through Yosemite today.

Flora and Fauna – With elevations ranging from 2,000ft to 13,000ft, Yosemite offers biodiversity. Its lower elevations are covered in ponderosa and Jeffrey pine, California black oak, willows, alders and cottonwoods; lodgepole pine, white bark pine, and red firs grow on higher slopes; white firs and quaking aspen can be found at many elevations. Wildflowers carpet much of Yosemite, blooming at lower elevations in the spring and moving up the mountainsides as the season progresses. Yosemite's animal population includes mountain lions, black bears, badgers, weasels and deer mice. Visitors may encounter mule deer, California ground squirrels and coyotes in areas frequented by humans. Common birds include Stellar's jays, Brewer's blackbirds, juncos and robins. The park also contains the Sierra Nevada's only known nesting grounds of endangered **peregrine falcons**.

America's Wonderland – Yosemite today encompasses 1,170sq mi, some 94 percent of which is officially designated wilderness. Most facilities are concentrated in relatively small Yosemite Valley, where annual visitation can exceed three million people. Grappling with this situation, the park service has taken measures to protect overused areas, and ongoing studies seek to determine better ways of conserving the environment while accommodating the visiting public. In 1984 Yosemite was named a UNESCO World Heritage Site.

★★★ YOSEMITE VALLEY

Described in Muir's writings as the "incomparable valley," the park's premiere attraction is a 7mi-long by .5mi-wide depression lying at 3,950ft, rimmed by sculpted granite peaks that tower 2,000ft and 3,000ft above and are veined by waterfalls that flow freely in spring and early summer. Now threaded by the Merced River and carpeted by meadows and woodlands, Yosemite Valley exhibits the characteristic U-shape of a chasm gouged by glaciers.
Note: Roads in Yosemite Valley can become extremely congested during the summer, and sights in the valley's eastern portion are inaccessible by private vehicle. Visitors are strongly encouraged to park in one of the many day-use parking lots at Curry Village and take the free **shuttle** *to points of interest. Shuttles (daily year-round; departures every 10-20min) make a circuit of valley. Parking is limited at Yosemite Village.*
Post numbers refer to post designations on site.

Visit *At least 1 day.* *Map p 244*

Enter the valley at the intersection of Hwy 120 (from Big Oak Flat entrance) and Hwy 140 (from Arch Rock Entrance, description p 247); .8mi after this junction the road splits into two, one-way thoroughfares separated by the Merced River.

★★★ **El Capitan** – *Post V18.* An open meadowland to the north of the road affords a superb **view** of this Yosemite landmark. The tallest unbroken cliff in the world, "the Chief" measures 3,593ft from base to summit. Composed of an extremely hard granite that resists weathering, its polished, yellow-hued surface attracts sightseers and rock climbers, who can often be spotted high up on its face.

Curry Village – *Post V22.* Nestled directly beneath Glacier Point, this group of shops, eateries and accommodations is the center of visitor facilities in the eastern end of the valley. The village was established in 1899 by David and Jennie Curry as Camp Curry, offering inexpensive tent accommodations.

Yosemite Village – The administrative and cultural heart of the park, the village contains the valley's main visitor center, museums, shops and food concessions. At **Yosemite Valley Visitor Center**, geologic and natural history displays and slide presentations tell the story of the area. The **Yosemite Theater** *(rear of the visitor center)* features live dramas, musicals and films, and is renowned for **Conversations With a Tramp**, a one-man dramatization depicting John Muir.

Yosemite Museum – *Open daily year-round.* ♿ This museum displays Miwok artifacts in addition to changing exhibits of art and photography, generally of Yosemite scenes. **People of the Ahwahnee** *(behind the museum; hours vary; check at visitor center)* interprets the Native lifestyle in 1872, some 20 years after contact with Europeans; the re-created Miwok village features reproductions of Ahwahneechee bark structures.

Ansel Adams Gallery – *Open daily year-round. Closed Dec 25.* ♿ *☎209-372-4413.* A commercial craft and photography gallery, this establishment was founded by Harry Best in 1906 as Best's Studio. It is now named for Best's son-in-law, **Ansel Adams** (1900-1984), America's preeminent landscape photographer. Adams' photos of the Yosemite wilderness are considered classics; prints made from his original plates are for sale in the gallery.

Practical Information

Area Code: 209

Getting There

By Car – Yosemite's four principal entrances *(map p 246)* are: Big Oak Flat (Hwy 120); Arch Rock (Hwy 140); South (Hwy 41) and Tioga Pass (Hwy 120). Ranger and information stations at all four entrances. Recommended winter route: Hwy 140. From **San Francisco** (193mi): I-580 east to I-205 east to Hwy 120 east to Big Oak Flat entrance. From **Los Angeles** (313mi): I-5 north to I-99 north; at **Fresno** take Hwy 41 north to South entrance. From other points via **Merced**: Hwy 140 east to Arch Rock entrance.

By Air – Closest airport: Fresno Air Terminal (FAT) 95mi; bus service from Fresno to Yosemite *(below)*.

By Bus and Train – Yosemite Gray Line (☎443-5240) service from Fresno (218mi) and Merced (82mi). Closest Amtrak station: Merced; fare includes bus transfer (☎800-872-7245).

Getting Around

Limited short-term public parking located at Yosemite Village, Lower Yosemite Falls and Merced River picnic areas; extensive day-use parking at Curry Village. Temporary parking permitted at scenic roadside turnouts at the southwestern entrance to Yosemite Valley. Narrated **bus tours** of the park (2-8hrs); tickets and departures available from Yosemite Lodge, Curry Village, the Ahwahnee Hotel and Yosemite Village; advance reservations suggested, ☎372-1240. Maximum speed limit 45mph. Off-road driving not permitted. Chains may be required on some park roads in winter.

General Information

Visitor Information – Yosemite National Park is open daily year-round. $5/car. **Yosemite Valley Visitor Center** (Yosemite Village, shuttle stops 6 and 9); open daily year-round. **Tuolumne Meadows Visitor Center** (south of Tioga Rd), open Memorial Day–Sept. **National Park Service**, PO Box 577, Yosemite National Park CA 95389 ☎372-0264 *(disabled traveler information p 251)*.
The *Yosemite Guide*, a free quarterly publication available throughout the park, contains information on park activities.

Accommodations – Reservations for hotel rooms and campsites are strongly recommended. The Ahwahnee Hotel and High Sierra Camps should be reserved a year in advance.
Accommodations available at the Ahwahnee Hotel ($208), Wawona Hotel ($65-$85) and Yosemite Lodge ($75-$90). Tent cabins, cabins and rooms at Curry Village ($35-$50), Tuolumne Meadows Lodge ($35) and White Wolf Lodge ($30-$55). **High Sierra Camps** (Jul–early Sept) offer dormitory-style cabins in conjunction with 4-7 day guided hikes (breakfast and dinner included). Room reservations available through **Yosemite Reservations**, 5410 East Home Ave, Fresno CA 93727 ☎252-4848, ☎454-2000 (winter). Lodging also available in nearby towns of Oakhurst, Fish Camp, Lee Vining and Bass Lake. *Rates quoted are average prices for a double room.*
Reservations required for most **campgrounds** through MISTIX outlets nationally, no more than 8 weeks in advance (MISTIX, PO Box 85705, San Diego CA 92138-5705 ☎800-365-2267). Campsites can also be obtained at Curry Village and Big Oak Flat entrances. Limited year-round camping available. Housekeeping Camps (campsites with shelters and cots) also available (open spring–fall, contact Yosemite Reservations). Additional information: Campground Office *(National Park Service address above)* ☎372-0200 or 372-0265.
Permits required for **backcountry camping**. Requests processed Mar–May, attention: Wilderness Permits *(National Park Service address above)*.

Useful Numbers

Police/Fire	**911**
Medical Assistance (non-emergency)	531-2000
Dental Assistance	289-1212
Lost and Found	372-4720
Road and Weather Info	372-0200
Road Service (repair and towing)	372-1221
Ski Conditions (Badger Pass)	372-1000

Recreation – More than 800mi of trails provide excellent **hiking** and **backpacking**. Park stores and visitor centers sell several types of trail maps. Organized hikes, and **rock climbing classes** through the Yosemite Mountaineer School (☎372-1244). Guided **horseback** trips (2-8hrs) organized through stables in the park (☎372-1248). **Bicycle** rentals at Yosemite Lodge and Curry Village. Bikes allowed on roads and bike paths only. **Fishing** allowed on the park's waterways; California license required (available at the Sports Shop in Yosemite Village and at the Wawona store).
Both **downhill** and **cross-country skiing** and instruction at Badger Pass. Rentals at the Badger Pass Ski Lodge. Free Ski shuttle departs twice each morning from Curry Village, the Ahwahnee Hotel and Yosemite Village; tickets available at Yosemite hotels (reserve the night before). Outdoor **Ice Skating** rink at Curry Village operates Nov–Mar ☎372-1441.

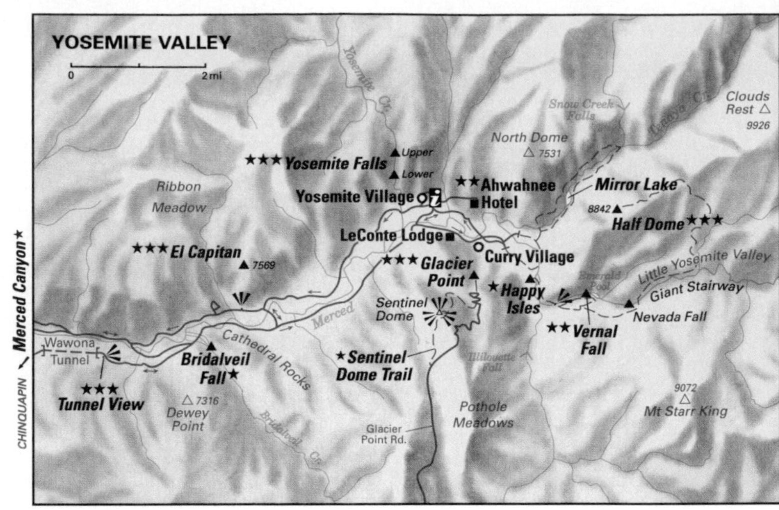

★★ **Ahwahnee Hotel** – *.8mi east of Yosemite Village center.* This massive granite and wood hotel (1927) is Yosemite's largest, most elegant structure. Considered by Ansel Adams to be "one of the world's distinctive resort hotels," it reflects the rustic style popular in national parks during the early 20C. The interior features Native American rugs and motifs echoing the geometric patterns of the Art Deco style. Floor-to-ceiling windows and large wrought-iron chandeliers enhance the majestic proportions of the cavernous **dining room** (130ft long by 34ft high).

★★★ **Yosemite Falls** – *Trailhead .5mi west of Yosemite Village center.* A paved trail *(.5mi round-trip)* provides a stunning approach to these falls, formed as the waters of Yosemite Creek plunge 2,425ft in three stages. From the traihead, both the **lower fall** (320ft), and the wispy **upper fall** (1,430ft) can be seen above, though the middle cascade (675ft) is only partially visible from this viewpoint. On clear, full moon nights in late spring, the phenomenon that John Muir called "moonbows" can sometimes be seen reflected in the falls.

A strenuous trail leads up the west side of the falls to a vantage point above the upper fall *(7mi round-trip; trailhead accessible from Yosemite Lodge shuttle stop).*

LeConte Memorial Lodge – *Post V21.* The sheer walls of Yosemite Valley are echoed in the vertical design of this granite, Tudor Revival structure; a steeply pitched roof and a floor-to-ceiling fireplace dominate the interior. Built in 1903 as a Sierra Club reading room and public information center, the lodge continues to serve these functions today. Named for club activist Joseph LeConte, it was relocated here from Curry Village in 1919.

★ **Happy Isles** – *Post V24.* As the Merced River tumbles into the valley here, it encircles these two small islands, accessible by footbridge. A **nature center** by the river displays life-size dioramas of woodland scenes featuring taxidermically preserved animals. Behind the nature center an interpretive boardwalk trail leads through a pleasant fenn, or marsh.

Vernal Fall Trail – *3mi round-trip; trailhead at Happy Isles bridge.* This paved trail ascends the steep, picturesque canyon of the Merced River before crossing a bridge *(.7mi)* from which extends a view of 317ft **Vernal Fall**★★. This wide, impressive cascade is part of the "Giant Stairway," a steep rock course that links Little Yosemite Valley, in the alpine highlands, to the main valley floor. Slab-sided boulders at the river's edge *(.9mi)* provide a closer **view** upriver of the fall. From here, the often slippery trail continues beside the river, soon reaching the man-made, 500-step Granite Stairs, which climb to the brink of the fall, with lovely Emerald Pool on the right.

The 594ft **Nevada Fall** lies a strenuous climb farther up the Giant Stairway *(7mi round-trip from Happy Isles)*; and the trail continues to join a steep cable trail to the top of Half Dome *(below; 16.8mi round-trip from Happy Isles).*

Mirror Lake Hike – *2mi round-trip; trailhead at post V26.* A paved trail follows the west side of Tenaya Creek to this small lake, which reflects nearby cliff faces in its surface. Half Dome towers above it to the east. A loop trail *(3mi)* continues beyond the lake, circling through the marsh meadows formed by Tenaya Creek and returning down the opposite side of the lake.

★★★ **Half Dome** – This unique geologic landmark rises 4,800ft above the northeast end of the valley. Scientists believe that glacial action initially cracked what was once a full granite dome along a vertical weakness, leaving only half the formation in place. Relatively rare, domes such as those found throughout Yosemite are formed as surface rock exfoliates (or falls away) in concentric scales like an onion skin.

★★★ Excursion to Glacier Point *4 hrs. 60mi round-trip.*

This scenic drive leads to Glacier Point, a sheer rock cliff towering above Curry Village. From this lofty perch, some of Yosemite's most renowned vistas extend down on the valley and across to the peaks on its northern side. From the valley floor, an arduous trail *(4.8mi)* climbs 3,200ft to the point's summit *(trailhead at post V18).*

From Yosemite Village, follow signs to Hwy 41 east, also called the Wawona or Fresno Rd.

★ **Bridalveil Fall** – *Post W1.* A short paved path leads to the base of this filmy fall, formed as Bridalveil Creek plunges 620ft from a small valley above.

★★★ **Tunnel View** – *Post W2.* From the turnout at the north side of the Wawona Tunnel extends a classic view into Yosemite Valley. El Capitan dominates the northwest end, and on the south side rise humped Cathedral Rocks, Bridalveil Fall, Cathedral Spires, Sentinel Rock, and in the distance, the distinctive shapes of Half Dome and Clouds Rest. The Mariposa Battalion used this approach to the valley in their historic 1851 march *(p 241)*.

Beyond the Wawona Tunnel, Highway 41 hugs the forested eastern slopes above the Merced River Canyon.

At the Chinquapin crossroads (post W5), turn east onto Glacier Point Rd (may be closed Nov-May) and continue 1.9mi to turnout (post G1).

This **view** overlooks the **Merced Canyon**★, where the dramatic effects of climate are clearly visible. The canyon's dry north side is sere, while the wetter south side rolls in green, lightly forested hills.

★ **Sentinel Dome Trail** – *2.2mi round-trip; trailhead .1mi beyond post G8.* A generally level trail leads through upland meadows to a paved fire road at the base of granitic **Sentinel Dome**. *Follow the road to the right around the side of the dome and ascend its gently sloping north side.* The top of the dome affords a panoramic **view**★★★, which includes Yosemite Valley from El Capitan to Half Dome, and above it, Little Yosemite Valley, Cloud's Rest, and the peaks rolling north toward Tuolumne Meadows. To the east rise the peaks of the Clark Range.

★★★ **Glacier Point** – *Post G11.* ✗. One of the nation's most spectacular viewpoints, this rocky peak hovers 3,000ft above the valley floor. From here, Vernal and Nevada Falls, Half Dome and Little Yosemite Valley are visible to the northeast, while Yosemite Falls ribbon a cliff face to the northwest. From early in the 20C until 1968, Glacier Point was the site of a nightly tradition called the Firefall. A red-bark bonfire was built here, then shoved off the cliff face in a glowing cascade to entertain spectators gathered in Curry Village below.

J. Warden/Travel Image

Yosemite Valley

★ SOUTH YOSEMITE *At least 1/2 day. Map p 246*

Wawona Area – Since the mid-19C, the Wawona area has attracted travelers to its Mariposa Grove of Big Trees. **Galen Clark**, a homesteader who settled here in 1856, was one of the first white men to "discover" these giant sequoias, and he fought to have them preserved under the 1864 Yosemite Grant. Clark also established Wawona's first lodging house, which he eventually sold to the three **Washburn Brothers** from Vermont. Clark later became the official guardian of Yosemite, while the Washburns went on to develop Wawona as a major resort area. This portion of Yosemite was not incorporated into the park until 1932, and a number of private cabins still stand along the Merced River.

★ **Pioneer Yosemite History Center** – *Post W10. From the parking lot off Hwy 41 and adjacent to the Wawona Hotel grounds, walk away from the road and toward the old gray barn. Open daily year-round. Period reenactments mid-Jun–Labor Day Wed–Sun.* ♿ Most of these historic structures, depicting life in late 19C Yosemite, were moved to this location from various parts of the park in the 1950s and 1960s. The gray barn, built by the Washburn brothers in the late 1880s to service stages

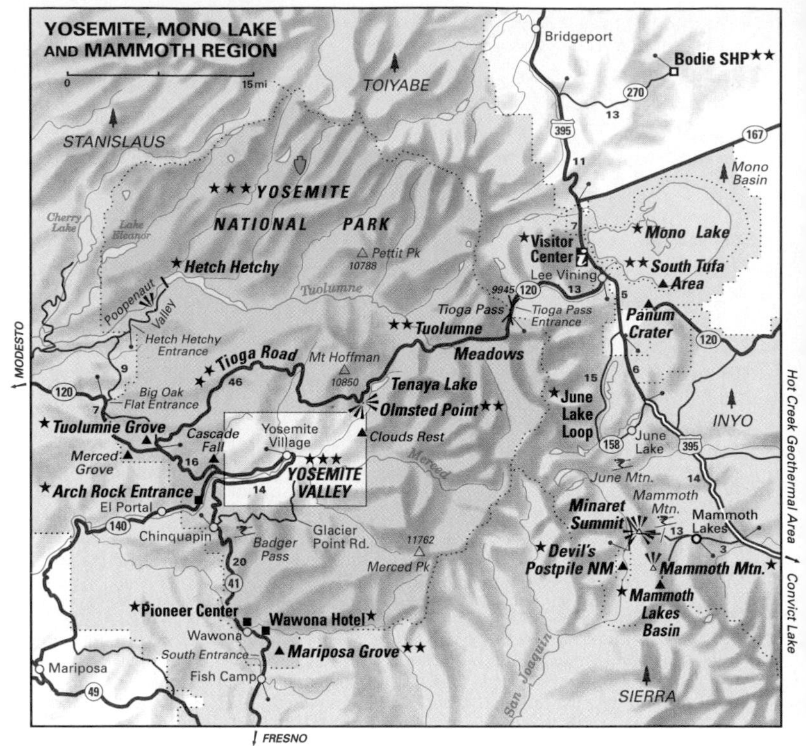

traveling the Wawona Road, is now used as a horse stable. To the left of the barn lies a long structure housing historic carriages. *Carriage rides (10min) around the immediate Wawona area offered at various times during the week. For information inquire at the book/souvenir shop attached to the carriage house.*

The covered bridge across the Merced River was built by the Washburn brothers in 1875 and served as the main thoroughfare across the river until 1931. The cluster of 19C structures on the west side of the river includes three private cabins, a blacksmith shop, a cavalry office, a ranger patrol building and a Wells Fargo office. *Interpretive pamphlet ($.25) available in the kiosk beside the covered bridge.*

★ **Wawona Hotel** – Built by the Washburn Brothers in the 1870s, this complex of Victorian clapboard buildings bespeaks the brothers' New England roots. The 2-story white frame hotel is fronted by a comfortable veranda; behind it and to the east lie clapboard cottages filigreed with gingerbread ornamentation. To the west is the **Thomas Hill Studio**, a small,19C Victorian cottage used by the respected landscape artist. *Open periodically for art exhibits. Check* Yosemite Guide *for schedule.*

★★ **Mariposa Grove of Big Trees** – *2mi east of South entrance. Vehicles not permitted; parking available at post S2. Tram departs Jun–Sept daily 9am–6pm. 1hr. $6.* Spread over 250 acres, this grove encompasses roughly 400 mature giant sequoias *(p 226)*, making it by far the largest of the three groves within Yosemite. The tram ride offers interpretive tours through Mariposa Grove, stopping at major attractions. Alternatively, a hiking trail loops and branches through Mariposa's upper and lower groves.

Fallen Monarch – This tree fell several hundred years ago, but the amazingly resistant sequoia heartwood of its trunk has not decayed. With their ability to resist destruction by fungus, fire and insects, fallen sequoias can exist on the ground for 2,000 years or more.

Bachelor and Three Graces – These four trees press close together, exemplifying the manner in which sequoias, though enormous (the Three Graces each measure over 200ft), can grow in dense stands.

Grizzly Giant – Leaning at a 17° angle, this 2,700-year-old tree is one of the largest and most ancient in the park, measuring 209ft tall and 96ft around at its base. The gigantic branch visible halfway up its trunk has a 7ft diameter and is believed by scientists to be larger than any tree east of the Mississippi River. The **California Tunnel Tree** *(50 yards downhill)* is an example of the late-18C–early-19C fashion for boring tunnels through the bases of these enormous trees.

Fallen Wawona Tunnel Tree – *Upper grove; about 2mi.* Internationally known, this giant had a 10ft by 26ft tunnel cut through it in 1881. Its fame drew large numbers of visitors and their vehicles, and the impact of so much disturbance to the tree's shallow root system finally took its toll. In the winter of 1968-1969, the tree succumbed under the weight of a heavy snow.

Mariposa Grove Museum – *Upper grove, about 1.8mi. Open during operation of tram (above).* Housed in a replica of the original log cabin that Galen Clark built here in 1864, the museum features an exhibit on the natural history of the giant sequoias.

★★ TIOGA ROAD *3 hrs. 46mi one-way. Map p 246. Closed Nov-May.*

This west-east road across the Yosemite high country passes through lovely coniferous forests, spectacular granitic terrain and rolling alpine meadowland, and ranks as one of the most scenic wilderness drives on the continent.

Begin at intersection of Tioga Rd and Big Oak Flat Rd, just east of Crane Flat.

The road initially winds through evergreen forests. After about 14mi, the forests become sparser and the vista begins opening into the stone-clad landscape of the High Sierra, with 10,850ft Mount Hoffman towering to the east and the Clark Range visible on the southeastern horizon.
After 1.7mi, the road passes between granitic cliffs that are prime examples of the processes of glacial polish and exfoliation. A roadside turnout 6mi beyond (T18) identifies and gives the natural history of five of the park's most common coniferous trees. After 3mi, **Clouds Rest** (9,926ft) looms into view to the east. Its summit is frequently shrouded in clouds, especially in spring and fall.

★★ **Olmsted Point** – *1.4mi from Clouds Rest viewpoint.* This renowned viewpoint, with its breathtaking Sierra vistas, is named for Frederick Law Olmsted. Panels explain geologic processes and identify visible peaks, such as Half Dome and Clouds Rest. A trail *(.25mi)* leads to a dome overlooking Tenaya Canyon, from Half Dome to Tenaya Lake.

Tenaya Lake – *1.8mi.* This large glistening alpine lake is skirted by white-sand beaches and shaded picnic spots. Named for the Ahwahneechee chief, the lake formed in a depression gouged by the Tuolumne Glacier. Area Natives called it "Lake of the Shining Rocks" because of the polished granite cliffs surrounding it.

★★ **Tuolumne Meadows** – *6mi.* ✗. This famed, sprawling alpine meadowland lies at 8,600ft and is braided by the Tuolumne River and its branches. Considered the heart of the high country, Tuolumne offers a visitors center, lodging, restaurants and numerous backcountry trails. Both the 211mi John Muir Trail and the 2,350mi Pacific Crest Trail *(p 260)* pass through here, the latter extending from the Canadian American border in the state of Washington to the US border with Mexico.
Just east of the visitor center the road runs below sharply angled Lembert Dome to the north and follows the Dana Fork of the Tuolumne River to Dana Meadows. Here it exits the park at 9,945ft **Tioga Pass**, the highest roadway pass in the state.
After leaving the park, Highway 120 passes Tioga and Ellery Lakes, then descends sharply along the north face of spectacular Lee Vining Canyon and continues on to its junction with US 395 *(13mi).*

ADDITIONAL SIGHTS

★ **Arch Rock Entrance** – Yosemite's most picturesque entrance is named for the two enormous boulders under which Highway 140 (the Merced Road) passes as it enters the park. Beyond the arch, the road winds through Merced Canyon *(p 245)*, following the scenic boulder-strewn course of the Merced River toward Yosemite Valley. **Cascade Fall** *(2mi north of entrance)* tumbles off the canyon walls beside the river in spring and early summer.

★ **Tuolumne Grove of Big Trees** – More intimate and less developed than the popular Mariposa Grove *(p 246)*, this stand contains 25 mature giant sequoias *(p 226)* scattered amid a forest of ponderosa pine, incense-cedar and sugar pine. Either this grove or the nearby **Merced Grove**, the smallest in the park *(accessible via a 2mi hike down a fire road off the new Big Oak Flat Rd)*, was apparently discovered by members of the Joseph Walker party when they crossed the Sierra in 1833.

Visit – *From Yosemite Valley, follow Hwy 120 west 9.5mi to Crane Flat. Turn right onto the Tioga Rd for .5mi, then left onto the Old Big Oak Flat Rd. Vehicles not permitted in the grove.* A narrow, scenic one-way road passes through Yosemite's only standing tunnel tree. Now dead, this sequoia was tunneled in 1878, making it the first such tree in the park. A short interpretive trail *(20min)* leads past about a dozen of the grove's giant sequoias.

★ **Hetch Hetchy** – Once flowing through a valley that nearly matched the Yosemite Valley in natural beauty, the Tuolumne River was dammed in 1923, forming this reservoir to provide water and hydroelectric power for the city of SAN FRANCISCO. In the early 20C, John Muir and the Sierra Club launched a futile conservation battle opposing the dam. Construction commenced in 1919, and the scenic valley was submerged by 1934. The term *hetch hetchy* derives from a Miwok word for one of their foodstuffs.

Visit – *Access via Hetch Hetchy entrance. From Yosemite Valley, exit the park via Hwy 120 (Big Oak Flat entrance, turn right on Evergreen Rd and right on Hetch Hetchy Rd.* The Hetch Hetchy Road twists and winds above the Poopenaut Valley, actually the canyon of the Tuolumne River. A turnout *(4.8mi)* offers a **view★** of the valley. At the reservoir, a bridge *(foot traffic only)* crosses O'Shaughnessy Dam and provides access to the northern side of the reservoir, where scenic trails follow the water's edge or lead into the sprawling, pristine wilderness of north Yosemite.

EXCURSION

★ **Mono Lake** *1/2 day. Description p 118.*

"Even suicide is cheaper out here. The California motorist will, on the average, knock off three pedestrians a month."

Groucho Marx, 1949

CALENDAR OF EVENTS

Listed below is a selection of California's most popular annual events; some dates may vary each year. For detailed information, contact the California Office of Tourism ☎ 800-862-2543.

Date	Event	Location
Spring		
1st weekend in Mar	**Los Angeles Marathon**	*Los Angeles*
early Mar	**Santa Barbara International Film Festival**	*Santa Barbara*
	Snowfest	*Tahoe City*
3rd week in Mar	**Nabisco Dinah Shore LPGA Golf Tournament** *(p 138)*	*Rancho Mirage*
late Mar	**Academy Awards** *(p 90)*	*Los Angeles*
mid-Apr	**Ramona Pageant**	*Hemet (Inland Empire)*
	Toyota Grand Prix of Long Beach	*Long Beach*
Sunday before Easter	**Blessing of the Animals**	*Los Angeles*
late Apr–mid May	**San Francisco International Film Festival**	*San Francisco*
1st weekend in May	**Cinco de Mayo**	*Los Angeles*
2nd weekend in May	**Russian River Wine Fest**	*Healdsburg*
mid-May	**Bay to Breakers Marathon**	*San Francisco*
	Calaveras County Fair & Jumping Frog Jubilee	*Angels Camp*
Summer		
late May	**Luther Burbank Rose Parade & Festival**	*Santa Rosa*
	Sacramento Jazz Jubilee	*Sacramento*
1st weekend in Jun	**Ojai Music Festival**	*Ojai (Central Coast)*
mid-Jun	**Napa Valley Wine Auction**	*St. Helena*
	Playboy Jazz Festival	*Hollywood*
July 4	**Fourth of July Parade & Fireworks Show**	*Huntington Beach*
Jul–Aug	**Festival of Arts & Pageant of the Masters** *(p 135)*	*Laguna Beach*
last two weeks of Jul	**Bach Festival**	*Carmel*
late Jul	**City of San Francisco Marathon**	*San Francisco*
	Gilroy Garlic Festival	*Gilroy*
	International Surf Festival	*Torrance (Greater L.A. Area)*
	US Open Sand Castle Competition	*Imperial Beach (San Diego Cty)*
early Aug	**Steinbeck Festival**	*Salinas*
	Old Spanish Days	*Santa Barbara*
late Aug	**Concours d'Elegance**	*Pebble Beach*
Fall		
early Sept	**City's Birthday Celebration**	*Los Angeles*
	Sausalito Art Festival	*Sausalito*
2nd weekend in Sept	**Russian River Jazz Festival**	*Guerneville (North Coast)*
mid-Sept	**Danish Days**	*Solvang*
	Mexican Independence Day	*Los Angeles*
	Monterey Jazz Festival *(p 121)*	*Monterey*
late Sept	**Valley of the Moon Vintage Festival**	*Sonoma*
mid-Oct	**International Festival of Masks**	*Los Angeles*
Winter		
early Dec	**Christmas in the Adobes**	*Monterey*
	Victorian Christmas	*Nevada City*
Dec 16–24	**Las Posadas**	*Los Angeles*
Jan 1	**Tournament of Roses Parade & Rose Bowl Game** *(p 141)*	*Pasadena*
mid-Jan	**Palm Springs International Film Festival**	*Palm Springs*
late Jan–Feb	**AT&T Pebble Beach National Pro-Am Golf Tournament**	*Pebble Beach*
	Chinese New Year Celebration & Golden Dragon Parade	*Los Angeles*
	Chinese New Year Parade & Festival	*San Francisco*
mid-Feb	**Bob Hope Chrysler Classic Golf Tournament**	*Riverside County*
	Ferrari Concours d'Elegance	*Beverly Hills*

Practical Information

Los Angeles skyline from Mulholland Drive, *C. Curran*

Consult the main section of the guide for detailed practical information about the following areas: ***Catalina Island*** *(p 41),* ***Channel Islands National Park*** *(p 44),* ***Death Valley National Monument*** *(p 46),* ***Disneyland*** *(p 51),* ***Lassen Volcanic National Park*** *(p 76),* ***Los Angeles*** *(p 86),* ***Monterey*** *(p 121),* ***San Diego*** *(p 165),* ***San Francisco*** *(p 187),* ***Santa Barbara*** *(p 217),* ***Sequoia and Kings Canyon National Parks*** *(p 227),* ***Yosemite National Park*** *(p 243).*

PLANNING YOUR TRIP

The following state and regional tourism offices provide information and brochures on points of interest, seasonal events and accommodations, as well as road and city maps.

Tourism Offices *(map of California tourist regions p 10)*

California Office of Tourism	PO Box 1499, Dept 5E Sacramento CA 95812 (North America only)	 916-322-2881 800-862-2543
San Diego County	**San Diego Convention & Visitors Bureau** 1200 Third Ave, Suite 824 San Diego CA 92101-4190	619-236-1212
Inland Empire	**Inland Empire Tourism Council** PO Box 1593, Upland CA 91785	909-624-5651
Orange County	**Anaheim Area Visitor & Convention Bureau** 800 W. Katella Ave, Anaheim CA 92802	714-999-8999
Deserts	**Barstow Area Chamber of Commerce** PO Box 698, Barstow CA 92311	619-256-8617
	Palm Springs Tourism Division 401 S. Pavilion Way Palm Springs CA 92262 (North America only)	 619-778-8418 800-347-7746
Greater Los Angeles Area	**Los Angeles Convention & Visitors Bureau** 633 W. Fifth St, Suite 6000 Los Angeles CA 90071	213-624-7300
Central Coast	**Monterey Peninsula Visitors & Convention Bureau** 380 Alvarado St, PO Box 1770 Monterey CA 93940	408-649-1770
	Morro Bay Chamber of Commerce 895 Napa St, Suite A-1 Morro Bay CA 93442	805-772-4467
	Santa Barbara Conference & Visitors Bureau 510 State St, Suite A Santa Barbara CA 93101	805-966-9222
Central Valley	**Fresno City & County Chamber of Commerce** 808 M St, Fresno CA 93721 (worldwide)	 800-788-0836
	Sacramento Convention & Visitors Bureau 1421 K St, Sacramento CA 95814-3915	916-264-7777
	Stockton-San Joaquin County Convention & Visitors Bureau 46 W. Fremont St, Stockton CA 95202	209-943-1987
High Sierras	**Lake Tahoe Visitors Authority** 1156 Ski Run Blvd South Lake Tahoe CA 96150	916-544-5050
	Mammoth Lakes Visitors Bureau 3399 Main St, PO Box 48 Mammoth Lakes CA 93546	619-934-8006
San Francisco Bay Area	**San Francisco Convention & Visitors Bureau** 201 Third St, Suite 900 San Francisco CA 94103-3185	415-974-6900
	San Jose Convention & Visitors Bureau 333 W. San Carlos St Suite 1000, San Jose CA 95110	408-295-9600
Gold Country	**Calaveras County Visitor Center** PO Box 637, Angels Camp CA 95222 (US only)	 209-736-0049 800-225-3764
	El Dorado County Chamber of Commerce 542 Main St, Placerville CA 95667 (US only)	 916-621-5885 800-457-6279
	Nevada City Chamber of Commerce 132 Main St, Nevada City CA 95959	916-265-2692
North Coast	**Redwood Empire Association** 785 Market St, 15th Floor San Francisco CA 94103	415-543-8334
Shasta-Cascade	**Shasta Cascade Wonderland Assn** 14250 Holiday Rd, Redding CA 96003 (US only)	 916-243-2643 800-326-6944

Outside the US – Foreign visitors can also request additional tourist information from the nearest US embassy or consulate in their country of residence.

US Embassies (selected)

Australia	Moonah Place, Canberra ACT 2600	6-270-5000
Canada	100 Wellington St, Ottawa ON K1P ST1 Canada	613-238-4470
Mexico	Paseo de la Reforma 305, Colonia Cuauhtemoc, 06500 Mexico *(Information on entering Mexico p 180)*	52-5-211-0042
United Kingdom	24/31 Grosvenor Square, W. 1A 1AE, PSC 801 Box 40, FPO AE 09498-4040	44-71-499-9000

Disabled Travelers – Recent Federal law requires that existing businesses (including hotels and restaurants) increase accessibility and provide specially designed accommodations for the disabled. It also requires that wheelchair access, devices for the hearing impaired, and designated parking spaces be available at newly constructed hotels and restaurants. For further information, contact **Disability Rights Education and Defense Fund**, 2212 Sixth St, Berkeley CA 94710 ☏ 800-466-4232 (US only) or 510-644-2555.
All **national parks** have restrooms and other facilities for the disabled (such as wheelchair-accessible nature trails or tour buses). Disabled persons are eligible for the Golden Access Passport, which entitles the carrier to free admission to all national parks, and 50% discount on user fees (campsites, boat launches); contact the National Park Service, Office of Public Inquiry, PO Box 37127, Washington DC 20013-7127 ☏ 202-208-4747. California **state parks** offer permanently disabled persons a 50% discount on campsites and day-use fees at most state-operated facilities; contact Disabled Applications, Dept of Parks and Recreation, PO Box 942896, Sacramento CA 94296-0001 ☏ 916-653-6995. Requests for Federal and state discounts must include: copy of ID card; vehicle registration card with disabled-person license number; SSI or SSA letter, or doctor's certification.

Foreign Visitors – Canadian citizens must show a passport or a birth certificate to enter the US. Naturalized Canadian citizens should also carry their citizenship papers. Citizens of countries participating in the Visa Waiver Pilot Program (VWPP) are not required to obtain a visa to enter the US for visits of less than 90 days. For a list of countries participating in the VWPP, contact the US consulate in your country of residence. Citizens of non-participating countries must have a visitor's visa. Upon entry, non-resident foreign visitors must present a valid passport and round-trip transportation ticket. Inoculations are generally not required (contingent upon country of residence and countries recently visited). Check with the US embassy or consulate before departing. Many countries have consular offices in Los Angeles or San Francisco.

Health Insurance – Before departing, visitors from abroad should check with their insurance company to ascertain if their medical insurance covers doctor's visits, medication and hospitalization in the US. Prescription drugs should be properly identified, and accompanied by a copy of the prescription.

US Customs – All articles brought into the US must be declared at the time of entry. **Exempt** from customs regulations: personal effects, one liter of alcoholic beverage (providing visitor is at least 21 years old), either 200 cigarettes, 50 cigars or 2 kilograms of smoking tobacco; and gifts (to persons in the US) that do not exceed $100 in value. **Prohibited items**: any plant material; firearms and ammunition (if not intended for legitimate sporting purposes); items from restricted countries; meat or poultry products. For further information regarding US Customs, contact the US embassy or consulate before departing. It is also recommended that visitors contact the customs service in their country of residence before departing to ascertain re-entry regulations.

Currency Exchange – Most main offices of national banks offer currency exchange and charge a small fee for this service; contact main or branch offices for exchange information and locations. Private companies generally charge higher fees.

Plant Material – All plant material entering the state of California must be declared and inspected for diseases at Agricultural Inspection Stations located at state borders. Up to $10,000 fine for smuggling.

WHEN TO GO

California's diverse regions experience dramatic variation in climatic conditions. Although coastal areas are subject to relatively little change in temperature between summer and winter, temperatures tend to increase with distance from the coast, and drop quickly as elevation increases. California's rainy season generally occurs between October and April, characterized in the south by infrequent, yet sudden downpours, and in the north by gentle showers occurring more frequently over a relatively extended season.

San Diego County – Coastal temperatures are cool, increasing as one moves inland. Seasonal variations are slight, and it seldom rains. Most days are sunny, breezy and comfortable, but light jackets may be necessary at night near the coast and in winter. **San Diego:** *Jan temps 46°-65°F/ 8°-18°C, avg precip 2in. July temps 64°-75°F/ 18°-24°C, avg precip 0-1in.*

Inland Empire/Orange County – The weather is mild and comfortable year-round along the coast; summer brings burning temperatures to lower inland areas. The San Bernardino and San Jacinto mountains offer cool relief from summer heat and haze. Rain generally falls in late winter and early spring. **Laguna Beach:** *Jan temps 42°-66°F/ 6°-19°C, avg precip 2in; Jul temps 59°-76°F/ 15°-24°C, avg precip 0-1in.* **Santa Ana:** *Jan temps 45°-69°F/ 7°-21°C, avg precip 2in; Jul temps 63°-83°F/ 17°-28°C, avg precip 0-1in*

Deserts – Spring and fall are good times to visit high desert areas; temperatures are warm during the day, cool at night. Summers are hot, with cooler nights. Avoid low desert areas in summer: temperatures are dangerously high and many amenities and attractions close between May and September. Wildflowers bloom gloriously in March and April. Summer daytime temperatures are searing in Palm Springs, but tourists are few, and many resorts drastically lower their prices. **Blythe:** *Jan temps 40°-66°F/ 4°-19°C, avg precip 0-1in; Jul temps 82°-109°F/ 28°-43°C, avg precip 0-1in.*

Greater Los Angeles Area – The coast is warm and pleasant year-round, though long sleeves are necessary at night, even in summer. Inland areas of the Los Angeles Basin are hot and hazy during summer and early fall. Rain usually falls between January and March. Tourism is heavy year-round, but peaks during spring and summer holidays; television show tapings, studio tours and other Hollywood sights are particularly crowded at this time. **Los Angeles:** *Jan temps 45°-63°F/ 7°-17°C, avg precip 2in; Jul temps 62°-75°F/ 17°-24°C, avg precip 0-1in.*

Central Coast – Coastal temperatures are moderate year-round. Fall is an excellent time to visit, with warm temperatures, clear weather, and fewer visitors. Long sleeves during the day and sweaters and light jackets at night are recommended. Late spring and summer may bring fog to the coastline. Visitors crowd the Pacific Coast Highway (Highway 1) during the summer months. Accommodations may be difficult to find on the Monterey Peninsula during major golf tournaments and music festivals *(p 248)*, so plan accordingly and reserve early. Spring and fall are the best times to visit inland areas, which are subject to fierce summer heat. **Santa Barbara:** *Jan temps 40°-63°F/ 4°-17°C, avg precip 4in; Jul temps 57°-74°F/ 14°-23°C, avg precip 0-1in.*

Central Valley – Colors abound between February and April when fruit and nut orchards bloom. Summer temperatures are high, but humidity is low, evenings are cooler, and the heat is moderated by breezes in the central portions of the valley. Winter brings **tule fog**, a thick, ground-hugging cloud cover that obscures visibility on highways and brings cold and dampness. **Sacramento:** *Jan temps 37°-53°F/ 3°-12°C, avg precip 4in; Jul temps 57°-93°F/ 14°-34°C, avg precip 0-1in.*

High Sierras – The winter sports season begins as early as late October and may extend through mid-April, depending on the amount of snowfall; advance reservations are usually necessary on weekends. Popular tourist areas such as Yosemite Valley and Lake Tahoe are quite crowded in summer; temperatures in the former often reach 90°F. Nighttime temperatures during the summer can drop below freezing at higher elevations. Waterfalls in the region, fed by melting snow and winter rain, are most impressive in spring; fall brings colorful aspens, crisp temperatures and fewer visitors. **Bishop:** *Jan temps 20°-54°F/ -7°-12°C, avg precip 1in; Jul temps 56°-97°F/ 13°-36°C, avg precip 0-1in.* **Fresno:** *Jan temps 36°-55°F/ 2°-13°C, avg precip 2in; Jul temps 63°-98°F/ 17°-37°C, avg precip 0-1in.*

San Francisco Bay Area – Seasonal temperature variation is slight in San Francisco and along the coast, but weather can change suddenly throughout the day from warm and sunny to foggy and chilly. Thick fogs are particularly characteristic of the summer months. Shorts and other light clothing are hardly ever comfortable in San Francisco—it's best to dress in layers. Inland Bay Area cities are warmer, with pleasant summer temperatures. Rain falls between November and April, usually in periods of several days followed by days of clear skies. Tourism increases during summer months. **San Francisco:** *Jan temps 41°-55°F/ 5°-13°C, avg precip 4in; Jul temps 54°-71°F/ 12°-22°C, avg precip 0-1in.*

Gold Country – Blooming flowers and comfortable temperatures make spring a glorious time to visit. Summer can be very hot. Deciduous trees show their colors between September and November (later at higher elevations) and local farm stands offer fresh produce; jackets or sweaters are necessary. Winter brings rain and chilly temperatures. **Auburn:** *Jan temps 36°-54°F/ 2°-12°C, avg precip 8in; Jul temps 61°-94°F/ 16°-34°C, avg precip 0-1in.* **Blue Canyon:** *Jan temps 30°-43°F/ -1°-6°C, avg precip 14in; Jul temps 59°-77°F/ 15°-25°C, avg precip 0-1in.*

North Coast – Late spring and early fall are the best times to visit the Wine Country and southern areas of the North Coast. Rain falls between October and April. Reserve accommodations well in advance in the Wine Country during the fall harvest season of September and October. **Healdsburg:** *Jan temps 38°-57°F/ 3°-14°C, avg precip 11in; Jul temps 52°-89°F/ 11°-32°C, avg precip 0-1in.*
The northernmost reaches of California's coast are prone to fog, rain and chill, especially during late fall and winter, so plan to see the redwoods in spring, summer and early fall. **Eureka:** *Jan temps 41°-53°F/ 5°-12°C, avg precip 7in; Jul temps 52°-60°F/ 11°-16°C, avg precip 0-1in.*

Shasta-Cascade – Summer and early fall bring opportunities for outdoor recreation. Summer temperatures are high in the southern areas near the Central Valley. Skiing and other snow sports occur at Mt Shasta from November to March. Winter temperatures are cold in the northern areas and higher elevations. **Red Bluff:** *Jan temps 37°-54°F/ 3°-12°C, avg precip 4in; Jul temps 67°-98°F/ 19°-37°C, avg precip 0-1in.* **Mount Shasta:** *Jan temps 25°-42°F/ -4°-6°C, avg precip 7in; Jul temps 51°-85°F/ 11°-29°C, avg precip 0-1in*

GETTING THERE & GETTING AROUND

By Air – Most international flights arrive at Los Angeles International Airport (LAX–*p 86)* and San Francisco International Airport (SFO–*p 187)*.

By Train – With access to over 200 communities in California, the Amtrak rail network offers a relaxing alternative for the traveler with time to spare. Advance reservations are recommended to ensure reduced fares and availability of desired accommodations. First class, coach, sleeping accommodations and dome cars with glass ceilings that allow a panoramic view are available; fares are comparable to air travel. Major long distance routes are: *Coast Starlight* from Seattle to Los Angeles, 36hrs; *California Zephyr* from Chicago to San Francisco, 2 days; *Sunset Limited* from Miami to Los Angeles, 2 days. Travelers from Canada should inquire with their local travel agents about Amtrak/Via Rail connections. **All-Aboard Pass** allows travel over any distance during 45 days (limited to three stops). **USARailPass** (not available to US or Canadian citizens or legal residents) offers unlimited travel within Amtrak designated regions at discounted rates; 15- and 30-day passes available. Schedule and route information: ☎800-872-7245 (North America only; outside North America, contact your local travel agent).

By Bus – Greyhound, the largest bus company in the US, offers access to most communities in California at a leisurely pace. Overall, fares are lower than other forms of public transportation. **Ameripass** allows unlimited travel for 7-, 14- or 21-days. Owing to lack of sleeping accommodations, some travelers may find long-distance bus travel uncomfortable. Advance reservations are suggested. Disabled riders are encouraged to notify Greyhound two days before departure if assistance will be needed. Schedule and route information: ☎800-231-2222 (US only) or 402 330-2055.

By Car – **Road Conditions** ☎800-427-ROAD (CA only). California has an extensive system of well-maintained major roads. In remote areas, some roads are unpaved and require extreme caution. During the winter months tire chains may be required on roads at higher elevations. It is also recommended that visitors planning on traveling long distances or through remote areas pack an **emergency car kit** containing such items as first-aid supplies, bottled water, non-perishable food, blanket, flashlight, tools and matches. **Gasoline** is sold by the gallon (1 US gal = 3.8l). Gas stations are usually found in clusters on the edge of a city, or where two or more highways intersect. In rural areas they are found on the major roads traveled by tourists. Self-service gas stations do not offer car repair, although many sell standard maintenance items. Foreign visitors are not required to obtain an International Driver's License to drive in the state of California; a valid license issued by the country of residence is sufficient. Drivers must carry vehicle registration and/or rental contract, and proof of automobile insurance at all times.

Rental Cars – Agencies offering worldwide reservation services include: **Avis** ☎800-331-1212, **Budget** ☎800-527-0700, **Hertz** ☎800-654-3131, **Thrifty** ☎800-331-4200, **National** ☎800-328-4567.

Road Regulations – The maximum speed limit on major freeways is 65mph (105km/h) in rural areas and 55mph (90km/h) in and around cities, unless otherwise posted. Speed limits are generally 35mph (57km/h) within cities, and average 25-30mph (40-48km/h) in residential areas. The use of **seat belts** is mandatory for all persons in the car; child safety seats are required for children under 4 years or 40lbs (available at most rental car agencies). Motorists are required to bring their vehicles to a full stop when the warning signals on a **school bus** are activated. Unless otherwise posted, it is permissible to turn right on a red traffic light after coming to a complete stop. **U-turns** are allowed only in residential areas.

In Case of Accident – If you are involved in an accident resulting in personal or property damage, you must notify the local police and remain at the scene until dismissed. If blocking traffic, vehicles should be moved if possible.

ACCOMMODATIONS

Luxury **hotels** are generally found in major cities, **motels** in clusters on the edge of town, or where two or more highways intersect. In rural areas, motels are found on roads frequently traveled by tourists. **Bed & breakfasts** can be found in residential areas of cities and villages. Many **resorts** are located throughout the state.
Local tourist offices provide detailed accommodation information *(telephone numbers listed under blue-banded entry headings in the main section of this guide)*. In season and during weekends, advance reservations are recommended. Always advise reservations clerk of late arrival; rooms, even though reserved, may not be held after 6pm. Off-season rates are usually reduced.

Hotels/Motels – Major hotel chains with locations throughout California include (toll-free numbers valid worldwide except where noted):

Best Western	800-528-1234	**Radisson**	800-333-3333
Embassy Suites	800-362-2779	**Ramada Inn** (North America only)	800-228-2828
Hilton Hotels	800-445-8667	**Sheraton**	800-325-3535
Holiday Inn	800-465-4329	**Residence Inn**	800-331-3131
Hyatt	800-233-1234	**Travelodge**	800-255-3050
Marriott	800-228-9290		

Also consult *Discover California's Accommodations*, a free directory available from the California Hotel and Motel Association, PO Box 160405, Sacramento CA 95816 ☎916-444-5780.

Accommodations range from luxury hotels ($145-$250/day) to more moderate hotels ($60-$90/day) to budget motels ($40-$65/day). Rates vary with season and location; rates tend to be higher in cities and in coastal and vacation areas. Many hotels and motels offer packages and weekend specials. Amenities include television, restaurant, swimming pool, and smoking/non-smoking rooms. The more elegant hotels also offer in-room dining and valet service. *All rates quoted are average prices for a double room.*

Bed & Breakfasts – Referral services: Eye Openers, PO Box 694, Altadena CA 91003 ☎213-684-4428 (all of California); Bed & Breakfast International, PO Box 282910, San Francisco CA 94128-2910 ☎415-696-1690 (San Francisco, Wine Country, Monterey); Megan's Friends, 1776 Royal Way, San Luis Obispo CA 93405 ☎805-544-4406 (Central Coast). Most B&B's are privately owned and located in historic structures ($90-$145/day). Continental breakfast is usually included; private baths are not always available. Smoking indoors may not be allowed.

Camping – *National & state park listings p 256.* Campsites are located in national parks, state parks, national forests, and in private campgrounds. Amenities offered range from full RV hookups to rustic backcountry sites ($7-$35/day). Advance reservations are recommended, especially during summer and holidays; some campgrounds do not accept reservations year-round.
Wilderness camping is available on most public lands. A Wilderness Permit (free) is usually required, advance reservation suggested. Topographic maps of most wilderness areas are available. Contact desired location or the addresses below for further information.

Campground Information – For **California State Parks**: Dept of Parks and Recreation, PO Box 942896, Sacramento CA 94296 ☎916-445-6477. Campsite reservations: MISTIX ☎800-444-7275 (US only) or 619-452-8787. For **California National Parks**: Western Region Information Office, National Park Service, Fort Mason, Bldg 201, San Francisco CA 94123 ☎415-556-0560. Advance reservations for groups of 6 or less can be made (at least 8 weeks in advance) for Death Valley National Monument *(p 46)*, Joshua Tree National Monument *(p 68)*, Sequoia & Kings Canyon National Parks *(p 226)*, Whiskeytown National Recreation Area *(p 147)* and Yosemite National Park *(p 241)* through MISTIX ☎800-365-2267 (US only) or 619-452-8787. For **California National Forests**: USDA Forest Service, 630 Sansome St, San Francisco CA 94111 ☎415-705-2874. National Forest Campsite Reservations: MISTIX ☎800-283-2267 (US only) or 619-452-8787. For **private campgrounds**: California Travel Parks Associa-tion, PO Box 5648, Auburn CA 95604 ☎916-885-1624.

Hostels – A simple, economical alternative, hostels average $4-$20/night; amenities include community living room, showers, laundry facilities, full service kitchen and dining room and dormitory-style rooms (blankets and pillows are provided, but guests are required to bring their own linens). Membership cards are recommended. There are 22 certified American Youth Hostels in California. Advance reservations are suggested during peak travel times. **American Youth Hostels**, 733 15th St, NW, #840, Washington DC 20005 ☎202-783-6161.

Guest Ranches – Primarily located in the mountain regions, guest ranches offer such amenities as meals, equipment, guided pack rides and horsemanship instruction. Rates average $650-$700/wk. Ranches in California that are affiliated with the *Dude Rancher Association* are: Coffee Creek Ranch, HC9 Box 4940, Trinity Center CA 96091 ☎800-624-4480 (North America only) or 916-266-3443; Honeywell Circle H Guest Ranch, Box 368, Bridgeport CA 93517 ☎619-932-7710.

Resorts – Located throughout the state, California resorts offer a wide range of amenities, including health and fitness programs, beauty and weight control programs, thermal treatments, tennis, skiing and golf. Facilities range from rustic cabins to luxury suites ($97-$300/day).

BASIC INFORMATION

Business Hours – Monday to Friday 9-10am to 5:30pm; some retail shops may stay open until 9pm on Thursday. Shopping centers: Monday to Saturday 9:30am–8 or 9pm, Sunday 11am–6pm. Banking hours: Monday to Thursday 10am–3pm, Friday 10am–5pm; some close later on Friday. Banks in larger cities may open on Saturday morning.

Electricity – Voltage in the US is 120 volts AC, 60 HZ. Foreign-made appliances may need AC adapters and North American flat-blade plugs.

Liquor Law – The legal age for purchase and consumption of alcoholic beverages is 21; proof of age may be required. Liquor stores, and many grocery and drug stores sell liquor. Almost all grocery stores sell beer and wine. Hours of sale: 6am–2am. Sale of alcoholic beverages prohibited between 2am–6am.

Mail – First class rates within the US: letter $.29 (1oz), post card $.19. Overseas: letter $.50 (1/2oz), postcard $.40. Inquire at post offices for further information.

Major Holidays – Most banks and government offices are closed on the following legal holidays *(*many retail stores and restaurants remain open on these days)*:

January 1	**New Years Day**
3rd Monday in January	**Martin Luther King's Birthday***
3rd Monday in February	**Presidents' Day***
Last Monday in May	**Memorial Day**
July 4	**Independence Day**
1st Monday in September	**Labor Day***
2nd Monday in October	**Columbus Day***
November 11	**Veterans Day***
Last Thursday in November	**Thanksgiving Day**
December 25	**Christmas Day**

Measurement – California follows the US Customary system of measurement. Weather temperatures are given in Fahrenheit (°F), liquids are measured by the pint, quart or gallon, and weight is measured in ounces or pounds. All distances and speed limits are calculated in miles. Some useful examples of metric equivalents are:

1 gallon (gal) = 3.8 liters	1 mile (mi) = 1.6 kilometers
1 pint (pt) = .5 liters	1 foot (ft) = 30.5 centimeters
1 pound (lb) = .4 kilograms	1 inch (in) = 2.5 centimeters
1 ounce (oz) = 31.1 grams	

Smoking Regulations – Many California cities have ordinances that prohibit smoking in public places or confine smoking to designated areas.

State Sales Tax – The general sales tax in California is 7.25%. Most metro areas add additional sales tax of .25%-1.25%. Unprepared food items are exempt from taxation.

Telephone – Instructions for using public telephones are listed on or near the phone. The cost for a local call is $.25 (any combination of nickels, dimes or quarters is accepted). Coins should be inserted before dialing. Some public telephones accept credit cards. All public phones will accept long-distance calling cards. Most hotels add a surcharge for local and long-distance calls. For further information dial "0" for operator assistance.

Time Zone – California is on Pacific Standard Time (PST), 3hrs behind Eastern Standard Time (EST). Daylight Savings Time (clocks advanced 1hr) is in effect for most of the US from the first Sunday in April until the last Sunday in October.

Tipping – It is customary in restaurants to tip the server 15% of the bill. At hotels, $1 per suitcase should be given to the porter. Taxi drivers are usually tipped 15% of the fare.

NATURE & SAFETY

Earthquake Precautions – Although severe earthquakes are infrequent, earth quake preparedness is a fact of life in California. As earthquakes cannot be predicted, it is advisable to know in advance what precautions to take. If you are **outside** when an earthquake strikes, stay clear of trees, buildings or power lines. If you are in a **vehicle**, decrease speed, pull to the side of the road and stop. Do not park on or under bridges; sit on the floor of the vehicle if possible. If you are in a **building**, stand inside a doorway or sit under a sturdy table. Remain in a safe place until shaking stops and be alert for aftershocks. If possible, listen to the radio or TV for advisories.

Wildlife – In most natural areas of California, tampering with plants or wildlife is prohibited by law. It is prudent to avoid direct contact with any wildlife; very often an animal that does not shy from humans is sick and poses a potential threat.

Bears – Active from early April through mid-December, bears are accustomed to people and will approach campsites and cars (especially if food is nearby). Improper storage of food is a violation of Federal law, subject to fine. Food storage guidelines: hang food 12ft off the ground and 10ft away from tree trunk, or store in a locking ice chest, car trunk or in lockers provided at some campgrounds. If a bear approaches do not move toward it, or attempt to retrieve your belongings. Try to frighten the bear by yelling and throwing rocks in its direction. Never approach a mother with cubs, as she will attack to protect her young.

Desert Safety – When traveling through the desert areas of California, particularly in summer, it is essential that certain precautions be taken. Before traveling through remote areas, notify someone of your destination, and your planned return time.

B. Ross/First Light

Dry lake bed, Mojave Desert

For Your Vehicle – Since service stations tend to be far apart, keep gas tank at least half full, and carry plenty of radiator water. If vehicle is running hot, turn off the air conditioning. If it overheats, pull to the side of the road, turn on the heater and slowly pour water over the radiator core (do not turn off vehicle). Refill radiator after engine has cooled. In the event of a breakdown, do not leave the vehicle to seek help. Stay with your vehicle and wait for passing traffic. Stay on marked roads. Unpaved roads are suitable for 4-wheel drive vehicles only.

For You – Temperatures in July and August can reach over 120°F (48°C). It is imperative that visitors carry plenty of water and drink it freely, at least once an hour. Do not lie or sit in the direct sun. Always wear loose-fitting clothes, broad-brimmed hat and sunglasses. Be watchful for sudden storms that can produce flash floods.
Heat exhaustion is caused by overexertion in high temperatures. Symptoms include: cool, clammy skin and nausea. If experiencing any of these symptoms, rest in the shade and drink plenty of fluids. Symptoms of **heat stroke** include: hot dry skin, dizziness or headache; victim may become delirious. If experiencing any of these symptoms, try to lower the body temperature with cold compresses (do not use analgesics) and seek medical assistance.
Abandoned mines are common in desert areas, and all are potentially dangerous. Never enter tunnels without a flashlight. Watch for loose rock, and do not touch support timbers.

Mountain Safety – When driving in mountainous areas, visitors should exercise caution. Mountain roads tend to be narrow, steep and twisting. Observe cautionary road signs and posted speed limits. Many mountain roads receive little traffic, and in the event of an accident, help could be long coming.
Altitude sickness is caused by overexertion at high elevations. If planning to hike or camp, visitors should allow 1-4 days to acclimate to the reduced oxygen level and lowered atmospheric pressure. Symptoms include: headache, swelling in feet and legs, and general weakness. If experiencing any of these symptoms, rest and eat high-energy foods (such as raisins, trail mix or granola bars). Seek medical assistance if symptoms become more severe or do not disappear in 2-5 days.

Ocean Swimming – *Beach listings p 258.* Waters along the California coast can be deceptively tranquil. Large waves can appear suddenly, even on the calmest days. Exercise caution when near the water's edge. Most public beaches do not have year-round lifeguards, and care should be taken when swimming at an unguarded beach. Never swim alone. Children should be supervised at all times. Swimmers may find big waves and rip tides (strong, narrow, seaward flows) all along the California coast. Cold water borne by the California current makes swimming uncomfortable north of Point Conception (near Lompoc). If caught in a rip tide, swim parallel to the shoreline until out of the current.
Be watchful of the incoming tide when exploring beaches and tidepools. Avoid sea urchins, which may be venomous; jellyfish, which sting on land or in the water; and stingrays, which often bury themselves in shallow water (obtain medical treatment immediately if stung).

SPORTS & RECREATION

National and State Parks – California has 19 national and 275 state parks, all offering a variety of activities. Entrance fees range from $2–$6; some state parks are free. Both national and state parks offer season passes *(disabled travelers p 251).* The busiest season is from Memorial Day to Labor Day, although central and south coast parks may be busy year-round. Most of the parks have information centers equipped with trail maps and informative literature on park facilities and activities. Park rangers often lead nature hikes or excursions to sights within the parks.
Regulations: gathering downed wood, or cutting wood for fires is prohibited; campfires are limited to firepits; hunting is prohibited in most parks; all pets must be leashed, and may be prohibited from certain park areas; current proof of rabies vaccine is usually required; an additional fee of $1 per pet may be charged; all plants and animals within the parks are protected.

Symbols on the following charts indicate: ⛺ camping; picnic area; hiking; swimming; fishing; food service/supplies.

National Parks

Western Region Information Office, National Park Service, Fort Mason, Bldg 201, San Francisco CA 94123 ☎ 415-556-0560.	camping	picnic area	hiking	swimming	fishing	food service/supplies
Channel Islands Natl Park *(p 44)* ☎ 805-644-8157 1901 Spinnaker Dr, Ventura CA 93001	•	•	•	•		
Death Valley Natl Monument *(p 46)* ☎ 619-786-2331 Death Valley CA 92328	•					•
Devil's Postpile Natl Monument *(p 116)* ☎ 619-934-2289 PO Box 501, Mammoth Lakes CA 93546	•	•	•		•	
Golden Gate Natl Recreation Area *(p 191)* ☎ 415-556-0560 Building 201, Fort Mason, San Francisco CA 94123	•	•	•	•	•	
Joshua Tree Natl Monument *(p 68)* ☎ 619-367-7511 74485 Natl Monument Dr, Twentynine Palms CA 92277	•	•	•			
Lassen Volcanic Natl Park *(p 76)* ☎ 916-595-3262 PO Box 100, Mineral CA 96063	•	•	•	•		•
Lava Beds Natl Monument *(p 78)* ☎ 916-667-2282 PO Box 867, Tulelake CA 96134	•	•	•			

Muir Woods Natl Monument *(p 127)* ☎ 415-388-2595 Mill Valley CA 94941	•					
Pinnacles Natl Monument *(p 160)* ☎ 408-389-4578 5000 Highway 146, Paicines CA 95043	•	•	•			
Point Reyes Natl Seashore *(p 145)* ☎ 415-663-1092 Point Reyes CA 94956		•	•	•		•
Redwood Natl Park *(p 153)* ☎ 707-464-6101 1111 2nd St, Crescent City CA 95531	•	•	•	•	•	
Santa Monica Mts. Natl Recreation Area ☎ 818-597-9192 30401 Agoura Rd, Agoura CA 91301	•	•	•	•		
Sequoia & Kings Canyon Natl Parks *(p 226)* ☎ 209-565-3341 Ash Mountain, Three Rivers CA 93271	•		•		•	•
Whiskeytown-Shasta-Trinity Natl Recreation Area *(p 147)* PO Box 188, Whiskeytown CA 96095 ☎ 916-241-6584	•	•	•	•	•	•
Yosemite Natl Park *(p 241)* ☎ 209-372-0200 PO Box 577, Yosemite Natl Park CA 95389	•	•	•	•	•	•

Selected State Parks *(state historic parks listed in index p 262)*

Dept of Parks and Recreation, PO Box 942896 Sacramento CA 94296 ☎ 916-653-6995.	△	⛩	!	≈	➤	Ꭓ
Año Nuevo SR *(p 222)* ☎ 415-879-0227			•		•	
Anza-Borrego Desert SP *(p 34)* ☎ 619-767-5311	•	•	•			
Armstrong Redwoods SR *(p 240)* ☎ 707-865-2391		•	•			
Auburn SRA ☎ 916-885-4527	•	•	•	•	•	
Austin Creek SRA ☎ 707-865-2391	•	•	•			
Bothe-Napa Valley SP ☎ 707-942-4575	•	•	•	•		
Calaveras Big Trees SP *(p 63)* ☎ 209-795-2334	•	•	•	•	•	
Castle Crags SP *(p 126)* ☎ 916-235-2684	•	•	•	•	•	
Clear Lake SP ☎ 707-279-4293	•	•	•	•	•	
Crystal Cove SP *(p 134)* ☎ 714-848-1566			•	•	•	
Cuyamaca Rancho SP *(p 179)* ☎ 619-765-0755	•	•	•		•	
D. L. Bliss SP *(p 73)* ☎ 916-525-7277	•	•	•	•	•	
Del Norte Coast Redwoods SP *(p 154)* ☎ 707-464-9533	•	•	•			
Donner Memorial SP *(p 230)* ☎ 916-587-3841	•	•	•	•	•	
Emerald Bay SP *(p 74)* ☎ 916-525-7277	•	•	•	•	•	
Garrapata SP *(p 42)* ☎ 408-667-2315			•	•		
Henry Cowell Redwoods SP *(p 222)* ☎ 408-335-9145	•	•	•			•
Humboldt Lagoons SP *(p 153)* ☎ 707-488-2171	•	•			•	
Humboldt Redwoods SP *(p 150)* ☎ 707-946-2409	•	•	•	•	•	
Jedediah Smith Redwoods SP *(p 154)* ☎ 707-464-9533	•	•	•	•	•	
Julia Pfeiffer Burns SP *(p 43)* ☎ 408-667-2315	•	•	•			
Kruse Rhododendron SR *(p 129)* ☎ 707-847-3221			•			
MacKerricher SP *(p 130)* ☎ 707-937-5809	•	•	•		•	
Malibu Creek SP ☎ 818-706-1310	•	•	•		•	
McArthur-Burney Falls Memorial SP *(p 148)* ☎ 916-335-2777	•	•	•	•	•	•
Mendocino Headlands SP *(p 118)* ☎ 707-937-5804					•	
Montaña de Oro SP ☎ 805-772-2560	•	•	•		•	
Morro Bay SP *(p 44)* ☎ 805-772-2560	•	•	•	•	•	•
Mount Diablo SP ☎ 415-837-2525	•	•	•			
Mount San Jacinto SP ☎ 714-659-2607	•	•	•			•
Mount Tamalpais SP ☎ 415-388-2070	•	•	•		•	•
Palomar Mountain SP ☎ 619-765-0755	•	•	•		•	
Patrick's Point SP *(p 153)* ☎ 707-677-3570	•	•	•		•	
Pfeiffer Big Sur SP *(p 43)* ☎ 408-667-2315	•	•	•	•	•	•
Plumas-Eureka SP ☎ 916-836-2380	•	•	•		•	
Point Lobos SR *(p 42)* ☎ 408-624-4909	•	•				
Prairie Creek Redwoods SP *(p 154)* ☎ 707-488-2171	•	•	•		•	
Providence Mountains SRA ☎ 805-942-0662	•		•			
Richardson Grove SP *(p 150)* ☎ 707-247-3318	•	•	•	•	•	•
Robert Louis Stevenson SP *(p 38)* ☎ 707-942-4575		•	•			
Russian Gulch SP *(p 130)* ☎ 707-937-5804	•	•	•		•	
Salt Point SP *(p 129)* ☎ 707-847-3221	•	•	•		•	
Salton Sea SRA *(p 140)* ☎ 619-393-3052	•	•	•	•	•	
Smithe Redwoods SR *(p 150)* ☎ 707-247-3318					•	•
Sugar Pine Point SP *(p 72)* ☎ 916-525-7982	•	•	•	•	•	
Tomales Bay SP ☎ 415-669-1140		•	•	•	•	
Torrey Pines SR *(p 70)* ☎ 619-755-2063			•			
Van Damme SP *(p 129)* ☎ 707-937-5804	•	•	•		•	

Symbols on the following chart indicate: $ admission/parking fee; restroom; swimming; lifeguard; camping; disabled facilities; surfing; scuba/snorkeling.

Selected Beaches *(listed in geographic order)*

	$	restroom	swimming	lifeguard	camping	disabled facilities	surfing	scuba/snorkeling
North Coast								
Crescent Beach ☎ 707-464-6101		•	•			•		
Enderts Beach *(p 154)* ☎ 707-464-6101		•	•		•			
Agate Beach		•						
Little River SB			•					
Manchester SB ☎ 707-937-5804	•	•	•		•			•
Fish Rock Beach ☎ 707-884-4222	•	•	•		•	•		•
Goat Rock Beach *(p 153)* ☎ 707-875-3483		•				•		•
Sonoma Coast SB's *(p 128)* ☎ 707-875-3483		•				•		•
Pt Reyes Natl Seashore Beaches *(p 145)* ☎ 415-663-1092		•	•			•		
Stinson Beach *(p 128)* ☎ 415-868-0942		•	•	•		•		
Muir Beach *(p 127)* ☎ 415-556-0560		•	•		•			
Rodeo Beach ☎ 415-331-7325		•	•			•		
San Francisco Bay Area								
Baker Beach ☎ 415-556-8371		•				•		
China Beach ☎ 415-556-7894		•	•	•		•		
Ocean Beach *(p 204)* ☎ 415-556-0560		•				•	•	
Montara SB ☎ 415-726-6238		•						
Francis Beach ☎ 415-726-6238	•	•	•		•	•		
San Gregorio SB ☎ 415-726-6238	•	•				•		
Pescadero SB ☎ 415-726-6238		•	•			•		
Lighthouse Field SB ☎ 408-429-3429		•	•			•		
Santa Cruz Beach Boardwalk *(p 221)* ☎ 408-426-7433	•	•	•	•				
Seacliff SB & Pier ☎ 408-688-3222	•	•	•	•	•	•		
Sunset SB ☎ 408-724-1266	•	•			•			
Central Coast								
Zmudowski SB ☎ 408-384-7695		•	•				•	
Salinas River SB ☎ 408-384-7695		•	•					
Carmel City Beach *(p 40)* ☎ 408-624-3543		•				•		
Pfeiffer Beach *(p 43)* ☎ 408-385-5434		•				•		
William R. Hearst Mem. SB ☎ 805-927-2020	•	•	•					
San Simeon SB ☎ 805-927-2035	•	•	•		•	•		
Morro Strand SB ☎ 805-772-2560	•	•	•		•			
Pismo SB ☎ 805-489-2684		•	•					
Gaviota State Park ☎ 805-968-3294	•	•	•	•	•	•		
Refugio SB ☎ 805-968-1350	•	•	•	•	•	•		
El Capitan SB ☎ 805-968-1411	•	•	•	•	•	•		
East Beach *(p 218)* ☎ 805-965-0509		•	•	•		•		
Carpinteria SB ☎ 805-684-2811	•	•	•	•	•	•	•	
Point Mugu SP ☎ 805-499-2112	•	•	•	•	•	•		
McGrath SB ☎ 805-654-4744	•	•	•	•	•	•		
Oxnard SB ☎ 805-984-4642	•	•	•			•		
Port Hueneme Beach Park ☎ 805-986-6555		•	•			•		
Greater Los Angeles Area								
Leo Carillo SB ☎ 805-499-2112	•	•	•	•	•	•	•	•
Zuma Beach County Park ☎ 213-457-9891	•	•	•	•			•	•
Point Dume SB	•	•	•				•	•
Malibu Lagoon SB ☎ 213-457-9891	•	•	•	•		•		
Las Tunas SB ☎ 213-457-9891			•	•				•
Will Rogers SB ☎ 213-394-3264	•	•	•	•		•	•	•
Santa Monica SB ☎ 213-394-3264	•	•	•	•		•	•	
Venice City Beach ☎ 213-394-3264	•	•	•	•		•		
Dockweiler SB ☎ 213-372-2166	•	•	•	•	•	•		
Manhattan SB ☎ 213-372-2166	•	•	•	•		•	•	
Hermosa Beach ☎ 213-372-2166		•	•	•			•	•
Redondo SB ☎ 213-372-2166	•	•	•	•		•		
Torrance County Beach ☎ 213-372-2166	•	•	•	•		•	•	•
Cabrillo Beach ☎ 213-832-1179	•	•	•	•		•	•	•
Long Beach City Beach ☎ 213-437-0375	•	•	•	•		•		
Belmont Shore ☎ 213-434-6781	•	•	•	•		•		
Topanga SB ☎ 213-451-2906	•	•	•	•		•	•	

A. Pitcairn/Grant Heilman Photography

Selected Beaches (continued)	$							
Orange County								
Seal Beach *(p 133)* ☎213-430-2613		•	•	•		•	•	
Bolsa Chica SB *(p 134)* ☎714-846-3460	•	•	•	•	•	•	•	•
Huntington City Beach *(p 134)* ☎714-536-5280	•	•	•	•	•	•	•	
Huntington SB *(p 134)* ☎714-536-1454	•	•	•	•		•		
Newport Beach & Pier *(p 134)*	•	•	•	•		•	•	
Balboa Beach & Pier		•	•	•		•		
Corona Del Mar Beach ☎714-644-3047	•	•	•	•		•	•	
Crystal Cove State Park ☎714-494-3539	•	•	•	•	•	•		•
Main Beach *(p 135)*		•	•	•	•	•		
Salt Creek Beach ☎714-661-7013	•	•	•			•	•	
Doheny SB ☎714-496-6172	•	•	•	•	•	•	•	
San Clemente SB	•	•	•	•	•	•	•	
San Diego County								
Ocean Beach Park ☎619-221-8901		•	•	•		•	•	
San Onofre SB ☎714-492-4872	•	•	•	•	•	•	•	
Oceanside City Beach ☎619-966-4530	•	•	•	•		•	•	
Carlsbad SB ☎619-729-8947		•	•	•		•	•	•
South Carlsbad SB ☎619-438-3143	•	•	•	•	•		•	
Encinitas Beach ☎619-944-3380			•					
Moonlight SB *(p 182)* ☎619-944-3380		•	•	•		•	•	
Swami's ☎619-944-3380		•	•	•		•	•	•
San Elijo SB ☎619-753-5091	•	•	•	•	•	•	•	•
Cardiff SB ☎619-729-8947	•	•	•	•		•	•	
Del Mar City Beach	•		•	•			•	
Torrey Pines City Beach			•					
Torrey Pines SB *(p 70)* ☎619-755-2063	•	•	•	•		•	•	
La Jolla Shores Beach-Kellogg Park		•	•	•		•	•	•
Marine Street Beach			•				•	•
Windansea Beach			•				•	
Mission Bay Beaches *(p 176)* ☎619-276-8200		•	•	•		•		
Ocean Beach City Beach			•					
Coronado City Beach ☎619-522-7342		•	•	•			•	
Silver Strand SB ☎619-435-5184	•	•	•	•	•	•	•	
Imperial Beach		•	•			•	•	

Boating – California offers many opportunities for fresh water and ocean boating. Most oceanside communities have boat rental agencies, many of which offer sightseeing cruises. Agencies on larger lakes also rent sailboats and powerboats. "The Delta," where the San Joaquin and Sacramento rivers flow into the San Francisco Bay, is a popular **houseboating** area, as is Shasta Lake *(p 147)*; boats can be rented through local agencies. In addition to state law, many cities and counties have special laws restricting speed or activities. Check with local agencies. For more information contact California Dept of Boating and Waterways, 1629 S Street, Sacramento CA 95814 ☎916-445-2615.

Golf – *Dates of selected PGA tournaments p 248.* California claims more than 600 public and private courses. The Monterey Peninsula courses feature white sands, stately forests and steep cliffs overlooking the Pacific. The Palm Springs area, known for its desert resorts, offers more than 70 courses in a predominantly dry climate. Southern California courses tend to have damp greens and slower fairways, which many golfers find challenging. Contact local tourism office *(p 250)* for the location of public greens.

Hiking/Biking – Many trail systems lace the state, and national and state parks also boast abundant opportunities for hiking and biking. The **John Muir Trail** (210mi/339km) extends from Mt Whitney to Yosemite National Park; the **Pacific Crest Trail** extends between the Canadian and Mexican borders, with 1,615mi/2,605km in California (wilderness permits required, contact the National Forest Service, National or State Park offices for maps & information *p 256*). In addition, some 195mi/314km of former railroad tracks throughout California have been converted into paved and dirt paths for bikers and pedestrians (contact Rails-to-Trails Conservancy, 1400 16th St NW, Washington DC 20036 ☏ 202-797-5400 for maps and information). For more information on biking and hiking trails, and on local mountain biking regulations, contact local tourism office *(p 250)*.

When hiking in the backcountry stay on marked trails. Taking shortcuts is dangerous and causes erosion. If hiking alone, notify someone of your destination and planned return time.

Bicycles are prohibited on most unpaved trails. Riders should stay on paved paths and roads (on public roads, stay to the right and ride in single file). Bicyclists are encouraged to wear helmets and other protective gear.

Both hikers and bicyclists are cautioned to be well equipped (with such items as detailed maps of the areas to be explored), and alert to current weather conditions, particularly in higher elevations.

Hunting & Fishing – Licenses are required to hunt and fish in the state of California. One-day non-resident fishing licenses are available in fishing supply stores (some offer rental equipment). Non-resident hunting licenses tend to be considerably more expensive than resident licenses. Most fish are in season year-round, whereas most game can only be hunted seasonally. **Deep sea fishing** excursions depart along the coast from cities with major ports; contact local tourism office *(p 250)* for information. Rifles and shotguns may be brought into the state for hunting or sporting purposes (no permit required). Contact the department of Fish & Game for regulations on transporting game out of the state, 3211 S St, Sacramento CA 95818 ☏ 916-227-2244.

Nature Tours – Guided specialty tours of California offering in-depth exploration of flora and fauna, guided biking, rock climbing or hiking can be arranged through: California Nature Conservancy, 3152 Paradise Dr, #203B, Tiburon CA 94920 ☏ 415-777-0862; Sierra Club Outings, 730 Polk St, San Francisco CA 94109 ☏ 415-923-5630, outings restricted to members only, $35/year membership fee; Wild Wheel Bicycle Tours, 15559 Union Ave, Suite 140, Los Gatos CA 95032 ☏ 408-267-8518; Vertical Adventures, PO Box 7548, Newport Beach CA 92658 ☏ 714-854-6250.

Snow Skiing

Cross-Country Skiing – Almost all of California's cross-country skiing resorts are in the High Sierra region. Most resorts offer equipment rentals, food service, and warming huts along the trails (serving warm beverages and light snacks). In higher elevations, public trails run throughout the state park and national park systems, most offering few amenities.

Selected Cross-Country Resorts

	☏	Total Trails	Trails		
			Beg.	Int.	Adv.
Bear Valley	209-753-2834	74mi	40%	40%	20%
Clair Tappan	916-426-3632	4mi	30%	60%	10%
Diamond Peak	702-832-1177	22mi	40%	40%	20%
Eagle Mountain	916-389-2254	43mi	25%	50%	25%
Kirkwood	209-258-7000	50mi	20%	60%	20%
Leland Meadows	209-881-3236	31mi	n/a	n/a	n/a
Nordic Ski Resort	(US only) 800-227-9900 415-967-8612	52mi	60%	20%	20%
Northstar	916-562-1010	40mi	20%	55%	25%
Royal Gorge	916-426-3871	196mi	45%	35%	20%
Sequoia Ski Touring Center	209-565-3381	25mi	25%	25%	50%
Squaw Creek	(worldwide) 800-327-3353	19mi	70%	30%	0%
Tamarack	619-934-2442	34mi	50%	25%	25%
Tahoe Donner	916-587-9484	40mi	34%	31%	35%
Tahoe Nordic	916-583-9858	40mi	30%	40%	30%

Downhill Skiing – **Ski conditions** ☎ 415-864-6440. The primary ski area in California is the High Sierras region (particularly around Lake Tahoe), although smaller resorts can be found in the Shasta-Cascade region and San Bernadino Mountains. Most ski area communities offer a variety of accommodations including bed & breakfasts, alpine lodges and major hotel chains. In addition, many places feature discount packages for stays of 3 or more days, which can include lift tickets, equipment rental, meals and transportation to the slopes.

Selected Ski Areas *(listed by tourist region, map p 10)*

	☎	Vertical Drop	Total Runs	Runs Beg.	Runs Int.	Runs Adv.	Snow Making
Gold Country							
Bear Valley Mtn Reba	209-753-2301	1900ft	60	20%	50%	30%	Y
Dodge Ridge	209-965-3474	1,600ft	29	20%	60%	20%	Y
Greater Los Angeles Area							
Kratka Ridge	818-449-1749	750ft	12	30%	30%	40%	N
Mount Baldy	909-981-3344	2,100ft	26	20%	40%	40%	Y
Mount Waterman	818-440-1041	1,000ft	23	30%	30%	40%	N
High Sierras							
Alpine Meadows	916-583-4232	1,802ft	100	25%	40%	35%	Y
Boreal	916-426-3666	600ft	41	30%	55%	15%	Y
Diamond Peak	702-832-1177	1,840ft	30	18%	49%	33%	Y
Donner Ski Ranch	916-426-3635	800ft	45	25%	50%	25%	Y
Granlibakken	916-583-4242	300ft	1	25%	75%	0%	N
Heavenly Valley	916-541-1330	3,500ft	79	25%	50%	25%	Y
Kirkwood	209-258-6000	2,000ft	68	15%	50%	35%	N
Mammoth Mtn *(p 116)*	916-934-2571	3,100ft	150	30%	40%	30%	Y
Northstar	916-562-1010	2,200ft	52	25%	50%	25%	Y
Sierra at Tahoe	916-659-7535	2,212ft	40	20%	60%	20%	Y
Sierra Summit	209 233-2500	1,679ft	25	10%	65%	25%	Y
Soda Springs	916-426-3666	652ft	16	30%	50%	20%	N
Squaw Valley	916-583-6985	2,850ft		10%	35%	55%	Y
Sugar Bowl	916-426-3651	1,500ft	47	20%	30%	50%	Y
Tahoe Donner	916-587-9444	600ft	11	50%	50%	0%	N
Inland Empire							
Bear Mountain	909-585-2519	1,665ft	27	25%	50%	25%	Y
Mountain High	714-972-9242	1,600ft	42	25%	60%	15%	Y
Ski Sunrise	619-249-6150	800ft	10	30%	45%	25%	Y
Snow Summit	909-866-5766	1,200ft	38	10%	65%	25%	Y
Snow Valley	909-867-2751	1,141ft	35	35%	35%	30%	Y
Shasta-Cascade							
Mt Shasta Ski Park *(p 125)*	916-926-8610	1,100ft	21	20%	60%	20%	Y

Whale, Seal & Sea Lion Watching – Whales can be seen along the California coast year-round as they migrate from the northern Pacific Ocean to Baja California. Gray whales migrate from December through May; prime locations for sightings include: Mendocino Headlands State Park *(p 118)*, Point Reyes National Seashore *(p 145)*, Carmel *(p 39)*, Santa Barbara *(p 217)*, San Pedro *(p 80)*, Palos Verdes Peninsula *(p 113)*, and Cabrillo National Monument *(p 177)*. Humpback and blue whales migrate from June through November; prime locations for sightings include: Point Reyes National Seashore or Davenport Bluffs (near Santa Cruz). California sea lions, harbor seals & elephant seals can be found lounging along the coastline year-round; prime locations for sightings include: Cliff House *(p 207)*, Año Neuvo State Reserve *(p 222)*, the 17-mile drive *(p 124)* and Cabrillo National Monument.

Selected agencies for whale-watching **cruises** include:

Oceanic Society Expeditions, Fort Mason Center, Bldg E, San Francisco CA 94123-1394 ☎ 415-441-1106. Cruises depart from San Francisco and Half Moon Bay late Dec–Apr, 3hrs & 7hrs, $32 & $48. Cruises to the Farallon Islands Jun–Nov 8hrs 30min–10hrs, $58.

Davey's Locker, 400 Main St, Balboa CA 92661 ☎ 714-673-1434. Cruises depart from Balboa end of Dec–Mar, 2hrs 30min, $12.

Sea Landing, 301 West Cabrillo Blvd, Santa Barbara CA 93101 ☎ 805-963-3564. Cruises to the Channel Islands late Dec–Feb, 9hrs, $59. Cruises from Santa Barbara Mar–May, 2hrs 30min, $22.

Natural Habitat Adventures, One Sussex station, Sussex NJ 07461 ☎ 800-543-8917 (North America only) or 201-702-1525. 5-day tours of San Ignacio Whale Camp depart from San Diego, $1395.

INDEX

Hollywood — City, town, region or other point of interest
Accommodations — Practical information
Muir, John — Person, historic event or term
98, **123**, *127* — Page reference, **principal reference**, *illustration*

Missions, **Wineries** and main sights in **Los Angeles**, **San Diego** and **San Francisco** are grouped under separate headings. Sight names appear with their tourist region abbreviations: Central Coast (CC), Central Valley (CV), Deserts (DT), Gold Country (GC), Greater Los Angeles Area (GLA), High Sierras (HS), Inland Empire (IE), North Coast (NC), Orange County (OC), San Diego County (SDC), San Francisco Bay Area (SFA), Shasta-Cascade (SC).

State Parks are listed in the chart on page 257.

A-B

C-D

E-F-G

H-I-J

K-L

M-N

O-P

Q-R

S

T-U-V

W-Y

MANUFACTURE FRANÇAISE DES PNEUMATIQUES MICHELIN
Société en commandite par actions au capital de 2 000 000 000 de francs
Place des Carmes-Déchaux – 63 Clermont-Ferrand (France)
R.C.S. Clermont-Fd B 855 200 507

Dépôt légal 5-1994 — ISBN 2-06-159801-3 — ISSN 0763-1383

Printed in the United States of America 05-94-110 by Hart Graphics, Austin, Texas